From the Series Editor:

Macmillan USA is excited and proud to announce that *Sams Teach Yourself Lotus Notes and Domino R5 Development in 21 Days* is part of our new integrated series of books on Lotus Notes and Domino R5.

As illustrated in the User Pyramid (see facing page) this series is not merely a collection of books but a carefully planned succession of tutorials and reference material. Our building block approach to Lotus Notes and Domino R5 gives corporations the ability to identify the right book for each of their users. Individuals "graduate" to the next level of proficiency with confidence that the topics and depth of coverage are appropriately expanded and enhanced.

The lead authors in our series are Certified Lotus Notes Professionals (CLP) and/or Certified Lotus Notes Instructors (CLI) with real-world product experience. They represent the professional Lotus Notes and Domino community, and they understand your need to augment skills commensurate with new product releases and evolving user community needs.

I hope you enjoy our series of R5 books as much as we have enjoyed our collaborative efforts to deliver them to you. Thank you.

Sincerely,

Jane Calabria

Series Editor

Where do you start with something as big as Lotus Notes and Domino? This is my problem as I sit to write a page or two about them. These products have been in development for over 15 years, been through five major revisions, support six different programming languages, communicate over seven different protocols, run on 11 different platforms, and have more than 30 million customers. There's so much here, where do you start?

Let's start at the beginning. Back then, Lotus Notes was much smaller than it is today, of course, but even then, it had big ambitions: a client/server application with an integrated development environment that enabled the creation of groupware applications. Not only were these big ambitions, but they also were ahead of their time. In fact, Lotus Notes has so often been ahead of the industry, that often the best words to describe it came about after Notes needed them. Client/server, integrated development environment, groupware, intranet, application server: these are all words that describe Notes and Domino, but were coined after Iris Associates (the Lotus subsidiary that develops Notes and Domino) had built the product they describe.

As much as Notes and Domino have grown over the years, they have remained true to their roots. In fact, the architecture laid out by the original developers is still in place today, working as well as ever. The fundamental concept of databases containing notes, which contain named, typed, items is the same as it was in version 1. The same document-centric focus is there: many structures that would be separately developed in other systems are simply another database of documents in Notes and Domino; email, server logs, discussion forums, and address books are all examples. These underlying principles form the heart of the infrastructure services provided by Domino, and it is these services that give Domino its deep power. The continuity of the architecture is what makes Domino such a lasting product.

My own involvement with Notes and Domino began in the team that built the first version of the Domino Web server. At the time, there was a lot of discussion about "the battle between Notes and the Web." Back then, it seemed like a real issue: the Web did many things that Notes had always done (client/server, document-focused, linking among documents, enabling information sharing and collaboration), and was growing phenomenally. Browsers were widely and inexpensively deployed. Many companies were racing to market with support for this new, exciting technology. How could an old product like Lotus Notes hope to keep up with these new innovations? It looked like the end was near.

Of course, the end didn't come: Lotus introduced the Domino Web server, and showed that the architecture of Notes was flexible and powerful enough not to battle the Web, but to embrace, extend, and empower it. The Domino Web server took the deep power of the Notes architecture and engine, and added Web technologies on top to provide a powerful combination that had the best attributes of both worlds: a sophisticated infrastructure with years of development and customer expertise, and widely available protocols to give Domino applications the broadest possible reach. It was (and is) an attractive combination.

At the same time, the Web introduced a wider audience to the concepts behind Notes, and terminology cropped up that allowed more people than ever to appreciate the power of Notes and Domino. Once again, words were coined to succinctly express concepts that Lotus had been talking about all along. Suddenly everyone knew what an "intranet" was, and Lotus was able to explain that intranets (and extranets) were what Notes had been building for all these years. Notes became more popular than ever, partly because of the new functionality in the Web server, and partly because all the Web hype educated people about what Notes had always done.

With the recent release of R5, Notes and Domino have taken the marriage of old depth and new breadth even further. More protocols than ever are implemented on top of the latest revision of the powerful Domino engines. Once again, the power deepens at the same time as the reach broadens.

Enough about us. Where do you fit into this picture? You will be a Domino application developer. Application developers are in many ways the most important customers of Domino, because they are the ones that will build the applications that the 30 million customers will be using. First and foremost, Domino is an application development environment.

At this point, you may be asking yourself the same question I faced above: "Where do you start with something this big?" This book is designed to answer that question. By laying out a course of instruction over 21 days, this book gives you an orderly introduction into the vast world of Domino application development.

There is, of course, a great deal to learn. Enjoy!

Ned Batchelder, Architect, Iris Associates

SAMS
Teach Yourself
Lotus Notes®
and Domino™ R5
Development
in 21 Days

SAMS

A Division of Macmillan Computer Publishing
201 West 103rd St., Indianapolis, Indiana, 46290 USA

Sams Teach Yourself Lotus Notes® and Domino™ R5 Development in 21 Days

Copyright © 1999 by Sams Publishing

International Standard Book Number: 0-672-31416-9

Library of Congress Catalog Card Number: 98-86480

Printed in the United States of America

First Printing: October 1999

01   00   99   4   3   2   1

Trademarks

Warning and Disclaimer

EXECUTIVE EDITOR
Dean Miller

DEVELOPMENT EDITORS
Nancy Warner
Sean Dixon

MANAGING EDITOR
Lisa Wilson

PROJECT EDITORS
Sara Bosin
Susan Ross Moore

COPY EDITOR
JoAnna Kremer

INDEXER
Greg Pearson

PROOFREADER
Andrew Beaster

TECHNICAL EDITOR
Leigh Weber

TEAM COORDINATOR
Cindy Teeters

SOFTWARE DEVELOPMENT SPECIALIST
Adam Swetnam

INTERIOR DESIGN
Gary Adair

COVER DESIGN
Aren Howell

COPY WRITER
Eric Borgert

LAYOUT TECHNICIAN
Timothy Osborn

Contents at a Glance

Contents

About the Authors

Dorothy Burke is an R5 Certified Lotus Instructor (CLI) and a Certified Lotus Notes Professional(Principal level). She teaches Domino system administration and application development and has been an independent consultant and trainer since 1988. Dorothy has contributed to several MCP books, including *Special Edition Using PowerPoint 97, Easy Lotus Notes R5*, and, along with Jane Calabria, has co-authored many Que books on the topic of Lotus Notes and Domino, Microsoft Windows, and Microsoft Word, Excel, and PowerPoint.

Jane Calabria has authored 13 Macmillan Computer Publishing books on the topics of Lotus Notes and Domino, Microsoft Windows, Microsoft Word, Excel, and PowerPoint. She and her husband, Rob Kirkland, own Stillwater Enterprises, Inc., a consulting firm located near Philadelphia, Pennsylvania. Jane and Rob are preeminent authors, speakers, and trainers on the topic of Lotus Notes and Domino, and they conduct national training sessions and seminars. Jane is co-author of the *Professional Developer's Guide to Domino* and is an R5 Certified Lotus Notes Professional (Principal level) and a Certified Microsoft User Specialist. She is also the Series Editor for the Macmillan USA series of Lotus Notes and Domino 5 books.

Co-authoring efforts by Jane and Dorothy include the *Certified Microsoft Office User Exam Guide*(s) for Microsoft Word 97, Microsoft Excel 97, and Microsoft PowerPoint 97, as well as *Microsoft Works 6-in-1, Microsoft Windows 95 6-in-1, Microsoft Windows 98 6-in-1*, and *Using Microsoft Word 97*. Their Lotus Notes and Domino titles include the *Ten Minute Guide to Lotus Notes 4.6*, the *Ten Minute Guide to Lotus Notes Mail 4.6*, and *Lotus Notes and the Internet 6-in-1*. New titles for release 5 of Lotus Notes and Domino also include *Teach Yourself Lotus Notes R5 Client in 24 Hours* and *Teach Yourself Lotus Notes R5 Client in 10 Minutes*.

Dedication

To Chris Novak, Senior Technical Solutions Manager, IBM. Thank you for Camp Spring Creek, for your endless energy, and for the whistle!

Acknowledgments

We are very excited about the release of Notes and Domino R5! Lotus Development Corporation has historically designed powerful and exciting products, and they continue to surprise and delight us with new features, new functionality, and new direction for Lotus Notes and Domino. Those of us whose businesses have come to rely on this product are never disappointed at new release time.

Just as we are delighted with this new release of Notes and Domino, we are thrilled with the Macmillan USA *series* approach to Notes and Domino books. We'd like to thank Al Valvano (Executive Editor), John Pierce (Publisher), Karen Reinisch (Executive Editor), and Don Essig (Acquisitions Editor) of MCP for creating a Series Editor position for the Notes/Domino R5 books and for re-engineering, redesigning, and rethinking their business practices to better support the Lotus Notes and Domino community.

As Dorothy Burke, Rob Kirkland, and I began this book, Rob and I were presenting an R4 "boot camp" in Atlanta, Georgia. We spent our summer working with Chris Novak, of IBM Software Group's World-Wide Network Integrator Alliance program. Chris develops regional, national, and international software alliances for IBM/Lotus by creating and strengthening the Alliance member's BESTeam and Lotus Business Partner locations. Part of Chris's work is to develop Certified Lotus Notes professionals and IBM Certified Specialists/Experts by establishing "boot camp" environments for his Alliance clients.

These types of programs enable us to keep our finger on the pulse of Notes/Domino training and to understand the needs of students who are new to Notes, as well as those who are experienced Notes professionals. Our boot camp students grill us constantly (morning, noon, night, weekends) with probing and insightful questions regarding Domino programming and administration. We believe that these students help us to produce comprehensive teaching materials such as *Sams Teach Yourself Lotus Notes and Domino R5 Development in 21 Days*, and we thank the staff of GE Capital IT Solutions (GECITS) for allowing us to conduct "Camp Spring Creek."

Dorothy, Rob, and I benefit greatly from our experiences as trainers and consultants, and we believe this helps us in our authoring efforts. But books are not written by the authors alone. We would like to thank the editorial staff of *Sams Teach Yourself Lotus Notes and Domino R5 Development in 21 Days* for their invaluable contributions. Our MCP contributors—Dean Miller, Publisher; and Sean Dixon, Development Editor—systematically created a comprehensive guide from many pages and thoughts presented by harried authors working under difficult deadlines with beta product. Leigh Weber, the Technical Editor, made golden our beta words—testing, querying, and confirming the technical acumen we present to you.

Special Contribution

Rob Kirkland is an R5 Certified Lotus Notes Instructor (CLI), a principal Certified Lotus Notes Professional System Administrator, a principal Certified Lotus Notes Application Developer, a Certified NetWare Engineer (CNE), and a Microsoft Certified Product Specialist (MCPS) for Windows NT. Rob is a preeminent author, speaker, and trainer on the topic of Lotus Notes and Domino. He conducts national training sessions and seminars. Rob is the author of New Riders" Domino System Administration and co-author of the *Professional Developer's Guide to Domino* He is also a contributing author to several Que books, including *Using Windows NT Workstation*, *Intranet Publishing*, *Running a Perfect Intranet*, and *Intranet HTML*. As a consultant, he designs, installs, maintains, and troubleshoots Domino networks, designs Domino applications, and subdues unruly hardware and software.

Tell Us What You Think!

As the reader of this book, *you* are our most important critic and commentator. We value your opinion and want to know what we're doing right, what we could do better, what areas you'd like to see us publish in, and any other words of wisdom you're willing to pass our way.

As an Associate Publisher for Sams Publishing, I welcome your comments. You can fax, email, or write me directly to let me know what you did or didn't like about this book—as well as what we can do to make our books stronger.

Please note that I cannot help you with technical problems related to the topic of this book, and that due to the high volume of mail I receive, I might not be able to reply to every message.

When you write, please be sure to include this book's title and author as well as your name and phone or fax number. I will carefully review your comments and share them with the authors and editors who worked on the book.

Fax: (317) 581-4666

Email: opsys@mcp.com

Mail: Dean Miller
           Associate Publisher
           Sams Publishing
           201 West 103rd Street
           Indianapolis, IN 46290 USA

Introduction

Who Should Read This Book

This book is designed for

- **The first-time Domino developer**—Experience with using Lotus Notes is extremely helpful—and recommended. Experience with using a Web browser is also recommended. Previous Notes/Domino development experience is not necessary.
- **Experienced Web developers new to Domino**—Experienced Web developers will find this book helpful as their introduction to the Domino development environment.

Experienced Notes/Domino developers should consider Que's *Special Edition Using Lotus Notes and Domino R5* to learn about the new features and functions of Notes and Domino R5. Professional and certified Notes and Domino should consider Sams' *Lotus Notes and Domino Development R5 Unleashed*, which covers the more advanced features of Domino application development and includes detailed information on scripting and programming languages.

Introduction

The new Domino R5 Designer enables developers to work in a single interface while developing applications for both the Notes client and the Web browser. The new user interface for Designer Release 5.0 is task-oriented and includes support for Web standard constructs such as framesets, JavaScript, and HTML pages.

With all its new capabilities, the R5 Designer is a powerful, streamlined developer's tool, and here you'll learn the basics of Domino application development—and more! You'll use "Notes-centric" features such as Lotus's formula language, and you'll be introduced to LotusScript as well as to "Web-centric" tools such as basic JavaScript, HTML, and incorporating Java applets.

You'll learn how to plan, design, and outline a workflow application and how to create forms, pages, views, and frames. You'll also learn about some more advanced topics such as agents, data manipulation, and layout regions. As you work through the lessons in this book, building your skills, you will develop a fully functional workflow application that uses multiple databases. You'll set up routing and depositing of documents, a document library, and a discussion database, and you'll write agents to notify, process lists, and create dynamic Web input forms.

How this Book is Organized

Sams Teach Yourself Lotus Notes and Domino R5 Development is divided into 21 days. Each day is a lesson, with each lesson taking approximately one hour to complete. It is recommended that you complete this book in the order in which the lessons are presented because each lesson builds on skills learned in previous lessons.

At the end of each lesson you will find a Summary and Workshop section. The summary section provides a synopsis of the topics learned in the lesson. You also find a Q&A section, where we present both questions that are often asked by students in class and the responses we give as instructors. The workshop is next, and is designed to guide you in building a workflow application as described in Hour 1, "An Introduction to Lotus Notes and Domino 5 Development." If you complete each workshop in order, you will develop a fully functional, secure application that is ready for rollout.

The following lessons comprise *Sams Teach Yourself Lotus Notes and Domino R5 Development in 21 Days*:

On Day 1, "An Introduction to Lotus Notes and Domino R5 Development," you will learn about Domino, its capabilities and features, and the programming tools you can use in Domino Designer. Also learn how to plan an application, sketch your plan, and create your first database.

On Day 2, "Forms 101: The Essentials of Form Design," you will be introduced to the types of forms you can create in Domino applications. You learn how to create forms, insert tables, add static text, and create window titles, as well as how to name, save, and store forms.

On Day 3, "Take a Field Trip: Add Fields," you will enhance your forms with fields. You learn about the types of Domino fields, as well as how to determine which field types work best for your application.

Day 4, "Formulas 101: The Basics," introduces you to Lotus formula language. You will learn how to write formulas that automate, calculate, and convert data, just to name a few.

On Day 5, "Forms 102: Enhance Form Appearance and Design," you will improve the look of your forms by formatting text and paragraphs, using styles, creating sections, and inserting graphics. Also learn how to set background colors.

Day 6, "Take in the View: Create Views and Folders," introduces you to the design of *views*, the method used to present the contents of a database to the using community. You start here with basic views, learn about the types of views that are available, modify views, and determine which documents will display in your view. Views are a dynamic, powerful feature of Domino and a unique, powerful tool for the Web.

On Day 7, "Sleep Soundly: Secure Your Application," you will learn about what is perhaps one of the greatest strengths of Domino—its security features. You learn the functions and terminology of Domino security as well as how to control access to a database, a form, a view, a document, or even a single field of information.

On Day 8, "Create Pages and Frames," you will learn the differences between pages and forms, how to create pages, and how to create frames using FrameSet Designer. Here, you also learn about HTML in pages, forms, and fields.

Day 9 is called "Forms on Steroids: Increase Form Performance." After you make your forms *look* good, you want to make them *work* well. Creating subforms, setting up inheritance, and hiding objects are just a few of the skills you learn on Day 9 to increase your users' productivity.

On Day 10, "Advanced Views," you will put views to work by learning to sort and categorize, add formulas for response columns, create column totals, and view indexes. Here, too, you learn how to import and export from views as well as tweak your document display.

Day 11 is called "Help the User: Design Interface Enhancements." You want to make it as easy as possible for users to contribute to your application. Day 11 teaches you how to add actions, buttons, hotspots, and links to make your application user-friendly.

On Day 12, "Beautify Your Application," you learn more skills to improve and optimize the appearance of your application. Create nested tables, layout regions with graphics and fields, and image maps and navigators to assist the user in maneuvering through your application.

On Day 13, "Put on Your Propeller Beanie: Advanced Formulas," you will learn more advanced formula writing procedures to create dialog boxes, access data from other views and databases, and prompt users for input information.

Day 14 is called "The Not So Secret Agents." Designing forms and views is hardly the end of application development. You need to plan now what happens to data after your application has been populated. How will you find, retrieve, and use information from your application? Here you learn how to create agents to automate reporting, searching, and updates of information.

On Day 15, "Incorporate Workflow," you will learn strategies for automating workflow. Learn how to mail-enable your application and how to create agents that detect defined events and respond to them automatically.

Day 16 is called "List Processing." Notes excels at handling lists of information. On Day 16 you learn how to manipulate lists and create dynamic tables.

On Day 17, "Embed Objects in Your Applications," you will learn how to embed spread-sheets, Domino elements, and Java applets in your application.

On Day 18, "Introduction to JavaScript," you learn what JavaScript is and how to use it in your applications.

On Day 19, "Introduction to LotusScript," you learn the basics of LotusScript, just enough to get a start.

On Day 20, "The Last Minute Details: Outlines, Icons, Help," you will learn to use Outlines to organize your application and to help users navigate your application.

On Day 21, "Roll Out and Maintain Your Application," you put the final touches on your application: create design templates, create help for the users, design database icons, pilot your application, and train the users.

Conventions Used in This Book

Note

A note presents interesting information relating to the surrounding topic.

Note

A tip offers advice, shows you an easier way to perform a specific task, or provides inside information regarding the surround topic.

Caution

A caution advises you of potential hazards or problems and helps to steer you clear of those problems and hazards.

NEW TERM   A new term explains new terms and definitions.

Sources for Further Information

There are several sources and Web sites available to provide you with additional information you might want before, during, and after completion of this book.

The Lotus Development home page is www.lotus.com. From the Lotus home page, you will find pointers to pages that are of interest to developers. Lotus often sponsors discussion databases for developers, and you might also visit the Iris site at www.iris.com. Iris Associates are the developers of Lotus Notes and Domino. At this site, you'll find a wealth of Domino and Notes information.

Visit the Java Web site at www.java.sun.com to learn more about Java, JavaScript, and Java applets.

As a reference during your development, you'll benefit greatly from what we call the "Lotus Yellow Books." These books, published by Lotus, include the *Programmer's Guide*, Parts 1 and 2, and the *Application Developer's Guide*. They are included in the shrink-wrapped Domino Designer package, both in printed form and as part of the Help database. You can also purchase them separately, either directly from Lotus or from any Lotus Authorized Education Center.

When you have completed *Sams Teach Yourself Lotus Notes and Domino R5 Development in 21 Days*, consider moving up to Sams *Lotus Notes and Domino R5 Development Unleashed* by Debbie Lynd and Steve Kern, a powerful and complete application developer's reference and tutorial. You can also find additional application development information and learn about the new R5 Notes Client and Domino R5 Servers in Que's *Special Edition Using Lotus Notes and Domino R5* by Randy Tamura.

WEEK 1

Plan and Design a Simple Application

1

2

3

4

5

6

7

DAY **1**

An Introduction to Lotus Notes and Domino R5 Development

What are Lotus Notes and Domino?

Lotus Notes and Domino are a set of programs designed to enable groups of people to work together efficiently. The original and still premier "groupware" product, they are now also a powerful set of tools for gathering, organizing, and disseminating information. They are an email system, a system of discussion forums, an information repository, a group project tracking system, a business process automation system, a knowledge management tool, and a Web application system. Because such applications need to be flexible and customizable, Notes and Domino include a powerful set of application development tools. The most prominent of these, Domino Designer, is where you will be spending your time in this book.

Notes and Domino, combined, constitute a client/server program. Lotus Notes is the client program. It resides on the user's computer and communicates with the server, retrieving data, presenting the data to the user, and sending newly created data to the server.

Lotus Domino is the server program. It resides on a separate computer, accessible by LAN, WAN, or modem to all users in the group. The Domino server is the custodian of Notes databases. It permits—or denies—the users access to its databases according to access control lists that it maintains for each database. Perhaps one user can add content to a database, another user can only read the content, and a third user might be denied access altogether.

Starting with Release 5.0, there is a third piece of the Notes/Domino software team— Domino Designer. In the past, all application development took place inside the Notes client. Domino Designer is an add-on to the Notes client, and it provides a separate development environment in which to design and write Domino applications. By separating the design and user tools, Lotus optimized the design of each for its audience.

History and Evolution

Early on, Notes and Domino worked only with each other. That is, the server (known prior to Release 4.5 as the Notes Server) could only serve data to Notes clients, and the Notes client could only access Notes data either locally or on a Notes server. This made sense when computer networks were small and isolated from each other.

However, the surge in popularity of the Internet (fueled largely by the advent of the World Wide Web in the 90s) has changed the playing field. We now have easy access to a worldwide network of computers, and that access is rapidly changing the way we work, shop, and play, and the way businesses interact with their customers and business partners. For many of us, email is now as indispensable as the telephone, the World Wide Web is more convenient than the local mall, and we get more news from our computers than we do from newspapers, magazines, or television.

Lotus has responded to this situation in a number of ways. First, they began, with Release 4.0, to incorporate the major Internet standards into both the client and the server. Second, as of Release 4.5, they renamed the server (from "Notes Server" to "Domino Server") to signal its new Internet functionality. Third, they began marketing Domino as not just the premier groupware product, but as a great Internet application server as well. Finally—and this is most important to you, the application developer—they have streamlined the process of developing Domino/Notes/Web applications.

1

The net result of all this is that, as of the current release (Release 5.0), the Notes client and the Domino server are no longer exclusive partners. They now have lives entirely independent of each other, in that Notes can function just fine without Domino and Domino can serve data to all sorts of clients other than Notes.

The Notes client can retrieve mail from POP3 and IMAP mail servers and deliver it directly to SMTP servers. It can also communicate directly with Web, News, FTP, Gopher, LDAP, and Finger servers. Finally, it is a Personal Information Manager with address book, email, calendar, task management, and information management features. Some people use it even though they don't have access to Domino servers.

The Domino server is a Web server, a POP3 mail server, an IMAP mail server, an LDAP directory server, an NNTP News server, and, oh yes, a Notes server. It gives access not only to Notes databases residing on itself, but also to files in its file system and a wide array of non-Notes databases residing on other computers.

You, as the developer, can develop Notes databases using Notes's proprietary tools—the Notes Formula Language and LotusScript (Lotus's version of BASIC)—or non-proprietary tools such as HTML 4.0, Java, and JavaScript. Domino supports CORBA/IIOP, so you can develop true client/server Domino applications for non-Notes clients. Furthermore, Domino provides both proprietary and third-party tools for connecting your applications to non-Notes data sources.

The R5 Product Line

To summarize, the R5 product line includes three basic products: the Domino server, the Notes client, and the Domino Designer application development environment, which is an add-on to the Notes client.

There are actually several Domino servers, which offer differing levels of functionality:

- **Domino Mail Server**—This low-end server offers basic email and collaboration services.
- **Domino Application Server**—This is the standard Domino server, similar to the Domino server of earlier releases. It includes the features of the Domino Mail Server, to which it adds Web application services and connectivity to data sources external to Domino.
- **Domino Enterprise Server**—This includes all the capabilities of the other servers and adds server clustering for increased data availability.

There is only one Notes client, but it has two possible add-on functions. The first, Domino Designer, is the application development interface where you will be spending your time in the rest of this book. The other, Domino Administrator, is yet another set of optional screens, where Domino system administrators maintain Domino servers and Notes clients. You have to buy a Notes license or a Domino Designer license as a separate purchase. The Domino Administrator license, on the other hand, is not a separate purchase; rather, it is included with every server license.

Setting Up: What You Need for Development

Veteran Notes programmers can generally use almost any tool they want to develop Domino applications, and for Release 5 Lotus has made more programming options available than ever before. But this book is aimed at the new Notes programmer who wants to learn the basics of Domino application development. For this reader, the needs are simple. You need a Windows 9x PC or a Macintosh PowerPC with Domino Designer and maybe—depending on who will use your application—one or more browsers installed on it. At some point, but not initially, you also need a Domino server on which to test your application. Depending on your application and, again, who will be using it, the server might have to be on a LAN, connected to one or more other computers running Notes or various Web browsers. But that's all in the future. Initially you just need the one workstation.

Hardware

To develop Domino applications, you of course need a computer on which Domino Designer can run. This must be either a Pentium-class PC running Windows 95, Windows 98, or Windows NT 4.0, or a Macintosh Power PC running System 8.5.1. If the computer runs Windows 95 or Windows 98, it needs at least 8MB RAM (16MB recommended). If it runs Windows NT, it needs at least 16MB RAM (32MB recommended). As we publish this, the Macintosh version is still in beta, and requires 32MB physical RAM (64MB recommended) and 64MB virtual RAM (80MB recommended). It will need less RAM when it goes gold. For marketing purposes, software makers always lowball the RAM requirements. So, we suggest that you double the recommended RAM requirement. You also need at least 70MB (236MB recommended) free disk space for the Notes and Domino Designer program and data files. Again, in reality you will be much happier if you have lots more free disk space than the minimum requirement. Also, the underlying operating system should include any patches that have been released for it. You should check the Notes/Domino release notes for exact requirements.

If you plan to develop applications that users can access through a Web browser, your computer also needs to be running the TCP/IP protocol stack. This means that your computer needs either a LAN adapter installed in it or a modem installed in or attached to it because the TCP/IP protocol stack must bind to a LAN or modem driver or it won't install. On most modern computers this won't be a problem because they almost always include at least a modem as part of the base price of the computer. But if your computer does not have a modem or a LAN adapter in it, you can't use it to test browser access to your applications.

Most of the functionality that you will develop can be tested right on your own Notes workstation. However, some Notes functions work differently on a Domino server than they do on a Notes workstation. Also, your prospective users might run browsers that you can't install on your computer for whatever reason. So, occasionally you might need access to a Domino server to fully test your application.

A bare-bones Domino server can run on a computer of the same specifications as for Domino Designer, with two exceptions. First, Domino server won't run on a Macintosh. Second, it requires a minimum of 48MB RAM (96MB recommended) if it is running under Windows 95, Windows 98, or Windows NT, and a minimum of 64MB (128MB recommended) if it is running under any of the other platforms. Also, you need at least 300MB free disk space to hold the program and minimal data files. Lotus actually recommends 750MB and up for a production server. If you are setting up a Domino server purely for test purposes, you can glide by with the minimum requirements, but don't expect the server to do anything quickly.

Finally, if you have enough RAM on your Windows workstation, you can actually install both Domino server and Domino Designer on it and run them simultaneously. The trick to doing this (besides having lots of RAM and disk space) is to make sure that the two programs don't share the same data directory or notes.ini file (although they *can* share the same program directory). As long as they use different data directories and notes.ini files, Domino Server and Domino Designer act as though they are on two different computers, connected by a LAN.

To set up your computer to run this way, simply install a Domino server, and then install Notes and Domino Designer. Specify different program directories if you have ample disk space, or the same program directory if disk space is tight. Specify different data directories in either case. For example, the program directory might be c:\lotus\domino, and the data directories might be c:\lotus\domino\serverdata and c:\lotus\domino\clientdata.

The Install program for both Notes and Domino will install notes.ini in the program directory (unless you're upgrading from an earlier version, in which case notes.ini might wind up in the Windows directory). Therefore, you have to move notes.ini between installs, so the second install won't overwrite the first install's notes.ini file. Move notes.ini to the data directory. You will also have to change the command line of your shortcuts to reflect the change in notes.ini's location. For example, if, in our example in the previous paragraph, Domino server's notes.ini is in the program directory, the short-cut's command line will say merely:

```
c:\lotus\domino\nserver.exe
```

But if the notes.ini is in the data directory, the shortcut's command line should say:

```
c:\lotus\domino\nserver.exe =c:\lotus\domino\serverdata\notes.ini
```

Also, when the Install program asks where you want to put your program shortcuts (it offers to put them in a folder called Lotus Applications), be sure to specify two different folders. Otherwise, the second install might overwrite the shortcuts that the first install created. That would force you to re-create the icons by hand. If you *do* have to create icons by hand, the command line needs to look (using the preceding sample directory names) like this:

Lotus Domino Server	`c:\lotus\domino\nserver.exe`
	or
	`c:\lotus\domino\nserver.exe =c:\lotus\domino\` `serverdata\notes.ini`
Lotus Notes	`c:\lotus\domino\notes.exe`
	or
	`c:\lotus\domino\notes.exe =c:\lotus\domino\` `clientdata\notes.ini`

In the preceding table, for each shortcut, use the first command line if notes.ini is in the program directory. Use the second command line if notes.ini is in the data directory.

Software

If you plan to develop applications that people can access via a Web browser rather than a Notes client, you want to test your applications not only in Notes but also using the Web browsers that your users will be using. You can test your applications as either Notes or browser users would experience them from within Domino Designer itself. It actually includes an internal HTTP stack so that it can become a mini-Domino Web server for test purposes.

To take advantage of this capability you must install the browsers on your workstation. Designer recognizes the presence of some browsers on your system and automatically sets itself up to enable you to test your application using those browsers. The browsers include Netscape Navigator, Microsoft Internet Explorer, and Lotus Notes's own internal browser, the Web Retriever. If you need to test using other browsers, you have to run them from the operating system to do so.

You might also want to test your application with multiple browsers because all browsers aren't created equal. They don't all support the same feature set, and they don't all support given features the same way. For example, some support frames, and others don't. The ones that do support frames might not render them the same way, or might not support them in the same way that others do.

The only sure way of knowing how your application will perform for a given user is to test it using the same browser that users will use. That might mean installing multiple versions of multiple browsers on your computer. One problem with this is that you can't install UNIX or Macintosh browsers on your Windows PC. Another problem is that you can't simultaneously carry multiple versions of Internet Explorer on your computer. You either have to test different versions serially or install different versions on different computers.

If you need to test with multiple versions of Internet Explorer or with browsers that run under different operating systems, you have to set them up on multiple computers. Then you either have to run Domino Designer on each of those machines in turn, or you have to set up a Domino server running the Domino HTTP service so that those other computers can access your application.

A less insane approach to this problem is to find out from their publishers exactly which features different browsers claim to support. Then you can design your application around the limitations of the browsers your users will be using. You can find this sort of information on the publishers' Web sites or in release notes accompanying the browser software. This won't solve the problem of different browsers supporting a given feature differently, but you can also find documentation of these kinds of problems at the Web Standards Project, `www.webstandards.org`.

Know the Domino Database Architecture

Domino databases bear only the most superficial resemblance to standard relational databases. They do have records and fields in them, as do relational or standard databases, but all resemblance ends there. In a relational database, all data reside in tables. Each record is a row in the table, and each field is a column in the table. This means that every record in a table has the same set of fields as all the other records. It also makes for a rigid database design and is best suited to data in which all records are uniform in character, that is, in which all records hold the same type of data.

Domino records, known as *documents* or *notes*, look and feel more like word processor documents than database records. All Notes documents contain fields of one kind or another. But Domino fields do not have a fixed length, and the length of any one field varies from document to document, depending on the field's actual contents. Also, no two documents in a database need to incorporate the same array of fields: Document A might have fields one, two, and three; document B might have fields one, two, and four; and document C might have fields five and six. Additionally, a document might acquire fields one and two when it is created, and then have fields three and four added at a later date. Thus, the flexibility of Domino databases makes them suitable for tracking extremely diverse pools of data, such as the types of data that office workers typically generate.

When you create, edit, or read a Domino document, you do so using a template known as a *form*. Forms define what fields can be added to a document when it is created or edited, what fields can be seen when you are reading the document, and how the document is formatted.

You can use one form to create a document and another to read it. Or I can read a document with Form A while you read it with Form B. The result might be that I, the salesperson, see some fields and you, the manager, see others. Domino databases typically have multiple forms.

To find information in a Domino database, you can either browse views or you can use the full text search engine to locate documents. A *view* is a tabular listing of a specific set of documents in the database, which places field information in columns. Each row in a view represents a different document.

Database Components

A Domino application consists of one or more databases. A Domino *database* is a collection of documents (sometimes called *notes*) and indexes. A database contains four kinds of documents:

- **Header documents**—Header documents contain the database's title, its properties, and its replication settings, among other things.
- **The Access Control List (ACL)**—The ACL contains the access rights of servers, people, and groups.
- **Design documents**—Design documents contain the design elements of the database, such as forms, views, and agents.
- **Data documents**—Data documents contain the production data that the database was designed to contain. Data documents are what is usually meant when you hear about the "documents" in a Notes database.

Certain elements are of particular importance in defining a database:

- **Forms**—Forms provide the structure for entering and displaying data. They look like word processing documents because they usually contain a lot of formatted text, and maybe some graphics. But they also contain fields where users enter variable data.

When a user creates a new document, he opens a form, reads it, and fills in the fields. When the user saves the document, usually only the contents of the fields are saved; the form is discarded. When a user opens an existing document, Notes retrieves both the document and a form. The form provides the static text and formatting and dictates the appearance of the document; the document itself provides the variable data, contained in the fields.

A given document can be created with one form and viewed with another, which makes it look much different to the reader than it looked to the creator. Or two users, for example a manager and a salesperson, might use two different forms to view the same document. The two forms might display different sets of fields, so the salesperson might see only a subset of the data, whereas the manager sees all of it (see Figures 1.1 and 1.2).

The designer of the database creates all its forms. (Alternately, the designer can accomplish the same thing using one form with hide-when formulas.)

FIGURE 1.1

This document displays data using a form designed to collect information from salespeople who open new clients.

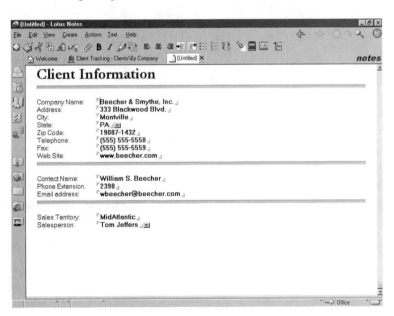

FIGURE 1.2

FIGURE 1.2

The same document displayed with a form designed for viewing by other office personnel. Note that the salesperson and territory information do not show on this form because that information is needed only by the manager.

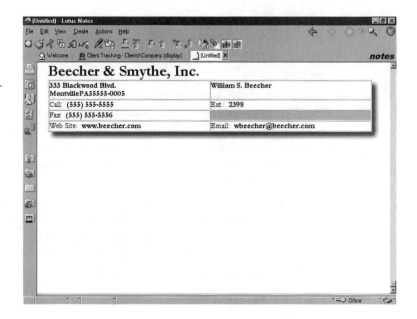

- **Documents**—Documents are the business end of a database in that they store the production data that the database was designed to contain. Documents store the information that is entered into the fields on a form in the database.

- **Fields**—Fields are specific areas on forms where users enter data or that compute data from other information. Fields have names and they contain a particular type of data: for example, text, numbers, or time/date information. The information in fields is typically all that gets stored when a user saves a document.

- **Views**—Views are tabular lists of documents (see Figure 1.3). Views function as tables of contents for the database. Each row represents information from a single document. Each column displays information from a single field or a group of fields, or the result of a formula that uses field information. Most Domino databases include multiple views, enabling you to use the one most suited to your current need. For example, you can view documents by date, by subject, or by author.

Current view

FIGURE 1.3

The current view is By Territory. You can tell from the tab (Client Tracking —Clients\By Territory) and the highlighted view name on the left side.

Other views listed for database

Navigation Pane

View Pane

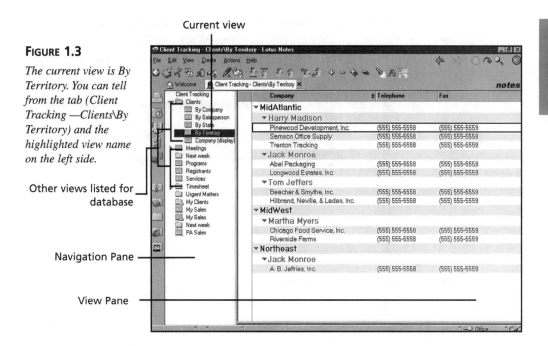

Forms and views are the heart of any database. A database is generally unusable if it does not have at least one view and one form. There are many other database components, however, that seem less essential but that are no less useful in making a database functional. Some that you will use include the following:

- **Folders**—Folders are like views, but with one crucial difference: A view includes a *definition* of what documents will appear in it, and a folder does not. The designer of a view decides at design time what documents are to appear in it. The user decides at runtime what documents are to appear in a folder by actually moving documents into the folder.

- **Subforms**—Subforms are reusable parts of forms. One subform can be attached to multiple forms to save the form designer from having to re-create that part of the form over and over again.

- **Shared fields**—Shared fields are reusable field definitions. Like subforms, they can be used in multiple forms to save the form designer the trouble of having to redefine the shared field again and again.

- **Actions**—Actions are programmable buttons that are associated with forms or views (see Figure 1.4). They provide a convenient way for users to carry out simple tasks. For example, in Figure 1.4 a user might click the Edit Document action button to put the memo into Edit Mode.

FIGURE **1.4**

*When you are looking
at this mail message,
you see several com-
ponents found in
Domino databases.*

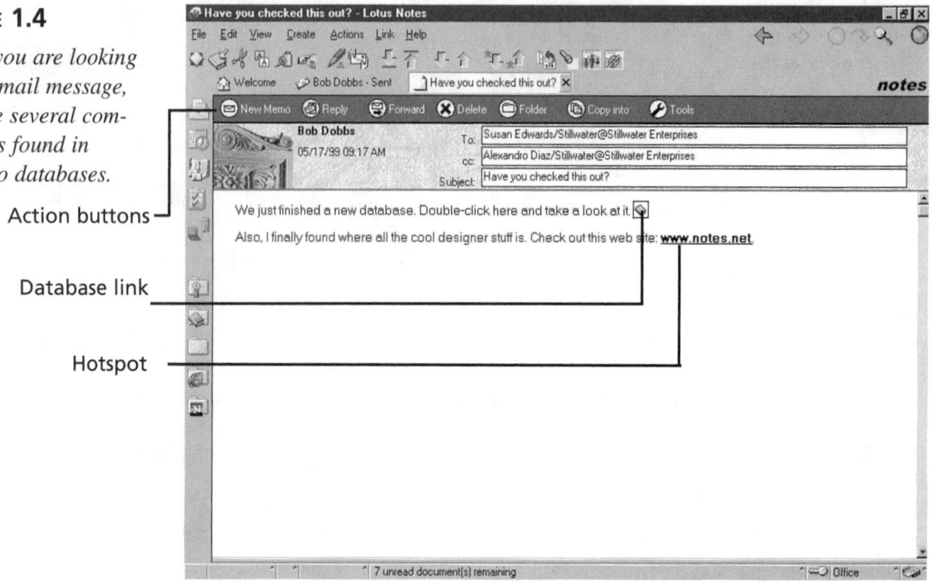

Action buttons

Database link

Hotspot

- **Shared Actions**—Shared actions are actions that are reusable in more than one form or view.

- **Hotspots**—Hotspots are areas of a form that, when clicked, run a program. See Figure 1.4.

- **Links**—Links are areas of forms or views that, when clicked, retrieve another database, view, document, or part of a document. Links can retrieve all sorts of documents, not just Notes documents. See Figure 1.4.

- **Agents**—Similar to actions in that they are small programs that users can run, agents automate tasks that are otherwise difficult or tedious for the users to carry out manually. Agents are different from actions in that they are not associated with any one view or form. Agents are usually *iterative*, meaning that they can carry out the same task again and again, on a whole group of documents.

- **Navigators and image maps**—Navigators and image maps are graphical images that contain hotspots (see Figure 1.5). If you click on a particular part of the picture, a program runs. Click on another part of the picture and another program runs. Navigators are separate Notes design elements that can appear in their own window or be embedded in a form. Image maps can only be embedded in a form, a page, or a document.

FIGURE 1.5

The simple navigator shown in this database becomes an image map when viewed in a Web browser. Clicking the hotspot opens the view in the view pane.

Hotspot

Navigator

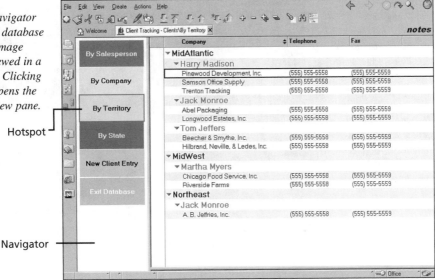

- **Pages**—Pages are like forms without fields. The database designer creates them, and they can contain text, pictures, hotspots, links—anything but fields. Designers use them to create Web pages.

- **Framesets**—Framesets are predefined arrangements of screen areas in which different documents, pages, views, folders, and navigators can appear (see Figure 1.6). They give the designer great flexibility in arrangement of objects on the screen. Designers can create multiple framesets and use them in different contexts.

- **Outlines**—Outlines are graphical representations of an application (see Figure 1.7). Users can click on the components of an outline to open specific views, documents, Web pages, or other objects. Designers use outlines to organize an application and to present site maps to users.

FIGURE **1.6**

*The Lotus
Development
Corporation site
(www.lotus.com,
viewed here in
Netscape Navigator,
not Notes) is a
Domino site.
Framesets are used on
this home page. Visit
this site often for new
and updated informa-
tion and features of
Domino (in fact, the
screen as we show it
here has probably
been changed since we
caught it).*

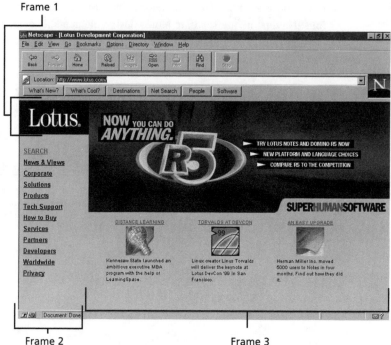

FIGURE **1.7**

*This is the outline of a
mail file. Outlines help
developers to organize
application compo-
nents. You'll learn
more about outlines
on Day 20.*

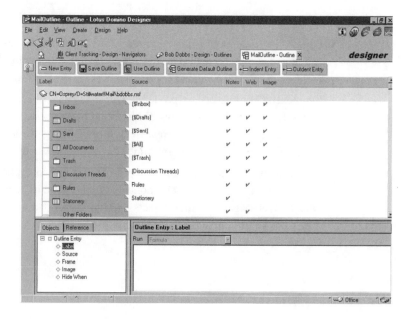

- **Resources**—These are miscellaneous shared objects. They include graphic images, Java applets, script libraries, shared fields, shared actions, and other miscellaneous objects. They can be referenced from within forms, pages, and, in some cases, views, agents, and other databases.

Objects, Properties, and Events

Notes, Domino, and Domino Designer were created with object-oriented programming tools; thus, they consist of bunches of objects that you manipulate as you use the product. Likewise, the Domino Designer is an object-oriented programming environment, and Formula Language, LotusScript, and the other programming languages that are used in Notes are all object-oriented. We program in Notes by attaching programs to objects. Objects have properties and events associated with them. We set the properties of objects, and we attach programs to the events associated with objects.

To understand what this means, it helps to realize that everything we do in everyday life involves manipulation of objects. The chair you are sitting in is an object. If it were a programming object, we might say that it is an *instance* or *member* of a *class* of objects called Chairs. The one you are sitting in has certain properties. It is hard or soft. It is gray, black, or maybe brown. It has arms or it doesn't. Events that are associated with a chair might include the acts of swiveling it or rolling it across the room.

The chair exists in a hierarchy of objects. That is, it is contained in a bigger object, the room in which you are sitting; and it contains smaller objects—the arms, seatback, wheels, legs, and cushion.

Likewise, a Notes database is an object. It has properties, such as a filename and a title. It has associated events, such as Open and Close. It is contained within the larger object of the Notes program itself. It contains smaller objects—documents, forms, views, and so on—which in turn contain smaller objects. For example, documents contain fields, pictures, and text. Each object has properties that can be set and events that can be programmed. When you program in Notes, that is exactly what you do.

You need to understand object-oriented programming when you get into the advanced features of Domino and when you use scripting languages such as LotusScript and JavaScript. As evidenced by the application you will build throughout this book, you can build Domino applications without this knowledge. For the most part, these tools are beyond the scope of this book. However, when you're ready to move on to more advanced programming, you'll want to learn about LotusScript and JavaScript. Here, at the introductory level of programming, we simply want you to be aware that you are working with an object-oriented program.

Raise Your Awareness: Think Applications

Domino applications are virtually the paradigm of groupware. Domino is perhaps the only product that was developed to embody a comprehensive definition of groupware. It includes messaging, shared databases, and a powerful set of integrated programming tools designed for rapid development and deployment of customized groupware applications. Typical Domino applications include electronic mail, information repositories, discussion databases, reference and broadcast databases of the type seen on the World Wide Web, project tracking databases, and automation of workflow.

Domino applications combine three key ingredients. They start with sharable, distributed, document-oriented databases. They include messaging in the form of fourth-generation (hypertext-enabled) electronic mail and the capability of Domino databases to pass messages to one another. They finish up with a rich, integrated, easy-to-master set of programming tools with which users can combine the first two features into flexible solutions to their business problems. The three key ingredients are

- **Shared document databases**—The heart of Domino is its shared document database technology. Domino databases consist of collections of documents contributed by users or added automatically by the system in response to various events. Domino databases are sharable in the sense that multiple users can add to and access them simultaneously.

- **Messaging**—All Domino databases can be mail enabled, meaning that they can be made to send documents to one another via Domino's built-in store-and-forward messaging capabilities. A byproduct of this is Notes Mail, which is Domino's built-in email system. Notes clients can communicate with one another via Notes Mail, and with non-Notes users through mail gateways.

- **Development tools**—In addition to its document databases and messaging capability, Domino provides a rich programming environment. Domino Designer 5 offers you a selection of programming languages, ranging from simple (the Notes @function language) to more powerful and complex (LotusScript, an ANSI BASIC-compliant language that is similar to Visual BASIC but that includes object extensions; the Lotus Notes API, a library of C/C++ functions; and more).

Shared document databases, messaging, and powerful development tools combine to permit the quick creation and customization of Domino applications to accomplish a variety of purposes, including publication of information, tracking of projects, and workflow.

Applications can consist of one or many databases, and databases can utilize all or some of the previously introduced components. Domino applications can be classified as follows:

- **Broadcast databases and reference libraries**—Domino is an ideal vehicle for storing masses of information that need to be available to masses of users (Web browsers and Notes clients). Documents can store virtually any type of information, including embedded files created in other applications. Domino provides powerful tools for locating information in its applications. These include various easily-defined, user-customizable views of applications and a full-text indexing and search engine. These databases might be populated by people adding individual documents or by programming that converts incoming data from, say, a newsfeed into Domino applications (see Figure 1.8). In this capacity, Domino duplicates the capabilities of World Wide Web servers.

FIGURE **1.8**

The Manuscripts database that you'll be creating today stores Notes documents that include embedded files or attachments from Microsoft Word, Excel, PowerPoint, and Paintbrush. It is based on the Microsoft Office Library template.

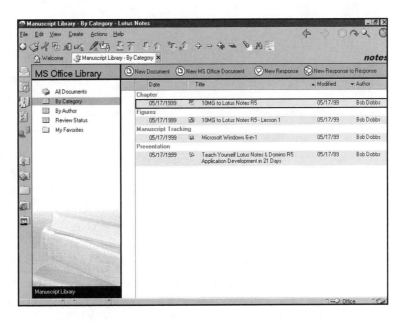

- **Discussion databases**—Domino documents can be defined as main documents or responses. As a result, one type of Domino application is the discussion database (see Figure 1.9), in which one person starts a discussion by creating a main document and other people continue the discussion by creating responses. The responses appear indented beneath the documents to which they respond in a view, making it easy for the reader to follow a discussion thread. In this capacity, Domino duplicates the functions of bulletin board systems, discussion forums in CompuServe, and UseNet newsgroups and List Servers on the Internet.

FIGURE 1.9

This discussion database is based on the Discussion template. Here, users create main topics and responses. Discussion databases are a hallmark of Notes and Domino applications.

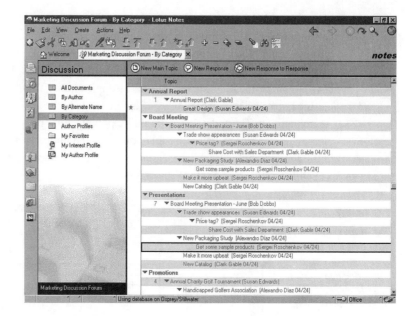

- **Tracking databases and workflow applications**—This is where Domino stands out from the groupware crowd. In a tracking database, groups of people who are collaborating on a project add documents that describe their activities (see Figure 1.10). Every member of the group can keep track of the progress of the project by referring to the database. In workflow applications, programming and messaging are added to the tracking database so that the members of the group can be notified by Domino when they have to perform some activity that is crucial to the project.

Domino workflow applications typically incorporate both messaging and shared database features to accomplish their goals. An example of a simple workflow application is an expense reporting application. At the end of a sales trip, a salesman fills out an expense report form in Notes Mail. When the salesman saves and closes the expense report, Notes mails it automatically to an expense tracking database on a Domino server; Notes also mails a message to the appropriate manager, notifying him that the expense report requires his review and approval.

The message that is received by the manager includes a link to the expense report in the tracking database. By double-clicking the link, the manager opens the expense report. The manager approves the report by placing an X in a box marked approved. When he saves the expense report, Notes affixes his signature to it, and then generates another message and mails it to the accounting clerk responsible for paying the expenses, and so the cycle continues.

FIGURE 1.10

This database uses the TeamRoom template, which allows discussion, assignments of tasks, and tracking of projects. Notice that this view displays current assignments.

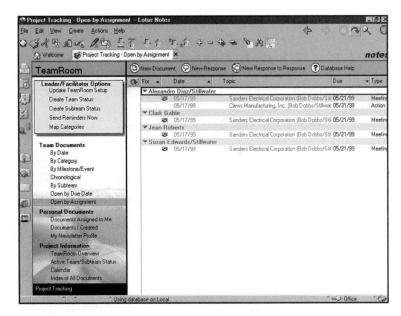

If either the manager or the accounting clerk neglects a pending task, Domino can be programmed to send a reminder. If the person who is designated to complete a task is unavailable for any reason, Domino can (if you program it that way) automatically send the notice to a substitute.

Because all the evolving information is stored in a central tracking database, anyone involved in the transaction can see its status simply by looking in the database. Form routing programs typically mail the expense report to the manager and then to the clerk. In such a system, the salesperson who submitted the expense report has no way of checking the status of his expense check other than to track down his manager and the accounting clerk and ask if they have processed it yet. With Domino, he merely has to open the expense report in the tracking database. If his manager has approved it, the report reflects that fact. If the clerk has not issued the check, the report reflects that fact as well.

Ready? Choose Your Programming Tool

You can use a wide variety of programming tools when creating Domino applications. By "tools" we mean programming languages, programming environments, and non-programming development tools. You will be using the most basic tools because this is a book for beginners. That is, you will use Domino Designer as your programming environment, and for the most part you will write formulas using the formula language, with maybe some HTML, JavaScript, or LotusScript thrown in where they provide functionality that Notes formulas cannot provide. Furthermore, you will learn how to import Java applets into your Notes databases. However, you need to know what other tools are available and under what circumstances you might use them.

Development Tools

You can develop Domino applications using Lotus's formula language, LotusScript, HTML, CGI programs, JavaScript, Java, C, C++, or BASIC. You can use Domino Designer as the environment in which you work, or you can use any Java, C, C++, or BASIC programming environment as long as you have access, from within that program, to the Notes/Domino classes. You can also use non-programming development tools such as Lotus DECS (Domino Enterprise Connection Services), NetObjects Fusion, and Microsoft FrontPage, and third-party scripting IDEs such as NetObjects ScriptBuilder.

The Notes formula Language is modeled on the @function macro language, with which users of Lotus 1-2-3 spreadsheets are probably familiar. With it, you write formulas in algebraic format (you know, (a+b)/c, that kind of thing). You manipulate Notes objects with predesigned functions known as @functions and @commands. You attach the formulas to objects in Notes databases. For non-programmers, using the formula language is the easiest way to get started writing Domino applications. It is powerful enough to accomplish all but the most esoteric Domino development chores.

LotusScript is a very powerful, BASIC-compatible scripting language with access to the Notes/Domino object classes, making it object-oriented. With it you write *scripts*, which are programs (short or long, simple or complex) that are attached to objects in Notes databases.

HTML (HyperText Markup Language) is a set of *tags* or *codes* that you can insert in a text document. An HTML interpreter (such as Lotus Notes or a Web browser) converts the tags to formatting or hotspots; or it treats them as commands to perform some action, such as retrieving a file from another computer. Standard Web pages are written in HTML. When you see them in a browser they appear as formatted text with pictures and hotspots embedded in them. But most browsers also enable you to see the *source* documents, which are the raw text documents with the tags still embedded. If you insert HTML tags in Notes forms, views, or documents, Notes or Domino passes them through to a Web browser, which interprets them.

CGI (Common Gateway Interface) is not a programming language, but rather a standardized method by which programs can pass data back and forth. Most Web servers process information that is sent to them by Web users by passing the information to another program for processing. After processing the information, the external program passes the results back to the server, and the server then sends them back out to the Web user. CGI is the method the Web server and the other program use to pass the data. Any programming or scripting language can use CGI rules to retrieve data from and pass it back to a Web server.

Domino servers generally don't need to use CGI because they process most information internally. However, Domino servers *can* use CGI, so if you know how to write CGI scripts or you have a functioning library of CGI scripts, you can incorporate them into your Domino applications.

JavaScript is an object-oriented scripting language that was created as an extension to HTML and consists of short programs (scripts) that Web programmers insert in their HTML pages. The benefit of JavaScript is that the browser—not the server—executes the scripts. That takes some of the programming burden off the Domino server and helps to minimize network traffic because the browser doesn't have to request a new page from the server every time some minor change occurs on the page in the browser. You can use JavaScript in Notes wherever you can add HTML.

Domino Enterprise Connection Services (DECS) is a forms-based tool that enables you to pull data from other (non-Notes) data sources (for example, from ODBC-compliant RDBMSes) into your Notes databases in real-time. It generally requires no programming; you simply fill in the fields in Notes forms. But to gain full benefit from DECS, you need to know how to write statements in SQL (Sequenced Query Language), which is the standard language for reading and writing relational databases. If DECS can't serve your data access needs sufficiently, there are add-on products from both Lotus (Lotus Enterprise Integrator) and third parties (for example, Replic-Action from Casahl Technology and Notrix from Percussion Software) that provide even greater connectivity between Notes databases and third-party data repositories.

C, C++, and BASIC are complete programming languages that professional programmers use to write all kinds of applications running on all kinds of computers. You can write programs in these languages in any text editor, although most programmers use special editors designed specifically for writing programs in these languages. Lotus has written libraries of code that give programmers who are using these languages access to the Notes object classes. This in turn enables us to write programs in these languages that can manipulate Notes databases and the data in them. These libraries are known generically as APIs (Application Programming Interfaces) and are trademarked by Lotus as the Hi-Test Tools for C, C++, and Visual BASIC.

Domino applications that are written in these languages generally work independently of Notes and Domino. That is, they are standalone, executable programs in their own right, whereas you write formulas, scripts (LotusScript and JavaScript), and HTML directly in Notes databases, from inside Domino Designer.

Then there is Java, a relatively new, object-oriented programming language that seems to be taking the programming world by storm. It is similar to C and C++ in its syntax, but (for esoteric reasons that we won't go into) is much easier to use and better suited to applications that are intended for use on TCP/IP networks (the Internet, intranets, and extranets). With respect to Notes, Java is a hybrid. That is, you can program some Notes objects in Java in Domino Designer. Alternately, you can write Java programs in stand-alone programming interfaces by using the Notes Object Interface (NOI), a set of Notes object classes written for Java. You can use Domino Designer to write Java agents, or use a Java programming environment of your choice (such as IBM Visual Age for Java, the Sun JDK, or Symantec's Visual Cafe) to write Domino Java agents, Java applets, or applications that interact with Notes databases. Agents or applets that are written in Java (but outside of Domino Designer) can be imported into Notes databases and attached to objects in them. Java applications that are written to work with Notes databases can stand alone like programs written in C, C++, and BASIC. The more people do business on the Internet and the more integrated Notes and Domino become with the Internet, the more important Java becomes as a tool for programming Domino applications.

Finally, you can build Web sites, Web pages, or Web scripts using third-party products such as NetObjects Fusion, Microsoft FrontPage, and NetObjects ScriptBuilder, and then import the finished Web sites or components into Domino applications. Lotus's goal is to make Domino application development easy for you by enabling you to use any tool you know, be it a Lotus tool or a third-party tool.

Which Programming Tool Should You Use?

Now that you know of so many ways to develop Domino applications, which tools should you use? In general, that depends on what you want to do and what tools you know *how* to use. Lotus has made so many tools available because they want you to be able to use the tools with which you are most comfortable.

To develop applications that are to be used by people inside Lotus Notes, the formula language and LotusScript are the preferred tools. The formula language is the only tool you can use for some programming chores. For example, you have to use it to define the values of computed fields. This is not a problem, however, because the formula language is generally the easiest of all the tools to learn and use. It is the one you will learn and use most thoroughly in this book.

1

There are many tasks that both the formula language and LotusScript can perform. Generally you will prefer the formula language in such situations because it usually takes less coding and executes faster. But if you are a whiz at LotusScript and you prefer to use it over the formula language in a given situation, God will not strike you dead because of it.

However, we generally reserve LotusScript for doing things that the formula language can't do. For example, the formula language provides no way to programmatically manipulate a database's Access Control List. As another example, the formula language can't write to an external database. But LotusScript can do both of these things.

If you plan to write applications that Web users will use, you might want to use HTML, CGI, or JavaScript in your applications. You might also want to embed Java applets in your applications or write Java agents.

Notes and Domino support HTML 4.0, and just about every HTML construct is represented in the Notes UI. But you might occasionally find that you can enhance the look or performance of a Web application by adding HTML tags to it directly. Or you might want to use non-standard HTML, DHTML, or XML. You might also want to import existing HTML documents into a Notes database. Or, if you are simply adept at writing HTML and you want to take advantage of that skill in Notes, it will accommodate you.

The same thing goes for CGI scripts. Domino doesn't need to use them, but if you know how to write them and you want to do so, or if you want to use existing CGI scripts, Notes will accommodate you.

JavaScript and Java actually enhance the way your applications perform on a Web browser, if it is capable of executing JavaScript and Java applets, of course—not all browsers are. Applications run faster because the browser executes the actions that are programmed in JavaScript and Java. A browser that couldn't execute JavaScript and Java applets would not benefit from them at all, or it might have to ask your Domino server to carry out those tasks and send it a new page—all at the expense of time and increased network traffic.

The external tools—the Hi-Test Tools for C, C++, Visual BASIC, and the Java NOI—are pretty much only of use for very high-level Notes application development or for developing specialized Domino clients. For example, you might want to write a Domino server add-in program—one that runs on the server and allows Domino to provide specialized services—or you might want to write a program that enables its users to gain some sort of specialized access to Notes data. These are the tasks that are reserved for these tools, and they are way beyond the scope of this book.

On the other hand, third-party tools such as NetObjects Fusion, NetObjects ScriptBuilder, and Microsoft FrontPage are widely known and used. If you happen to have expertise in one of these, you can leverage that expertise by building parts of your application in them, and then importing the results into Domino.

Finally, if you have to pull data from non-Notes data sources such as relational databases or transaction systems, or if you have to push data from Notes to these other data repositories, you can use either built-in tools or the add-ins that are available from Lotus and from third parties. The built-in tools include @functions (which you will learn about in this book), LotusScript and Java classes, and DECS. Add-in tools, which provide additional functionality and speed over DECS, include Lotus Enterprise Integrator and such products as Replic-Action from Casahl Technology and Notrix from Percussion Software.

Introduction to Domino Designer

Your main development tool is Domino Designer 5. In this integrated application development environment, you will create, manage, and deploy interactive applications to the Domino server.

You can launch the Designer from your Start menu or from your Notes client by clicking the **Launch Designer Client** Button on the Bookmark Bar (see Figure 1.11). If this is the first time you've launched Designer, the List of Recent Databases Bookmark Pane (on the left) is empty. Otherwise, all the databases you opened recently in Designer are listed (see Figure 1.12).

FIGURE 1.11

Launch Designer from your client using the Launch Designer Client bookmark.

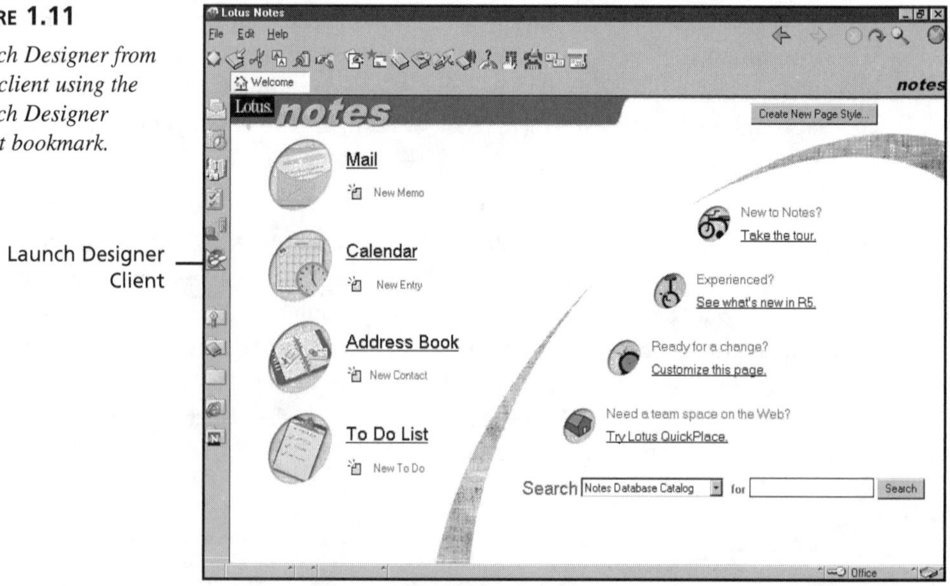

Launch Designer Client

Launching Designer in this fashion might not mean a lot to you. Another way to access Designer is to look at a database in design mode. Do this by right-clicking any database in your View Pane, such as your mail database, and select **Open in Designer** from the pop-up menu. Figure 1.12 illustrates a mail database opened in Designer.

FIGURE 1.12

The mail database is opened in Designer and displays the Forms view. To quickly close the database and return to the client, press Esc.

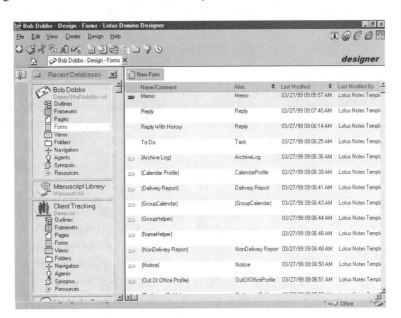

You'll be working in Designer throughout this entire book, and you learn more about this window in Day 2, "Forms 101: The Essentials of Form Design."

Set: Plan Your Application and Workflow

The most important part of application development is the planning stage. Good planning can help avoid midstream and last-minute changes that make it necessary to redesign whole sections of your application. When you plan well and have your client (users) sign off on your plan, you save time reworking an application. However, even the best-laid plans are subject to some changes, so development requires a flexible calendar and attitude.

Interview the Using Community

Working with the end user community during the planning and development stages is key to a successful application. As trainers, far too often we've trained end users in applications that were developed by consultants working by and with management, only to discover that the application is not well-suited, comprehensive, or applicable to the needs of the field personnel. Whether you are developing in-house for your employer or developing as a consultant for a client, it is imperative that you have access to and open communication with the user community to ensure a successful project. For example, management and accounting departments might always refer to and access vendor information by a vendor number, whereas people in the field might use vendor names or even shortened versions of those names (such as GE). In developing an application for use by many departments, you can enable the end user to enter—or search the application for—vendor names by acronyms.

The more you understand the reason that your group has chosen Domino as their tool, their goals for the application, and the existing workflow, the less time you'll spend back at the drawing board. Look at what methods and practices the using community is currently employing to get to their end result.

Following are the most basic steps to planning an application:

1. Establish the needs of users through interviews and by analyzing their current information access and manipulation. Don't forget interviews with the sales and marketing staff if the application includes information that will be accessed via the Web.

2. Sketch out a design for the application on paper.

3. Gather user feedback on your design, make note of any modifications to the plan, and obtain approval to incorporate or institute those changes.

4. Create the first database file.

5. Design the forms and define the fields on the form (some developers prefer to complete step 7 here so that the hide-when formulas work early in the form design phase).

6. Create the views.

7. Set up the Access Control List to specify the user access levels for the application, databases, views, forms, fields, and so forth.

8. Create the About Database, Using Database documents, and any *pages* you need.

9. Create the database icon (for Notes clients).

10. Set up a pilot program to test the application with a small group of users.

11. Make the necessary modifications to the application, based on user feedback.

12. Grant access rights to the remainder of the community.

13. Roll out the application, and provide training if necessary.

Review Workflow Needs

Workflow is the process of completing a task. It includes how information is shared and the series of steps taken along the way to completion.

When you are considering workflow it is useful to draw a picture, or flowchart, of the process. Figure 1.13 is an example of a flowchart for a multiple database application. In the first database, new project ideas are entered. Based on the availability of consultants and project managers, the project is accepted and sent to the active projects database or killed and sent to the archive database. After an active project is completed, it is sent to the archive database. This is representative of the kind of sketch you create in your planning process.

Sketch a Plan

Sketching an application is one of the simplest ways to demonstrate the workflow needs and design for the application. If you application includes mail-enabled features or multiple databases, create a flowchart of your application. It's essential to have an idea of how the application is going to work as a whole before you decide on the details. Figure 1.13 displays the application you will build during the Workshop you find at the end of each day.

This application is designed to support the project needs of a publishing company; in this case we use the example of Macmillan Computer Publishing. Our application tracks a manuscript, much like this book, from its inception to its completion. Here, you see the workflow of this project, as well as the number of databases involved. Databases are represented by cylindrical figures.

In Figure 1.13, our application workflow begins in the upper-left corner. A discussion database is used to enter proposed titles for new manuscripts. Opinions about proposed titles are gathered from the editorial staff. Managers then pass along the best of the projects and suggested titles to the Executive Committee. Executive Committee members notify the database of approvals and rejections, and after a project is approved, information is mailed to the Titles database. If a project is rejected, it is sent to the archive database. When a project arrives in the Titles in Development database, managers assign editorial staff and notices are automatically sent to the staff members' mailboxes. As the project matures, portions of the manuscripts are stored in the Manuscript library database, and notification of completion is sent to the Titles in Development database. After projects are completed, the project is automatically moved to the Completed Titles database for use by the marketing team. The Marketing team creates information to be posted to the Web, and book information is then published to the Web by the Completed Titles database.

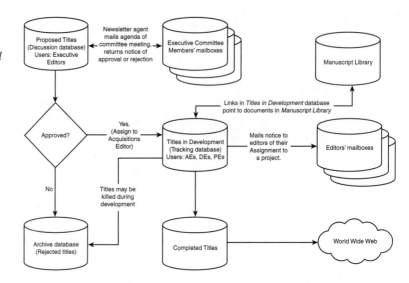

After you have sketched the flow of your design, you need to plan the individual elements of the application. Following is a list of important issues to consider when designing forms, views and fields for an application. You learn more about forms in Day 2, but
this bulleted list is designed to get you thinking in terms of Domino applications.

- What forms do you need?
- What fields of information will be contained in those forms?
- Who will populate the forms?
- What will trigger the creation of a document? For example, a salesman closing a
  sale might be the trigger for the creation of an order document. Triggers can be
  external, that is, the closing of a sale, or they can be internal, the end of a month
  when a sales report is automatically generated.
- What will the forms look like?
- What information needs to be included in which views? This is critical for helping
  users to quickly and accurately find the document they are looking for.

Of course, some of these considerations might be difficult for you to assess at this early
stage in your introduction to Domino development, but try to think of all your application needs before you begin.

1

Go! Create a Database

An application begins at the creation of the first database. When you create the database, you determine which of the following three methods to use:

- **Create a database using a template**—Using a template saves you design time. For example, the approval cycle template described later contains elements you otherwise have to build from scratch, such as views, forms, and agents.

- **Copy an existing database**—Using an existing database that contains views, forms, and other Notes elements that are similar to those you need in your database can save you time. You copy the database, but not its documents, and then you customize the database components to meet your specific needs.

- **Create a new database from a blank template**—Using a blank template enables a designer to create a database "from scratch." If the database is so different than any existing templates or databases, it's easiest to start fresh.

Domino includes several database design templates. You can choose one that is similar to the design you want to create. Templates save you time because you only have to modify the design to fit your needs.

Table 1.1 is a partial list of the application templates included in Domino R5. For this table, we chose to describe the templates that we find ourselves using most often.

Table 1.1   Notes Templates

Template	Type	Description
Discussion	Discussion	An electronic conference room for groups to share ideas. Includes archiving capabilities, interest profile (users can automatically mail themselves document links to topics of interest).
Docu Library	Reference	An electronic library to store reference documents. Includes author-initiated review cycle and archiving capabilities.
Microsoft Office	Reference	Document library for Microsoft Library Office Automatically launches, stores, and supports review cycles of documents created with Office products.

continues

Table 1.1 Continued

Template	Type	Description
Personal Journal	Discussion	An electronic diary for creating and organizing private ideas and documents. Includes graphic navigators.
Resource Reservations	Tracking	Schedules and tracks the use of conference rooms. Can customize to track other shared resources.
TeamRoom	Collaboration	Provides a workflow enabled forum for groups of people to manage projects together. (Not available in Domino Mail Server.)
Search Site	Search tool	Provides multi-database searching, however, it is primarily a tool for backward compatibility with Release 4. In Release 5, it is replaced by Domain Catalog Searches. (Not available in Domino Mail Server.)

You've finally come to the point where you can begin to create your application! The first step is to create a database from a template, from scratch, or from another database. Following are the instructions for each scenario. You might want to try all three methods. If you decide that you don't need three databases, it's simple to delete the databases. Simply highlight the database and choose **File**, **Database**, **Delete**.

Create a Database from a Template

Use the following steps to create a database based on a Domino template:

1. Choose **File**, **Database**, **New** from the menu. The New Database dialog box appears (see Figure 1.14). Local should appear in the Server list box. Accept this selection.

Caution

Make it local!   Always create a new database on your own workstation hard disk or in a personal directory or folder on your network to prevent users from accessing the application before you're finished designing it.

FIGURE 1.14

The New Database dialog box with a template selected. To learn more about a template before you commit to it, click the About button to see the About Database document. This document, if it is available, contains descriptive template information.

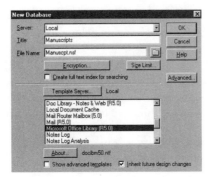

2. In the Title box, type the name of the database as you want it to appear on the database icon and in the list of databases for the server. The maximum length is 96 characters. Try to keep it short and simple so it's easy to see and to remember.

3. Enter a filename in the File Name space or use the one that Notes has entered. Depending on the operating system your computer uses, you might be limited to eight characters for the filename (we always find that it's better to stay with this limit with database filenames). Notes automatically adds a period and the file extension NSF.

4. Ignore the **Encryption** button. It is for use by *users* who take individual copies of sensitive databases out of the office with them on their laptops. You learn more about encryption on Day 7, "Sleep Soundly: Secure Your Application."

5. Ignore the **Size Limit** button and the **Create Full text index for searching button** for now. These are considerations you take when you are ready to roll out the database as described in Day 21, "Roll Out and Maintain Your Application."

6. From the list of available templates, choose the one on which you are basing your application.

Tip

Template files are stored locally *and* on the server. You might have different templates on your server than those on your workstation. Click the **Template Server** button and select your server to see if the templates on the server differ from those that are available on your workstation.

7. Do not check **Inherit future design changes.** You learn more about design inheritance on Day 21. Click **OK** and close the dialog box.

> **Inherit future design changes**   When you base a new database on a template, you effectively make a copy of the template, as well as its forms, views, and so on. If you choose to inherit future design changes, changes to the original template overwrite changes you made to your database. Therefore, if you don't want to lose your customization of the database, choose not to inherit design changes.

Create a Database From Scratch

If you must, you can create a database from scratch. Remember that this is working the hard way in that you have to design everything in the database from the ground up. One of the exercises in our workshop involves creating a database from scratch; we've included it for your experience, not because we couldn't find a template to suite our needs. In your work environment, when everything seems to be needed yesterday, you are advised to use templates whenever you can. If no template meets your needs, so be it. To create a database from scratch, choose **File**, **Database**, **New** and follow steps 2–5 of "Create a Database from a Template," selecting a **—Blank—** template to start the application from scratch. Click on **OK** to close the dialog box.

Create a Database From Another Database

Just as basing your design on a template saves time, copying an existing database can also save design time. After you make a copy of a database, you can modify the copy to meet your needs, adding forms, fields, views, and so on. To create a database based upon an existing database, select the database by clicking on it, or opening it from the menu, then choose **File**, **Database**, **New Copy.** The copy database dialog box appears as shown in Figure 1.15

FIGURE 1.15

The Copy Database dialog box. Choose Database design and documents only if you want to copy all the documents into your new database.

Copy Database "Proposed Titles"	
Server: Local	OK
Title: Rejected Titles	Cancel
File Name: Rejected.nsf	Help
Encryption...	Size Limit...
Copy:	
○ Database design and documents	
● Database design only	
□ Access Control List	
□ Create Full Text index	

Following steps 3 and 4 of "Create a Database from a Template," give your database a title and a filename. Ignore the **Size Limit** and **Encryption** buttons for now. This is only important at the time of roll out (see Day 21). Select **Database design only** unless you want to copy all the documents into your new database.

Disable **Access Control List** because you'll want to create your own ACL for the database. Another reason to disable the Access Control List (ACL) is that you might not have designer access to the database you're copying, and you'd be denied access to your new one if you copied the ACL. For more on the ACL, see Day 7). Ignore **Create Full Text index**—you don't need this now and it is discussed further on Day 21. Click **OK** to close the dialog box and you're on your way!

Note | **Copying gives you rights!**—Seven levels of database access exist. Only people who are designated as Managers or Designers can change the design of a database. However, when you *copy* a database to your hard drive you are, by default, the Manager.

Access Database Properties

Properties boxes provide additional information about Notes and Domino components and enable you to perform and set features and functions of a particular component. For example, you can change the title of a database or the color of text in a Properties box. An invaluable tool for learning about and using Notes and Domino, Properties boxes are available for many types of components such as databases, fields, text, forms, views, and so forth.

The beauty of Properties boxes is that they can be left open while you work. Unlike a dialog box, which must be closed before you continue working in an application, Properties boxes are context-sensitive. Open a Properties box for a database and you see database property information. Keep that box open and click on a view or a document, and the Properties box changes to display the view or document properties.

To view the Properties of a component, right-click the component and choose x Properties, where x is the name of the component (see Figure 1.16).

FIGURE 1.16

The database Properties box for the mail database contains a great deal of information about the database. Click the Design tab to view the template on which the database was based.

You learn more about Properties boxes throughout this book, and you will use Properties boxes each time you design a new component for your application.

Summary

In today's lesson you learned that Domino *applications* can be delivered to both Notes Clients and Web browsers, and that the Notes R5 client is a universal client—useful for accessing Domino applications as well as Web pages. You also saw that the success of any application begins with careful and thorough planning and preparation.

Many programming tools are available to you as a Domino developer, but your primary development environment is the Domino Designer. Domino applications can consist of one database that can be an information repository. They can also consist of many databases and track complex workflows. Finally, databases can be created from scratch, from design templates, or from existing databases.

Q&A

Q Because Domino applications can be delivered to Notes Clients as well as Web Browsers, do I need to differentiate or define my audience during the planning stage?

A As a developer, all your design work is done in the Designer regardless of audience. However, when you are designing for the Web you need to consider the following:

- Databases might appear differently when viewed from a Notes Client and from a Web Browser. Browsers control some display qualities.

- Web browsers don't have Notes menus, so browsers can't perform tasks such as creating forms and editing documents without additional design elements added to the database by you. In other words, you'll add buttons for creating forms and editing documents. You learn how to add these buttons later, but when you are planning and sketching forms, add these kinds of buttons for future reference.

Q **You make Domino sound like the answer to all business problems and needs. Is this really true? Are there applications that are not well suited for the Domino environment?**

A You probably need to think about developing your application with a program other than Notes in the following situations:

- **When the application involves continual access to real-time**—Notes is not structured for continuous connections and immediate updating of information: for example, high volume transaction-based systems needed for stock trading, and certainly not where currency is measured in milliseconds.

- **The application requires complex calculations**—Notes can handle mathematical functions, but not the complex, processing-intensive calculations that are common to scientific or financial services. This is the province of spreadsheets or programming languages.

- **Your application needs query-based or report-based access**—Notes uses views and full-text search to locate data in a database. It doesn't support SQL query techniques, and it doesn't have a report writer.

Workshop

The purpose of this workshop is to guide you in putting your new skills to work. Here, we provide information on our application as illustrated in Figure 1.17. Each day, you will add components to your application until you have built an application similar to ours. Today, you start by creating some of the application databases. These databases are created by using templates and by building from scratch:

- **Proposed Titles**—Create this database from scratch, using the Blank template. Use the filename Proposed.nsf. In this database, new titles will be proposed, discussed, and either accepted or rejected for publication.

- **Rejected Titles**—Copy the Proposed Titles database to create this database. Use the filename Rejected.nsf. This database will hold the rejected book titles as an archive.

- **Manuscript Library**—Create this database from a template (Microsoft Office Library). Use the filename Manuscpt.nsf. As new pieces of manuscript arrive from the authors and editors, they are stored in this database. As they arrive, notification is sent to the editors and to the tracking database, Titles in Development.

By creating these databases, you have made a good start on your application (see Figure 1.17). You will create the remaining databases on future days as you learn new skills that will be applied to the other databases.

FIGURE 1.17

The databases you created in the work-shop are the beginning of our workflow application.

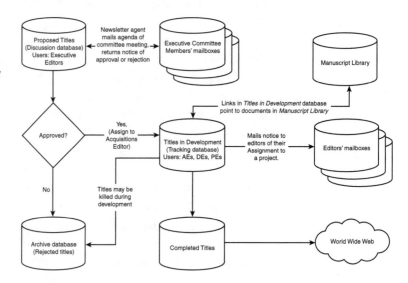

On the accompanying CD, you find examples of the databases that represent this work-shop. When you complete the workshop, compare your databases to ours or use ours as a study guide. The CD contains folders labeled Day1, Day2, Day3 and so forth and each contains completed workshop databases for the corresponding workshop. In today's folder (Day 1) you find:

PTDay1.nsf the Proposed Titles database at the end of Day 1

MSDay1.nsf the Manuscript database at the end of Day 1

RTDay1.nsf the Rejected Titles database at the end of Day 1

DAY 2

Forms 101: The Essentials of Form Design

Before you create a Domino form, consider sketching the form on paper. Pay close attention to the layout of the form in relation to how it will be used, and consider what the users will see in one screen of information. Keep in mind the following design tips:

- The most important field information needs to be at the top of your form so that users can quickly read through documents without having to scroll the page for the most important or critical information on the form.
- Present a consistent look with the forms in your application. For example, always put important and basic information (header type information such as customer name) in the same location on each of your forms. This helps users when they need to locate information using different forms.
- Group related information together. For example, if your form contains customer information, group his address and contact information together, his purchasing history together, and so forth.

- Space the text and fields on the form so that they are easy to read. We strongly recommended that you use tables to organize your form and present a clean, uniform look. Tables also help you to align fields.

- Avoid centering text, except at the top of a form or in table columns. Centered text can get lost in other locations on the form.

- Use colors to differentiate text that is *static*, or permanently displayed on the form, from text that is the result of users entering data in a field.

- Add graphics and colored backgrounds for variety in your application, and to help users differentiate between forms.

- Plan which fields you want to include on the form, what types of information needs to be entered in those fields, and which fields need to be computed. You learn about computed fields on Day 3, "Take a Field Trip: Add Fields," but for now, think of computed fields as those whose value will be calculated. Domino computes fields in order: from the top of your form to the bottom, and from the left of your form to the right. Therefore, fields that are dependent on the contents of other computed fields must be placed to the right of or below those other computed fields.

- Consider who will access this form. Web browsers do not include "Notes" menus; therefore, you need to create methods for Web users to create and edit new documents. Prepare for this by adding buttons to your sketched form and labeling them something such as "Edit document." This will be a reminder to you to include this functionality in your design process.

When you have the design mapped out, you can begin to create your forms.

Types of Forms

The first design decision you need to make about a form is its *type*: whether this form will be a *Document*, a *Response*, or a *Response-to-Response*. When you create the form itself (see "Create a Form" later in this lesson), you set the document type in the Form Properties box. This isn't necessarily the first action you take when creating the form, but it is certainly a decision you need to make prior to creating and saving the form. Types of forms are as follows:

- **Document**—Use this type of form to create main documents, that is, documents that are not in response to any other documents. For example, in a discussion database, users would use a form of type Document to compose Main Topics. This is the type of form users will use most frequently.

- **Response**—Use this type of form to create documents that are in response to main documents. For example, in a discussion database, users would use a form of type Response to compose responses to main topics. Response documents are "children" and main documents are "parents" in a response hierarchy.

- **Response-to-Response**—Use this type of form to create documents that are in response to main documents, response documents, or other response-to-response documents. For example, in a discussion database, if someone wanted to respond to a response, they would have to use a form of response-to-response type to do it. If they tried to respond using a Response form, their response would be to the main document, not the response. Response-to-response documents can be children, grandchildren, or great-grandchildren in a hierarchy.

2

NEW TERM   **Hierarchical view**—A view that clearly displays the response hierarchy, in which the original main topic is the parent, the response to the parent is the child, and the response-to-response is the descendent of either the main topic or the response. A hierarchical view shows the responses and response-to-response documents indented under the parent document to show how the descendents relate to the parent in a conversation.

If the preceding definitions make your head spin, don't feel bad about it. These definitions make everyone's head spin. Part of the confusion arises from your confusion about the difference between forms and documents. Designers create forms. Users use the forms to create documents. The three kinds of forms allow users to create three kinds of documents: one kind that stands alone and two kinds that respond to others. Documents stand alone. Responses respond to documents. Responses to responses can respond to documents, responses, or other responses to responses.

We care about these distinctions in hierarchical views, which display the response relationships among documents. In non-hierarchical views, on the other hand, the response relationships disappear—we can't tell which documents respond to which, and we don't care.

Figure 2.1 displays the form types in a discussion database hierarchical view.

However, response hierarchies aren't limited to discussion databases. Use them wherever you want to develop a hierarchical view later. An example of how these types of forms are used is in a database designed to track customer information. In this scenario, you gather information about a customer company, as well as about each person you have contact with at the company. You want to store information about your activities with respect to each customer or contact. In this example, you start by creating a form called "Customer Profile," which includes basic information about a customer. This form is the form type *Document*.

FIGURE 2.1

*A hierarchical view
shows a main docu-
ment with the response
document indented
beneath it, and the
response-to-response
document indented
beneath the response
document. The main
purpose of using these
different forms is to
establish this hierar-
chy. The user is usually
not aware that a form
is a response-to-
response type.*

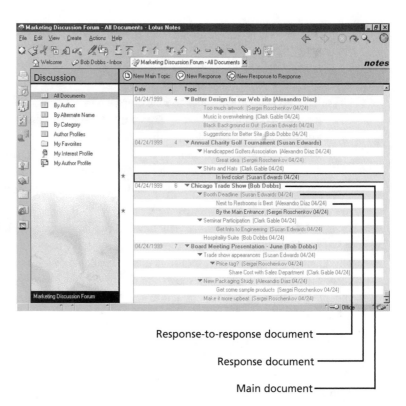

Response-to-response document ⎯⎯⎯⎯

Response document ⎯⎯⎯⎯

Main document ⎯⎯⎯⎯

Because there might be more than one contact per customer, you'll want to create a second form, "Contact Profile," that contains information about a contact. Each Contact
Profile relates to a particular company; therefore, the Contact Profile form is naturally a
form of type *Response*. Because you use a Response form, Contact Profiles display
beneath their parent, the Customer Profile forms, and can inherit information from that
form so that users don't have to fill in existing information, such as the company name
and address. Using a response form, each Contact Profile that is created is automatically
associated with some Customer Profile. When you create a new Contact Profile (person
information), you first have to select the Customer Profile (company information).

Finally, you want to create forms for different types of actions, such as a meeting or
phone conversation record. Because these activities can be associated with either a
Customer *or* a Contact, they would be of form type *Response-to-response*, allowing them
to display indented beneath the Customer Profile or the Contact Profile or another Action
document.

Note

> You'll find lots of terms in Notes and Domino that have two meanings. *Document* is a type of form, yet *document* is a collection of filled-in fields (similar to a record) that can display in different types of forms: response, response-to-response, and documents. Even from the beginning of our experiences with Lotus Notes, it seemed as if no one at Lotus was watching the company's use of terms; as a result, students got pretty confused. We noticed in the Release 5 documentation that Lotus began to call the form type Document a *main topic form*. That's a step in the right direction; however, they didn't change this name officially, and the Properties box still uses "document" as the form type label. Whew! Help screens tell you to create a *main topic form*, but the Properties boxes call it a *document*. Besides terms that have double meanings (*navigator* is another one), Lotus confused everyone when they renamed the server products in release 4.5; then we had to deal with "Domino" and "Lotus Notes." Even now, there are times when we aren't always certain if an object or feature should be called a *Notes* feature or a *Domino* feature. On the up side, working with the product and getting hands-on experience helps to clear up confusion. The hundreds of Certified Lotus Professionals that we have trained have proved to us that in the end, we all get over it.

Forms are stored in the database and are used to display document information—they act like a template to display information in the manner that best suits your needs. You can have many forms in a database, each designed for a specific purpose. Depending on your needs, you don't necessarily have to create all three types of forms.

You saw how the different types of forms are well suited for discussion databases and tracking databases, but what do you use when you have no need for this type of hierarchy? Suppose you have a form in which the salespeople supply customer information—a sort of everything-you-ever-wanted-to-know about this customer (Customer Info). The order department might have access to this information, but might need to know only the customer's address and phone number. A separate form for the order department might display only relevant information (Customer Address). A third form can be designed for the purchasing department, including information about your customers' products and services—inherited from the Customer Info form. All three of these forms can be of the type *Document*.

Form Components

Now that you know the *types* of forms you can create, you need to know what can be contained within a form, or the components of a form. The most obvious component is the *field*. Forms without fields aren't forms at all; they're *Pages*. Consider this: Forms are essentially templates or frameworks for entering and viewing database information, and the content of a form changes from document to document (for example, from customer to customer). Pages contain uniquely composed information that is static and that does not change at all. So, without fields, is a form a form? We think not!

Forms, however, do not contain fields alone. Domino forms can contain many elements that help to structure data in a document. These elements include the following:

- **Actions Buttons and Hotspots**—Used to automate tasks by providing a single-click environment for the users.

- **Applets**—Java Applets Programs that are written in Java, for instance an animated logo, that can only run inside of a Java-enabled program such as a Web browser (for example, the R5 Notes client). Contrast to a Java application, which is a stand-alone program.

- **Attachments**—Files that are attached to forms can be detached or viewed locally by the user, and they can be launched from every document created with that form.

- **Embedded objects, Controls, and elements**—Embedded objects (OLE) can be viewed and updated in a form and created in a different OLE-supported product. Embedded controls allow a browser to upload files and view the schedules of specified users. Embedded elements are Domino/Notes elements such as the outline, view, folder pane, navigator, and date picker.

- **Fields**—Fields are defined by their type, with each type of field containing a particular type of data such as number fields or text fields. You learn more about fields on Day 3. Fields can also exchange data with other products (as in Notes/FX fields).

- **Pictures**—Pictures (graphics) that are placed on a form appear in every document that uses that form. Graphics can be converted to imagemaps by adding hotspots. You learn more about Graphics on Day 12, "Beautify Your Application."

- **Horizontal Rule**—A horizontal line used to separate parts of a form or to make a form more visually interesting.

- **HTML (Hypertext Markup Language)**—A collection of instructions or tags that tell a browser program how to display a document (for example, when to bold or italicize). HTML tags typically appear embedded within a document, set apart from the document text by angle brackets.

- **Imagemaps**—A graphic that contains hotspots.

- **Layout Regions**—Used on a form or subform, a fixed length design area in which related elements can be dragged and moved easily and can be displayed in ways not possible elsewhere on the form. Layout regions are not supported in Web browsers.

- **Links**—Links are similar to Web hyperlinks in that they take the user to other databases, views, documents, or URLs. Links can be designed to automatically launch when a user opens a document that uses your form.

- **Sections**—Collapsible areas of a document. Helpful for managing large documents. When collapsed, sections display one line of information; when expanded, sections reveal their entire contents.

- **Subforms**—As its name implies, a subform is a form within a form, stored as a single object in Domino. Subforms can appear in forms based on conditions (formulas); for example, if a user places an X in a field to indicate that they are a first time visitor to your site, a subform opens in the current form, asking them to supply registration information.

- **Tables**—Tables that are placed on forms appear in every document created with that form. Tables are useful for organizing information, aligning fields, and positioning other elements on the form. Tables can be "invisible" to users if the designer opts to omit borders. Tables can contain nested tables, and tables have numerous formatting options. You learn more about advanced table formatting on Day 12.

- **Text**—Text can be placed anywhere on a form. Text that is placed directly on the form and is not contained within a field is referred to as *static* text because it does not change. Text formatting options are numerous; you learn about advanced text formatting on Day 5, "Forms 102: Enhance Form Appearance and Design."

Create a Form

To create a form, first open the database in which you are going to add your form. Choose **Create**, **Design**, **Form** from the menu. The Design Window appears as shown in Figure 2.2.

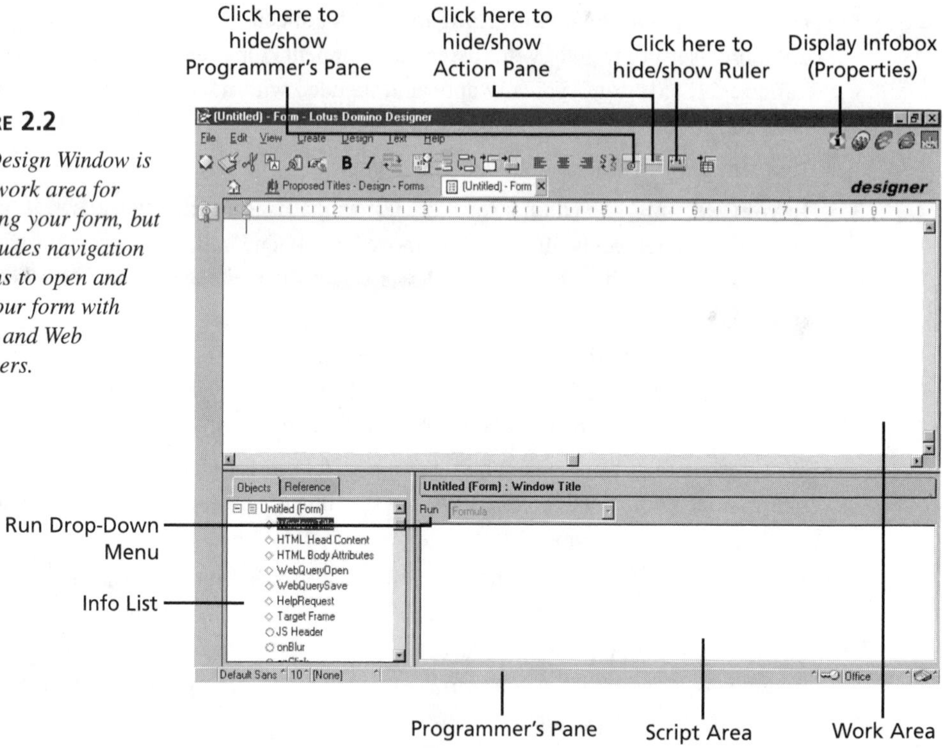

Click here to   Click here to
hide/show   hide/show   Click here to   Display Infobox
Programmer's Pane   Action Pane   hide/show Ruler   (Properties)

FIGURE 2.2

*The Design Window is
your work area for
building your form, but
it includes navigation
buttons to open and
test your form with
Notes and Web
browsers.*

Run Drop-Down
Menu

Info List

Programmer's Pane   Script Area   Work Area

Caution

Hide or show the Programmer's Pane, by clicking the icon on the SmartIcon
bar whose pop up label says "View Show/Hide Design Pane". This label is
incorrect. Clicking this icon actually shows and hides the Programmer's Pane.
The icon label is apparently left over from Release 4.6, in which the pane
formerly known as Designer is renamed in Release 5 to Programmer's.
Whew! If you hide the Design Pane and want to get it back, click the Recent
Databases icon on the Bookmark Bar. Hopefully, Lotus will fix this soon.

You are now in the design window. The Work pane is a blank page that will become your
form. This is similar to looking at a blank document in a word processing program.

Just below the Work Pane is the Programmer's Pane where you associate programming
code (the left pane) to an object within a design element (right pane) In the script area,
the Run field is grayed out unless the selected object can be programmed in more than
one language. For example, certain events can only be programmed using Lotus Formula

Language, whereas others can be programmed with Formula Language, simple actions, LotusScript, or JavaScript. Watch the Run field as you add objects to your form and as you move around your form. It's context-sensitive and changes as you select different objects in your form. When programming is attached to an object, the programming appears in the formula pane. You'll learn more about the Run options later.

The Task Button reflects the name of your form (untitled), followed by the object name (Form). When you name your form, the form name replaces (untitled) on the task bar and any place in Designer that refers to this form.

It's easy to create your very first form by placing the static text on the form and adding the fields later. We suggest this because you haven't yet learned about fields and field options. Place your form heading information first and then use tables to align the balance of the form, placing static text in one cell and leaving room for a field in the cell to the right of the static text or below the static text. You learn about fields on Day 3, so you'll be revisiting your form then to add the fields.

Note

You can size the Programmer's Pane by dragging on its top border. To make it disappear from the screen, double-click on the border or choose **View, Design pane** from the menu. Do the same thing to make it reappear (the border is right above the status bar). Also, display SmartIcons (see Figure 2.2) by choosing **File, Preferences, SmartIcon Settings**, and checking the **Icon Bar** checkbox.

Name your form and assign its basic properties. To do this, you need to open the Form Properties box (see Figure 2.3). Choose **Design, Form Properties** from the menu; right-click the Work Pane window and choose **Form Properties** from the shortcut menu. (See Figure 2.3.)

Note that lots of people refer to Notes Properties boxes as Infoboxes. In fact, Lotus calls Properties boxes both *Properties box*es and *Infoboxes* interchangeably. When you right click an object, you can choose to view it's properties from the pop up menu. But if you hold your mouse over the navigation buttons on the top right of Designer, you find an icon labeled "Display Infobox". It's all the same—*Properties box*es and infoboxes.

Form Names and Synonyms

Enter the name of the form in the Form name box, and then click once on the small check mark button at the end of the box. By clicking that button you activate a check of your syntax. The form name can be up to 64 characters long for a simple name, and another 64 characters for each name viewed in a cascaded menu, for a total of 32 bytes, which is different than 32 characters. However, you should keep the name short, simple, and descriptive. You can use any combination of letters, numbers, spaces, and punctuation. Be aware that Notes form names are case sensitive, so you need to give all forms unique names or Domino does not know which form to use at runtime.

FIGURE 2.3

The Form Info tab of the Form Properties box (aka InfoBox)contains the form name and a place to enter comments.

Check to include form in Search Builder dialog box to help find items by form name

Check to not store in the document the name of the user who creates it

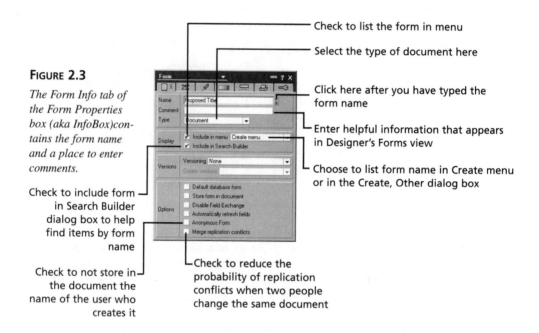

Check to list the form in menu

Select the type of document here

Click here after you have typed the form name

Enter helpful information that appears in Designer's Forms view

Choose to list form name in Create menu or in the Create, Other dialog box

Check to reduce the probability of replication conflicts when two people change the same document

The form name affects those who will be using the form to create documents. As a Notes user, you are accustomed to creating documents by accessing forms listed under **Create** on the Notes menu bar. As a Notes designer, you determine whether and how your Notes forms are to appear on that menu (see "Selecting Form Properties" in this lesson). In naming your form, consider how the form name will appear on the Create menu:

- **Accelerator Keys (Alt+key combinations)**—By naming all forms with a unique first letter, you can enable users to move quickly through menu choices by typing the underlined letter of a menu entry, combined with **Alt**. The default accelerator key is the first letter of the name. If you create two forms that begin with the same letter, the form's default accelerator key becomes the first letter that is not used by a preceding form. This can be awkward for your users. If you can't assign form names with different first letters, include an underscore (_) in the form name just before the letter you want to use as the shortcut. Make sure you don't use the same letter more than once in the same menu list. For example, in Figure 2.3, the name of the form is "Proposed Title." Normally, the underscore appears under the *P* because that is the first letter of the form name and no other entry on the Create menu starts with the same letter. However, by typing the form name as "Proposed _Title" the menu changes, as in Figure 2.4.

FIGURE 2.4

Entering the form name as "Proposed _Title" changes the T *to the accelerator key.*

- **Order**—The names on the Create menu are normally listed in alphabetical order. If you want the forms in a different order, you'll have to put numbers or letters in front of the names. Numbers work well for fewer than nine forms, but when you add more than nine, the form named "10" appears in a list before the form named "2" because the sort order is alphabetical. In such a case, use letters instead, as shown in Figure 2.5. (You might not be able to add more than nine entries because more entries would be grouped under "Other," which you would then click to see a complete list of forms.)

FIGURE 2.5

Using numbers or letters in the form name sets the order in which forms appear in the user menu.

- **Cascading**—If you have several forms with the same words at the beginning, or forms that are response forms to a parent document, you might want to create a *cascading* menu to group them together. In the form name of each form, enter the main name followed by a backslash (\), and then enter the name that you want to appear on the cascading menu. For example, if you have a "Book Proposed Title" form and "Book Response" for replies about books, you might name them "Books\Proposed Title" and "Book\Response." Book appears on the **Create** menu, and when you click **Book**, a cascading menu displays "Proposed Titles" and "Response" (see Figure 2.6). Just be sure to enter the beginning name the same way because *Book* appears as a different entry from *book*.

FIGURE 2.6

You can also use cascading to force a custom ordering on the menu so that you group names instead of numbering or lettering them.

- **Synonyms**—Synonyms are alternate form names that don't appear on the menu but that can be used in formulas. For example, a form named "Book\Proposed Title" might work well for users but not for the designer who has to type out that name in a formula. Make a practice of using synonyms. To create a form name synonym, enter a vertical bar (|) after the form name and then enter the synonym (Book\Proposed Title|Title), as shown in Figure 2.7. By the way, it's also okay to use multiple synonyms: Just precede each synonym with another vertical bar. Synonyms must be unique within a design class; that is, a view and a form can have the same synonym, but not two forms, within one database.

FIGURE 2.7

Using a form synonym enables you to change a form name without having to change formulas in which you've referenced the form.

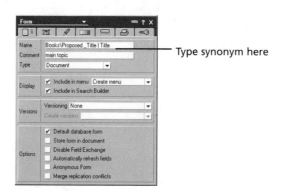

Type synonym here

A short form name is no excuse for omitting synonyms. For example, say a form called "Orders" is part of a database you completed and rolled out six months ago. Today, the order department expands its services and now wants to call the existing "Orders" form "Domestic Orders." A design request has been made for you to create an "International Orders" form, which needs new fields added to support international commerce. Renaming the "Orders" form "Domestic Orders" can have an unpredictable effect on the documents created with the form "Orders," particularly if you

used the form name in any formulas. Creating a synonym—
"Orders|Orders"—enables you to continue to use "Orders" in your formulas,
and renaming the form "Domestic Orders|Orders" has no negative effect.

2

- **Consistency**—When you have multiple databases with similar forms that contain the same information, standardize the names so that users can recognize them easily. For example, "Client Contact," "Client Call Report," and so forth. In fact, you might want to define a company-wide standard for naming forms (and all other Notes objects).

After you've named your form, save it. There are several ways to save the form:

- Choose **File**, **Save** from the menu or press **Ctrl+S**. This saves the form but enables you to continue working on it without closing the Designer window.
- Choose **File**, **Close** from the menu, or press **Esc**. This closes the window and Designer and then prompts you to save the form with the question, "Do you want to save this form?" Answer **Yes** to save it, **No** to close it without saving it, or **Cancel** to go back to the form without saving or closing it.

After you save your form, you can see the form listed in the forms design view (see Figure 2.8). To do so, expand Design in the Navigator Pane and choose **Forms**. You see your form in the View pane. Double-click to open it in Design mode.

Insert Tables

We always use tables on our forms. Tables organize information on the form and are especially useful for creating side-by-side paragraphs or evenly spaced fields. Tables are particularly important when creating forms for Web users. They help with the alignment of fields and text when Domino converts your Domino form to a Web form.

When we use tables, we like to use a few small tables as opposed to one big one. In this way, editing is an easier task and tables can be broken into sections on the form.

Tip

Tabs, indents, outdents, and extra spaces are not supported on the Web. If you are designing forms for Web use, rely on tables to lay out the text and fields.

To add a table to your form, position your cursor where you want the table to begin. Choose **Create**, **Table** from the menu. The Create Table dialog box appears (see Figure

2.9). Enter the number of Rows and Columns you want in the table. You can always insert and delete rows and columns later if needed. Select the Table Width you want the table to use: **Fits Window** (adjusts width of table to current size of window) or **Fixed width** (stays the size you set the column widths). Click the button for the Table Type you want to create; **Standard** meets most needs. Click **OK** to insert the new table into your form.

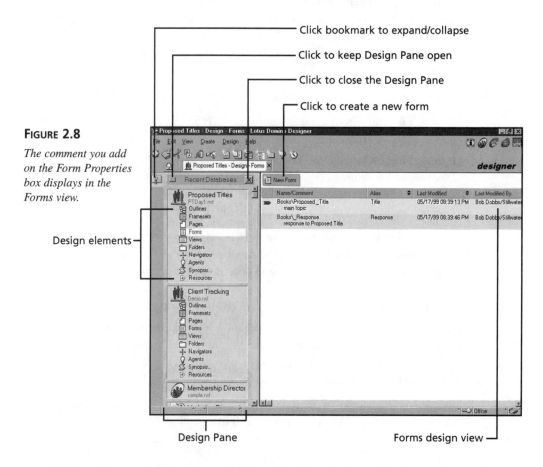

FIGURE 2.8

The comment you add on the Form Properties box displays in the Forms view.

Click bookmark to expand/collapse

Click to keep Design Pane open

Click to close the Design Pane

Click to create a new form

Design elements

Design Pane

Forms design view

Table cells can contain static text (the text that doesn't change in a form), fields, and graphics. They can be formatted in many ways—with predefined styles, colors, fill colors, border styles, and drop shadows. Domino even supports the use of nested tables, tabbed tables, a table that shows a different row every two seconds, and animated tables that show a different row based on the value of a field.

FIGURE 2.9

Our tables frequently involve two columns— one for the static text and another for the fields. This helps line up the fields and keep the field responses across from the field labels.

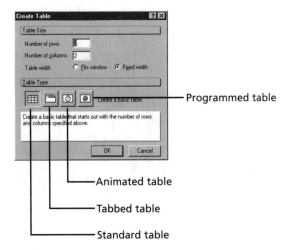

2

Programmed table

Animated table

Tabbed table

Standard table

Add Static Text

Static text is the text that appears on the form but isn't part of a field. It tells the user what he is to enter in a field and provides instructions on how to complete the form. To enter static text, position your cursor where you want to place the static text on the form and simply type the text. Use word processing techniques to edit text and move around the form. For example, you have to insert hard returns (press the Enter key) several times to insert text in a blank area of the form, other than at the first line. Use the **Tab** key to indent text, and use the alignment SmartIcons (left, right, center) to align text. Again, consider the use of tables instead of tabbing around the form for placement. One of the most efficient methods for applying formatting options to your text is to use the Text Properties box (see Figure 2.10). The Text Properties box displays the current text formatting selections. In it you can change font sizes, colors, attributes, and so forth without having to access several menus. To open the Text Properties box, choose **Text, Text Properties** from the menu or right-click within the text. Shrink the Text Properties box to provide useful tools while taking up minimal space (see Figure 2.11).

The text formatting options are all listed in the Properties box, so you don't need to access the menu in Designer. When you click an option in the Properties box, Designer applies the formatting immediately, enabling you to see the effects of your change without having to close the Properties box. If you don't select text prior to opening the dialog box, Designer applies the formatting options you select to the next text you type at the insertion point.

FIGURE 2.10

The Text Properties box remains open until you close it, which enables you to format text throughout your form without opening and closing dialog boxes or menus.

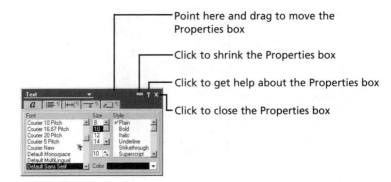

Point here and drag to move the Properties box

Click to shrink the Properties box

Click to get help about the Properties box

Click to close the Properties box

FIGURE 2.11

Even when you shrink the Text Properties box, you have access to many text attributes. There are also buttons for creating attachments and tables and for importing pictures.

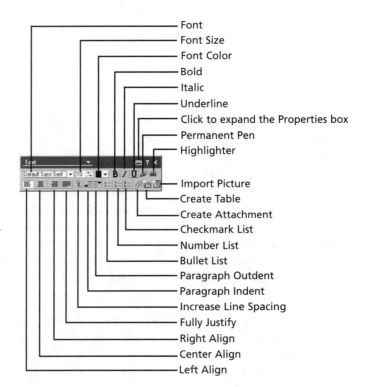

Font
Font Size
Font Color
Bold
Italic
Underline
Click to expand the Properties box
Permanent Pen
Highlighter
Import Picture
Create Table
Create Attachment
Checkmark List
Number List
Bullet List
Paragraph Outdent
Paragraph Indent
Increase Line Spacing
Fully Justify
Right Align
Center Align
Left Align

The default font in Notes is Helvetica (Helv). Lotus recommends a sans serif font such as Helv because it's easier to read onscreen. But if the documents that are created from the form are likely to be printed, you might want to use a serif font such as Times New Roman because serif fonts are considered easier to read in print than are sans serif fonts.

If you plan to use the form on the Web, remember that Helv and Times New Roman aren't supported on the Web. The look of your page depends greatly on the default font of the user's Web browser and the fonts available on the user's computer. When you use Arial instead of Helv, you're specifying a font that is available to all Windows users.

 Serif/Sans Serif—Serifs are the short, horizontal bars at the tops and bottoms of text characters. If a typeface has serifs, it's known as a serif typeface or serif font. If it does not have serifs, it's known as a sans serif font.

Be judicious in your use of font types, colors, and sizes. Decorative fonts might be difficult to read in small sizes. Simple is best. Stick with Arial and Times New Roman for Windows users.

2

> **Tip**
>
> Don't go crazy with font styles and colors. Keep forms easy to read—a good rule of thumb is no more than three different fonts per form. More than that and eyes will cross!

Much of the text Properties box contains formatting options that are pretty easy to understand and apply. Like a word processing program, if you select text first and then change formatting in the Properties box, the formatting changes are applied to the selected text. If you change properties before you type text, the formatting is applied to the next text you type at the current insertion point. Your word processing and Notes client skills will be very helpful to you when it comes to working with text. You will learn more about formatting text on Day 5.

Edit Tables

It's common to insert a table and then realize that you need more rows or columns. After a table has been inserted, you can add columns and rows using the process described in Table 2.1.

TABLE 2.1 Adding or Removing Columns or Rows

To achieve this	Do this
Add a column	Click in the column to the right of where you want your new column to appear. Choose **Table, Insert Column**.
Add a column at the right of the table	Choose **Table, Append Column**.

continues

TABLE 2.1 continued

To achieve this	Do this
Add a row	Click in the row just below where you want the new row to appear. Choose **Table, Insert Row**.
Add a row at the bottom of the table	Choose **Table, Append Row**.
Add more than one column or row	Position your cursor where you want to insert the columns or rows. Choose **Table, Insert Special**. Specify the number of columns or rows and then select **Column(s)** or **Row(s)**. Click **Insert**.
Delete a column or columns	Click in the column or select the columns you want to remove. Choose **Table, Delete Selected Column(s)**.Click on **Yes** to confirm the deletion.deletion.
Delete a row or rows	Click in the row or select the rows you want to remove. Choose **Table, Delete Selected Row(s)**. Click on **Yes** to confirm the deletion.
Delete a specified number of columns or rows	Place your cursor in the first column or row of the ones you want to delete. Choose **Table, Delete Special**. Specify the number of columns or rows you want to delete, select **Column(s)** or **Row(s)**, and click **Delete**. Choose **Yes** to confirm the deletion.

Caution

When you delete a column or row, the contents of the column or row are also deleted. To keep the text for use in the table but delete a column or row, cut and paste the text elsewhere on the form before deleting rows or columns. Then, paste it back into your table.

To change the width of a column, click inside the column and drag the column marker on the ruler, as shown in Figure 2.12.

If you're using tables to manage your form layout (as we recommended), you might not want users to see the borders on some or all of your tables. Or you might want horizontal borders only. Borders can be placed around the entire table, on groups of cells (such as a column or a row), or around individual cells (see Figure 2.13). Additionally, borders have several formatting options, such as embossed borders and extruded borders. Use one of the following methods to set border options:

Column marker being dragged   Table Layout page of Table Properties box

FIGURE 2.12

Dragging the column marker enables you to set the column size visually. For precise widths, use the settings on the Table Properties box.

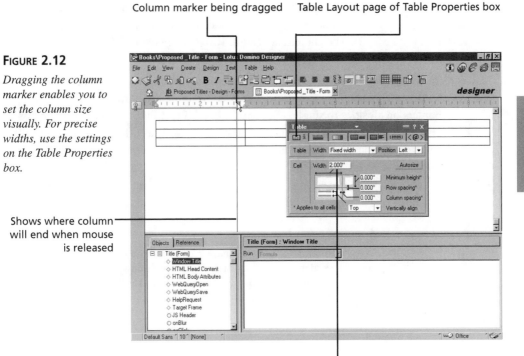

Shows where column will end when mouse is released

Enter new column width here

FIGURE 2.13

Click the Table Borders tab of the Table Properties box to change the outline borders of the table. Change individual cell borders on the Cell Borders (shown). Hold your mouse over the tabs in the Properties *box* to *see the tab labels pop up.*

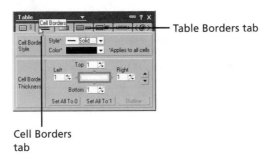

Table Borders tab

Cell Borders tab

2

- Choose border styles and colors on the Cell Borders tab of the Table Properties box. Note that the color and style affect all cells in the table, not just selected cells (see Figure 2.13). The choices are **Solid**, **Ridge**, and **Groove**. Try each one to see which you prefer.

- To change the thickness of borders, select the cells you want to change and set the border thickness on the Cell Borders tab of the Table Properties box. To set the borders on all sides to single, click on the **Set All to 1** button. If you want no borders, click on the **Set All to 0** button. Remember that this affects the selected cells, and a cell is considered selected when your cursor resides in it. Select a border thickness for each side of the selected cells by choosing a thickness from zero to ten for each side. The sides of the cell correspond to the measurements in the property box (left, top, right, bottom).

Note

Our Tech Editor and Notes Guru, Leigh Weber, wanted us to point out that if you set all borders to zero, your table displays a non-printing grid while you are in design mode. This is a welcomed feature for those of us (and you?) who have used earlier versions of Notes.

Tip

Right-align the static text in your tables so that all the colons line up. Then set your table borders to zero. See Figure 2.14 for an example.

FIGURE 2.14

A table was used to right-align the text on this form. After the fields are entered, the borders can be removed so users won't even realize there is a table there.

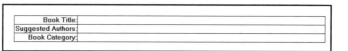

In addition to border options, the Properties box contains formatting options for the placement of your table, alignment of text within cells, and the width of your table. The Tables that follow list the options found in the Table Properties box, except for the

HTML page which can be found in Day 8, "Create Pages and Frames." The icons on the tabs in the Properties box represent the following:

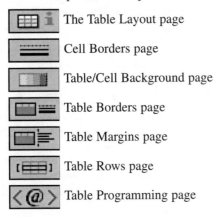 The Table Layout page

Cell Borders page

Table/Cell Background page

Table Borders page

Table Margins page

Table Rows page

Table Programming page

The Properties box is very manageable and can be expanded and collapsed or moved around your screen while you work (see Figure 2.15). You can also change the Properties box to view properties of other components in your database, such as the form, by clicking the triangle in the title of the Properties box and selecting a component from the drop-down menu.

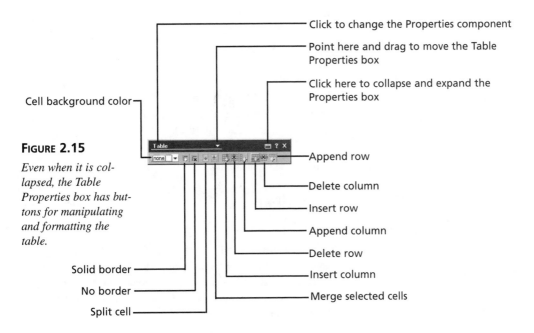

Click to change the Properties component

Point here and drag to move the Table Properties box

Click here to collapse and expand the Properties box

Cell background color

FIGURE 2.15

Even when it is collapsed, the Table Properties box has buttons for manipulating and formatting the table.

Append row

Delete column

Insert row

Append column

Delete row

Solid border

No border

Insert column

Merge selected cells

Split cell

Remember that changes you make in the Properties box can affect the entire table or the selected cells, rows, or columns (such as changes you make in the Table Layout Page as listed in Table 2.2). If you make a change to the table and change your mind, close the form without saving it. Also remember to save your form frequently as you make changes to it while in Designer. This enables you to exit the form without saving your most recent change, and without losing the changes with which you are happy.

Note | Please note that the table features and functions available in this release of Domino Designer are quite extensive. We could almost write an entire book on creating tables. Take time to explore some of the table features that we have not covered here, and don't overlook the Lotus Notes Help database (not just the Designer Help Database) for help with creating tables.

TABLE 2.2 Tables Properties Box—Table Layout Page

Items marked with * are default settings

Section	Item	Description
Table	Width	Choices include Fit to window, Fit with margins and Fixed width (*). Changes here are applied to the entire table.
	Position (displays when Fixed width is selected)	Determines where the fixed width table is to be placed on the page; Left (*), Right, or Center.
Cell	Width	Sets individual *column* widths, affecting the currently selected column. (You cannot set the width for a single cell using this feature, instead choose Autosize).
	Fixed width (use for Fit to window or Fit with margins tables)	Sets a fixed cell width for the currently selected column.
	Autosize	Automatically sizes cells according to the widest cell in the table, regardless of which cell you click on. Works with Fixed Width tables only. Autosize is specific to individual cells. To Autosize a cell, enter the text in the cell, place your cursor in the cell and click Autosize.

Section	Item	Description
	Mininum height	Sets minimum height for all cells. When you change this field, a check mark and an X appear. Click the check mark to save your changes, X to cancel.
	Row Spacing	Adjusts the spacing between the text and row borders for all cells. When you change this field, a check mark and an X appear. Click the check mark to save your changes, X to cancel.
	Column spacing	Adjusts spacing between text and column borders for all cells. When you change this field, a check mark and an X appear. Click the check mark to save your changes, X to cancel.
	Vertically Align	Aligns text to the top (*), center or bottom of a cell.

Note: Table sizing options work differently when the table is contained in a rich text field that resides inside of a *frame*. Frames can differ in size and because of that a Fit to window or Fit with margins table adapts to the frame size in which they were created. For example, a Fit to window table fills the frame, from margin to margin, within a rich text field. A Fit to margins table fills the frame completely from left to right, extending beyond the margins of the rich-text field that contains the table. A Fixed width table creates a column width that is fixed, regardless of the frame size in a document. You learn more about frames on Day 8.

To create or edit cell borders, click the Cell Borders tab of the *Properties box*. The changes you make here affect selected cells, so select your cell(s) before you select options in the *Properties box*. Table 2.3 lists the options found on the Cell Borders page of the Table Properties Box.

TABLE 2.3 Tables Properties Box—Cell Borders Page

Section	Item	Description
Cell Border Style	Style	Sets border style for all cells. Choices include: Solid (*), Ridge (raised border), and groove (raised border), and groove (indented border).
	Color	Sets border color (Black) for all cells. Customize the color by clicking the color wheel in the upper right corner of the Color box.

continues

TABLE 2.3   continued

Section	Item	Description
Cell Border Thickness	Left	Adjusts border thickness for the left side of the selected cell(s). Minimum value is zero (no borders) maximum value is 10.
	Top	Adjusts border thickness for the top side of the selected cell(s).
	Right	Adjusts border thickness for the right side of the selected cell(s).
	Bottom	Adjusts border thickness for the bottom side of the selected cell(s).
	Set All to 0	Removes borders from all sides of currently selected cell(s).
	Set All to 1	Sets borders for all sides of the currently selected cell or cells to 1.
	Outline	Outlines the entire table if more then one cell is selected. Clears all internal borders (sets to 0) leaving the outer borders at the thickness they were before this option was selected.
	Master spinner	This increases or decreases all of the cell border thicknesses at the same time. They are incremented/decremented by one.

To help you work your way around a table and decide which borders are which, look at a table layout from left-to-right like this; the left table margin is the starting point for the outside border. A table is laid out left margin, outer border, border thickness, inner border, left most column of table, remaining columns, inner border, border thickness, and outer border.

Tables and table cells can also contain background images and colors as described in the following Table 2.4.

TABLE 2.4   Tables Properties Box—Table/Cell Background Page

Section	Item	Description
Table Color	Style	Sets a color style (* None) for the table, options include alternating rows and columns.
	Color	For all choices except None.
	And	The alternate color for Alternating Rows and Alternating Columns.
	Body	Available when not alternating, not solid, and not None. The color to be used for the main part of the table, whereas color is used for the remaining part of the table.

Section	Item	Description
Cell color	Color	Sets color (* None) for selected cells. To select a color and style for all cells, click Apply to All in the Cell color section.
	Style	Sets style for selected cells. To select a color and style for all cells, click Apply to All in the Cell color section.
	Apply to All	Applies color and style selection to all cells.
	To (color, only present if one of the style gradients is selected)	Sets the final color for the gradient for each selected cell.
Cell image	Source	Enter the filename for the file (or a selection formula) to be used as a wallpaper for the selected cell(s).
	Repeat	Determines how the wallpaper image (source) appears within a cell, such as centered, or sized to fit. Choices are: Repeat once, Repeat vertically, Repeat horizontally, Tile (*), Center, and Size to Fit.
	Unnamed Preview area	Shows the selected cell image as a thumbnail. It does not show the effect of the repeat setting.
	Apply to All	Applies the cell image to all cells in the table.

The table border is the outer top/bottom/left/right line on the table. Cell borders may hide the table border if the cell border is thicker than the table border. The following Table 2.5 describes the settings found on the Table Borders page of the *Properties box.*

TABLE 2.5   Tables Properties Box—Table Borders Page

Section	Item	Description
Border Style	None	The type of line used as the border of the table. Choices are: None(*),Solid, Double, Dotted, Dashed,Inset, Outset, Ridge, and Groove.
	Color	The color of the border.
Border effects	Drop shadow	Check box, if set will display a dropped shadow on the bottom and right side of the table. Default is NOT checked.right side of the table. Default is NOT checked.
	Width	If Drop shadow is selected this defaults to 12. Range is 0 to 96.

TABLE 2.5 continued

Section	Item	Description
Drop down list: Thickness (*		The thickness of the outer border. The border may start a certain distance away from the table itself (see inside).
	Top	The thickness of the border. Zero means none.
	Right	The thickness of the border. Zero means none.
	Left	The thickness of the border. Zero means none.
	Bottom	The thickness of the border. Zero means none.
	Spinner	This increases or decreases all of the cell border thicknesses at the same time. They are incremented/decremented by one.
Drop down list: Inside		The amount of space between the inside table border and the outside table border.
Drop down list: Outside		The amount of space between the outer edge of the table border and other design elements on the form or text wrapping around a table in a rich text field.

Changes that you make to a table margin are affected by *absolute* and *relative* measurements. Absolute represents the inches/centimeters from the left-hand edge of the paper, or, for an embedded table, the offset from the containing cell's left border. Relative is the window width. Table 2.6 lists the settings and options found on the Table Margins Page of the Properties box.

 Caution   Settings for the table margins and table type can cause a lot of confusion. Fit to margins and Fit to window using relative setting(s) resizes the table width on screen as the overall window width changes. The Fit to window and Fit to margins with absolute value for *right* margin stays (in the designer) the absolute size even when the window is too narrow. So? Fit to window is only true to its implied name when *right* is 100% relative.

TABLE 2.6 Tables Properties Box—Table Margins Tab

Section	Item	Description
Table margin	Left	Sets left absolute or relative margin if table width is Fit withmargins or Fit to window.
	Absolute/ Relative	Sets the left margin in absolute (inches) or relative (percentage).
	Right	Sets right absolute or relative margin if table width is Fit with margins or Fit to window.
	Absolute/ Relative	Sets the right margin in absolute (inches) or relative (percentage).
Table Wrap	Outside table	Wraps text around the outside of the table (grayed out unless Fixed width is selected in the Table Layout Page. This allows text and tables to be side-by-side.
	Inside table	Causes text to flow from one cell to the next, horizontally in table. When all cells in the row are full, remaining text is dumped into the last cell of the table column.
	At height	Available when Inside table is selected for table wrap. Specifies the height of the cell space for text to fill before it flows into the next cell. Click check mark to save.
Compatibility	Use R4 spacing within table	Makes tables compatible with Notes R4 users.

Our last discussion here of table properties brings us to the Table Rows page of the Properties box. Here, you can program which rows to display, different than displaying one row at a time with a tabbed table, because a tabbed table ultimately displays all rows in the table when the cycle is finished. Table 2.7 describes available options and features found on the Table Rows page.

TABLE 2.7   Tables Properties Box—Table Rows Page

Section	Item	Description
Special table row display	Show all table rows	Displays entire table at all times (default)
	Show only one row at a time	Displays table one row at a time. The table is reduced to one row with tabbed pages representing each row in the table. Users click on a tab and that row appears. Provide the tab name in the Tab Labelfield, below.
Which row to display	Users pick row via tab buttons	Available when **Show only one row at a time** is selected under Special table row display. The table is reduced to one row with tabbed pages representing each row in the table. Users click on a tab and that row appears. Provide the tab name in the Tab Label field, below.
	Switch row every x milliseconds	Available when **Show only one row at a time** is selected under Special table row display. Advances rows every x milliseconds. The default setting is 2000 (2 seconds).
	Switch rows programmatically	A field controls which row to display. Find an example of this use in Appendix E, "Formulas and Scripts by Task."
	Also show tabs so user can pick row	Available when Switch rows programmatically is selected under Which row to display.
For selected row	Tab Label	Text here displays as the name on the tab for the selected row. Select a row first by clicking on the tab, type the Tab Label, click the check mark.
Transition when switching rows	Effect	Available when Switch Row every _ seconds is selected. Determines the method used when one row is transitioned to another, such as **Dissolve**, or **Rolling**. Can be set separately for each row.
	Cycle through rows	Available when Switch Row every x seconds is selected. Determines how the cyle from row to row takes place, for example, Continually, or Advance on Click. It is set once for the entire table.

Tip

It's easier to view tabbed rows if you choose a different color for each row. To advance rows with a mouse click; in the **Which row to display** section, select **Switch row every 0 milliseconds** then, in the **Transition when switching rows** section, choose **Advance on Click** in the Cycle **through rows** box.

Set Form Properties

Like tables, forms contain properties that you set which affect the form appearance, performance and security. Here, you begin to explore some of the form properties and their settings.

Set Form Properties

After you've named the form, you want to select other properties associated with forms. In the form Properties box you'll set options for the type of form, how users will access the form, and whether you want to apply versioning. Open the Forms Properties box or, if the box is open, use the drop-down menu to change the component to Form. On the Basics tab, select the form **Type:**, and choose **Document**, **Response**, or **Response-to-response**. The default setting is Document.

By default, both Display options—**Include in Menu** and **Include in Search Builder**—are enabled. If you don't want this form to appear on the Create menu, disable the **Include in Menu** option. If you want it to appear only under Other on the Create menu, select **Create - Other dialog** from the drop-down list box next to **Include in Menu**. Enabling **Include in Search Builder** causes the form to appear in the list of available forms when you create an agent or view. If you deselect both options, you effectively hide your form from users. Why might you do this? It might be a form that contains static text only, or computer fields, and requires no input from the users; therefore, the users need not have access to that form from the Create menu. You learn more about views on Day 6, "Take in the View: Create Views and Folders," and more about agents on Day 14, "The Not So Secret Agents."

Enabling *versioning* causes Notes to (optionally or automatically) maintain a history of document changes. Versioning is not often needed; when you want versioning, however, the following choices are available:

- **New versions become responses**—Shows the original document first, with all successive versions below. Use this when the original document is the point of reference. This option also prevents replication and save conflicts.

- **Prior versions become responses**—Lists the latest revision first in the view. Make this selection when the latest update is what you want to focus on, and older versions become back up or reference documentation. You can't prevent replication or save conflicts with this choice.

- **New versions become siblings**—Lists the original document first, but all successive versions are listed below it as main documents. Use this when you don't expect every main document to be revised because it is hard to find updates in the view. This prevents replication or save conflicts of the main document.

When you choose one of the versioning options, the Create versions field, appearing just below Versioning, becomes active, offering you two additional choices (see Figure 2.16). If you select **Automatic - File, Save**, Notes automatically creates new versions as new documents whenever users save a document. If you choose **Manual - File, New Version**, a new document is created only when users select **File, Save as New Version** from the menu. (With this option, users have control over when they create new versions.)

FIGURE 2.16

Editing a document creates a new version document as a response, a main topic, or a sibling. You decide whether this occurs automatically or manually.

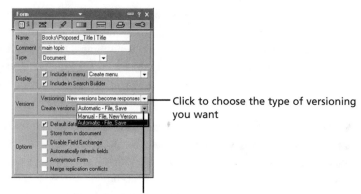

Click to choose the type of versioning you want

Select whether versioning occurs manually or automatically

Enable **Anonymous Form** when you want to create a form that doesn't record the names of the people who create or edit documents. This is applicable for a voting ballot form, an instructor evaluation form, or an anonymous complaint or suggestion form.

To avoid replication conflicts, enable **Merge replication conflicts**. With this enabled, replication conflicts only occur if the same field in the same document is modified by more than one person at the same time.

NEW TERM **Save Conflict**—Occurs when two users who are accessing the same database on the same server edit the same document at the same time.

Replication Conflict—Occurs when two users who are using different replica copies of the database edit and save the same document, and then the database is replicated. One version of the document becomes the main document; the other becomes the "Replication or Save Conflict" document. Someone, usually a designated manager of the database, has to resolve the conflict by editing one of the documents to include the changes made in the other, and then delete the other document.

Not all the selections you make on the Basics tab of the Properties box apply to or work well for Web browsers. Always keep your audience in mind. **Versioning, Anonymous forms,** and **Merge replication conflicts** are options that are not supported in Web browsers.

Select Form Background Properties

Color and graphics can be added to forms in the Form Background tab of the Form Properties box (see Figure 2.17). To add a background color, choose a color from the **Color** drop-down list. Be aware that certain colors can be hard on the eyes. We recommend that you avoid vibrant, dark colors. Pastel shades make good form backgrounds, particularly when you select dark colors for your text.

FIGURE 2.17

Not all users have monitors with 256 or more colors available. Any pastels or muted colors you pick might therefore be translated to the ones in the top two rows of the color choices. If you know that the monitors are limited in colors, restrict your backgrounds to the colors in those rows.

Click here to mix or pick your own custom colors

When adding color to text, table borders and backgrounds, form backgrounds, and so on, you are using the Notes palette of colors. Consider changing to the Web palette to get greater color fidelity. Choose **File, Preferences, User Preferences** from the menu. Under Advanced Options on the Basics page, select **Use Web Palette.** Click **OK**.

Background properties are, by default, ultimately controlled by end users, who can change a background color or import a document-specific background graphic when they create documents from your form. Why? Because background properties can slow down the display of a document, especially when accessed through a Web browser. If you don't want users to change the background properties when they create documents with this form, deselect **Allow users to change these properties** on the Form Background tab of the Form Properties box.

Backgrounds can also include graphics, such as a logo or a picture. You learn more about adding graphics and using image resources on Day 5.

Identify the Default Form

Every database needs a *default form*. Why do you need a default form? Suppose you intentionally—or unintentionally—delete or rename a form. Documents that were originally created by that form still exist in the database. To display these documents, Domino uses the default form of the database. Documents displayed in the default form might appear differently than in the form with which they were created, but at least some of the data can be seen. There can be only one default form in a database.

To set a form as the default form, click the **Form Info** page of the Form Properties box and check **Default Database Form**.

If you don't identify a default form, an error might occur in your application if someone tries to open a document with which no form has been associated, or if the form has been deleted. The default form is identified by an icon that precedes its name in the list of database forms (see Figure 2.18).

Store Forms with Documents

Documents are collections of field data; forms are the format or layout used to display the fields to the user. By default, a form is not stored in the document that is created using the form. Forms are stored in the database and called upon by Domino to display associated documents.

But what happens when you mail a document to a database (or to a user's mail database) and the receiving database does not contain the form that was used to create the document? Domino displays the document in the receiving database's default form, and the end result would likely be unusable or unreadable by the recipient because the default form in the receiving database isn't likely to have the same fields.

Domino addresses this scenario with an option on the **Form Info** tab of the form Properties box called **Store form in document**. Checking this box results in the form itself being stored in the document, enabling any user to view the document in its intended form.

FIGURE 2.18

When you copy or mail documents from one database to another, if a form with the same name does not exist in the target database, the target database default form is used. Be aware that "Form1" in the source database might be completely different in layout and field names than "Form1" in the target database.

Indicates the default database form

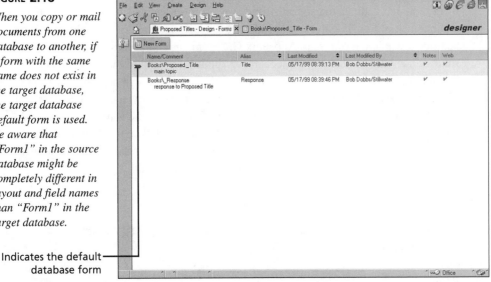

It is recommended that you avoid using this feature. Consider that storing a copy of the form in each document that is created with it uses vastly more disk space than storing just a pointer to the form. Also note that storing the form in a document makes it impossible for the user to switch to another form, and very difficult for the designer to force the use of another form.

There are two alternate solutions to this problem. One calls for you to use the same set of fields and the same field names that are used in the default form in the destination database. That way, documents created with your form can be adequately viewed in the destination database.

The other solution calls for you to copy your form to the destination database or its design template. You will learn about design templates on Day 21, "Roll Out and Maintain your Application." But for now, you've learned that storing forms with documents has its pros and cons.

Create a Window Title

The window title determines what text appears in the title bar when users are creating, reading, or editing a document using your form. "Untitled" is the default window title. Descriptive window titles are very helpful to users and should be created by the designer.

Window titles can be static or they can be dynamic, depending on the state of the document (editing, reading, and so forth), and they can even include such information as the author's name. To create dynamic window titles you need to write formulas; you'll find additional window formulas in Appendix G, "Formulas and Scripts by Task." To create static window titles, click the **Objects** tab in the Info List list of the Programmer's Pane. Expand the objects under your form name by clicking the **+** sign next to your form name. Then select **Window Title**. In the formula box, enter the text you want to appear in the form title bar and surround the text with quotes. Oh, and by the way, congratulations— you've just written your first Domino formula! You learn lots more about formulas on Day 4, "Formulas 101: The Basics." Figure 2.19 shows the formula in the Script Area of the Programmer's Pane and the resulting document window title.

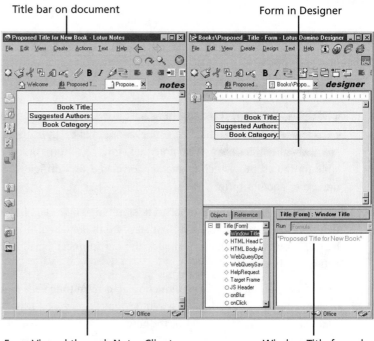

FIGURE 2.19

The text that makes up the Window Title formula, appears on the title bar when the user selects Proposed Title from the Create menu, and starts the new document.

Title bar on document   Form in Designer

Form Viewed through Notes Client   Window Title formula

View and Edit Forms

As you design your form, you also want to test it to make sure all elements are working as expected. Testing the form becomes much more critical when you add fields and formulas (as you begin to do On Day 3; there, too, you will see how to test the form).

To view your form as if you were the end user, have the form opened in design mode and choose **Design**, **Preview in Notes** or **Preview in Web Browser** from the menu (see Figure 2.20). Press the **Esc** key to close the Notes or Web browser window after you have previewed your form.

Tip

When you want to test the form, one quick way to open Notes or a browser to test it is to use the navigation buttons in the upper-right corner of the Designer window. These buttons include Notes and any browser software you have on your system. These buttons also give you the advantage of opening additional browsers to view your work. This works if you are working on a local database. You need to have your Web browser configured and working before you click these icons.

FIGURE 2.20

When designing for both Notes and Web users, you should check both previews to see that your design works for both types of users.

2

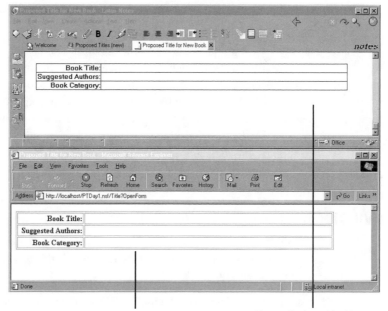

Form displayed in Web Browser   Form displayed in Notes

Summary

In today's lesson you learned that forms are templates through which documents are created and viewed. You also learned that forms can contain many different Domino objects and events including—but not limited to—fields, tables, graphics, attachments, and actions.

Some considerations must be taken when users who are accessing your forms are doing so through Web browsers because not all form properties and objects are supported for the Web. As you develop forms, you can view them through a Web browser and a Notes client without leaving your design environment.

Finally, databases can and often do contain many forms for many purposes. Forms control which parts or fields a user sees, and documents can be created in one form but viewed in others.

Q&A

Q **If the form type Document can inherit information from another form type Document, why do I need Response and Response-to-response documents?**

A The main objective of the response and response-to-response type document is to facilitate a hierarchical view. To follow a discussion thread, you need to see how the discussion unfolded: which document started the discussion (main topic) and which documents respond to that first document (response and response-to-response). If you don't need a view that displays this kind of thread, you don't need to create response document types. By the way, inheritance can also occur *between databases*—something you want to keep in mind when you are building an application. You learn more about this on Day 9, "Forms on Steroids: Increase Form Performance."

Workshop

The purpose of our workshop is to guide you as you put your new skills to work. In this workshop, you'll create three forms for the Proposed Titles database you created on Day 1. These three forms are

1. **Proposed Title (synonym "Title")**—This is the main document in which a new book is proposed. It needs to also be the default database form.

2. **Response (synonym "Response")**—This is a response document in which the user gives an opinion of the proposed title and makes suggestions about the book.

3. **Comments (synonym "Comments")**—This is a response-to-response document that enables users to express opinions about the proposed book or about the responses of other users.

Here's what you need to do for this workshop:

1. Create these three forms and name them so that they maintain the order as listed above. Hint: use letters to keep the order. Also, you want the letters underscored in the menu as hotkeys.

2. Enter the static text on each form, using the information in Table 2.7 as a guideline for the text you'll need. You don't have to use the same wording. Use tables to keep your text aligned.

TABLE 2.7 Form Add Static Text

Form Name	Information To Include on Form
Proposed Title	Book Title
	Suggested Authors
	Book Category
	Book Description
	Discussion Period
	Assigned Acquisition Editor
	Status
	Document Author
	Date Created
Response	Opinion
	Comments
Comments	Opinion
	Comments

3. Select the background for each form and format the text to make it both easy to read and attractive (see Figure 2.21).

4. Create a Window Title for each form to help your users identify the form easily when they have it open (see Figure 2.22).

5. As shown in Figure 2.23, add a static text title to the top of the form to help users identify it (not everyone checks the Window Title).

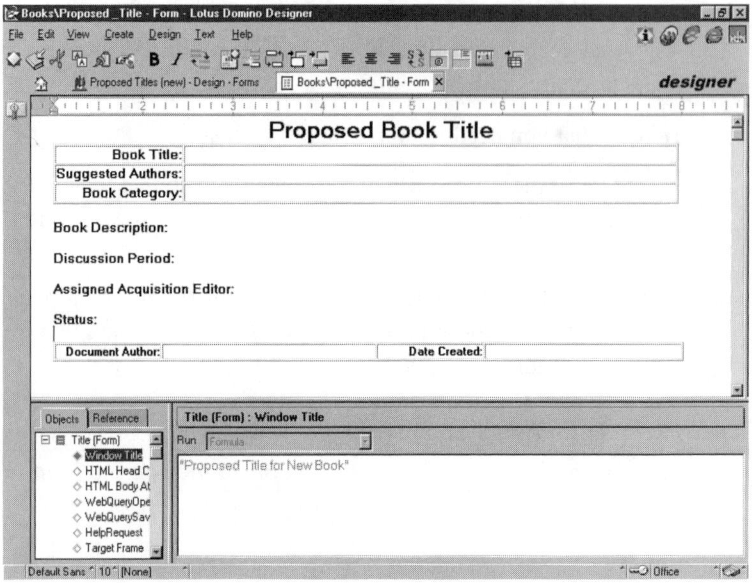

FIGURE 2.21

In our version of the Proposed Title form, we used tables to organize the text.

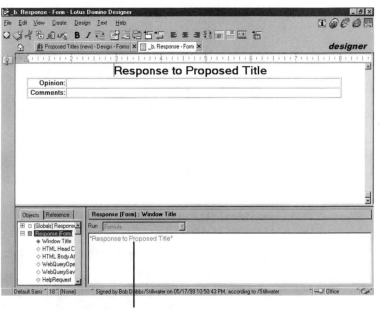

FIGURE 2.22

The Window Title helps the user differentiate this form from the Comments form, which is very similar. Always remember to put quotes around text when you enter it in the Formula pane. Note that the Window Title you see in the designer's window is not the window title that appears in the Notes client

Window Title Formula

FIGURE 2.23

Giving different color backgrounds, colored text, Window titles, and static text titles helps users tell which form they're using, especially when two forms are as similar as the Response and Comments forms.

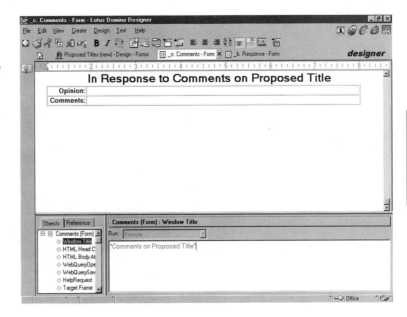

6. Save each form and test it to see how it looks in Notes and on the Web.

Tip

Testing response documents. In order to create a response and response-to-response document in Notes, you must first select a main document. So, to truly test your form in Notes, you need to start the Notes client, open the Proposed Titles database, create a main document (or two), and then create response documents. After you open the Notes client, use buttons on the Windows taskbar to switch between the Designer and the client.

DAY **3**

Take a Field Trip: Add Fields

The heart of a database is its fields, and certainly fields are the heart of any form. In fact, a form without fields is basically unusable for gathering information from users.

In Domino, fields are the areas on forms where users enter data. When a user saves a new document, it is only the fields—their definitions and contents—that get saved. The other parts of the form—the static text, the graphics—usually do not get saved with the new document.

This lesson introduces you to fields. Here, you learn how to create and define them and how to set their options.

About Fields

Adding fields to your form is a multistep process. When you add fields, you also need to add static text to help users determine what information is to go into your fields. Fields display on your form, but not field *names*. Users might have no clue as to what information is to be entered into each field on your form without special-use static text called *labels*.

After you create a field, you need to define the field by supplying the following elements:

- The field name
- The data type
- Whether the field is computed or editable
- The field display options
- Optionally, one or more formulas
- Optionally, the kind of field this is: shared or single use

All fields have names and a data type (such as text or numbers). Most fields are visible to users and are *editable* (filled in by users) or *computed* (filled in by formula or script). Some fields are invisible and are present to hold values that other fields use in computations. Visible fields typically have static text labels so users know what data goes in them. Editable fields might also have help information associated with them to further clarify to users what is to go in them. Fields that the users don't fill in are usually—although not necessarily—computed, and generally do not need labels or field help.

Computed fields must always have formulas that define their values. Editable fields have optional formulas that might provide default values or clean up or validate the data that is entered by the user.

Display options include how the field looks to the user and whether the field can be seen at all. A field might appear only when the document is being read or edited; it may appear only when certain people have the document open; or it can be encrypted, with its contents appearing only to people who have a copy of the encryption key.

Furthermore, Domino fields can be unique to a form or they can be shared among many forms within a database. Display options and text attributes determine how a field value appears in a given document.

Fields can also contain default values. For example, in a yes/no field, you can assign a default value of yes. When a user creates a document using a form that contains this field, he needs to change the value of the field to no; otherwise, the value is yes. You learn more about field formulas on Day 4, "Formulas 101: The Basics," but today you learn about the other basic field elements.

Fields can be very simple in their design, for example a text field in which a user supplies, say, a customer name. Fields can also be very complex, containing compound formulas and display options. For example, a field might calculate a salesperson's commission structure, based on a customer's location, and display the commission structure only when the document is viewed by the salesperson or his manager—and maybe only the salesperson or manager can access a particular form (the commission structure form).

As you can see, there are many decisions to be made about each field you add to your form. Of course, field properties, values, types, and all elements of a field, including its formula, can be changed at any time during the development of your application. You can even change these attributes after your application is rolled out, but it is best to try to perfect your field performance before you grant the user community access to your application. When possible, make a list of the fields you need prior to adding them to your form; it can help you as you design your fields. Determine which field values depend on other field values, which fields are to be populated by the users, and which fields you need to calculate (these will need formulas).

Field Properties

As you add fields to forms, you will work in the Field Properties box. Throughout today's lesson you will learn about the options that are found in the Field Properties box, which is context sensitive. The information on tabbed pages changes depending on selections and type of field. The icons that are located on the tabbed pages of the field properties box represent the following:

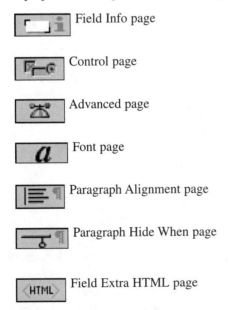

Field Info page

Control page

Advanced page

Font page

Paragraph Alignment page

Paragraph Hide When page

Field Extra HTML page

Field Labels

A *field label* is the static text that defines a field's contents. You learned about static text on Day 2, "Forms 101: The Essentials of Form Design," and you might have already added labels to your form in anticipation of adding fields. Some developers like to add labels as they add their fields. It really isn't important which comes first, the label or the field. It is, however, extremely important that you add labels, as evidenced in Figure 3.1.

FIGURE 3.1

In the new document shown at the top, the absence of address labels makes it difficult for users to know what information is to be added in which fields. In the form at the bottom, new labels have been added Because these labels are contained within one paragraph, they can be hidden later from the reader but remain visible to anyone editing the document.

Label to left of field   New document without address labels

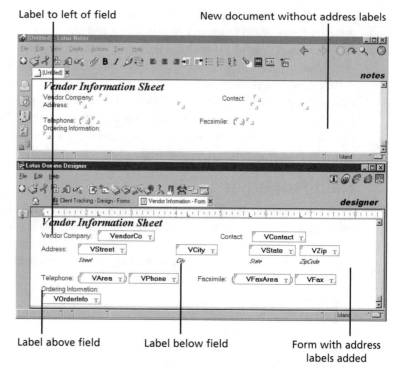

Label above field   Label below field   Form with address
                                                        labels added

As you can see in Figure 3.1, labels can be added to the form to the left of, above, or below fields. Alternately, the fields can be embedded in a sentence. We recommend that you decide which method you prefer and be consistent in placing labels on your forms so that users become accustomed to your style of field labeling.

Single Use Fields Versus Shared Fields

If you know ahead of time that you will be using the same field definition in more than one form, you might want to create a shared field rather than a single use field. *Single use fields* are defined within one form; their definitions are stored in that form. *Shared fields* are defined separately from any form; their definitions are stored as *resources* for your database (see Figure 3.2). The purpose of a shared field is to enable you to reuse the field definition in multiple forms within a single database. For example, you might want all your forms to collect information about the authors of the documents that are created with them (for example, the author's name and department). You can define "Name" and "Department" fields on every form, or you can save yourself time and effort by defining shared fields called "Name" and "Department," and then just drop them into each form as you create it.

Note

The shared field's *value*—its contents—is not part of its definition and is therefore not necessarily the same from form to form. This difference often trips up new developers. Remember that when you use a shared field, you are sharing its definition—*not* its value!

FIGURE 3.2

State is a shared field. Shared fields are found under the Resources view of the Design Pane.

Shared field

Shared Fields view

Design Pane

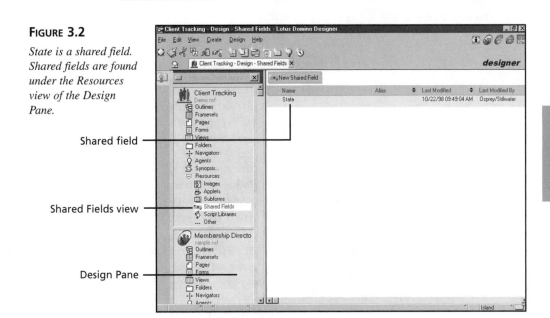

When you need to reuse a single field in many forms, using a shared field is an efficient method. You learn how to create a shared field later in this lesson. Keep this in mind, though: If you need to reuse *multiple* fields and the *associated static text* in multiple forms, consider designing a subform instead of many shared fields. A *subform* is a partial form within a form that enables you to reuse fields and design elements across many forms. You learn more about subforms on Day 17, "Embed Objects in Your Applications."

If you aren't sure which fields need to be shared fields, don't worry about it. It is easy to convert a field from single use to shared and vice versa. You'll learn how to do both on Day 17.

Field Names

Every field must have a field name (see Figure 3.3). You can name a field by entering its name in the Name field of the Field Properties box. As has already been stated, field names do not appear on forms, so they're not useful to users. Field names are used by Domino to identify the field.

FIGURE 3.3

When you first create a field, the field type defaults to text, editable. Consider including a clue in the field name to remind you of the form name. This will help you later as you begin using field names in formulas and searching for fields and forms as you diagnose application problems.

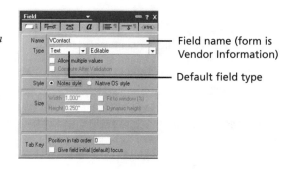

Field name (form is Vendor Information)

Default field type

> **Note**
>
> Note from authors: Field names are truly a personal preference and style decision. If you decide to identify the form name in your field name, try to keep the field name short by using a very short abbreviation for the form name. Whatever you decide, be consistent.

The name of each field within a form must be unique. For example, a client form might have several address fields: one for the street address, one for PO Box, one for the city, and so on. A logical name for each of these fields is "address." However, Domino requires a unique name for each field. Consider naming these fields Address1, Address2, and City so that each is unique.

Creating unique field names is only one part of naming convention rules. Additional field naming restrictions dictate that

- Field names contain a maximum of 32 characters.
- Field names cannot begin with the $ or @ symbols or a number (but they can contain numbers) because these symbols are reserved for special use by Notes. Lotus uses $ as the first character of the names of internal fields it creates; if you begin your field names with $ you risk stepping on an internal field with the same name, which can have unpredictable results. Lotus uses the @ symbol for creating formulas.
- Field names cannot contain spaces. If a field name consists of multiple words, run the words together and capitalize the first letter of each word (for example, CourseDescription or CustomerName). Alternately, you can use an underline

character (_) to mark a space. However, the first method is recommended because your field names will be shorter. The first method is also the way that almost all Domino programmers name fields, so you'll be in good company if you use the first method.

You use field names in formulas, so keep your field names short, easy to remember, and descriptive. In the following examples, a formula produces a listing of a customer name and address. The first example uses very descriptive field names; the second example uses descriptive but shorter field names. Which would you prefer to write?

```
CustomerStreetAddress1 + CustomerStreetAddress2 + CustomerCity
+ CustomerState + CustomerZip
```

or

```
CustAddress1 + CustAddress2 + CustCity + CustState + CustZip
```

You can, of course, make this formula even shorter by naming the fields Address1, Address2, and so forth, leaving off the "Cust" part of the naming convention. But be careful when you make field names too short. Say, for example, that customer information is contained on a form that also has a field that indicates which of your company's offices services the customer. In this case, you might need to display the customer address as well as the branch office address. If you name the customer address fields Address1, Address2, and so forth, what do you name your branch office address fields? There is the potential for confusion here. In this scenario, a slightly longer, descriptive naming convention is most useful:

CustAddress1

CustAddress2

CustCity

BranchAddress1

BranchAddress2

BranchCity

In this example it's easy to tell what data each field will contain, and it's easy to recognize the field names when you begin to write formulas.

Field names are entered on the Field Info tab of the Field Properties Box. Table 3.1 describes the items found on the Basic tab.

Table 3.1 Field Properties Box, Field Info Page

Item	Description
Name	Enter the name you want to assign to the field.
Type (first field)	Select the data type of the field: text, date/time, number, dialog list, checkbox, radio button, listbox, combobox, rich text, authors, names, readers, password, or formula. You learn more about Data types later today.
Type (second field)	Select the type of the field: editable, computed, computed for display, computed when composed (for the formula data type there is a Literalize Fields choice, and a password data type has no second choice).
Allow Multiple values	Check to be able to select or enter more than one piece of data.
Compute after Validation	Check this for a computed field when you want to wait until all editable fields have been validated (confirmed to have required field data) before determining the calculated field value.
Style	Choose Notes or Native OS (operating system). If you choose Native OS, the field appears on the form as a fixed size outlined box, as opposed to a Notes style, which appears as a bracketed space.
Size (available only when Native OS style is selected)	Sets the width and height of the field box. To get the look of the native control without being restricted by a fixed size, choose the accompanying Dynamic height option, which increases the size of the entry box up to three lines as needed. Select Fit to Window (%) to set the width of the field to a percentage (1 to 100) of the overall width of the window.
Web Access: Display	Sets how a rich text field displays in a Web browser. Using HTML translates the contents of the field using HyperText Markup Language formatting codes, which may limit the display. Using Java Applet displays a toolbar with formatting choices the Web user can use to format the rich text in the browser.
Position in Tab Order	Controls the order in which editable fields are visited when the user presses the Tab key. When you enter a number that number also appears as a notation in the lower left corner of the field.
Give field initial (default) focus	Choosing this option positions the user's cursor in the field upon opening a form that contains that field.

Just because you follow the rules for naming conventions doesn't mean that you can give your fields any name you want. You also need to be aware of Notes *reserved* field names.

These are field names that Notes expects to be used for specific purposes. If you try to use one of these field names for a purpose other than the reserved purpose, the outcome is unpredictable. For example, don't create a field called "SendTo" unless you intend for it to hold the names of mail addressees.

Table 3.2 lists the most of the reserved field names. When creating fields, use these field names to perform only the functions listed in the table.

Table 3.2   Commonly Used Reserved Field Names

Reserved Field Name	Definition and Use
Reserved Fields for Mailing Documents	
MailOptions	Gives users the option of mailing a document
SaveOptions	Controls whether documents are saved
Sign	Attaches creator's electronic signature on saving the document
Encrypt	Encrypts mail
SendTo	Contains names of users who are to receive a mail memo if the document is mailed
CopyTo	Contains names of users who are to receive a copy if the document is mailed
BlindCopyTo	Contains names of users who are to receive a blind copy if the document is mailed
DeliveryPriority	Determines delivery priority (high, medium, or low) if the document is mailed
DeliveryReport	Returns a delivery report to recipient if the document is mailed
ReturnReceipt	Returns a receipt to sender when recipient reads mail
MailFormat	Routes mail via cc:Mail
Reserved Names for Embedded Elements	
$$ViewBody	Contains the name of an embedded view and replaces itself with that View.
$$ViewList	Replaces itself with an embedded folder pane.
$$NavigatorBody	Contains the name of an embedded navigator and replaces itself with that Navigator.
$GroupScheduleRefreshMode	Sets a value for refreshing an embedded group scheduling control.
$GroupScheduleShowLegend	Displays a color legend (1) or does not display a color legend (0).

continues

Table 3.2 Continued

Reserved Field Name	Definition and Use
Reserved Fields for Use in Billing Applications	
$ChargeRead	Creates a billing record when the user opens a document that contains this field.
$ChargeWrite	Creates a billing record when a user creates, copies, edits, or saves a document that contains this field.
Reserved Fields for General Use	
Categories	Categorizes documents.
$VersionOpt	Allows choice of version control options on a document-by-document basis.
FolderOptions	Places new documents in folders.
SecretEncryptionKeys	Holds a list of encryption keys.
HTML	If a browser requests this document, only the contents of this field are to be delivered.
$$HTMLHead	Passes HTML information to the HTML HEAD tag.
$$Return	Use this to override the default response to the Submit button on a Web browser. This field value displays as the response.
Internal Fields on Forms	
$Title	Contains the name of a form when the form is stored with a document.

At this early stage of the game, you might not fully understand the use and description of each of the fields listed in Table 3.2, but don't fret. As you learn more about development, you'll find examples throughout the book that further explain the use of some of these reserved fields.

In addition to reserved fields, Domino uses Internal fields, which Domino creates automatically when you create a document of any kind, including design elements such as forms and views. You can see a document's internal field names and their values by selecting a document in a view, choosing **Document Properties** from the **File** menu, and then choosing the **Fields** tab (see Figure 3.4). The internal field names all begin with a dollar sign ($) and appear at the very top of the list of fields. Select a field name from the list on the left. Its value appears in the window on the right.

FIGURE 3.4

The Document Properties box displays all the fields that are contained in the document. For each field, including the reserved fields, you can see the data type and a sequence number that implies how often the field has been updated, and sometimes the contents of the field. Highlight the $UpdatedBy field to see who last updated the document.

3

Some internal fields that are of particular interest to application developers include:

- **$Ref**—This field appears only in response documents and holds the UNID of its parent document. Notes uses this field to build hierarchical views.
- **$UpdatedBy**—This field appears in all documents that have been saved at least once, but not on documents created with a form marked as Anonymous. It contains the names of everyone who saved the document. It is useful if you need to know who made changes in a document.
- **$Revisions**—This field appears in all documents that have been revised at least once. It holds the date and time of each revision of the document.

Field Data Type

After you name a field, you must determine its *data type*. You specify a field type by selecting it from the Type drop-down list on the Field Properties box (see Figure 3.5).

The data type dictates the kind of data a field holds. Domino uses nine data types. It's important that you select the appropriate data type for each of your fields. For example, if a field is to hold numbers that you will use in calculations, you need to define the field's data type as Number. If you leave the data type as Text, you can enter numbers in the field, but you cannot use those numbers in calculations.

FIGURE 3.5

Choose the type of data you want to collect in the selected field. It is commonly recommended that you don't use more than one rich text field in a form, although in some cases you might add a second one to hold an attachment or for special security purposes. Remember that data contained in a rich text field cannot be included in a view.

Table 3.3 lists Domino field data types and their descriptions.

Table 3.3 Field Data Types

Data Type	Use
Text	To contain letters, punctuation, spaces, and non-mathematical numbers (such as phone numbers and zip codes).
Date/Time	To hold date and time information that appears as numbers separated by punctuation, that is MM/DD/YYYY HH:MM:SS.
Number	To hold numbers that are intended to be used in numerical computations. Numbers can be decimal, percent, scientific, or currency (which has full international currency support).
Dialog list	Displays a list of choices in a dialog box. You decide whether users can choose more than one option or add choices not on the list.
Checkbox	Displays a list of choices as checkboxes. Users can select more than one value.
Radio Button	Displays a list of choices from which users can only select one.
Listbox	Displays a box in native O/S style that has spinner buttons (small up and down arrows) that users click to display one of the options in the list.
Combobox	Displays a drop-down box from which users select an option.
Rich Text	For use when text must be formatted, or to contain graphics, pop-ups, buttons, attachments, tables, and embedded objects (such as spreadsheets, presentations, project manager files, and more). Note that rich text fields can't be displayed in a view, and their values can't be returned in most formulas.

Data Type	Use
Authors	List of people—names, group names, or roles—who can edit the document, provided that they also have author or higher access to the database.
Names	User or server names as they appear in the Notes ID. Note that this is often used to display the creator of a document or to maintain a list of users who edit a document.
Readers	To limit the read access of a document to those users named in this field.
Password	To create a password field that displays characters as asterisks.
Formula	Used to populate a subscription list and used in the headlines.nsf database.

Note that fields of type Dialog list, checkbox, radio button, listbox, combobox, Names, Authors, Readers, and Password are really just specialized versions of the Text data type. They all hold text.

Field Events

Fields are Domino objects and have associated events. The events that are associated with a given field depend on its properties. For example, an editable field has, among others, a default value event, an input translation event, and an input validation event (all of which you'll learn about on Day 4). A computed field has, instead, only a value event (because it is computed, it needs nothing more than a value). These are all events that can be used with formula language, and they have a diamond icon associated with them. Other items in the list are used with JavaScript and LotusScript, but we won't be concentrating on them until Days 19 and 20.

To see field events, open a form in Design mode and select any field. If no fields exist yet in the form, add one by choosing **Field** in the Create menu. In the Info List, choose the **Objects** tab. Then scroll down the list of objects until your field name appears. Indented beneath it are its events (see Figure 3.6). If no events appear, click the plus sign to the left of the field name.

Field (Object)

FIGURE 3.6

Editable fields have at least three events— Default value, input translation, and input validation.

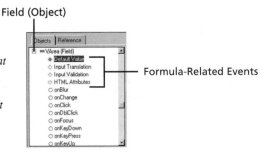

Formula-Related Events

Computed Versus Editable Fields

All fields are editable when they are first created, but you can make them computed. *Editable Fields* are fields in which users enter data manually. *Computed Fields* are fields in which the value of the field is determined by a formula; users cannot add data directly to computed fields.

There are three kinds of computed fields:

- **Computed**—The value is calculated when the document is created, and then it is recalculated every time a document is saved or refreshed. The value is stored in the field.

- **Computed when composed**—The value is calculated when the document is created, and it is never recalculated. The value is stored in the field.

- **Computed for display**—The value is recalculated when a document is opened for reading or editing. The value is not stored in the field but is recomputed every time you display the document.

You indicate the editable or computed option by choosing it from the drop-down list on the Field Properties box (see Figure 3.7).

FIGURE 3.7 FIELD PROPERTIES BOX

In this example, DocAuthor is a computed when composed field type. The name of the document author is captured when the document is created.

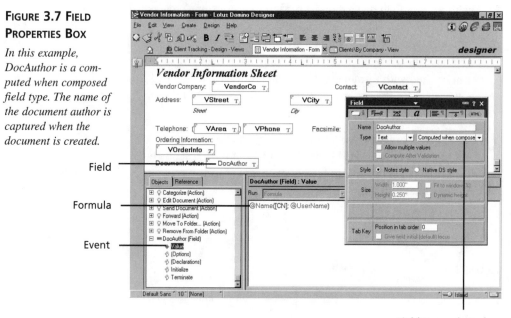

Field type selected

Field Display Options

Display options affect how, if, and when the contents of the field are to appear to the user. You can select display options in the Field Properties box, where they appear on several of the panels, including the Control, Paragraph Alignment, and Font tabbed pages.

Some display options are really text display options that appear in the Field Properties box just for your convenience. These include all the options on the Font, Paragraph Alignment, and Paragraph Hide When panels. The settings in these panels default to the settings of the surrounding text. When you change the settings in the Paragraph Alignment or Paragraph Hide When panels, you change them not just for the selected field but also for the paragraph in which it appears. Likewise, if you change those settings in the Text Properties box while the cursor is in the same paragraph as the field, the changes appear in the Field Properties box as well. Table 3.4 describes the field display options that are found in the Properties box.

Table 3.4   Field Properties Box: Font and Paragraph Alignment Pages

Tabbed page	Item	Description
Font	Font	Select a typeface.
	Size: (first box)	Select a point size.
	Size: (second box)	Enter or use spinners to select an unlisted point size.
	Style	Select a text style: Plain, Bold, Italic, Underline, Strikethrough, Superscript, Subscript, Shadow, Emboss, or Extrude.
	Color	Select a color.
Paragraph Alignment		Click a horizontal alignment button—left, center, right, full, no wrap.
	First line	Click a first line indent type button—no indent, indent first line, hanging indent.
	Indent	Appears when indent first line is selected. Enter measurement for indent.
	Outdent	Appears when hanging indent first line is selected. Enter measurement for outdent.
	List	Select a type of list paragraph— bullet, circle, square, checkmark, number, alphabet (uppercase), alphabet (lowercase), Roman (uppercase), Roman (lowercase), or none

continues

Table 3.4 continued

Tabbed page	Item	Description
	Spacing: Interline	Select spacing between lines of text—single, 1 1/2, or double.
	Spacing: Above	Select spacing between the current paragraph and the one above it—single, 1 1/2, or double.
	Spacing: Below	Select spacing between the current paragraph and the one below it—single, 1 1/2, or double.

Other display options are driven by the data type. Several data types have their own display options, including Number, Date/Time, Dialog list, checkbox, and so forth. Display options appear on the Control tab of the Field Properties Box (see Figure 3.8).

FIGURE 3.8

In a number field type, the options on the Control tab of the Field Properties box set how the number appears. In this example, the number is a calculated vendor number and the number of decimal places is fixed at zero.

Field display options also include Hide-When options, which enable you to hide a field and its label from certain readers, or from all readers when a document is previewed, opened for reading, printed, and so forth. You learn more about Hide-When options on Day 9.

On the Advanced page you can enter some text in the Help Description field that tells the user what to do to complete the field. The user sees this help text at the bottom of the screen above the Status bar when the cursor is in the field.

Number Field Display Options

In the Control panel of the Field Properties box for Number fields you can choose from four basic number formats: Decimal, Percent, Scientific, and Currency. The differences between the four formats are illustrated in Table 3.5.

Table 3.5 Differences Between Number Display Formats (using default decimal settings and American currency)

Format	If the user enters	Notes will display
Decimal	123.456	123.456
Percent	1.234	123.4%
Scientific	123.456	1.23E+02
Currency	123.456	$123.46

In the preceding table, the scientific notation 1.23E+02 is the computer equivalent of 1.23456x10^2.

Depending on which format you choose, you have other display options, as set forth in Table 3.6. For a text field, the Control Page contains only one option: **Show field delimiters**. This option, when checked, displays brackets around a blank field (if you chose to display the field using the Notes style), helping the user see where the field begins and ends. If you chose to display the text field using the Native OS, the control option that appears is whether or not to use the Tab key to move to the next field.

Table 3.6 Field Properties Control Page: Display Options for Number Fields

Section	Option	Description
Number Format	Decimal Percent Scientific Currency	You select the general number type. Percent shows the % sign and displays .01 as 1% and 1.00 as 100%. Scientific displays with one digit before the decimal point and the exponent, so 123 is 1.23E+02. Currency displays the currency indicator, which for the USA is $123.45. Decimal appears as written, but with the number of decimal places specified.
Decimal Places	Varying	If you check this, Notes displays the number of decimal places required by the number, instead of a fixed number of decimal places. It is available only for Decimal and Percent formats.
	Fixed	Enter a value or use the spinners to tell Notes how many numbers to the right of the decimal point to display, even if they are zeroes.

continues

Table 3.6   continued

Section	Option	Description
Border Style (Only if Notes style field)	Show field delimiters	If checked, the usual brackets are shown for the beginning and end of a field. If not checked and you are using Notes style, there is nothing to indicate the field size or location.
Preferences for display formatting	Use preferences from	You can choose User setting or Custom. If you choose User setting, the number is displayed using a thousands separator and decimal symbol, as designated in the client's preferences. If you choose Custom you can designate the Decimal symbol and the Thousands separator for this field.
Additional display formatting	Parentheses when negative	If you select this option, negative numbers display within parentheses. Otherwise, they are preceded by a minus sign.
	Punctuated at thousands	If you select this option, numbers display the thousands separator at every third digit, moving to the left from the decimal point.
Currency symbol (Only available for Currency formats)	Currency Symbol	You can either select a currency symbol from a list of national currencies or you can choose Custom. If you choose Custom, two other fields appear. In the first you can enter a currency symbol (plus other characters such as spaces wanted). In the second you can choose, from a list of Countries, which country the currency symbol is for.
	Symbol follows number	By default Lotus displays the currency symbol to the left of the number. Select this option to display the symbol to the right instead.
	Space next to number	By default Lotus displays right the currency symbol next to the number. Select this option to have the symbol and number separated by a space.

Date/Time Field Display Options

In the Control page of the Field Properties box for Date/Time fields you can control just about every aspect of the display of dates and times. As you change the display rules, examples appear in the Sample box of dates and times as they would display according to each rule. The initial choices you can make appear in Table 3.7. Custom date and time display options appear in Table 3.8. Note that date/time settings may vary, depending upon the international settings in the client.

Table 3.7 Field Properties Control Page: Initial Time/Date Display Options

Option	Choice	Comment
On display		
Use preferences from	User's settings Or Custom	The default is User's settings, which means that all dates and times display on each client according to the client's own display preferences. If you choose Custom, a whole array of choices appears, which are set forth and explained in Table 3.8
	Sample	This shows a sample date/time, with all the settings selected.
Display Date		
Display Date	Checkbox	If you select the Display Date checkbox the control options Show and Special are activated.
Show (available only if Display Date is selected)	There are nine options for combinations of weekday, month, day and year	You select the date display control. If you selected User's settings, the order of the month, day, and year is controlled by your international settings for your Notes client or OS.
Special (available only if Display Date is selected)	Show Today when appropriate	Depending upon the date value, this field can display Yesterday, Today, Tomorrow, or a date value. This takes precedence over all the other settings.
	Always show 4-digit year	Shows all years as four digits. This takes precedence over the 4-digit 21st century value.
	Show 4-digit year for 21st century (This is the default)	Shows only years before 1950 and after 1999 as four digits. 1950–1999 are shown as two digits.

continues

Table 3.7   continued

Option	Choice	Comment
	Show year only when not this year	If the date entered is within the current year, the year component of it is not displayed. This takes precedence over the 4-digit year settings.
	None	If you don't check any of the options for Special, the display depends on the default of your user settings.

Display Time

Option	Choice	Comment
Display Time	Checkbox	If you select the Display Time checkbox the options Show and Time Zone are activated.
Show (available only if Display Time is selected)	All Hours, minutes, and seconds Hours and Hours only	You select which parts of time you want to display. The order and whether it uses the 24 hour clock or AM/PM depends on your client international settings. Please note that All adds hundredths of a second.
Time Zone (available only if Display Time is selected)	Adjust time to local zone	Displays all times as local time. If a user in the U.S. Eastern time zone enters 4 p.m., a user in the Pacific time zone sees it as 1 p.m.
	Always show time zone	Displays times in the local time of the user who entered it. All users see the time entered in the previous row as 4 p.m. EST. The user in the Pacific time zone has to do the conversion to local time in his head.
	Show only if zone not local	Displays the time zone only if the user viewing the information is in another time zone. In the preceding example, the user in the Eastern time zone sees 4 p.m. The user in the Pacific time zone sees 4 p.m. EST.

On Input

Option	Choice	Comment
Require user enter 4-digit years	Checkbox	If checked, a user is not permitted to save the document if he or she enters the year as only two digits.

Require user enter alphabetic months	Checkbox	If checked, a user has to enter the months by their names, not their numbers. It uses a first match, so *m* gives you *March* in English. You have to enter *au* to get *August* instead of *April*.

Border Style (for Notes style fields only)

Show field delimiters	Checkbox	Shows the start and end brackets when checked. The field has nothing to delineate it when this box is not checked.

Table 3.8   Field Properties Control Page: Custom Date/Time Display Options

Option	Choice	Comment
	Display Date	
Format. This defines the order of the fields you selected in Show and Special.	YMDW	Displays dates in Year, Month, Date, Weekday order. This is the convention in Japan.
	WMDY	Displays dates in Weekday, Month, Date, Year order. This is the convention in the United States.
	WDMY	Displays dates in Weekday, Date, Month, Year order. This is the convention in the U.S. Military and in Europe.
Separators	You can enter spaces, dash, parentheses, slash, period, comma, and most punctuation in this field.	These three fields are used to separate the date parts. The separators work in the same left to right order as the display date format. For YMDW, the first separator field is between Y and M. For WMDY, the first separator field is between W and M.
Day	d	Do not fill single-digit dates with a leading zero. For example: January 1, 2000

continues

Table 3.8   continued

Option	Choice	Comment
	dd	Fill single-digit dates with a leading zero. For example: January 01, 2000
Month	m	Display months as numbers. Do not fill single-digit months with a leading zero. For example: 1/31/2000
	mm	Display months as numbers. Fill single-digit months with a leading zero. For example: 01/31/2000
	mmm	Display months as words, abbreviated (Jan, Feb, and so on).
	mmmm	Display months as words, written out (January, February, and so on).
Year	yy	Display years in two-digit format if the year is between 1950 and 1999, inclusive (98, 99, and so on).
	yyyy	Display years in four-digit format (1998, 1999, 2000, and so on).
Display Time		
Format	12-hour or 24-hour	24-hour uses military time, so 11:00 p.m. is displayed as 23:00
Separator	Defaults to a colon (:)	You can substitute any non-alphanumeric character, or up to three characters.

Other Field Display Options

Keyword fields offer choices of words or phrases and include the following field types: dialog list, checkbox, radio button, listbox, and combobox. Set display options for these keywords field types in the Control page of the Field Properties box. One of these options includes entering the list of words used in these fields for users to select or choosing a method to produce that list automatically. The display options are illustrated in Figure 3.9 and described in Table 3.9.

FIGURE 3.9

Depending on the field type, options you can set include the style of border, the width and height, the number of columns, whether multiple values can be selected, and if values that are not on the list can be added.

Radio buttons shown in one column with an inset border

Dialog list that enables you to select more than one value and add values that aren't on the original list

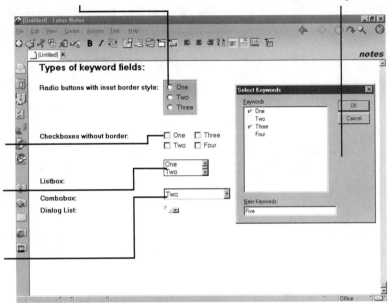

Checkboxes shown in two columns without a border

Listbox has a height of 0.5 inch instead of the standard 0.250 inch

Combobox that has a width of 1.5 inches, instead of the standard 1.0 inch

Table 3.9   Field Properties Control Page: Dialog list, Checkbox, Radio button, Listbox, and Combobox Options

Option	Description
Display	
Border Style (Radio buttons and checkboxes only)	Three choices: **None**—no border shows **Single**—border line around the choices **Inset**—border and internal area is set to gray
Number of columns (Radio buttons and checkboxes only)	Enter or use spinners to select the number of columns to spread out the choices. The values are set in top-to-bottom, and then left-to-right order.
For Dialog list	Show field delimiters (checkbox). If this is checked, the field has begin and end brackets on the form.

continues

Table 3.9   continued

Option	Description
Choices: The Options Vary Depending on Field Type	
Dialog list	Enter choices (one per line) Use formula for choices Use Address dialog for choices Use Access Control List for choices Use View dialog for choices
Checkbox, Radio button, Listbox, Combobox	Enter choices (one per line) Use formula for choices
Option: Enter choices (one per line)	You type in the values. Do *not* put them in quotes. **Sort**—Sorts in ascending order the entries you entered. **List Window…**—Presents a dialog box to enter the values. The dialog box enables you to sort, accept, or reject what you entered.
Option: Use formula for choices:	Enter the formula in the box below this choice. **Formula Window…**—Presents a dialog box to enter the formula. The dialog box includes buttons to access Fields & Functions, to accept or reject the changes, and to obtain help.
Option: Use Address dialog for choices	When you click the helper entry key it presents the address selection dialog box. The appropriate version displays, based on the field accepting single or multiple values.
Option: Use Access Control List for choices	When you click the helper entry key it presents the ACL information for the current database. The appropriate version displays, based on the field accepting single or multiple values.
Option: Use View dialog for choices	This option enables you to show the user information from a view from any database on the current server to which the user has read access. The additional fields you can set are **Database**—Shows you the databases known to your Notes client. You cannot type in the name. **View**—A list of all views, including hidden views. All columns of the view are displayed to the user to select from. **Column**—The column whose value you want to retrieve from the selected row in the view. The leftmost column is column 1.
Options section: Values Vary Based on Field Type and Choices	
Allow Values Not in List (for Dialog list and Combobox only)	Check this box to allow the user to type in their own value.

Option	Description
Look up names as each character is entered	This option is only available when the choice is Use Address dialog for choices, and when you do not use the helper entry key. Domino tries to guess who you want to select based on the letters you enter before you pause. If you don't like the selection, just keep typing.
Display entry helper button (for Dialog list only)	Check this to show the small arrow that appears next to the field. When users click on the helper entry key, a dialog box displays. The alternative way to display the dialog is to press Enter when the cursor is in the field, but that method is not obvious.
Refresh fields on keyword change	Check this to refresh all the document fields when you change the selected keyword. This is advised when you have other fields on the form that calculate or hide/unhide based on the keyword choice.
Refresh choices on document refresh	Check to have this field change the choices that are presented to the user. This usually has impact only when the Choices setting is Use formula for choices. For example, Company field value tells the document to refresh. This field, Contacts, has the setting Refresh choices on document refresh checked. The choices for Contacts are based on the Company field. This way the user is shown only contacts for the selected company.

3

Create Fields

When you are ready to add a field to your form, follow these steps:

1. With the form opened in design mode, position your cursor on the form in which you want the field to appear. Place your field following or underneath your field label. For example, if you have a label text that says "Customer name," place your cursor a few spaces after the static text or in the adjoining cell of a table.

Note

To create a shared field, choose **Create, Design, Shared Field**. Then define the field as you define any field. If you have already created the field and decide that you want to make it shared, select the field, and then choose **Design, Share this field**. To learn more about using shared fields in other forms, see Day 17

2. Choose **Create**, **Field** from the menu.

3. On the **Field Info** page of the Field Properties box, enter the name of the field in the Name box. (for example, a field for entering a first name might be called Fname). Figure 3.10 shows a field name entered in the Field Properties box.

FIGURE 3.10

The field name is a short descriptive name that indicates the contents. In this case, the name also includes "Resp," which indicates that it is a field on the "Response" form.

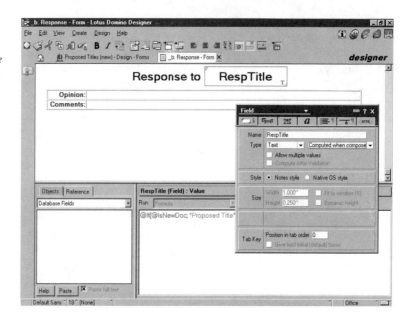

4. Select the Type of field. If necessary, refer to Table 3.3 for field types.

5. Choose whether the field is to be **Editable**, **Computed, Computed for display**, or **Computed when composed**.

   If you pick a keyword type of field (combobox, listbox, and so forth), list the keywords you want to appear on the Control Page (see Figure 3.11). Check **Allow values not in list** if you want users to have the capability to use words that are not included in your dialog list. If you allow values that are not included in your list, those new values are not added to your original list. Check **Allow multiple values** on the Field Info page for dialog list or listbox fields if you want to enable the users to pick more than one keyword (not available for radio buttons).

FIGURE 3.11

*When entering choices
for keywords use syn-
onyms to force the
order of the keywords
in radio buttons,
checkboxes, listboxes,
comboboxes, and dia-
log lists. In this exam-
ple, the left side is the
form in Designer,
Priority is a radio but-
ton field, and the Field
Properties box shows
the choices on the
Control page. On the
right is the document
with the radio buttons
in the listed order,
instead of appearing
alphabetically as they
would normally.*

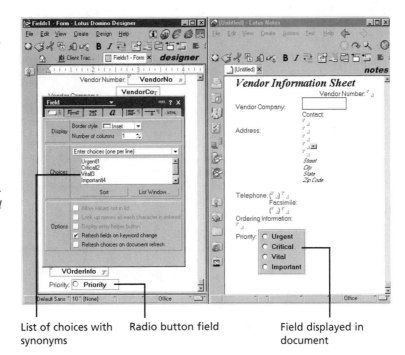

List of choices with
synonyms

Radio button field

Field displayed in
document

On the Control tab of the Field Properties box, select your desired display options
(see Figure 3.12).

FIGURE 3.12

*Radio buttons, check-
boxes, listboxes, and
comboboxes are easy
for users to fill out but
take up space on the
resulting documents.
Only the result of a
dialog list choice
shows when a user
reads a document.*

Result in document

Choices in dialog list

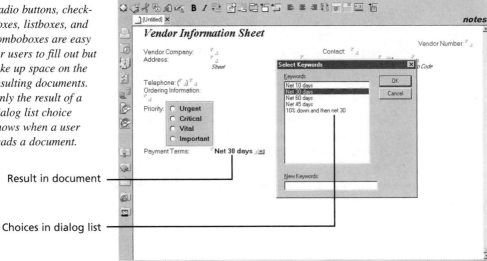

6. Click once on the **Advanced** tab of the Field Properties box (see Figure 3.13) and enter any helpful text in the Help description box (for instance, "Select the location closest to your home"). If the user has selected **View**, **Show**, **Field Help** from the menu, this help description appears at the bottom of the screen when the cursor is in the field.

> **Tip**
>
> Field Help text displays on one line of the status bar when a user clicks in a field. You can use 200 characters for field help (although Lotus recommends 70 to accommodate lower resolution, smaller monitors), including numbers, spaces, and punctuation. Because field help is displayed on the status bar, it is often overlooked by users. Consider placing important help information directly on your form and hiding that information when a document is in read mode. You learn more about hiding information on Day 9.

FIGURE 3.13

Seventy characters are available for your help text, but keep your message brief. Add emphasis with capitalization.

7. If the field is computed, you must enter a formula or script in the Script Area (see Figure 3.14). Select the appropriate type of entry you are going to make from the Run drop-down list. When you enter a formula or script you must type the text and then click on the green check to accept the entry. You'll learn more about formulas in the next lesson; scripts are covered on Days 19 and 20.

8. Beginning again at step 1, continue to add fields to your form.

In the example shown in Figure 3.15, a computed field is inserted at the top of the form to display the name of the program, which is entered in the ProgramName field. The text attributes for the display field are set at 24-point bold, italic Times New Roman. Most of the fields are editable text fields, except for the ProgramFacilityMap field—which is a rich text field (so that a picture of a map can be stored there)—and the Radio Button field ProgramFacilityName. Each field on this form starts with "Program" for the purpose of avoiding confusion when other forms are used to inherit information from this form. By using the form name in the field name, you'll know which fields came from which forms. Note that *Program* is a long word to be included in a field name; remember that field names need to be as short as possible. It is easier to use "P" for Program, or "Pro." Program was spelled out for the sake of this example. You also see static text on this form, such as "Cost of Program" and "Program Name."

FIGURE 3.14

A formula can be as simple as a field name, or it can be quite complex. This formula is a @Function that returns the original creator's name.

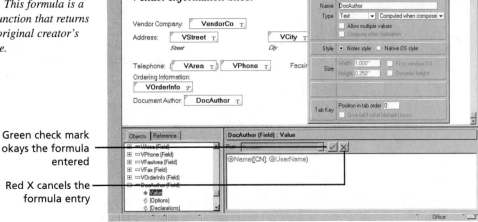

Green check mark okays the formula entered

Red X cancels the formula entry

FIGURE 3.15

The ProgramName field will later be hidden when the document is read, and the ProgramNameDisp field will be hidden when the document is edited. For that reason, each of these fields are in separate paragraphs.

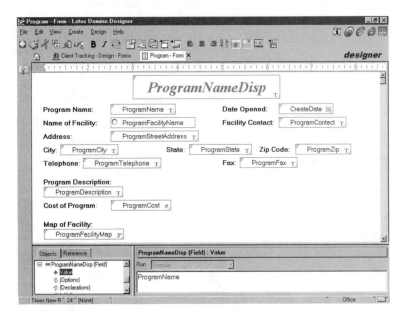

Edit Fields

You can edit or change a field name, field properties, and formulas for fields at any time by opening the properties box and making changes.

It's important to note that changes you make to the field properties boxes can create unwanted results. For example, changing a field's data type from text to date/time can result in conflicting data type messages if you decide to change a form field after documents have been created and after users have already entered text. The existing documents won't open until you resolve the conflicts by returning the field to its original data type.

Tip

To make sure that your fields behave the way you planned, choose **Design, Preview in Notes**, or choose **Design, Preview in Web Browser** from the menu. You have to save the file when you are queried by Notes. When the form and its fields appear, enter some sample data to see how your fields work. You can save the test document to help in your view tests later, or you can close it without saving it.

Summary

In today's lesson you learned that fields are the areas on forms in which users enter data. Entering fields requires that—at a minimum—you supply a field name and a field type. If you do not supply a field name, fields names are entered on your form by Domino and named "untitled," "untitled1," "Untitled2," and so forth. You can accept Domino's naming convention, but it's virtually useless when you need to determine a field's purpose.

Speaking of purpose, we purposely avoided showing you methods of hiding fields and information at this stage of development. It's a good idea (as we stated earlier, and feel that we can't stress enough) to wait until later in development before you hide objects. This gives you the chance to see fields and field results at work in your form.

You also learned that fields are objects, and that they have events associated with them. Take the time to create different types of fields and note their events. As you progress through this book, you learn more about field types and events, but it's a good idea to familiarize yourself with event names now.

Q&A

Q **What happens if I actually roll out an application and realize after rollout that a new field needs to be added to a form?**

A Edit the form and add the field. Documents that were created prior to the addition of the new field do not display the new field until they are placed in edit mode. If the field is computed, you can write an agent to update existing documents (you learn about agents on Day 14, "The Not So Secret Agents").

Q **If I decide to delete a field from a form after an application is rolled out, what happens to documents that were created with this field in the form? Does the field disappear from existing documents?**

A Just as you have to place saved documents in edit mode to see new fields, you have to place documents in edit mode for deleted fields to disappear from display. However, the field remains in the underlying document. Take heed: Before you delete a field, you need to be certain that you have not used this field in any formulas or views that will be affected by the deletion of this field. We recommend writing an agent to delete the field (again, you learn about agents on Day 14).

Q **What if I need to add a hidden field? Because you haven't covered hiding fields here, should I wait to add fields to my form that need to be hidden?**

A Fields can be hidden, and they can be hidden based on the user's task—when a document is being printed, when a document is being read, and so forth. It's a good idea to wait to hide fields until you are near the end of your development cycle. By waiting, you allow yourself the opportunity to see the fields in action when you test your documents. You learn about hiding fields on Day 9, but you can add fields to your form now and hide them later. A heads up here: It is recommended that you place fields that you intend to hide near the bottom or the top of your form. When you select information to hide, Domino measures this information in units of paragraphs. So if you think you have fields that are hidden for one purpose and fields that are hidden for another purpose, be sure to include a paragraph break between them (a hard return). Note that each *cell* of a table is considered a separate paragraph. Also, you learn on Day 4 that some calculated fields need special handling when it comes to placement on forms.

Q I want to add field help documentation, but the Properties box help field isn't large enough at 70 characters and I don't want help text filling up my form. Is there any other way to assist the user in filling out a field?

A Consider the use of a pop-up annotation to the field label to place help information directly on the form. This is useful when the information you want to provide does not fit in the help description field on the Properties box. To place pop-up text on a label, select the label text and choose **Create, Hotspot, Text Pop-up** from the menu. Type your help information in the HotSpot pop-up dialog box and indicate whether the pop-up is to appear when the mouse is held over the field or when the field is clicked. You learn more about HotSpots on Day 12, "Beautify Your Application," in the section "Add Hotspots".

Workshop

In this workshop, you will add fields to the forms you created for the Proposed Titles database on Day 2. Your tasks will include

- Create fields
- Name fields
- Set field type
- Specify display options
- Add field help
- Save the form
- Test the form

All the fields you are entering will be editable fields until Day 4, when you learn how to enter formulas. Because you created the forms based on your own design, you continue to control the appearance of the text and therefore the text formatting of the fields.

Add Fields to the Main Topic Form

Open the Proposed Title form in Designer. Using the static text you placed on the form as a guideline, add the fields listed in Table 3.10 to the form. You might have to adjust the position of your static text or even your fields; use cut and paste to move text or fields. Additional static text might also be needed. Be sure to add help text for your fields. Test your form by choosing **Design, Preview in Notes**. Note that all the names of our fields begin with the letter *T*, used to help us identify the field as one contained in the form "Title".

Table 3.10   Fields to Add to Proposed Title Form

Static Text	Field	Type/ Options	Choices
Book Title	TBookTitle	Text, Editable	
Suggested Authors	TProposed Authors	Text, Editable Allow multi-values	
Book Category	Tbook Category	Dialog list, Editable Allow multi-values Allow values not in list	Communications/ Internet
			Graphics & Desktop Publishing
			Operating Systems
			Word Processing
			Spreadsheet
			Database
			Presentation
			Accounting
			Suites
Book Description	TDescription	Text, Editable	
Discussion Period	TReviewStart	Date/Time, Editable	
		Show only month, day and year	
To	TReviewEnd Editable	Date/Time,	

continues

Table 3.10 continued

Static Text	Field	Type/ Options	Choices
		Show only month, day and year	
Assigned Acquisition Editor	TAcqEditor	Dialog List, Editable	
		Use Address dialog for choices	
Status	TStatus	Radio Button, Editable	Accepted|1
			Rejected|2
			Hold for Further Discussion|3
			Under Discussion|4
Document Author	TdocAuthor	Names, Editable	
Date Created	TCreateDate	Date/Time, Editable	
		Show only month, day, and year	

Note that the TStatus field has synonyms added to the choices.

After you finish adding fields, save your form; it should resemble the one shown in Figure 3.16. Remember that response documents can be tested only after you select a main document in the Notes client, so you'll need to create a main document or two before you test the response.

FIGURE 3.16

The Proposed Title form with the fields added.

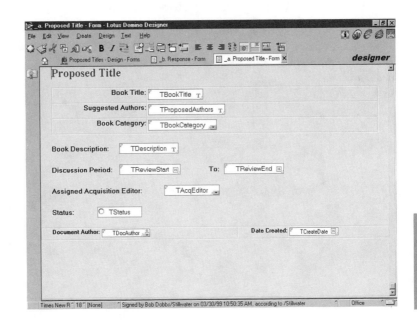

Add Fields to the Response Document

The Response form has two lines of static text: Opinions and Comments. You are going to enter three fields on this form:

- **ROpinion**—This is an editable checkbox. The keywords include Great Idea, Fantastic, Worthy, Some good points, Needs more work, Needs further development, Rethink this.
- **RRespComments**—Text, editable field meant to collect a short summary of the user's remarks.
- **RBody**—Rich Text field (editable by default). Place below the RRespComments field to collect a full opinion of the book, with details.

After you enter the fields and define them, add the field help. Save and test the form.

The Comments form also has an opinion field, and the choices work for both. To save yourself some duplicate work when you create that form, click on the ROpinion field and choose **Design**, **Share This Field** from the menu.

When the form is complete, it looks similar to the one in Figure 3.17.

FIGURE 3.17

*The Response form
after adding the fields
and sharing the
Opinion field.*

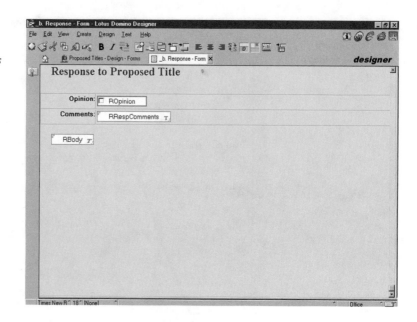

Add Fields to the Comments Form

The Comments form has only two fields:

- **ROpinion**—This is the shared field you created in the last section. To insert it at your cursor's position, choose **Create, Insert Shared Field** from the menu. Select **Opinion** in the Insert Shared Field dialog box and then click **OK**. You can still assign text attributes to the field.

- **CCommentBody**—This is a rich text field in which the user can enter text, format the text, add graphics or attachments, or embed objects.

Save the form and test it (you have to open a response document to do this, so test from the client). When it is complete, it resembles the form shown in Figure 13.18.

FIGURE 3.18

FIGURE **3.18**

*The Comments form
with the Opinion
shared field and
CommentBody rich
text field added.*

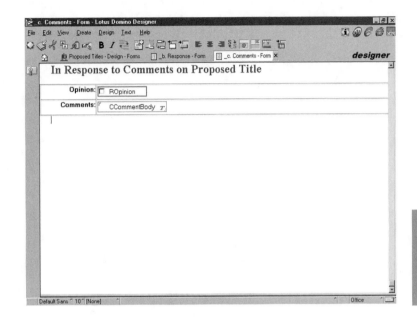

These three forms are works in progress. You will add more static text and fields on
future days.

To see our examples of this application, open the folder on the CD called Day3 and open
the database file named PTDay3.nsf. Our forms may not look exactly like yours, but we
don't object if you improved on the looks of the forms. Use this database to check that
you have the correct fields and field types.

DAY 4

Formulas 101: The Basics

A *formula* is an expression that performs a function (`@sum (Commission, Bonus)`), expresses a fact (`1+2=3`), sets a principal or rule (`@ProperCase ("ClientName")`), or determines a method for doing something (`if x= "Yes," SaveDocument`). Formulas can appear practically everywhere in Notes databases. Here are a few examples: Formulas can appear in fields to calculate, format, or validate a field value. They can be contained in views to select which documents appear in which views or to calculate and format the data that appears in view columns. Formulas can also be used in forms or views to determine which forms certain users use to read documents. You attach formulas to the events that are associated with various Notes objects. Then, when those events occur, Notes runs the formulas and applies the results.

In this lesson you learn about formula construction—how to build formulas, formula syntax, and the Lotus @Function programming language. Although this chapter concentrates on the use of formulas in fields, the skills you learn here apply to all formulas used throughout Domino databases.

Don't be discouraged by the size of this chapter—it is one of the longest lessons in the book. This is because we've provided many tables that contain information that is critical to writing formulas. We could have placed the tables in an appendix at the end of the book, but we wanted you to be able to find these tables within their respective topics.

Understand Formulas

A formula can be as simple as a field name or concatenation of field names, or as complex as a multiple statement with combined functions. Formulas consist of any or all of these components: constants, variables, operators, keywords, and functions.

 Concatenation—The stringing together of field names and text constants. In this example, the values of the City, State, and Zip fields are concatenated with punctuation:

```
City + ", " + State + " " + Zip
```

Depending upon the value of the City, State, and Zip fields, this formula might result to:

```
Philadelphia, Pennsylvania 99888
```

Do not confuse concatenation with addition. They both use plus (+) signs, but addition is a *mathematical* function.

You can use formulas to perform a variety of tasks in Domino applications. Table 4.1 illustrates just a few of the many uses of formulas in a Domino database.

Table 4.1   Where to Use Formulas

Use Formulas in	In order to
Forms	Compute field values
	Format data for display
	Hide fields under specified conditions
	Set the window title
	Provide a default value
	Translate input
	Validate input
	Perform actions
Views	Select documents for the view
	Determine column values
	Perform actions
Actions	Perform menu commands
Security	To control access to sections, fields, and text

Enter Formulas in Fields

You create formulas by entering them in the Programmer's Pane. But first you have to select the object—and the associated event—to which you want to attach your formula. You can select an object by clicking it either in the Work Pane, where it appears visually, or in the Info List, where it appears in a list. Selecting an object in the Work Pane causes it to be selected in the Objects list.

When you have found the object in the Objects list, you can select the associated event for which you want to write your formula. An object's events appear indented beneath the object. There can be one or many events associated with a given type of object. If you don't see any events indented beneath the object you want to program, but the object has a plus sign (+) to its left, click the plus sign. The list of events appears.

After you have selected the event, you can enter the formula in the Programmer's Pane, to the right of the Info List. For example, select a field in your form, select an event listed under your field in the Info List (such as Value or Default Value), and then type the formula in the Programmer's Pane as shown in Figure 4.1.

FIGURE 4.1

Select the object (field) event (such as value) and enter your formula in the Programmer's Pane. When you are finished entering your formula, click the green check mark in the Programmer's Pane.

Object selected in Work pane

Event in Info List

Formula in Script Area

Click to accept formula

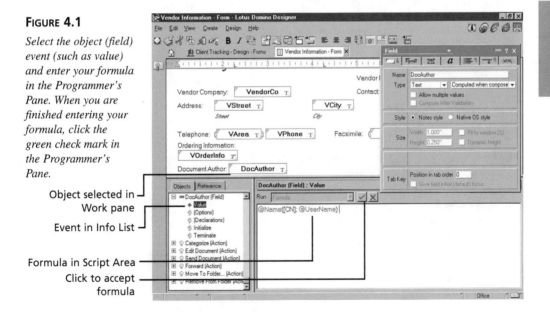

4

If you make a mistake in your formula syntax, Domino notifies you. This notification can be in the form of a dialog box (see Figure 4.2) or in a message that appears in the bottom of the Programmer's Pane (see Figure 4.3). Note that in formulas containing @Functions, there is no space between the @ sign and the name of the function.

FIGURE 4.2

Errors in syntax, such as the incorrect number of arguments in an @If formula or mixing data types in the same formula, should cause Designer to alert you with a dialog box. However, some errors aren't detected automatically and might not become obvious until you test the form. Errors for incompatible data types may appear in the field when you save the test document.

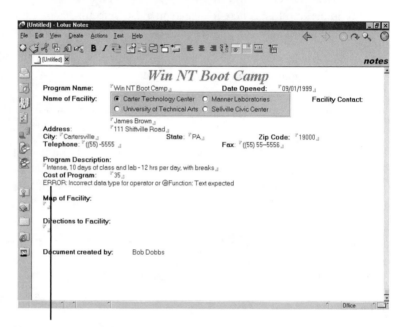

Error appears at field

FIGURE 4.3

An error message appears, suggesting that an operator or semicolon is missing, and the incorrectly used comma is displayed in red. One of the most common errors in writing formulas is missing or mistyped semicolons.

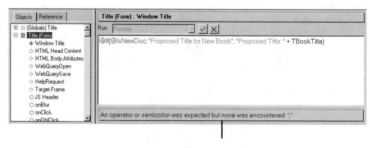

Error message

Finally, you need to test your formula by choosing **Preview in Notes** from the Design menu. This shows you a new document based on the form in Edit mode. You can then fill out the fields and refresh the document to see the results of your formula. You can also choose Preview in Web Browser if you want to know how the formula will work in a Web browser (see Figure 4.4). If the form in which you are working is a Response or Response to Response form, you can't preview it this way because you have to select a document to respond to. In this case you have to save the form, switch to a view in which you can select a document, and then create a new document with this form.

FIGURE 4.4

Previewed in a Web browser, two fields display information. One is a computed when composed field that captures the date the form is created, and the other shows a default value that can be changed by the user.

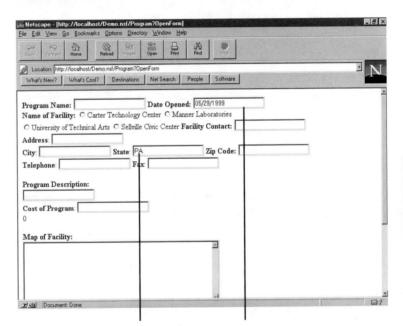

Editable field displaying default value   Computed when composed field

Formula Syntax

All programming languages have syntax rules, and Notes formulas are no exception. You have to know where to put spaces, when to use quotation marks, when to capitalize letters, and where to place parentheses. If you make a syntax error, Designer displays an error message. For the most part, you can rest assured that if your formula is not entered with correct syntax, Designer will tell you about it.

But you can't depend on Designer to ensure that all formulas you write will work properly. Syntax is only part of knowing how to write a formula. There are times when Designer will pass a formula on syntax, but the formula might not do exactly what you intended because it is logically incorrect.

For example, let's say that you want the field "Salesperson" to default to the value of the field "CreatedBy." In this case, you are using the field name as a variable, so do not enclose it in quotation marks. Therefore, the formula for the field Salesperson is simply CreatedBy, the name of the field whose value you want to accept. That's it—the whole formula.

Alternately, you might want the field Salesperson to accept, say, the name of the sales manager as the default. In this case the formula is the sales manager's name in quotation marks, for example, "Calabria." The text between the quotation marks becomes the value of the field.

You can see that quotation marks are needed to identify text in a formula, and no quotation marks are needed to identify a *field name*. But what happens if you forget the quotes around Calabria? Domino accepts Calabria as a field name, and no syntax error message results when you enter the formula. Of course, the field contents will be blank because there is no field (or other variable) called Calabria. Conversely, if you put quotes around a field name, the formula resolves to the literal field name, "CreatedBy." Whoops! Figure 4.5 shows some examples of what can happen when you misplace or misuse quotation marks in a formula.

FIGURE 4.5

Putting quotes around field names or leaving the quotes off text causes problems; in this document title, the name of the field appears instead of the name of the company. The telephone number also suffers from the same error. The state had to be entered because the default state name didn't appear—no quotes around the text!

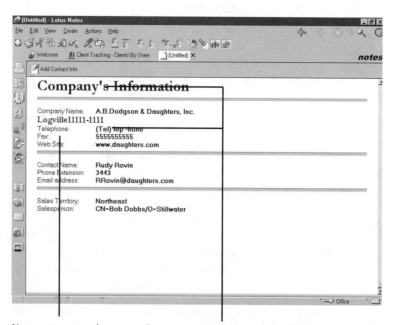

No quotes around text   Quotes were put around the field name

If this little scenario doesn't convince you that formula syntax is critical to the success of your application, what will? Of course, this is just a very small example of the importance of syntax. Formulas also contain parentheses, brackets, commas, spaces, colons, and semicolons, all of which play a very important role in Domino's capability to resolve your formulas.

Table 4.2 details what you need to know and remember about syntax.

Table 4.2 Formula Syntax Rules

Use	Rules	Example
Upper- and Lowercase	Formulas are not case sensitive. However, most Notes programmers follow these conventions:	
	KEYWORDS in uppercase	`SELECT Form = "Person"`
	@Functions in mixed case	`@ProperCase(Lname)`
	@Commands in mixed case	`@Command([Compose] ;"memo")`
	Variables in mixed case	`CreatedBy`
Colons (:)	Use to separate elements in a list	`"A" : "B" : "C"`

Data types	The use of mixed data types is not permitted in formulas. That is, you cannot combine text with numbers, text with date/time values, or numbers and date/time values.	`@Text ( @Now )`
		
		`@TextToNumber ( Price )`
		
		`@TextToTime ( TextDate )`

	To combine data types, use data conversion @Functions.	

continues

Table 4.2 Formula Syntax Rules

Use	Rules	Example
Logical operators AND (&) OR (¦) NOT (!)	Expressions on each side of an operator are evaluated separately. Therefore, they must be complete expressions (this doesn't apply to NOT, which applies only to the expression on the right).	Correct: `Category = "Database" ¦` `Category = "Spreadsheet"` Incorrect: `Category = "Database" ¦ "Spreadsheet"`

Parentheses
( )
	Enclose all @Function arguments in parentheses. Also, use parentheses to enforce order of execution. Use the same number of open and closed parentheses.	`@If(State = "PA";`
		`@Success;`
		`@Failure("Please`
		`enter your state"))`
		
		`(PhilaIncome + NYIncome)/12`

Quotation marks	Use to enclose text strings.	`CompanyName + ",` `Inc."`
	Use to treat a number as text.	`"610-555-8899"`
	Do not use around field names.	`CompanyName`

Semicolons (;)	Use to separate multiple statements in a formula and multiple arguments in an @Function.	`Total := Qty *`
		`Price; @If(Total>40;`
		`"Y"; "N")`

Use	Rules	Example

Spaces	Use any number of spaces to separate formula elements.	`@If  (  Key  =`
		`"One"  ;  "Yes"`
		`;  "No"  )`

	Use one space to follow a keyword.	`SELECT Form =` `"Inquiry"`

	Use spaces within text constants wherever they normally fall.	`@If(State = "PA";`
		`@Success;`
		`@Failure("Please`
		`enter the state"))`

Square brackets [ ]	Use to enclose date/time constants.	`[01/03/96 10:33:12]`

	Also used for keyword arguments in @Functions.	`@prompt(`
		`[OkCancelEdit];"`
		`Enter Your`
		`Name";"Type your`
		`name in the box`
		`below";@UserName)`

Text constants	Must be in quotes with appropriate spaces.	`Address :=Street +`
		`@NewLine + City +`
		`", "; State + "`
		`" + Zip`

	Use case as it is to appear.	

Constants in Formulas

Constants are values that don't change. As their name indicates, constants always remain the same. Constants can be numbers, text, or date/time. Text constants are always enclosed in quotation marks. Date/Time constants are always enclosed in square brackets. Number constants are not enclosed in any punctuation.

Number constants include numerals from 0–9, + (plus), - (minus), exponent (E), constant (e), and/or decimals (.).

Text constants are any set of characters that appear in a formula in quotation marks (" "), such as `"Philadelphia"`.

If you want to include quotation marks in a text string, you must precede the quotation mark with a backslash (\) (see Figure 4.6).

Date/time constants are any set of characters in Notes date or time format that appear in a formula in square brackets ([ ]), such as `[09/05/96]`.

FIGURE 4.6

Here, an error message appears below the Programmer's Pane because a backslash is needed before the quotation mark that precedes the word Great.

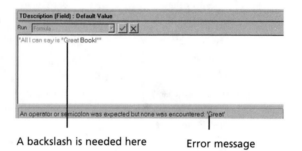

A backslash is needed here   Error message

Operators in Formulas

Formulas can contain algebraic expressions:

```
x + y
```

is a formula, where *x* and *y* are variables, or *operands*. The plus (+) is the *operator*. You use operators to assign values to variables, to modify values, or to combine values into new values. There are five types of operators: arithmetic, assignment, comparison, string, and logical (see Table 4.3).

Tip

Order of Calculation—Arithmetic operators evaluate in the following order: expressions within Parentheses, Exponents, Multiplication and Division, and then Addition and Subtraction. For example

```
6 + 4/2 = 8
(6 + 4)/2 = 5
```

Formulas can contain combinations of operands and operators. Operands in Notes can include field names and other variables, constants, or @Functions. Table 4.3 lists types of formula operators and examples of their use.

Table 4.3   Formula Operators

Type of Operator	Example	Results
Arithmetic		
+ (Addition)	`Cash + Accounts Receivable`	Adds the two elements
- (Subtraction)	`Income . Expenses`	Subtracts the second element from the first
* (Multiplication)	`Price * Quantity`	Multiplies the two elements
/ (Division)	`Unit/Total`	Divides the first element by the second element
Assignment		
:=	`tempStatus:= STATUS`	Assigns a value to a temporary variable
Comparison		
= (equal)	`@If(Year = "1999"; "Current"; Year)`	If the Year is 1999, return "Current". Otherwise return the value of the field Year.
!=, =!, ><, <> (not equal)	`@If(Year != "1999"; "Old"; "Current")`	If the Year is not 1999, return "Old". Otherwise, return "Current".
< (less than)	`@If(Age < 21; "No"; "Yes")`	If Age is less than 21, return "No"; otherwise, return "Yes".
> (greater than)	`@If(Age > 54; "Discount"; "No Discount")`	If Age is greater than 54, return "Discount"; otherwise return "No Discount".
<=, =< (less than or equal to)	`SELECT Qty <= 20`	Selects documents where the field Qty is less than or equal to 20.
>=, => (greater than or equal to)	`@If(Price >= 200; "Sell"; "Hold")`	If Price is greater than or equal to 200, returns "Sell"; otherwise returns "Hold".

continues

4

Table 4.3 continued

Type of Operator	Example	Results
Concatenation		
: (list)	`"Van" : "Sedan" : "Wagon"`	The list operator concatenates values into a list.
+ (text)	`FName + " " + LName`	Concatenates the value of `FName` with a space and the value of `LName` to return something such as `"Joe Doaks"` if the value in `FName` is `"Joe"` and the value in `LName` is `"Doaks"`.
Logical		
! (NOT)	`SELECT !(Month = "March")`	Selects documents for all months except for March.
& (AND)	`SELECT Status = "Active" & Year = "1999"`	Selects only documents in which both the field `Status` is set to `"Active"` and the field `Year` is set to `"1999"`.
¦ (OR)	`SELECT Name = "Dorothy" ¦ Name = "Tom"`	Selects only documents in which either `"Dorothy"` or `"Tom"` appears in the `Name` field.

Note   As you can see in our examples, we use field names in formulas. In these examples, you see the importance of creating unique, descriptive, and short field names.

In the preceding table we pointed out that you must use a complete expression on either side of a logical operator. Compare the following two statements:

```
Name = "Dorothy" ¦ Name = "Tom"
Name = "Dorothy" ¦ "Tom"
```

The first example is correct usage because both `Name = "Dorothy"` and `Name = "Tom"` are complete statements that can individually be evaluated as true or false. The second example is incorrect because the second statement—`"Tom"`—cannot be evaluated as true or false.

If this seems unsatisfying to you—if it seems like you shouldn't have to write out the whole statement twice—take heart. You can use the list concatenation operator (:) instead of the OR operator as follows:

```
Name = "Dorothy" : "Tom"
```

Here we have combined the two expressions into a single expression, which says that the value of Name is true if it contains any member of the list.

Tip

Don't confuse the assignment operator (:=) with the equality comparison operator (=). Use the assignment operator to assign values to variables:

```
Temp1 := "Tom"
```

The preceding example assigns the value "Tom" to the variable Temp1.

Use the equality comparison operator to compare the values of the operands on either side of it:

```
Temp1 = "Tom"
```

The preceding example is true if Temp1 contains the value "Tom"; otherwise, it is false.

4

Variables

Variables have different values at different times. Domino recognizes three kinds of variables: field names, temporary variables, and environment variables. Field names are just what you think they are—the names of fields. When you use a field name as a variable, Notes uses the value of the field. Temporary variables are variables that you can set in a formula for use later on in the formula. They are stored in memory while the formula is being computed, and then they are dropped from memory. Environment variables are stored in a workstation's or server's notes.ini file and are, therefore, more permanent than are temporary variables. We discuss the use of field names as variables and temporary variables in today's lesson. We discuss environment variables on Day 13, "Put on Your Propeller Beanie: Advanced Formulas."

Field Names as Variables

Field names are the most commonly used variables. They can stand by themselves as formulas. For example, if you want to show the value of the field FacilityName in a view column, the formula for the view column is simply this: FacilityName. Field names can also be used in arithmetic formulas. For example, if the field NetPrice has $100 in it, and the field GrossPrice has the formula `NetPrice * 1.06` in it, the user sees $106 in the GrossPrice field.

Field names can be strung together with operators and text in a concatenation. Depending on the values in the fields, the following formula

```
FacilityCity + ", " + FacilityState + " " + FacilityZip
```

might produce `Philadelphia, PA 19103`. It concatenates `"Philadelphia"` with a comma and a space, `"PA"`, another space, and then `"19103"`.

You can also use field names as arguments for @Functions:

```
@If(FacilityCity = "Philadelphia"; "Home"; "Away")
```

This formula says return `"Home"` if the field FacilityCity contains `"Philadelphia"`; otherwise it returns `"Away"`.

Temporary Variables

A temporary variable is one that you set in a formula for use later on in the formula, and only in the formula. Use temporary variables to make long, complex formulas easier to read (see Figure 4.7). Following are two examples of the same formula:

```
Cost * 1.28 * 1.06
```

```
Price := Cost * 1.28;
Tax := Price * .06;
Price + Tax
```

The first example is terse and uninformative. The second example is longer, but it is much more readable because it tells the reader what it is doing. It includes three expressions, separated from each other by semicolons. The first expression creates a temporary variable (`Price`) and assigns to it the value of the field Cost multiplied by 1.28. The second expression creates a temporary variable (`Tax`) and assigns to it the value of Price multiplied by .06. The third expression adds the values of the temporary variables (`Price` and `Tax`) and returns the result to the field that contains this formula. You'll learn more about multiline formulas on Day 13.

FIGURE 4.7

This input translation formula takes the 10 digits of a telephone number (text field), in which the user entered 1234567890, *and formats it to read* (123) 456-7890.

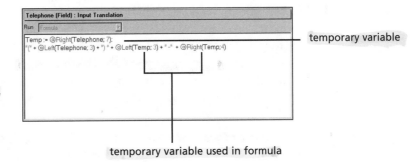

Telephone (Field) : Input Translation

Run [Formula]

Temp := @Right(Telephone; 7);
"(" + @Left(Telephone; 3) + ") " + @Left(Temp; 3) + "-" + @Right(Temp;4)

temporary variable

temporary variable used in formula

Formula Keywords

Formula keywords perform special functions in Notes formulas. Don't confuse them with keyword fields—they are different. By convention, we always enter them in uppercase. There are five of them, and they are used as follows:

- **DEFAULT**—Associates a value with a field. If the field already exists in a document, the field's actual value is used. If the field does not exist, Notes uses the value supplied by DEFAULT. In the following example, if the field Topic exists, its actual value is returned. If it doesn't exist, the DEFAULT value is returned:

```
DEFAULT Topic := MainSubject;
Topic
```

- **ENVIRONMENT**—Assigns a value to an environment variable in the user's notes.ini file or (on a Macintosh) the Notes Preferences file. The following formula converts the counter number to text and saves it as an environment variable called Order:

```
ENVIRONMENT Order := @Text(Counter)
```

The variable and its value appear in the notes.ini file as follows:

```
$Order=12
```

- **FIELD**—Assigns a value to a field in the current document. If the field doesn't exist, Notes creates it. If it does exist, Notes replaces the contents of the field with the assigned value. The formula in the following example creates a new field called FormalName that adds "Dr. " to the beginning of the name. It is not a visible field unless you add it to the form, but it exists in the document and you can use it in formulas:

```
FIELD FormalName := "Dr. " + LName
```

4

- **REM**—Enables you to insert a remark (documentation) into a formula. Notes ignores the remark when evaluating the formula. Its value lies in that, when you read the formula a year after you wrote it, it informs you what you were thinking when you wrote it. REM lines always end with a semicolon. Remarks must be in quotes and cannot include semicolons or other separators that are used in formulas:

```
REM "This formula assigns variables to calculate the correct date"
...
```

- **SELECT**—Defines a statement as a selection statement and tells Notes what documents to select. Use this in agents to tell the agent which documents to act upon. Use it in views to tell Notes or Domino what documents are to appear in the view. Use it in Replication formulas to tell what documents Notes or Domino is to replicate. The following example tells Notes or Domino to select all documents that have a Salesperson field that is equal to "Joe Doaks":

```
SELECT Salesperson = "Joe Doaks"
```

Understand @Functions

As you learned on Day 1, "An Introduction to Lotus Notes and Domino 5 Development," the Domino formula language helps you to write formulas in algebraic format and manipulate Domino objects using predesigned formulas known as @Functions (pronounced "at-functions") and @commands (pronounced "at-commands"). (You learn about @commands on Day 11, "Help the User: Design Interface Enhancements.") Use @Functions to do the following:

- Format text strings
- Generate and format dates and times
- Evaluate conditional statements
- Manipulate values in a list
- Calculate numeric values
- Activate agents, hotspots, actions, buttons or SmartIcons.

Using @Functions is the easiest way to write complex formulas in Domino. You might already be familiar with some @Functions and not realize it. If you've ever created a Lotus Spreadsheet, you're undoubtedly familiar with this @Function

```
@Sum(x,y)
```

where two variables (x and Y) are summed. There is one caveat: In Lotus spreadsheets, separate @Functions arguments with commas; in Notes, separate arguments with semicolons.

Note
> If you need help with @Function syntax or purpose, click the Reference tab in the Info List. Use the drop-down list to select Formula @Functions, highlight the @Function you need help with, and click the **Help** button or press **F1**.

Although some @Functions produce values on their own (such as @Created, which returns the date a document was created), many require *arguments*. Arguments are the variables a formula uses to perform the operation that is specified by the @Function. For example, in the formula

```
@Min(Retainer; Earnings),
```

"Retainer" and "Earnings" are the two arguments that @Min uses to return the smaller of the values. Notice that the arguments are enclosed in parentheses.

When an @Function uses arguments, the syntax rules are as follows:

- Separate multiple arguments with semicolons.
- Enclose all arguments in parentheses.
- Enclose keyword arguments in square brackets. These @Functions require keyword arguments: @Abstract, @Ascii, @Certificate, @Command, @PostedCommand, @DialogBox, @DocMark, @GetPortsList, @PickList, @Platform, @MailSend, @Name, @Prompt, @URLHistory and @URLOpen.

Tip
> There are three uses of *keyword* in Notes. A *keyword field* enables the user to choose a value from a list of keywords. A *formula keyword* appears in all CAPITAL LETTERS at the beginning of an expression and tells Notes that the expression is of a special type. A *keyword argument* in an @Function is a parameter that certain @Functions use to further specify the style of value to return. For example, in the formula @Name([CN];@UserName), CN tells @Name to return the common name of the user.

4

There are more than 200 @Functions in Domino, and they're all listed in the *Domino Designer Programming Guide - Volume 1: Formula Language*. They are also described in the Domino 5 Designer Help database. Finally, they are listed on the Reference tab in Designer (see Figure 4.8). We've provided an alphabetical list of the most frequently used @Functions in Appendix B, "@Functions." For more information on using Help databases and finding help online, see Appendix A, "Find Help."

FIGURE 4.8

*To add an @Function to your formula, click the **Reference tab** of the Info List, highlight the function, and then click **Paste**.*

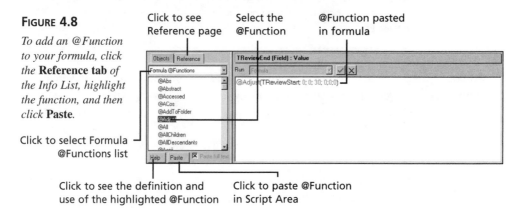

There are seven basic categories of @Functions: arithmetic operations, data conversion, date/time operations, list operations, logical operations, string manipulation, and special. The last is a catch-all category to hold the @Functions that don't fit neatly into any of the other categories.

Arithmetic Operations

Use arithmetic @Functions to make calculations using numeric values (refer to Appendix B, Table 2.1, for a listing of the more commonly used arithmetic @Functions).

How might you use an arithmetic function? Let's say you're trying to calculate pay for salespeople, but you want to pay whichever is the greatest: the commission on an individual's monthly sales or the salesperson's draw of $2,000. You want this amount to appear in the PayThis field of your form. To do this you might use the @Max function. This function returns the larger of two variables and is written in the following manner:

```
@Max(number; number)
```

If you know the actual figures, you can enter them into the formula to get the result you need for the PayThis field. The 2000 is the salesperson's draw, and the 7000 is the commission amount. The following @Max formula returns $7,000:

```
@Max(2000;7000)
```

However, you rarely know the two numbers in a comparison, so instead you want to use field names as variables in this formula. To do this, create a field called Draw, in which the salesperson's monthly draw amount is entered, and a field called Commission (see Figure 4.9 for an example of the formula you would create). Then, if the field for the monthly sales is named Sales, the formula to compute the commission is

```
Sales * 0.15
```

FIGURE 4.9

The manager wants to pay the salesperson the greater of the draw or the commission, and the @Max function provides that information.

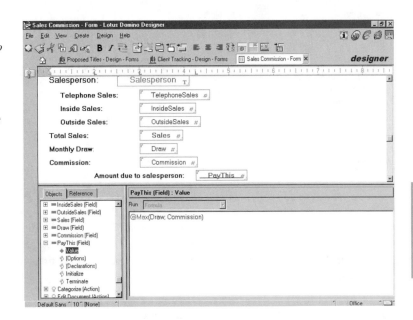

Round the number by making the commission formula look like this:

```
@Round(Sales * 0.15)
```

Now you can enter the formula for the PayThis field. This formula returns the higher number—the value in the Draw field or the value in the Commission field:

```
@Max(Draw; Commission)
```

Another situation in which you might want to use an arithmetic operation is if you need to calculate the monthly sales for each salesperson. To do this, you have to total the results of the three types of sales calls made (see Figure 4.10 to see a document created with this calculation), as in this equation:

```
@Sum(TelephoneSales : InsideSales : OutsideSales)
```

The @Sum function computes the total of a series of numbers. In the preceding example, @Sum totals the values in each field.

FIGURE 4.10

In this document for Jim Monroe, the @Sum formula calculates the Total Sales— a sum of the telephone sales, inside sales, and outside sales figures. The commission is 15% of that total, and the amount paid to Jim Monroe is his monthly draw, which is greater than his earned commission.

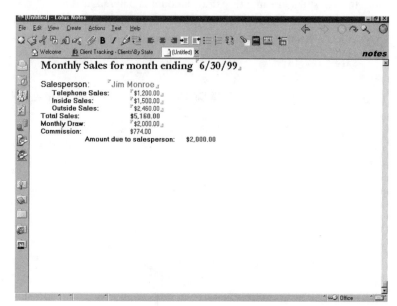

Table 4.4 Lists the most commonly used arithmetic @Functions and shows examples of formulas.

Table 4.4   Commonly Used Arithmetic @Functions

@Function	Example	Results
@Max(number; number)	@Max(5000; Actual)	Returns the larger of two numbers.
@Min(number; number)	@Min(Earnings; 10000)	Returns the smaller of the two numbers.
@Pi	2 * @Pi * Radius	Uses a predefined Pi value (3.14159265358979).
@Round(number)	@Round(Average)	Rounds a number to the nearest whole number.

@Function	Example	Results
@Round(number; factor)	@Round(Count;10)	Rounds a number to the nearest specified factor (in this case to the nearest ten).
@Sqrt(number)	@Sqrt(256)	Calculates the square root of a number.
@Sum(numbers)	@Sum(10; 30; 35) @Sum(Visitors : Employees : Contractors)	Totals numbers. Totals members of number list.

Other arithmetic operators include: @Abs, @Acos, @Asin, @Atan, @Atan2, @Cos, @Exp, @Integer, @Ln, @Log, @Modulo, @Sin, and @Tan.

Data Conversion

Domino does not enable you to concatenate values of different data types (for example, text and numbers). It does not enable you to do arithmetic or date/time calculations on text values. If you need to do these things, you first have to convert all the values to a single data type. You'll need to convert text to numbers, numbers to text, text to dates, or dates to text to ensure data type consistency within a formula. There are three @Functions that can do this for you:

- **@Text**—Converts numbers or date/time values to text
- **@TextToNumber**—Converts textual numbers to numeric numbers
- **@TextToTime**—Converts textual dates and times to date/time data type

Why might you need to convert data? Why not just set the field to the correct data type to begin with? Perhaps you want to use a field value for more than one purpose. For example, you might need the date a form was submitted or created to calculate due dates on a document, but in another field or in a view column you might want to include the same value in a concatenation formula. Or you might want to store a numeric value in an environment variable. Because environment variables are stored in a text file (notes.ini), they are necessarily text values. You have to convert a number to text to store it as an environment variable, and then convert it back to a number to use it in formulas.

4

> **Tip**
>
> Concatenating is stringing together or linking text, numbers or dates. For example, you use the following formula to concatenate fields which contain a city, state, and zip code to display all the information on one line:
>
> ```
> City + ", " + State + " " + Zip
> ```

When you concatenate a date/time or number field with text, you have to convert the date, time, or number value to text:

```
RegName + "registered on " + @Text(@Created)
```

If the field RegName contains the name of the registrant, the preceding formula returns that person's name plus the text "registered on" plus the date the registration form was created (which is the value that is returned by the @Created function). The result appears as follows:

```
Susan Frohm registered on 4/11/97 9:19:25 AM
```

Notice in the preceding example that the date and time are just plunked down without any punctuation. @Text enables you to format the value that it returns. When you use @Text(*value; format-string*), the format string you choose significantly affects the appearance of the returned value. For example, if you only want to return the date, and not the time, you can add a format string to the formula to specify the style in which you want Notes to return the date:

```
RegName + " registered on " + @Text(@Created; "D0S0")
```

This formula returns the following text:

```
Susan Frohm registered on 4/11/97
```

Here "D0" tells Notes to return the year, month, and day, and "S0" tells Notes to return only the date, not the time. This example is illustrated in Figures 4.11 and 4.12, where Susan has responded to a seminar offering the use of a registration form that collects her name and the date she registered. The information then appears in a view as a response to the seminar document.

FIGURE 4.11

In the registration form the RegDate field is a date field with the formula @Created.

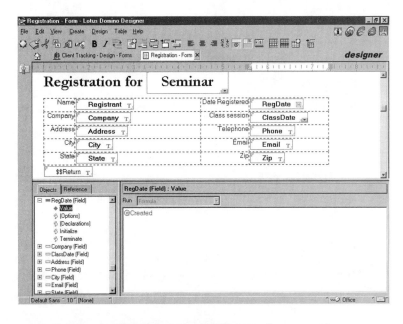

FIGURE 4.12

Because the concatenation formula for the column includes text, a text field, and a date field, the date field information had to be converted with an @Text formula. The format string "D0S0" makes the date show with month, day, and year, but without the time.

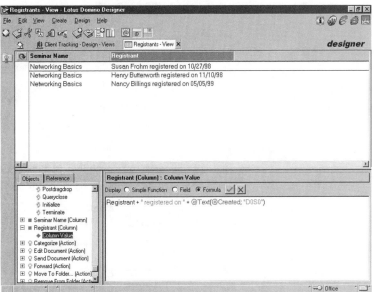

There are four categories of date/time format strings, as shown in Table 2.3 in Appendix B. Although you can include up to four components in your format string, you can only choose one from each category. For example

`@Text(Date; "D0S0")`

returns 8/19/96, where the `"D0"` tells Notes to return the year, month, and day, and the `"S0"` tells Notes to return the date without the time.

But

`@Text(Date; "T1S1")`

returns 10:15, where `"T1"` returns the hour and minute, and `"S1"` returns the time without the date.

There are also format strings for numbers, as shown in Table 4.5. You can combine any of these into a string. For example, `@Text(Price; "C,2")` returns `$25.00` when the value in the Price field is 25. Here the `"C"` represents currency and the `"2"` represents the number of decimal places. The comma tells Domino to separate thousands with a comma.

Table 4.5   Format-String Options for @Text function

Category	String	Returns
D	D0	Year, month, and day
	D1	Month and day (plus year if not current year)
	D2	Month and day
	D3	Year and month
T	T0	Hour, minute, and second
	T1	Hour and minute
Z	Z0	Always convert time to this zone
	Z1	Display zone only when it is not this zone
	Z2	Display zone always
S	S0	Date only
	S1	Time only
	S2	Date and time
	S3	Date, time, Today, or Yesterday
Number values	G	General number format (significant digits only)
	F	Fixed format (set number of decimal places)
	S	Scientific format (E notation)

Category	String	Returns
	c	Currency format (two decimal places)
	,	Punctuated at thousands (using U.S. format)
	%	Percentage format
	(	Parentheses around negative numbers
	Number	Number of digits of precision (as in "F2", which results in a fixed-format, two-digit number)

There are also a number of data conversion functions that determine what type of data a field contains. The function @IsNumber, for example, determines if the data type of a value is a number:

```
@IsNumber(Value)
```

Based on the preceding format, use a field name as the variable you substitute for Value in the function. If the value in the field is a number, the function returns "1" (true); if not, the function result is "0" (false). You might use a function like this if you aren't sure if the field is a number or text type field. If the field is a keyword type, for instance, the value in it is text regardless of whether it is a numeral.

Even if the field is a number field it can be blank, which Notes sees as NULL or "" and thus interprets as text. In that case you get an error message if you try to use that field in formulas in which the other elements are numbers. You can avoid that problem by making sure that the default value of the field is "0", but you might not want a bunch of zeros appearing across your documents. The alternate solution is to test if the field is a number and, if it is not, convert it to a number before the rest of the calculation occurs:

```
@If(@IsNumber(Price); Price * Qty; @TextToNumber(Price) * Qty)
```

In the preceding formula, the @If function poses a question: Is the value in the Price field a number? If the answer is yes, the first argument of the formula (@IsNumber(Price)) returns "1" (true). In that case, the second argument of the formula is returned, and the value in the Price field is multiplied by the value in the Qty field. If the value in the Price field is not a number, @IsNumber(Price) results in "0" (false) and the formula runs the formula in the third argument, @TextToNumber(Price) * Qty, and returns the result. The @TextToNumber function converts the contents of the Price field to a number, which can then be multiplied by the value in the Qty field. Table 4.6 lists data conversion @Functions.

4

Table 4.6 Data Conversion @Functions

@Function	Example	Results

@IsNumber(value)	`@If(@IsNumber`
	`(Price); Price`
	`* Qty;`
	`@TextToNumber`
	`(Price) * Qty)`
		Evaluates to 1 (true) if the value is a number. If Price is not a number field it gets converted to a number and then multiplied by Qty.

@IsText(value)	`@IsText(Price)`	Evaluates to 1 (true) if the value is a text string. Asks what data type the Price field is.
@IsTime(value)	`@IsTime(BirthDate)`	Evaluates to 1 (true) if the value is a time/date value. Asks if BirthDate field is in time or text format.
@Text(value)	`@Text(Count)`	Converts a value to a text string. Converts number data in Count field to text.

@Text(value; "format-string")	`@Text(Price;`
	`"C,2")`
	`@Text(@Today;`
	`"D0S0")`
		Converts a numeric or date/time value to a text string according to a specified format. (See Table 4.5 for Format String Options.)

@TextToNumber (string)	`@TextToNumber` `(Price)`	Converts a text string to a number.
@TextToTime (string)	`@TextToTime` `("09/05/96")`	Converts a text string to a date/time value.

Date/Time Operations

Use date and time @Functions to generate or manipulate time and date values. Some examples are @Created, which returns the date and time a document was created; @Modified, which returns the next-to-the-last time and date a document was last modified (and therefore works best in view columns); and @Now, which returns the current date and time.

Others return portions of the date and time; for example, @Today returns only today's date. You can combine time @functions. For example, if you use @Now to get the current date and time, you can combine it with @Time to extract the time portion:

```
@Time(@Now)
```

Or, use the @Date function to return only the date portion of the result:

```
@Date(@Now)
```

If you want to see only the month portion of the date in a field, use the @Month function. This returns the month as a number. In the following formula, if the date in the SaleDate field is in December (which results in 12), the words "Holiday Savings Month" appear. Otherwise, the words "No Discounts" appear:

```
@If(@Month(SaleDate)= 12; "Holiday Savings Month"; "No Discounts")
```

Similarly, the @Day function pulls out just the day of the month, and @Year results in the year portion of the date.

The @Weekday function results in the number of the day of the week, where Sunday is 1 and Saturday is 7. If you assign a temporary variable in your formula to replace the number with the name of the weekday, you can change your formula to add the weekday:

```
Weekday := @Select(@Weekday(DueDate); "Sunday"; "Monday"; "Tuesday";
"Wednesday"; "Thursday"; "Friday"; "Saturday");

"Your report is due on " + Weekday + ", "
+ @Text(@Month(DueDate ; "D2S0" )) + "."
```

This formula returns the following:

```
Your report is due on Monday, 6/30.
```

The @Select(*Number*; *Value*) function returns the value that appears in that number position of the values listed. Because @Weekday returns a number, in this case 2, the @Select function result is the second choice in the list (Monday). Plugging the Weekday temporary variable into the previous formula adds the day of the week to the resulting text.

Up to this point, the value in the DueDate field has been a date entered by the creator of the document. You can also calculate the due date based on a beginning date. To do this, we use @Adjust, which is a very useful @Function. For instance, if you want the due date to be 30 days from the date the document was created, you might enter a formula like this in the DueDate field:

```
@Adjust(@Created; 0; 0; 30; 0; 0; 0)
```

The @Adjust function follows this syntax:

```
@Adjust ( time-date ; year ; month ; day ; hour ; minute ; second )
```

4

The first (time-date) argument is a starting date or time. It might be a time constant (which would appear in square brackets), it might be a variable that contains a time value, or it might be a formula that returns a time or date, such as @Created or @Today.

The other six arguments each represent one of the six components of a date/time value—year, month, day, hour, minute, and second, in that order—and they accept integer values. A zero in one of those positions results in no change for that component of the date/time value. A positive integer adds that amount to the date/time value. A negative integer subtracts that amount. You cannot leave any argument blank; arguments two through seven must all have a zero or a positive or negative number in them. In the preceding example, we add 30 days to the value in the date-time argument and return the resulting date.

Going back to the seminar registration example that was illustrated in Figures 4.11 and 4.12, you might want the office to confirm a registration within 24 hours. To flag registrations that are less than 24 hours old, you can add a column in the view that marks a registration as *new* and adds the registrant's name. For that column you can add the following formula (see Figure 4.13):

```
@If(@Now < @Adjust(@Created; 0; 0; 0; 24; 0; 0); "New - "; "")
+ Registrant + " registered on " + @Text(@Created; "D0S0")
```

FIGURE 4.13

Using the @Adjust function in the view column formula sets a limit on the amount of time the word New appears before the registrant's name.

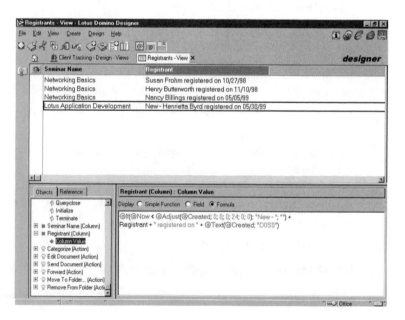

Table 4.7 lists some of the frequently used date and time @Functions, shows examples, and explains what the @Function does.

Table 4.7 Commonly Used Date and Time @Functions

Function	Example	Results
@Adjust (time-date; year; month; day; hour; minute; second)	`DueDate := @Adjust (BillDate; 0; 0; 30; 0; 0; 0)`	Adjusts a date/time value by the negative or positive values of the remaining arguments.
@Created	`@If(@Created > [01/01/96]; "New"; "")`	Returns the date and time the document was created.
@Date	`@Date(@Created)`	Returns only the date portion of a date/time value.
@Modified	`"Last Edited: " + @Text(@Modified)`	Returns the date and time the document was last edited and saved.
@Month	`@If(@Month(Issue) = 6 ¦ @Month(Issue) = 7 ¦ @Month(Issue) = 8; "Summer"; "Schoolyear")`	Extracts the month from the date/time value (1=January, 12=December).
@Now	`@Text(@Now; "T1S1")`	Returns the current date and time.
@Time	`@Time(@Modified)`	Returns only the time portion of a date/time value.
@Today	`@If(DueDate < @Today; ""; "Late")`	Returns the current date.
@Tomorrow	`@If(DueDate = @Tomorrow; "Due Tomorrow"; "")`	Returns tomorrow's date.
@Weekday (time-date)	`@If(@Weekday(@Today) = 1 ¦ @Weekday(@Today) = 7; "Weekend"; "Work Week")`	Computes the day of the week and returns the number for that day. (1=Sunday, 7=Saturday)
@Year (time-date)	`@Year(CreateDate)`	Extracts and returns the year from the time-date value
@Yesterday	`@If(Date = @Yesterday; "Yesterday"; Date = @Today; "Today" ; "")`	Returns yesterday's date.

4

List Operations

Use list @Functions to manipulate and calculate lists and the items in them. For example, let's say a field on a meeting form requires the names of the people attending the meeting. On the form, this is a names field that opens the address book so the person creating or editing the document can add as many names as they want. But you want a count of the number of attendees to appear on the document. In the field in which you want your head count, use an @Elements(*list*) formula (see Figure 4.14), where *list* is the name of the field in which the names of the attendees appear:

```
@Elements(Attendees)
```

FIGURE 4.14

The MtgNumber field automatically counts the number of people attending the meeting based on the list of names in the Attendees field.

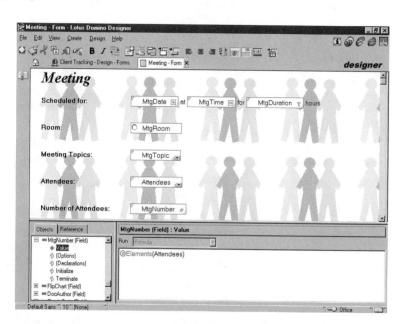

NEW TERM **Refreshing fields**—If the values in other fields are dependent on the choices you make in a keywords field, select **Refresh fields on keyword change** from the Control tab of the Field Properties box. Then, when you make a change in keywords, all the fields that are dependent upon that choice are also updated immediately.

On the same form, you can include a field for the topics of discussion. If Health Benefits is one of the topics under discussion, a special flip chart has to be provided for the meeting. In a field that indicates whether a flip chart is needed, you might include an

@IsMember(*TextValue*; *TextListValue*) formula (see Figure 4.15), where the *TextValue* is the text string you are searching for and *TextListValue* is the list in which it might be found. If you need a Yes or No answer in the field, you might enter a formula like this:

```
@If(@IsMember("Health Benefits"; MtgTopic); "Yes"; "No")
```

FIGURE 4.15

The FlipChart formula returns "Yes" *if Health Benefits is a meeting topic.*

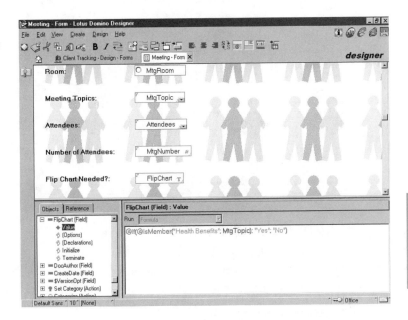

The MtgTopic field can list a number of topics, in order of importance. Let's say that in your Meetings view, you do not want to list all these topics, but you want to show the first three. In the Topic column you can enter @Subset(*List*; *Number*) to specify what field the list is in (*List*) and how many entries you want to return in the column (*Number*):

```
@Subset(MtgTopic; 3)
```

In the example shown in Figure 4.16, the first meeting actually has a fourth topic (Quarterly Reports), but that doesn't appear in the view because the @Subset formula limits the list to the first three topics.

FIGURE 4.16

The Column formula limits the topics displayed to the first three selected by requesting a subset of the chosen topics. The second argument of the @Subset function determines how many topics are displayed in the view.

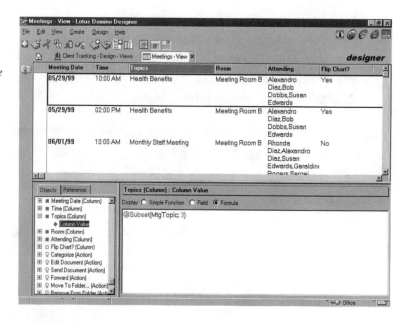

Logical Operations

There is only one logical operation @Function—@If—but it is a very important @Function. Use @If to evaluate conditions and produce true or false results. The basic @If function is written as follows:

```
@If(condition; action; else-action)
```

In an @If formula, if the condition evaluates as true the *action* is returned. If the condition evaluates as not true, the *else-action* is returned.

A second form of @If enables you to evaluate multiple conditions in succession, and returns the action for the first condition that evaluates as true. The syntax of this form of @If is as follows:

```
@If(condition1; action1; condition2; action2;
[... ; condition99; action99;]; else-action)
```

You can include up to 99 condition/action pairs. When Domino evaluates multiple arguments, it evaluates the first argument first. If that argument resolves to true, it returns the first action, and then stops. If the first argument is false, it moves on to the second condition and repeats the process. It continues in this fashion until it reaches a true statement, and no further evaluation occurs. If none of the conditions test as true, the else-action is the result. Keep in mind that there must be an odd number of arguments for an @If formula.

You can also nest @If statements inside other @If statements. This enables you to evaluate a complex set of conditions and take varying actions depending on which combination of conditions is true. For example

```
@If ( conditionA ; @If ( conditionB ; actionAB;
else-actionBnotA ) else-actionNotAorB )
```

This has the following effect: If conditions A and B are true, return actionAB; if A is true and B is false, return else-actionBnotA; if both are false, return else-actionNotAorB. The formula is evaluated left to right. The first condition that is true causes its action to process, and no further evaluation takes place. Only if none of the other conditions are true does the else-action process. For example, you want to calculate the payroll tax from the following table:

Paid by Commission

Commission amount	Tax Rate	Draw Amount	Tax Rate
0–1,000	15%	0-1,500	20%
1,001–5,000	25%	1,501-4,000	28%
>5,000	35%	>4,000	39%

You have a field PayType that has either the value "Commission" or "Draw". Here is the formula:

```
@if( PayType = "Commission";  @if( Commission > 5000;
Commission * .35; Commission > 1000; Commission * .25;
Commission * .15 ); PayType = "Draw"; @if( Draw > 4000;
Draw * .39; Draw > 1500; Draw * .28; Draw * .20 ); 0 )
```

 Tip

Although nesting is possible and you can use it, making the formula can sometimes be confusing. Alternately, you might want to consider using a temporary variable for each @If formula you want to nest within the final expression. It's easier to read and understand later, especially if you have to troubleshoot the formula.

4

Nested If Statement—An @If formula that constitutes one of the conditions of another @If formula

In Figure 4.17 you see a view that lists the services of a consulting and training organization. The service type appears in the first column. In the second column, the designer wants to show the values of different fields, depending on the type of service showing in the first column. This formula reads

```
@If(ServiceType = "Application Development";
ServAppDev; ServiceType = "Contract Classes";
ServContract; ServiceType = "Network Planning";
ServNetwork; ServiceType = "Programming";
ServProgramming; ServiceType = "Server Migration";
ServMigration; ServiceType = "Tutorials";
ServTutorial; "Other")
```

FIGURE 4.17

An @If formula determines what appears in the view column based on the choice made in another field on the form (ServiceType).

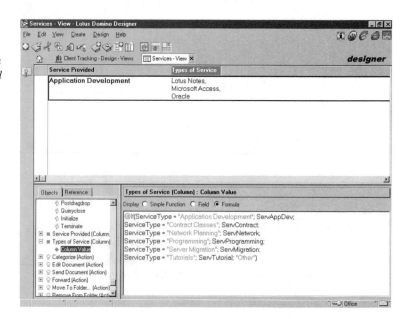

String Manipulation

When you're working with text you might need to select part of a text string, or you might have to format the text string in order to get the results you want. That's what string manipulation @Functions are for. They only work on text fields. They can take variables or constants as arguments, including case-sensitive arguments, but they require quotation marks around arguments that are constants.

One typical use of a string manipulation function is working with telephone numbers (which, you'll recall, are text because you don't use them in arithmetic computations). The telephone number as entered by the user of the document includes the area code, but you need to pull the area code out separately to work with it elsewhere. Provided that the user didn't enter parentheses around the area code, the area code is represented by the first three digits of the phone number. Use an `@Left(string; n)` formula, where `string` is the text from which you need to pull the information and `n` is the number of characters (starting at the left end of the text string) that you want. Using the area code example, the formula is

```
@Left(Phone; 3)
```

You can also use the @Right function to get a specified number of characters, counting from the right end of the text string. But what if you don't know the specific number of characters (in a person's last name, for example)? Both @Left and @Right have an alternate form that returns the characters to the left or right of a specified text substring. For example, to get the last name of the person's name entered in the Contact field, you write the following formula:

```
@Right(Contact; " ")
```

This formula returns all the text to the right of the space that separates the first and last names.

You can also format the text in a field. After all, you never know when users will use all caps, all lowercase, or mixed case. If you want a particular case, force it with a function: @UpperCase to make the text string all caps, @LowerCase to make the text string all lowercase, or @ProperCase to capitalize the beginning letter of each word. For instance, if you want the state abbreviation to be in all caps, write a formula:

```
@UpperCase(State)
```

You can use string manipulation functions to search for and replace text. The `@Matches(string; pattern)` function finds text in the `string` that matches the `pattern`. You can use the asterisk (*) wildcard for multiple characters or the question mark (?) for single characters. In the following formula, if the state name begins with `"new"` it appears with the first letter of each word capitalized (as in New Jersey):

```
@If(@Matches(State; "new *"); @ProperCase(State); "")
```

To replace text, use the `@ReplaceSubstring(sourceList; fromList; toList)` function. Let's say your company often refers to your Northeast sales territory as the New England territory, so that language keeps creeping into your sales territory field. You can write a formula to translate that incorrect entry into the one you want. The Territory field is then the *sourceList*, "New England" is the *fromList*, and "Northeast" is the *toList*:

@ReplaceSubstring(Territory; "New England"; "Northeast")

If you want to specify Northeast as the sales territory if one of the states in that area appears in the State field, you might want to use @Contains(*string*; *substring*) to see if one of those states is mentioned in that field:

@If(@Contains(State; "ME" : "NH" : "VT" : "MA" :
"RI" : "CT"); "Northeast"; "")

Table 4.8 lists some of the commonly used string manipulation @functions, provides sample formulas, and explains how the @Function works in the formulas.

Table 4.8 Commonly Used String Manipulation @Functions

Function	Example	Results
@Contains(string; substring)	@If(@Contains (Request; "urgent" : "important" : "immediate") ; "High priority"; "Medium")	Determines if Request contains any of the listed values that are within quotes, and if so returns High Priority; otherwise returns Medium.
@Left(string; n)	@Left(Phone; 3)	Extracts the area code from the Phone. 6105551212 returns 610.
@Left(string; substring)	@Left(AuthName; " ")	Returns the characters to the left of substring. Returns the author's first name.
@Length(string)	@Length(Title)	Returns the number of characters in a string or list.
@LowerCase	@LowerCase (Category)	Changes COMPANY to company.
@Matches(string; pattern)	@Matches(Name; "* Smith")	Finds all names equal to Smith. Use wildcard "*" for multiple characters and "?" for single characters.
@NewLine	Street + @NewLine + City + ", " + State + " " + Zip	Inserts a carriage return into a text string.
@ProperCase	@ProperCase (JobTitle)	Capitalizes the initial letter of each word in a string. director of merchandising returns Director Of Merchandising.

Function	Example	Results
@Replace(Source; From; To)	`@Replace` `(Location;` `"Canada";` `"NORTH")`	Replaces all Locations from Canada with `NORTH` if Location is a list of locations.
@Right(string; n)	`@Right(Phone; 7)`	Extracts the rightmost n characters from a string. When Phone is `6105551212` returns `5551212`.
@Right(string; substring)	`@Right(AuthName;` `" ")`	Returns the characters to the right of substring. Returns the author's last name.
@Trim(string)	`@Trim(FullName)`	Changes `"Joe Doaks "` to `"Joe Doaks"`.
@UpperCase	`@UpperCase(State)`	`Pa` becomes `PA`.

Special Functions

There are a number of @Functions that don't fit any straightforward category. They perform useful tasks such as accessing information about the user environment, about the document hierarchy, or about the database and views. Some of them are listed in Table B.2 in Appendix B.

Several of these functions determine if certain documents are main documents, response documents, or response to response documents. These functions are particularly useful in specifying what documents appear in a view, as discussed on Day 16, "List Processing," and include @AllChildren (all responses to parent documents) and @AllDescendents (all response and response to response documents). To have the Seminars view display all the Seminar forms and the registration requests (responses), the selection formula for the view is

```
SELECT Form = "Seminar" | @AllDescendants
```

When combined with an @If function, the @IsResponseDoc function sets a condition that can be true or false. Therefore, if a document is a response document, this formula calls for the title text to include the words `"Response to"` in addition to the value of the Subject field. If the document isn't a response document, only the Subject appears:

```
@If(@IsResponseDoc; "Response to " + Subject; Subject)
```

The @IsNewDoc function determines whether the document is a new one. This can be useful in creating a Window title for a form (the default is to use the name of the form).

4

The Window title appears in the title bar of a document. If you want the title to be different when the document is first created than when it's edited, @IsNewDoc provides the true/false condition you need for an @If function:

```
@If(@IsNewDoc; "New Meeting"; @Subset(MtgTopic; 2))
```

This formula puts the words "New Meeting" in the title bar of the Meeting window if the document is being created. Otherwise, it enters the first two elements of the contents of the MtgTopic field when the document is being read or edited (see Figure 4.18).

Window title formulas

At times, you want the name of the user to appear on forms they create or edit. If you enter the formula

```
@UserName
```

Notes returns the name that is associated with the current user ID, or Dorothy Burke. But if your organization uses hierarchical names, you might get a result like this:

```
Dorothy Burke/Consulting/R&A/US
```

To define which portion of this name you want, you need to use an @Name([action]; name) function such as:

```
@Name([CN]; @UserName)
```

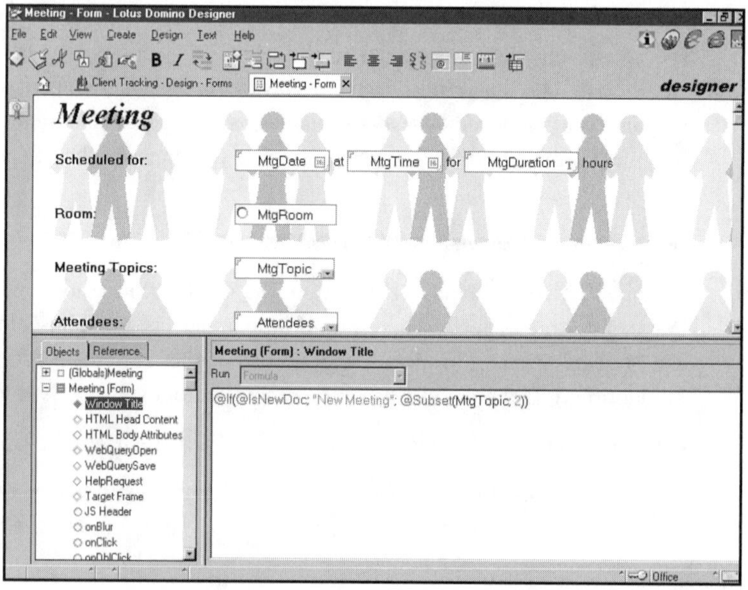

FIGURE 4.18

The Window Title formula for the Meeting form tests for a new document (not yet saved) and displays the title "New Meeting" if the document is new.

This returns the common name (`[CN]`) portion of the user name, or just `Dorothy Burke`. There are several actions that can be used with @Name to return certain portions of the hierarchical name:

- **[Abbreviate]**—Returns the hierarchical name without the component labels. For example, @Name ([Abbreviate]; @UserName) returns Dorothy Burke/Consulting/R&A/US.

- **[C]**—Returns the country. For example, `@Name([C];@UserName)` returns `US`.

- **[Canonicalize]**—Expands an abbreviated name, adding components and labels to complete the full name. For example, `@Name([Canonicalize]);@Username]` returns `CN=Dorothy Burke/OU=Consulting/O=R&A/C=US`.

- **[CN]**—Returns the common name. For example, `@Name([CN];@Username)` returns `Dorothy Burke`.

- **[G]**—Returns the given name. For example, `@Name([G];@UserName)` returns `Dorothy`.

- **[O]**—Returns the organization name (in this example, `R&A`).

- **[S]**—Returns the surname (in this example, `Burke`).

There are additional parameters that meet the X.400 naming standard. Please refer to Domino documentation for additional keyword arguments.

> **Tip**
>
> **Hierarchical names**—Notes uses hierarchical names to uniquely identify all users and servers, so the John Smith who works for ABC Corporation in the Sales Department (John Smith/Sales/ABC) doesn't get the mail for John Smith in the Marketing Department (John Smith/Marketing/ABC). The components of the hierarchical name are the common name (CN), the four levels of organization units (OU1, OU2, OU3, OU4), the organization (O), and the country (C). When the level abbreviation appears with the names, that is the *canonical* form (CN=Dorothy Burke/OU1=Sales/O=ABC Corporation). Your Notes Administrator determines how many organization units your organization has and how they're organized.

Table 4.9 lists some special functions that you might find useful in writing formulas. Sample formulas appear for each with an explanation of the results expected.

Table 4.9 Commonly Used Special Functions

Function	Example	Results
@AllChildren	`SELECT Form = "Inquiry" ¦ @AllChildren`	Includes all responses to parent documents.
@AllDescendents	`SELECT Form = "Suggestion" ¦ @AllDescendents`	Includes all response and response to response documents to parent documents.
@IsNewDoc	`@If(@IsNewDoc; "New Inquiry" ;InqCategory)`	Returns 1 (true) if the document hasn't been saved yet.
@IsResponseDoc	`@If (@IsResponseDoc; "Response to " + Subject; Subject)`	Returns 1 (true) if a document is a response.
@Name([action]; name)	`@Name([CN]; @UserName)`	Returns a portion of the hierarchical name where [CN] = common name [O] = organization [OUn] = organizational unit (where n is 1,2,3, or 4) [C] = country
@UserName	`@Right(@UserName; " ")`	Returns the name of the current user.

Editable Field Formulas

Although you can change the information contained in editable fields, you can still use formulas for those fields. Unlike computed fields that only contain one formula (the event: *Value* formula), each editable field can involve up to three formulas: a *default value* formula, an *input validation* formula, and an *input translation* formula.

Default Value Formulas

Use default value formulas to make it easier for your users to enter information in documents. By providing a default value, you give users freedom to accept this value and skip the field or to change the value if they want. For example, suppose you have a field in which the user is asked to enter his or her state, but most of the users are located in the same state. If you make the default value formula for the state field ("PA" for Pennsylvania), users can accept it or change it if they need to.

Tip

> **Default Values**—You can use a text string (in quotes), a field name, or a for-
> mula (such as @Now to put in the current date) as a default value formula.
> Notes evaluates a default value formula only once—when the document is
> created.

To enter a default value formula, select the field on your form, highlight the Default
Value event in the Objects window, and enter the formula in the Programmer's Pane.
Click on the green check mark and save the form.

Input Translation

To standardize the input from your users to a desired format, use an input translation formula. Input translation formulas convert user entries when the document is saved, based
on the formula you put in the field. This gives your documents consistency while letting
the users have the freedom to enter the text as they choose.

For example, the following input translation formula makes sure that the state entered
into the field State is always capitalized:

```
@UpperCase(State)
```

To enter an input translation formula, select the field on your form, highlight the Input
Translation event in the Objects window, and enter the formula in the Programmer's
Pane. Click on the green check mark and save the form.

Input Validation

To create a field in which users are required to enter data, add an Input Validation formula. If users try to save a document in which a field's Input Validation formula does not
resolve to true, an error message appears. The error message contains text that you provided in your formula.

For example, if you did not provide a default in the State field and want to force users to
enter the state, you include the following input validation formula:

```
@If(State = ""; @Failure("Please enter the state
where the facility is located"); @Success)
```

In the example, State is a field name. If the user leaves it blank (""), the user is not
allowed to save the document and sees the @Failure message "Please enter the state
where the facility is located" in a dialog box; otherwise, the input is accepted
(@Success). The user's cursor is placed in the field that generates the error if the field is
an editable field.

4

By the way, we used @Failure and @Success in this formula. Validation formulas are just about the only place you will ever use these two @Functions, and almost every validation formula you ever write will be in one of the two following formats:

```
@if ( FieldName = NULL ; @Failure ( … ) ; @Success )
```

or

```
@If ( FieldName <> NULL ; @Success ; @Failure ( … ) )
```

Notice that these are just inverses of each other. Most of the time it won't matter which of these two formats you use; they work equally well. But occasionally you might encounter a situation where one works better than the other.

FIGURE 4.19

When a user fails to enter data in a required field for which you created an input validation formula, a dialog box appears when the user tries to save the document. The message in the dialog box is the text argument you entered in the @Failure function.

Tip

When you are writing formulas that look for empty fields, use double quotes with no space in between, as in

```
@If(State = ""; @Failure("Please enter the state
where the facility is located"); @Success)
```

Alternately, use the keyword NULL to indicate blank fields. This is strictly a personal preference. Using the keyword NULL can make it easier to read your formulas, as in this example:

```
@If(State = NULL; @Failure("Please enter the state
where the facility is located"); @Success)
```

To enter an input validation formula, select the field on your form, highlight the Input Validation event in the Objects window, and enter the formula in the Programmer's Pane. Click on the green check mark and save the form.

Notes evaluates input validation formulas when the document is saved or recalculated, but after any input translation formulas have been evaluated.

Build Computed Fields

Fields that are not editable are *computed*. The user cannot input in these fields or change the result. There are three classifications of computed fields: *computed*, *computed for display*, and *computed when composed*. The differences might not be obvious in the formulas because they involve factors such as when the calculation occurs and whether the data in the field is saved with the document.

Computed

The formula in a computed field is calculated whenever the document is created, saved, or refreshed. The data in a computed field is saved with the document.

A typical computed field is an arithmetic operation:

```
Price * Qty
```

The formula multiplies the value in the Price field by the value in the Qty field. Because this formula requires input from other fields that appear before it on the form, Notes calculates the result when the document is saved or refreshed if you select the Compute After Validation check box.

> **Tip**
>
> In calculating field values, Domino works from the top of the document down, going from left to right. For that reason, you want to place fields that input data that is needed for computations above or to the left of the field that contains the formula that calculates the result.

Computed for Display

Forms designed for rapid input might not be pleasing to the eye when they are read. For example, your form might have a set of fields lined up one below the other to collect the

4

name, address, city, state, and zip code because this makes data entry much easier. When a user reads the document, however, it's much easier if the data is collected to read as the address on an envelope.

To accomplish this, you leave the input fields visible for creating or editing a document, and hide them for reading. Then you create a field to format the information as a normal address block. You hide this field when the document is created or edited, but make it visible when the document is read (learn more about hide-when on Day 9, "Forms on Steroids: Increase Form Performance"). The field that displays this information for reading purposes only should be a computed for display field. Following is an example of a name and address formula:

```
Fname + " " + Lname + @NewLine + StreetAddress
+ @NewLine + City + ", " + State + " " + Zip
```

This formula produces an address that looks like this:

```
John Rath
1414 Tenth Avenue
Amosville, NY 14321
```

Computed for display fields are recalculated every time the document is opened or refreshed, but only for the current session. The data from the field is not saved with the document. You don't need to save it. The data is already saved in the individual fields that are referenced in the display formula.

Display formulas are typically the names of other fields in the document or concatenations of field names with text (see Figure 4.20). In order to quickly distinguish these fields when working with forms, we typically include the letters *disp* as part of the field name. For instance, you collect the name of the person in the Name field, but you display it in a table that only appears when the user is reading the document. In the table where you want the Name information to appear, create a computed for display field called NameDisp or DispName and create a formula that is just `Name`.

Because the data from computed for display fields isn't stored in the document, you can't reference those fields when you build views.

Some information is automatically saved in documents even if you don't have a field for it. This includes the name of the form, the name of the user who created the document, and the date and time the document was created. When you want to display this information in your document but you don't need to save it again for use in calculations, use a computed for display field type.

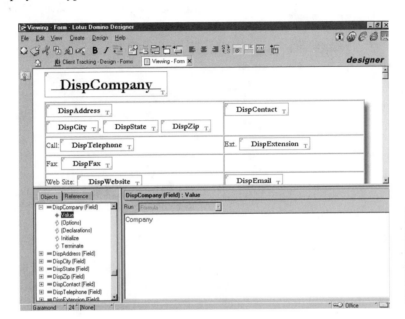

FIGURE 4.20

This form has a display area where each field is computed for display. The formula of the selected field, DispCompany, is Company.

Computed When Composed

Computed when composed fields are calculated once—when the document is created. The data in these fields is saved with the document. Use computed when composed fields to store information about the document's original values. Computed when composed fields are typically used when a document inherits data from another document (you'll learn about inheriting data on Day 9).

Formulas that appear in computed when composed fields might include field names from a parent document, @Created to capture the date the document was created, @UserName to store the name of the person who created the document, or the type of operating system the user has (see Figure 4.21).

FIGURE 4.21

The Platform field is a computed when composed field that captures the name of the operating system used on the user's computer. In the @Platform([SPECIFIC]), the SPECIFIC parameter also captures the version of the software.

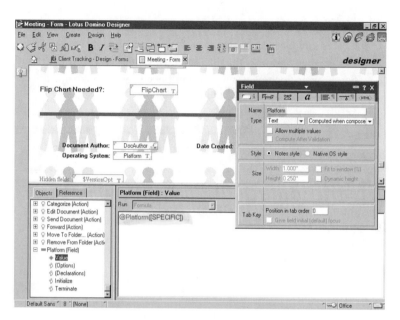

Summary

In today's lesson you learned the basics of creating formulas. Although formulas are used everywhere in Notes, our emphasis in this lesson was on using them in fields on forms. You'll soon get a chance to use them in views, folders, agents, and many other places.

Formulas often use @functions. @Functions are predefined formulas that run data that you supply as arguments through a computation and then replace themselves with the result. We've listed many commonly used @Functions in this lesson, but be aware that there are too many to mention in one lesson (and keep your attention at the same time).

Formulas can appear in both editable and computed fields. They are optional in editable fields but required in computed fields. You can use them in three different ways in editable fields: to set a default value, to translate an entered value, and to validate an entered value. By *translate* we mean clean up the value the user entered. By *validate* we mean ensure that the user entered valid data.

Q&A

Q How do I decide whether to use an input translation formula or an input validation formula?

A Use an input translation formula to clean up the user's input. For example, `@ProperCase ( @Trim ( fieldname ) )` removes excess spaces and capitalizes the first letters of words in *fieldname*. Use an input validation formula to make sure the user has entered valid data. For example, if the user left a required field blank, the validation formula won't allow the user to save the document. Input validation formulas almost always use an @If function to test the validity of the field contents.

Q What's the most common error that new programmers make with formulas?

A Syntax errors. Study the syntax rules carefully and make sure you follow them carefully. You lose a lot of time searching for errors if you are a sloppy typist.

The most common error is to try to mix data of more than one type. You cannot concatenate a number or a date with text. You have to convert the number or date to text first, using @Text. You cannot do arithmetic with a number that is in text format. You must convert it to numeric format first, using @TextToNumber. You cannot do date arithmetic with a date that is in text format. You must convert it to date/time format first, using @TextToTime. Some programmers like to name fields a two letter suffix representing the data type in the field name, such as DT for Date/Time, or NO for Number. If you do this, you might not want to take our advice for using some type of code that represents your form in the field name.

Q Can I write long sections of code?

A Yes, you may write many lines of code to accomplish a decision or calculation. Just separate each line from the next with a semi-colon. You'll learn more about writing longer and more complex formulas on Day 13, "Put on Your Propeller Beanie: Advanced Formulas".

Workshop

In this workshop you continue to build the Proposed Titles database in your workflow application. You will begin adding formulas for both computed and editable fields. Because we originally made all the fields editable, there will be some changes in field types.

Add Formulas for Computed Fields

Open the Proposed Title form in the Proposed Title database. Using Table 4.10 as a guide, change the following fields to indicate the type of Computed field. Then enter the formula to compute the desired value for the field.

Table 4.10 Computed Fields in Proposed Title Form

Field	Type	Desired Result
TReviewStart	Computed when composed	The date the document was created
TReviewEnd	Computed	Date 30 days after the ReviewStart date
TDocAuthor	Computed when composed	The common name of the user who created the document
TCreateDate	Computed for display	Date document was created

The title of the form needs to be changed to display the title of the book. Add a display field in place of the title on the form that reads "Proposed Book Title" if the document is new, and "Proposal for *Name of Book*" if the document isn't new. Retrieve the *Name of Book* information from the TBookTitle field (see Figure 4.22).

FIGURE 4.22

By using a display field, you can include information elsewhere on the form, where it might be helpful to the reader.

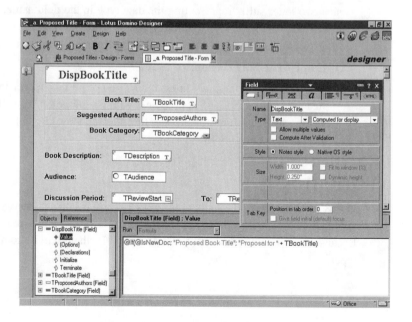

Click in the middle of the form (not on a field) and edit the Window Title formula for the form (this formula is similar to the one you just created for the display field). The current window title is text you entered earlier. Now, change the formula to read "Proposed Title for New Book" if the document is new. Otherwise, have the window title display "Proposed Title:" followed by the title of the book.

Add Formulas for Editable Fields

Using the information in Table 4.11, add default value, input translation, and input validation formulas for the editable fields in the Proposed Title form. If the Default Value, Input Translation or Input Validation columns are blank, don't create a formula.

Table 4.11   Creating Formulas for Editable Fields

Field	Default Value	Input Translation	Input Validation
TBookTitle		Make sure that the title has the first letter of each word capitalizedand the rest of the letters in lowercase.	This is a required field. Write a formula to tell users they must fill out the field.
TProposedAuthors			
TBookCategory			This is a required field. Write a formula to tell users they must fill out the field.
TDescription			
TAcqEditor			
TStatus	The status should automatically display "Under Discussion" unless it is changed.		

Add a radio box field and appropriate static text to the form, close to the description of the book, called TAudience. The choices for the field are Computer Illiterate, Beginning, Intermediate, Advanced, and Super Advanced. Only one category can be chosen by the user. The field is a required field, so add an input validation formula.

Save and test the form. Create a few documents that can be used later as examples when you create your views. Make sure you test the validation formulas by leaving fields empty when you save the documents at first.

To see our examples of this application, open the folder on the CD called Day4 and then open the database file PTDay4.nsf.

DAY 5

Forms 102: Enhance Form Appearance and Design

Forms can be enhanced with text and paragraph formatting as well as with the addition of sections that help users to manage long documents. Graphics add interest to forms and can be imported or pasted into forms, depending on their format. Of course, graphics can slow down the display and print time of a form. If you know that many users will retrieve the forms by modem or other slow medium, you might want to minimize the use of graphics in your forms.

In this lesson you learn how to enhance your form appearance with sections, graphics, background graphics and colors, styles, and headers and footers.

About Form Sections

Make long forms manageable for your users by incorporating collapsible sections. Sections can be collapsed or hidden, and they enable you to group and organize fields on your form; that is, you can place fields and static text in a logical grouping order. For example, on a customer information form, fields containing the customer address can be grouped into a section called Address, as shown in Figure 5.1.

FIGURE 5.1

Here, the customer address fields are grouped in a section called Address. At the bottom, the Address section is collapsed, and at the top it's expanded.

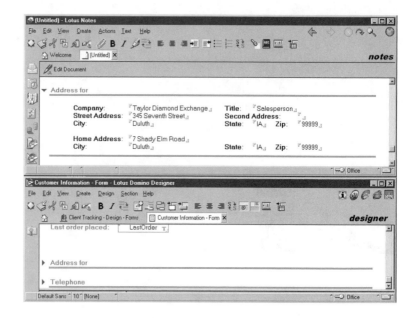

When you create a section, you first select the information that is to be contained in that section. If the existing layout of your form doesn't allow contiguous selection of the information you want to contain in a section (see Figure 5.2), you need to reposition your static text and fields before you can create a section.

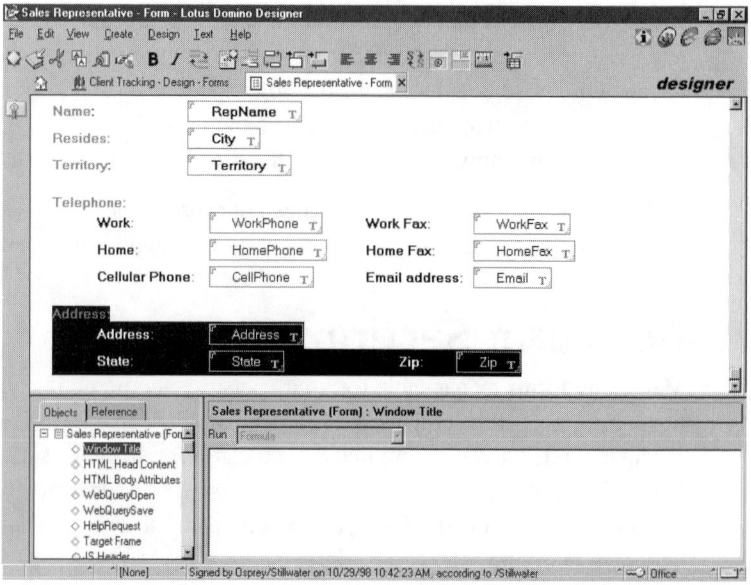

FIGURE 5.2

Here, placing the sales representative's address in a section isn't possible with the current form layout because the City field isn't grouped with the other address fields. Add a computed for display field down by the address with the value of City as its formula so that the address in the section is complete.

If you've been following our design tips ("keep related information together on the form"), creating sections on your form will be a breeze. If you followed our advice regarding tables, your forms contain tables. Tables can be contained within a section (as can graphics and any objects a form contains), but a section cannot be created within a table. So, if your long form contains one long table, you can't use sections until you split the table apart. Unfortunately, Domino does not support splitting tables. Your only workaround is to create mini tables and cut and paste your fields and static text into the new tables. If you need to rearrange your form, do it now before you continue with creating sections.

Sections come in two flavors: *Controlled Access* and *Standard*. These two sections differ in two ways. A Controlled Access section enables you to restrict who can edit the fields in it. You can also set the section expand/collapse options based on who is accessing the document—editors or non-editors.

Caution

> Don't confuse expand/collapse options with hide when options. If a section is hidden with a hide-when formula, it's hidden and the user doesn't know it exists. If a section is collapsed, a title appears and the user can expand it to see the information it contains.

To create a controlled access section, you must have some idea of who can and can't access the section. This doesn't necessarily mean that you need to know every user's name but you need to understand groups, roles, and *access levels*. You learn about the Domino Access Control Levels on Day 7, "Sleep Soundly: Secure Your Application," and you learn about controlled access sections on Day 9, "Forms on Steroids: Increase Form Performance." In this lesson we will concentrate on adding standard sections to a form.

5

Even though we're not going to create controlled access sections here, you still need to know the difference between editors and non-editors for this lesson. An editor is one who has the rights to edit a document, and a non-editor can only read a document.

Add Standard Sections to a Form   *NOT GOOD IN BROWSER!*

To add a standard section to a form, open your form in design mode and highlight the area of the form you want to include in the section. From the menu, choose **Create, Section, Standard.**

By default, Domino uses the first line of the paragraph as the section title. You can change the section title by accessing the Section Properties box. Here you set a new title by adding the title text or creating a formula for the title. For example, you can create a title that includes information from fields in the section. In this example, the section title includes a text constant and the customer name:

```
"Address information for " + Client
```

This example creates a title for each branch location of the client:

```
"Address information for " + Client + ", " + Branch
```

To access the properties box, right-click the section and choose **Properties**. The icons that are found on the tabbed pages of the Section properties box are

  • Section Title and Border

  • Expand/Collapse

  • Font

  • Section Hide When

Enter a formula for the title, click the **Formula** Radio button on the Section Title and Border page, and enter your formula in the Title box as shown in Figure 5.3.

FIGURE 5.3

Use a formula to pull information from fields on the form and include it in the section title.

Table 5.1 lists the options that are found in the Section Properties box that you want to review and possibly change when you first create a section.

Note   Properties for hiding sections are discussed on Day 9 in the section, "Hide Objects," and the HTML page of the Section properties box is covered on Day 8, "Create Pages and Frames," in the section "HTML in Forms."

Table 5.1   Section Properties Section Title and Border Page

Option	Choice	Comment
Title	Text	Enter the text for the section title. Do not use quotes around the title.
	Formula	Enter the formula for the section title. When including text constants in the formula, enclose the text constants in quotes. Click the **Formula Window** button if you need more room to enter the formula or need a list of fields or functions to use in the formula; enter the formula there and click **Done** to return to the properties box.
Border	Style	Select the border style from the drop down list. The border encloses the section title, not the entire section. However, a separator line is placed at the bottom of the section.
	Color	Select the border color from the drop-down list.

A section's title can be hidden when the section is expanded. If you leave the default title (being the first line of text in the section), we recommend that you choose this title option. If you don't, expanded sections display the title twice, as shown in Figure 5.4. You can find this option on the Expand/Collapse tabbed page of the Section Properties box.

FIGURE 5.4

Select **Hide title when expanded** *on the Expand/Collapse page of the Section Properties box to prevent titles from appearing twice when sections are expanded.*

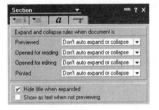

Note
Don't confuse hiding a section *title* when the section is expanded with hiding the *section*. The options on the Section Hide When page of the Section Properties box determine when a section is hidden.

The expand/collapse options in the properties box enable you to control the section's appearance according to the mode a document is in. For example, you can force a section to be expanded when a document is opened in Edit mode and when a new document is being created, but collapsed when a document is opened in Read mode.

You can also make section titles appear only in Preview mode by choosing Show as text when not previewing. When a document is in any other mode (Edit or Read), the section title disappears, but the section contents are displayed. Why would you do this? You can create a much more concise version of the form for preview, especially if the section titles have nice formula titles. For a meeting notice, for example, the section title can show date/time and place of meeting, whereas in edit mode there are separate fields to select/set the time, date, and place.

Caution   Do not confuse the option called Show as text when not previewing with the Previewed field on the Expand/Collapse page of the Section Properties box. The Previewed choice you make to expand or collapse the section when in Preview mode does override the Show as text when not previewing selection.

To set expand and collapse options for your section, open the Section Properties box and click the Expand/Collapse page. There are three expand/collapse rules available in each of the drop-down menus of the Expand/Collapse page:

- **Don't auto expand or collapse**—Whether the section appears expanded or collapsed when the document is opened depends on whether it was expanded or collapsed when the document was last saved.
- **Auto-expand section**—The section is always expanded when the document is opened.
- **Auto-Collapse section**—The section is always collapsed when the document is opened.

Choose which rule to apply when the user is previewing the document, has the document in read or edit mode, or is printing the document as shown in Figure 5.5.

Sections can be nested within sections. For example, you might have a Customer section of a form, which, when expanded, shows three more sections: one for address and phone information, one for contact information, and one for SIC information. When the main section is collapsed, only the title (in this case, "Customer") shows.

FIGURE 5.5

Auto-collapse the section for reading to make the document open quickly. Auto-expand for editing to make all the fields available for entries. Normally, you auto-expand the section for printing, but you might want to leave it collapsed if the section contains proprietary or confidential information that you don't want printed.

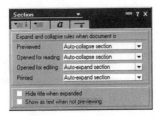

Format and Edit sections

Sections can be moved, added to, deleted, or removed as described in the following list:

- **To move a section**—Place your cursor in the section head and cut and paste it to its new location.

- **To remove a section, but keep its contents**—Click the section and choose **Section, Remove Section** from the menu.

- **To delete a section and its contents**—Click the section and choose **Edit, Clear** from the menu.

- **To add data to the beginning or middle of a section (but not the end)**—Just expand the section and add the data.

- **To append data to the end of a section**—Choose **Section, Remove Section** from the menu and redefine the new section. Alternately, temporarily add a border to your section (see Figure 5.6), and Domino inserts a horizontal line at the end of the section. Place your cursor before the horizontal line and append your information.

5

Change the style and the color of a section's border by making selections in the Section Properties box. Choose a border style and color on the Section Title and Border page of the properties box (see Figure 5.6).

FIGURE 5.6

Select the border style you want to use (choose the empty one if you don't want a border). The default border is none.

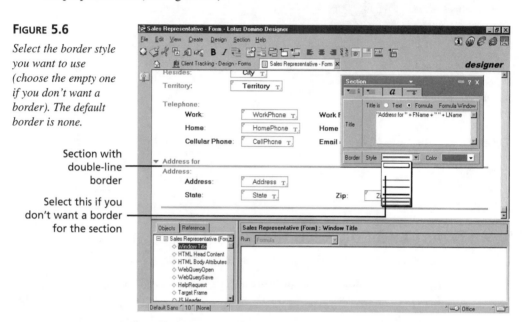

Section with double-line border

Select this if you don't want a border for the section

Insert a Horizontal Rule

Like sections, a *horizontal rule* (line) can help you group information on your form. Like most Domino design elements, horizontal rules have their own properties box in which you can select different formatting options such as color, height, and width.

Figure 5.7 shows how horizontal rules can help to visually organize a form. To insert a horizontal rule, position your cursor where you want the rule to appear in your form and choose **Create, Horizontal Rule** from the menu.   *NO WEB!*

After your rule is inserted, you can change its appearance by selecting options in the Horizontal Rule Properties box, as shown in Figure 5.8.

Color and size settings for the rule, as they are found on the Horizontal Rule Info tab of the Horizontal Rule Properties box, are described in Table 5.2.

FIGURE 5.7

Horizontal rules can be decorative, as at the top, or they can be utilitarian (a separator of text), as at the bottom.

Thick, 3D horizontal rule with gradient coloring

Thin horizontal rule without 3D

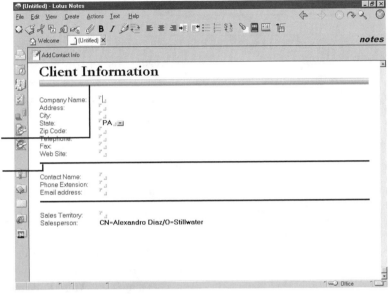

FIGURE 5.8

When you add a horizontal rule, it automatically has a 3D style, no color, fits to the available width, and is 0.073 inches high. The current settings change the rule to 0.15 inches high, with 3D style and gradient coloring going from medium blue to dark blue.

5

Table 5.2   Horizontal Rule Properties—Horizontal Rule Info Page

Option	Description
Size: Width (left box)	For Absolute values, specifies in inches or centimeters (depending upon your international settings) the width of the rule. For Relative values, a percent value, where 100 is the full width of the window and 50 is half the width.
Size: Width: (right box) Absolute	Specify the width of the rule in inches or centimeters.

continues

Table 5.2 continued

Option	Description
Size: Width: (right box) Relative (%)	Sets the width within the available window width based on percent.
Size: Height	Height (thickness) of the rule in inches or centimeters (depending upon your international settings).
Fill: Color	Basic color of the rule.
Fill: (no name) Solid/Gradient	The two icons located next to Color are for solid color (left) or gradient color (right). Click on gradient to open gradient color selections.
Fill: To (for Gradient only)	The final color at the bottom of the rule.
Fill: No 3D shading	Gives the rule a flat-line look.

If you make the length of a horizontal rule less than 100% of the width of the user's screen, you can center it by placing the insertion point on the line occupied by the horizontal rule, and then, in the menu, choosing **Text**, **Align Paragraph**, **Center**.

The HTML properties of the Horizontal rule are covered on Day 9.

Format Paragraphs and Text

You learned about text formatting on Day 2, "Forms 101: The Essentials of Form Design," when you added static text to your form. You also learned that users can only apply formatting options to rich text fields. Therefore, any text and paragraph formatting you apply to your form cannot be changed by the user, except in rich text fields, in which users can always format or reformat text.

But what you might not have come to realize is that the form is itself essentially one big rich text field. After all, you've already added static text and tables that have individual formatting options applied. With this thought in mind, we want to introduce some additional formatting options you can apply to your form. Have you considered applying text formatting options to fields?

Like a word processor, Domino treats text formatting in units of characters (text) and paragraphs. Character formatting options include font selection, font color, and font sizes—all the things that influence the look of the characters. Paragraph formatting includes such options as paragraph alignment, inter-line and inter-paragraph spacing, bullets, and numbers—all the things that influence the look of the paragraph.

To format characters, select the text first (a single character, a word or group of words, a paragraph, or a field), and then apply formatting options using icons on the toolbar or options in the Text Properties box.

If you do not first select the text to be formatted, Notes assumes that you intend to apply your formatting selections to the next text you type at the current cursor position. If you move the cursor without typing anything, Notes ignores your formatting selections.

Work with Paragraphs

Paragraph formatting includes numbers, bullets, alignment, and the application of styles. In most cases, when you format paragraphs, you place your cursor in the paragraph and select formatting options. If you apply formatting while you are typing, you need to des-elect formatting options at the point in your form at which you want to stop, say, bullets or numbering.

To align paragraphs, place your cursor in the paragraph (optionally, highlight the entire paragraph) and then apply the formatting changes using icons on the toolbar or options in the Text Properties box. Remember that paragraphs are defined by hard returns—text that follows a hard return does not accept the formatting changes you make unless you included it in a selection prior to making formatting changes. Paragraph alignment options include flush left, flush right, centered, justified and no wrap. You can apply paragraph alignment to static text as well as to fields. Select the field or the static text and choose alignment by clicking the text alignment icons on the toolbar or by setting the alignment options on the Paragraph Alignment page of the Properties box (see Figure 5.9).

5

FIGURE 5.9

Alignment selections can be made using the SmartIcons or the Properties box. Use No Wrap for repeat characters (asterisks, underscores, dots) to keep them from wrapping to the next line in a smaller window.

Align Left ⌐   ⌐ Align Right

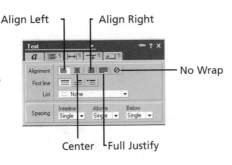

No Wrap

Center └Full Justify

To indent paragraphs, select one of three indenting options on the Paragraph Alignment tab of the Properties box (see Figure 5.10). Choices include indenting the first line of the paragraph, outdenting the first line of a paragraph (which creates a hanging paragraph), and no indent.

FIGURE 5.10

*Click the **return to normal button** to remove any first line indents. Enter the amount of indent (in inches or centimeters) when you select one of the other options.*

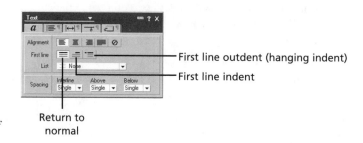

First line outdent (hanging indent)
First line indent

Return to
normal

To add bullets or numbers to paragraphs, use the drop-down List menu found on the Paragraph Alignment Page of the text properties box (see Figure 5.11).

FIGURE 5.11

*Choose one of the List options to add bullets or numbering to selected paragraphs. When a paragraph has bullets or numbering assigned and you press Enter, the next paragraph has the same bullet or the next number. To turn the bullets or numbers off for a paragraph, select **None** as the List option.*

Paragraph line spacing can be set for the spacing between lines in a paragraph (Interline) as well the spacing before (Above) and after (Below) a paragraph. Choose these settings on the Paragraph Alignment page of the Text Properties box, as shown in Figure 5.12.

You can set paragraph margins and tabs by choosing the Paragraph Margins page of the Text Properties box. Settings here work just like a word processor. If you change paragraph margins, the margin settings are retained, even when you press the Enter key. However, if you change paragraph margins by selecting a paragraph after you type, the new margin settings affect only the selected paragraph. Choices for margins include setting Absolute and Relative margins, with absolute being an actual measurement (inches or centimeters) and relative representing a percentage of the width of the window.

By default, tab stops are set at 1/2 inch intervals. Tabs can be set individually, in which you type the actual position in inches or centimeters, preceded by the alignment indicator—*r* for right, *l* for left, *c* for center, and *D* for decimal and separated by a comma (for example, R3.5, C5, L7). The simplest way to set tabs is to right-click on the ruler at the position at which you want the tab setting. From the pop-up menu, choose the tab type (left, center, and so forth) you desire. This also works like a word processor.

FIGURE 5.12

Set the Interline, Above, or Below options to Single, 1 1/2, or Double.

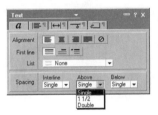

Use Styles

Another useful paragraph formatting option is the use of paragraph styles. By creating a paragraph style, you can reapply formatting options without having to set individual components each time, such as the font, the paragraph alignment, the font color, and so forth. To create a paragraph style, format a paragraph with the properties you want to save in your paragraph style, open the Text Properties Box, and click the **Paragraph Styles** page. Click on **Create Style**. The Create Paragraph Style dialog box appears as shown in Figure 5.13. Type a name for your style and select one or more of the following options:

- Check **Include font in the style** if you want to save the font as part of the named style
- Check **Make style available for all documents** if you want to use the named style for other forms or documents.
- Check **Assign style to the Style Cycle key [F11]** so it becomes one of the styles that is available when users press F11 to cycle through paragraph styles.

FIGURE 5.13

*After you create a
style, you apply it to
selected text by press-
ing* **F11**. *Alternately,
select the text, choose*
Text, Apply Style *from
the menu, and then
select the style from
the submenu.*

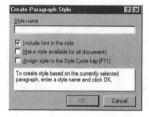

After a style has been created, apply it to other paragraphs by selecting the paragraph
and choosing one of the following methods:

- Press **F11** until you see the style you want applied to the text (this works only if
  you included the style in the cycle list when you created it).
- Choose **Text, Apply Style** from the menu and select a style from the submenu.
- Click the **Paragraph Styles** indicator on the status bar and select a style from the
  pop-up list.

To change the properties of a paragraph style, open the Paragraph Styles page of the Text
Properties box, highlight your style, and click the **Redefine Style** button. To delete a
style, click the **Delete Style** button.

Add Graphics

Graphics are a very popular addition to forms, but you do not want to overwhelm users
and resources (memory, processors, and so forth) with graphics. Keep the size, position,
and colors of graphics within reason. Remember, the purpose of a form is to gather and
disseminate information—not entertain the using community. Graphics can enhance the
purpose of the form by making the form more pleasing to the user's eye.

Graphics can be a great way of letting users know which form they are using when creating documents. This is also true of background colors and, of course, headings on forms.

Domino accepts several graphics formats, including .PIX, ANSI metafiles (.CGM,
.CGF), JPEG files (.JPG), TIFF 5.0 files (.TIF), and .BMP, .GIF, and .PCX files.
Graphics can be *imported* as pictures or objects, pasted into forms from other forms or
applications (but only bitmap graphics such as .BMP, .GIF, and .TIF can be pasted), or
used as Navigators or image maps. Graphics can also be used as an *Image Resource*, that
is, an object that is shared and that can be used in other forms in the database. Here, we
discuss importing graphics files and using them as backgrounds. You learn more about
shared resources, navigators, and image maps on later days.

NEW TERM Graphics fall into two categories—*bitmap* and *vector*. Graphic formats such as .CGM and .WMF are vector drawings. Those drawings build curves using mathematical equations, so the curves come out smooth. Vector graphics usually occupy less disk space then equivalent bitmap graphics and can be resized at will. Bitmap graphics consist of a set of pixels (dots) such as those on your computer monitor, and each pixel is mapped to a color. How the pixels are mapped makes up the picture. Bitmap graphics don't resize well because when you resize a bitmap graphic you actually make each pixel in it either larger or smaller. If you don't resize the graphic in even multiples of its original size, not all pixels are resized the same, and, depending on the subject, you might end up with an ugly result. Even if you do resize a bitmap by, say, making it four times its original size, you end up with a blocky looking graphic because all you have done is made the pixels bigger.

One of the easiest ways to add a graphic to your form is to paste the graphic. As we already stated, only bitmap files can be pasted into your form and maintain their original quality. To paste a .BMP, .GIF, or .TIF file, copy the graphic to the clipboard, position the cursor on your form where you want to place the graphic, right-click the mouse, and choose **Paste** from the pop-up menu.

To import a file into your Domino form, position the cursor in the location at which you want the graphic to appear, and then choose **Create, Picture** from the menu. The Import dialog box appears as shown in Figure 5.14. Select the type of file you want to import from the Files of type drop-down list, select your file name, and click Import.

FIGURE 5.14

*The Import dialog box appears when you choose **Create, Picture** or **File, Import** from the menu. The only difference is that the types of files you can choose to import are restricted to graphics formats when you select **Create, Picture**.*

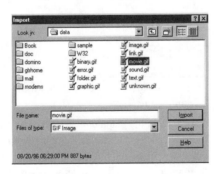

After you've added a graphic to your form, you can change its size by selecting the graphic (click on it) and dragging the sizing handles.

Tip

> If you incorrectly size a graphic and you want to return it to its original pro-
> portions, don't use **Undo**. Instead, select the picture by clicking it, open the
> Picture Properties box, and select **Reset width and height to 100%**.

You can also change the picture properties by right-clicking the picture and opening the
properties box from the pop-up menu. Here, you can change the height or width of the
picture and add text that displays while a picture is loading in a Web application (see
Figure 5.15).

FIGURE 5.15

*You change the height
and width of the pic-
ture by entering per-
centages. Keep the
percentages the same
to maintain the aspect
ratio (ratio of height
to width) and avoid
distortion of the
picture.*

Table 5.3 lists options found in the dialog box that you might want to select or set for
your picture.

Table 5.3   Picture Properties, Picture Info Page

Item/Option	Description
Source	The resource name with browse and formula buttons, or a reference to an inline image.
Text Wrap	How text and the graphic relate to each other within a paragraph. There are seven choices that combine wrap or don't wrap with float image or specific alignments. Wrap refers to how text flows around the graphic. Float and align define where the graphic is in relation to the text: top, middle, bottom, baseline, left, or right.

Item/Option	Description
Scaling (%): Width	The width of the picture in relation to its original size (100% is the original width).
Scaling (%): Height	The height of the picture in relation to its original size (100% is the original height).
Scaling (%): Reset	Resets the graphic to the size it was when originally imported or pasted.
Alternate Text:	Alternate text used for graphic reader programs (for the visually impaired).
Caption:	The text to associate with the graphic.
Caption: Display caption:	Either below the image or centered on the image.
Hotspots: Number:	The number of hotspots that currently overlay this graphic.
Hotspots: Add hotspot:	Press one of the three add buttons to define the shape of the hotspot you are about to add: Polygon, circle, or rectangle.

For pictures that don't have a strong definition around the edge, you might want to add a border. When you click the **Picture Border** tab of the Picture Properties box (see Figure 5.16), you can select a Border style (Solid, Dotted, Double, and so forth), pick a color for the border, and set its Thickness. To give the picture a sense of 3D, add a drop shadow and give it a width that is greater than zero so that it's visible (see Figure 5.17).

FIGURE 5.16

Add borders and drop shadows to your graphics to give them definition by setting options on the Picture Border page of the Picture Properties box.

5

FIGURE 5.17

The graphic at the top of the document has top and bottom solid borders and a drop shadow.

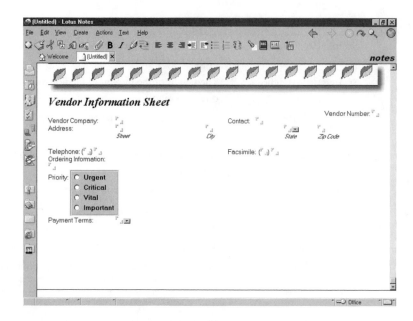

Create Non-Scrollable Headers

Not to be confused with headers (as in headers and footers), which are used for printing and are covered later in this day, a *non-scrollable header* creates a frame at the top (or bottom) of the Notes document (see Figure 5.18). This feature is similar to the header that is used in the mail template, where the area of the form that contains the addressees, sender, and subject line remains onscreen while you scroll through a mail message.

Note

It's misleading for Lotus to call these elements *non-scrollable* headers in light of the fact that you can set scrolling options for these features in the Form Properties box. It's also confusing that Lotus has two kinds of headers, and that they really don't clearly differentiate between the two types with definitive names. We wish that they had called them *screen headers* and *printed headers*. In this book, we refer to them using the Lotus term *non-scrollable headers* and our own term, *printed headers and footers*, and we're hoping this helps to eliminate confusion between these two very different features.

Non-scrollable header ⌐

FIGURE 5.18

The non-scrollable header remains at the top of the document even when you scroll through the remainder of the document. Notice that there is a scroll bar next to the "non-scrollable" header but it only scrolls up and down within the area you defined as the header.

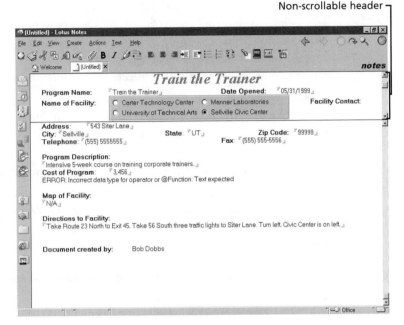

Headers can contain any elements a form can contain, including graphics and tables.

When a form contains a header and a background graphic (see "Create Background Graphics" later in this day), the background graphic is displayed only in the header area of the document when it is viewed through the Notes Client. You cannot add two background graphics to a form. Therefore, you cannot have a different background graphic for the header and another for the remainder of the form.

5

To create a header for your form, first position your cursor where you want the header to end. We liken this process to the way you split a window or freeze panes in a spreadsheet program.

Open the Form Properties box and click on the Header tab (see Figure 5.19). Click **Add header to form** to create the header. Other settings on this page include

- Set the **Height** (optional) in number of pixels or as a percentage of the form height. Use the drop-down menu to choose between **Percent, Pixels**, and **Content** (dynamically resizes the header to show all content, even user entered data, on the form. When using content the Height number field is inactive). If you don't change these fields, the header appears in the Notes client exactly as you defined it when you positioned your cursor and checked Add header to form on the Header page. Note that changes you make here are not reflected in Designer; although a line appears to denote the non-scrollable area from the main area, you must preview the form in the Notes client to see the affects of Height changes.

- Choose to always display scroll bars by clicking the **Yes** Radio button in the **Scrolling** area of the Header page; never display scroll bars by clicking the **No** button; or click **Auto** to display scroll bars automatically when the content of the header exceeds the allotted space.

- Enable users to resize the header area by selecting **Allow Resizing**.

- The header border is the separator line between the header and the form. Turn the header border off by setting Border: Width to zero. Otherwise, set the border thickness and color in the **Width** and **Color** areas. Add 3D styling to the border by selecting **3D Shading**.

FIGURE 5.19

If you select Auto scrolling as a header option, the scrollbar appears only when the contents of the non-scrolling header are longer than the allotted area.

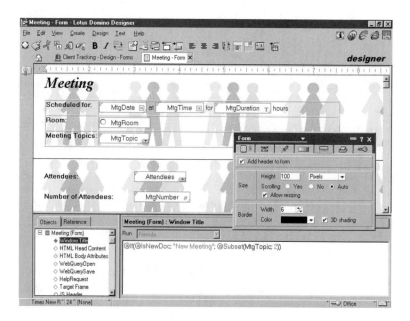

Figure 5.20 shows a form that contains a border with a graphic (not a graphic background), a table, and a thick border.

FIGURE 5.20

The non-scrolling header in this document contains a table, a graphic, and text. In Designer, you can't see the thickness of the border or the color.

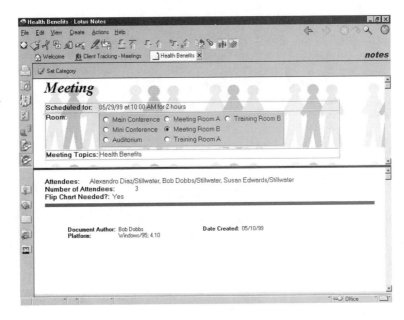

Tip

Don't use scrollable headers in a mixed environment. Note that the browser ignores scrolling and non-scrolling headers and presents the form as one form. If your form is to be accessed by both Notes clients and Web browsers, consider using frames instead. You learn more about frames on Day 8.

5

Create Background Graphics

Pictures can be used as background graphics, where text and other objects appear on top of the tiled graphic itself (see Figure 5.21). To create this effect, import or paste a graphic image into your form. Whether you paste or import depends on the graphic file you intend to use. Only bitmap files can be pasted; other file formats must be imported. You can import BMP (bitmap), CGM, GIF, JPEG, PCX Image, and TIFF 5.0 Bitmap files.

To *paste* a bitmap image as a form background, copy the picture into the Windows clipboard and, in Designer, open the Form Properties box. Click the **Form Background** tab and click the **Paste** button in the Graphic or Resource section.

To *import* a picture as a form background, open the Form Properties box and click the **Import** button on the Form Background page (see Figure 5.22). The Import dialog box appears (refer to Figure 5.14 earlier). Select the file you want to import and click the **Import** button.

FIGURE 5.21

When using a background graphic, be sure that it doesn't make it too difficult to read the text in the document.

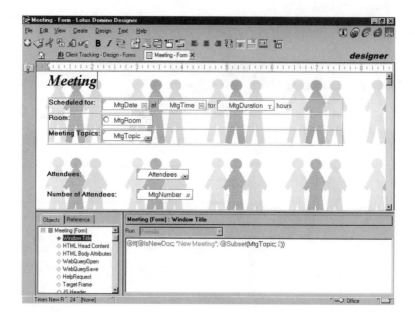

Another method for using graphics is to create an Image Resource from a graphics file. This method enables you to share, or reuse, images quickly and efficiently because the image is stored in one location, available throughout the database. Therefore, if you need to change the graphic, you change it in one location only. You learn more about Image Resources on Day 17.

When you have image resources available to you and want to use one for your form background, click the **Folder** button in the Graphic or Resource section of the Form Background page. Select an image from the list in the Insert Image Resource dialog box and then click **OK**.

FIGURE 5.22

For background graphics, you must use the Paste or Import buttons in the Graphic or Resource section of the Form Background page of the Form Properties box. Using File, Import or Create, Picture only places one image on the form and does not place it behind the text.

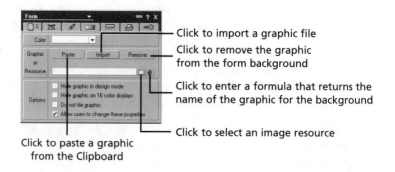

Click to import a graphic file

Click to remove the graphic from the form background

Click to enter a formula that returns the name of the graphic for the background

Click to select an image resource

Click to paste a graphic from the Clipboard

Note   Do not use File, Import, or Create, Picture to insert a picture as a form background. These commands insert the picture into your form, but not as a form background.

In the Options section of the Form Background page are four options for you to choose:

- **Hide graphic in design mode**. Turns the background graphic off while you're working in Designer, which means less distraction and faster refresh times while you work.

- **Hide graphic on 16 color displays**. Users who have monitors that only display 16 colors can't see the lighter pastels you should be using for background graphics. Instead, lighter colors are either translated to a bright equivalent or disappear altogether. A pale yellow, for instance, will display as bright yellow on a 16 color display. With brighter colors in the background, users won't be able to see the text. To prevent this problem, select this option. Users who have displays that show more colors will see the background properly.

- **Do not tile graphic**. If the graphic you choose for the background is smaller than the entire screen, Designer automatically repeats it across and down the form. Select this option if you don't want the graphic to repeat.

- **Allow users to change these properties**. When you select this option, users have control over the background for the documents they create based on the form. If they don't want to see the background, they can turn it off.

Plan for the Printed Form

Just as you have considered how your form will appear in the hands of users by previewing your form in Notes and in a Web browser during the design process, you need to consider how your form will print. This is particularly important if you are creating forms for the purpose of printing, where having a hard copy is a part of the application process. But even if printing is not your major consideration, consider that people *do* print Web pages to read offline and, necessary or not, it is still a fact of life. So you want to look at your form or a test document in Print Preview mode (see Figure 5.23) during the design process to ensure that the form will be as useful in hard copy as it is on the computer screen.

5

FIGURE 5.23

By looking at the Two-Page preview of a document, you see that it automatically breaks to a second page when the document won't fit on one page.

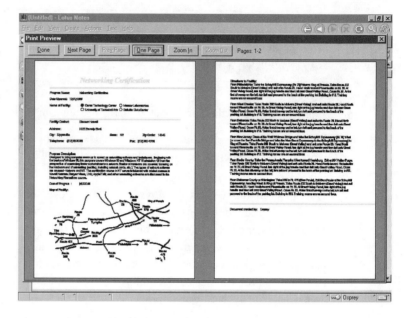

You can preview documents you've created with the form, or you can preview the form itself in Designer by choosing **File**, **Print** from the menu. The Print dialog box appears, as shown in Figure 5.24.

FIGURE 5.24

*Click the **Preview** button in the Print dialog box to preview the current document or form.*

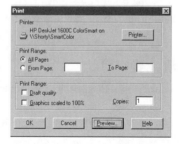

Tip

In most applications, the shortcut keystroke **Ctrl+P** prints a document, bypassing the Print dialog box. In Domino, **Ctrl+P** brings up the Print dialog box, from which you can press the letter *P* to Preview the document. No real shortcut exists to preview directly, and no menu choice exists for previewing directly.

Print preview illustrates your document as it will appear when it is printed (see Figure 5.25). Print preview displays one page or two, and has navigation buttons for viewing the document (**Next Page**, **Prev Page**, **Zoom In** and **Zoom Out**). If you've set the print options to auto-collapse a section when printing, the section is collapsed in print preview mode, even if the section is open in your Designer window.

Navigation buttons

FIGURE 5.25

The navigation buttons in Print Preview provide methods for magnifying and reducing the view of the document or form, moving from page to page, or seeing one or two pages at one time.

Section automatically expanded for printing as part of form design

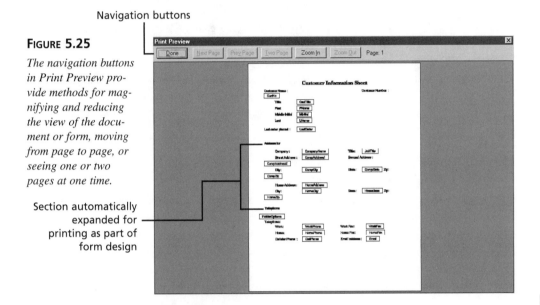

Ready, Set, Print

If you discover that your form is unacceptable when you preview it, use the following table (Table 5.4) as a guide to troubleshooting and reformatting the form so that it is better suited for printing.

Table 5.4 Troubleshooting Printing Problems

Problem	Solution
The text in the document is too wide for my printed page	Open the Paragraph Margins tab of the Text Properties box. Make sure both the Left and Right margins are Absolute and have measurements that fit within the width of a printed page.
Tables don't fit within left and right margins of the printed form	On the Table Layout tab of the Table Properties box, change Table Width to Fixed Width and then set the size of the columns so they aren't wider than the space between the margins.

continues

Table 5.4 continued

Problem	Solution
Page break is in unwanted position on the form	1. View page breaks by selecting **View**, **Show**, **Page Breaks f**rom the menu.
	2.Insert manual page breaks by choosing **Create, Page Break** from the menu.
	3. (optional) Remove unnecessary blank lines and change the font size to a smaller font
Sections do not show as expanded in Print Preview	Check the Section Properties Expand/Collapse page. Make sure the Printed: options are set to Auto-Expand the section. Do not confuse the print options with the Previewed options. The Previewed options are not *Print* Preview options.

Add Headers and Footers

Another consideration for the printed form is the use of headers and footers. Headers and Footers are created on the Printing page of the Form properties box (see Figure 5.27). There you determine the text, font, font size, font style (not to be confused with paragraph styles, which you just learned), and fields to use, such as date, time, and page number. Creating a header and footer for printing is very similar to the process you use when you create headers and footers in your word processing program.

Tip

Headers and footers can also be set in the Database Properties box for all the documents in the database and in the Document Properties box by the user for the open or selected document.

FIGURE 5.26

*Click the **Header** or **Footer** Radio button to select the one for which you are entering text.*

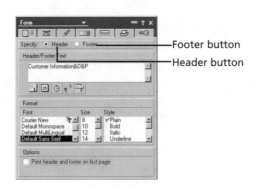

Table 5.5 lists the options that are found on the Printing page of the Form Properties box. Remember that if you need to hide information when a document is printed, you can create a section and use the Expand/Collapse properties of the section to hide it when you are printing, as described earlier in this lesson. (Alternately, you can use the Hide When property, covered in Day 9.)

Table 5.5 Form Properties, Printing Page

Item	Description	Comments
Header	Click Radio button to create header	Toggle between header and footer using the Radio buttons
Footer	Click Radio button to create footer	Toggle between header and footer using the Radio buttons
Header/Footer Text	Type header or footer text in the text pane. Add pipe separators (|) for center and left alignment.	
	Inserts code for page number: **&P**	This inserts just the numeral for the page. Type any text you want to appear with it in the text pane; for example, "Page &P" becomes "Page 1" when the first page prints.
	Inserts code for date: **&D**	Inserts the current system date, such as 10/31/98.
	Inserts code for time: **&T**	Inserts the current system time, such as 10:00:00 PM
	Inserts code for tab: |	Tab stops are predetermined and permanent; center and right.
	Inserts code for form or document name: **&W**	Inserts the title of the form if it has been saved and assigned a title.
Format: Font	Select the font to use for the header or footer	
Format: Size	Determine font size for header or footer	
Format: Style	Determine font style for header or footer	
Options: Print header and footer on first page	Deselect if you want no header and footer on the first page	If page numbering is included, the second page is numbered 2 even though no header and footer appear on page 1

Use the Tab icon as shown in Table 5.5 to align text in your header or footer. When you click the Tab icon, it inserts a pipe into your header or footer text (|). Tabs determine the placement of the text using preset, permanent tab stops—center and right. The placement of these tabs establishes the placement of the text on your document. The default placement of header and footer information is flush left. Use one pipe for each tab you want to insert preceding text. Following are examples of using the tab insert:

```
Customer Information¦&D¦&P
```

Left justifies the words `Customer Information`, center justifies the date, and right justifies the page number.

```
¦Customer Information
```

Center justifies the text `Customer Information`.

```
¦¦&P
```

Right justifies the page number.

Form Properties Not Suited for Web Browsers

Throughout this book, we point out Domino objects, functions, and properties that are not supported on the Web. Here, we've compiled a table (Table 5.6) that lists form properties that are not supported on the Web to help you find these items in one location. If your application is a Web application, don't use the features. If your application is a mixed application, usable by both Notes and Web users, we will show you in later lessons how to display these features to Notes users but hide them from Web users.

Table 5.6 Form Properties Not Supported on the Web

Form Properties Page	Item	Comment
Form Info	Versioning	See Day 2 for more information on this feature
	Anonymous forms	See Day 2 for more information on this feature
	Merge replication conflicts	See Day 2 for more information on this feature
	Store form in document mode	Although edit mode is not supported, read mode is. But don't use this for documents that need to be created or edited on the Web.

Form Properties Page	Item	Comment
	Disable field exchange	
	Automatically refresh fields	
Defaults	On Create: Inherit entire selected document into rich text field	Because Web browsers can't select documents, default value formulas cannot reference a selected document. Other On Create Inherit options are supported.
	On Open: Show context pane	
	On Close: Present mail send dialog	
Launch	Auto Launch options (First Attachment, First Document Link, First OLE object)	
Security	Default encryption keys	
	Disable printing/ forwarding/copying to clipboard	

5

Summary

In this lesson you learned how to make your forms more usable and more attractive to users. You learned that sections can make long forms more manageable to users, and that graphics can make forms more interesting and appealing. Pasting a graphic into a document and adding a background graphic are two of many ways to incorporate graphics into your Domino application. If neither of these methods suits your needs, keep in mind that you will be learning about pages, navigators, and layout regions, which also support graphics and might be the Domino features you want to use to incorporate your graphics.

You also learned the difference between screen headers and printed headers and how to set up each kind. Try to remember that these are two very different kinds of headers, and that if you add a graphic background to your form it only displays in the screen header.

Print Preview is a new feature in Domino R5, and we suggest that you take full advantage of this feature, previewing your work often. In the word processing world, we've come to take print preview for granted. It has been a feature of Notes/Domino that we have longed for, for many years. We can assure you that people still print documents even though, as programmers, we do our best to automate their world and try to eliminate the necessity for printed material. If you ignore the printed document, you might have to face redesign later to satisfy the needs of the using community.

And speaking of needs, it isn't enough to design for function alone. You might develop the most functional application in the universe, but if it's not easy for users to work with, they won't use it and it will end up on the cutting floor, so to speak. If you have the opportunity, visit with your using community often during your design process, show them your forms, and have them test a few. Staying close to the users now can save you lots of redesign work later.

Finally, in this lesson you learned which features of forms are not suitable for use in Web applications. We try to point these features out in every lesson, but do keep in mind that Day 8 concentrates heavily on supporting the Web client.

Q&A

Q How can I create a background graphic that is not tiled?

A The simplest method is to select the **Do not tile graphic** option on the Form Background page of the Form Properties box.

You can create a layout region and use the graphic as a background for just that region (see Day 12, "Beautify Your Application"). That leaves the remainder of the form without a graphic background, and you determine where on the form the layout region appears. A layout region is an interesting way to create a banner with a graphic background as the title area of the form.

Another way is to create the graphic in such a way that it is the same size as the screen. That depends on your capability to work with graphic programs to enlarge or add extra pixels to your picture. When it is so large, there is no room for it to tile. Be careful here, though. If your screen is smaller than that of another user, the background tiles. If your screen has a much higher resolution than that of your user, only a portion of the graphic is seen by them and you might cause excessive scrolling during data entry.

Q I want a section to have a colored background; how can I do this?

A You can't assign colored backgrounds to sections; however, you can create a table with a table background and no borders. When the section is expanded, it has a background color, but no color appears behind the section title.

Q I want the printed footer to say page x of x—how can I do this?

A Unfortunately, you can't do this unless you know the total number of pages and enter the page numbers as text.

Workshop

In this workshop you enhance the forms you created for the Proposed Titles database. This workshop will engage your creativity, so you don't have to adhere as strictly to the examples that are shown as you have in past workshops. As long as the field names and form titles remain the same and the formulas remain as written to date, you can employ your ingenuity to create attractive and easy to use forms.

Do the following to the Proposed Title form:

- Create a standard section on the form that includes the TReviewStart, TReviewEnd, TAcqEditor, and TStatus fields and their associated static text.
- Make the title of the section "Management Information," and then format the section border and title as you want. Collapse the section for reading and preview. Expand the section for editing and printing.
- Place a horizontal rule immediately after the title of the form. Format the rule as you want. Add any other horizontal rules you deem necessary.
- Add a background graphic to the form from clip art you have available, or create one in any available graphic program and paste or import it into the form.
- Change any paragraph alignment, indenting, or spacing you want to enhance the form.
- Add a non-scrollable header to the form.
- Make adjustments to make the form printable, including adding a header with the form title and the date, and a footer with the page number.

In Figure 5.27, you see the adjustments we made to our form.

5

FIGURE 5.27

*A Management
Information section,
horizontal rules, a
non-scrollable header,
and a graphic back-
ground are visible
enhancements to the
form. The graphic was
drawn in Windows
Paint.*

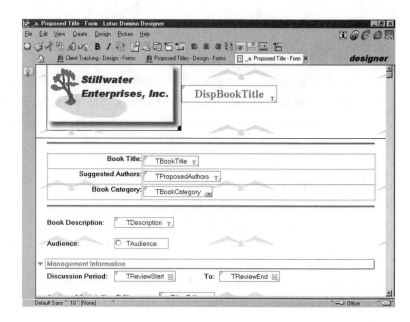

Now add enhancements to the Response and Comments forms.

DAY 6

Take in the View: Create Views and Folders

Views perform like a table of contents to a database, listing the documents of a database in rows and information from or about those documents in column format. A sorted or categorized list of documents, views also provide access to the documents in a database, acting as pointers to the documents. Without a view, documents cannot be accessed.

Experienced Notes users take views for granted—they have been an integral part of the software from the beginning—but even the most experienced Web user will find Notes views unique. Notes-like views are not native to other HTTP servers, and no other server performs like Domino, giving users the capability to create content and see that content listed among other documents upon saving. Domino was the first to create views dynamically on the Web and, we contend, it remains the best. If you're an experienced Web developer, think of views and folders as index files that automatically update and contain programming features and graphics.

To create shared forms and views, you must have a minimum of Designer access to the database, and it is typically the application developer who creates most of a database's shared views and folders. Designer access is the default ACL setting for creating different types of views, as well as for specifying who can access those views. However, the end user can create views, and in certain cases, so can someone who has Editor access to the database. The end user has the right (by default) to create private views—views available to that end user only. An Editor, if given specific rights in the database Access Control List (not by default), can create shared views. You learn more about shared and private views a little later in this day.

Folders are populated by end users who can drag and drop documents into them and, unlike views, require no selection formulas. As a Designer, you can create folders for users, but you cannot populate the folder through the use of a selection formula. However, you can create and run actions or agents to populate folders after the folders have been created.

 Note

> Unlike the folders you find in your operating system, Notes folders are *not* directories. When you place documents in three different folders, you are not creating three copies of the document—you are only displaying that document in the folder. If you delete a document, you delete it from the database and from all three folders. However, if you remove a document from a folder, you have not deleted it from the database.

This lesson concentrates on the basic design of views for the Notes client; on Day 10, "Advanced Views," you learn about enhancing views for the Web client. Today you learn

- The types of Notes views
- How to create a view
- Determining which documents to display in the view
- Setting view properties
- Adding and defining columns
- Creating folders

Types of Views

Views display documents in rows and columns. Each row represents a document, and each column displays information from the document. Columns can contain an actual field value or the result of a formula. Every database must have at least one view; therefore, Domino creates a default view for each database (see Figure 6.1).

FIGURE 6.1

In the list of views in the Designer, the default view for a new database has no name except the label "untitled," but it is marked by the default icon.

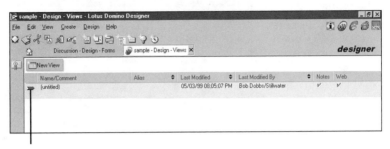

Default icon

This *Domino-generated* default view has no meaningful column headers (see Figure 6.2), and documents are represented by a number that reflects the order in which documents were added to the database (1, 2, and so forth). It isn't the most useful view, but without this default view you couldn't access documents during the design process. Because database design typically starts with forms and the creation of *test* or *dummy* documents, and then proceeds to the creation of views, the default view is—at the very least—temporarily important and useful.

FIGURE 6.2

The default view has only one column, which displays document numbers. The numbers represent documents in the order they were created. The number 1.1 is a response document, and 1.1.1 is a response-to-response document.

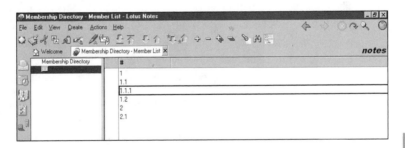

6

When you are ready to create your first view, you can edit the default view or start from scratch with a new view. Figure 6.3 shows an edited default view, designed to be more functional for the end users.

Sorting triangles (ascending and descending)

Column headers

FIGURE 6.3

This view is categorized by sales territory and then by salesperson. Each column displays information from a field within the document. The companies are sorted alphabetically, but the user can reverse that by clicking the small sorting triangle on the column header.

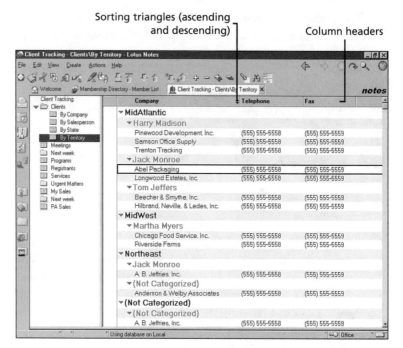

The database Designer determines exactly which documents are displayed in a view. Many databases contain several views, enabling users to view documents in different ways (see Figure 6.4). In a client tracking database, for example, you might create a view that displays documents by company name, one that displays documents by salesperson, and yet another that displays documents by customer location or region.

Views can be as simple as a single-column sorted view or as complex as a multiline-per-row view. Views can be collapsible or categorized, and the contents of the view can be determined by a formula that identifies the user accessing the view and returns contents pertinent to that user. You (the Designer) determine such features, as well as how users access the view, which view is the default view for the database, the view colors, numbers of lines per row, row spacing, how documents are sorted or categorized, which documents to include in the view, and so forth. Figure 6.5 illustrates a view and calls out many of the view properties you can set.

FIGURE 6.4

This database can display client documents in one of four ways: by company, by salesperson, by state, and by sales territory. The By Company view is shown here, as evidenced by the checkmark in the menu, the name on the task button, and the window title.

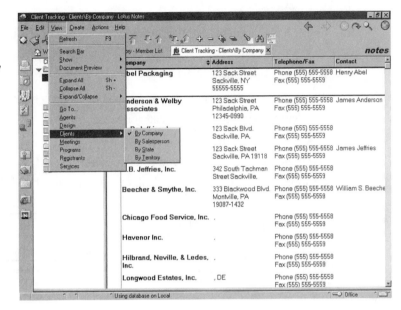

1 1/2 line spacing between rows

FIGURE 6.5

This view is categorized by salesperson. Alternating row colors, 1 1/2 line spacing between rows, and multiple lines of text in rows make the view easy to read.

Category text is formatted as bold

Alternating row colors

Multiple lines in a row

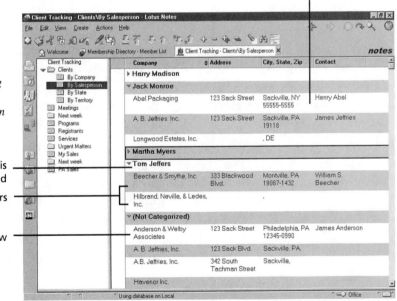

6

As you prepare to create a view, consider planning the view on paper first (see Figure 6.6). Answer these questions and then sketch your view based on the databases you created in previous lessons:

- Who will access this view?
- What forms will be used when users access documents from the view?
- How will the view be sorted or categorized?
- How will response documents display?
- What information will display in column titles?
- What fields of information will display in each column?

FIGURE 6.6

Here is a plan for a view that shows what columns need to be included and what information to show in each column.

Books - By Category				
Category	Title	Authors	Audience	Submitted by
TBookCategory (categorized by this column)	TBookTitle	TProposedAuthors	TAudience	TDocAuthor + "on" + @Text (@created, "DOSO")
		Response document ROpinion + "by" + Author + "on" + @Text (@created, "DOSO")		

If your database will be accessed by Notes clients as well as Web clients, you might want to create alternate views to enhance the display for each platform. For example, Web clients don't have access to the Notes menu system, so depending on your application, additional design elements might be needed to enable Web clients to create documents and open views.

Next, determine what type and style of view you will create. Domino has three flavors of views: *Private* views, *Shared* views, and *Shared, Private on first use* views. Private views are created by the end user for use on one workstation only—the one on which the view was created. As a designer, you will create Shared views and Shared, Private on first use views. These views are further defined in the following section.

In designing views, you'll work with some new icons on the toolbar that you might have seen or used in previous lessons while creating forms and fields. The following list illustrates those icons:

 Design View

 Create Folder

Design View Properties

Create Insert New Column

Design View Selection Conditions

View Show/Hide Design Pane

Shared Views

Shared views are available to all users with Reader access and above; they are stored in the database, on the server. Most views you design will be shared views. In addition to Designers, users with Manager access to the database can create shared views. Users with Editor access can also create shared views if the Manager has selected "Create personal folders/views" in the Access Control List for the database (learn more about this on Day 7, "Sleep Soundly: Secure Your Application").

Shared views are further defined by their specific type:

- **Shared**—A shared view is stored on the server and is available to all users with sufficient access rights (Readers and above).

- **Shared, contains documents not in folders**—A shared view that displays only those documents that are not kept in any folder.

- **Shared, contains deleted documents**—A special view that contains a list of "soft deleted" documents. Normally, documents that are deleted are permanently removed from the database when a view is refreshed or the database is closed. However, the designer or database manager has the option to Allow soft deletions, which can be selected on the Advanced tab of the Database Properties box. *Soft* means the deleted documents are recoverable. The database manager or designer must also set the number of hours to pass before documents are permanently deleted from the database. To make soft deletions work, the designer must create a Shared, Contains Deleted Documents view that contains the deleted documents. Those documents remain in the view for the specified period. To retrieve the deleted documents, the user needs to undelete them using an action created by the application designer. That action must use the @UndeleteDocument function.

- **Shared, private on first use**—These views are initially stored on the server and are created by someone with a Designer or Manager Access. When this type of view is accessed, it becomes a private view when the user saves it. This type of view provides a method for distributing customized personal views to many users.

6

For example, you design a sales tracking system so each salesperson can keep track of their own clients. You make the view shared, private on first use. As each salesperson calls up that view, it becomes a private view for that person and shows only that person's information. Each salesperson has the same view structure, but doesn't see anyone else's sales contacts. Create this view by using @UserName in the selection formula to customize the display for each user (see Appendix E, "Formulas and Scripts by Tasks," for an example).

> **Caution**
>
> Shared, private on first use views do not inherit design changes after they've been saved. If you add a column to the view, users need to delete their private versions of the view and open the newly modified, shared, private on first use view. Don't use this type of view as a security feature; if you omit documents from this view, a user can still create a private view that includes them. All shared, private on first use views are stored on the server until their first use. Where they are stored after that is determined by the "Create personal folders/views" option in the Access Control List (ACL). Refer to Day 7 for more information on the ACL.

- **Shared, desktop private on first use**—This is the same type as Shared, private on first use, but with one difference: This view is stored in the user's Desktop.dsk file on their local drive instead of on the server.
- **Private**—A private view is available only to the person who created the view. Where these files are stored depends on the user's rights to create private folders/views in the access control list for the database. If the user has those rights, the user's private views are stored in the Notes database. Otherwise, they're stored in the Desktop.dsk file on the user's workstation.

> **Note**
>
> The Desktop.dsk file is stored on the workstation and stores the information that personalizes your workspace. It contains the list of database icons in your bookmark bar, in addition to storing your private views.

Private Views

Private views are exactly that—private (see Figure 6.7). When you create a Private view you are the only person who has access to that view. Create a private view by following the instructions found in "Create Views," selecting **Private** as the View Type in the Create View dialog box.

FIGURE 6.7

The private views appear at the end of the list of views and have a dashed line under the view icon. Although you can prepare a private view for yourself in your own Notes client, as a developer you will be more concerned with shared views.

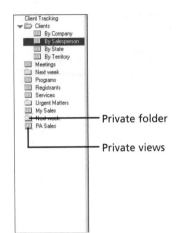

Private folder

Private views

Users can create their own private views to any database, and this helps them to organize documents using personal preferences. Users select **Create**, **View** from their Notes client menu to create these views. If the Access Control List grants users the rights to create private folders and views, private views are stored on the server. If the ACL does not grant this right, private views are stored in the user's Desktop.dsk.

You (the Designer) can also create a Private view for yourself from your Notes client by choosing **Create**, **View** from the menu.

View Styles

After a view *type* has been selected, a view *style* must be chosen: *standard outline* or *calendar*. A standard outline view is much like the view you see in your Notes mail database, with documents organized by rows and columns. In a standard outline view, one column is typically used to organize documents in some kind of order, such as alphabetical order or date order. For example, the Notes R5 Client Inbox view displays mail organized by the sender, as shown in Figure 6.8

A calendar view groups documents by date (see Figure 6.9). This type of view is useful for schedules, appointments, and meetings. Users can choose between viewing formats of 1 Day, 2 Days, 1 Week, and so forth (you determine which formats they can choose).

6

FIGURE 6.8

To open a document, Notes users double-click on a row in the view. In the Inbox, the Who, Date, and Size columns can all be sorted by the user because the designer enabled sort triangles to the column headers.

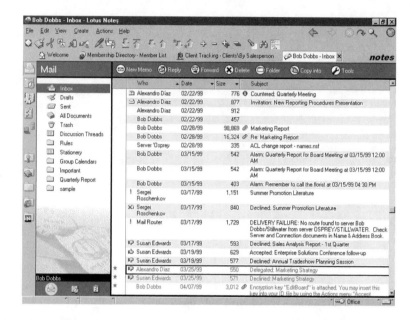

Click one of these numbers to change view format

FIGURE 6.9

Calendar views display in 1 day, 2 day, 7 day, 14 day, or 31 day formats. This is the 7 day view.

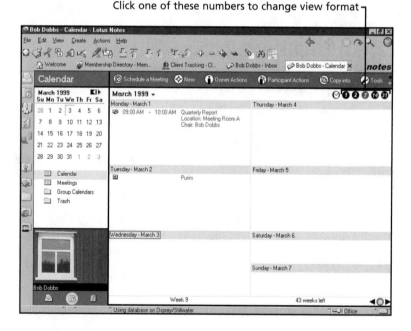

Create a Standard View

Lotus refers to outline views as *standard* views, and they are the most commonly used type of view. One of the columns in the view is usually set as the organizing column, such as a Date column that organizes documents in chronological order.

Caution Although you can change a standard view to a calendar view, you must set the first column of the view as a date column and have at least two columns in the view. You will be warned that changing to the calendar view will permanently change some of the view attributes. Converting a calendar view to a standard view is fairly straightforward.

Use the following steps to create a view

1. Open the database in Designer and click **Views** in the Design Pane.

2. Click the **New View** button on the Action bar (see Figure 6.10).

Click here to pin the
Design pane open

Click here to create
a new view

FIGURE 6.10

Select Views from the Design Pane and then click on the New View button on the Action bar. The Design Pane is pinned open in this figure.

Click here to see a
list of views

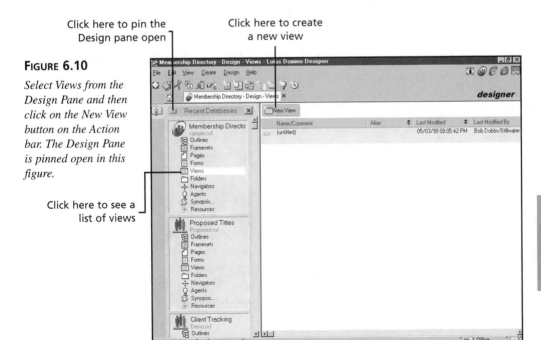

6

3. The Create View dialog box appears (see Figure 6.11). Enter the **View Name**. Like forms, you can use synonyms (also referred to as an *alias*) in your view names. A view name can be 64 characters long and include any combination of characters, such as letters, numbers, spaces, and punctuation.

4. Choose the **View Type**. Domino assumes you want a Shared view; to create another type of view, select a different view type from the View Type drop-down list.

FIGURE 6.11

When entering a View Name, you can use up to 130 characters (including the alias), but you won't see all the characters in the menu. About 32 characters are visible on the menu.

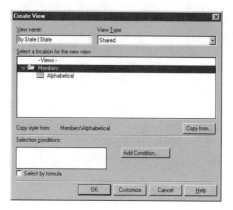

5. Decide where the view will appear in the list of views in the Navigation Pane of the database. In the **Select a Location for the New View** box, select the view under which you want this view name to appear. Choose **Views** to have this view listed alphabetically with the other views. If you select another view name, that name will display a twistie in the database Navigation Pane and your new view name will appear under it (see Figure 6.12).

FIGURE 6.12

By selecting another view while choosing a location for your new view, you create a cascaded list of views, as if you'd typed the view name with a backslash (Books\By Authors)

6. Click the **Copy From** button. The Copy From dialog box appears (see Figure 6.13). From the list in the **Copy Style From** box, choose the view whose attributes (columns, formulas, category and sort settings, and so on) you want to use as a template for your new view. Select **Default** to use the attributes of the database's

default view (this doesn't appear as a choice if you've named the default view); choose **Blank** to build your view from scratch. Click **OK** to close this dialog box and return to the Create View dialog box.

FIGURE 6.13

Save time by selecting a view to copy and build upon that has similar characteristics to the one you want to create.

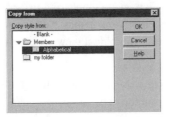

7. Unless you enter a formula or set a condition in the **Selection Conditions** box, this new view will display all the documents in the database. However, you do not have to enter your selection criteria in this dialog box. The criteria can also be set while you are designing the view (we'll cover selection conditions and formulas later in this lesson).

8. Click **OK** to close the Create View dialog box. Your view now appears in the list of views for your database (see Figure 6.14).

Default view

FIGURE 6.14

The new view you created appears in the list of views for the database. Here, the (untitled) view was modified and named "Members\Alphabetical," but is still the default database.

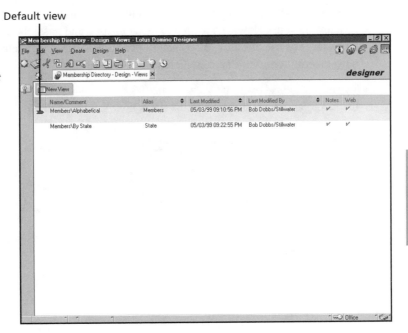

6

View Names, Aliases, and Synonyms

As was indicated in the preceding exercise (create a view), view names can contain up to 130 characters (including the alias). The name you give your view is visible to Notes users in the folders pane and in the View menu, appearing in alphabetical order. Web users see the view name in the Views list. View names are case sensitive and appear in the View menu in alphabetical order. If you hide a view, of course, users do not see the view name in any menus or lists.

Keep view names as short and descriptive as possible. When you can name a view by indicating how documents are sorted in the view, as in "By Date" or "By Category," users find the view name very descriptive. Naming conventions and view names need to be consistent across databases to help users. For example, don't call a view that lists documents chronologically by date "chronologically" in one database and "by Date" in another; choose one descriptive name and stick with it.

Like forms, views can have aliases (synonyms) that are used to change or translate the view name without causing formulas to stop working. For example, say you create a view called "By Customer Invoice" for your users, with the alias "invoice." Months after your application is rolled out, the user community requests that you change the view name to "Customer Invoices By Date." Provided that you used your alias, "invoice," in all formulas, changing the view name will not affect any formulas in the database that contains the alias. However, it's a good idea to copy and paste the original name as a second alias. The use of aliases also enables you to work more efficiently because you don't have to write formulas that contain lengthy view names.

To create an alias, open the View Properties box (choose **Design, View Properties** from the menu) and type your alias in the **Alias** box (see Figure 6.15).

FIGURE 6.15

Be short but descriptive in naming views for users, but create an even shorter alias. Using the view alias in a formula enables you to change a view name if necessary.

Tip

You want to use a view alias in your programming after you have assigned it. But what happens if you or another programmer makes a change to the database using the view name instead of the alias? This can crash lookup formulas that use the alias! To address this potential hazard, add a second alias, using the view name. For example, the view name "Customer Invoices" is used in a formula instead of the alias "Invoices." Change the View name to include "Customer Invoices" as a second alias, so that the view name reads Customer Invoices|Customer Invoices|Invoices. Lotus suggests that you always keep the original alias (in this case, "Invoices") as the rightmost alias in the view name. You might also want to use this method when you change a view name as an added precaution.

Changing a View Name

You can edit view names and aliases when the view is open in the Designer by changing their names in the Properties box. If you change the name of a view, it's a good idea to copy and paste the previous name into the Alias box, placing it to the left (first) of any other aliases and using a pipe (|) as a separator. That way any formulas or scripts that refer to the view by that name will still have a pointer to the view.

Display and Hide View Names in Menus and Lists

All shared views you create for your database appear alphabetically in the users View menu as well as the Views list. You might want to change the order of appearance of view names in the View menu. Take the example of a customer order tracking database, where an alphabetical list of views is

Contacts

Information

Orders

Status

But in this example, used primarily for viewing customer orders and status, we can best serve the using community if the views in the menu and view list display as follows:

Orders

Status

Contacts

Information

6

To force a change in the order of view names in a menu, number or letter the view names. For example

1. Orders
2. Status

and so forth. Using this naming convention, views appear in the View menu and the View list in the assigned order. If you start a name with a hyphen (-), the view appears before both numbered and lettered views.

View names that appear in the View Menu have accelerator keystrokes assigned (an underlined letter, as shown in Figure 6.16). Domino assigns accelerator keys using the first letter in the name of the view that has not already been assigned to a preceding name in the menu. If the first letter is in use, Domino assigns the second letter as the accelerator key; if that is being used, the third, and so forth. For example, in a database that contains three views called Books\by Author, Books\byCategory, and Books\by Title, Domino assigns the following accelerator keys:

by Author

by Category

by Title

These accelerator keys might not be particularly helpful to your user community, in which case you need to redefine the accelerator key. To do this, type an underscore in the view name prior to the letter you want to assign as the accelerator key, as shown here:

by _Author

by _Category

by _Title

In this example, the view names appear in the menu as follows:

by Author

by Category

by Title

If you want to hide a view from users, surround the view name with parentheses, as shown in Figure 6.17. This view will not display in the users View menu or in the View list. Using the parentheses also overrides the **Show in View Menu** option on the **Options** page of the View Properties box, if it's selected. If you don't use the parentheses but you deselect the **Show in View Menu** option, you only hide the view from the menu. It still shows in the Navigation Pane.

FIGURE 6.16

As the designer, you can assign accelerator keys to your view names. Be careful, however, not to use an accelerator key that is already in use elsewhere in the menu.

FIGURE 6.17

Using parentheses hides the view from both Notes and Web users. You do this for views you need as lookups or for calculations, but that you don't want the users to see.

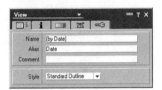

You also have the option of hiding a view from either Notes clients or Web clients. You do this from the list of views in the Designer (see Figure 6.18). Select the view from the list and open the Design Document Properties box (choose **Design, Design Properties** from the menu). On the Design page, select **Web Browsers** or **Notes R4.6 or Later Clients** under Hide Design Element From, depending on which type of client should not see the view. Note that when you make one of these selections the check mark in the **Web** or **Notes** column disappears.

In considering the order of view names in the View menu, determine whether you need a *cascading view* to help your users (see Figure 6.19). A cascading view groups related menu items under one item, which is particularly helpful when you have a long list of views or views that need to be grouped together. To see an example of a cascading view on your copy of Domino, start the Notes client, open your Personal Address Book, and click the **View** menu. Cascading views can be found under **Advanced** on this menu.

To create a cascading view, type a backslash (\) after the view name in the Properties box, as shown in Figure 6.20.

6

Design tab

FIGURE 6.18

To hide the view from Web users or Notes clients, or both, select the appropriate option on the Design Document Properties box.

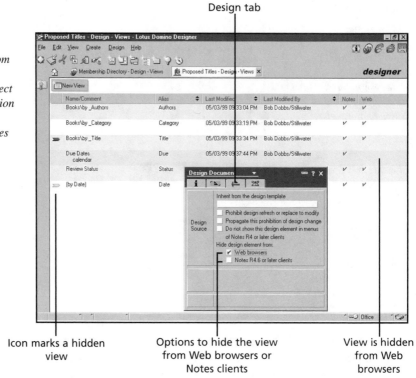

Icon marks a hidden view

Options to hide the view from Web browsers or Notes clients

View is hidden from Web browsers

FIGURE 6.19

*Here a cascading view makes use of accelerator keys, so the user types **Alt+V** to access the view menu, and then types **A** twice, **Enter** to display the cascade menu, and finally the letter of the desired view, such as **L** for Locations.*

FIGURE 6.20

"Books" will appear on the View menu and "by Authors" will display on the cascading menu.

Select a Default View

At least one view in a database must be designated as the default view. The default view is the one users see when they open the database for the first time. Typically, the default view displays all the documents in the database and has unrestricted access. When a user creates new views or folders, the default view provides the template unless the user specifies otherwise.

In Designer, you immediately see which view is the default view because an icon appears next to the name in the list of views.

To indicate the default view for the database, open the view in design mode and right-click to display the View Properties box. Click the **Options** tab and place a check mark next to **Default When Database is First Opened**, as shown in Figure 6.21.

Note

Don't confuse Default view, which is the view seen when the database is first opened, with Default design view. When you select the View property Default design for new folders and views, you make the current view the template for all newly created views and folders. In other words, new views and folders will have the same design—columns, actions, backgrounds—as the default design view unless you specify otherwise in the Create View or Create Folder dialog boxes.

FIGURE 6.21

Assigning a view default status doesn't affect the order of appearance of view names in the View menu or Navigation Pane. Users aren't even aware of which view is the default view.

6

Select Documents to Display

By default, a view displays all the documents in the database. There are two ways to specify which documents you're going to display in your view: the Search Builder or the selection formula.

There are two places in the Designer where you can set selection conditions for a view. One is in the Create View dialog box (see Figure 6.22), where you either choose **Add Condition** to open the Search Builder or check **Select by Formula** and enter a formula in the Selection Conditions box.

FIGURE 6.22

*When you check **Select by formula**, you enter the formula in the Selection conditions box. Click **Fields & Functions** to see a list of database field names or the @functions and @commands. Then click **Paste** to paste the selected field or function into your formula, or click **Help** to find out more about a function. If you need more room to write your formula, click **Formula Window**.*

The second place to set selection criteria is in the Programmer's Pane when you have a view open in the Designer (see Figure 6.23). Click the middle of the Work Area or select View Selection from the Objects list. From the **Run** drop-down list, select **Easy** to set conditions using the Search Builder or **Formula** to enter a selection formula in the Programmer's Pane.

FIGURE 6.23

In Run, specify how you want to select documents—by formula (Formula) or by using the Search Builder (Easy). When this was opened, the selection formula SELECT @All *displayed. This formula selects all the documents in the database.*

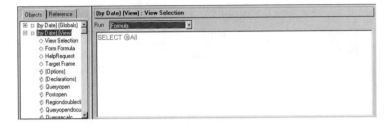

To use the Search Builder window

1. In the Create View dialog box, after you've specified the view name, type, and location, click on the **Add Condition** button. In the Designer, with the view open, select the View Selection event in the Objects list and choose **Easy** from the **Run** drop-down list in the Programmer's Pane. Then click **Add Condition** to open the Search Builder dialog box (see Figure 6.24).

FIGURE 6.24

When you select a condition in the Search Builder dialog box, the rest of the fields change.

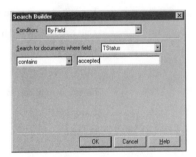

2. From the **Condition** list box, choose how you want to select documents for the view: **By Author**, **By Date**, **By Field**, **By Form**, or **By Form Used**.

3. Depending on your choice of condition, the remainder of the dialog box changes (see Table 6.1 for details about the choices). For instance, if you selected **By Author**, the conditions you set up are for the author of the document to contain or not contain the names you specify. If you select **By Field**, you specify what field and what text string it does or does not contain. Make the appropriate selections and enter any necessary values.

4. Click **OK**.

6

Table 6.1 Selection Conditions in Search Builder

Condition	Select	Enter or Select
By Author (documents must have an Authors field)	Contains Does not contain	Enter author names or choose from Directory. Separate names with commas.
By Date	Date created Date modified	Select: Is on Is after Is before Is not one Is in the last n days Is in the next n days Is older than n days Is after the next n days Is between (you specify two dates) Is not between (you specify two dates) Enter a date or the number of days (n)
By Field	Field name	Select: Contains Does not contain Enter text
By Field (for date/time field)	Field name	Select: Is on Is after Is before Is not one Is in the last n days Is in the next n days Is older than n days Is after the next Is between

Condition	Select	Enter or Select
		Is not between
		Enter a date or number of days (*n*)
By Field (for number field)	Field name	Select:
		Is equal to
		Is greater than
		Is less than
		Is not equal to
		Is between (specify beginning and ending numbers)
		Is not between(specify beginning and ending numbers)
		Enter a value
By Form (doesn't work with forms stored in documents)	Form name	Enter or select field values for multiple fields
By Form Used	Form name	Select one or more forms from the list

Selection formulas always begin with the keyword SELECT. To select (or include) all the database documents in your view, enter

```
SELECT @All
```

You might want to display only the documents created with a specific form. You might enter a formula such as this:

```
SELECT Form = "CourseDescription"
```

To enter a selection formula for a view in the Create View dialog box, check **Select By Formula** at the bottom of the Create View dialog box; then enter the formula in the **Selection Conditions** box (click **Formula Window** if you need more space). If you need help with the formula syntax or the field names, click the **Fields & Functions** button. Select **Fields** or **Functions** (see Figure 6.25). Choose the field or function you want from the list and click **Paste** to put it into the formula. Click **Help** for more information on how to use a function. After entering your formula, click **OK** to close the dialog box.

6

FIGURE 6.25

*When you select a
function, click **Help** or
press **F1** to open a
window with addition-
al information about
the function.*

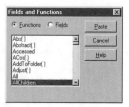

When you enter a selection formula in the Programmer's Pane, you must first select
Formula from the Run drop-down list. For assistance with field names and functions,
click the Reference tab on the InfoList. From the drop-down list, choose **Database
Fields**, **Formula @Commands**, or **Formula @Functions**, depending on the type of
assistance you need. Then select the item you want from the list and click **Paste** to put it
in your formula at the position of your cursor. For functions, click **Help** or press **F1** to
see more information on the syntax and use of the function. When your formula is complete, click the green check mark in the Programmer's Pane (see Figure 6.26).

FIGURE 6.26

*A selection formula
such as* SELECT Form =
"MemInfo" *will display
main documents unless
you combine it with the*
@AllChildren *or*
@AllDescendents
function.

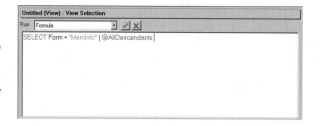

Tip

Even if you started your view using the Search Builder and specifying selection conditions, that will change to the equivalent formula when you click
the **Select by Formula** option in the Create View dialog box or choose
Formula from the Run drop-down list in the Programmer's Pane.

Insert, Delete, and Move Columns

Unless you create a view based upon an existing view, your new view has only one column. That column displays the document number assigned to each document in the order
the document is saved, as shown in Figure 6.27.

FIGURE 6.27

A column displaying document numbers to end users is not of particular use. Adding columns and displaying different and more meaningful information in those columns is what the users need here!

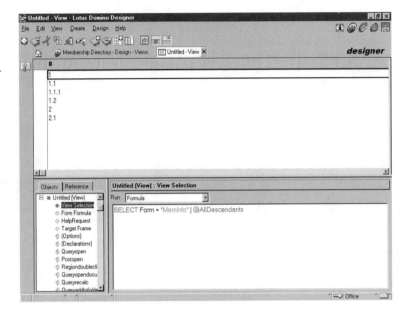

Take one of the following actions to create a new column:

- Double-click the column heading to the right of any existing columns.
- Choose **Create**, **Insert New Column** from the menu. This makes a new column to the left of the currently selected column.
- Choose **Create**, **Append New Column**. This makes a new column to the far right of any existing columns.

Caution When you make changes to your view design, you need to refresh the screen to see how the documents in your view are affected. Press **F9** or click the Refresh icon in the left corner.

6

After your new column is inserted, double-click the column header to open the Column Properties Box (see Figure 6.28). Set the width of the column by entering a value in the Width box, by using the up and down spinner arrows on the Width field, or by dragging the column heading boundary.

Figure 6.28

Dragging the column boundary enables you to visually set it wide enough for the text in the column. As you drag, the mouse pointer becomes a two-headed arrow and a vertical line stretches down the screen to show the width of the column.

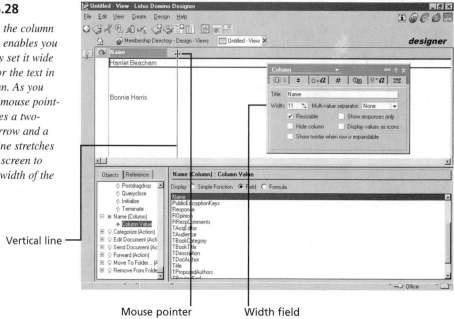

Vertical line

Mouse pointer   Width field

To remove a column, click on the heading to select the column and press the **Delete** key. Answer **Yes** to confirm the deletion.

To move a column, select it and cut it. Answer **Yes** to permanently remove the column. Click on the column head that you want to appear just to the right of the column you're inserting. Then paste the column.

Assign Titles and Values to Columns

Column titles are created in the Column Properties Box, as shown in Figure 6.29 (double-click the column header to open Column Properties). The information you type in the Title box is the information that appears in the column header. The purpose of the column title is to help the user understand what the column displays; adding a column title is optional. Where narrow columns are used for sorting or categorizing purposes, you might decide not to enter a title.

FIGURE 6.29

The column title is optional, but convention is to put one whenever possible. Here, you see the same title in the Properties box and in the header.

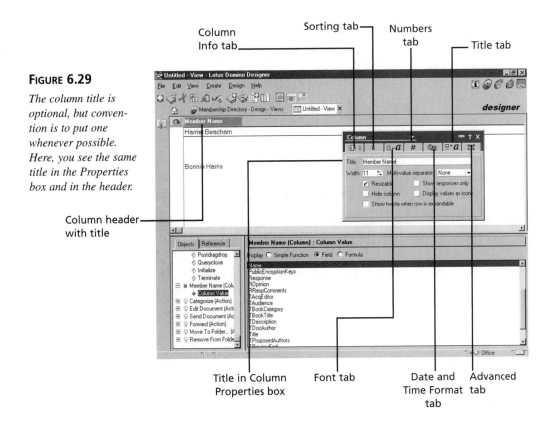

Column Info tab

Sorting tab

Numbers tab

Title tab

Column header with title

Title in Column Properties box

Font tab

Date and Time Format tab

Advanced tab

You can also set the **Width** of the column on the Column Info page of the Column Properties box, or you can drag the border of the column to change its width (as was mentioned previously). If you use the drag method, the Width field will reflect that change. To enable the user to size the column as needed, check **Resizable**.

When you know the column needs to list more than one value, such as a list of cities, click Multi-Value Separator and choose **Space**, **Comma**, **Semicolon**, or **New Line** (if you pick **None**, the values run together).

To set the contents of the column, you can select a simple function (see Figure 6.30), choose a field name, or enter a formula in the Programmer's Pane. The formula can be as simple as a field name or a concatenation, it can calculate a value, or it can be an @Function.

6

FIGURE 6.30

The Simple Functions display data that Notes stores in the document automatically, such as the creation date.

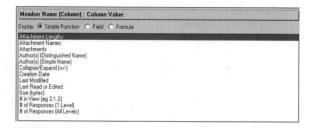

For example, if you want to add a column that shows the date the document was created, choose the **Simple Function** option for display and select the Creation Date from the list. To show a field value, choose **Field** and then select the fieldname from the list that appears.

For columns that have number values, you need to format the number—even if the number field was formatted in the document. On the Numbers page of the Column Properties box, select the type of number format you want applied to the column—**General**, **Fixed**, **Scientific**, or **Currency**. Where applicable, enter the number of Decimal Places you want displayed. Select **Percentage** to display the number as a percentage. Enable **Parentheses on Negative Numbers**, unless you want to indicate negative numbers with a minus sign. Select **Punctuated at Thousands** to use your preferred method of punctuation to indicate the thousands break in the number (in the United States, this option adds a comma).

On the Date and Time Format page of the Column Properties box, you set the formatting for dates and times in the column. From the Show drop-down list, select **Date and Time**, **Date Only**, **Time Only**, or **"Today" and Time**. From the Date Format and Time Format lists, choose the format for displaying the date or time. The Time Zone list offers choices to either adjust the time for the local time zone, show the time zone with the time, or show the zone only if the time is not local.

Note

When selecting date formats, the last two at the bottom of the list are consistent with four-digit year displays.

Use the Font page of the Column Properties box to set the font of the column contents. The Title page has font property settings for the column headers.

If you want your column to display information from more than one field, or to display a calculation on field values, you must enter a formula. Select the **Formula** option and then enter your formula. The formula can be as simple as a field name or a concatenation of fields, or it can be a complicated set of conditional statements, depending on what you need to appear in the column (see Day 10). For example, to display the city and state information in one column, you might use a formula such as this:

```
City + ", " + State
```

Preview Your Work

As you develop your view, you want to preview the results of your work from your users' perspective. Take a look at your view in Internet Explorer, Netscape Navigator, Domino (with Notes as the browser), or the Notes client by selecting one of the icons located on the right end of the menu bar of Designer. To preview in the Web browsers, you must have a version of that software installed on your workstation:

 Display Infobox (Properties box)

 Notes Preview

 Domino Preview

 IE Preview (Internet Explorer)

 Netscape Preview

Create a Calendar View

You use a calendar view when you want to group documents by date, such as schedules, meetings, and appointments. Calendar views have choices that users can select to display the view as one day, two days, one week, two weeks, or one month at a time (see Figure 6.31). They feature point-and-click navigation among days, months, and years. Users can add and edit entries, as well as print the calendar view.

When you opt for a calendar view, the View Properties box changes. It adds a Date and Time Format tab, and there are changes on the Style page. All these differences are discussed in the following section, "Set View Properties."

6

 Tip

Before you convert a standard outline view to a calendar view, you must first make changes to the design of the standard outline view. First, insert or create the first column, based on a field that results to a time/date format. Choose a Sort option in the Column Properties box and make sure you specify both a date and time, even if the time is 00:00. Second, create a second column based on a field with a number value that specifies the duration, in minutes, of a calendar entry. Third, create a document selection formula for the view and select all documents containing the time/date field. Finally, change the style in the View Properties box to **Calendar**.

FIGURE 6.31

Your calendar in the Mail database shows all the features of a calendar view.

Set View Properties

As you add views to your database, you work extensively with the View Properties box. Throughout this lesson you learned about the items found in the View Properties box.

Unlike the *Field* Properties box, which is context sensitive and changes as you move your cursor from field to field in a form, the tabbed pages on the View Properties box do not change while it is open. This is because you can only access this Properties box after you have opened a view in design mode, and only one view can appear in design mode at a time.

Table 6.2 lists the options in the View Properties box, related to Standard views to help you find and set the options you need. Table 6.3 sets out the Properties that relate only to Calendar views.

Table 6.2 Properties for Standard Views

Tab	Property/Option	Description
View Info	Name	Enter a name for the view as you want it to appear on the menu, using any combination of letters, numbers, spaces, and punctuation.
	Alias	Another name, or synonym, for a particular view that you want to use in formulas and script.
	Comment	Additional text describing the view, which appears only in the list of views in the Designer.
	Style	Standard Outline or Calendar.
Options	Default when database is first opened	Sets that view as the default view for the database.
	Default design for new folders and views	Unless otherwise specified, Notes copies the design from that view when creating new folders and views.
	Collapse all when database is first opened	In a view that has categories, collapses all categories so none of the underlying documents display when you first open the database.
	Show response documents in a hierarchy	Indents response documents under their parent documents. Response-to-response documents are further indented under the response documents.
	Show in View menu	Select to have view name displayed in View menu.
	On Open:	Sets the initial display of the view when you make a selection: Go to last opened document. Go to top row. Go to bottom row.

continues

6

Table 6.2   continued

Tab	Property/Option	Description
	On Refresh:	When changes are made to the database, your choice determines when the user sees the new changes:
		Display indicator—not refreshed automatically, shows indicator instead so the view can be manually refreshed.
		Refresh display—refreshes automatically on
change.		
		Refresh display from top row—refreshes from the top down.
		Refresh display from bottom row—refreshes from the bottom up.
Style	Color: Background	Sets the background color for the view (lighter colors are suggested).
	Color: Column totals	Sets the color of the text for column totals.
	Color: Unread rows	Determines the color for unread documents.
	Color: Alternate rows	Color that alternates rows with background color.
	Show column headings	Determines whether headings show, and if yes what type of headings:
		Beveled headings
		Simple headings
	Lines per heading	Determines number of lines of text display in the column headers (1–5).
	Lines per row	Determines how many lines of text display in one row (1–9).
	Shrink rows to content	For multiple line rows, shrinks height of row to fit actual lines of text in the longest entry in the row.
	Row spacing	Sets the amount of space between rows:
		Single
		1 1/4
		1 1/2

Tab	Property/Option	Description
		1 3/4
		Double
	Show selection margin	Leaves a space to the left of the rows for selecting multiple documents.
	Extend last column to window width	Fills out last column to avoid empty space in the view.
Advanced	Refresh index	Determines when a view is refreshed:
		Auto, after first use—built the first time a user requests to view it and then is automatically built again whenever the user opens it.
		Automatic—updates the view automatically regardless of whether it's opened
		Manual—relies on the user to refresh the view.
		Auto, at most every _____ hours—updates the view automatically at a specified interval.
	Discard index	Determines when to delete indexes automatically for a particular view:
		Never
		After each use
		If inactive for _____ days
	Unread marks	Determines how unread marks are indicated:
		None
		Unread documents only—displays asterisks for unread main or response documents; unread marks don't appear next to collapsed categories.
		Standard (compute in hierarchy)—displays asterisks for unread main and response documents any for any collapsed categories containing unread main or response documents.
	For ODBC Access: Generate unique keys in index	Creates needed keys when accessing external data using ODBC (Open Database Connectivity). This is beyond the scope of this book.

6

continues

Table 6.2 continued

Tab	Property/Option	Description
	For Web Access: Treat view contents as HTML	When viewed in a Web browser, any HTML formatting attributes you specify in the column formula will display. Looks like a standard view in Notes.
	For Web Access: Use applet in browser	Enables Web browser users to resize columns, collapse and expand views without regenerating the page, select multiple documents, scroll vertically to see additional documents, use F9 to refresh the view, and use the Delete key to mark documents for deletion.
	Active Link	Sets color for active links.
	Unvisited Link	Sets color for unvisited links.
	Visited Link	Sets color for visited links.
	Restrict initial index build to designer or manager	First time indexing can only be done by the database manager or designer, as defined in the ACL.
	Don't show categories having zero documents	Categories that have no documents associated with them won't display in view.
Security	May be used by	Restricts who can read the view (must have at least Reader access to the database):
		All readers and above—default setting—everyone with Reader access can see the view.
		Specified names—only the selected names can read the view (do not create for the default view of the database).
	Available to Public Access Users	Select to make the view available to users with public access read or write privileges in the ACL for this database.

For calendar views, some of the view properties are not enabled. They are dimmed (unavailable) in the View Properties box. The fields on the Style page are different, more in keeping with the calendar style (the items that are the same for both views are not shown in Table 6.3). A Font page and a Date and Time Format page are added to the properties box for the Calendar style view.

Table 6.3 Properties for Calendar View

Tab	Property/Option	Description
Style	Color: View background	Sets background color for the entire view.
	Color: Date background	Sets color that marks dates.
	Color: Unread rows	Sets color that marks unread rows.
	Color: Busy rows	Sets color that marks rows for busy times.
	Styling: Show conflict marks	Determines whether conflict marks (line in margin) appear when two items are scheduled during the same time period.
	Non-month colors: Background	Sets background colors for view when not in month format.
	Non-month colors: Text	Sets color of text used when not in month format.
	Today	Sets color used to mark today's date.
	Day separators	Sets color used for day separators.
Font	Text type drop-down	Determines item to which font will be applied:
		Time Slots/Grouping
		Header
		Day and Date
	Font	Sets typeface.
	Size	Sets point size for text.

continues

6

Table 6.3 continued

Tab	Property/Option	Description
	Style	Sets style of font:
		Plain
		Bold
		Italic
		Underline
		Strikethrough
	Text color	Sets color of text.
Date and Time Format	Enable Time Slots	Turns on display of time slots.
	Show Daily Bitmaps (only available if time slots enabled)	Turns on display of time slot icon so user can turn time slots on and off.
	Start Time (only available if time slots enabled)	Sets beginning time displayed on calendar.
	End Time (only available if time slots enabled)	Sets last time displayed on calendar.
	Duration (only available if time slots enabled)	Sets length of interval between times displayed: 15 minutes, 30 minutes, 1 hour, or 2 hours.
	Allow user to override times (only available if time slots enabled)	Enable to allow user to set their own start and end times and intervals.
	Enable Time Grouping	Turns on time grouping.

Tab	Property/Option	Description
	Initial format	Sets calendar view format displayed when calendar view is opened:
		Default
		1 Day
		2 Day
		1 Week
		2 Weeks
		1 Month
	Allowed formats:	Sets which formats the user can select to display the view:
		1 Day
		2 Day
		1 Week
		2 Weeks
		1 Month

Choose a Folder

Folders and views are similar in design, but whereas the contents of a view are determined by a selection formula, the user decides the contents of a folder. Users determine the contents of folders by dragging documents from a view into folders or by using Move to Folder or Copy to Folder commands.

Folders display documents in rows, just like views. Like views, the columns each show one type of information about the listed documents based on a formula, a simple function, or a field name. In fact, you base the design of a folder on a view.

Like views, there are three types of folders:

- **Private folders**—Any user with reader access to a database can create a folder for his own use. A private folder isn't shared by other users in the database. It's a good idea for users to create their own folders to store documents to which they frequently refer.

6

- **Shared folders**—A shared folder is stored on the server and is available to all users with sufficient access rights. Only users with designer or manager access to the database can create shared folders (a user with Editor access can create shared folders if the database manager selects "Created shared folders/views" for that user).

- **Shared, private on first use folders**—These folders are initially stored on the server and are created by someone with designer or manager access to the database. After someone uses the folder, it automatically becomes a private folder for that person and is stored on that person's desktop.

Create a Folder

Use the following steps to create a folder for the open database:

1. From the menu in the Notes Client or Designer, choose **Create**, **Folder**. Or, in Designer, select **Folders** from the Design Pane and then click the **New Folder** button on the Action bar. The Create Folder dialog box appears (see Figure 6.32).

FIGURE 6.32

*The design of your new folder will be based on the view or folder listed next to Copy Style From, unless you click **Copy From** and make a different choice.*

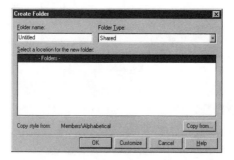

2. Enter a **Folder Name** (use the same rules for naming folders that you used for views).

3. From the **Folder Type** drop-down list, select the type of folder you're creating:

    - **Private**—Available only to the user who creates it.

    - **Shared**—Available to all users who have access to the database.

    - **Shared, private on first use**—Creates a shared view available to all users. However, when the user opens the folder the first time, a private copy is created for that user and is available only to that user. The folder is created in the database if the user has access to it. If not, the folder is created in the desktop file (Desktop.dsk).

- **Shared, desktop private on first use**—Creates a shared view available to all users. However, when the user opens the folder the first time, a private copy is created for that user and is available only to that user. The folder is created in the desktop file.

4. Select the folder under which you want your new folder to show in the Navigation Pane or click **Folders** to store your folder at the top level.

5. Click on **Copy From** to open the Copy From dialog box (see Figure 6.33). Select the name of the view or folder on which you're basing the design of this folder (if you don't select a view or folder to copy from, the design of your new folder will be based on the default view for the database). To design the folder from scratch, select **Blank**. Click **OK** to return to the Create Folder dialog box.

FIGURE 6.33

*Select **Blank** to design your folder from scratch; choose a view or folder name to use that design as the basis, or template, for your new folder.*

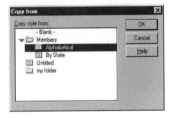

6. Click **OK**.

For example, Figure 6.34 shows a shared, private on first use folder named "Close Contacts." This is created for users to store names of members they refer to often. The design of the folder is based on a "Members\Alphabetical" view that displays all the member information documents.

Note Our Tech Editor thought you should know that although Figure 6.34 is correct in having both the Shared, Private on first use and the Private folders display, he believes this is a bug. In all prior versions of Domino/Notes, the Navigator changed from showing the folder as shared to showing only *one* folder as private.

6

FIGURE 6.34

The Navigation Pane shows a shared folder named "Local Chapter" and a private folder called "My Committee" (note the dashed line under this folder that indicates it's private). The two "Close Contacts" folders are the shared, private on first use folder and the private folder that appeared after opening the first "Close Contacts" folder.

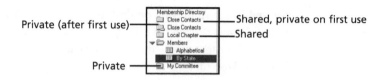

Private (after first use) — Shared, private on first use
— Shared

Private —

Summary

Views provide listings of documents contained in a database. There are two flavors of views: standard (outline) and calendar. Calendar views are based on dates and have a calendar-like appearance. Standard views consist of rows that represent documents and columns that contain information drawn from the documents.

Views can be shared, private, or shared, private on first use. Shared views are available to all users of the database. Private views are available only to the user who creates the view. Shared, private on first use views are available to all users until the first time the view is opened. At that time, a copy of the view becomes a private view for that user.

The designer determines which documents are displayed in a view by setting simple conditions or creating selection formulas. Selection formulas begin with the keyword SELECT and define selection by form name or field contents.

View design involves view properties such as view name and alias, background color, alternating row colors, the number of lines of text in a row or heading, refresh options, and security options (who can see this view).

The designer defines what columns show in the view and uses simple functions, field names, or formulas to set the contents of the columns.

Folders are similar to views, except the user decides which documents are displayed in the folder by adding, moving, or dragging the documents into the folder.

You haven't learned all there is to know about folders and views, and you will learn more on Day 10. On Day 10 you also learn more about views and how views work, and how to optimize views for Web clients.

Q&A

Q **A user opened a shared, private on first use view. Now I've made design changes to the original view. Will the user see those changes?**

A No. In order for the user to see a view with the new changes, the private view must be deleted. Then the user must open the newly revised shared, private on first use view.

Q **Users are complaining that there are delays when trying to open a particular database. Could my view designs cause that?**

A One possible cause might be too many views. Views take additional space on disk and redundantly store information from documents in them. You need to consider consolidating some of the views. Another problem might be that you set the view indexes to be refreshed too frequently. Unread mark processing might also delay the opening because the database must update this information on opening. You might consider disabling unread marks on the database. A possible problem might be due to a large number of changes in view contents (many deleted or new documents), which means the index has been discarded and has to be rebuilt when the view is opened. Another minor solution might be to collapse your categorized views on opening (you'll learn more about this on Day 10).

Q **I designed a Calendar view but it won't open.**

A The first column of a calendar view must contain date/time data. The field you use to define that column must contain both date and time information, even if the time is 00:00. The selection formula for the view should select all documents containing the time/date field. Plus, the first column must be sorted. The calendar view's second column must be formatted as a number column that represents the duration of the entry in minutes.

6

Workshop

In this workshop session, you'll be working with the Proposed Titles database. You'll be setting up views for that database and some folders. In later sessions, you might be enhancing these views and folders.

Create Views

You will create the following shared views (standard style) to include in the Proposed Titles database:

Books\by Authors. Alias: Authors.

Books\by Title. Alias: Title. This is the default view.

Books\by Category. Alias: Category.

Review Status. Alias: Status.

The Books\by Authors and Books\by Categories views are similar in design to the Books\by Title, so create Books\by Title first and complete its design before starting the other views. Copy from its design to build the other views. Review Status will be built from scratch.

The Books\by Title view will display the main documents (Proposed Title), response documents, and response-to-response documents. All the other views will contain only the main documents.

You can select whatever background colors and row attributes you think are appropriate for each of these views. All views should appear on the View menu.

Another view, called Due Dates (alias Due), will be a calendar view. It will only include main documents. To make the calendar view work properly, you'll need to add a field to the Proposed Title form called Duration. Put it near to the end of the form in a separate paragraph. You'll hide that field later from all users, but leave it visible for now so you can check how it works. Make it an editable number field. Set the Number Format as Decimal, and make the Decimal Places Fixed with 0 places. For the Default Value formula, enter 60 (for 60 minutes). Make sure you *don't* select **Show Conflict Marks** on the Style page of the View Properties box. In the Date and Time Format View Properties, enable time slots and make the initial display the 31-day (1-month) format.

Define Columns

Table 6.4 lists the column definitions for these views.

Table 6.4   Columns in Views

View Name	Column Name	Column Contents
Books\by Title	Title	TbookTitle
	Author(s)	TproposedAuthors
	Audience	Taudience
	Submitted by	TdocAuthor + " on " + @Text(@Created; "D0S0")
Books\by Authors	Author(s)	TproposedAuthors
	Title	TbookTitle
	Audience	Taudience
	Submitted by	TdocAuthor + " on " + @Text(@Created; "D0S0")
Books\by Category	Category	TbookCategory
	Title	TbookTitle
	Author(s)	TproposedAuthors
	Audience	Taudience
	Submitted by	TdocAuthor + " on " + @Text(@Created; "D0S0")
Review Status	Status	Tstatus
	Title	TbookTitle
	Author(s)	TProposedAuthors
	Acquisition Editor	@Name([CN]; TAcqEditor)
	Review Period	@Text(TReviewStart; "D0S0") + " to " @Text(TReviewEnd; "D0S0")
Due Dates	Untitled	TreviewEnd (format as time only)
	Untitled	Duration
	Untitled	TBookTitle

6

Open the client and look at the views you created. See any problems? Did the Status column in the Review Status view show up with numbers? If you remember, we used synonyms when we entered the choices for the Status field. The synonyms are displayed in a view:

1 Accepted

2 Rejected

3 Hold for Further Discussion

4 Under Discussion

To make these words appear instead of the numbers, you must enter a column formula that translates the numbers to text for your view:

```
@If(TStatus = "1"; "Accepted"; TStatus = "2";
"Rejected"; TStatus = "3"; "Hold for Further Discussion";
TStatus = "4"; "Under Discussion"; "")
```

Other problems might occur because you did not complete all the fields in your sample documents. Try making additional documents, using different status settings. Also, check any formulas you entered to be sure you entered them correctly.

Create Folders

Create two folders for the Proposed Titles database. Name the first one **Most Promising Titles** and make it a shared folder based on the Books\by Title view. The alias for the folder should be **Promising**.

The second folder will be shared, private on first use. Call it **My Suggestions**, with **Suggestions** as the alias. Select **Folders** as the location. Use Books\by Title as the view on which you base the design. In this folder, the users can store any titles they personally suggested.

Test both folders from the client. Drag documents into both. Note that when you open the My Suggestions folder it becomes a private view.

Today's sample database on the accompanying CD is found in the folder called Day6. The file name is PTDay6.nsf.

DAY 7

Sleep Soundly: Secure Your Application

Security is always a concern for organizations. From a personal point of view, you don't want anyone else to be reading all your mail, so you want your mail file to be protected from entry by unauthorized individuals. The same thing applies to the applications you create. Not all applications should be equally available to everyone in the organization. For example, an employee handbook that contains policies on sick days, vacation days, disability, pay raises, and employee evaluations might be available for everyone in the organization to view. But only a limited number of people (probably a group within the personnel department) should be able to change the policy documents.

Your initial planning of application design should include who can and who can't access the databases and the database documents and views. You set up the access levels for users as you create the components of an application based on this plan, with additional consultation with the person or group requesting the application and with the Domino system administrator.

On this day you'll learn about

- Levels of access
- Where security is applied
- The use of roles and groups in setting security
- Setting access for each of the design elements

Understand Domino Security

Security in Domino defines who can see, create, or edit documents, views, folders, agents, or databases. Setting up security is the joint responsibility of the Domino administrator and the application designer.

With Domino, security is set at many levels. A user who can open a database cannot necessarily open all the documents in that database, or even create documents. This multi-level system makes Domino security flexible to meet the needs of controlling a large and diverse group of users.

Encrypted Fields

Domino security begins at the field level. The designer can encrypt individual fields that only specified individuals can view or edit. If the document uses a *private key* (a key is a hexadecimal number, but it acts like a key to a door—you can't get in unless you have a key to unlock the door), the specified individuals receive an encryption key from the designer. They must use that encryption key in order to enter data in the encrypted field. For example, the encrypted field might be one that gives approval to issue a check, so only those individuals who have the power within the organization to sign checks should be able to change the entry in the field.

 Caution Web users can see encrypted fields. You will have to use another method to restrict access to that information if you have Web users.

Encryption keys can also be public (associated with a person's document in the Public Address Book). Public keys are used to decrypt mail documents.

Only one encryption key is needed for all the encrypted fields in a document. You can't specify a particular key for a particular field.

Document Encryption

Users that possess the correct encryption key can read the encrypted information in the document. Users without the proper key can only read the information that is not encrypted—they can see all the other fields in the document.

Encrypted documents can't be edited by users who don't have the correct encryption key. However, these users can still create new documents as long as they remove the encryption key from the Document Properties box before saving the document.

Authors can remove encryption or change the keys from their own documents, provided that they have the proper access to edit their own documents and they have both the current and new encryption keys.

Users can't get around the encryption by copying the database. Even if the database is copied at the operating system level (for example, through the Windows Explorer), the data remains encrypted.

Caution

The full text search has an option for indexing encrypted fields. If used, this option enables any users with access to the database to see the encrypted data. Also, if the database has been indexed by someone who has an encryption key, the index can be read as an ASCII text file at the server.

Controlled-Access Sections

Using controlled-access sections, you can limit accessibility to an area of a document to specified individuals or groups. Without the proper permission, a user cannot change any of the fields in the section. You'll learn how to create controlled-access sections on Day 9, "Forms on Steroids: Increase Form Performance."

Readers, $Readers, and Authors Fields

Access to the document itself is controlled by fields that are assigned the Readers or Authors data types, as well as by a field named $Readers, which Notes itself can insert into the document. A field of Readers data type *restricts* who can read a document. A field of Authors data type *expands* who can edit a document. The Readers data type, the $Readers field, and the Authors data type work as follows:

- **Readers data type**—Normally, all users with Reader or higher access to a database can read all documents in the database. But if a field of Readers data type

7

exists in a document and it isn't empty, only the users listed in that field (or in any Authors fields or in a field named $Readers, if it exists) can read the document. No other users can read the document or even see it in a view or folder, no matter what their level of access to the database. If there is more than one Readers field, a user needs to appear in only one of them (or in an Authors field or the field named $Readers, if it exists) to read the document and see it listed in views and folders.

- **$Readers field**—The Document Properties box has a section under the Security tab named "Who can read this document." If you restrict readership in that section, a field named $Readers appears in the document. Its contents include all entities (users, servers, groups) checked off in that section. Only entities listed in that field (and any fields of Readers or Authors data type) can read the document or see it listed in views or folders. If you remove the restrictions in "Who can read this document," the $Readers field disappears from the document.

  The Form Properties box has a similar section named "Default read access for documents created with this form." There you can set default readership restrictions. If you do, a corresponding $Readers field appears in the form and in all documents created or edited with the form.

- **Authors data type**—Normally, only users with Editor access or higher can edit a document. But if a field of Authors data type exists in a document, any users with Author access to the database who are listed in the field can edit the document. Members of Authors field can also read any documents with restricted readership (because you can't edit what you can't read).

When you use an Authors field, it enables users with Author access to edit a document. An Authors field is a list of *potential* editors for the document. If you want to see who actually edited a document, look for the contents of the $UpdatedBy field (which you can see in Document Properties, under the Fields tab).

The names you enter in Readers and Authors fields should be fully distinguished names (for example, Bob Dobbs/Sales/Stillwater, instead of just Bob Dobbs). If you use only common names, you confer the rights on all users with the same common name—even cross-certified users from other organizations. Unless this is your intention, use fully distinguished names.

To create Readers or Authors fields in a form, you assign a data type of Readers or Authors to the field (see Day 3, "Take a Field Trip: Add Fields," for more information on data types for fields). You specify the readers or authors by entering the names or roles as the value or default value of the fields. If the Readers or Authors field is computed, use a formula that returns the names of users, servers, groups, or roles (make sure your formula evaluates to valid names). The other option is to allow users to populate the list by providing an editable text field or a keywords field.

Following are some things you need to keep in mind:

- A user with ACL Author access can only edit a document he created unless there is at least one Authors field in the document that contains the user's name. If there is an Authors field in a document but it is empty, users with ACL Author access can't edit it; only an Editor or above can edit it.

- If you place a Readers field on a form but leave it blank, there are no document access restrictions. However, if one name is added, only that user can read the document despite the ACL rights of other users.

- If you're using an editable Readers field, make sure you include yourself in the default value formula so there is at least one reader.

Note

When you have an editable Readers or Authors field, it's a good idea to have a validation formula to ensure that at least one name is present when the document is saved. You might even add a validation that your name must be in the field; otherwise you could delete the default value and remove the document restrictions.

- Readers and Authors fields only work in databases that are located on a server. This can cause problems for you if you're developing the database locally, but you can get around it by selecting the Advanced Access Control List property **Enforce a Consistent Access Control List across all replicas of this database**.

- On documents that have more than one Readers field, all entries in all the Readers fields have read access to the document.

- Only one Authors field is needed to control author access for the entire document, although you can have more than one. You might want one Authors field that automatically computes the name of the person creating the document (by making the default formula @UserName), and another that is editable (so the creator can add or remove names).

- If the name of a user or server appears in an Authors field but not in the Readers field in the same document, that user or server still has reader access. After all, you can't edit a document if you can't read it.

Even without using Readers and Authors fields in a form, you can limit who can use a form to read or create documents by setting the form security. Views have security

7

settings also, so you can control who sees a view. However, view or form security are sometimes considered not to be "real" security because users can see the same documents and column values by creating a private view. They can also open the Document Properties box for any document and make changes to document access. Form and view security are more of a convenience because they keep most users from seeing what you don't want them to see.

Electronic Signatures

One way to add further security to documents is to attach electronic signatures. An electronic signature assures the reader that the author's identity is genuine, and guarantees that the information in the document has not changed since the author mailed or saved it.

Electronic signatures can only be attached to forms that are mail-enabled or that have controlled-access sections. Then you have to create a field that is sign-enabled. If the field is within a controlled-access section, it applies to the entire section and is generated when the document is saved; otherwise, the signature is only generated when the document is mailed. It is possible to have more than one field in a document that has a signature.

Electronic signatures are not supported on the Web.

Access Control Lists (ACL)

Every database and database replica has a *unique* Access Control List (ACL) that defines who has entry to the database and what each entrant can do within the database—open, read, edit, and create documents, as well as design database elements and manage the database. The ACL is configured to suit each database need and the need for users to see and use the data.

Domino defines seven levels of access to a database:

- **No Access**—This denies access to the database altogether. If you have No Access, you can't even add the database bookmark to your bookmark pages. The only exception is when **Read public documents** or **Write public documents** is checked in the ACL refinements.
- **Depositor**—Depositors can create new documents, but they can't read or edit any of the documents in the database—including the ones they created themselves. You might be granted this access level to cast a ballot in a voting database or submit an

evaluation of a training session, for example. The only exception is when **Read public documents** or **Write public documents** is checked in the ACL refinements.

- **Reader**—A reader can read the documents in the database, but can't create or edit documents. You might have this level of access to a company policy database so that the user can read policies but can't create or change them.

- **Author**—As an author, you can create and read documents. You cannot normally edit or delete any document that you did not create. However, if any document—regardless of whether you created it—has a field of data type Authors in which your name appears, you can edit that document.

- **Editor**—If you have editor access, you can do everything an author does, *and* you can edit any documents in the database. For example, a manager who approves the expense reports that are submitted by others needs editor access to those documents.

- **Designer**—A designer can do everything an editor does, but she can also create or change any design elements of the database—forms, fields, views, folders, agents, or actions. In order to create a new call report form in a database, for instance, you need designer access.

- **Manager**—Someone with manager access can do everything a designer can, in addition to being able to modify the access control list—add new users to it, delete users from it, and modify the degree of access enjoyed by other users. The Manager can also modify the database's replication settings and delete a database from the server. The Manager does not necessarily have to be the Domino administrator, but certainly must be in a position of trust with the group that is using the application.

A newly created database inherits its ACL settings from its Design Template, if it has one. Otherwise, a new database's default ACL entries are shown in Table 7.1.

Table 7.1 Default Access Level Settings

Entry	Access Level
Default	Designer
Local Domain Servers group	Manager
Other Domain Servers group	Manager
(person who created the database)	Manager

7

> **Tip**
>
> Immediately after you create a database, change the Default setting to be Author, Reader, or No Access. Make sure you remain the Manager until it's time to roll out the application. Change the OtherDomainServers group so that it is set to No Access immediately upon creating the database. Add the entry **Anonymous** to control Web access separately from Notes client access (just enter the name in the ACL—don't make a group). Set Anonymous to No Access, Author, or Reader, depending upon the use of this database over the Web.

During the design phase of the database, the ACL settings aren't critical, although you might want to make yourself manager so that you can, in turn, make changes to the ACL. However, before the database is put on the server, it's very important to decide who gets what level of access and set the ACL accordingly. Otherwise, the default ACL will enable any user to change the very design of your database. You do not want unauthorized tampering with design and data elements during development, especially if you are adding encryption keys to any part of the database. At rollout time, you set the finalized ACL.

If you replicated the database to your server for testing purposes, make sure you change the Replication Settings to temporarily disable replication. Then deselect that option when you are ready for users to replicate.

Server Access

The Domino system administrator also works with ACLs, determining who can access a server, who can copy or create new databases to that server, and who can create replicas on a given server. The system administrator also maintains a list of those from whom access has been taken away, such as terminated employees.

Levels of access are granted based on the user ID file that is created for each user when they are registered by the system administrator. The user ID file contains the user's common name, password, software license, public and private keys for identification to the servers and for mail encryption, certificates, and encryption keys (if any) to enable them to edit encrypted fields. This information is used to satisfy the conditions that enable the user to access the server and the applications on it.

Web Security Considerations

Some Domino security measures—such as electronic signatures and encrypted fields—do not work in Web browsers, but overall Domino security will work. For example, Domino can authenticate Web users and restrict them to or from particular databases.

By creating a person document in the Domino Directory for each Web user, the system administrator can create an HTTP password that must be entered by the Web user before gaining access to any databases on the server. Access to the server automatically grants the user reader access to the databases.

When no authentication is required at the server level, Web users are anonymous users (they have no Notes ID). Access to individual databases can still be controlled for these users; you just create an anonymous entry in the ACL and assign a level of access. If you don't, the anonymous users automatically get the same level of access assigned to **Default**. To prevent an anonymous user from viewing a database, assign No Access as the default access or to Anonymous.

Following are some other ways to prevent anonymous users from viewing information are:

- In the Advanced page of the Access Control List dialog box, select the appropriate access level from the Maximum Internet Name & Password drop-down list.
- Use hide-when formulas to hide portions of documents from Web users (see Day 9 to learn more about hiding objects). Specify that either the username of the current user has to be the same as the author of the document or that the user's role is not $$WebClient (see discussion about user roles in the "User Roles" section later in this lesson).
- Deselect **Available to Public Access Users** on the Security tab of the Form Properties box to prevent access to documents based on that form.
- Select the **Web Access: Require SSL Connection** option in the Database Properties box. The Secure Sockets Layer (SSL) is a security protocol that provides privacy for communications and authentication over the Internet. Web users must include an SSL certificate in their browser configuration.

Set the Database ACL

To see or change ACL settings (you can only change settings, of course, if you have Manager access), choose **File, Database, Access Control** in the menu while the database is open or while its bookmark is highlighted. The Access Control List dialog box appears. It has four different panels, which you can access by clicking the four icons on the left side of the dialog box. We only care about the first panel at this time (see Figure 7.1).

7

FIGURE 7.1

The Access Control List automatically gives manager access to the creator of the database, so you have full access during the design process.

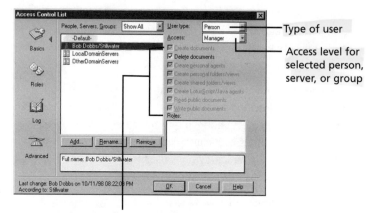

Type of user

Access level for selected person, server, or group

Select or deselect to further define access
(grayed ones are automatically granted)

The People, Servers, Groups window lists all users by default, but you can limit the display by changing the setting of the People, Servers, Groups field from Show All to one of the access levels. The types of users listed include people, servers, and groups (which might themselves include people, servers, or other groups). The very first listing is for **Default**. This listing covers any user not otherwise listed either individually or as a member of a listed group. Two other listings, **LocalDomainServers** and **OtherDomainServers**, are server groups. These are automatically assigned Manager level access, which is needed to replicate databases. Never leave OtherDomainServers at the Manager level. If servers outside the domain need to replicate the database, they need to be individually named and given sufficient access (that should be the Domino Administrator's decision).

To see the level of access that is granted to a listed user, select the user in the list. That user's access level appears in the Access field in the upper-right corner of the dialog box. Also, if a User Type has been specified, that also appears in the upper-right corner.

In addition to giving a general level of access to a user, you can refine that access by checking the boxes on the right side of the dialog box. Depending on the general level of access, you might be able to take away the right to create or delete documents; to create personal agents, views, or folders; to create shared views or folders; to create LotusScript or Java agents; or to read or write public documents.

To add a user to the ACL, click the **Add** button. The Add User dialog box appears (see Figure 7.2). Either type in the name of a person, server, or group, or click the user icon to choose people or groups from a list. If you type in the usernames, be sure to enter their *fully distinguished name* (Bob Dobbs/Stillwater), not just their *common name* (Bob Dobbs). This ensures that the ACL works correctly. Also, if there is more than one Bob Dobbs in the organization, they both can't have the same distinguished name (Domino requires a unique name for each user when you're using hierarchical naming) so each Bob gets the proper level of access to the database.

FIGURE 7.2

Type the fully distinguished name of a user or the name of a group in the Person, server, or group text box.

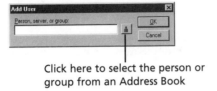

Click here to select the person or group from an Address Book

If you click the user icon to choose from a list, you will see the Names dialog box, which displays a list of people, servers, and groups from any Address Book to which you have access (see Figure 7.3). You can select people, servers, or groups in the left-hand window, and then click the **Add** button to copy the names to the right-hand window. After you have added the names that you want to the right-hand window, click **OK**. The dialog box closes and the selected names appear in the Access Control List dialog box.

FIGURE 7.3

*To select more than one name, click before the name to place a check in the margin. Then click the **Add** button.*

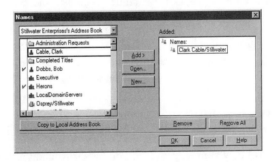

Select each newly added user and specify a User type and an Access level. Refine the access level by checking or removing check marks from the checkboxes. Add a person to a Role, if any appear in the Roles box, by clicking on the Role to make a check mark appear (you'll learn more about roles later in this lesson).

You can also rename someone (for ACL purposes only). Select the user to be renamed, and then click the **Rename** button. When the Rename User dialog box appears, type the user's correct name or pick it from a list.

7

Note

Why might you have to rename a person? Most of the time it's because you entered the name incorrectly in the first place—which is an argument for selecting it from an Address Book. You don't give someone a new name here, for example, because of a recent marriage or divorce. That's done in the Administration Process, which is under the Domino Administrator's control. The Administration Process provides an alias in the Address Book, so the old name is recognized as being the same as the new one.

Finally, you can remove a user from the Access Control List. Select the person you want to remove, and then click the **Remove** button.

Create Groups

Listing individual names in the access control lists can backfire on you. For example, if someone leaves the company or is replaced, you have to remove that person's name in every ACL in which they are named and add the new person. However, if you use *group-names* in the ACL, you only have to update the group once in the Address Book when the membership changes. If the individual is a member of more than one group, of course, each group must be changed. Chances are, this is still less work than if you had to delete the user from every ACL of which he or she is a member.

Putting groups into the ACL has several advantages: first, the ACL becomes simpler to maintain. Second, groups can be controlled by other individuals who should *not* be given Manager access to a database (for training and security reasons). Third, you, as the database designer, can get out of the daily maintenance of access by having the user community control access via the group definition. The same applies to the Domino Administrator. As to the changes for someone leaving the company, that should be done via the Administrative Process, which is controlled by the Domino Administrator.

Creating a group is fairly simple, provided you have sufficient access to the Domino Directory. Otherwise, you might have to ask the Domino administrator to do it for you.

You open the Groups view of the Domino Directory and click the **Add Group** action button to open a new group document (see Figure 7.4). The Group name needs to be descriptive but brief.

Group types include *Mail only* (for mailing lists), *Access Control List only* (for use exclusively for the ACL), *Servers only* (for specifying servers, such as LocalDomainServers), *Deny List only* (to deny access to servers), and *Multi-purpose* (for more than one of the other purposes, such as mail and ACL). If you choose Multi-purpose you can later use the group either in an Access Control List or as a mailing list. If you choose Access Control List only, you cannot add this group to the To, cc, or bcc fields of a mail message. That doesn't mean you should make every group a multipurpose group. On the contrary, you want to define groups as narrowly as possible. Only use multipurpose where the same list is used for both ACL and mailing purposes.

FIGURE 7.4

The Group can be either Access Control List only or Multi-purpose for you to use it in the ACL to specify access levels.

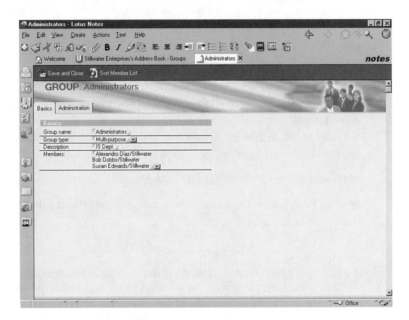

In the Description field, enter any descriptive text you want. What you type here needs to be of help to anyone who looks at this document to understand the purpose of this group.

Enter the fully distinguished names of the members of the group in Members or select their names from an Address Book list. Selecting the names gives you the correct spelling (as far as the Domino Directory is concerned) and enables you to quickly select multiple users by checking the names before clicking **Add**. Save and close the group document.

Even if you haven't specified a complete list of members, you can begin using the group to specify access to your databases. More members can be added or removed later.

You add a group name to the ACL the same way you add an individual. Click **Add** and select the name from an Address Book list. Enter or select the name of the group and click **OK**. Select the Access for that group and click **OK**.

7

> You don't always have access to create groups in the Domino Directory, even
> when you are an application developer. During the design period, create the
> group in your Personal Address Book (if you're developing locally). Specify
> the group as needed throughout the application. When you're ready to add
> the database to the server, ask the Domino administrator to add the group
> to the Domino Directory. If you are doing your development on a server—
> some organizations have a specialized development server—put the group
> in the Domino Directory from the beginning.

User Roles

When you want to define access for a group of people for your current application only,
consider assigning *roles*. A role defines a group of users in the Access Control List but is
not used in the ACL itself. For example, the role of Supervisor can be created for people
who have author access in the ACL. When a formula such as

```
@If(@UserRoles = "[Supervisor]"; @UserName; "")
```

appears in an Authors field on a form, the user can edit that document if she is assigned
the Supervisor user role in the ACL.

> A good reason for using roles is that, as the developer, you don't know what
> users or groups will work with your application. When you set security on
> forms, views, and sections, to whose names will you give access? You can
> define roles as the programmer, use them in the Security tab for the form or
> view, and then let the database manager associate the appropriate users,
> groups, and servers with the roles.

There is no particular access associated with a role, but you can use role names in formulas and fields to define who can read or edit documents and who can see views. Role
names are text strings and they are always enclosed in square brackets ([Approvers]).

For example, if you want to hide an area of your documents from Web users, use a formula such as

```
@UserRoles != "[$$WebClient]"
```

as the hide-when formula.

Before you can start creating formulas, you need to create the user role in the ACL and then assign users to that role. Open the ACL for the selected or open database by choosing **File, Database, Access Control** (see Figure 7.5).

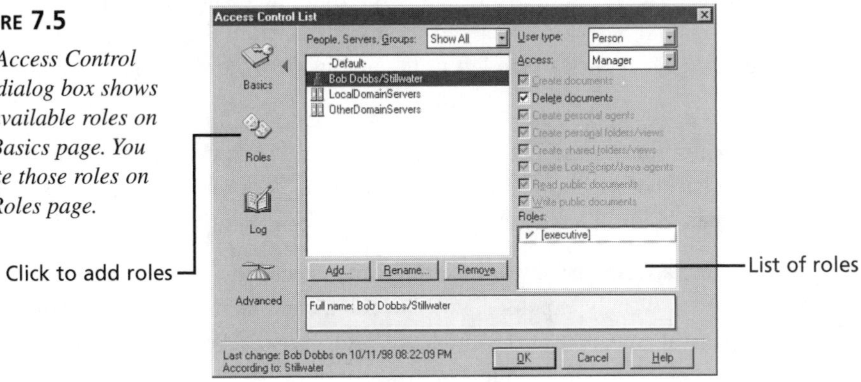

FIGURE 7.5

The Access Control List dialog box shows the available roles on the Basics page. You create those roles on the Roles page.

Click to add roles ⟶

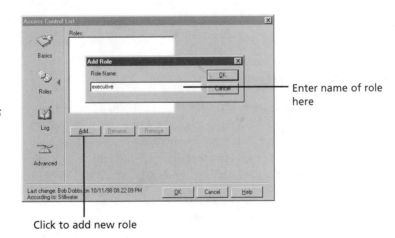

⟶ List of roles

Click the Roles icon to switch to the Roles page of the Access Control List dialog box (see Figure 7.6). Click **Add** to add a new role to the ACL. Select the role name and click **Rename** to give it a new name (be aware that this will not carry over to existing formulas) or **Remove** to delete the role name from the list.

FIGURE 7.6

*Choose **Add** to open the Add Role dialog box. In the Role Name text box, type a short descriptive name for the role (the limit is 15 characters) and click **OK**.*

Enter name of role here

Click to add new role

7

Now that you've created a role, you need to assign users to that role. The users must already be listed in the ACL in order to have roles assigned to them. User roles can also be assigned to groups, to servers, and to server groups.

To assign a role to a user or group, you need to return to the Basics page of the Access Control List dialog box. Select the user's or group's name from the list of people, servers, and groups. Then click to the left of the role in the Roles box to place a check mark there.

Use the @UserRoles function to get a text list of the roles the current user has in the database. On the basis of this information, you can grant the user access to forms and views or see hidden fields or sections.

When programming a form or view, for example an expense report form in which employees enter their weekly expenses, you can add a computed subform that holds the fields for the approval signature of the employee's supervisor. You only want the supervisor and the payroll personnel to see the Approval subform. You've added the supervisor to the Approvers role, and the payroll personnel are already in the Payroll role. The formula for the computed subform might look like this:

```
@If(@Contains(@UserRoles; "[Approvers]" : "[Payroll]"); "Approval"; "")
```

The @UserRoles function only works on a database that is on a server (or a local database in which the "Enforce a consistent ACL" option is selected in the ACL); it returns an empty text string ("") if the database is local. You can't use this function for column, selection, mail agent, or scheduled agent formulas.

Set the View ACL

You can determine who can see or use a particular view by establishing a *view read access list*. This is not a real security feature—any user with reader access can create a private view. Rather, it is more a convenient method to set up your database so certain users don't have to see views that don't apply to them, for example in a client database with a view read access list of individual salesperson clients displayed.

Make sure you don't apply a view read access list to the default view; any users you exclude from seeing that view will have to view all their documents through another view. Also, be sure to *not* restrict access for any servers that need to replicate the database so that any design changes get replicated.

The view read access list is defined in the View Properties box. Open the view in Designer, and then open the Security tab of the View Properties box (see Figure 7.7). **All readers and above** is normally selected. To specify users who can see the view, deselect that option and select the users, servers, roles (already defined), or groups from the list. If a user or group isn't on the list, click the user button and select the name from the Address Book. Select **Available to Public Access Users** if you want the view to be visible to anonymous Web users and Notes users with No Access or Depositor access.

FIGURE 7.7

The open view contains management information, so only a few individuals can see the view. Notice that the server group LocalDomainServers is selected, so replication can occur smoothly.

Set the Form ACL

Normally, anyone with reader access to the database can read all the documents. You can restrict who can read documents based on a particular form by creating a *read access list*. As a designer, you set the default read access for documents created by the form; as a creator of a document, you set the document property that determines who can read the document.

Avoid setting reader access to the database default form, or take great care if you do set a reader access list. If a form in a database is corrupted, the users might be able to read the documents created with that form by using the default form. However, if the users don't have read access for that default form, they cannot read any of the documents created with the corrupted form.

You can also define a *form create access list* to control which users can use the form to create and edit documents. Users with Reader access and No Access to the database can't create and edit documents in *any* case; users with Editor access and above who are in the read access list for the form or document can still edit documents. However, if you don't add someone who has read access to the database to the read access list, that person still can't read documents using this form. Authors not listed in the create access list can't create new documents using the form despite their level of access to the database.

7

Being included in the read or create access lists cannot increase a user's current level of access as defined in the ACL, but it does limit those who have higher levels of access.

Define the form read access and create access lists in the Form Properties box. With the form open in the Designer, open the Security tab of the Form Properties box (see Figure 7.8).

FIGURE 7.8

Controlling who can read and who can create documents using the form might not be sufficient. Select the option **Disable printing/forwarding/copying to Clipboard** *to make sure the information is not passed on to users who don't normally have access.*

To define the *form* read access list, deselect **All Readers and Above** (a reserved $Readers field is added to the form, containing the list of people and servers entered in the list box). To define the form create access list, deselect **All Authors and Above**.

In the appropriate list, click each user, group, server, or role to place a check mark before the names you want to include in the access list (if a destination server is not included in the $Readers field, the document won't replicate).

If the names you want to include in the access list aren't displayed, click the user icon to choose names from the Domino Directory. To remove names, click the name again to remove the check mark.

Select **Available to Public Access Users** to make documents that use the form accessible to anonymous users from the Web and Notes users with No Access or Depositor access.

Control Document Access

The Database Designer controls the read and create access for documents by setting those access levels in the form or by putting Readers and Authors fields on the form.

The creator or editor of a document can also set a read access list for a document. With the document open or selected, open the Security tab of the Document Properties box (see Figure 7.9).

FIGURE 7.9

Setting a document read access list only works if the database is stored on a server.

To give access to specific users, groups, or servers, deselect the **All Readers and Above** option. Then select the user, group, server, or role to which you want to grant read access (the server must have read access to replicate the document). If the user, group, or server you want isn't listed, click the user button and select it from an Address Book.

Use Encryption

To keep some users from seeing or editing all the fields in a document but still allow them to see the remaining fields, you use *document encryption*. Encryption enables only authorized users to access selected fields.

In order for users to access the encrypted fields within an encrypted document, they must already have read and edit access to the document, and they must have the encryption key used to encrypt the data stored in their user ID.

Users who have at least read access but not the encryption key can see all the data in the document that isn't encrypted, but the encrypted fields appear blank. Even objects embedded in rich text fields are not visible to users without the proper key, although attachments are accessible to anyone with reader access.

How does a user get an encryption key? If the document uses a *public* encryption key (such as a mail message uses), the user already has the key. It's part of his Person document in the Domino Directory. Each user has a public and a *private* key. The public key is stored in the Person document. Both keys are stored in the user ID file. Any encrypted document that is sent to the user is encrypted using the public key, and the user decrypts it using his private key.

7

There are also *secret* encryption keys. These are generally created by the application developer. The system administrator or database manager distributes them to the appropriate users when the database is deployed. The users then merge the keys with their user ID files.

Create an Encryption Key

The first step in encrypting a document is to create the secret encryption keys that you need, although you can use one that already exists. Choose **File, Tools, User ID** from the menu. Enter your password, if it is requested. Click the Encryption icon and choose **New**. When the New Encryption Key dialog box appears (see Figure 7.10), enter a descriptive name for the key in the Encryption Key name text box.

FIGURE 7.10

Be sure to include comments that help identify how the encryption key is to be used.

To set the type of security used to create the key, select **North American** if the users are going to use the key in only the United States and Canada. If the users' office is located outside of the United States or Canada they must choose **International**. Users outside North America (whose office is located in the United States or Canada) can only use the North American security if they have a North American license.

It's a good idea to include information about the database, form, and fields that will use the key in the Comments area. You might need that information later. Click **OK** to close the dialog box and return to the User ID dialog box (see Figure 7.11).

Enable Encryption for a Field

To encrypt a document, you must have at least one encrypted *field* in the document. You can have more than one encryptable field, and each field can have a different encryption key. However, any user who possesses one of the encryption keys can read all the encrypted fields.

Enabling encryption for a single field only involves a few steps. First, you create or select a field. Then, in the Field Properties box, open the Advanced page (see

Figure 7.12). From the Security Options drop-down list, select **Enable Encryption for This Field.**

FIGURE 7.11

The User ID dialog box lists the encryption keys stored in your User ID. At any time after you create a key, you can mail or export it to another user. You can specify a password when you export it and restrict the recipient from giving it to another user.

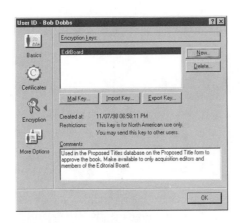

FIGURE 7.12

Choosing Enable Encryption for This Field is only one step in encrypting a document. For example, it does not associate the field with a specific encryption key.

Encrypt the Document

There are three different ways to associate the encryption key with the document:

- **Forced Encryption**—Set the Form Properties so all the encryptable fields are automatically encrypted whenever someone saves a document composed with that form. This is convenient for the users, but gives them no choice in picking a key.

- **Optional Encryption**—Create a keywords field (dialog list, checkbox, radio button, listbox, or combobox field) on the form. The choice made by the user selects the appropriate key. Use this method to allow some variation in the keys the users want, as long as the list of possible keys is predictable.

- **Manual Encryption**—Enable the author or editor to assign the keys themselves from the Document Properties box.

To force encryption of all the encryptable fields when someone saves a new document composed with a form, you need to open the form in Designer and change the Form

7

Properties. On the Security tab of the Form Properties box (see Figure 7.13), select the encryption keys you want to use from the Default Encryption Keys drop-down list.

FIGURE 7.13

Users who create and save documents with this form must have at least one of the default encryption keys you selected.

Unless the author or editor changes the encryption keys associated with the document or disables encryption, the document is automatically encrypted when it is saved. Documents created before you add the encryption keys remain unencrypted; however, you need to manually encrypt them.

Authors can remove encryption or change the associated keys from their own documents if they are allowed to edit their documents and they have all the associated encryption keys. Editors can remove encryption from and change the keys associated with any document.

Users who don't have the correct encryption key in their Notes User ID can't edit encrypted documents. They can create new documents, but they must remove the encryption key from the Document Properties box before they save the document. It is saved unencrypted.

Optional encryption enables the user to select from a list of encryption key options. You create a text or keywords field (dialog list, checkbox, radio button, listbox, or combobox field) and give it the reserved field name SecretEncryptionKeys. The field formula must evaluate to the name of an encryption key. For a keywords field, use the name of the encryption key as the synonym:

```
Encrypt this document ¦ "ManagerKey"
```

Either make a text field computed or write a default value formula for an editable field (use a null value for the Don't Encrypt option):

```
@If(Status = "Classified"; "ManagerKey"; "")
```

When you don't force encryption or provide an encryption option in the document, the author or the editor can decide when to encrypt the document and which key to use. From a view, they select the document and open the Document Properties box. Then, on the Security tab, they can choose a Secret Encryption key from the drop-down list (see Figure 7.14). If the document is going to be mailed, you can encrypt it with a user's public key. Select or enter the user's name under Public Encryption Keys.

FIGURE 7.14

Be careful when using the Public Encryption keys to include yourself, at least until you finish the design process.

Distribute the Key

Finally, you must distribute the encryption keys to the people who need to use them. Users must have a copy of the encryption key so that they can save documents. The database manager is in charge of distributing secret encryption keys to all users who need them. You need to send the encryption key to the database manager. There are two ways to do this: Either export the key to a file or send it through Notes Mail.

To copy the encryption key to a .KEY file, choose **File, Tools, User ID** from the menu. Enter your password. Click the Encryption icon in the User ID dialog box, and then select the encryption key. Choose **Export Key**, and the Export Encryption Key dialog box opens (see Figure 7.15).

FIGURE 7.15

Choose Export Key to create an encryption key file for distribution, or choose Mail Key to send the key to a specific user or group of users.

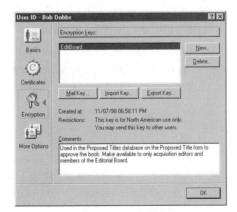

7

We recommend that you assign a password to your encryption key; enter it in the Password box and then type it again in the Confirmation box (see Figure 7.16).

FIGURE 7.16

*Enter a password to protect the encryption key file. Click **Restrict Use** to designate the person who can use the encryption key file, so the file can't be passed on to other users.*

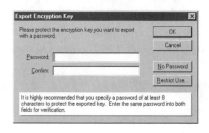

To restrict the use of the key file, choose **Restrict Use**. Enter the fully distinguished name—and spell it correctly—of the only person who is allowed to use the import file. To make certain that only that person has use of the file, deselect **Allow That Person to Export the Key or Forward It to Others**. Click **OK** to return to the User ID Encryption Key Export dialog box.

Click **OK** after you set the password, or choose **No Password** if you want. A dialog box appears, in which you specify where you want the key file stored (somewhere accessible to other users of the network) and what filename you want to give it. Click **Save**. The file automatically has an extension of .KEY.

At the receiving end, the user chooses **File, Tools, User ID** from the menu and enters his password. He clicks the Encryption icon and then selects the encryption key. Then he clicks **Import Key**. He selects the encryption key file from the agreed upon location in the file system, and clicks **Open**. If a password was entered, the Provide Password dialog box appears. He enters the password and clicks **OK**. The Accept Encryption Key dialog box appears. The user clicks **Accept**. This merges the key into his user ID.

To distribute the key via Mail, click **Mail Key** from the Encryption page of the User ID dialog box. Enter the name of the recipient and the person who gets the carbon copy. Click OK. The recipient opens the document and chooses **Actions, Accept Encryption Key**.

Add Signatures

When you sign a document, Notes attaches to the document a unique electronic signature based on your user ID. This signature verifies that the information was entered by you as the last person who edited that document or section.

Designer combines the data in a sign-enabled field with the private key from the sender's User ID to create a unique electronic signature. Designer stores the signature, along with the public key and the list of certificates from the sender's ID, in the document.

If a user with Editor access in the database ACL changes a field in a document, Notes replaces the existing signature with the signature of the editor when the document is mailed. If the document contains several sign-enabled fields, Designer uses data from each sign-enabled field to generate a signature. After mailing, a change in any field causes verification to fail when the recipient opens the document.

Consider this scenario to understand how this works: Harry saves a mail-enabled document with his signature. His user ID's private key and the data in the sign-enabled field create the unique signature. The document is mailed to Beverly, who opens the document to read it. Notes checks to see if the document was signed, checks the signature against the data to see if it's the same, and then checks the certificates in the document generated by Harry's ID against Beverly's ID to see if they have a trusted certificate in common or a common certifier. If the signature and data are verified by Notes, a message appears, indicating who signed the document. If the data has been modified, a message appears, saying the document has been changed or corrupted since it was saved (meaning this is not the same as what Harry created). If the signature can't be verified or Harry and Beverly don't share a trusted certifier, the message indicates that the signature can't be verified—meaning Harry might not have created this document or it might not be the same document as when Harry saved it.

Electronic signatures are generally used for mailed documents or with access-controlled sections. If used with mailing, there are four requirements that must be met:

- The form must contain a SendTo field; you can create a LotusScript program that uses the Send method of the NotesDocument class with a recipients argument.

- The form must have at least one sign-enabled field.

- The form must be mail-enabled by using a Send Document form action, the form property On Close: Present mail send dialog, a MailOptions field with the value 1, an @MailSend formula, or a LotusScript program that uses the Send method of the NotesDocument or NotesUIDocument class.

- The sender must activate signing during mailing by choosing **Sign** in the Mail Send dialog box. Alternately, include a Sign field on the form that has a value of 1, use the [Sign] flag in an @MailSend formula, or create a LotusScript program with SignOnSend property set to TRUE.

The signature is generated at the time the document is mailed.

7

You might want to attach signatures to access-controlled sections. To do this, the following two requirements must be met:

- The form must contain an access-controlled section.
- There must be at least one sign-enabled field in the access-controlled section.

The signature applies only to the controlled-access section and is generated when the document is saved. To generate multiple signatures on a form, such as in routed approvals for a workflow application, create multiple sign-enabled fields in separate access-controlled sections.

To sign-enable a field, open the form in Designer and create or select a field. Open the Field Properties box and select the Advanced tab. From the Security Options drop-down list, select **Sign If Mailed or Saved in Section** (see Figure 7.17).

FIGURE 7.17

To use Sign if mailed or saved for a section requires a controlled-access section.

Summary

Domino and Notes have multiple levels of security. The Domino Administrator limits who has access to the server, which is the highest level of security. The Access Control List (ACL) sets the levels of access to a database: No Access, Depositor, Reader, Author, Editor, Designer, or Manager.

Within the ACL, roles can be assigned to groups, individuals, servers, and server groups. When used in formulas or script, the user roles can also limit access. Functions such as @UserRoles are often used in hide-when formulas to restrict who sees what on a form.

Access levels can also be assigned to groups, which are created in the Domino Directory. Changing the membership of groups is easier than adjusting the ACLs of several databases, so creating groups is often considered a security measure.

Access to a view is set in View Properties, on the Security page, where you specify a reader access list. Forms have reader and author access lists, which you set on the Security page of the Form Properties box.

Fields and documents can be encrypted, but you must create the encryption key and distribute it to the authorized users.

Q&A

Q I noticed that the checkbox for deleting documents can be checked off for the manager in the ACL. Why might you do that? Can't someone with manager access just go in and change that?

A Well, you're right about that. But by removing that right you protect managers from accidentally deleting documents. They have to first give themselves the right, and then delete the document.

Q What is the Execution Control List?

A The ECL protects your workstation, so only certain people are allowed or certain organizational certifiers are required to execute Notes scripts and formulas on your workstation. For example, unless you grant permission in the ECL for an agent created by an application developer to run particular scripts on your workstation that access files on your hard drive, the agent will not run. If you click the **Security Options** button in your User Preferences, you will see the Execution Control List (ECL) for your workstation.

Q If I don't want the users to see a particular view, what can I do?

A You can specify only the users you want to see the view in the reader access list on the Security page of the View Properties box. To hide the view from the menu, deselect **Show in View Menu** on the Options page of the View Properties box. To totally hide the view from everyone, enclose the Name of the view in parentheses on the View Info page of the View Properties box. Even deselecting the **Create Personal Folders/Views** option for anyone else in the database ACL won't stop users from creating their own views to see the same information.

Workshop

In this workshop, you will once again be concentrating on the Proposed Titles database. You will set up the security for the database, starting with the ACL through creating encryption keys.

Set the ACL

In the Access Control List for the database, set the default access setting to **Author**. Make sure **Create Documents** is selected. This means that all users can at least create

7

documents. Make sure that your name is listed and that you have Manager access (you'll need that level of access until you roll out the application on the server). The LocalDomainServers group and your Domino Administrator should also have Manager access. Although this doesn't make much difference while you are working locally, the ACL will be ready when you roll out the database.

Create a group (use your own Address Book if you don't have access rights to the Domino Directory) called **EditBoard**, and add that group to the Access Control List with Editor access. Add any names you want to use to test your applications to that group.

Create a user role in the Access Control List called **AcqEditor**. Assign that role to your name, and to two other people who will have management of books as their position.

To be sure that all users can edit their own title suggestions, open the Proposed Title form and change the **TDocAuthor** field to an Authors type field.

The Review Status view is meant for management purposes only. Assign reader access for that view to yourself, the EditBoard group, and the role [AcqEditor].

Create a new Encryption Key called **EditBoard**. Mail the key to the members of the EditBoard group, but don't allow them to send the key to anyone else. In the Proposed Title form, enable encryption for the TStatus field. Then select EditBoard as the default encryption key for the form and disable printing, forwarding, and copying to the Clipboard.

Sample files for today's lesson are found in the Day7 folder of the accompanying CD. Use the following files:

- PTDay7.NSF is the Proposed Titles database at the end of Day 7.
- Document.key is the document key needed to open the encrypted fields in the sample database. You'll have to import it into your ID if you want to open encrypted documents in PTDay7.nsf.

WEEK 2

Embellish and Refine Your Application

8

9

10

11

12

13

14

DAY **8**

Create Pages and Frames

Pages and frames give you the capability to design interesting and interactive Web sites, while incorporating the data collection and display capabilities of Notes applications. Even more exciting, pages and frames are available to the Notes *client*, which means your Notes databases can have the same appearance and flexibility as your Web site.

Pages display information (see Figure 8.1), much as documents do, but users cannot create pages and cannot enter data on them. However, users can use the links on pages to reach other pages, documents, views, databases, or Web sites.

A frame contains one page, form, view, folder, navigator, or page from the Web. A group of frames is a *frameset*. When you see a screen in your browser that is divided into one or two areas, those areas are frames. The whole browser screen is a frameset, which is a group of frames (see Figure 8.2).

FIGURE 8.1

This home page will eventually be displayed in a frameset, which is why it consists only of links.

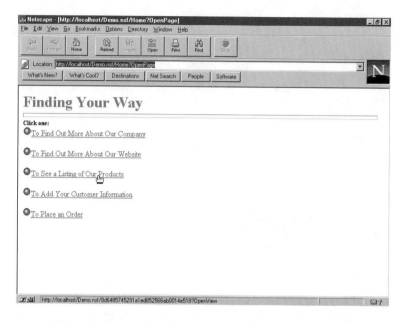

FIGURE 8.2

This two-frame frameset shows the home page from Figure 8.1 on the left and the linked page for entering customer information on the right.

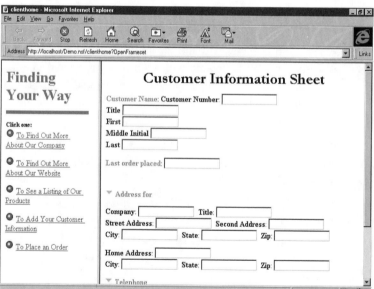

In this lesson you learn about

- Creating pages
- Specifying frame contents

- Setting up framesets
- Using outlines
- Exploring HTML (hypertext markup language) and its use in pages, frames, and forms

Create a Page

Like a form, a page displays text and graphics. It can contain horizontal rules, navigators or imagemaps (see Day 12, "Beautify Your Application"), animation, some ActiveX controls, certain embedded objects, embedded controls (outline controls, navigators, views, or folders), or applets (see Day 17, "Embed Objects in Your Applications"). It can also contain links to other pages, documents, views, databases, or URLs. However, a page cannot contain fields and subforms.

Pages differ from documents (which are created from forms) in several ways. First, users can't create pages or enter data into pages because pages can't contain fields. Second, because a view is a list of documents, pages won't display in a view. Pages are accessed through links or from a frameset where one of the pages is displayed in a frame.

You might be asking yourself, "Why create a page instead of a form, when a document holds more Notes elements than a page?". Use a form to collect information, and use a page to display information that does not require input from fields. The application developer designs pages (unless they are inherited from a template). An application that includes pages typically has a home page that provides links to other documents, pages, views, or databases in the application.

Use the following steps to create a page:

1. Open the application database in the Designer.
2. Select **Pages** in the Design Pane.
3. Click the **New Page** button on the Action Bar. A blank, untitled page opens. Like a form, this is one big rich text field. You can add text, HTML, applets, and graphics as you do in a form.
4. Choose **Design, Page Properties** from the menu to open the Page Properties box (see Figure 8.3).
5. On the **Page Info** tab, enter a title for the page in the Name box.
6. Although the Comment box is optional, you need to always enter a comment defining the purpose of the page to assist you or other designers in the future.
7. If you have included HTML (Hypertext Markup Language) code on your page, HTMLcheck **Web Access: Treat page contents as HTML** (see the "Add HTML" section later in this day for more information on this selection).

8. (Optional) Under Link Colors, select the default colors for active, unvisited, and visited links on the page.

9. Save the page.

FIGURE 8.3

You enter the name of the page on the Page Info tab of the Page Properties box, as well as determining whether to show the contents as HTML and picking colors for the links on the page. The other tabs include Background, where you set the background color or image of the page; the Launch tab, which contains the name of the frame and frameset where the page is displayed; and the Security tab, where you decide who can access the page.

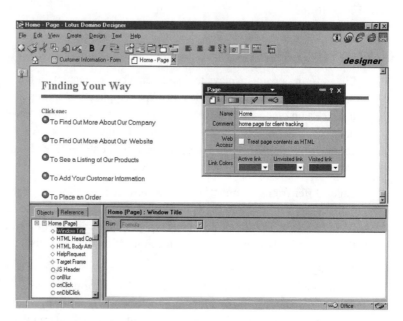

If you decide later that you don't want to include a page in your application, open the Pages view from the Design Pane and then select the page you want to delete. Choose **Edit, Clear** from the menu, and then click **Yes** to confirm the deletion.

Enhance Your Page with Graphics

Graphics certainly make your pages look better. They can also act as signposts to let users know what the page represents (in Figure 8.4 you see a picture of a house that makes it obvious that this is the home page). However, keep in mind that a page with graphics takes more time to display and print.

Adding graphics to a page works the same way it does for forms. You either copy a bitmap graphic (BMP file) to the Clipboard and then paste it onto the page at your cursor position, or you import a file.

FIGURE 8.4

To help users identify this page as the Home page, a picture of a house is displayed.

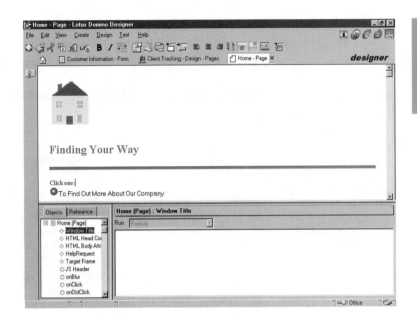

Imported graphic files must be in one of the following formats: BMP (bitmap), JPEG, GIF, PCX Image, or TIFF 5.0 bitmap. Position your cursor where you want the file to appear. Choose **File, Import** from the menu. Select the graphic file you want to import and click **OK**.

Graphics can also be shared resources. A *shared resource* is a single file that you store in a central location for use in multiple pages or forms. If you have shared image resources available, choose **Create, Image Resource** from the menu and then select the name of the image file. Click **OK** to display the image on your page at the cursor's location. If the only databases you are working with are ones you created while completing lessons in this book, you won't have any shared image resources available, but you will learn on Day 17 how to add graphic files to the database's shared resources. In that case, what you want to remember from this lesson is that shared resources can be used in pages.

The Picture Properties box (choose **Picture, Picture Properties** from the menu) has a number of options to set, many of which are the same as paragraph properties for text. Most of the options are on the Picture Info tab. The Text Wrap choices determine how the text on the page or form wraps around the picture (see Figure 8.5). The Scaling options set the height or width of the picture (in percentage of original size). Specify Alternate Text to show in the browser when the picture is loading. Caption options define the text that appears with the picture and its position in relation to the picture. The Hotspots are used for imagemaps, and we'll discuss them on Day 12.

The Picture Border tab of the Picture Properties box contains options for adding a border to the picture, selecting the border color, setting the border thickness, adding a drop shadow to the picture, and specifying the width of the drop shadow.

FIGURE 8.5

Choose a Float option to let the text wrap around the graphic. However, this option might not be supported in all browsers. An alternative is to put the graphic in a table, with the cell next to it containing text.

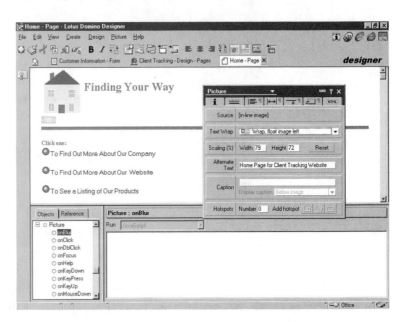

Tip

A Web browser that supports sizing and scaling shows the graphic in the size and scale you specified in the Picture Properties. However, a Web browser that doesn't support sizing and scale shows the graphic in its original size. To have the picture show in the correct proportions, set the size in a photo editor or graphics package before importing or pasting it on your page.

Add a Page Background

Like a form, a page can have a background color or graphic that adds interest to the page. As you have probably experienced yourself while surfing the Internet, pages with background graphics take more time to load in a browser than pages without background graphics. Weigh the use and need for background graphics carefully before you add them to your page.

Use the following steps to add a background to your page:

1. With the page open, choose **Design**, **Page Properties** from the menu to open the Page Properties box.

2. Select the **Background** tab of the Page Properties box (see Figure 8.6).

FIGURE 8.6

Page elements appear in front of the page background. Therefore, it's useless to set a page background color if you use a background graphic.

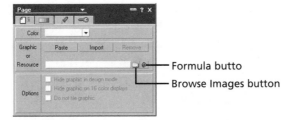

Formula butto

Browse Images button

3. To use a colored background, choose from the Color drop-down list. We recommend that you use the paler colors for your background color, with dark type for easy reading.

   To use a graphic background, do one of the following:

   - If you have copied the graphic to the Clipboard, click **Paste**.

   - Click **Import** and specify the location and name of the graphic file to import. The graphic must be a BMP (bitmap), JPEG, GIF, PCX Image, or TIFF 5.0 bitmap graphic file.

   - Click the **Browse Images** button (also called the **Folder** button) and select one of the database's image resources. Click **OK**.

   - Click the **Formula** button (also called the **@** button) and enter a formula that evaluates to the name of a graphic file. Click **Done** when the formula is complete.

4. (Optional) Background graphics can slow the page refresh as you are working in Designer, or you might find the image distracting. Select **Hide Graphic in Design Mode** if you don't want to see the graphic as you're working.

5. (Optional) On monitors that don't display 256 or more colors, the graphic image you select might display poorly. To avoid this, select **Hide Graphic on 16-Color Displays**.

6. (Optional) A background graphic that is the same size as the user's window only appears once in the page background, but smaller graphics tile (repeat) to fill the entire background—especially when the user has a larger screen than the one used to create the graphic. Select **Do Not Tile Graphic** to avoid tiling the background image.

7. Save the page.

The Designer color palette is extensive, and some colors provided in Designer don't translate well to Web browsers, so you might want to limit your choices to the Web Palette colors. To access the Web Palette, choose **File, Preferences, User Preferences** from the menu. Under Additional Options, select **Use Web Palette** (see Figure 8.7).

FIGURE 8.7

There are fewer colors available in the Web color Palette than in the Designer color palette, but the colors will successfully display in Web browsers.

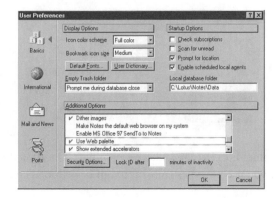

After you add a background graphic, you might find that it's too busy and you can't read the text that runs over it. To delete the page background, click **Remove** on the **Background** tab of the Page Properties box.

Create a Home Page

A home page is the entry hall to your application. You want to provide one when you have Web users entering your site or application, but it's also helpful to Notes or internal users because it's a great starting point to help users find other elements of the application.

What information do you include on your home page? We suggest—at the very least—that you include links to help users navigate to the other parts of the site (see Day 11, "Help the User: Design Interface Enhancements," to learn about links). You might also want to include some of the following, or at least a link to a page that contains this information:

- A short description of your company, product, or service
- A statement of the purpose of the site
- A way to search for information
- Information to help new visitors
- A *what's new* list for frequent visitors so they know what's changed since their last visit
- If needed, a way for users to register so they can participate in restricted areas of the site

8

Although many home pages on the Web are HTML files created with Web authoring graphics and text packages, Domino and Designer help you make attractive and useful pages—without using HTML. Or you can combine Designer features with HTML.

The home page is simply a page with a purpose. You create it like any other page. It can be one page in a database designed for an application, or it can be stored in its own database (for possible security purposes). A home page usually has open access, but you might want to limit access to other parts of the site or to other databases in a multiple-database application.

For a home page for multiple databases, have the System Administrator set the Home URL to specify a URL that identifies the page. When the home page is set to launch when a database is opened, the Home URL is just the name of the database (/dbname.nsf).

Design Frames

Add flexibility and ease to your application by giving it the capability to present more than one page or more than one type of information at one time. For example, one side of the screen can display a list of links to other pages, whereas the main portion of the screen might display a list of products your company is selling. When the user clicks a link to another page, the new page appears in the main pane, but the list of links stays where it is.

These separate parts of the screen are called *frames*. This is the same technology and design element you see when you are surfing the Net. Each frame can show a separate page, document, view, folder, navigator, or page from another Web site. A collection of frames is a *frameset*. You use the Frameset Designer to set the configuration of the frames, and the Frames Properties box to control what the frames display.

Use Frameset Designer

In the Frameset Designer, you choose the arrangement of frames you want to use, or adjust the number or sizing of the frames. Before you set up your frames, you need to already have the pages or elements that you want to display in the frames created.

It helps to start by creating a paper and pencil design of the Web site, where you can decide which frameset layout and combination of pages works best. Then create the pages you need with the frameset layout in mind. Finally, create the frameset.

Use the following steps to create a frameset:

1. Select **Framesets** from the Design Pane.

2. Click the **New Frameset** button on the Action Bar. The Create New Frameset dialog box opens (see Figure 8.8).

3. Select the Number of frames in your initial configuration—2, 3, or 4.

4. The four arrangements for the frames display the number of frames you chose. Click on the Arrangement you want to use for your frameset.

5. Click **OK**.

FIGURE 8.8

Although the number of frames and the frame arrangement is set in the initial configuration, you can adjust the configuration in the Frameset Designer.

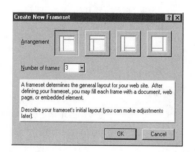

The action buttons in the Frameset Designer (see Figure 8.9) enable you to further refine your configuration:

- **Split into Columns**—Vertically splits the selected frame (click in the frame to select it) into two frames.

- **Split into Rows**—Horizontally splits the selected frame into two frames.

- **Delete Frame**—Removes the selected frame.

- **Remove Frame Contents**—Removes the contents of the selected frame.

> **Tip**
>
> Following are some Frameset Shortcuts. Use **Shift+Insert** to split into columns, **Insert** to split into rows, **Ctrl+Delete** to delete a frame, and **Delete** to remove frame content. Cycle through the frames using **Tab**, or use **Shift+Tab** to go backwards. Refresh the content of a selected frame by choosing **Frame, Refresh Frame Content**.

Choose **Frame, Frameset Properties** from the menu to open the Frameset Properties box (see Figure 8.10). On the **Basics** tab, enter a name for the Frameset. Choose **File, Save** from the menu to save the Frameset.

FIGURE 8.9

Quickly adjust the height or width of the frames in the Frameset Designer by dragging the frame borders.

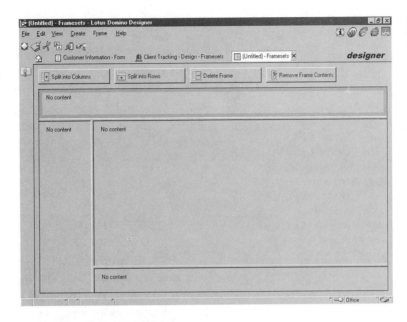

FIGURE 8.10

The Name is the title of the frameset, but the Alias is the synonym— the name you use internally to refer to the frameset. The Title is the name that appears in the Windows tab when the frameset is launched.

Set Frame Properties

The properties of a frame establish the name of the frame, the contents of the frame, the frame size, scrolling instructions, and borders.

You select a frame by clicking in it. Then choose **Frame, Frame Properties** from the menu to display the Frame Properties box (see Figure 8.11).

On the **Basics** tab of the Frame Properties box, enter a name for the frame. Under Content, specify what is to display in the frame. This includes the Type of contents— URL, Link, or Named Element for the frame—and the value and type of element (only for Named Element).

Frame Border tab
Frame Size tab ⌐   ⌐ Advanced tab
Basics tab ⌐   ⌐Additional HTML tab

FIGURE 8.11

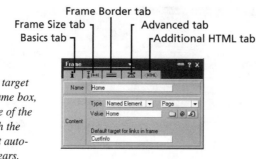

In the Default target for links in frame box, enter the name of the frame in which the linked element automatically appears. Then, when a user selects a link in this frame, the resulting page appears in the target frame.

For example, to display the home page of the Lotus Web site, choose URL as the type of source and enter the URL as the Value (`http://www.lotus.com`). To display a page from the current database, choose Named Element as the type, and specify Page and the name of the page as the Value. If you choose Link as the type, you need to already have a link copied to the Clipboard. When you click the Paste button, the kind of link (database, view, document, or anchor) appears in the kind box and the name of the linked item appears as the Value.

To have the choice you make in the currently selected frame appear in one of the other frames, enter the name of the other frame in the Default target for links in frame box.

Although you can drag the borders of the frames to set the size, the **Frame Size** tab of the Frame Properties box (see Figure 8.12) enables you to set the Width and Height of the selected frame. *Percent* sizes the frame as a percentage of the frameset (50% is half the width of the frameset). *Relative* sizes the frame relative to the other frames in the frameset (in a two-frame frameset, frames with the same relative size are equal in size; frames with unequal numbers, such as 3 and 5, are sized in proportion so one frame is 3/8 the width of the screen and the other is 5/8 of the screen). *Pixel* sizes the frame exactly in pixels (the dots on the screen).

Here, too, you decide whether you want to add scrollbars to the frame. You either turn them **On** or **Off**, but if you choose **Auto** the scrollbars appear only as needed. Selecting **Default** also turns on the scrollbars only as needed because the default is **Auto**.

FIGURE 8.12

*Choosing **Yes** for Allow Resizing gives users the capability to adjust the size of the frame, whereas **No** keeps the borders as you set them.*

Whether the borders show on the selected frame or on all the frames, how wide the borders are, and the color of the borders are all determined on the Frame Border tab of the Frame Properties box. You must deselect **Default** for the Border Width in order to specify a width in pixels. The Border Width and Border Color are the same for all frames in the frameset, but the 3D border can be turned on or off for each frame. To use the 3D border for all the frames in the frameset, click **Apply to All Frames**.

On the Advanced tab, deselect **Default** to set the Frame Spacing (minimal space between frames, in pixels), Margin Height, and Margin Width (margins are the space between the frame border and the frame content, in pixels). The defaults for these values are all 1. These properties aren't supported in the Notes client.

When you want a frameset to open automatically when the database is opened, change the properties by opening the Database Properties box (choose **File, Database, Properties**) and selecting the **Launch** tab (see Figure 8.13). Select the frameset that contains the home page from the **When Opened in the Notes Client** list or **Open Designated Page** from the When Opened in a Browser list. Then specify the frameset or page to use.

FIGURE 8.13

Set the launch option for Notes from When Opened in the Notes Client and for Web clients under When Opened in a Browser.

Add HTML

Hypertext Markup Language enables you to save a document with formatted text, graphics, rules, sound, and video (if you have the necessary hardware) in a text-only ASCII file that any computer can read. HTML works with *tags*, which are keywords that indicate what type of content follows. These tags appear between angle brackets (< >). A Web browser interprets the HTML tags and then shows the properly formatted document on the screen.

Domino automatically converts your Notes documents and pages to HTML for you on-the-fly. However, some Notes attributes don't translate into HTML code, so you might need to include HTML code in your forms and pages. A list of frequently used HTML codes appears in Appendix D, "Frequently Used HTML."

HTML in Pages

There are several ways to bring HTML to your page. One is to import the contents of an existing Web page, either prepared in Designer or elsewhere. With the page you are designing open, choose **File, Import** from the menu. Select the file that contains the HTML and click **OK**. The contents of the imported Web page now appear on your new page, and you can add to it, edit it, or delete unwanted portions.

You don't always have to import the entire file; you can paste the portion you want into your new page. Select the content from the existing Web page, copy it to the Clipboard, switch to your new page, and paste it where your cursor is.

 Caution   If you import or copy from a Web page, make sure it's your own or one you have permission to copy, or you might be infringing on someone's copyright.

Another alternative is to turn the entire contents of your page into HTML. With the page open, choose **Page, Page Properties** (see Figure 8.14). When the Properties box appears, select the **Page Info** tab. Enable the option **Treat Page Contents as HTML**. Domino converts all the data on the page to HTML, ignoring any embedded navigators or folders and any embedded views that don't have the Treat View Contents as HTML option selected (the applets won't show in this case). You can add HTML code to the page also.

8

FIGURE 8.14

*After you select **Treat Page Contents as HTML**, Domino treats the entire page as HTML code when it renders the page and embedded Java applets won't display.*

Any HTML code entered directly on the page or pasted on it can be marked as HTML so the Designer will serve it properly. Select the text and choose **Text, Pass-Thru HTML** from the menu, or create a Named Style called HTML and apply it to the text.

One example of using HTML in a page is for referencing a graphic file. Domino renders any pasted or imported graphic as a GIF on-the-fly, but if it's a graphic you use on several different pages or forms, Domino gives it a different name each time. Using an HTML reference points to the same file, with the same filename each time:

```
<img src = "/images/logo.gif">
```

There are two HTML events associated with pages. The HTML Head Content event defines the <HEAD> tag attribute that Domino assigns to the page. Click the name of the page from the InfoList Objects list, and then select HTML Head Content (see Figure 8.15). In the Programmer's Pane, write the HTML code. For example, to specify a graphic file such as your logo to use as a form background, write

```
"BACKGROUND=/images/logo.gif"
```

FIGURE 8.15

This code displays the logo.gif graphic as the background for the page.

The other event is HTML Body Attributes, which defines the attributes of the body text on the page. Click the page name in the InfoList Objects List, and then select HTML Body Attributes. Enter the HTML code in quotes in the Programmer's Pane.

HTML in Forms

Domino automatically converts the data in the documents to HTML on-the-fly. To add HTML directly on the form used to create the documents, enable the **Treat Document Contents as HTML** option on the **Defaults** tab of the Form Properties box (see Figure 8.16).

FIGURE 8.16

To have all field content (including hidden fields) converted to HTML, select Generate HTML for All Fields, and deselect Treat Document Contents as HTML. This is important when you have calculations based on hidden fields because the result doesn't display correctly on the Web otherwise.

If you choose not to use the Treat Document Contents as HTML property for the form, you can add a $$HTMLHead field to the form to pass HTML information such as Meta tags and JavaScript to the Head tag Domino assigns each document for the Web. Although the field can be of any data type, we recommend a hidden computed-for-display text field. Meta tags are frequently used to note keywords for Web search engines, to help Web users find your site if it meets their search criteria. A $$HTMLHead field might use the following formula to create a Meta tag for a furniture catalog Web site:

```
"<meta name = \"keyword\" content = \"furniture\">"
```

Small portions of HTML code can be entered or pasted on the form. Select the text and choose **Text, Pass-Thru HTML** from the menu to mark the text as HTML. Or create a Named Style called HTML and apply it to the text.

In form design, the HTML Head Content event defines the <HEAD> tag attributes Domino assigns to Web documents. Click the name of the form from the InfoList Objects list, and then select HTML Head Attributes. In the Programmer's Pane, write the HTML code. For example, to specify a graphic file such as your logo to use as a form background, write

```
"BACKGROUND=/images/logo.gif"
```

To attach HTML formatting attributes to editable fields, use the HTML Attributes field event. Click the field you want to format in the InfoList Objects list and select HTML Attributes from the event list. Write the HTML code in quotes in the Programmer's Pane (see Figure 8.17). To set the maximum size of a field, you might write

```
"SIZE=30 MAXLENGTH=120"
```

SIZE limits the width of the field to 30 characters. MAXLENGTH limits the total number of characters to 120.

FIGURE 8.17

Using the HTML Attributes event for the field, you can define its length and width, which differs from the unlimited field length available to all Notes clients.

When working with a rich text field, you use ROWS and COLS to set how many rows long and columns wide the field can be:

```
"ROWS=10 COLS=25"
```

You can also set how many items of a keywords field can show before a scrollbar appears. The following code allows a maximum of two rows before the scrollbar shows:

```
"ROWS=2"
```

If the form you are creating is intended to collect information from the Web user, create a field called $$Return. When the user submits the form, Domino returns a URL that takes them to another Web page, displays a personalized message, or runs a CGI script to execute a program. Without the $$Return field, the user only receives the message Form Processed after clicking the **Submit** button. To include a personalized message, create a formula for the $$Return field (see Figure 8.18), such as this one, which thanks the user:

```
@Return("<H2>Thank you, " + Name + ". A confirmation
➥email will be on its way to you shortly.</H2>")
```

The <H2> and </H2> assign and end the HTML heading style H2. This sets the type as a larger, bold font (see Figure 8.19).

FIGURE 8.18

The @Return formula for the $$Return field as it is entered in the Programmer's Pane.

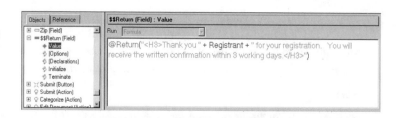

FIGURE 8.19

This is the personalized message received by the Web user after submitting a registration form.

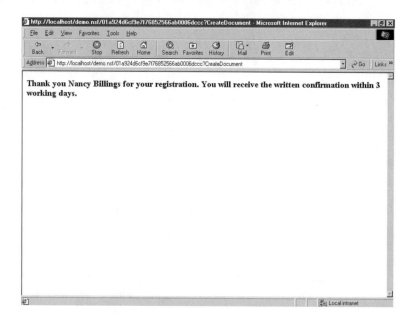

HTML Fields

Making a form that works both for Web users and Notes clients can be time consuming. One method is to use a field named HTML on the form, which passes the HTML directly to the browser. This is very cool because with the inclusion of this field, Domino ignores all other fields in the document and passes only the contents of the HTML field to the browser.

The HTML field can be computed or editable, although the latter is the better choice if you need to modify the HTML for each document instead of creating it once for the form. You use HTML code as the field value or default value. If the field value is less than 15K, use a text field; use a rich text field for more.

8

To control the HTML from the form, enter the HTML code directly in the Programmer's Pane as the value or default value for the field. That code will be the same for every document. To have the code vary from document to document, create each document from the form and enter the HTML code for that document in the editable HTML field.

This solution is similar to the form property Treat Documents as HTML, except that it converts only the HTML field value to HTML. Web clients see only the HTML information. The other fields are available to Notes clients who open documents created with the form.

Tip

If you have existing HTML documents that you want to pass to Web users in their entirety and unchanged, create a form that contains a text or rich text field called HTML. If the HTML field is rich text, you need to also include at least one other text field so the document can appear in a view because rich text fields do not appear in view columns. The form should also include other fields, as many (and of whatever data types) as you want. Next, create documents based on the form by pasting or importing your HTML documents in the HTML field of each new document, and save the new documents. The result of importing and pasting is the same, but importing a file is more convenient because you don't have to open the file first, select its contents, copy it to the clipboard, and then switch back to Notes and paste. Rather, you just pick the file from a list in a dialog box and click the import button.

Domino and the Web

When you are designing applications specifically for the Web or applications that serve both Notes clients and Web clients, you need to know that not all features of Domino translate or work well on the Web. We have highlighted some of those features here, but for a complete list, search the Designer Help file for "Web, Unsupported."

As you work through this book, you will learn about lots of tools and issues regarding Domino and the Web. For example, you will learn about Domino URLs and how to use CGI scripts as well as JavaScript and frames. Here, we want to take a brief look at some of the Domino attributes that don't translate well to the Web or don't appear exactly as they do in Notes. Remembering this list, found in Table 8.1, will be helpful to you as you develop applications that will be accessed by Web browsers.

Table 8.1   Notes Features Attributes that Don't Work on the Web

Attribute	Level of Support on Web
ActiveX, OLE Objects	Displayed, but edits not saved.
Attachments	Supported if not created with API.
Buttons	Not supported on the form except for first one, which is the submit button. Action buttons are supported (except for six system actions and actions scripted with LotusScript).
Collapsible Sections	Sections appear, but section borders and lines do not.
Font (typeface)	Text is displayed with the user's Web browser default font.
Font Size	The font size is mapped to one of eight HTML font sizes.
Font Styles	All are supported except shadow, emboss, and extrude.
Graphics	Supports up to 256-color bitmaps, platform-independent.
Hotspots	Supported except for text pop-ups.
Indents and Outdents	Not supported.
Interline Spacing	Not supported.
Layout Regions	Not supported.
Named Styles	Carries only the font size for mapping.
Paragraph Alignment	Left, Center, and Right are supported. Full Justification and No Wrap are not.
Rich Text formatting	All formatting disappears in rich text fields when they are edited on the Web and then submitted.
Spaces, extra	Supported if you use monospaced fonts.
Tables	Supported, but empty cells aren't displayed. If there is a border assigned to the top left cell, a border is applied to the entire table. All table borders are double lines.
Tabs	Not supported.

Summary

Framesets are a design element that enables you to divide the screen into 2–4 separate areas called frames. In each frame, a different page, document, view, database, or Web page can appear. You specify the size of each frame within the frame set, the type of borders, whether the borders are user-adjustable, and what the target frame is for any links or jumps from the current frame.

Pages, which can appear in frames, are design elements similar to forms, except that they have no fields and users can't create documents from them. They exist to display information only. However, pages can contain links to other pages, framesets, databases, views, documents, and URLs.

HTML code puts formatting instructions directly into pages and forms, without having Domino translate it. It provides specific control for the appearance of applications that are used on the Web.

Q&A

Q In some of the older databases we have from R4.5, our company used the About Database document as the home page for the databases that make up our Web site. Do I need to convert all those old databases?

A No, you can still launch the database with the About Database document as the home page and use links from there to navigate to the rest of the application.

Q Our old Web application has HTML code to create frames. Should I keep that or replace it with framesets?

A If you want to change the appearance of the frames or specify different contents, you'll find it's easier with framesets. The first time you need to make a change in the frame setup in the application, change over to framesets for your application. Then your Notes users will also see the frames.

Q When I preview my new frameset in Internet Explorer, the frame that contains my Domino view also displays previous, next, expand, collapse, and search icons. Where did that come from?

A Those are automatically added when you use a Domino server to show Web pages. These elements (next, expand, and so forth) help users to navigate a Domino view displaying in a Web browser.

Workshop

In today's workshop, you'll continue to work in the Proposed Titles database. This is an internal database, designed for use by Notes clients. Although it needs to be functional, there's no reason not to make it easy to use as well—not to mention good looking. The tasks you will practice include

- Creating a home page
- Designing a frameset

- Specifying contents for a frameset
- Adding some HTML code to pages and forms

Create a Home Page

Create a home page for the database. Name it Home Page, with an alias of Home. Add a logo, if you want to, or another graphic. Color the background, or add a graphic there. Make sure you leave some room to add an outline later.

Add links to the views in your database so you can open them from the Home Page. You can also include folders.

Research some Web sites that have information on or sell computer books. You might also want to include some software company sites in your research. Narrow down your choices to three or four. On the Home Page, add some URL links to those Web sites.

Keep in mind as you design the Home Page that this page will appear in a frameset. It will continue to display as the other frames around it change.

Create a Page

Create a second page, called Banner, that has the name of the database. Under the database title, enter **Make suggestions for titles you'd like to see us publish and comment on the suggestions of others.** Again, you are in control of the page appearance. Make it look right—it's going to be at the top of the frameset.

Create a Frameset

Create a frameset and call it Main. The frameset needs to have three frames. One will hold the Home Page, one the Banner, and the third the Books\By Title view. The frame that holds the view should be the target frame for the Home Page frame.

Name each frame. Set the look of the frameset to suit yourself. Then test it. You might need to adjust your views or pages or frames after you see how it looks.

Add HTML

Although most of the users will be using this database from a Notes client, a few will use browsers. There are some elements that don't translate well to browsers. You might want to add HTML tags to control the size of the headings on your pages (to make them the same size on each page) or add a horizontal rule (<hr>).

In the forms, set size limits on the comment fields, such as RRespComments in the Response form and CCommentBody on the Comments form.

View the database from a browser, or from more than one browser if you have more than one. Again, you might have to adjust it. If you're worried that the codes show in Notes, don't; we will learn how to hide paragraphs on Day 9, "Forms on Steroids: Increase Form Performance."

The accompanying CD contains the following sample file for today's lesson. Locate these files in the folder called Day8:PTDay8.nsf, the Proposed Titles database at the end of Day 8.

8

DAY **9**

Forms on Steroids: Increase Form Performance

Forms are the foundation of your application. It is in the forms that you determine what information you are going to collect and display in your application. But forms go beyond fields and enhancing the appearance of your data; forms can display *different* information to *different* sets of users.

On this day, you learn how to

- Inherit data from a parent document
- Create profile forms using reserved and internal fields
- Hide objects and design elements
- Set document launch options
- Limit who can edit sections
- Add computed text to your form
- Use the Editor applet with Web forms

Inherit Information

As you learned in Day 2, "Forms 101: The Essentials of Form Design," there are three types of forms: Document, Response, and Response-to-Response. The relationship between the documents created with these types of forms is one of parent-child-descendant. The *document* form creates parent documents, *responses* are the child documents, and *response-to-response* documents are the descendants.

Each response and response-to-response document keeps information about the parent document to which it's responding (see the section "Internal and Reserved Fields" later in this day). Because of this relationship, you can create fields and formulas that pull information from the parent document into the response document or response-to-response document—the document *inherits* the information from the parent document.

This inheritance does not happen automatically, nor does it happen by accident. For each response or response-to-response form you create, you must enable inheritance in the Form Properties box. On the Defaults tab (see Figure 9.1), select the option **Formulas inherit values from selected document**.

FIGURE 9.1

When you select Inherit Entire Selected Document into Rich Text Field, the entire contents of the parent document are incorporated into the response document. Selecting Formulas Inherit Values from Selected Document pulls only desired information into the response document.

Inheritance occurs only when you select or open a document (the *source*) and then create a document that has inheritance enabled (the *target*). You don't have to use response documents to inherit information; inheritance can also occur between main documents—as long as inheritance is enabled and there is a valid source document.

After you enable inheritance, you need to create or specify the fields that are to inherit the information from the parent document. These fields need to be either editable or computed when composed fields. Use an *editable* field when you want the default value to be one that's inherited but you want the user to have the option to change that information. The inherited information is not necessarily saved in this case. Use a *computed when composed* field when you want inheritance to occur only once—when the document is created. The inherited information is stored in the document when the document is saved. The user cannot change this data.

The formula for a field that inherits data should reference the name of the original field. We recommend that you use the same field name in both the original and the inheriting document, although that is not required—it just makes writing formulas easier. Where we don't use the same name, we incorporate the name of the original field into the new field name, such as *ResponseTitle* for a field that inherits data from the Title field on the parent document.

For example, let's say a parent document has a *Subject* field. When the user creates a response, you want the subject from the main document to appear as the subject of the response document. To make this happen, enable inheritance for the response form. Then create a field called *Subject*. Make the subject field a text field that is computed when composed. The formula for the field is Subject. If you're not sure how this works, look at your mail database. When someone sends you a memo and you reply, the subject from the first memo becomes the subject (with *RE:* preceding it) of the reply memo (see Figure 9.2).

FIGURE 9.2

The subject of this reply is the same as the subject of the message to which it's responding, except for the Re: *that precedes it.*

Inherited subject

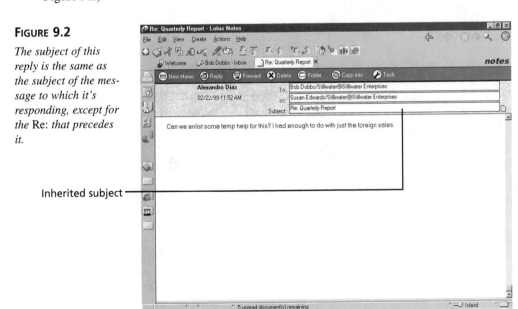

In applications where you set up response and response-to-response forms, you can create views that make it easy to differentiate between the parent, children, and descendants (see Day 10, "Advanced Views").

Users might have more difficulty finding related documents when you use a document form to set up inheritance from another document form because the resulting documents don't display a hierarchy. To help the users find the related document, create a link to it. To do this, create a rich text field to display a document link in the form that is to inherit information. Open the Form Properties box and click the **Defaults** tab. In the On Create field, enable the Inherit Entire Selected Document into Rich Text Field option (see Figure 9.3). From the drop-down list, select the name of the rich text field you created to hold the link, and then choose **Link** from the As drop-down list. If you want, you can also select the On Open option called Show Context Pane and then choose **DocLink**.

FIGURE 9.3

To provide the user with information about the parent document, incorporate the entire contents of the parent into the new document or create a document link to the parent.

The advantage of creating the link is that you save disk space. Instead of including the full contents of the parent document in the inheritance-enabled document, only a pointer to the parent document is saved. In addition to saving space, you save the users time by making the reference to the parent document available.

Determine What Happens When Documents Open

What happens when a user creates or opens a document depends on two sets of options. One set is the Auto Launch setting on the Launch tab of the Form Properties box. The Auto Launch options determine what opens first when you open the document that was created using the form. These choices include the first attachment, the first document link, the first OLE object, a URL, images, the audio recorder, media clips, drawings, charts, and more. The default option is None.

The other set includes the On Open options you set on the Default tab of the Form Properties box for the form used to create the document (see Figure 9.4).

FIGURE 9.4

Make information collection documents always ready for data entry by having them open in edit mode.

In some circumstances, you might want documents such as surveys, profiles, or client information sheets to always open in edit mode—ready to fill in. When you create the form for those documents, open the Form Properties box and select the **Defaults** tab. Under On Open, enable **Automatically Enable Edit Mode**.

The other On Open option is Show Context Pane. Two choices are presented when this option is selected: Parent or Doclink. When you enable the Show Context Pane option and select **Parent**, the users see two panes in the document window—one is the document they are creating, and the other is the parent document (see Figure 9.5). This is only useful when the document being opened is a response or response-to-response document because the users can refer to the original document while creating a response.

An alternative to having the entire contents of the parent document display in the context pane is to display only a document link to the parent document. The users click the document link icon to open the parent document if it's not already displayed. To use this option, select Doclink when you enable Show Context Pane.

You can also control the opening of items related to the document at the time the document is opened. These items can include attachments, document links, embedded objects, URLs, Lotus Freelance or Microsoft PowerPoint presentations, Image documents, media clips, documents, spreadsheets, video clips, and more.

You add an attachment to a form the same way you do in a document (choose **File, Attach** on the menu). The attachment is available in every document based on that form. For example, you can attach a set of rules related to the contents of the document, a set of codes used to assign numbers or names to items in the document, or a glossary of terms. To have the attachment automatically launch when users open the document, click the **Launch** tab on the Form Properties box (see Figure 9.6) and select **First Attachment** from the Auto Launch drop-down list. Don't mistake this to mean that the attachment launches when you create a new document—that doesn't usually happen unless the attachment has a "launch when" choice. Instead, the attachment launches when the user opens an existing document.

FIGURE 9.5

This newly created response document displays a context pane with the contents of the parent document.

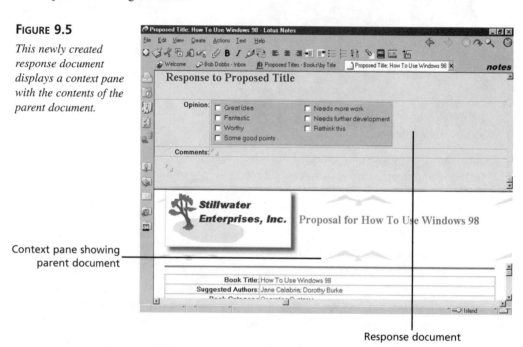

Context pane showing parent document

Response document

Launching a document link works in the same way. Create the link in the form and then select **First Document Link** from the Auto Launch list.

For items such as presentations, video clips, media clips, and documents, you select the object you want to automatically launch from the Auto Launch list. A set of options appears:

- **Launch Object in Place**—Enables the user to use the object directly from Notes instead of having to launch the object's application and then switch to that application. The Notes menu adjusts to the corresponding application.

- **Present document as modal dialog**—Displays a dialog box when the user returns from the object. The form appears in the dialog box. If this option isn't selected, the form appears full pane when the user returns from the launched object.

- **Create Object in Field**—Specifies where you want the object stored. Your selections include None, First Rich Text Field, and the names of any rich text fields that already exist in the form.

- **Launch When**—Specifies that the object is to launch when the user is Creating, Editing, or Reading the document. You can choose one, two, or all options.

- **Hide When**—Tells Notes when to hide the object—when the user opens the document to create it, opens the document to edit it, opens the document to read it, closes the document after creating it, or closes the document after editing it. Some of the choices might be unavailable, depending on the Launch When option. You can select more than one option.

9

FIGURE 9.6

Select the type of item you want automatically launched when the user opens a document. When necessary, specify whether it launches in Notes or in its related application, in which field the object is stored, when the object is launched, and when it is to be hidden.

As you will learn on Day 17, "Embed Objects in Your Applications," you can embed objects such as Excel spreadsheets or charts, in your forms. These can also be automatically launched when the document is created or opened, if you select **First OLE Object** from the Auto Launch drop-down list on the Launch tab of the Form Properties box.

Automatically launching a URL when a document opens is a little different from the other options on the Auto Launch list. You must create a text field named URL in the form (there can be only one auto launch URL field per form). From the Auto Launch list on the Launch tab of the Form Properties box, select **URL**. The user who creates the document enters the URL to be launched in the URL field. The URL automatically launches when users open the document.

There is one more set of launch options that appear on the Launch tab. To always have a form launch in a particular frame in a certain frameset, you specify the name of the Frameset and the Frame in the Auto Frame options.

Create a Profile

In a discussion database, the User Profile document stores specific information about users of the database (see Figure 9.7). Profile documents store user or database values to which your application needs quick access. The information in profile documents is cached whenever the database is open.

FIGURE 9.7

This simple User Profile collects information on the user's name, platform, email address, and areas of interest.

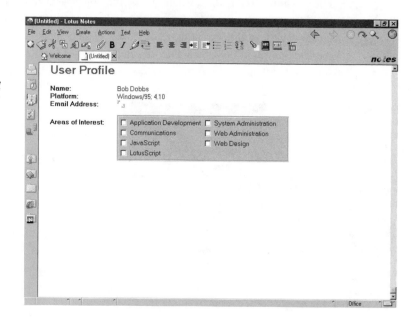

Although profile documents resemble other documents in the database, they do not display in views and aren't included in the count of documents in the database. Users can't use the Create menu to create a profile document. Instead, the application developer must provide an action or agent that uses an @Command formula or LotusScript to create or edit the Profile document.

A database can have one or multiple Profile documents, provided they match the key the designer specifies. The number of profile documents in a database depends on the design—only one profile based on a specific form can exist for each user of a database. Alternately, one profile can exist for the database if the form is available to all users (the person creating a profile document that is available to all users must have at least Author access in the database ACL). A single profile document can store settings that apply to all the documents in the database, such as a job order number variable. As each new document is created, Domino checks the profile document for the settings stored there, so the job order number for each document is unique. An example of a multiple profile document database might be a specialized discussion database in which each user has his own profile that governs who the user can answer as well as the appearance of the answer.

To use profile documents in your application, you need to create a form or use an existing form to act as the basis for the profile. Any form will do because it isn't the form itself that marks the document as a profile, but rather how documents created from the form are displayed and how values are exchanged. In the Form Properties box, deselect **Include in Menu** on the **Basics** tab. Add the fields that are to hold the information you need for the profile, and then save the form. Do not include the form in any view.

For the application, you create a button, action, or agent that uses @Command([EditProfile]) in a formula to create or retrieve a document (you'll learn more about actions, buttons, and agents on Day 11, "Help the User: Design Interface Enhancements," and Day 14, "The Not So Secret Agents"). The action or agent might be available from the menu; or, you can add an action button to a view or form or a hotspot button to a form.

For example, to create the User Profile for the current user, the formula for the agent or button is written as:

```
@Command([EditProfile]; "Author Profile"; @UserName)
```

The form name is a required argument, but the name of the user is optional. You only need it where you have to specify a profile that is specific to that user. When the button, action, or agent is activated, it opens the specified profile document in edit mode or creates the profile document if none exists.

To retrieve field values from a profile document, use the @GetProfileField(*profilename*; *fieldname*; *username*) function. This function not only retrieves the field value, but also caches it for the remainder of the session. The *profilename* argument is the name of the profile document. The *fieldname* argument is the name of the field that contains the value you are trying to retrieve. The *username* argument is optional. Make it the name of the user associated with the profile document, the name of a field that contains that information, or the @UserName function to capture the name of the current user.

For example, in a discussion database, the User Profile document contains a list of the user's areas of interest in the Interest field. To get the contents of that field for the user Robert Jeffers when he is the author of the current document, you write a formula such as this:

```
@GetProfileField("User Profile"; "Interest"; @UserName)
```

To set field values in the profile document, use the @SetProfileField(*profilename*; *fieldname*; *value*; *username*) function. The *profilename* argument is the name of the profile document that has the field you want to access (the *formname* used in the [EditProfile] command). The *fieldname* is the name of the field you want to change. The *value* argument is the value to which you want to set the field. The *username* argument is optional; it is the name of the user associated with the profile document.

One reason for setting a profile field value is to capture the type of platform being used by the current user and add that information to that user's profile. For example, the following formula sets the value of the PlatformType field to the platform being used:

```
@SetProfileField("User Profile"; "PlatformType"; @Platform; @UserName)
```

Profile documents can't be deleted using an @function. You must use LotusScript to delete a profile document.

Hide Objects

Making forms easy to use and visually pleasing is an important part of form design. Design, at times, can seem incompatible with your need to collect information and make the form functional. When you design a form for data entry, you want the fields to line up for easy tabbing and entry, but that spreads the information out too much for comfortable reading. The solution is to create a computed for display field that brings all that information together. Hide the data entry fields when the document is read, and hide the display field when the document is being edited.

Another reason to hide fields and text is to display only what the user needs at a given time. Users enter or select a particular area of interest in a field, and as a result the fields and text displayed after that choice relate specifically to that subject. For example, a survey on hobbies has a list of hobbies. When someone chooses sports, a field and static text appear, requesting that the user select the particular sports in which he is interested (see Figure 9.8). Another person might select painting, and then is requested to select the type of medium she uses (see Figure 9.9). The sports fan doesn't see any information about painting, and the painter doesn't see anything about sports.

Hide items from view by using the Hide-When properties of the item. Text and fields are hidden by paragraphs (defined by the ending carriage return). That means you can't hide the first part of a sentence and leave the remainder visible. Although you usually select the text or fields before you hide them, everything else in the paragraph is also hidden at the same time.

FIGURE 9.8

When the hobbyist chooses sports, only fields and text relating to sports appear.

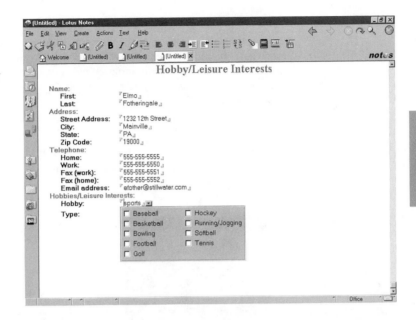

9

FIGURE 9.9

When the hobbyist chooses painting, she sees only text and fields relating to painting.

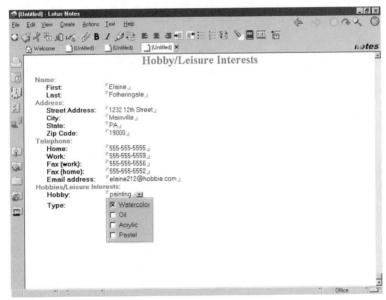

Tip

You can't hide one item and not hide another item on the same line (in the same paragraph). However, you can hide one cell in a row of a table while the others remain visible. You can even hide one paragraph in a cell and leave visible the other paragraphs in the cell. Consider reformatting your form with tables to hide only part of one line.

When you open the Field or Text Properties box, click the **Paragraph Hide When** tab (see Figure 9.10). Table 9.1 gives you an overview of the options on the Paragraph Hide When tab.

FIGURE 9.10

When you select a hide-when option, the selected item is visible at any other time.

Table 9.1 Paragraph Hide-When Options

Option	Use to make the text/fields:
Hide paragraph from:	
Notes R4.6 or later	Invisible to Notes clients
Web Browsers	Invisible to Web clients
	(These two choices hide the paragraph regardless of any options selected below.)
Hide paragraph when document is:	
Previewed for reading	Invisible when a user opens the Preview Pane to read that document
Opened for reading	Invisible when a user opens the document to read it
Printed	Invisible when the document is printed
Previewed for editing	Invisible when a user opens the Preview Pane to edit that document
Opened for editing	Invisible when a user creates or edits the document

Option	Use to make the text/fields:
Copied to the clipboard	Impossible to be cut or copied to the clipboard (Select as many of the above options as needed.)
Hide paragraph if formula is true	Invisible if the formula in the formula window evaluates as true

Tip

You can't access hidden text to edit it. However, if the text was hidden by selecting Notes R4.6 or later to hide it from Notes clients, you can choose **View, Show, Hidden from Notes** to view and edit the text from a Notes workstation.

Hide-when formulas resemble @If functions, except you use only the first argument and not the entire @function. Figure 9.11 shows the Field Properties box, showing the formula that hides all but the sports-related fields and text when Sports is chosen as the hobby.

FIGURE 9.11

In creating the hide-when formula, you have to think in negatives. Test your formula to be sure you wrote it correctly.

Tip

When you plan to hide or display fields based on the selection made in a keywords field, enable the **Refresh Fields on Keywords Change** option that appears on the Control tab of the Field Properties box. Otherwise, your hidden fields and text won't appear immediately after a selection is made in the keywords field.

Hide-when properties can be applied to many form features—layout regions, sections, actions, buttons, pictures, embedded objects, and more. You must select the item and then open the Paragraph Hide When tab of the Properties box to set the options.

Hide Forms and Other Design Elements

Hiding isn't limited to objects on forms. Forms, views, navigators, folders, subforms, and agents can all be hidden. This is particularly useful when you have Notes and Web clients. You can have two versions of a design element, one for each environment, either of which you can hide when the client is from the other environment. Give both elements the same name or alias. Domino then displays the proper version of the element, based on the client's system.

For example, you have one form for use by the Web client and another for your Notes clients. The Notes form has a layout region; the Web form uses a table instead because layout regions aren't supported, as you learn on Day 12, "Beautify Your Application." Both forms are named "Employee Application." The Web clients can't see the Notes form (with different aliases), but the same fields are available because they were format-ted as a table. The Notes clients get the more visually appealing layout region, but they don't see the extra HTML codes used on the Web form.

To hide a design element, view the list of design elements for the database by displaying the Design Pane or choosing **View, Design** from the menu. Select the type of design ele-ment you want to hide (agents, folders, forms, navigators, pages, subforms, views). Then select the name of the particular element you want to hide. To hide a form, select Forms from the Design Pane and then select the form you want to hide.

Choose **Design, Design Properties** (or **Agent, Agent Properties** for agents) to open the Design Document Properties box, and select the Design tab (see Figure 9.12).

FIGURE 9.12

In the Design Document Properties box, choose the appro-priate option to hide the design element based on the user's environment.

Under Hide Design Element From, select **Web Browsers** if the element is designed for Notes clients or **Notes R4.6 or later clients** if the element is designed for Web clients.

Caution   Your server won't be able to access documents in hidden views or forms using URL commands. Hidden design elements are also hidden from the server.

When the purpose of hiding a design element is to keep all users from seeing it but still have it accessible for background processes, don't use the Hide design element options. Instead, put parentheses around the name of the element in the element's Properties box. For example, if you create a view to use for your lookup formulas (see Day 13, "Put on Your Propeller Beanie: Advanced Formulas"), you don't want it to be available to your users. In the View Properties box, write the name of the view in parentheses (see Figure 9.13).

FIGURE 9.13

In the Properties box, write the element's name with parentheses around it to hide it.

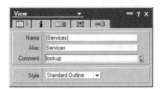

Increase Section Performance

Sections enable you to group portions of a form under a single heading and only display the heading when the section is collapsed. The user can then expand the section by clicking the heading. You learned to create sections on Day 5, "Forms 102: Enhance Form Appearance and Design."

In defining a section, you determine whether the section is collapsed or expanded when a document is previewed, read, edited, or printed.

You can also specify when the section is viewed. Using hide-when options, you can hide the section from Notes clients or Web clients when the document is previewed, read, edited, printed, or copied (see the previous section, "Hide Objects"). By creating hide-when formulas, you set more specific parameters on when the section is visible—even using roles to limit who sees the section.

But regardless of whether the section is visible, there are times when you want to restrict who has access to the section. In that case, you need to create an access-controlled section.

Access controlled sections are useful in workflow applications, where you restrict who can edit or sign parts of a document. You learned about signing, or *signatures*, on Day 7, "Sleep Soundly: Secure Your Application."

If a document requires more than one approval signature, create a different section for each required signature. Then you can define access to each section by a user role. It might even help to add text that notes who can have access, for example, "For Managers Only."

As with the creation of a standard section, you start by selecting the text, fields, and other elements that you want to include in the section. Then you choose **Create, Section, Controlled Access** from the menu.

The text in the first line of the section automatically becomes the section title. You can change that in the Form Section Properties box (choose **Section, Section Properties** from the menu to open it). In the Title Text box (see Figure 9.14), delete the current text (if you don't want to use that as the title) and then type the title you want to appear on the section. Unless you want to use the default field name assigned to the section, change the name in the Section Field Name box. As with a standard section, you can also set a border style and color.

FIGURE 9.14

To be able to specify the section in formulas, enter a field name for the access-controlled section in the Form Section Properties box.

To define who has access to the section, determine who the editors of the section are. Start by clicking the **Formula** tab of the Form Section Properties box (see Figure 9.15). If you select **Editable** as the type, the document creator determines who the editors of the section are. When you select **Computed**, **Computed when composed**, or **Computed for display**, you define the editors with a formula that you type in the Access Formula box (you can create a formula for an editable field, to set a default value).

An access formula can be the name of the document author:

```
@UserName
```

FIGURE 9.15

This formula defines editors as any user that has the Managers user role in the Access Control List.

Or, it might be a list of names or a user role, or evaluate to a username or a text list of names. Names need to be enclosed in quotes and separated by colons (:) when you list more than one:

```
"Jane Calabria/Stillwater" : "Dorothy Burke/Stillwater"
```

User roles need to be enclosed in square brackets and in quotes, as you see in Figure 9.15.

A user that you specify as an editor must have at least editor access to the database to edit the section. All users not specified as section editors, no matter what their ACL level, can be no more than readers of the section. Also, if a user is listed in an Author field in the document, but not in the section editor list, that user cannot edit the section.

One way to define a list of editors is to create a field in advance of the section and write a formula that calculates the list of editors. The formula can evaluate to the user's name, use a lookup formula to find the name from a view (see Day 13), use the value of another field that contains approver's names, or specify a group name or role from the ACL. The section editor formula is then the name of that field.

To create a permanent list of editors, use a computed when composed section so the list is frozen at the time the document is created.

Caution
When you are testing the local copy of the database during the design phase, it might appear that your section restrictions don't work. Section restrictions are only available when you are connected to a server.

If the section field is editable, the creator of the document defines who the editors are by selecting the section and then choosing **Section, Define Editors** (only available when the document is being edited). The Edit Section dialog box appears (see Figure 9.16). The creator selects **All Users** or **Only the Following Users**. With the latter selected, the creator clicks **Add** and selects a user from an address dialog box. Repeat for each user you want to add. Choosing **OK** closes the dialog box.

9

FIGURE 9.16

FIGURE **9.16**

If the document cre-ator doesn't want to grant editor access to all users, he must select the names of those who can edit the controlled-access sec-tion.

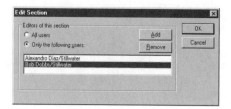

Select the Expand/Collapse tab on the Form Section Properties box to define how the section appears to editors and non-editors. Choose **For Editors** from the drop-down list (see Figure 9.17), and determine under what conditions the section is expanded or col-lapsed. You can select Auto Expand, Auto Collapse, or Don't Auto Expand or Collapse for each document condition (Previewed, Opened for Reading, Opened for Editing, and Printed). Then select For Non-Editors and do the same for those users without editor access to the section. When specifying options for non-editors, you also have the option to Hide Title When Expanded so that the title disappears when the section opens.

FIGURE **9.17**

When you select For Editors, you specify that the section be auto-expanded when previewed, read, edit-ed, or printed.

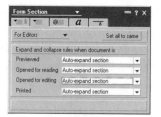

Create Computed Text

In creating forms for your Web or Notes applications, you might decide you want to use dynamic text—text that changes based on specified conditions. To do this, you need to generate text that is based on formula results. You use the formula to specify the condi-tions under which the text appears. Then you want to create computed text.

To add computed text, place the cursor where the text is to appear in the form and then choose **Create, Computed Text** from the menu. The text **<Computed Value>** appears at your cursor location and the Computed Text Properties box opens. All the Computed Text properties involve adding text attributes, HTML, or hiding the text.

In the Programmer's Pane, enter a formula that evaluates to the text you want to appear. For example, you might want a line of text to act as a reminder to the user, based on the user's role in the Access Control List. For example, if the user is a manager, you want to remind him to complete the Approval section of the form; if not, you don't want the reminder text to appear. The formula in that case might be

```
@If(@IsMember("[Manager]"; @UserRoles);
"Please fill in all the information required in the
Approval section"; "")
```

Although you, the application developer, can add computed text to a form in the design mode, a user can also add computed text to a document's rich text field when the document is in edit mode.

Work with Internal and Reserved Fields

There are some fields that Notes automatically adds to forms or reserves for special uses. As a developer, you can make use of these fields to extract information or have specific actions take place.

Internal Fields

Not all the fields in documents are created by developers. Some are generated by Notes for document identification and control. The names of most of these internal fields begin with a dollar sign ($). Although you can't assign these names to fields you create, you can use the information stored in these internal fields when you build formulas (see Table 9.2 for a partial list of these internal fields).

Caution

> Our Tech Editor cautions that the mail and calendar and directories have many fields that are used and special to them. Do not use those names for your own fields. Also, if you are building mail enabled applications, see the Domino 5 Designer Help documents "Predefined Fields with Built-In Functionality" and "Checking Field Values in a Document."

Table 9.2 Internal Fields—A Partial List

Field Name	Description
$File	Shows an entry for each attachment in a document (a single attachment might create multiple $File entries)
FolderOptions	Puts new documents in folders
Form	Shows which form was used to create the document or the one with which it was most recently saved

continues

Table 9.2 continued

Field Name	Description
$FormUsers	Results of Compose Access set on a form
$Links	Shows an entry for each link in a document
PostedDate	Indicates that a document was mailed and displays the date and time it was mailed
$Readers	Lists authorized readers if document has a reader access list
$Ref	Appears on response forms and contains the document ID number of the parent document
$Revisions	Lists the date and time of each editing session since the first time the document was saved
$Title	The name of the form, if a form has been stored in the document (in which case the document can also have $Info, $Body, and $WindowTitle fields)
$UpdatedBy	List of all users who have modified the document (doesn't appear on an anonymous form)
$VersionOpt	Controls version tracking for documents

To see what internal fields are stored in a document, right-click on a document in a view and select **Document Properties** from the drop-down list. Select the **Fields** tab (see Figure 9.18). When you click the field name, the right side of the properties box provides information about the field and its contents.

FIGURE 9.18

By selecting the $UpdatedBy field, you see that the form was last updated by Bob Dobbs.

 Caution

Do not use internal field names when defining fields on your forms, or you might change the functionality of the form. Safer yet, totally avoid using dollar signs ($) at the start of field names. Also, don't change the values of the internal fields, or you might corrupt documents—and possibly the database.

Some of the @Functions already use the information stored in internal fields—such as @IsResponseDoc, which refers to the $Ref field, or @Modified, which uses the information in the $Revisions field.

You can use these internal fields in your formulas. For example, in a view selection formula to designate the form you want to include in the view, use the internal Form field:

```
SELECT Form = "Seminars"
```

Reserved Fields

Reserved fields use names that have predefined functions. You can create a field and give it one of these names, but if you try to use it for some other purpose, Notes might consider it an error.

Many of the reserved field names are used with mail-enabled forms such as SendTo, CopyTo, BlindCopyTo, DeliveryPriority, DeliveryReport, ReturnReceipt, MailFormat, MailOptions, SaveOptions, Sign, and Encrypt. We'll discuss these in depth on Day 15, "Incorporate Workflow."

Use the reserved field SecretEncryptionKeys to give users the option of encrypting a document without having to do it manually (see Day 7, where you learned about encryption).

Some other reserved fields you might find useful are

- **FolderOptions**—For putting new documents in folders
- **HTML**—To pass HTML directly to the server
- **$VersionOpt**—To control version tracking for documents
- **$$HTMLHead**—To pass HTML information to be hosted within the <HEAD> tag for a document
- **$$Return**—For use in sending messages to Web users after they submit a document

A full list of reserved fields is available in Designer Help.

Categorize Documents in a View

To categorize documents in a view, create a form that has a field with the reserved field name Categories. The Categories field can be text or keywords, computed or editable. An editable field must have a default value formula. Select **Allow Multiple Values** on the **Field Info** page of the Field Properties box to permit the user to select more than one category; if Categories is a keywords field, you might want to also select **Allow Values Not in List**.

When you create the view that shows the categories, create a categories column as your first column (as you learned on Day 6, "Take in the View: Create Views and Folders"). Make the column one character wide and don't enter a column title. On the Sorting page of the Column Properties box, select **Ascending** and **Categorized** (you'll learn more about these choices on Day 10). The formula for the column is simply the field name Categories.

You can create subcategories for your view if you enter them as keyword choices in the Categories field on your form. Keyword choices such as "Personnel\Health Benefits" and "Personnel\Vacation and Personal Days" appear as shown in Figure 9.19. The backslash (\) after the main entry denotes the subcategory name.

FIGURE 9.19

By using keywords choices for your Categories field that have backslashes (\) marking the subcategory text (such as "Personnel\Health Benefits"), you can create subcategories that display in your view.

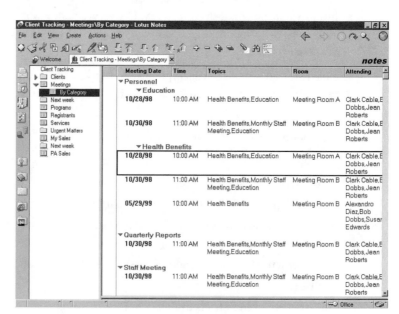

Note The All by Category view and the system Action "Categorize" show the user the existing list of all categories from all documents that contain the Categories field. It's also possible to add new categories. This is a convenient way to update documents one by one, but it is not the only way to categorize a view. You can categorize any view using any text field on any form, not just the Categories field.

See Different Versions of Documents in a View

After a document is saved, it's difficult to tell if it has been modified. When versioning is in effect, instead of the new version of the document replacing the original, the modified document can become a response document to the original, the original can become a response document to the new version, or the new version can become a sibling to the original document. That way, the user can see both the original and the modified document.

Note

When a document is a response to a main topic, it's considered a *child* of the *parent* or main topic document. A response-to-response document is a *descendent* of the parent document. Response documents and response-to-response documents are usually shown in a view as indented under the parent document. A *sibling* is equal to the main topic document and is not indented.

Versioning can be set on the **Form Info** tab of the Form Properties box (see Figure 9.20). The choices available include None, New Versions Become Responses, Prior Versions Become Responses, and New Versions Become Siblings.

FIGURE 9.20

Select a versioning option for the form that displays either the new or prior versions of the documents as responses.

Another method is to use a $VersionOpt field to control version tracking for documents. A $VersionOpt field must have a value between 0 and 6 and can be either a computed text field or an editable keywords field (computed for display and computed when composed types don't work). If you use a keywords field, do not select Allow Multiple Values or Allow Values Not in List. Use synonyms in your keywords choices ("Don't track versions | 0"). Add a formula for a computed field or a default value formula for an editable keywords field.

The $VersionOpt values evaluate as follows:

0—No version tracking.

1—New versions become responses if users choose File, Save as New Version when they save the document.

2—New versions automatically become responses when saved.

3—Prior versions become responses if users choose File, Save as New Version when they save the document.

4—Prior versions become responses when saved.

5—New versions become siblings when users choose File, Save as New Version when they save a document.

6—Newversions automatically become siblings when saved.

Add New Documents to Folders

To automatically put new documents into a folder without using an action, create a field with the reserved name FolderOptions. Define it as a computed text field (computed when composed and computed for display fields don't work), a computed numbers field, or an editable keywords field. Do not select Allow Multiple Values or Allow Values Not in List.

The FolderOptions field must contain a value of 1 (Prompt user to choose folder) or 2 (Save to current folder). If it has a value of 1, the user sees the Move to Folder dialog box (see Figure 9.21). Any folder that's open is selected by default. The user selects a folder and clicks **Add** to put the new document in a folder (clicking Cancel saves the document without putting it in a folder).

If the FolderOptions field has a value of 2, Notes automatically adds the document to the open folder.

When you're using a computed field, use a formula that evaluates to 1 or 2. For a keywords field, add synonyms after the text ("Select a Folder | 1" and "Save to Open Folder | 2"). Set a default value formula that evaluates to 1 or 2.

Access Fields on Other Documents

When you have response documents that inherit values from their parent documents, use the unique document ID of the parent document (see Figure 9.22) to establish the link between the two documents as long as they are within the same database or a replica of that database.

FIGURE 9.21

The Move to Folder dialog box appears because the FolderOptions value is 1.

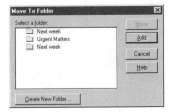

FIGURE 9.22

The Document Properties box shows the unique Document ID for the selected document. The first two lines are the unique ID (excluding OFF and ON); the rest of the characters make up other parts of the document's ID.

Note

Each document in Notes is assigned a unique 32-character combination of letters and numbers that identifies that document in all replicas of the database—the *Unique Document ID (UNID)*. If a document in your local replica of a database has the same unique ID number as a document in the server copy of the database, the two documents are replicas of each other. To see a selected document's unique ID, open the Document Properties box and select the Document IDs tab.

There are several functions that deal directly with the unique document ID. The @DocumentUniqueID function returns the 32-character hexadecimal number that uniquely identifies the document. Used in a field formula, @DocumentUniqueID creates a link to the current document; this link is lost if the document is mailed because it only works from within the original database.

Because the UNID is unique to each document, it's useful when you need to lookup documents. For example, a response document has an internal field, $Ref, that tracks the UNID for the parent document. To access fields on that parent document, you might want to create a hidden view of documents sorted by unique ID and then perform an @DbLookup function on that view to get your information (you'll learn more about @DbLookup on Day 13). In the hidden view, the first column should be the ID numbers converted to text, as shown in Figure 9.23, where you can plainly see the following column formula:

```
@Text(@DocumentUniqueID)
```

FIGURE 9.23

The view column formula calls for the unique document ID.

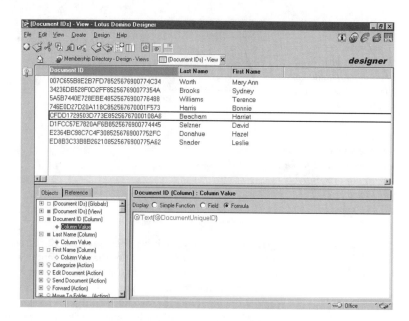

As part of your lookup formulas, you find the document in the view by its ID, but you request information from one of the other columns in the view or by specifying the name of the field whose value you want to retrieve.

Each response document has a $Ref internal field, which contains the unique ID of the parent document. Another reason a hidden view might show IDs is to provide a way of finding the parent document for a particular response, especially if you need to get updated information from the parent. Again, this involves lookup functions that are covered on Day 13. There are, of course, other methods of getting field information from a parent document, such as using the @GetDocField and @SetDocField functions mentioned below. With LotusScript you can directly open a document without using a lookup view if you know the UNID. Also, the @Command([OpenDocument]) function allows you to directly open a document if you know the UNID.

Another function that uses the unique document ID is @InheritedDocumentUniqueID; this returns the unique ID of the current document's parent document. Use this function only for response documents created with a form whose field values inherit from the selected document. When used in a field formula, this function creates a link to the current document.

The @GetDocField(*documentUNID*; *"fieldname"*) function returns the contents of the specified field on the document whose unique document ID is specified in the first argument of the formula.

Although a response document can inherit some field information from the parent, that information is gathered only when the response is composed. Any data that's changed in the parent document afterward is not updated in the response. However, you can use an @GetDocField formula. The @GetDocField function enables you to obtain the updated information even after the registration document is created.

For example, in the Proposed Titles database you've been building, the title of the book might change. That title might be carried over to the response documents, but the responses that have already been created do not reflect the change in title. Enter a formula similar to the following in the field where you want the book title to appear on the response document:

```
@GetDocField($Ref; "TBookTitle")
```

The reserved field $Ref contains the unique document ID of the parent document (the Proposed Title document), so the formula pulls the book title directly from that document.

The @SetDocField(*documentUNID*; *"fieldname"*; *newValue*) sets the value of the specified field on the document whose unique document ID is the first argument of the formula.

For example, in a club's Membership database, information on proposed new members is submitted in a Membership Information document. On that document is a hidden, editable keyword field (called Status) with four selections: Under Consideration, Accepted, Rejected, or Probationary. The default is Under Consideration. A response document, called Application, contains information not used for the membership directory that is needed for determining whether a new member meets the qualifications for the club. The results of the membership committee's decision are also recorded there. If the member is accepted, the committee secretary clicks the Approval button on the Application form. That automatically changes the Status field on the parent Member Information document to Accepted, and as a result the Member Information document appears in the Membership List. The formula for the Approval button might be

```
@SetDocField($Ref; "Status"; "Accepted")
```

Return Information with CGI Variables

When a Web user saves or opens a document, the Domino Web server collects information about the user using Common Gateway Interface (CGI) programs The collected information includes the user's name, the type of browsers used, and the user's IP address.

CGI variables are a set of standard variables that CGI programmers can use when writing scripts. CGI variables are the vehicle by which a Web client delivers information about itself to CGI scripts running on Web servers. If fields named for CGI variables appear in an input form, the Web browser automatically enters the values of those variables into the fields, and when the Web user submits the form, the included CGI variables are returned along with the user-entered data. Domino can then use the information when processing a form received from a Web user.

You can capture this information in a Web application by adding CGI variables to your application. Create CGI variable fields (they should be text fields) by naming them with the CGI variable name whose data you want to collect. Because the user submitting the form does not fill in these fields manually, you want to mark them hidden. To do so, open the Field Properties box for each such field. Mark the fields *Hide When Previewed for Editing* and *Hide when Opened for editing* so users cannot enter information into the field.

You also need to create an agent whose script contains a CGI variable as a DocumentContext property. You learn more about agents on Day 14. Talk with your Domino Administrator regarding CGI variables and agents. To learn more about using CGI, see *Special Edition Using CGI, Second Edition*, by Jeffry Dwight, Michael Erwin, and Robert Niles.

The CGI variable names that Domino recognizes includes those in Table 9.3.

Table 9.3 CGI Environment Variables

Variable	Description
Auth_Type	Returns the protocol-specific authentication method used to validate the user, but only if the server supports user authentication and the script is protected.
Content_Length	Returns the length of the content, if and as reported by the browser.
Content_Type	Returns the content type of the data for queries that have attached information, such as PUT and HTTP POST queries.
Gateway_Interface	Returns the server's CGI version number.
HTTP_Accept	Returns the MIME types that the client accepts.
HTTP_Referer	Returns the URL of the page from which the user opened this form.

9

Variable	Description
HTTP_User_Agent	Returns the name and version of the browser used to create this form.
HTTPS	Returns ON if the server is running the SSL protocol; otherwise returns OFF.
Path_Info	Returns the portion of a URL that trails the name of the HTTP server.
Path_Translated	Returns the same as Path_Info, but in terms of the physical pathname, not the virtual pathname.
Query-String	Returns the portion of a URL that trails the question mark.
Remote_Addr	Returns the IP address of the browser's host.
Remote_Host	Returns the hostname of the browser's host.
Remote_Ident	Returns the username of the browser's host.
Remote_User	Returns the name by which a Web user authenticated.
Request_Method	Returns the HTTP command the browser used to make the current request.
Script_name	Returns the virtual pathname of the script being executed.
Server_Name	Returns the server's hostname or IP address.
Server_port	Returns the server's HTTP port number.
Server_protocol	Returns the name and version number of the protocol being used by the browser to make this request.
Server_Software	Returns the name and version of the HTTP server program.
Server_URL	Returns the version of CGI with which the server complies.

Summary

In an application that uses a response hierarchy, it's important to carry information over from the main document (the parent) to the response to that document—and from the response to the response-to-response document. By enabling inheritance on a form, fields can pull data from the parent document. That makes the relationship between parent and response more evident and more useful.

Because some parts of forms, views, databases, and pages are geared to a specific audience or are only to appear in particular circumstances, the capability to hide objects and elements is important. Text, fields, pictures, sections, embedded objects, tables, and more can all be hidden based on whether the user is reading, editing, previewing, or printing a document. When a Web user opens a document, all the Web features are visible. When a Notes client opens a document, all the HTML code is invisible. The designer controls the circumstances under which items are hidden, including selecting from predefined options.

Internal fields used by Notes and reserved fields that exist for a designated purpose help the developer collect data—such as the unique document ID for a parent document—and use that data in writing formulas.

Access to sections of a document can be limited by the access level of the user or by user roles. Computed text can appear based on other conditions in the document. Both add greater functionality to forms.

Q&A

Q **When I try to test my response form in Designer, I get an error message. Also, although I have my application set up so Web users can respond to main topics, information from the parent document doesn't appear in the response.**

A You can't use **Design, Preview in Notes** to test response documents. You must open the database in the Notes client, select a parent document, and then create the response. Inheritance doesn't work in Web browsers because there is no way to establish the parent-child relationship between documents.

Q **I'm having a lot of trouble hiding fields that should be hidden based on a choice in a dialog list.**

A Make sure that you set the field property Refresh Fields on Keyword Change for the dialog list field. It's one of the most common errors in hide-when. This property is on the Control tab of the Field Properties box. The other common error is selecting the wrong set of hide-when options. You have to read the Field Properties box carefully; just before the options it says Hide paragraph when document is. If you want the paragraph or field to be invisible during reading, select the Opened for Reading set of options. Many people get them backwards, as they do the formulas. Most of the time the formulas are negative—you hide the field or paragraph when something isn't selected. When in doubt, reverse the settings and see if that works. Also, in hide-when formulas, make sure you write the text exactly as it appears in the critical field (*Sports* is not the same as *sports*).

Q **Profile documents can't be seen in a view. How do I view what's on a profile document?**

A You can examine the profile form in Designer to see its fields. If you are working with user profiles, try creating a form with fields that pull information from the profile using the @GetProfileField function. Also, use the @Command([EditProfile]) function to open the profile for editing.

Workshop

In this day, the workshop concentrates on making the forms in the Proposed Titles database more functional, especially in setting up relationships between parent and response documents. Some of the tasks you'll complete include

- Setting up inheritance for the response and response-to-response documents
- Creating user profiles for contributors to the discussion
- Hiding text and fields based on selections in the forms
- Adding access controlled sections where approval is required
- Working with some internal and reserved fields to make inheritance function correctly

Make the Response Forms Inherit Data

The Response form needs to inherit the title of the book from the Proposed Title form. You need to do the following tasks to accomplish this:

- In the Proposed Titles database, open the Response form and enable inheritance.
- The static text at the top of the form displays the text "Response to Proposed Title." Add a TbookTitle field to that text so it shows the title of the book, such as "Response to Proposed Title: Windows 98 6-in-1." Have the inheritance occur when the document is composed.
- The Window Title for this form displays the text "Response to Proposed Title." Change the Window Title formula to use the actual title of the book that the response is about, such as "Response to Windows 98 6-in-1." Base it on the TBookTitle field, which inherits information from the parent document.

The Comments form should also inherit information. For the Comments form, take the following steps:

- Open the Comments form and enable inheritance.
- Change the static text at the top of the form to display the book title, such as "Comments on Windows 98 6-in-1." Have the inheritance occur when the document is composed.
- The Window Title for this form should also display the book title, such as "Comments on Windows 98 6-in-1." Have the inheritance occur when the document is composed.

Set Up the User Profile Form

To be able to use information about the contributors in the Proposed Title form, you need to create a profile form for the users. For that form, called Profile, deselect the **Include in Menu** property on the Form Info tab of the Form Properties box. On the Defaults tab, select **Automatically Enable Edit Mode** as the On Open option.

Add four fields to the form, with the appropriate static text and the title "User Profile" at the top of the form. The fields are listed in Table 9.4, along with a description of what is to be in the fields.

Table 9.4 Fields for Profile Form

Name	Compute the common name of the user
Platform	Compute the platform (Windows, Macintosh, and so forth) of the user.
Position	Have the users select their job title or position from a dialog list. Choices can include Acquisitions Editor, Author, Copy Editor, Editorial Assistant, Executive Editor, Production Editor, Publisher, Publisher Assistant, Support Personnel, and Technical Editor. Make it possible for the users to add their title to the list.
Group	Have the users select which publishing group they work with from a dialog list. The choices can include Business, Communications, Computer Basics, Educational, Network & Operating Systems, or Suite Software. Again, allow the users to add other groups to the list.

Make sure no view will display the Profile form. You might have to change some of your view selection formulas.

To bring the profile information into the Proposed Title documents, open the Proposed Title form and add a field just below the TDocAuthor field in the same cell. Call it TProfileInfo. For right now, make the field an editable text field. Because profile documents need to be created using the EditProfile function so they can be cached, you'll add the final formulas when you learn about actions on Day 11.

Hide a Field

In order to create a calendar view for the Proposed Title documents on Day 6, you added a field at the bottom of the Proposed Title form. That is the Duration field. Hidden fields are typically placed at either the top of the form or the bottom, depending on whether you need the fields calculated before the other fields in the document or after. To help identify such fields, we recommend that you add some static text such as "Hidden Fields" and apply a color to the text and fields (we use red text in 8- or 9-point type). At first, you don't hide the fields—you want to see if they work before you hide them.

Hide the Duration field from all readers and editors. It should only be visible to you in Designer.

Create an Access Controlled Section

The Management Information section in the Proposed Titles form should only be available to the EditBoard group you created earlier. In order to make this an access controlled section, you need to remove the section first—after noting what fields and text are included in the current section. Select the section head, and then choose **Section**, **Remove Section**. Then you start again, but you create the access controlled section instead of a standard one.

Give the access controlled section the same title, Management Information, but add MgmtInfo as the field name. Set the border style and color to suit yourself, and apply text formatting to the head to suit yourself as well. On the Formula tab, enter **EditBoard** as the formula. Set the Expand/Collapse options so everything is automatically collapsed for non-editors and either expanded or not for editors.

There is one problem. You now want to give permission to a group of people to edit a section on the form. However, there is an authors field in which only the author of the document is listed. You need to change the formula of that field to the following so the members of the EditBoard group can edit the documents:

```
"EditBoard" : @Name([CN]; @UserName)
```

Use an Internal Field to Update Responses

Inheritance should work for any new response documents you create, but your older response documents won't inherit the information. Also, if someone decides that the book title ought to be changed, any modification won't carry to the response document. You need to modify the TbookTitle field in the Response form. Change the field type to Computed and the formula to get the TbookTitle field from the parent document.

Hint: Write the formula so that it checks first if the document is new (just being created) because in that case it only needs to inherit the TbookTitle field. However, if the document is not new, it needs to get the field information from the parent document. You'll need to ask for the parent document by its document ID, which is found in the $Ref field in a response or response-to-response document.

After you set this up in the Response form, do the same for the Comments form.

To see our examples of this application, open the folder on the CD called Day 9. Open the database called PTDay9.nsf.

DAY 10

Advanced Views

Views display lists of documents and, with some enhancements, they can provide users with information at the view level rather than acting solely as a pointer to documents. An example of such information lies in the Inbox view of your mail database. In that view, icons represent important information such as whether there is an attachment to a mail memo (a paper clip displays) and if the email is considered important or urgent by the sender (red exclamation mark displays). Consider displaying icons in your application to provide visual signals to the users about the documents in the view.

You learned about categorizing documents on Day 9, "Forms on Steroids: Increase Form Performance." In addition to using categories, views need to list documents in some order—alphabetical, reverse alphabetical, date, numerical; therefore, sorting the documents is important. Even more important is giving users the capability to sort the documents themselves.

Some of the other enhancements you'll learn about today include

- Hiding columns to enhance the sorting or display of icons
- Displaying response documents in a view
- Showing totals, averages, and percentages in a view
- Controlling how the documents display

Sort and Categorize Views

You control the order of appearance for the documents in a Notes view. Documents can be sorted in *ascending* (A–Z, 1–10, youngest to oldest) or *descending* (Z–A, 10–1, oldest to youngest) order, using the contents of one or more columns as the sorting criteria. Domino can sort the documents automatically, and you can also make your application more user-friendly by allowing the users to sort the columns in a view.

Categorization goes hand-in-hand with sorting. You learned to create categories on Day 9 using the internal Categories field, but a view can be categorized by any field. Categorizing groups sorted columns and creates headings for the documents in each category. It's possible to collapse category headings, and users can expand the categories when they need to see the documents in a particular category. This is very useful for views that contain large numbers of documents.

Keep in mind the following properties of sorting and categorizing:

- Sorting in Domino generally occurs in the following order: numbers, letters, accented letters, and then punctuation and special characters. For a non-case sensitive sort, the sort sequence is A, a, accented a's, accented A's, B, b, accented b's, and then accented B's, C, c, and so on. Some punctuation occurs before letters (apostrophe and dash), most after.
- Sorting is not case sensitive by default.
- If there are two or more sort columns, the order of the sort is determined in column order from left to right, so place your most important sort column to the left of the other sort columns.
- Place categorized columns to the left of any other sort columns.

 Note

> When you are sorting dates, make sure that the field is a date/time field and not a date written in a text field. If it is a text field, use an @TextToTime conversion formula in the column formula to convert the text to a date. Then the dates will sort properly.

Sort a Column

The order of the documents in a view is dependent on the sorting settings you specify for each column. The settings in the leftmost columns truly determine the order because the view sorts by the first column on the left. The settings for the next column to the right refine the order, and so on.

The only exception is user-defined sorting. For example, the first column is a name, sorted alphabetically, and the second column is a date, which the user can sort in ascending or descending order. If the user changes the sort order of the date column, that change overrides the alphabetical sorting in column one. The documents then display in date order.

Use the following steps to set a sort order for a column:

1. Open the view in design mode.

2. Double-click the header of the column you want to sort.

3. In the Column Properties box (see Figure 10.1), select the **Sorting** tab.

FIGURE 10.1

Case-sensitive and accent-sensitive sorting are turned off by default.

10

4. From the Sort options, choose **Ascending** or **Descending**. Ascending order displays documents in alphabetical order (A–Z) for a text column, numerical order (0–9) for a number column, or oldest to youngest for a date/time column. Descending order is just the reverse.

5. Select **Standard** as the Type.

6. (Optional) If the field or formula for the column results in multiple values, select **Show Multiple Values as Separate Entries** to display the document in a separate row for each value (if a column formula results in three values, the document shows three times in the view). If this option is deselected, the view displays all values in the same row, and the first value is the one on which Notes bases the sort order of the document in the view.

7. (Optional) Enable **Case Sensitive Sorting** to sort lowercase letters before uppercase letters. In other words, *name* sorts before *Name*, which sorts before *NAME*.

8. (Optional) Enable **Accent Sensitive Sorting** to sort non-accented characters before accented characters; for example, a word beginning with *E* appears before a word that starts with *É*.

9. If you want your users to sort documents as they wish, check **Click on Column Header to Sort**. Then select **Ascending**, **Descending**, or **Both** from the list box. These choices add small triangles to the column headers (see Figure 10.2). Selecting **Change to View** adds a small arrow to the header; when users click the header, the specified view opens.

FIGURE 10.2

Users click on these triangles to sort the view in ascending or descending order (or both), based on the contents of the column. A single triangle indicates that the user can only change the sort order in one direction.

Sorting triangles   Set user sorting options here

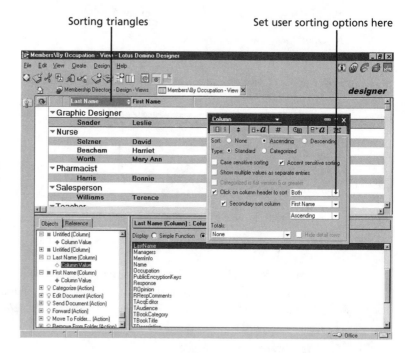

10. (Optional) To have the sort order of the documents depend on two columns with the one on the left usually being the primary sort column (as in last name, first name), select **Secondary Sort Column**. For example, as seen in Figure 10.2, the Last Name column sorts in ascending order, but the First Name column is the secondary sort column. Therefore, when two people with the same last name are listed, the first name determines which document comes first in the list. When you specify a secondary sort column, you must also set the sort order of that column.

11. Save the view.

Categorize the View

When you want the documents in a view grouped by categories, double-click the column head that contains the category information. Then, in the Column Properties box, select the **Sorting** tab. Select a Sort order, and then set the type to **Categorized**.

Click the **Column Info** tab of the Column Properties box and check **Show Twistie When Row is Expandable**. This provides users with a visual aide on expandable rows in the form of a small triangle called a *twistie*. Users click on the twistie to expand a collapsed row or to collapse an expanded row.

In the view shown in Figure 10.3, the first column of the view is only one character wide and the value assigned to the column is the field Occupation. The twistie shows that the row is expandable. This column is sorted in ascending order and is categorized. It's placed first, so the view is sorted by occupations.

FIGURE 10.3

The first column of this view is categorized. You don't see a border between the column header for the first column and the Last Name column because the designer deselected the Resizable option on the Column Info tab of the Column Properties box.

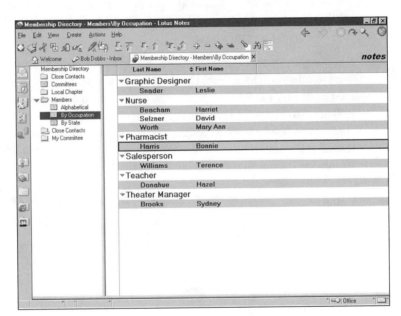

Although the first categorized column on the left takes precedence, you might want to categorize other columns to group some documents together within the larger category. Those categories can also show twisties.

A category column is usually set to a width of 1 or 2. Generally, you want to deselect **Resizable** on the **Column Info** page of the Column Properties box.

To make the category text stand out in the view, click the **Font** tab and select a different text color and bold style.

Another way to make the categories stand out is to collapse all the categories when the user opens the view. You do this by selecting **Collapse All When Database Is First Opened** on the **Options** tab of the View Properties box. The users can then expand the individual categories as needed.

Occasionally, you might have a view in which categories that don't have documents associated with them appear. That usually occurs when the user doesn't have read access to the documents. You don't want your users to be confused by empty categories. Select the Advanced tab of the View Properties box and enable **Don't Show Categories Having Zero Documents**.

Hide Columns

Use a hidden column when you want to sort your view based on a particular field but you don't want to show the field values in your view. To hide a column, select it by clicking the column header, and then choose **Hide Column** from the Column Info page of the Column Properties box.

For example, in a view that shows upcoming trade meetings sorted in date order, you want to categorize by month. However, when you set up a column for months, the months display as numbers. When you convert the dates to text, the months don't display in order—April comes first! The way to handle this is to have two columns: one that shows the numerical value (you sort based on this column), and another that shows the text for the month. The numerical column is the first column, and it's the one you hide. Categorize the month text column. Figure 10.4 displays this view.

FIGURE 10.4

If the months were listed alphabetically, June and July would both come before May. The first sort in the view is on a hidden column on the left, which is sorted in date order.

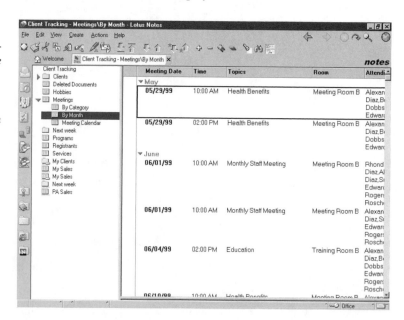

The formula in the hidden column is

```
@Month(MtgDate)
```

The formula in the categorized column is

```
@Select(@Month(MtgDate); "January"; "February"; "March"; "April";
"May"; "June"; "July"; "August"; "September"; "October";
"November"; "December")
```

Another situation in which you have to deal with a numerical return when you need to display text is that of keyword synonyms. *Synonyms* are internal names that Notes stores as the value of the field (instead of the keyword itself). This enables you to use shorter names and to change the keywords without affecting formulas that reference the synonyms.

A very popular use of keyword fields is to enable users to select a priority of High, Medium, or Low from a keyword field. Categorizing in ascending order on that field in a view produces High, Low, and Medium. To produce a sort of High, Medium, and Low, assign synonyms to each keyword as follows: High|1, Medium|2, Low|3.

Although keyword synonyms don't appear on forms, the keywords text value displays on the form even though internally the synonym is stored on disk. However, the keyword synonyms *do* appear in views. The contents of the Priority column show numbers (the synonyms). If you use a formula to change the numbers into their text equivalents, they won't sort in the priority order. Therefore, you want to hide the column so users can't see these numbers, and set the Sort to Standard. In a new column to the right you display the text equivalents, with the column sorted as ascending and categorized.

The formula for the column that displays the text might be

```
@If(Priority = "1"; "High"; Priority = "2"; "Medium";
Priority = "3"; "Low"; "")
```

Display Icons in Columns

Visual signals such as icons in columns make your view look "cool" and can quickly tell your users what type of document is in that row.

For example, the icons in the mail database (see Figure 10.5) indicate what mood stamp was used and what mail is important, and indicate that attachments are included.

10

FIGURE **10.5**

*The icons in the Inbox
tell the user something
about the mail he's
receiving even before
he opens a document.*

Joke mood stamp

Invitation

Invitation declined

Invitation countered

Attachment

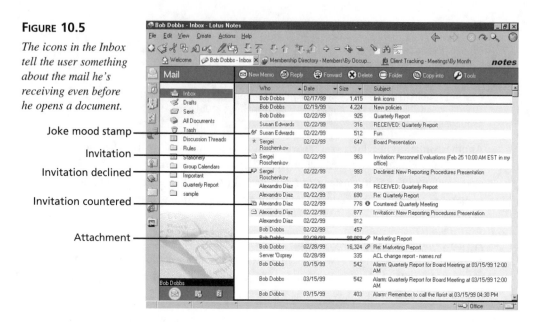

To place icons in a column, check **Display Values as Icons** on the Column Info page of
the Column Properties box. Then enter a formula to show the icons. The formula must
result in a numerical value that's equivalent to one that is assigned to an icon.

Where do the values come from and what do they mean? In Domino 5 Designer Help,
there is a table of available icons (see Figure 10.6) in the document "Displaying an Icon
in a Column." You pick the icon you want and find the number of that icon. Enter the
number in your formula.

How can you use icons in a meaningful way? Well, in a Membership database, you
might want to indicate which members were accepted for membership (see Figure 10.7).
The Accepted field on the Membership Information form is a radio button field with two
choices—Yes or No. The column formula for the icons column is

```
@If(Accepted = "Yes"; 83; Accepted = "No"; 84; "")
```

You might notice in Figure 10.7 that the names of the members appear in alphabetical
order, even though they are listed with the first name followed by the last name. There is
no elaborate formula here: There's a hidden column between the icons and the names
that contains the last name. That hidden column is in ascending order.

FIGURE 10.6

The table of column icons appears in a Help document. The number at the top of the column is the number of the first icon in that column.

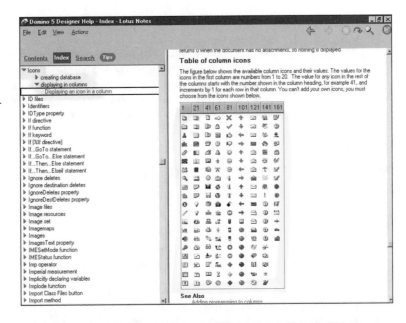

10

FIGURE 10.7

The thumbs-up icon is 83, and the thumbs-down icon is 84.

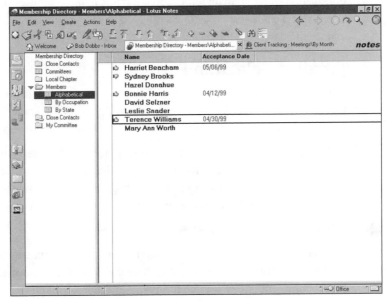

Note

> You can't display .gif images in lieu of icons, but you can create views that use .gif images for the Web. The column needs HTML code. Here is an example: [<img src=" + GifFile + " border=0>], where the GifFile field contains the filename of the .gif image. You also need to select **Treat view contents as HTML** in the Advanced Tab in the View Properties box. You learn more about .gifs in views later in today's lesson.

Display Responses in Views

In applications that use response and response-to-response documents, you want to show those documents in a view in such a way that your users can immediately identify them as being responses instead of main documents. That is why you want them displayed in a hierarchy, with the response documents indented beneath the main topic. The response-to-response documents are further indented.

If you choose to show all the documents in a view, you'll notice that blank spaces appear in some columns or for entire rows. That's because the column formulas call for field information from the main topic, and the fields in the responses have different names. When you include responses in a view, you have to set up special response columns to display the data from the response documents.

Create a Selection Formula

The first step in displaying response documents in a view is to write a selection formula for the view that includes the responses (see Day 6, "Take in the View: Create Views and Folders," for a review on determining which documents to display in a view).

If your database only includes the main topic form and the response forms, using SELECT = @All displays all the documents in the database. However, when the database includes other documents, your selection formula might specify a particular form and its descendents (responses and response-to-responses). Following is an example:

```
SELECT Form = "MainTopic" | @AllDescendants
```

Alternately, write the selection formula to exclude all documents that aren't the main topic or its descendents. In the case where the only other form in the database is the Profile form, you might use the following selection formula:

```
SELECT Form != "Profile"
```

Table 10.1 lists the most common functions for writing formulas involving response documents.

Table 10.1 Using @Functions for Response Documents in View

Function	Example	Results
@AllChildren	SELECT Form = "Inquiry" | @AllChildren	Includes all responses to parent documents
@AllDescendents	SELECT Form = "Suggestion" | @AllDescendents	Includes all response and response-to-response documents for parent documents
@IsResponseDoc	@If(@IsResponseDoc; "Response to " + Subject; Subject)	Returns 1 (true) if a document is a response

Show Responses in a Hierarchy

One way to distinguish response documents from main documents in a view is to show the response documents in a hierarchy.

As you can see in Figure 10.8, the responses are indented—and response-to-response documents are indented further—under the main topics. To create this hierarchy in your view, open the View Properties box, select the **Options** tab, and enable **Show Response Documents in a Hierarchy**.

FIGURE 10.8

In this view, the responses are shown in a hierarchy. The responses are indented under the main documents, and the responses-to-responses are indented under the responses.

Main document
Response
Response-to-Response

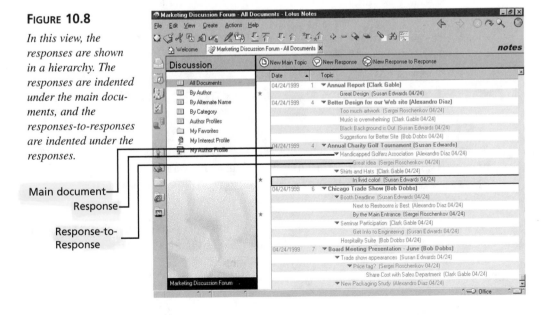

Add a Responses Only Column

The view in Figure 10.8 also contains a Responses Only column that defines what field data to display from the response documents. There can be only one Responses Only column per view.

 After you create the new column in your view, open the Column Properties box and select **Show Responses Only** on the Column Info page.

> **Tip**
>
> Because columns to the right of the Responses Only column display only data referring to the main document, where you insert the column is important. Cut and paste the column elsewhere if you don't place it correctly the first time. All columns to the left of the Responses Only column will show data for both main and responses. Make certain the columns before the Responses Only column have formulas that select the correct information from either the Main or response document.

The formula for a Responses Only column usually consists of a concatenation of text and fields from the response documents. A typical response formula might be

```
ROpinion + " by " + DocAuthor + " on " + @Text(CreateDate; "D0S0")
```

When you have both response and response-to-response documents with different fields, you might want your formula to distinguish between the two document types:

```
@If(Form = "Response"; ROpinion + " by " + RDocAuthor + " on " +
@Text(RCreateDate; "D0S0"); "Comment by " + CDocAuthor + " on " +
@ Text(CCreateDate; "D0S0"), "")
```

Create Column Totals, Averages, and Percents

When database documents contain number fields—such as item prices, expense reports or numbers, income, and so forth—use views to display averages, percents, and totals. These view calculations work only on main documents; response documents are not included in the calculation.

To see how this works, create a column in a view to display a numeric value. Then, in the Column Properties box, select the **Sorting** tab (see Figure 10.9). From the Totals drop-down list, choose an option other than **None**:

Average Per Document—An overall average calculated by totaling the main documents and dividing that value by the number of main documents.

Average Per Sub-Category—An average for each category. The documents are totaled within each category, and that value is divided by the number of documents in that category.

Percent of Parent Category—Displays the parent category's percentage in relation to the total for all the main documents. The subcategory's percentage is shown in relation to the parent category.

Percent of All Documents—Displays the category's percentage in relation to the total for all the main documents.

Total—A grand total for all main documents, it displays at the bottom of the list of documents in the view.

FIGURE **10.9**

*Select **Hide Detail** **Rows** to suppress totals for the detail rows in each category and subcategory.*

Select the **Style** tab of the View Properties box and choose a color from the Column Totals drop-down list to make your totals more easily distinguished from other information in the view (see Figure 10.10). After you choose a color, the detail rows in the view display a different color for the total column than for the category and subcategory rows. If you only want to display the totals at the category and subcategory levels, select the total column and enable **Hide Detail Rows** on the Sorting tab of the Column Properties box.

In Figure 10.11 you see a view that displays totals, but the totals for the detail rows are hidden.

Column Totals color

FIGURE 10.10

The color of the totals is controlled as a View property, although the other text in the column is a Column property.

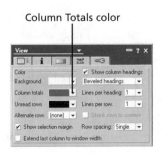

FIGURE 10.11

Totals appear for the categories (project name) and subcategories (consultant). The totals for the individual documents do not appear because Hide Detail Rows is selected.

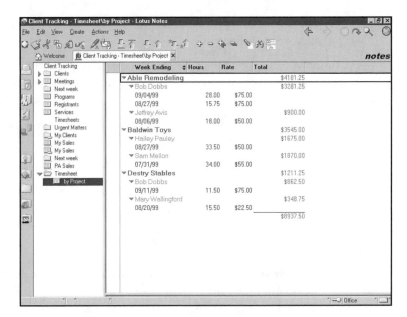

Create View Indexes

A *view index* is an internal filing system that builds the list of documents to display in a view or folder. Updating view indexes is important in keeping views and folders synchronized with document updates. Don't confuse this with the full text index of a database, however.

A *full text index*, with which you are probably more familiar, is an index of all the text in a database and is necessary to perform advanced searches for text. The initial full text index is usually created by the Designer or Manager of the database. Thereafter, the server automatically updates the index daily, although users can update the index before doing a search. Users control the full text index for any database that they store locally.

There are two server tasks that deal with indexes—Update and Updall. Update runs continually after server startup and checks its work queue for views and folders that require updating. Every 15 minutes, Update updates all view indexes in the database, which allows it to include any database changes made during that 15 minute interval. First it updates all the view indexes in the database, and then it updates all databases that have full text indexes that require immediate or hourly updates. When Update detects a corrupted view or full text index, it deletes the view index or full text index and rebuilds it to correct the problem. Although Update runs on *all* databases every 15 minutes, individual database indexes can be updated almost instantaneously—or at least in far shorter intervals.

Updall can be run as needed, but by default it runs daily at 2:00 a.m. Updall updates any view indexes or full text indexes on the server, discards view indexes for views that haven't been used for 45 days (the default), and purges deletion stubs from databases. When view or full text indexes are corrupt, Updall deletes and then rebuilds them.

Update and Updall are managed by the Domino Administrator.

If you have trouble with a view that won't show the correct documents or won't open, the Updall process might need to be run. Before you contact the Domino Administrator, however, try using the keyboard shortcuts for updating or rebuilding views, as shown in Table 10.2.

Table 10.2   Shortcuts to Update or Rebuild Views

Press	To
F9	Update the open view to display current information in documents.
Shift+F9	Rebuild the current view (might fix problems with just that view).
Ctrl+Shift+F9	Rebuilds all views in a database that aren't built yet and updates all other views. Use if you can't run the Updall task. However, you can't do anything else until the process is complete. Updall needs to always be run first, if possible.

You might be asking yourself why you need to understand the Updall and Update tasks, other than to fix a view you're working with as a Designer. As a Designer, you might need to fix a view with which you're working. Furthermore, you *do* need to set some database properties, in cooperation with the Domino Administrator, that determine how frequently these tasks run (primarily Updall).

To set the frequency of the full text index update on a database, open the Database Properties box either by opening the database and choosing **File, Database, Properties** from the menu or by right-clicking the bookmark and selecting **Database, Properties**. Click the **Full Text** tab (see Figure 10.12).

FIGURE 10.12

This database is set to immediately update the full text index when a change is made to the database.

Click **Count Unindexed Documents** to see how many documents aren't indexed and decide whether you need to update the index. If an update is needed, click **Update Index** to start updating the full text index. This button is gray if the index hasn't been created. In that case, click **Create Index**. To set the frequency of the updates (with the Domino Administrator's permission), choose an option from the Update Frequency (Servers Only) drop-down list (this does not apply to local copies of databases):

Immediate—Updates occur when changes are made in the database. Lotus recommends that you use this option for small or infrequently modified but frequently read databases. Our Tech Editor advises you do the least frequent updating and not base your choice on database size. Some very large databases require Immediate updating, so users have faith in the system. Change this setting if the database performance slows.

Hourly—Updates occur every hour. Use this option for small or infrequently modified but frequently read databases. Change this setting if the database performance slows.

Daily—Updates at 2:00 a.m. every day by default. For large databases, you don't want the updating of the index to slow performance during working hours.

Scheduled—Choose this to set the time of day you want the task to run. For a large database, you might want the process to run at a different time than the default schedule used by other databases. To implement the schedule, a program document must be created on the server. Work with the Domino Administrator on this.

If the database doesn't have a full text index, click **Create Index** in the Database Properties box. The Create Full-Text Index dialog box appears (see Figure 10.13). In addition to setting the frequency of the server updates, the dialog box offers four options:

Index Attached Files—Select this to be able to search all documents, including the attachments. Select **Raw Text Only** for a faster—but less comprehensive—search (it searches just the ASCII text of the attachments). Choose **Binary Attachments** for a slower but more comprehensive search. In most cases, the time penalty is very small between these choices.

Index Encrypted Fields—With this selected, Notes searches all words in fields, including the encrypted fields. Warning: This can give someone a way to guess at the encrypted information using searches. You shouldn't select this option without some careful consideration.

Index Sentence and Paragraph Breaks—Select to be able to search for words in the same sentence or paragraph.

Enable Case-Sensitive Searches—Selecting this option means that Notes differentiates between words based on the capitalization (case), so if you're searching for *Home* the results won't include *HOME* or *home*.

When you click **OK**, Notes begins creating the index.

FIGURE 10.13

Enabling the checkbox options makes a more accurate full text index, but also increases the size of the index.

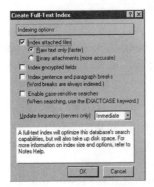

A full text index *does* take up disk space—about 20% the byte size of the database. Indexing a large database can therefore consume a measurable amount of disk space. In addition, Notes only indexes documents that are 6MB or less in size (including attachments). Very large documents might, therefore, cause problems during indexing. In such a case, consult your Domino Administrator about what to do.

Control How Documents Display

A *document* is a set of field data stored in a database. The *form* determines how that data is presented to the user. Therefore, the document is dependent on a form—but not necessarily the form that was used to create it—to display its data.

The name of the form used to create a document (or its alias) is kept in the Form field of the document. To see the form name, select the document in a view and then right-click it. Choose **Document Properties** from the shortcut menu. Then select the **Fields** tab of the Document Properties box (see Figure 10.14).

FIGURE 10.14

The form used to create the selected document is called "Timesheet" or has that as an alias.

When a document opens, Notes uses the following rules to determine how to display the document:

1. **A form is stored with the document**—The stored form is used to display the document (its name is stored in the $Title internal field).

2. **The view has a form formula.**

3. **The form used to create the document is available (the name of that form is stored in the Form internal field in the document)**—The original form is used to display the document unless there is a form stored in the document or a form formula that governs the form to use.

4. **The form used to create the document isn't available, there isn't a stored form, and a form formula doesn't exist**—The default database form is used to display the document.

Default Forms

Each database should have a *default form*. When the database is opened in Designer, the default form has an arrow icon pointing to it in the list of forms (see Figure 10.15). A default form is necessary: If a form is deleted or corrupted, a document uses the default form to display its data.

FIGURE **10.15**

The default form in this database is the Member Information form.

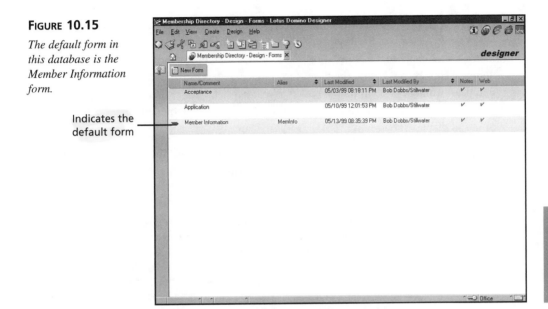

Indicates the default form

When creating or editing a form, you can make it the default form by selecting the **Default database form** property from the Form Info page of the Form Properties box (see Figure 10.16).

FIGURE **10.16**

Only one form can be the default form of a database, so selecting this option removes default status attached to any other form in the database.

Store Forms in Documents

One way to ensure that your documents display information using the correct form is to store the forms used to create the document in the documents themselves.

Storing forms in documents can take up system memory, in addition to requiring more hard disk space (up to 20 times more disk space, depending on the number of design elements, static text, embedded objects and graphics on the form). We don't recommend doing it. However, there might be reasons you have to do it. One reason, for example, is that the document is going to be mailed to another database or a user. That database or user might not have the original form, so the form must be included with the document or it will display incorrectly.

To store a form in a document, open the form and choose **Design, Form Properties** from the menu. On the Form Info tab, select **Store Form in Document** in the Options section.

> **Tip**
>
> When you store a form in a document, the name of the form is stored in the $Title field, an internal field. Other information is kept in the $WindowTitle, $Info, and $Body fields when you store the form in the document. If you want to convert a document with stored form information to a regular document, you need to write an agent that removes these fields: $Title, $WindowTitle, $Info, and $Body. The agent should add a Form field to the document with the name of the form you now want to use.

You also need to make sure that stored forms are acceptable for the database. With the database open, choose **File, Database, Properties** from the menu. On the Database Basics page of the Database Properties box, select **Allow Use of Stored Forms in This Database**.

Form Formulas

Another way to control which form is used to display a document is to write a form formula for the view in which the document is listed. Form formulas are optional.

> **Tip**
>
> Our Tech Editor, Leigh Weber, wants us to tell you that the whole form formula feature of Notes is very elegant. During his review of our manuscript, he sent us this comment and we'd like to share it directly with you: "Author: I think it is very important to tell the reader that Notes default behavior is very powerful. You can create a view that has all of the documents each using one of many forms in the database displayed in one nice view, AND when the user requests to open a specific document Notes uses the correct form. POWERFUL! -lsw"

The selection formula for a view might be

```
SELECT Form = "Customer Information"
```

All the documents in that view are created with the Customer Information form. The Form field in each document contains "Customer Information."

However, if you want to show the same documents using one form when creating the document and another when reading it, you create a form formula. For example

```
@If(@IsNewDoc; "Data Entry"; "Customer Information")
```

In this situation, the Data Entry form is used when creating the document, possibly because it is set up to easily tab from one field to another so the user can quickly enter data. When the document is opened in read mode, the Customer Information form is used. Its appearance is enhanced, and field data is combined for ease of reading.

When you use a form formula, it applies only to that view. In all other views, the documents display with the form that appears in the Form field of the document (if there isn't a stored form in the document). Unlike selection and column formulas, which run on the server or workstation containing the database, a form formula runs on the user's workstation.

Use the following steps to enter a form formula:

1. Open the view in Designer.
2. In the Info List, click the **Objects** tab (if it's not currently displayed).
3. In the list of objects you see the name of the view followed by "(View)". Click the plus sign (+) in front of that object to expand the list (see Figure 10.17). The plus becomes a minus sign (-).
4. Select **Form Formula**.
5. Write the formula in the Script Area. Keep in mind that a form formula must result in the name of a form or its alias.
6. Click the green check in the Script Area, and then test your formula.

Form Fields

The name of the form used to create a document appears in the internal Form field of the document, which you see when you open the **Fields** tab of the Document Properties box.

As was explained earlier, when a form is stored in a document, the name of the stored form appears in the $Title field (also visible in Document Properties). The $Info, $WindowTitle (if a window title is specified), and $Body fields store additional information (see Figure 10.18).

FIGURE 10.17

There is only one form formula per view, and the form formula only affects the documents opened from that view.

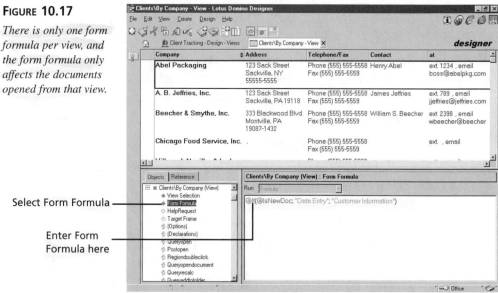

Select Form Formula

Enter Form Formula here

FIGURE 10.18

The Document Properties box for a document that has a form stored in the document. There is no Form field, but there is a $Title field. There are also $Body and $Info fields, but no $WindowTitle because a window title formula wasn't created for the form.

In order to remove a stored form from a document, you must delete the $Title, $Info, $WindowTitle, and $Body fields. Then you have to create a Form field that contains the title of the form. The best way to do that is to create an agent that has a formula similar to the following, where the Interest Profile is the stored form to be removed and replaced by the Interests form:

```
SELECT $Title = "Interest Profile";
FIELD $Title := @DeleteField;
FIELD $Info := @DeleteField;
```

```
FIELD $Body := @DeleteField;
FIELD $WindowTitle := @DeleteField;
FIELD Form = "Interests"
```

Views on the Web

Consider that not all Domino view properties are supported on the Web (see Table 10.3) and that you need to carefully evaluate views when you're designing for Web browsers.

Table 10.3   View Properties Not Supported on the Web

Feature	Note
Private Folders	Not supported in outlines on the Web
Private Views	
Show in View menu	
(found on the Options page of the View Property box)	Web users don't have view menus.
On Open:	
(found on the Options page of the View Property box)	Go To options not supported.
On refresh	
(found on the Options page of the View Property box)	Not supported.
View Style: **Unread rows**	
View Style: **Alternate rows**	
View Style: **Show selection margin**	
View Style: **Beveled headings**	
View Advanced properties: **Refresh index options**	
View Advanced properties: **Discard index options**	
Column Info properties: **Show twistie when row is expandable**	Triangles are always displayed.

10

The primary difference in views for Notes clients versus Web clients lies in the *selected* document in a view. On the Web, there is no such thing. Users can't select a document on the Web. So, inheritance becomes a potential problem; after all, if you can't inherit from a selected document, how can you inherit values *at all*? Inheritance on the Web must be drawn from the *document* itself, not the document in a view. Therefore, a document must be composed from within a document. Adding an action to a view to compose a document will, indeed, deliver a new blank document to the Web client. But the document will be blank, with no inherited values. Adding an *action* to a document to compose a document presents a new document with inherited values specified by the designer. Actions are also useful as a method of opening views. You learn more about actions on Day 11, "Help the User: Design Interface Enhancements."

Specifying the Link Column

Domino uses the first (leftmost) column in a view as the link column, making each entry a link. This doesn't always make sense to the users. For example, if you have a view that displays documents by date, followed by the document title, the date column becomes the link that Web users click to view the documents. Although there is nothing wrong with this example, it might be more appropriate for Web users if the document title were the link, not the date. To define which column links to documents, follow these steps:

1. Select the columns you want to display as linking columns.

2. Click the Advanced tab of the Column Properties box and select **For Web Access: Show values in this column as links.**

HTML and GIFs in Views

GIF images can be used in a view designed for the Web in the same manner that you use icons. For example, a column can contain a formula that displays a GIF file that contains a file labeled "New!" whenever a new document is displayed in a view.

GIFs can be inserted through the use of Passthru HTML code in a formula for a view. *Passthru HTML* is a reference to a file on your server. When a document converts the document to HTML or generates the view, the reference is passed through to the resulting HTML page. The formula containing the HTML Passthru might look something like this:

```
@If (@Now <@Adjust(@Created; 0; 0; 5; 0; 0; 0);
[<img src=figs/new.gif border=0>]
```

This causes the file named new.gif to appear in a column if a document is fewer than five days old, and to have no border around the image.

Animated GIF files can also be used in views, documents, or pages. Because views are created on-the-fly by Domino, you can't pass any graphics into a view, but you can place them there with HTML code.

Key to the use of GIFs is the location on the Domino server in which they are stored. They must be stored in the path set in the HTTP section of the Server Document. The default directory is the Icons directory, which, of course, can be changed in the server document if desired. Consult with your Domino system administrator if you use GIFs in this way, to ensure that your formula contains the right path to the file.

As you learned on Day 8, "Create Pages and Frames," you can use HTML almost anywhere in your application design. Store HTML formatting attributes in a column to override the default row and column settings. When the view is presented on the Web, the view uses the HTML formatting attributes you specified in the column formula.

To add HTML formatting, open the View properties box and click the Advanced tab. Select **For Web Access: Treat view contents as HTML**. Create a column and write the HTML code in the Script area as the formula for the column. The HTML must define all formatting and document linking for the view. To learn more about HTML formatting, see Appendix D, "Frequently Used HTML."

Tip

> A great way to control the display of views on the Web, and also in Notes, is to create a page or form that acts as a "view template" of sorts. You embed the view on the page or form, which can contain other design elements such as your company logo. You learn more about embedding views on Day 17, "Embed Objects in Your Applications."

Summary

The documents in a view can be sorted in ascending or descending order, or categorized to group related documents. Sorting and categorizing are controlled as properties of the columns in the view. Users can sort the view when you add sorting triangles to the column headers.

Because the values returned by some field formulas return numbers or text values necessary for sorting, columns that contain that information can be hidden to preserve the sort order. In doing this, another column is inserted to hold the text you want the user to see. The formulas for some columns might evaluate to numbers that correspond to a specific icon, which you set to display in that column to give the user a visible clue to the contents of the document.

When working with response hierarchies or parent-child documents, the child document can inherit some information from the original document. The parent document must be selected by the user when the child document is created, inheritance must be enabled for the child document, and the field formulas must specify the name of the original field. Inheritance occurs when the document is composed; otherwise, the field formulas must access the parent document using the unique document ID to update data from fields in the parent document.

Views can include totals, percentages, and averages based on the Totals properties you select for number columns in the view.

Two indexes control the display of documents in views—the view index and the full text index. Two server tasks are associated with these indexes—Update and Updall. Both tasks are important to preventing or fixing corrupted views.

How the data in documents displays is controlled by the form used to create the document, the form stored in the document, the form formula you create in the view, or the default form of the database.

Q&A

Q Do you need to specify a secondary sort when you have first name and last name columns?

A Secondary sort is valid only when someone clicks on the column heading. After you click on the column heading for last name, you have to specify the secondary sort if you want the result further sorted by first name.

Q What if I want to show the full name in the view but I want the view sorted by the last name?

A Create a hidden column to the left of the name column you display. If you have a last name field, specify that as the contents of the hidden column. Then sort the hidden column in ascending order. If you only have the full name in one field, try using the @Right function to get just the last name portion for the hidden column. Of course, that might not work if you also allow suffixes such as Jr., M.D., II, and so forth. For example, `@Right( FullName; " " )` will give everything after the last blank in the name; so, `"Sheila Galloway"` will return `"Galloway"`, but `"Sheila Galloway, Ph.D."` will return `"Ph.D."`

Q **I know I can use the Form field in selection formulas. Can I use the $Title field when the form is stored in the document?**

A Of course. You can use field values to select documents for views. For example, to display documents that have the Interest Profile form stored in the document, you might write a selection formula like this:

```
SELECT @All & $Title = "Interest Profile"
```

Workshop

The goal of today's workshop is to add more functionality to the views in the Proposed Titles database. Then you'll create and begin working on the Titles in Development database. This database, as you can see from the diagram in Figure 10.19, is the database to which accepted books will eventually be sent. It tracks the production cycle of the book, from assigning editors and authors to the final review of the book before printing.

FIGURE 10.19

In the flowchart of workshop application, the Titles in Development database works with the proposed titles that have been approved.

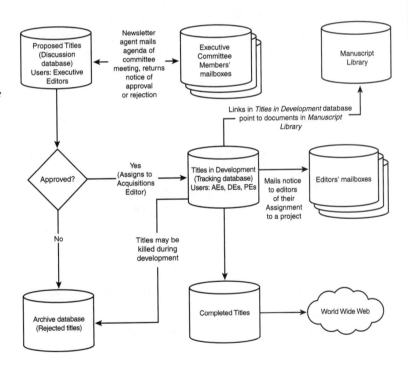

Tasks you will perform in this workshop include

- Sorting and categorizing views
- Displaying icons in view columns

- Hiding view columns
- Showing a response hierarchy in a view
- Adding a response-only column to a view
- Storing a form in documents
- Using form formulas

Sorting and Categorizing Views

Open the Proposed Title database in the Designer (or open the ending database from yesterday's workshop, PTDay9.nsf, which you'll find in the Day9 folder on the CD) and make the following changes to the Books\by Category view:

- Sort the first column, Category, in ascending order and make it categorized. Go to the Sorting tab of the Column Properties box to set these properties.
- Have twisties display for the Category column when the row is expandable. This is on the Column Info tab of the Column Properties box.
- Change the size of the Category column to 1 and turn off the Resizable property. These are also on the Column Info tab of the Column Properties box.
- Remove the Title from the column header. Just delete the name from the Title box on the Column Info page.
- If necessary, change the font and color of the Category column to distinguish the category text.
- Make it possible for the Author(s) column and the Audience column to be sorted by users.
- The Author(s) column can have multiple values. On the Column Info tab, change the multivalue separator to **New Line**.
- Change the View properties to allow five **Lines per row** (on the Style tab) and select **Shrink rows to content**. Each author in the Author(s) column is now visible on a separate line, with room to see five authors if needed.

The Books\by Authors view also needs to have some sorting and categorizing added:

- Sort the Author(s) column in ascending order and categorize it. Notice that the **Show multiple values as separate entries** option is automatically selected when you categorize the column.
- Remove the Title from the column heading, change the width to 1, and deselect **Resizable**.
- Select **Show twistie when row is expandable**.

Displaying Values as Icons

In the Proposed Titles database, open the Review Status view in the Designer. Make the following changes to the view:

- Sort the Status column in ascending order and make it categorized. Change the width to 1, deselect **Resizable**, and select **Show twistie when row is expandable**. Remove the name from the Title. Set the font to make the category text stand out.

- Create a column to the left of Title (click on the Title header and choose **Create, Insert New Column**). Don't give it a name. Make it only 2 wide, deselect **Resizable**, and select **Display values as icons**.

- In the formula for the new column, enter a formula that displays icons based on the numbers in the display chart in Help. Remember that TStatus used synonyms for the choices: "1" is Accepted; "2" is Rejected; "3" is Hold for Further Discussion; and "4" is Under Discussion. Your formula uses those values, for example @If(TStatus = "1"; 83; TStatus = "2"; 84; 0). The number 83 shows the "thumbs-up" icon, and 84 is "thumbs-down" icon.

10

Hiding a Column

As often happens when you use keyword synonyms, the choices appear in the desired order in the field, but not when you use the same field in the view. In the view, the synonyms themselves appear if you only use the field name as the column formula. That's why you used a formula that substituted text for the synonyms in the categorized column in the Review Status view. Because you are using the text and have sorted that column, the categories appear in this order: Accepted, Hold for Further Discussion, Rejected, Under Discussion. The order you want, though, is the order in which the choices appeared in the form: Accepted, Rejected, Hold for Further Discussion, and Under Discussion. The hidden column forces the order.

You need to insert a column to the left of the categorized column (click the column heading for the first column and choose **Create, Insert New Column**). Make that new column 1 wide, deselect **Resizable**, and select **Hide Column**. Sort it in ascending order. The formula for the column is the field TStatus. This works because sorting in a view starts with the left column first, and refines that sort as you move to the right. You can test it by changing the status of some documents. You might want to disable the encryption on the TStatus field before you do, though, so you don't have unexpected results—just remember to enable it again before rollout.

Showing a Response Hierarchy in a View

The Books\by Title view is the only one that "displays" response documents. Some might only appear as blank lines. Open the view and, in the View Properties box on the Options tab, select the option **Show response documents in a hierarchy**.

Adding a Response-Only Column to a View

The response and response-to-response documents in the Books\by Title view don't have the same fields as the main topic, except for the TBookTitle field. When you add a responses-only column, the formula is usually a concatenation of fields from these documents.

- Sort (ascending) and categorize the Title column. Remove the Title from the column heading, reduce the size to 1, and deselect **Resizable**. Select **Show twistie when row is expandable**. Choose a nice font and size to make the text stand out.

- Make the multiline separator for the Author(s) column a **New Line**.

- Change the View Properties on the Style tab to allow five **Lines per Row** and enable **Shrink rows to content**.

- Create a new column to the left of Author(s). Make it 1 wide and deselect Resizable. Enable **Show twistie when row is expandable** and **Show responses only**. Sort the column in ascending order. To make it obvious that the Response Only text is different, you might want to use a different font or size in this column.

- Because you are dealing with two forms—Response and Comments—that have different fields, use a formula that puts different text in the column based on the form used. Display the opinion and the comments (the short ones, not the body) for both forms. We even added text that appears when the comments are empty.

The formula we use for the response only column is

```
@If(Form = "Response"; "Opinion: " + ROpinion;
Form = "Comments"; "Comments: " + ROpinion;)
```

```
However, to practice true "defensive" programming, use this formula:
@If(Form = "Response"; "Opinion: " + ROpinion;
Form = "Comments"; "Comments: " + ROpinion;
"Unexpected Form Name"))
```

Because we made a correction to the TDocAuthor field in the last workshop, you might notice a problem in the Submitted by column of the view because it now displays the names of the Editboard group. While you are here you can correct it. In the column formula, replace the TDocAuthor field with `@Name([CN]; @UserName)`.

Storing a Form in Documents

At some later point in the development of the Proposed Titles database, the rejected Proposed Title documents will be sent on to the Rejected Titles database. Because you created the Rejected Titles database without any forms, you need to store the form in the Proposed Title documents. That way, the documents can be correctly read when they arrive in the Rejected Titles database.

Enable **Store form in document** in the Form Properties box for the Proposed Title form. Make sure, too, that in the Database Properties box the **Allow use of stored forms in this database** option is selected. Note that storing a form in the document breaks all the view selections because there is no longer a Form field. Therefore, if you have a selection form such as `Form = "Title"` or `Form = "Title" ¦ @AllDescendants`, the newly created documents with stored forms do not show up in the view.

Note

Although we have stored forms in documents in this database, there are better ways to deal with documents that are moved from one database to another to avoid all the side effects of stored forms. The best is probably creating a design template for the Proposed Titles database and then having the databases to which you are mailing documents inherit some of their design (like the form design) from that template. We discuss design templates on Day 21, "Roll Out and Maintain Your Application."

Using Form Formulas

You don't need to use a form formula in the Proposed Titles database, but you'll need it in the Titles in Development database. At some point, when a proposed title is accepted, it will be sent to the Titles in Development database. Because you've stored the form in the Proposed Title documents, that form will automatically be used to display the documents. However, the editors need to use a different form in the Titles in Development database. We'll enter a form formula now, although it won't replace a stored form, and remove the stored forms later.

- Create a new database called Titles in Development. Give it the file name Develop.nsf. Use a blank template when you create it.
- Create a new form called New Title and use New as the alias. Make it the default form.
- Add the following fields to the new form (you can even copy and paste them) and then save the form. Notice that you're using the same field names as those on the Proposed Title form. That way, the transferred document can be displayed using the new form. Add any necessary static text as labels.

  TBookTitle

  TProposedAuthors

  TBookCategory

  TDescription

  TAudience

  TAcqEditor

- Customize the default view for the new database. Name it Titles, with Titles as the alias. Create the following columns:

  Title—Sorted in ascending order, 20 characters wide. Field information: TBookTitle.

  Author(s)—Sorted in ascending order. Allow users to sort. Make the width 15, and select New Line as the Multiline separator. Field information: TProposedAuthors.

- Set the view properties to allow five **Lines per row** and enable **Shrink rows to content**.
- Add a form formula to the view to display the documents using the New Title form. Simply adding "New" as the form formula should be sufficient.
- Save the view. Close the database.

To see our examples of this application, open the folder on the CD called Day 10. Open the database called PTDay10.nsf to see the current version of the Proposed Titles database. To see the Titles in Development database, open the database called TDDay10.nsf.

DAY 11

Help the User: Design Interface Enhancements

Part of your job as a developer is to make users comfortable with your application. The easier it is to use, the more likely it is that users will work with it—and abandon their attitudes of "the way we did things before." Think carefully about your audience: Are all users computer literate? Is there anything you can do to automate tasks for them or avoid extra steps to prevent problems later?

In this day, you learn about the @Command functions that enable you to use menu commands from within a formula. You then use these functions to work with design elements that improve the user interface for your applications:

- Actions
- Buttons and Hotspots
- Links
- Domino URL commands to navigate your site

Use @Commands

The @Commands are a specialized class of @Functions used to execute menu commands and some additional specialized commands. Two design elements that employ
@Commands are actions and agents, both of which help automate the application for the
user. You can also use @Commands for SmartIcons, buttons, and hotspots.

When writing an @Command formula, always enclose the command name in brackets
([]). For commands that involve parameters, separate parameters with semicolons (;).

An @Command can contain a very simple command, using the following syntax:

```
@Command([CommandName])
```

For example, the command to close a window is

```
@Command([FileCloseWindow])
```

Other @Command formulas require an argument, or parameters, using this syntax:

```
@Command([CommandName]; parameters)
```

An example of this syntax is the @Command to create a new document using a specified
form:

```
@Command([Compose]; "Customer Information")
```

When you enter the formula in the Script Area, click the **Reference** tab in the Info List
and choose **Formula @Commands** from the drop-down list to see a list of the
@Commands you can use (see Figure 11.1). If you aren't sure which command to use,
select the command and click **Help** for an explanation of how to use the command.

FIGURE 11.1

*Select the @Command
from the Reference list
and click **Paste** to
place it in the Script
Area. Add any neces-
sary parameters and
then click the green
check mark. The dis-
played command adds
a horizontal scrollbar
to the screen.*

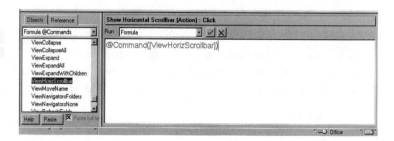

> **Tip**
>
> Don't know which @Command to use? Think about which menu command you want to use and look for an @Command with that name. For example, @Command([FileSave]) saves the file. There are some major exceptions to this because the @Commands inherited some language from older versions of Notes. Instead of *Create*, for instance, many of the commands you find on the Create menu use *Compose*, a menu command more familiar to users of R3.

Add Actions

One way to automate a task for a user is to create an *action*. The action can appear as a menu choice (in the Actions menu), as a button on the Action Bar, or as both. For Web users in particular, actions are important because Notes menu commands are not available to them in their Web browsers—but action buttons are.

Actions work in views or forms. They can be exclusive to a particular view or form, or they can be shared for use in more than one design element. You program them using simple actions, formulas (generally including @Commands), LotusScript, or JavaScript.

View and Form Actions

Actions you might want to create for a view include creating a new document, editing a document, printing a document, deleting documents, or categorizing documents. Helpful actions in a form might include actions that mail a document, save it, edit it, process an approval, or print the document.

Several built-in actions already exist for both forms and views: Categorize, Edit Document, Send Document, Forward, Move to Folder, and Remove from Folder. These are sometimes referred to as "system" actions, and they have asterisks (*) in front of their names in the Action Pane. They appear on the Actions menu by default, but not as buttons on the Action Bar, although you can make buttons for them. To see the list of system actions (see Figure 11.2) and any actions that have been created for the form or view, take one of the following steps:

- Click the **View Show/Hide Action Pane** SmartIcon (click again to close the pane).
- Choose **View, Action Pane** from the menu (repeat the menu command to close the pane).
- Drag the right edge of the Work Area toward the center of the screen (drag it back to the right edge or double-click the separator bar to close the pane).

11

View Show/Hide Action Pane SmartIcon

FIGURE 11.2

The Action Pane lists the system actions, plus any actions you added to the view.

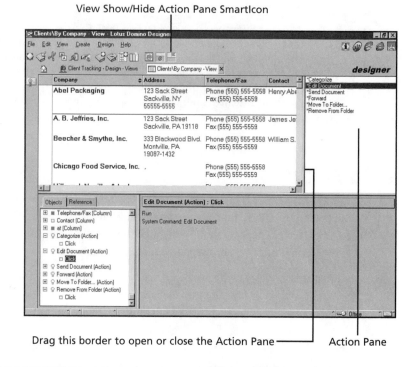

Drag this border to open or close the Action Pane ——— Action Pane

Caution

System actions work in the Notes client but not in Web browsers. If you want an Edit Document action button that works in a Web browser, for example, create a new action and write a formula for it.

Use the following steps to make an action button for one of the system actions:

1. Open the Action Pane.

2. Select the action from the list.

3. Double-click the action to open the Action Properties box (see Figure 11.3).

4. In the Display section, select **Include action in button bar**. If you also want the action to display on the Action menu, select **Include action in Action menu**. To have only a symbol appear on the button (no text), enable **Only show icon in button bar** (of course, you must select a graphic to display on the button). You also have the option to right-align the Action button, which makes the Action buttons start from the right with position 1 at the right hand side, position 2 to the left of position 1, and so on.

FIGURE 11.3

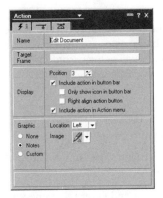

*By default, a system action doesn't appear on the Action Bar. To include a system action as a button, select **Include action in button bar**. Then you can choose a graphic for the button if you want.*

5. To set the order of the buttons on the Action Bar (going from left to right), increase or decrease the Position number. Position 1 is the first button on the left.

6. In the Graphic section, choose whether you want just text (**None**), one of the available Notes icon graphics (**Notes**), or one of the graphics stored in the shared images for the database (**Custom**).

7. If you selected Notes in step 6, choose **Left** or **Right** from the Location drop-down list to determine on which side of the button the graphic appears. Then click the Image drop-down arrow to see a selection of icons (see Figure 11.4). Click the one you want to use.

11

FIGURE 11.4

There is a wide selection of graphics available for your action buttons. Click one to select it.

If you selected Custom in step 6, choose **Left** or **Right** from the Location drop-down list to determine on which side of the button the graphic appears. Then enter the name of the graphic you want to use in the Image box; click the **Folder** button to select one of the shared database images from a dialog box; or click the @ button to write a formula that resolves to the name of a graphic.

Note

Become familiar with the Lotus use of Action button icons in the mail, discussion, and other databases. Associate the same icons with the same functions; otherwise, your users will get very confused.

Use the following steps to create a new action:

1. Open the view in which you want to create the action.

2. Choose **Create, Action** from the menu. The Action Pane automatically appears, as does the Action Properties box.

3. Select "(Untitled)" in the Name box and enter the name you want to appear on the action button.

4. (Optional) If you're working with framesets, enter the name of the Target Frame in which the action is to take place.

5. Follow steps 4–7 for creating a button for a system action.

6. To provide the instructions the button is to follow when clicked, make a selection from the Run drop-down list in the Programmer's Pane:

   Formula—Enter a formula, such as @Command([ViewHorizScrollbar), to show a horizontal scrollbar.

   Simple Action(s)—Click the Add Action button. In the Add Action dialog box, select the Action and complete the remaining fields (see Figure 11.5). Then click OK.

   LotusScript—Enter a script to perform the desired action.

   JavaScript—Enter a script to perform the desired action.

FIGURE 11.5

*To approve the membership application of a selected individual, create an Approve Membership action. Use the simple action method to set instructions for the button. Select **Modify Field** as the Action, choose **Accepted** as the Field, enter the Value **Yes**, select **Replace Value**, and click **OK**.*

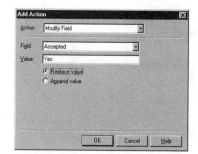

7. Save the form or view to save the actions.

When you open the form or view in the Notes client, the action buttons you created appear on the Action Bar of the view (see Figure 11.6).

FIGURE 11.6

The Approve Membership button displays on the Action Bar in the position you selected in the Action Properties box.

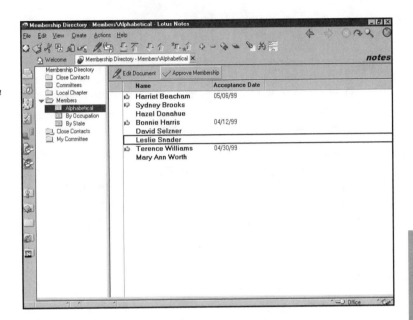

To have the action buttons display in a Web browser, use the Action Bar applet (see Day 17, "Embed Objects in Your Application"). Although the buttons display without the applet, they don't have the 3D appearance of buttons that the applet gives them.

> **Tip**
>
> To save space on the Action Bar, you might want to group some related actions together under a drop-down action button. For example, create an action called Approval\Approved that approves the membership of a selected individual. Then create another action called Approval\Rejected. In the Action Bar, you see the Approval button. When you click it, a menu drops down with the choices Approved and Rejected on it.

With form actions you are more likely to employ the hide-when properties to have different action buttons appear. For example, you don't need to see the Edit Document action button when you already have the document in edit mode, so you want to hide the button when editing (see Figure 11.7).

FIGURE 11.7

The Edit Document button only needs to be available when someone is reading or previewing the document.

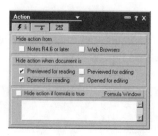

When you need to make changes to an action, open the Action Pane and double-click on the name of the action. Make your changes in the Action Properties box or the Programmer's Pane. Then save the form.

To delete an action, select it in the Action Pane and press **Delete**. To copy it, select it and choose **Edit, Copy** from the menu. Then open the form in which you need a copy of the action. With the Action Pane open, choose **Edit, Paste**. The name of the copied action appears in the list of actions.

You cannot delete system actions. Instead, deselect **Include action in button bar** and **Include action in Action menu**, effectively hiding the action from the user.

Shared Actions

Some actions, such as saving a document or printing it, are common to several forms or views in a database. Rather than create the same action over and over in each form or view, use a shared action. Shared actions are stored in the database as Resources.

Use the following steps to create a shared action:

1. Open the database in which you want to store the shared action.
2. In the Design Pane, click **Resources** and then click **Other**.
3. Select **Shared Actions** from the list of Other resources.
4. The Action Properties box automatically appears for the first shared action (see Figure 11.8). For other actions, choose **Create, Shared Action** from the menu to open the Action Properties box.
5. Make the appropriate selections in the Action Properties box and set the action instructions in the Programming Pane as you do for view or form actions.

FIGURE 11.8

The name of the shared action appears in the Work Area. Enter the formula or script in the Script Area or choose a simple action.

Action name in Work Area

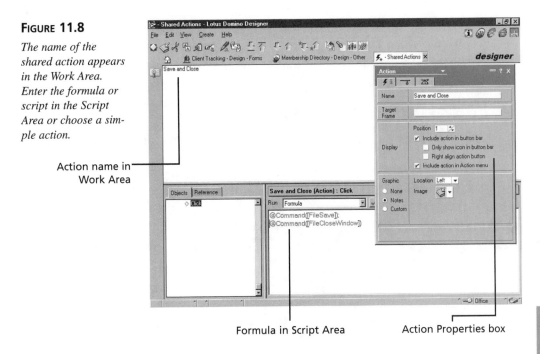

Formula in Script Area   Action Properties box

11

After you create the shared action (you can make more than one at a time, if needed), it's available for use throughout the database. Use the following steps to insert a shared action into a form or view:

1. Open the form or view.

2. Open the Action Pane and select any action, or click the **Objects** tab in the Info List and select any action.

3. Choose **Create, Insert Shared Action** from the menu.

4. From the Insert Shared Action(s) dialog box, select the action you want to insert into your form or view.

5. Click **Insert**. If you need to add more than one shared action, click the next one and then click **Insert**, and so on.

6. Click **Done** to close the dialog box.

7. In the Action Properties box, select the **Position** in which the shared action appears on the Action Bar.

8. Save the form or view. When you open the database in the Notes client, the action appears in the form or view.

Customize the Action Bar

You can set properties that affect the actual appearance of the Action Bar. To see the Action Bar Properties box (see Figure 11.9), open a form or view, select an action in the Action Pane or from the Info List Objects tab, and then choose **Design, Action Bar Properties** from the menu.

FIGURE 11.9

The alignment of the buttons, the background of the bar, the borders, how Web browsers see the bar, and the appearance of the buttons are all included in the Action Bar properties.

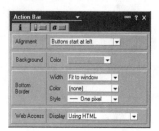

Table 11.1 explains the Action Bar properties and how they affect the appearance of the bar.

Table 11.1 Action Bar Properties

Tab	Property	Description
Action Bar Info	Alignment	Decide whether the buttons start on the left or right end of the bar.
	Background: Color	Select the color for the background of the bar.
	Bottom Border	Set the Width (None, Fit to Window, Fixed Width, or Under Buttons Only), Color, and Style (thickness) of the bottom border of the bar.
	Web Access: Display	Decide whether to use HTML or the Action Bar applet to display the bar on the Web.

Tab	Property	Description
Button Background	Button Size	Set the Height to Default (8 pixels for the Height), Minimum Size, Fixed Size (pixel spinner appears), or Background size (each button is the height of the Action Bar). Width can be Default or Background size (each button is the width of the entire Action Bar). Set Margin (around button) to Default (2 pixels) or Fixed size (pixel spinner appears).
	Button Border	Determine if the button borders show On Mouse Over, Always, or Never.
	Button Background	Select the Color for the button background or specify an image for the background.
Button Font	Font, Size, Style, Color	Set the Font, Size, Style (bold, italic, and so on), and Color of the button text.

Create Buttons and Hotspots

Action buttons aren't the only one-click automation you can add to your forms. A hotspot can be a picture or text. The user clicks the hotspot to perform an action, run a formula or script, or link to another database, database element, or Web site.

There are several types of hotspots:

Link—Opens a database element (view, page, frameset, form, document, folder, or navigator), a database, or a Web site.

Button—Performs a programmed task. Can be programmed with simple actions, formulas, LotusScript, or JavaScript.

Action Hotspot—Performs a programmed task. Can be programmed with simple actions, formulas, LotusScript, or JavaScript.

Text Pop-Up—Displays information in a pop-up.

Formula Pop-Up—Performs a programmed task. Can only be programmed using formulas, with the result showing in a pop-up.

11

Create a Button

Buttons can be added to pages or forms. You use buttons to open a related document, see a view, create a new document, open a database, import related data, and more.

Use the following steps to add a button to a form or page:

1. Open the page or form.

2. Click to place your cursor where you want the button to appear.

3. Choose **Create, Hotspot, Button** from the menu. The Button Properties box appears (see Figure 11.10).

FIGURE 11.10

Enter the label for the button, set the appearance of the text, and specify hide-when options.

4. Enter a Label for the button and specify the Width on the Button Info page.

5. Click the **Font** tab to select the font, font size, font style, and color for the button text.

6. (Optional) If you want to hide the button under certain conditions, click the **Paragraph Hide-When** tab and select the appropriate options (such as hiding a button when reading because it performs an action needed only when editing).

7. From the Run drop-down list in the Programmer's Pane, select the programming method you want to use: Simple Action(s), Formula, LotusScript, or JavaScript.

8. Enter the formula or script in the Script Area, or click **Add Action** to specify the simple action you want the button to perform.

Generally, you position the buttons next to text or a field relating to the button action. That means the button can be anywhere on the page or form. After the user scrolls past the button, they won't be able to see it to click it. Tasks you want to do from anywhere on the page or form should therefore be done with Action buttons. Hotspot buttons need to be more specialized.

Caution	Domino displays all actions, buttons, and hotspots even if they are created with @commands and @functions that aren't supported for Web applications. By default, Domino only supports one button for Web use—the Submit button, which closes and saves the document. If a Submit button doesn't exist, Domino places one at the bottom of the form. To Web-enable certain @commands and all buttons in a database, enable the database property for Web access, **Use JavaScript When Generating Pages**. If you don't set this property, Domino recognizes only the first button in a document and regards it as the Submit button.

Create an Action Hotspot

An *action hotspot* is text or an image that you click to perform an action, such as opening a view or document in a specified "target" frame, creating a new document, or bringing in data from a related document or another database. It's the Notes equivalent to a text or graphic hotspot in an HTML document, and you can program it to open a form in compose mode, open a document in Edit mode, delete a document, and anything else you can do with action bar actions.

Use the following steps to add an action hotspot to a form or page:

1. Open the form, navigator, or page.
2. Select text or an image to associate with the hotspot.
3. Choose **Create, Hotspot, Action Hotspot** from the menu.
4. The Action Hotspot Properties box opens (see Figure 11.11). On the Hotspot Info tab, enter the name of the target frame in the Frame box. The *target frame* is the frame in the frameset where the element opens, which you specify in the formula, simple action, or script for the hotspot. If the name of a frame isn't entered, the result of the action hotspot displays in the current frame or in a new window.
5. (Optional) If you don't want the action hotspot to be visible in all conditions, click the **Paragraph Hide When** tab and specify the conditions for hiding the hotspot.
6. From the Run drop-down list in the Programmer's Pane, select the type of programming you want to use for the hotspot: Simple Action(s), Formula, LotusScript, or JavaScript.
7. Enter the formula or script in the Script Area, or click **Add Action** to specify the simple action you want the hotspot to perform.

11

FIGURE 11.11

A label isn't needed for an Action Hotspot because you select text or a picture and make that selected item the hotspot. The text needs to indicate what happens when the user clicks it.

Create a Link Hotspot

A *link hotspot* is text or an image that you click to open a view, document, database, other named design element, or URL. Before you create a link hotspot that links to a database, view, document, or anchor link, you must have a link copied to the Clipboard (open the item and choose **Edit, Copy as Link**, and then select the type of link).

Use the following steps to create a link hotspot:

1. Open the page, navigator, or form.

2. Select text or an image for the hotspot link.

3. Choose **Create, Hotspot, Link Hotspot** from the menu. The HotSpot Resource Link Properties box opens (see Figure 11.12).

FIGURE 11.12

A link hotspot can link to a named element or a URL, or it can use a link that's been copied to the Clipboard.

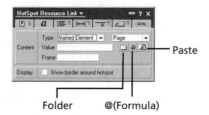

Paste

Folder   @(Formula)

4. On the Hotspot Info tab, select the Type of link hotspot you want to create:

> **Link**—To use the Link type, you must copy a link to the Clipboard before creating the hotspot (see the "Include Links" section later in this day). Click the Paste button on the Hotspot Resource Link Properties box to add that link as the Value for the hotspot.
>
> **Named Element**—Specify a design element (page, form, frameset, view, folder, or navigator) from the drop-down list. Enter the name of the element

in the Value box; click the Folder button and select the element from a dialog box; or click the @ button and enter a formula that results in the name of a design element.

URL—Enter the URL in the Value box, click the @ button to write a formula that results in a URL, or click Paste to paste a URL you copied to the Clipboard.

5. In the Frame box, enter the name of the target frame that displays the item to which the hotspot links.

6. (Optional) Select **Show Border Around Hotspot** if you want the hotspot to have an outline.

Create a Text Pop-up

A *Text Pop-Up* hotspot displays additional text in a box that pops up when the user clicks on the hotspot, or when the user's mouse goes over the hotspot area (depending on the setting). Pop-ups are most frequently used for glossary-like explanations of terms. Unfortunately, they don't work in Web applications.

When preparing a document with unfamiliar terms, it's a good idea to define the terms with pop-ups. The users who are familiar with the terms won't have to read through the definitions, but users who need a definition have only to click and hold on the hotspot to see the pop-up. The mouse pointer becomes a small hand when it comes across the hotspot.

You select the words that you want to make the hotspot. From the menu, choose **Create**, **Hotspot**, **Text Pop-Up**. The HotSpot Pop-up Properties box appears (see Figure 11.13).

FIGURE 11.13

In the HotSpot Pop-up Properties box, you enter the text for the pop-up.

The Hotspot Pop-up Info tab of the properties box has a large white Popup Text area in which you enter the text to appear in the pop-up. Click the check mark when the text is complete.

On the same tab, you determine when the user sees the pop-up text by selecting **On Mouse Over** (text pops up when the mouse crosses the hotspot) or **On Click** (text pops up only when the mouse is clicked and held on the hotspot) under Show Popup.

The other choices on the Hotspot Popup Info tab determine how the hotspot looks to the users. If you select **Border the Text**, a small box appears around the hotspot words. When you select **Highlight the Text**, the hotspot appears as if you had used the highlighter on it.

You format the hotspot text (the static text on the form) by changing the settings on the Font tab of the HotSpot Pop-up Properties box, if you feel the border or highlighting doesn't make it stand out enough.

Although you can't see the pop-up in Designer, it appears when the document is being created, read, or edited.

Create a Formula Pop-Up

Use a formula pop-up to provide information that is the result of the formula, such as @Time. Formula pop-ups don't use formulas that take action. The information appears in a pop-up when the mouse crosses the hotspot or when the user clicks the hotspot.

Use the following steps to create a formula pop-up:

1. Open a form.

2. Select the text or image you want to associate with the pop-up.

3. From the menu, choose **Create, Hotspot, Formula Pop-up**. The HotSpot Pop-up Properties Box appears (see Figure 11.14).

FIGURE 11.14

The hotspot can pop up when the mouse crosses it or when the user clicks on it, depending on the option you select from the properties box.

4. On the Info tab of the Properties box, determine when the pop-up appears: **On Mouse Over** or **On Click**.

5. Decide how the hotspot will look by putting a border around the text, by highlighting the text, or by doing nothing.

6. Click the Font tab if you want to set special font characteristics for the underlying hotspot text (not the text that pops up).

7. Click in the Script Area and write the formula for the pop-up result.

Include Links

Links are pointers to other documents, views, or databases. When the user clicks the link icon, the linked document, view, or database opens. Use links as a way of navigating your application, or to guide users to help information when it's needed.

There are four types of link icons available for inclusion in your documents. These are shown in Table 11.2, as are brief descriptions of each type of link.

Table 11.2 Types of Links

Link Icon	Type	Description
	Document Link	Connects to another Notes document, which can be a mail message or even a document in another database. When you click the icon, the linked document opens on the screen.
	Database Link	Connects to another database. When you click the icon, the database opens in the default view.
	View Link	Connects to a view, either in the same database or another database. When you click the icon, the view appears onscreen.
	Anchor Link	Connects to a specific location in a document. When you click on the icon, the document opens at a particular location within the document (marked by the link).

To create a link for your document, begin by opening or selecting the document, view, or database to which you want to link (use the task buttons and bookmarks to switch between documents and databases). If you want to create an anchor link, you must select text within a document as the location to which you want the link to jump. From the menu, choose **Edit, Copy as Link** and select the type of link you want to create—**Database Link**, **View Link**, **Document Link**, or **Anchor Link**. Links that are inappropriate for the selected or active item are dimmed (unavailable).

Then open the document, form, or page in which you want to place the link (for a document, turn on the edit mode and position your cursor in a rich text field). Choose **Edit, Paste** from the menu. The link icon appears.

You might want to include some introductory text with your link, such as "Click here to see a related document." Just position your cursor in front of the link icon and type.

By the way, a quick way to disseminate a new database is to create a mail memo to all the users and include a database link. When the users click on the link, the new database opens.

Links are also useful in creating applications for the Web because they provide hotspots to other pages, frames, framesets, forms, and views.

 Tip

> One quick way to see the linked document without clicking on the document link icon is to choose **View, Document Link Preview** from the menu. The linked document appears in a Preview Pane at the bottom of the screen.

Interface Enhancements for the Web

When a Web user needs to create, edit, or delete a document from within a browser, he can't just pull down the menu and choose a command. He must embed these functions in one of the following three ways:

- As actions on view and form action bars
- As action hotspots anywhere in a document, page, or form
- As HTML links anywhere in a document, page, or form

These all appear in a browser as HTML hyperlinks, clickable text, or graphics hotspots. The user clicks the hotspot to perform the designated function.

For example, the Web user clicks a hotspot to create a new document. This triggers the browser to retrieve a form from the Domino server and display it in edit mode to the user. The user fills in the fields on the form and clicks the Submit button; the browser sends the form to Domino using standard CGI methods. Domino stores the form in a Notes database.

For the most part, actions enable users to click an onscreen button to perform the same sorts of tasks for which they otherwise have use the choices in the Notes menu. Therefore, actions in a Notes database for Notes users are mostly a convenience feature.

Whereas they are a great enhancement to a Notes application, they are essential to the Web user. They provide the Web user with his only means of creating a new document, opening an existing document in edit mode, or deleting a document.

Note

Simple actions are not supported for the Web and cannot be customized. Domino only translates actions to HTML if they are defined with the @function/@command language. All others (including LotusScript) do not translate. Also, Domino can't translate an action to HTML if your @function or @command formula instructs Domino to do something it can't do. For example, if you add an Edit Document or Delete Document action to a view action bar, Domino can't perform the action because you can't select a document in a view using a browser. However, these actions can display on your view action bar. Use @Commands when you want to give Web users simple action capability, as in @Command([EditDocument]). Avoid using "Include action in Action menu" as an action property for Web users because Web users don't have an Actions menu. Instead, use the option Include action in Button Bar.

11

To create an action so the Web user can create a new document, use `@command([com-pose]);formname)` as discussed earlier in this lesson.

To create an action that performs, in a Web browser, some act upon an existing document, you have to add an action to the action bar of the form that Domino uses to display documents. You can't put this kind of action in a view action bar because there is no way for the browser to tell which document in the view it is to act upon. The kinds of actions that must appear in form action bars and not view action bars include the following:

- **Compose a response document**—@Command([Compose];"formname"), where formname is the name of the response form. Domino automatically treats the open document as the parent of the new response.
- **Edit an existing document**—`@Command([EditDocument])`.
- **Delete an existing document**—`@Command([EditClear])`.

Customizing Response Messages with the $$Return Field

When a Web user submits a form back to a Domino server, a default message—Form processed—appears on the screen. You can customize this response using the *$$Return* field. For example, you can cause Domino to respond as follows: "Thank you, Rob. One of our representatives will reply to you within one business day."

You do this by adding a computed field to the form that users submit, and naming that field $$Return. In the formula Pane, enter a formula defining the response message. The formula that responds with the preceding example's thank you message looks something like this:

```
@Return ("<H2>Thank you, " + FirstName + ". One of our representatives
will reply to you within one business day. </H2>").
```

The <H2> and </H2> tags tell the browser to display the text between the tags in a smaller font than the default, which is H3. The rest of this formula is standard Domino programming.

The following formula says, "Thank you, Rob", and displays a second line that contains a hotspot back to the site home page:

```
@Return ("<H2>Thank you, " + Rob + ".</H2><BR><H4>
<a href=/>Return to Home Page</a>")
```

The "Thank you" message is in a smaller typeface, <H2>. The hyperlink, "Return to Home Page", is in a larger typeface, <H4>.

By enclosing a URL in brackets, you can re-route the user upon submitting a form. The following formula skips the "Form processed" or "Thank you" message entirely and simply returns the user to a different Web page—that is, when the user clicks the Submit button. The browser sends the form to the Domino server, and then sends out a URL for some other HTML page, and Domino displays the form when it receives it.

```
[http://www.lotus.com]
```

You can also include HTML with a URL to link to another page, based on field values in the document.

You can use the same technique to run a CGI script. Simply enter the URL of the script you want to run instead of an HTML page:

```
"[http://inotes/cgi-bin/cgiscriptname.ext]"
```

Understanding Domino URL Commands

Browsers use URLs to access the components of Web servers. Domino Web servers recognize a superset of the standard URL syntax that includes references to Notes objects, actions that one can perform on them, and arguments that qualify the actions.

Basic Syntax of a Domino URL

The basic syntax of a Domino URL is as follows:

```
http://Host/NotesObject[?Action[&Argument...]]
```

where

Host is a Domino server, referred to by its DNS host name or its IP address.

NotesObject is a Notes object such as a database, a view, a form, a navigator, a document, and so on.

?Action is the action to be performed on the object. Examples include ?Open, ?OpenDatabase, ?OpenView, and ?EditDocument.

&Argument... is one or more qualifiers of the action. Each argument is preceded by an ampersand. An example is `http://Host/Database/View?OpenView&Count=10`. This opens the view referred to by `//Host/Database/View` and limits it to 10 rows of objects per screen.

About the Host Parameter

Domino URLs never refer to a Domino server by its Notes server name, but always by either its DNS hostname or its IP address, such as `Server1.Stillwater.com`.

About Notes Objects

You can refer to a Notes database by its filename or its Replica ID.

For example: `http://www.planetnotes.com/home.nsf`

You can refer to other Notes objects by their names (`http://Host/names.nsf/people`), universal IDs (`http://Host/names.nsf/PeopleViewUNID`), or NoteIDs (`http://Host/names.nsf/PeopleViewNoteID`), or in some cases by special identifiers (`http://Host/names.nsf/$defaultView`). You can also give a page (not a document) a text name such as Hotflash, and then open that page by referring to that name (`http://Host/dbname.nsf/HotFlash?OpenPage` or `http://Host/dbname.nsf/HotFlash`).

A Notes object's name and universal ID do not change from one replica of a database to another. An object's NoteID is unique within a database but might change from one replica of the database to another. Therefore, under most circumstances, you want to refer to an object by its name or universal ID, not by its NoteID.

An object's universal ID is a 32-digit hexadecimal number. It is also known as a unique ID or a UNID. An object's NoteID identifies its location within a database.

Special identifiers of Notes objects include $defaultView, $defaultForm, and $defaultNav, which retrieve the default object of each type. Another special identifier, $searchForm, retrieves the standard search form for use in initiating a full-text search on a database. Another, $file, retrieves a file from a Notes document. $icon retrieves the

11

database icon. $help retrieves the Using Database document. $about retrieves the About Database document.

If an object name has spaces in it, replace them with plus signs (+) because spaces are illegal in URLs. For example, refer to the By Date view in a database as `http://Host/Database/By+Date`.

If an object name uses a backslash (\), substitute a forward slash (/). This situation arises, for example, if a database is in a subdirectory or if a view or form is in a submenu.

For example, refer to c:\notes\data\sub1\filename.nsf as http://Host/sub1/filename.nsf, and refer to the Public Address Book view Server\Connections as `http://Host/names.nsf/server/connections`.

About Actions

Actions can be explicit or implicit. Examples of explicit actions include ?OpenDatabase, ?OpenView, and ?EditDocument. Examples of implicit actions include ?Open, ?Edit, and ?Delete. If a URL does not specify an action, Domino assumes defaults to ?Open.

About Arguments

Possible Notes Objects include

Server—However, Domino URLs never refer to servers by their Notes server name, but rather by their DNS hostname or their IP address.

Database—Refer to them either by their filename or their Replica ID.

View

Form

Navigator

Agent

Document

Field

Offset(within Field)

SubOffset (such as attachment name)

DatabaseIcon

DatabaseHelp

DatabaseAbout

IconNote

HelpNote

AboutNote

SearchForm

Frameset

Page

Examples of NotesObjectPath include the following:

Server

Server/Database

Server/Database/DatabaseIcon

Server/Database/IconNote/Field/Offset

Server/Database/DatabaseAbout

Server/Database/AboutNote/Field/Offset

Server/Database/View

Server/Database/View/Document

Server/Database/View/Document/Field/Offset

Server/Database/View/Document/Field/Offset/SubOffset

Server/Database/View/$searchForm

Server/Database/Form

Server/Database/Form/Field/Offset

Server/Database/Form/Field/Offset/SubOffset

Server/Database/Navigator

Server/Database/Navigator/Field/Offset

Server/Database/Agent

Server/Database/Frameset

Server/Database/Page

11

Ways to identify NotesObjects include

Server=	*Nothing*
Database=	/directory/fileName.nsf
View=	NoteID|NoteUNID|Name|$defaultView
Form=	NoteID|NoteUNID|Name|$defaultForm
Navigator	NoteID|NoteUNID|Name|$defaultNav
Agent=	NoteID|NoteUNID|Name
Document=	NoteID|NoteUNID
Field=	Name
Offset=	x.y
SubOffset=	Name
DatabaseIcon=	$icon
DatabaseHelp=	$help
DatabaseAbout=	$about
IconNote=	NoteID
HelpNote=	NoteID
AboutNote=	NoteID
SearchForm=	$searchForm

Possible Actions include

Nothing

ImplicitAction

ExplicitAction

ImplicitActions include

Open

Create (documents only)

Edit (documents only)

Save (documents only)

Delete (documents only)

Search (views only)

Possible ExplicitActions include

OpenServer

OpenDatabase

OpenView

OpenForm

OpenNavigator

OpenAgent

OpenDocument

OpenElement (such as attachments)

CreateDocument (Form Post Action only)

EditDocument

SaveDocument (Form Post Action only)

Delete Document

SearchView

Frameset

Page

Possible Arguments include

Start(OpenView)

Count(OpenView)

Expand(OpenView)

ExpandView(OpenView)

Collapse(OpenView)

CollapseView(OpenView)

FieldElemType(OpenElement)

FieldElemFormat(OpenElement)

SearchForm(Open the search form)

Query(SearchView)

OldSearchQuery

SearchMax(SearchView)

11

SearchWV(SearchView)

SearchOrder

SearchThesaurus

Frameset

Page

ParentUNID

Creating Custom Search and Search Result Pages

Domino uses four search forms for Domain searches. They reside in the Catalog (R5.0) template and are called Search Form, SearchResults, ResultEntry, and DetailedResultEntry. You can customize these forms to meet the needs of your organization by adding navigation buttons for result pages, determining the number of Hits to be returned, instructing Domino in the order of return (ascending, descending), and so forth.

Customizing search forms is fairly advanced and somewhat beyond the scope of this book, but after you complete all the lessons in this book, we're confident that you can create custom search results from the instructions provided in the Domino Designer Help database (see "Search forms, customizing search forms"). We mention it here because we think customizing the search forms for your Web site is a good idea because it adds polish and individuality to your site.

You might need to work with your Domino System Administrator when you customize search forms because the forms you create need to be copied or pasted into the domain catalog on the Domino server used for Domain Search.

Summary

By using @Commands, formulas for action buttons, hotspot buttons, action hotspots, and agents, you can access the menu commands for the user. The user clicks a button, and the command is carried out without touching the menu bar (which is very helpful for Web users who don't have access to the Notes menu).

Actions appear on the Notes menu, but by adding them to the Action Bar you also make them available to Web users. Hotspots and links provide navigational tools to documents, views, databases, and URLs. Pop-ups provide onscreen information and help for the user.

Use Domino URL commands to help Web users navigate your site. Submit responses can be easily customized, adding a personal touch to your Web applications. Remember that simple actions do not translate to the Web, and you want to use @commands on buttons and hotspots to help users create and edit documents and perform other functions otherwise found on the Notes menu.

Q&A

Q Do I have to create two action buttons to save a document and close it?

A No, create one button but combine both expressions in the formula and separate them with a semicolon:

```
@Command([FileSave]);
@Command ([FileCloseWindow])
```

Q I'm interested in the action buttons that have pull-down menus. Are there any limits?

A You can't go more than one level, so you won't have another menu cascading off the main list.

Q In some of our existing databases I see @PostedCommands functions. What are they?

A The @PostedCommands are very similar to @Commands. They even use the same keywords (commands). However, any command written using the @PostedCommand function executes after the rest of the formula has been evaluated. You can't use @PostedCommands in column, selection, hide-when, section, window title, field, or form formulas, or in agents that run on the server. They are intended for use in buttons, hotspots, action formulas, and SmartIcons.

One of the reasons you see these commands on some of your existing applications might be the age of the application. When applications that were designed originally in Release 3 of Notes were upgraded to Release 4, the @Commands were converted to @PostedCommands. This is especially true for an application where the formula was still executed in Release 3 because Release 3 couldn't execute Release 4 @Commands.

Workshop

In this workshop you are going to add automation to the application you've been building. This automation includes action buttons, hotspot buttons, link hotspots, and links.

Open the Proposed Titles database (or open the PTDay10.nsf from the Day10 folder on the CD and start working from there).

11

Add Form and View Actions

In the Proposed Title form, do the following:

- Using the system action Edit Document, add an Edit Document button to the Action bar. Hide this button when the document is in edit mode.

- Create an action button, Your Profile, that opens an existing Profile document in edit mode or creates a new one. The button should have a formula similar to `@Command([EditProfile]; "Profile"; @UserName)`.

- Because users will now complete their Profile documents, you can bring information from that form into the Proposed Title form. Change the TProfileInfo field to a computed text field. Add this formula to the field:

```
JobTitle := @GetProfileField("Profile"; "Position"; @UserName);
Dept := @GetProfileField("Profile"; "Group"; @UserName);
JobTitle + " from " + Dept
```

- Make another action button so the reader can respond to the proposed title. Call it Response.

- Make an action button called Set Status\Accept that changes the value of the Status field to Accepted (hint: use a simple action to modify the field, and don't forget to use the synonym). Then create another button called Set Status\Rejected to set the Status field value to Rejected. Hide both of these actions from anyone who is not a member of the EditBoard group.

- Save and close the form.

In the Response and Comments forms

- Create an Action button called Comment so readers of the response document can comment on it.

- Make the same button in the Comments form.

In the Books\by Title view

- Add an action button called Propose New Title to create a new proposed title.

- Add an action button called Response to respond to a selected proposed title or, if the selected document is a Response or Comments document, create a Comments document. Try using the @IsResponse document @function.

Create and Use Shared Actions

Create the following shared actions and add them to the designated forms or views:

- A Save and Close action to save the document and close the document window. Add to Proposed Title, Response, and Comments forms.

- A Print Document action to Print the document. Add to Proposed Title, Response, and Comments forms and to the Books\by Title view.

Add a Button to a Form

Open the Proposed Title form and add a button immediately below the "Discussion Period" and the Review date fields. When a user clicks the button, an additional 30 days are added to the review period and the TStatus field value is changed to Hold for Further Discussion.

Call the button Extend Review Period. Hide the button when the document is read, printed, or previewed. Write a formula to add 30 days to the TReviewEnd field and change the TStatus value. Hint: Use @Adjust to change the TReviewEnd date and @SetField to change the TStatus field.

Adding Links on the Home Page

On Day 8, "Create Pages and Frames," you created a home page for the Proposed Titles database. At that time, you were instructed to add view links to the different views in the database. If you were unable to do that because you needed to learn how to make the links, add those links now. Add another link to the Titles in Development database.

Also, add some URL links to Web sites that might be related, such as
`http://www.mcp.com`.

Use @Return

Add a Submit button to the Profile form that saves the document and closes the window. Use @Return to confirm to the user that the proper information has been received. Also, add another field called BrowserInfo to the Profile document to collect information on the type of browser used.

To see our examples of this application, open the folder on the CD called Day 11. Open the database called PTDay11.nsf.

11

DAY 12

Beautify Your Application

There's no reason why an application can't be practical and good looking at the same time. Those who have to work with your application will appreciate anything you do in your design that makes the application easy to use. A little thoughtfulness on your part can prevent your application from presenting itself as the boring, mundane set of screens often associated with data entry.

In today's lesson, you learn to combine brains and beauty by working with

- Animating your tables, adding tabs, and programming them.
- Using layout regions to arrange your fields, static text, and graphics.
- Adding navigators to pictorially guide your users around your application.

More Tables

Tables organize information into columns and rows and help users quickly view and digest important information—in addition to making it easier to enter data. In Domino, you can take tables a step beyond the ordinary by adding animation and, consequently, flexibility to your application.

As you learned on Day 2, "Forms 101: The Essentials of Form Design," Domino has four types of tables:

- The basic table
- The tabbed table that displays each row as a clickable tab
- The animated table that displays each row for two seconds
- The programmed table that displays one row based on a field value

Add Tabs

A tabbed table has tabs along the top of the table (see Figure 12.1), each of which opens a different row.

FIGURE 12.1

When you select a tab, the row associated with it appears. Add text and fields as needed.

You can create a tabbed table from scratch or convert an existing basic table into a tabbed table.

Use the following steps to create a tabbed table:

1. Open a page or form and click to place your cursor where you want the table.
2. Choose **Create, Table** from the menu. The Create Table dialog box opens (see Figure 12.2).

FIGURE 12.2

Click the appropriate button to select the type of table you want to create.

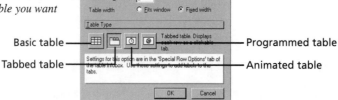

3. Enter the number of rows and columns you need.
4. Decide whether the table will be a fixed width or stretch to fit the window.

5. Click the **Tabbed Table** button to set the table type.

6. Click **OK**.

7. Click in any cell of the table. Then right-click and select **Table Properties** from the shortcut menu.

8. Select the **Table Rows** tab.

9. Add tab labels by clicking on the tab and entering the label in the **Tab Label** box.

Before you convert a basic table to a tabbed table, you'll probably have to reorganize it. The cells in the first column become the tabs, and the text in that column appears on the tabs as labels.

Use the following steps to add tabs to a basic table:

1. Click in any cell of the table. Then right-click and select **Table Properties** from the shortcut menu.

2. Select the **Table Rows** tab.

3. Under Special Table Row Display, select **Show Only One Row at a Time**. Additional options appear on the page (see Figure 12.3).

FIGURE 12.3

Each selection under **Which Row to Display** *changes the table to a different type—tabbed, animated, or pro-grammed.*

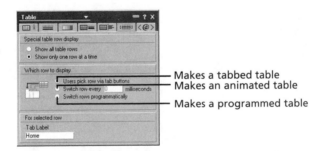

— Makes a tabbed table
— Makes an animated table

— Makes a programmed table

12

4. Select **Users Pick Row Via Tab Buttons**.

5. Add or change tab labels by clicking on the tab and entering the label in the **Tab Label** box.

Animate a Table

An animated table displays only one row at a time. As each row disappears and a new one appears, special animated effects (called *transition effects*), such as dissolving or wiping, display.

If you know you want to use an animated table to start, create one. In the Create Table dialog box (refer to Figure 12.2), select the **Animated Table** button.

Use the following steps to animate an existing table:

1. Click in any cell of the table. Then right-click and select **Table Properties** from the shortcut menu.

2. Select the **Table Rows** tab (see Figure 12.4).

FIGURE 12.4

The transitions you specify in Effect animate the table.

3. Under Special Table Row Display, select **Show Only One Row at a Time**.

4. Under Which Row to Display, select **Switch Row Every**. Although 2000 is the default, you can enter whatever length of time (in milliseconds) you want to pass before the next row displays in the table.

5. To set how the rows display as they switch, choose an **Effect** such as Rolling, Wipe, or Explode.

6. Determine when switching will occur by selecting an option from the Cycle Through Rows drop-down list:

   Advance on Click—Changes rows only when you click the table

   Continually—Cycles continuously, changing rows based on the switch row setting

   Once When Opened—Only changes rows when the document is first opened in read mode

   Once on Click—Only changes rows once, the first time you click the table

The animated effects only show when the document is in read mode. If you want to test your animation, you have to save your form or page and then test it (see Figure 12.5).

FIGURE 12.5

The home page displayed in this frame has an animated table that cycles between "Best Buys Guaranteed," "Quick Delivery," and "Excellent Service."

Animated table ——

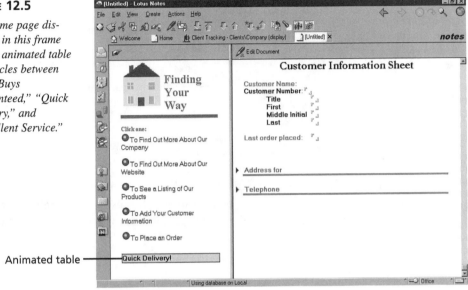

Program a Table

A programmed table resembles a tabbed table at first glance because only one row or tab is visible at a time. But instead of clicking on a tab to change the rows, the user clicks on an action, a link, or an outline entry to switch rows.

To create a new programmed table, choose **Create, Table** from the menu and select the **Programmed Table** button as the table type. Enter the number of rows and columns and click **OK**.

To convert an existing table to a programmed table, open the Table Properties box (choose **Table, Table Properties** from the menu), click the **Table Rows** tab, and select **Switch Rows Programmatically**. If you want the user to also be able to switch rows by clicking on a tab, enable **Also Show Tabs So User Can Pick Row**.

The programmed table and each row in it must be named. Click the **Table Programming** tab of the Table Properties box (see Figure 12.6). In the Name/Id field of the Table HTML Tags section, enter a name for the table. Then click in the first row of the table and enter a name for that row in the **Row Tags** field. Repeat these steps for each row.

12

FIGURE 12.6

Each row in the pro-
grammed table, as
well as the table itself,
must have a name.

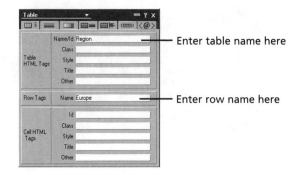

— Enter table name here

— Enter row name here

You need to create links, hotspots, actions, or outline entries to give the users access to the different rows of the table. When you refer to the table, use the field $*tablename*. For example, for a table named Region, the field name for the programmed table is $Region (see Figure 12.7).

Action hotspots

FIGURE 12.7

Each of the action
hotspots in the first
table is linked to a row
in the programmed
table. The formula for
the Europe hotspot
assigns Europe *as the*
value for the $Region
field. Europe is the
row tag for the first
row in the pro-
grammed table. The
@Command([RefreshHi
deFormulas] refreshes
only the hidden
formulas.

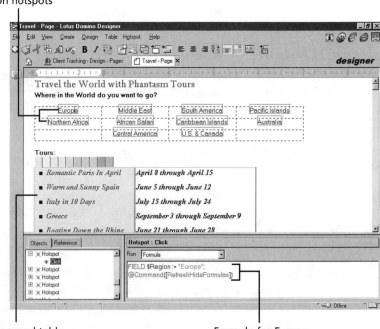

Programmed table

Formula for Europe
action hotspot

Nest a Table Inside Another Table

A *nested table* is a table within another table. Being able to put one table inside the cell of another makes it possible to make a cell look as if it's been split into rows or columns.

To create a nested table, place your cursor inside the cell of the existing table (make sure the document is in edit mode) and choose **Create, Table** from the menu. Specify the number of rows and columns you want in the nested table and select the type. Click **OK**.

Figure 12.8 shows an example of a tabbed table with a nested table. The nested table is a tabbed table with a tab for each day of the week. Inside that table, within each row is a basic table.

FIGURE 12.8

This tabbed table has another tabbed table nested inside, which in turn contains a nested table.

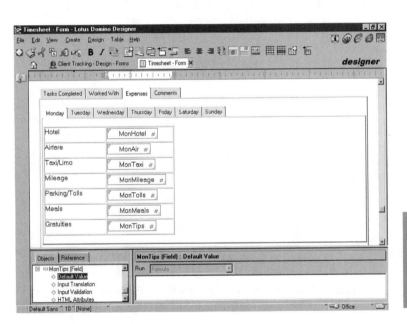

12

Create Layout Regions

A layout region is a design area on a form or subform that offers greater flexibility than working in the form itself. Layout regions can contain static text, fields (except rich text fields), graphics, and buttons. Within the layout region elements can be dragged to move them. Unfortunately, layout regions are not supported for Web applications.

To create a layout region on a form, place your cursor where you want the layout region to appear and then choose **Create, Layout Region, New Layout Region** from the menu.

If you need to adjust the look, position, or size of the layout region, click the region and choose **Design, Layout Properties** from the menu. The Layout Properties box opens (see Figure 12.9). Set a different Left setting to position the region horizontally. Specify the Width and Height to set the size of the region (or drag the *sizing handles*—the little black boxes along the border of the region—to change the height and width). To make the region "invisible," deselect **Show Border**. If you select **3D Style**, the layout region has a gray background, and fields and buttons look as they do in dialog boxes.

FIGURE 12.9

Left is the position of the left side of the layout region, in inches. The 1" position lines up with the left margin.

As you add elements to the layout region, you might have difficulty positioning them so they line up properly. Select **Show Grid** to see a series of dots lined up in columns and rows. These dots help you align your elements. The Grid Size specifies how far apart the dots are. For more help in positioning elements, select **Snap to Grid**. With Snap to Grid on, the elements you move seem to cling to the rows and columns of dots, making sure the element you're moving is lined up.

The Layout Properties box has a Layout Hide-When tab, which you click to select when the layout box is to be visible. The elements you add to the layout region can also be hidden according to the conditions you set in the Control or Field Properties boxes.

To make changes to the layout region, open the form or subform and select the layout region. Move or remove elements (click the element and press **Delete**). Change the size of the layout region or elements on the region.

Save the form to save the layout region.

Add Graphics

Before you add a graphic to a layout region, you must copy the graphic to the Clipboard. Then open the form or subform in which you want to insert the graphic. Click in the layout region to select it, and then choose **Create, Layout Region, Graphic** from the menu.

Point in the middle of the graphic and drag it to a new position within the layout region. For exact positioning, specify measurements in the Left and Top fields of the Control Properties box (choose **Design, Object Properties** to open it).

If you add the graphic after your text or fields are in place, it might cover up your other design elements. To remedy this, select the graphic and choose **Design, Send to Back** from the menu to place the graphic behind the other design elements in the layout region.

Add Static Text

You can't just start typing in a layout region like you can in a form. Select the region first, and then choose **Create, Layout Region, Text**. A text object appears in the layout region. Point to the center of the text item and drag it to the desired position in the layout region. Then type the text in the Text box of the Control Properties box (see Figure 12.10).

FIGURE 12.10

The Control Properties box controls the properties of the selected item in the layout region. In the case of text, you enter the text, and then set its alignment and position in the properties box.

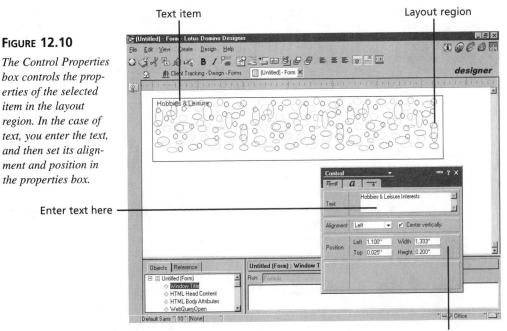

In the Control Properties box, you can set the exact position of the text item by entering measurements in the Left and Top boxes. You can also specify the Height and Width of the text object if you don't want to drag the sizing handles on the item to set its size. The text wraps within the area marked by the sizing handles. The Alignment (Left, Center, Right) is the horizontal alignment of the text within the text item area. Center Vertically centers the text from top to bottom within the text item area.

All the text within the text item shares the same font characteristics, which are set on the Font tab of the Control Properties box.

Add Fields

Be sure to select the layout region before you create a field that you plan to place within the region. Then choose **Create, Field** from the menu. When the field appears on the layout region, it has sizing handles (see Figure 12.11). Point in the middle of the field area and drag to move it; drag one of the sizing handles to make it bigger or smaller. Alternatively, set the position and size in the Control Properties box.

Sizing handle   Field

FIGURE 12.11

The Native OS style is automatically selected for the field because it displays as a white box in the layout region instead of showing brackets.

Size of field

Position of field in layout region

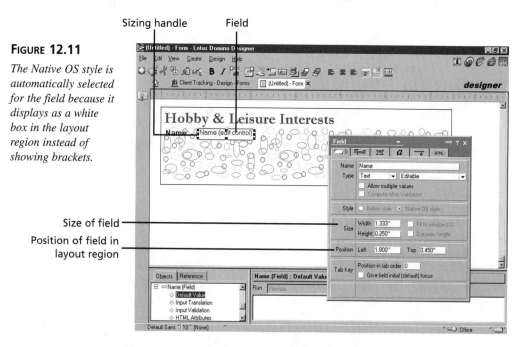

Fields in layout regions are a little different than fields in forms. In layout regions, fields can be displayed over text or graphics, the size of the field can be limited, and a text field can display multiple lines and have a scrollbar. In date/time fields that display times a time selector appears, and in date/time fields that display dates a date picker appears.

Insert Graphic Buttons

Using a graphic button is the way to add a hotspot to the layout region. Before you add the button, you have to copy the appropriate graphic to the Clipboard. Then select the layout region and choose **Create, Layout Region, Graphic Button** from the menu.

Position the button by dragging it to a new location, and size it by dragging the sizing handles.

You need a formula to direct the action of the button. Click the **Objects** tab in the Info List and select **Hotspot, Click** if it isn't already selected. Then click in the Script Area and enter the formula (see Figure 12.12).

FIGURE 12.12

This graphic button opens the frameset in the database that contains the home page.

Graphic button

Control Properties box

Hotspot click event selected

Formula

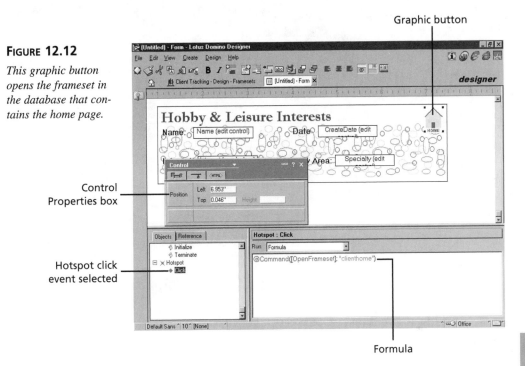

12

Set Tab Order

Because fields are not set out in the same "orderly" fashion as in a form, tabbing from one field to another as you enter text doesn't necessarily follow the usual left to right, top to bottom pattern.

For each field you enter in the layout region, assign a number in the **Position in Tab Order** field on the Field Info page of the Field Properties box. The tabbing follows the order of the numbers you enter.

Design Navigators

Navigators combine graphics and hotspots to make it easier to move around in an application.

Figure 12.13 shows a simple navigator that consists of some colored rectangles that are labeled so users know what opens when they click the hotspots.

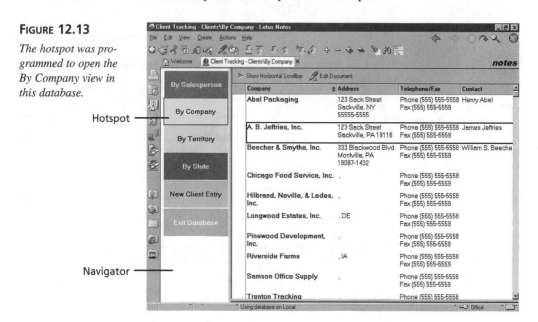

In a navigator, you combine several types of objects:

- Graphic backgrounds
- Hotspots—rectangles, circles, and polygons (the hotspot polygons aren't supported on the Web)
- Graphic buttons
- Buttons
- Text
- Shapes—rectangles, rounded rectangles, ellipses, polygons, and polylines

You create objects by drawing them with the tools in Designer or by importing or pasting objects from other applications.

Add actions to any navigator object you draw (you can't add actions for the items you pasted or imported). Simple actions you can use include opening another navigator, opening a view or folder, opening a URL, and opening a database, view, or document link. For any other actions, you need to write formulas or scripts.

Use the following steps to create a navigator:

1. Open the database in Designer and select **Navigators** from the Design Pane.

2. Click the **New Navigator** button on the Action Bar.

3. To open the Navigator Properties box (see Figure 12.14), choose **Design**, **Navigator Properties** from the menu.

FIGURE 12.14

On the Info tab, enter the name of the navigator, set the initial view or folder that opens with it, and pick a background color. On the Grid tab, click Snap to Grid to help align objects in the Navigator.

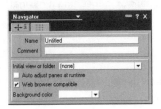

4. Enter a Name for the navigator.

5. (Optional) Select **Web Browser Compatible** if you want to be able to use the navigator on the Web.

6. (Optional) Select an initial view or folder to open along with the navigator.

7. (Optional) To keep users from having to adjust the size of the Navigation Pane if the navigator doesn't fit, select **Auto Adjust Panes at Runtime**.

8. Add graphics, text, and hotspots to the navigator.

9. Save and close the navigator.

Because the purpose of creating a navigator is to make it easier for your users to get around the application, you want to make sure that they see the navigator when they first open the database. In the Database Properties box (choose **File, Database, Properties**), click the **Launch** tab, and then select **Open Designated Navigator** from the When Opened in the Notes Client field. From the Type of Navigator field, select **Standard Navigator** (**Folder** opens the Folders and Views navigator). Then select the **Name** of the navigator.

For Web applications, select either **Open Designated Navigator in its own Window** or **Use Notes Launch Option** (if you are launching the database with the navigator open) from the When Opened in a Browser field. Before you do this, though, you must select **Web Browser Compatible** from the Navigator Properties box of that navigator.

12

When navigators are needed for Web applications, consider embedding or importing the navigator. This helps you to control the size and display of the navigator. If you simply select Web browser compatible as a navigator property, Domino converts the navigator to an HTML imagemap and your navigator displays full screen. Clicking a Polyline object has no effect on the Web, so avoid using those objects. See Day 17, "Embed Objects in Your Applications," for the details of embedding a navigator on a page or form.

Add Graphic Elements

Only one object can be pasted into a navigator as a graphic background. Graphic buttons, however, can be used to initiate actions.

The graphic objects you paste or import into the navigator must one of the following formats: BMP (bitmap), GIF, JPEG, PCX, or TIFF.

Use the following steps to paste or import a graphic into a navigator:

1. Copy the graphic to the Clipboard if you intend to paste it into the navigator.

2. Open the navigator.

3. Choose **Create, Graphic Background** from the menu to paste the graphic into the navigator background (to remove a graphic background, choose **Design, Remove Graphic Background**).

   Choose **Create, Graphic Button** from the menu to paste the graphic as a button on the navigator. Then drag the button to an appropriate location on the navigator.

   Choose **File, Import** from the menu. Select the file to import and click **OK**. Click **Graphic Background** to import the graphic as a background; click **Graphic Button** to import the graphic as a button.

Did one of your objects overlap or cover up another object? Select the "offending" object and choose **Design, Send to Back**. This does not, however, apply to hotspots, which are always on top of other objects.

A graphic button has a related action that you program. Select the button and choose **Design, Object Properties** to open the Graphic Button Properties box. Enter a Name for the button on the Info page, and select **Lock Size and Position** after you've moved the button to its location in the Navigator. On the HiLite page, choose whether you want the button highlighted when it's touched or when it's clicked. The programming of the graphic button involves selecting a simple action or writing a formula or script (see the next section, "Add Hotspots").

Designer also has a set of drawing tools that you can use to create graphic objects for the navigator (see Figure 12.15). They can be accessed from the Create menu or from the SmartIcons.

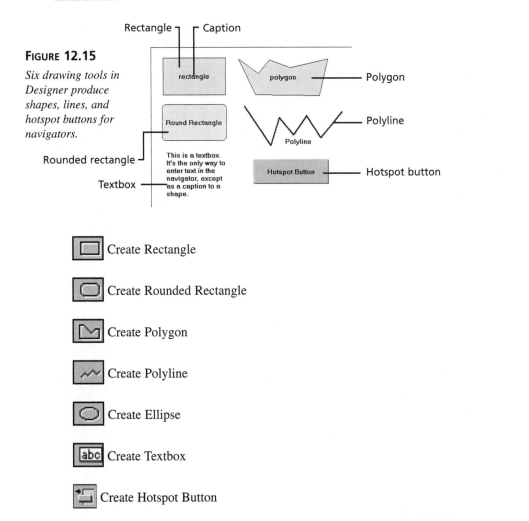

FIGURE 12.15

Six drawing tools in Designer produce shapes, lines, and hotspot buttons for navigators.

Create Rectangle

Create Rounded Rectangle

Create Polygon

Create Polyline

Create Ellipse

Create Textbox

Create Hotspot Button

After selecting a drawing tool, your mouse pointer becomes a *cross hair* (little cross). With shapes such as rectangles, ellipses, textboxes, and hotspot buttons, you click at one corner and drag diagonally to the opposite corner. With polylines and polygons, you click at the beginning of the object and then click again at each bend or angle you want; double-click to finish drawing. To draw a circle or square, hold down the **Shift** key as you drag.

If you need to draw several of the same object, hold down **Shift** and choose **Create** and then the type of object. When you're finished drawing the objects, choose **Create** and the type of object again.

Move objects by pointing in the center of the object and dragging it to a new position (unless it's locked in position). Drag the sizing handles (little black boxes) to change the size of shapes or the position of the angle points for polygons and polylines.

Each drawn object (except the polyline) has a name and caption—which you assign on the properties box for that object (choose **Design, Object Properties**)—that appear on the object. The properties include an option to lock the size and position of the object; font settings for the caption, color, and width of the border or line; background color and a choice of a solid or transparent background; and the option of highlighting the object when it is touched or clicked.

Each drawn object, including the polyline, can be programmed. The programming involves selecting a simple action or writing a formula or script (see the next section, "Add Hotspots").

Add Hotspots

Hotspotsin a navigator are areas that you click to make something happen. The something that happens is the result of the programming you add to the hotspot. It can be a simple action such as opening a view, the result of a formula such as creating a new document, or the result of a LotusScript program.

Although graphic buttons and the drawn objects in navigators are programmable, there are also tools for drawing hotspots. These are ideal for highlighting areas of a graphic background, such as a map, and using them to initiate an action.

The hotspots you draw are

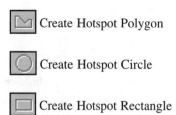

Create Hotspot Polygon

Create Hotspot Circle

Create Hotspot Rectangle

You draw hotspots as you draw shapes. Double-click the hotspot to open the Hotspot *ObjectName* Properties box (*ObjectName* is Circle, Polygon, or Rectangle). Give the hotspot a name or accept the one Designer created for you. On the HiLite tab, as you can see in Figure 12.16, you not only determine when the hotspot is highlighted but also select a border width and color for the hotspot.

FIGURE 12.16

Decide whether the hotspot is to be high-lighted when the mouse pointer touches it or when it is clicked.

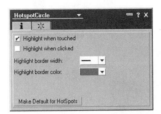

To program a hotspot (or a drawn shape or graphic button), choose Simple Action(s), Formula, or LotusScript from the Run drop-down list in the Programmer's Pane (see Figure 12.17). The available simple actions include Open Another Navigator, Open a View or Folder, Alias a Folder, Open a Link, or Open URL. You must specify the name of the navigator, view, folder, or URL. For links, you must already have copied the database, view, or document link to the Clipboard.

FIGURE 12.17

Use simple actions whenever possible, and reserve formulas and scripts for other actions, such as creating a new document or exiting the application.

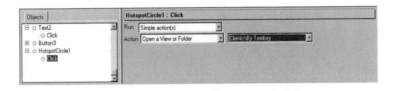

12

> **Tip**
>
> **Alias a Folder** replaces a current folder (if one is open) with one activated by the object the user clicks. For example, if you have your Important folder open and you click a navigator hotspot that's programmed to alias the folder Next Week, the Next Week folder replaces Important. Choosing **View, Go To** enables you to return to the original folder.

Imagemaps

A navigator is a standalone design element. An *imagemap* is a graphic that appears on a page or form, but it contains hotspots that perform actions when clicked. Imagemaps are often used to navigate through a database, in a similar manner to navigators. One advantage that imagemaps have is that you can include text and other page elements, and you can hide the imagemap using hide-when options. The navigator is a better choice when you plan to combine several graphics with text and action buttons.

Use the following steps to create an imagemap:

1. Open a page and paste or import a graphic.

2. Select the graphic and choose **Picture, Picture Properties** to open the Picture Properties box (see Figure 12.18).

FIGURE 12.18

*To size the graphic, drag the sizing handle in the lower-right corner or set the **Width** and **Height** percentages in the Picture Properties box.*

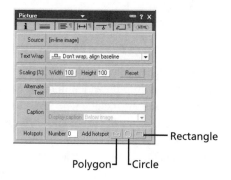

3. Set the size using the Scaling percentages. Enter Alternate Text if you plan to use the imagemap on the Web; the alternate text appears while the user waits for the graphic to display. Click the **Picture Border** tab to specify a border.

4. To add a hotspot to the graphic, click one of the three Add Hotspot buttons—**Polygon**, **Circle**, or **Rectangle**—or choose **Picture, Add Hotspot** and select the hotspot you want to add.

5. Click and drag to draw a circle or rectangle hotspot; click at each angle to draw a polygon, and then double-click to end the shape.

6. In the Hotspot *ObjectName* Properties box (*ObjectName* is the name of the type of object—rectangle, circle, or polygon), which appears when you draw the hotspot, enter a Name for the hotspot or accept the one Designer creates for you (see Figure 12.19).

FIGURE **12.19**

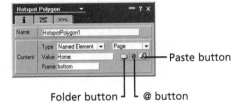

Paste button

Folder button — — @ button

7. In the Contents section of the Hotspot Info page, choose a Type:

   Link—Before you specify the link, copy a database, view, document, or anchor link to the Clipboard. Then click the Paste button to paste the link into the Value.

   Named Element—Specify the type of element (page, form, frameset, view, folder, or navigator). Then, in Value, enter the name of the element; click the **Folder** button to select the name from a dialog box; or click the @ button to write a formula that results in the name of an element.

   URL—Enter the Web address in Value; click the @ button to enter a formula that results in a URL; or click the **Paste** button to paste the address of a Web page currently in the Clipboard.

8. If the page is part of a frameset, enter the name of the target frame to display the link, URL, or named element.

Formatting Considerations for Web Applications

12

Not all table and navigator properties are supported on the Web. Furthermore, there are some formatting and text styles that are not supported on the Web, and it's a good idea to keep these in mind when you're developing for a Web or mixed group of users. Throughout this book, we've talked about Domino features and the effect they have on the Web; here, we want to remind you of some things to avoid when working with text and tables for Web users.

For a complete list of features that are not supported, see *Web, unsupported features, Overview of features to avoid using in Web applications* in the Designer Help database.

Table 12.1 lists Table, Text and Formatting features and properties that are not supported on the Web.

Table 12.1 Web, Domino Text and Table Features Not Recommended for Use on the Web

Feature or Property	Note
Table column spacing	Not supported but can affect the Width property of a cell, which is supported on the Web
Table minimum height	
Table row spacing	
Table width	Same as Window; is ignored on the Web
Cell border color	Cells are the same colors as the table
Cell border styles	Ridge and groove aren't supported
Cell border thickness	Only thickness settings less than 1 are supported
Table background	Only solid is supported; Gradients appear as first color
Cell image	
Table margins, left, right	
Table wrap	
Table compatibility	
Table, show only one row at a time	Transitions and switch rows every n milliseconds are not supported
Text, default fonts Helvetica and Times Roman	
Text alignment	Full justification and No Wrap aren't supported
Text alignment interline spacing	Any number other than a whole number isn't supported
Text alignment such as tabs, indents, outdents, and extra spaces	
Text effect: shadow, Emboss, and Extrude	

Summary

Tables go way beyond just rows and columns. A tabbed table shows a different row for each tab that a user clicks. Animated tables display a different row at specified intervals and incorporate transitions (such as wipe and explode) that add movement to your applications. Programmed tables show different rows depending on programmed conditions.

Layout regions offer flexibility in adding graphics, text, and fields. These elements can move to any part of the layout region. Fields in layout regions appear as empty white boxes to users, which makes it easier to read field data when a background graphic is applied to the layout region. Because they are not supported by Web browsers, it's helpful to be able to hide the layout region when a document is opened by Web users.

Navigators combine graphics, buttons, and hotspots to help users easily navigate a database. Graphics can be imported, pasted, or drawn with Designer's drawing tools. Programming can be in the form of simple actions, formulas, or LotusScript.

Imagemaps appear to be similar to navigators because they also combine graphics and hotspots. However, imagemaps must appear on forms or pages. Generally, imagemaps use one large graphic image on which several hotspots appear, such as a map. Navigators use several graphics, buttons, and hotspots.

Q&A

Q **Some of our users still prefer to use the Folders and Views navigator instead of the navigator I created. The database automatically launches the graphical navigator. What can I do? They're tired of having to go to the view menu to switch to Folders and Views.**

A I suggest you create a hotspot in your navigator to open the Folders and Views navigator. You program it with a simple action. If the users can simply click a hotspot to get the other navigator, they'll be happier. It's always a good idea to do this with a graphical navigator because some users are more accustomed to seeing folders and views, or they might have private folders or views they can't see from your navigator.

Q **I need to put an updated imagemap on my home page. Does that mean I'll have to redraw all those hotspots?**

A Select the picture that you are currently using for the imagemap and choose Picture, Replace Picture from the menu. Then specify the name of the updated image. You might have to move or reshape a couple of hotspots, but you won't lose them.

Q **I seem to have a lot of trouble lining up text and fields in layout regions. What can I do?**

A Try turning on Snap to Grid. That might help. Keep the type size and style in both your fields and your static text the same; otherwise they won't seem to line up. If you're a real stickler, watch your top and left position numbers to make sure your fields and text are at the same position.

12

Workshop

In this workshop, you enhance both the Proposed Titles and Titles in Development databases. If you haven't been building the databases as we go along, open the PTDay11.nsf database from the Day11 folder on the CD and the TDDay10.nsf database from the Day10 folder.

Add a Tabbed Table

In the Titles in Development database, open the New Title form. Add a tabbed table to the form that has four tabs: Acquisition Editor, Development Editor, Technical Editor, and Copy Editor. Each row of the table displays the name of the editor, the editor's phone number, and the editor's email address. The names of the fields are listed in Table 12.2.

Table 12.2   Fields for Tabbed Table

Editor	Editor's Name field	Editor's Phone Number field	Editor's Email Address field
Acquisition Editor	AcqEditor	AcqEdPhone	AcqEdEmail
Development Editor	DevEditor	DevEdPhone	DevEdEmail
Technical Editor	TechEditor	TechEdPhone	TechEdEmail
Copy Editor	CopyEditor	CopyEdPhone	CopyEdEmail

These fields are all Editable Text fields, except for AcqEditor. That field is computed for display, and the formula is the field name TAcqEditor. We added a different color to each row and set our fields to the Native OS style with 1.5" width and dynamic height.

Add an Animated Table

In the Proposed Titles database, open the Home Page and add an animated table at the bottom. Make the table one column wide and three rows deep. Choose a different background color for each row. Select a transition effect for the table (remember that animated tables won't work on the Web, so view it in Notes to see the animation). Enter the following text:

Books for Beginners and Books for Experienced!

Writers Who Are Experts in Their Field!

Every Major Subject Covered!

Add a Programmed Table

In the Titles in Development database, open the New Title form. Add a programmed table that is one column wide and has five rows. Name the table Series and name the rows Computer Illiterate, Beginning, Intermediate, Advanced, and Super Advanced. These are the choices available for the TAudience field. TAudience is the field that describes the target audience of the book. The programmed table changes rows based on the value in the TAudience field.

You need to add a field to control the Programmed table. Make it a computed text field called $Series, and enter TAudience as the formula. Make sure for TAudience that the option **Refresh fields on keyword change** is selected (on the Control tab of the Field Properties box).

On each row of the programmed table, create a standard table (a nested table) that has two rows and three columns. The top row of each table contains the column labels Page Count, Use Guideline, and Graphic Resolution. The second row contains three fields, one in each column. The field in the first column is an editable text field to capture the number of pages or page range. In the second column is an editable Listbox field that has choices for the types of books suitable for that audience (such as "Easy" for the computer illiterate). The third column field is a combobox that lists the possible display settings at which the figure illustrations can be captured: 640x480, 800x600, 1024x768, 1152x864, 1280x1024, and 1600x1200.

The naming of each of the fields in the tables has to be different for each row of the programmed table. For example, on the Computer Illiterate row, the fields are named PagesCI, GuideCI, and ResolnCI. On the next row, the Beginning row, they are called PagesB, GuideB, and ResolnB. For the Intermediate row, we added I at the end of Pages, Guide, and Resoln. We added an A for the Advanced fields and SA for the Super Advanced fields.

To make this easier, copy the fields from one table to another and then rename them. Pages is an editable field so it remains the same except for the name, and the choices for Resoln are the same for each table. Only the choices in Guide vary (use names that indicate what type of book this would be for the level user). We used the following choices:

GuideCI—Easy, Idiot's Guide.

GuideB—How to Use, 10 Minute Guide.

GuideI—Using, Teach Yourself in 24 Hours.

GuideA—Special Edition, Teach Yourself in 21 Days.

GuideSA—Unleashed.

12

Use your own names; make up some that aren't already used by publishers if you can.

As for formatting, we removed the borders from the programmed table but left them around the nested tables.

Use a Layout Region

Create a new form in the Titles in Development database. Call it Author Information, with an alias of Author. The purpose of this form is to store information about book authors.

Create a layout region on the form. Add the following fields and appropriate text labels to the layout region:

- **AuthName**—An editable text field for the author's name.
- **AuthAddress**—An editable text field for the author's complete mailing address. You probably want to select the Display options **Allow multiple lines** and **Show scroll bars** (both on the Control tab of the Field Properties box).
- **AuthPhoneWork**—An editable text field for the author's telephone number at work.
- **AuthPhoneHome**—An editable text field for the author's telephone number at home.
- **AuthEmail**—An editable text field for the author's email address.

Make the fields as large as you think necessary. How you position them and what static text you add are entirely up to you. Add a graphic to the layout region if you want to "spruce it up" a little.

Hint: It might help you to select **Show Grid** and **Snap to Grid** in the Layout Properties box.

Create a Navigator

In the Proposed Titles database, create a navigator that opens each of the views, and links to the Main frameset, which contains your home page. You want to also add a hotspot that creates a new title proposal.

Call the navigator Main. Set the initial view to display Books\by Title. Select the option **Auto adjust panes at runtime** (on the Info tab of the Navigator Properties box) so the user can see the entire navigator width.

Change the Launch options of the database to **Open Designated Navigator** when opened in the Notes client. Then select **Standard Navigator** as the Type of Navigator. Enter **Main** as the Name of the navigator.

Create an Imagemap

An imagemap requires a graphic to which you can add hotspots. We drew a simple one that you can use, called Imagemap.gif, that you'll find on the CD in the Day12 folder.

In the Titles in Development database, create a home page called Home. Paste or import a graphic to be your imagemap. Use the hotspot buttons to add hotspots that link to the Books\by Title view and the Review Status view in the Proposed Titles database. Create another hotspot to link to the Rejected Titles database. For the Titles in Development database, create a hotspot for the Titles view. If you're using imagemap.gif, you'll note that there is a place to put another hotspot for a nonexistent authors view. You can add that at a later time.

To see examples of the databases as completed to this stage, open the PTDay12.nsf and TDDay12.nsf databases stored on the CD in the Day12 folder.

12

DAY 13

Put on Your Propeller Beanie: Advanced Formulas

Accessing information that lies outside a document requires a few specialized @functions. On Day 9, "Forms on Steroids: Increase Form Performance," you learned about inheriting information from a parent document and the functions related to that. Today you delve into pulling data from the Notes.ini file, using dialog boxes to gather information from the user, and retrieving information from other documents via views.

This lesson covers

- More complex formulas that require temporary variables and multiple lines
- Tapping into the Notes.ini to store and retrieve environmental variables
- Working with prompts and dialog boxes
- Looking up information in views

Work with Multiline Formulas

Every formula must contain a *main expression*. The main expression resolves to a result or action. Throughout this book, most of the formulas you've created have been single statement or single line formulas that only consist of a main expression, as in the following example:

```
@If(@IsNewDoc; "Proposal for New Title"; TTitle)
```

This main expression includes @functions, constants (the text), and a variable (the name of the field).

Formulas that contain more than one statement are called *multiline formulas*. A multiline formula must have a main expression, which is the last statement of the formula. All lines in the formula, except the last one, must end with a semicolon (;). For example,

```
@Command([FileSave]);
@Command([FileCloseWindow])
```

This formula has two expressions, both resulting in actions, and their order of appearance in the formula sets the order of execution.

Formulas use field names as variables, but multiline formulas frequently use *temporary variables*. Temporary variables are storage areas to which you assign values during the formula. They only exist for the length of time of the execution of the formula, and their scope is limited to the formula. A formula statement that creates a temporary variable is not a main expression. The values assigned to temporary values are not saved in the document. You use temporary variables to make formulas more comprehensive. For example

```
Area := @Left(Telephone; 3);
Exchange := @Middle(Telephone; 3; 3);
Ext := @Right(Telephone; 4);
"(" + Area + ")" + " " + Exchange + "-" + Ext
```

This formula sets three temporary variables: *Area* is the first three digits of a telephone number, *Exchange* is the next three digits, and *Ext* is the last four digits. The main expression is the concatenation of these temporary variables with text to produce a phone number in the form (555) 555-5555.

Multiline formulas frequently use *keywords* that perform special functions in the formula, including the following:

> **DEFAULT**—Associates a value with a field. When the field exists in the document, the current value of the field is used. If the field doesn't exist, it's treated as if it does exist and the DEFAULT value is used. Written as DEFAULT fieldName := value.

ENVIRONMENT—Assigns a value to an environment variable (see the section on "Use Environment Variables" later in this lesson) in the user's Notes.ini file (or Preferences file in Macintosh). Written as `ENVIRONMENT variable := textValue`.

FIELD—Assigns a value to a field in the current document, replacing the current value in that field. If a field by that name doesn't exist in the document, it is created (it isn't added to the form, but you can use it in formulas). The value assigned the field is stored in the document. Written as `FIELD fieldName := value`.

REM—Adds comments to formulas to document the purpose for the formula or statement within the formula. Enclose the comment that follows REM in quotes. Written as `REM "comments"`. REM lines aren't processed by the application.

SELECT—Tests whether the current document is valid for processing. Used in view selection, replication, and agent formulas. Written as `SELECT logicalValue`.

A keyword is always the first word in a statement, and by convention is entered in uppercase. For example

```
REM "Creates a field to combine the first and last name of the client";
FIELD FullName := FName + " " + LName
```

Use Environment Variables

It's possible to store and retrieve values in the Notes.ini file (Windows, OS/2, and UNIX). These are *environment variables*. You might want to use an environment variable to store sequential numbers, such as job order numbers or purchase order numbers. Environment variables are also a way to pass temporary data between databases or formulas.

Environment variables are text, so you must convert any nontext values before you set them or after you retrieve them. If you use a text editor or LotusScript to add an environment variable, start the variable with $. Otherwise, you can't retrieve the variable using the @Environment function. For example, if you want to use Notepad to add a line to the Notes.ini that sets the beginning Invoice Number (which is 1001), the line you add is

```
$InvoiceNumber=1001
```

However, if you use @Environment to set the Invoice Number, the line in the Notes.ini also shows the environment variable starting with $. For example, you can use the following formula to add the Invoice Number variable to the Notes.ini:

```
OldInvoiceNumber := @Environment("InvoiceNumber");
NewInvoiceNumber := @TextToNumber(@If(OldInvoiceNumber = ""; "0";
OldInvoiceNumber)) + 1;
ENVIRONMENT InvoiceNumber := @Text(NewInvoiceNumber);
NewInvoiceNumber
```

13

There are a few functions that set or retrieve environment variables, plus the keyword
ENVIRONMENT. Table 13.1 lists these and briefly explains their functions.

Table 13.1 Working with Environment Variables

Use	To
ENVIRONMENT *variable* :=*textValue*	Set a named variable to a specified value, such as ENVIRONMENT JobNumber := @Text(NewJobNumber), which converts a number to text and saves it as an environment variable.
@Environment(variable)	Retrieve the value of a named variable, such as @Environment("JobNumber"), which retrieves the current job number in the Notes.ini.
	Use text or a text list for the variable.
@Environment(variable; value)	Set a named variable to a specified value, such as @Environment("JobNumber"; "0"), which sets the JobNumber variable in the Notes.ini to zero. The variable name must be passed in quotes.
@SetEnvironment(*variableName*; *value*)	Set an environment variable, such as @SetEnvironment("JobNumber"; @Text(NewJobNumber)), which sets the environment variable JobNumber (always show variable in quotes) to the value of the field NewJobNumber (converted to text).
	Use @SetEnvironment when setting an environment variable from within another function, such as @If or @Do.

Formulas that add or change environment variables do affect your Notes.ini file. When the formula is in a database that's on the server, the formula will run on the server under these conditions:

- It's a replication formula.
- It's a selection formula.
- It's a column formula.
- It's in an agent whose trigger is If New Mail Has Arrived or On Schedule.

In all other situations, the formula runs on the user's workstation.

Environment variables aren't consistent. For example, replica copies might access different Notes.ini files, depending on the server or workstation that is local to the replica copy. Also, server access is restricted administratively, which means your formula might not run on a server. A suggested alternative to environment variables is to create a database profile document in which you store the variable. In that case, the profile document is stored in the database. However, you still have the problem of different replicas if you need a consistent variable, such as a purchase order number, across all replicas.

Design Dialog Boxes for User Input

At some point in a workflow application you might want to alert your users of pending deadlines or the need to perform one step before proceeding to another. You might also require input from the user before the user continues with a particular project. Other than having the user fill in fields on a form, the only way to communicate and receive answers is to use a dialog box. There are two functions—@Prompt and @DialogBox—that help you do this.

@Prompt

When used in a formula, the @Prompt function displays a dialog box (see Figure 13.1). Based on the style you use in the formula, the dialog box can act as a simple alert or warning, or it can accept input from the user that determines later action.

You can use an @Prompt formula for fields, buttons, SmartIcons, manual agents, form actions, and view actions (see Figure 13.2). Sometimes @Prompt can even be used with window title and form formulas.

13

FIGURE **13.1**

This dialog box is the result of an @Prompt formula attached to a form action button.

Note

The @prompt function is not supported on the Web. Additionally, you can't use the @prompt function with column, selection, mail agent, or scheduled agent formulas.

FIGURE **13.2**

This formula produced the dialog box displayed in Figure 13.1. The user clicks the Add Contact Info action button and makes a choice of the type of contact document to create, and the form opens for that type of form, ready for user input.

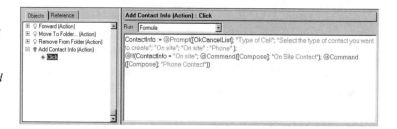

The syntax of an @Prompt formula is

```
@Prompt([style]:[NoSort]; title; prompt; defaultChoice;
choiceList; filetype)
```

style—The type of dialog box displayed (see Table 13.2).

[NoSort]—A keyword (optional) to include if you want the members of *choiceList* to appear in the order that you type them (otherwise, they're sorted alphabetically).

title—The text in the dialog box title bar.

prompt—The text displayed in the dialog box (required for all styles except LocalBrowse); only the first item in a list is displayed as the prompt (use @Implode to display the entire list).

defaultChoice—That value used as the default value for the user's input; not applicable to styles Ok, YesNo, YesNoCancel, LocalBrowse, or Password.

ChoiceList—The list of text values displayed in the dialog box's list box; separate the values with colons (:). Values can be text strings or @functions that return text strings. Required with styles OkCancelList, OkCancelCombo, OkCancelEditCombo, and OkCancelListMult.

Filetype—A text value that specifies the types of files to display initially: 1 for .NSF files, 2 for .NTF files, or 3 for all types of files. Required only with style LocalBrowse.

Table 13.2   @Prompt Styles

Dialog Box Style	Use to	Dialog Box Contains	Returns	Example
LocalBrowse	Let user select a file name from the local file system	Select, Cancel, and Network or Help buttons, and controls and displays for browsing the local file system	Text (file name the user selected or entered)	Prompt([Local @ Browse]; "Location of Picture File"; "3")
Ok	Show information	Title, prompt, and OK button	1 (true)	@Prompt([OK]; "Completed"; "You have finished your order successfully")
OkCancelCombo	Enables the user to select a value from a drop-down list	Title, prompt, list of choices, and OK and Cancel buttons	Text (the value the user selected)	@Prompt([OkCancel Combo]; "Reader Level"; "Please select the audience that would read this book"; "Beginner"; "Computer Illiterate" : "Beginner" : "Intermediate" : "Advanced" : "Super Advanced")

continues

13

Table 13.2 continued

Dialog Box Style	Use to	Dialog Box Contains	Returns	Example
OkCancelEdit	Enables the user to type input	Title, prompt, text box for input, and OK and Cancel buttons	Text (the text the user entered)	@Prompt([OkCancel Edit]; "Editor"; "Please enter the name of the Acquisition Editor"; @Name([CN]; @UserName)
OkCancelEdit Combo	Enables the user to select a value from a list of choices or type in a value	Title, prompt, list of choices with text box, and OK and Cancel buttons	Text (value the user selected or entered)	@Prompt([OkCancel EditCombo]; "Reader Level"; "Please enter or select the reader level for this book"; "Beginner"; "Computer Illiterate" : "Beginner" : "Intermediate" : "Advanced" : "Super Advanced")
OkCancelList	Enables the user to select a value from a list of choices	Title, prompt, list of choices, and OK and Cancel buttons	Text (the value the user selected)	@Prompt([OkCancel List]; "Reader Level"; "Please select the audience that would read this book"; "Beginner"; "Computer Illiterate" : "Beginner" : "Intermediate" : "Advanced" : "Super Advanced")

Dialog Box Style	Use to	Dialog Box Contains	Returns	Example
OkCancel ListMult	Enables the user to select more than one value from a list of choices	Title, prompt, list of choices, and OK and Cancel buttons	Text list of values user selected, separated by colons (:)	@Prompt([OkCancel ListMult]; "Reader Level"; "Please select the type of readers that should read this book"; "Beginner"; "Computer Illiterate" : "Beginner" : "Intermediate" : "Advanced" : "Super Advanced")
Password	Enables the user to enter a password without displaying it on the screen	Title, prompt, text box that accepts and hides user input, and OK and Cancel buttons	Text (password the user entered)	@Prompt([Password]; "Password"; "Please enter your password")
YesNo	Enables the user to make a yes or no decision	Title, prompt, and Yes and No buttons	1 (true, yes) or 2 (false, no)	@Prompt([YesNo]; "New Author Profile"; "Would you like to create a new Author Profile?")
YesNoCancel	Enables the user to make a yes or no decision, or cancel	Title, prompt, and Yes, No, and Cancel buttons	1 (true, yes), 2 (false, no), or -1 (cancel)	@Prompt([YesNo Cancel]; "Send this message?"; "Send this message to all members of the Editorial Board?")

13

An @Prompt formula returns a value if a value is entered by a user: 1 (true) if the user selects "Yes," or 0 (false) if the user selects "No." The OkCancelEdit style only returns the first 254 characters of the text entered. When the user selects "Cancel," formula evaluation stops, except for the YesNoCancel style that returns -1 if the user selects "Cancel."

@DialogBox

The dialog box you see as a result of an @DialogBox formula displays the current document using a specified form. The user uses the form to enter data for the document, and then chooses OK or Cancel when finished. The @DialogBox function is useful for actions. It doesn't work with column or selection formulas, in agents that run on the server, or for window titles or form formulas.

Displaying the current document using a different form means that if the specified form has the same field names as the current document, the field values from the current document display in the dialog box. (Rich text fields do not display, even if the field names are the same.) If the values in the dialog box change and the user chooses OK, the same changes appear in the fields of the same name in the document. Any values entered in fields in the dialog box that don't share a name with fields in the document are still stored in the document.

The syntax of an @DialogBox function is

```
@DialogBox(formname; [AutoHorzFit] : [AutoVertFit] : [NoCancel] :
[NoNewFields] : [NoFieldUpdate] : [ReadOnly]; sizeToTable;
noOkCancel; title)
```

> *formname*—The name of the form you want to use to display the current document.
>
> **[AutoHorzFit]**—An optional keyword that scales the dialog box horizontally to fit the layout region.
>
> **[AutoVertFit]**—An optional keyword that scales the dialog box vertically to fit the layout region.
>
> **[NoCancel]**—An optional keyword that you use to display only an OK button in the dialog box. Normally, the dialog box shows both an OK and a Cancel button.
>
> **[NoNewFields]**—An optional keyword that prevents the addition of fields in the dialog box form to the underlying document if they aren't in the underlying form.
>
> **[NoFieldUpdate]**—An optional keyword that prevents passing edits from the fields in the dialog box to the underlying document (such as when you're passing the edits on somewhere else).
>
> **[ReadOnly]**—An optional keyword that makes it impossible to write to the dialog box (for dialog boxes that only display messages or help screens).

SizeToTable—An optional Boolean parameter. Specify True to scale a table to fit into the dialog box.

NoOkCancel—An optional Boolean parameter. The OK and Cancel buttons don't display if you specify True.

Title—A text parameter that is the title of the dialog box. The title defaults to "Lotus Notes" unless you specify otherwise.

Although @DialogBox works with any form, it works best with forms that contain a single layout region (see Figure 13.3). The [AutoHorzFit] and [AutoVertFit] keywords are optional, but you use them to display the entire layout region in the dialog box without showing the rest of the form. For best results, deselect **Display Border** and select **3D Style** in the Layout Region Properties box. Use 9-point Helvetica for static text, fields, and buttons to closely match the look of the Notes user interface.

FIGURE 13.3

This dialog box displays a layout region from a form called Hobby & Leisure Interests (Layout2).

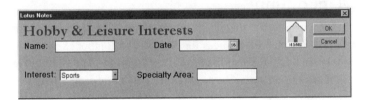

A table also adds to a dialog box, as seen in Figure 13.4.

FIGURE 13.4

Tables organize fields in dialog boxes, too.

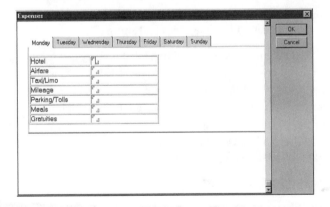

13

Retrieve Data from Other Views

Importing data into your document from another document, or even another database, requires a view that shows the documents you want to access. It might sometimes be necessary for you to create a special view to use with your lookups; use a hidden view when you don't want the user to see it (put parentheses around the view name in the View Properties box).

Make sure the view you use for @DbLookup formulas has a sorted column that the formula can use as the lookup key.

When referring to the view in the formula, use its full name or alias in quotes. If it's a cascading view, add another backslash (\) before the one in the name, such as `"Books\\By Category"`.

@DbColumn

The principal use for the @DbColumn function is for keyword formulas, so you don't have to type in all the choices for dialog lists, comboboxes, and so forth. Your application dynamically retrieves data from a view to display as the list of choices. The @DbColumn function returns an entire column of values from a view or folder.

When you refer to a column in your @DbColumn formula (and also in @DbLookup), you use the column *number* and not the column *name*. The column numbers start at the left, so the first column on the left is 1, the one to the right of it is 2, and so on. Do your counting in Design mode, where you can see all the columns in the view, including those that are hidden or used for categories and sorting.

In your column count, skip any columns that display a constant value (such as `Submitted by` or `64`). Columns that display a value because the column formula returns the same result for all the documents are not displaying a constant value; count these columns. Don't include columns in your count that display the results of simple actions or @functions, such as Collapse/Expand (+/-), # in View, # of Responses, @DocChildren, @DocDescendants, @DocNumber, @DocParentNumber, @DocSiblings, @IsCategory, or @IsExpandable.

The syntax for @DbColumn is

```
@DbColumn(class: "NoCache"; server : database; view; columnnumber)
```

  class—Text that indicates the type of database you are accessing. To indicate a Notes/Domino database, write **"Notes"** or **""**.

"**NoCache**"—An optional keyword. Only exclude "NoCache" from your formula if you want to cache the results of your formula for reuse. Caching the results saves time on repeated lookups to the same information, but it means you might be missing the latest updates. Make sure you include "NoCache" if you expect data to change frequently; don't include it if your data is fairly stable. This argument can also be replaced with a **NULL** or "", indicating that results should be cached (the default).

server : database—Text specifying the server location and the path and filename of the database. For the current database, use "" to specify both values. If the server is local but the database isn't the current one, use "" for the server only (""**:database.nsf**). From a workstation, it's a good idea to specify both. Where there are multiple replicas of the database, use the replica ID in place of the server and database. The replica ID must be text, and it must include a colon (:) between the two sets of eight hex digits. This returns the workstation replica information if one exists locally.

Tip

> When @DbColumn runs on a server and accesses a database on the server, the source database (the one containing the formula) must have at least reader access in the Access Control List (ACL) to the target database (the one containing the data to retrieve). If the security on the target database doesn't permit a default of reader access, it is possible to grant access to the source database by using the replica ID of the source database (check Database Properties to find the replica ID). Click **Add** in the ACL and enter the replica ID number. Then assign an access level to the replica ID.

view—The name (in quotes) of the view in which @DbColumn searches.

columnnumber—The number of the column within the view. Data must appear in the view for it to retrieve that information.

When you are creating a keywords field, such as a dialog list, use the @DbColumn formula to display your choices. In the Field Properties box, click the **Control** tab and select **Use Formula for Choices** from the Choices drop-down list. Enter the formula in the text box (see Figure 13.5).

Both @DbColumn and @DbLookup can be used to retrieve information from ODBC-compatible databases. That information is beyond the scope of this book. For details, consult *Special Edition Using Lotus Notes and Domino R5* by Randy Tamura.

13

FIGURE 13.5

The @DbColumn formula pulls company information from the Company view so users of the current form can select a company name.

@DbLookup

Starting with a key value, the @DbLookup function finds all documents in a specified view or folder that contain the key value in the first sorted column in the view or folder. The formula returns either the contents of a specified field or a column in the view.

The match between the key value and the value in the sort column must be exact (excluding capitalization). That means spacing and punctuation must also be the same.

Instead of specifying a text value as the key, use a field name in the formula. The value of that field in the current document is used as the key.

There are two ways of writing @DbLookup formulas. To retrieve the value in a particular field of a document (even if that field doesn't show in the view), write your formula using the following syntax:

```
@DbLookup(class : "NoCache"; server : database; view; key; fieldname)
```

To return the values displayed in a specified column of the view, write your formula using the following syntax:

```
@DbLookup(class : "NoCache"; server : database; view; key; columnnumber)
```

class—Text that indicates the type of database you are accessing. To indicate a Notes/Domino database, write **"Notes"** or **""**.

"NoCache"—An option keyword. Only exclude "NoCache" from your formula if you want to cache the results of your formula for reuse. Caching the results saves time on repeated lookups to the same information, but it means you might be missing the latest updates. Make sure you include "NoCache" if you expect data to change frequently; don't include it if your data is fairly stable. This argument can also be replaced with a **NULL** or **""**, indicating that results should be cached (the default).

server : database—Text specifying the server location as well as the path and file-name of the database. For the current database, use "" to specify both values. If the server is local but the database isn't the current one, use "" for the server only ("":**database.nsf**). From a workstation, it's a good idea to specify both. Where there are multiple replicas of the database, use the replica ID in place of the server and database. The replica ID must be text, and it must include a colon (:) between the two sets of eight hex digits. This returns the workstation replica information if one exists locally.

view—The name (in quotes) of the view in which @DbColumn searches.

key—A text parameter that determines which document is read in order to retrieve a value. The key must be found in the first sorted column in the view.

fieldname—The name of the field from which the data is retrieved. It might be different than what's displayed in the view. The lookup is slower if the field is stored in the document but not displayed in the view. If the view contains documents created with different forms, some of the documents that match the key might not include the field name.

columnnumber—The number of the column within the view. Data must appear in the view for it to retrieve that information. See the information about column numbers in the @DbColumn section of this lesson.

If you have some of the information you need, such as the name of a person or a company, use @DbLookup to find related information (see Figure 13.6).

FIGURE 13.6

This formula for the Contact field uses @DbLookup to match the value in the Company field to the first sorted column in the Company view (which holds company names) and return the value in column 4, which is the contact name.

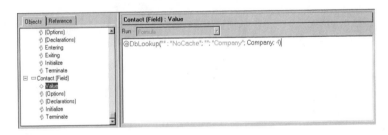

13

@PickList

The @PickList function displays a list of choices based on a view you specify or on the Address dialog box. When you specify a view, the user sees the view as the list of choices. The user picks a document and @PickList returns a value in the specified column for that document. When used with an Address dialog box, the users see a list of names from an Address Book, just as when they click the Address button to address a mail memo.

Note

Use the @PickList function in button, manual agent, paste agent, form action, and view action formulas. Don't use it for column, selection, mail agent, scheduled agent, hide-when, window title, or form formulas. It also doesn't work in Web applications.

Although @PickList looks up values in a view as @DbColumn does, it also enables the user to pick a value from one document. It's not limited to 64K of data, as @DbColumn and @DbLookup are, and it's faster than those two functions. Lookup results are never stored, as they can be with @DbColumn and @DbLookup. The user can type the first few characters of an entry to quickly locate it in the view.

When the view is a Calendar view, @PickList displays it in the two-day format with no time slots, starting with today's date. A date picker button enables the user to select other dates.

With the @PickList function, you also have the capability to display the Address dialog box (see Figure 13.7), which contains information from all the available Address Books.

FIGURE 13.7

Select the users to add to the field in the document that contains the @PickList formula, which is @SetField("Salespers on"; @PickList([Name]). *The Salesperson field already exists in the form.*

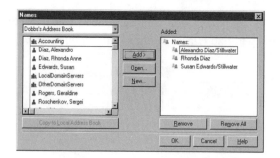

The general syntax for @PickList is

```
@PickList([Custom]:[Single]; server : file; view; title; prompt;
column; categoryname)
```

     [Custom]—An optional keyword that you use when you want to display a view in a dialog box.

     [Folders]—A keyword that returns a text list of all folder names in the database and from the desktop. When combined with [Single], the selection is limited to one. For example, @PickList([Folders] : [Single]).

     [Name]—An optional keyword used when you want to display the Address dialog box.

[NoDesktop]—A keyword that combines with [Folders] to exclude folders in the desktop from the selection. For example, @PickList([Folders]; [NoDesktop]).

[Private]—A keyword that combines with [Folders] to limit the selection to only private folders, both in the database and on the desktop. For example, @Picklist([Folders]; [Private]).

[Resource]—A keyword that opens a dialog box for selecting resources, usually for meetings. For example, @PickList([Resource]).

[Room]—A keyword for opening a dialog box for selecting a room, usually for meetings. For example, @PickList([Room]).

[Single]—An optional keyword that limits the selection to a single document, such as @PickList([Name]:[Single]), which enables the user to select one name from the Address dialog box.

[Shared]—A keyword that's combined with [Folders] to limit the select to only shared folders, such as @PickList([Folders]; [Shared]).

[Shared] : [Private]—A keyword combination used for folders to display a list of both shared and private folders. For example, @PickList([Folders]; [Shared] : [Private]).

server : file—A text list. *server* is the name of the server where the database is. *file* is the path and filename of the database you want to open, written in the proper notation for the operating system. Use "" to replace the *server:file* argument when referring to the currently open database. In place of the server and filename you can use the replica ID of the document, but only when it follows the [Custom] parameter. The replica ID must be text, and it must include the colon (:) between the two sets of eight hex digits. For example,

```
@PickList([Custom]; "8525662E:0051297B"; "Titles"; "Select a Title";
"Select the Title of the book you want "; 2)
```

view—The name of the view (in quotes) that you want to open in the database.

title—The window title for the dialog box, in quotes.

prompt—The prompt you want to display in the dialog box, in quotes.

column—A number corresponding to the column value you want returned from the @PickList formula. Unlike @DbColumn and @DbLookup, @PickList counts every column, no matter what type of formulas they contain.

categoryname—An optional text parameter that displays the specified category in the view. Of course, the view must be categorized before you can use *categoryname* in the formula.

13

In Figure 13.8, the dialog box displays a view, Meetings\By Category, from which the user selects a category for a new meeting. The action button Set Category has the following formula:

```
FIELD Categories := Categories;
@SetField("Categories"; @PickList([Custom]; ""; "Meetings\\By Category;
  "Categories"; "Select a Category for this meeting"; 1)
```

FIGURE 13.8

The dialog box displays a view because the formula for the Set Category action button includes an @PickList formula.

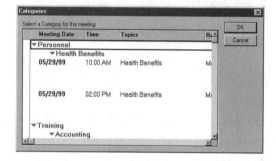

Summary

More complex formulas often require more than one line of text and frequently employ keywords such as FIELD, which assign a value to a field. A multiline formula contains two or more statements, one of which is the main expression that resolves to a result or an action. Temporary variables, which are in force only for the processing of the formula, help make multiline formulas easier to read.

Environment variables are set in the Notes.ini file. The @Environment and @SetEnvironment functions and the ENVIRONMENT keyword set and retrieve these variables.

To alert users to conditions or remind them of things they need to do in an application, use @Prompt to create a dialog box that appears with the text. The @Prompt formula can also create dialog boxes in which the user selects a response, and the result of that response is used in the application. The @DialogBox also creates dialog boxes, but uses layout regions on tables or forms to build the dialog box. The fields on the forms or in the layout regions become fields in the dialog box. Responses from the user are stored in the document.

Retrieving information from other documents involves working through a view using @DbColumn or @DbLookup. Use @DBColumn to provide a list of the text entries in a specific column; use @DbLookup to use the contents of one field to match a document in a view and then retrieve information from a field on the matching document. Lastly, @PickList enables the users to see the view or the Address dialog box from which they can make selections.

Q&A

Q I'm working on a Web application, and I need to use an Order Number in the application that changes for each order. Can I use environment variables for this like I can in Notes?

A No, Web users don't have access to a Notes.ini file, so none of the environment variable functions are supported on the Web. Try creating a database profile document that contains a field that holds the order number data. Then use @GetProfileField to retrieve that value and @SetProfileField to set it to a new number.

Q Can I create dialog boxes for my Web application using @DialogBox?

A You cannot use @DialogBox, @Prompt, or @PickList for Web applications.

Q How can I get the replica ID for a database so I can incorporate it in @DbColumn and @DbLookup formulas?

A The replica ID displays on the Database Properties box. However, you can't copy and paste it into your formula from there, and with so many digits you run the risk of typing it incorrectly. Instead, choose **File, Database, Design Synopsis**. Select **Replication**. Copy the replica ID from the synopsis and paste it into your formula.

Workshop

In this Workshop you will incorporate some of the advanced formulas in both the Proposed Titles and Titles in Development databases. If you haven't been developing your own databases along with us, you can use the PTDay12.nsf and TDDay12.nsf files in the Day12 folder of the CD to do this workshop.

The activities in this workshop include environment variables and the @Prompt, @DialogBox, @DbColumn, @DbLookup, and @PickList functions. In the process of doing these activities, you'll be using multiline formulas.

Use an Environment Variable

Management has decided that they need a book tracking number for each new book idea created in the Proposed Titles database. Create a new field on the Proposed Title form called **TrackingNumber** and place it near the bottom of the form. This field uses an environment variable that puts the variable in the Notes.ini file and then adds 1 to it each time a new Proposed Title document is added to the database.

13

After you have the formula working in Proposed Titles, open the Titles in Development database and add a field named **TrackingNumber** to the New Title form. When the new title is sent from the Proposed Titles database, the tracking number comes with it. To be sure, make the field TrackingNumber the formula for the field also.

@Prompt and @DialogBox

In the Titles in Development database, create a new form called Deadlines. Deselect the **Include in menu** and **Include in Search Builder** options on the Form Properties box.

Create a layout region and deselect the **Show border** option and select the **3D style** option on the Layout Properties box. In the layout region, add the following fields and the related static text. All the fields are editable date/time fields.

- **DueContract**—"Contract Due"
- **DueTOC**—"Table of Contents Due"
- **Due25**—"25% Due"
- **Due50**—"50% Due"
- **Due75**—"75% Due"
- **Due100**—"100% Due"
- **DueReview**—"Author Review Due"

Save and close the Deadlines form.

Open the New Title form in Designer. Create a basic table that is three columns wide and has eight rows.

In the first row of the table, enter the following labels as the column headings: **Submitted**, **Due**, and **Actual**.

In the first column, under Submitted, enter the following row heading labels: **Contract**, **Table of Contents**, **25%**, **50%**, **75%**, **100%**, and **Final Author Review**.

Each cell in the Due column contains an editable date/time field. The field names are **DueContract**; **DueTOC**; **Due25**; **Due50**; **Due75**; **Due100**; and **DueReview**. Make the default value formula for each of these fields the name of the field. For example, the default value for DueTOC is DueTOC.

Each cell in the Actual column contains an editable date/time field. The field names are **ActContract**, **ActTOC**, **Act25**, **Act50**, **Act75**, **Act100**, and **ActReview**.

Create a hotspot button just above the table and call it **Deadlines**. Add some static text next to the button, such as "Click on this button to enter deadlines". Hide the button and text when the document is read, previewed, or printed.

When the button is clicked by a user, a prompt appears that asks if the user wants to enter deadlines. If the user clicks **Yes**, a dialog box appears that is based on the Deadlines form. After filling out the information and clicking OK, the user sees the due dates in the table. If the user clicks **No**, nothing happens.

Save and test the form. Copy one of the Proposed Title documents and paste it into the Titles in Development database in order to have a document to test.

@DbColumn and @DbLookup

In order to use @DbColumn and @DbLookup, you need to create a new view in the Titles in Development database. Call it the Author Information view (alias "Authors"). The view should only display information from the Author Information documents. Add the following columns and sort the first column in ascending order:

- **Author Name**—Field: AuthName
- **Mailing Address**—Field: AuthAddress
- **Work Phone**—Field: AuthPhoneWork
- **Home Phone**—Field: AuthPhoneHome
- **Email**—Field: AuthEmail

Make the rows able to display multiple lines of text.

Save and close the view.

To be able to test your view, add two or three Author Information documents. Make sure you include some of the author names you used in some of the Proposed Title documents, particularly those for the documents you copied into Titles in Development for testing purposes.

Information from the Author Information view is going to be added to the New Title form using @DbColumn and @DbLookup functions to create a table. Open the New Title form. Create a basic table below the TProposedAuthors field. The table has two rows and four columns. The first row of the table contains the labels **Author Name**, **Work Phone**, **Home Phone**, and **Email Address**.

13

In the second row of the table, create four fields. Name them **NAuthName**, **NAuthPhoneWork**, **NAuthPhoneHome**, and **NAuthEmail**. Each of these fields is the computed text type. Use the name of the field as the formula. For example, the formula for the NAuthName field is NAuthName. In the Field Properties box, select **Allow multiple values** on the Field Info tab and **New Line** from the Display separate values with drop-down list on the Advanced tab.

Create a hotspot button above the table and call it **Add Author Info**. Add static text, such as "Click on this button to add author information to the table", and hide both the static text and the button when the document is being read, previewed, or printed.

For the hotspot button formula, create a formula that prompts the user for the names of the authors to look up, and uses @DbColumn to provide the list of choices. Then, using @DbLookup, assign values to the other fields in the table. Create temporary variables for the common parts of the @DbColumn and @DbLookup functions.

Because this formula is fairly complicated, we thought you might appreciate seeing ours:

```
REM "set temporary variables for lookup functions";
type := "Notes" : "NoCache";
db := "" : "Develop.nsf";
view := "Authors";
REM "add temporary variable for author name column";
acol := 1;
REM "get author names";
aname := @DbColumn(type; db; view; acol);
REM "display author list to users";
selnames := @Prompt([OKCANCELLIST]; "Select Author";
"Select an Author"; ""; aname);
REM "assign value to NAuthName field";
FIELD NAuthName := @Trim(selnames : NAuthName);
REM "set columns for other lookups";
awphone := 3;
ahphone := 4;
aemail := 5;
REM "look up field info and assign to fields";
luwphone := @DbLookup(type; db; view; selnames; awphone);
FIELD NAuthPhoneWork := @Trim(luwphone : NAuthPhoneWork);
luhphone := @DbLookup(type; db; view; selnames; ahphone);
FIELD NAuthPhoneHome := @Trim(luhphone : NAuthPhoneHome);
luemail := @DbLookup(type; db; view; selnames; aemail);
FIELD NAuthEmail := @Trim(luemail : NAuthEmail);
@Command([ViewRefreshFields])
```

@PickList

Another item you need for the Titles in Development database is a list of editors, so you can pick the editors you need in the New Title document. First, you need to create a form so we can make editor information documents. Then you'll create a view to display that information. Finally, you use that view to choose editors.

Create a form called **Editor Information** (alias "Editors"). Add four fields to that form:

- **EdName**—"Editor's Name". A dialog list field that pulls the name choices from an Address Book.
- **EdPhone**—"Editor's Phone Number". An editable text field.
- **EdEMail**—"Editor's Email Address". An editable text field.
- **EdType**—"Type of Editor". Use a dialog list to select the type of editing the person does: **Acquisition**, **Development**, **Copy**, or **Technical**.

Save the form and test it. Create at least one document for each editor type.

Create a view that displays the field information from the Editor Information documents. Call the view **Editor Information** (alias "Editors"). Put the columns in the following order: **Editor Type** (sorted and categorized), **Editor Name** (sorted), **Editor Phone**, and **Editor Email**. Save the view.

In the New Title form, create three Action buttons:

- **Assign Editor\Copy**—Put value in CopyEditor field.
- **Assign Editor\Development**—Put value in DevEditor field.
- **Assign Editor\Technical**—Put value in TechEditor field.

Use the @PickList function to provide the list of names, which is based on the Editor Information view.

To see how we handled the tasks in this Workshop, look at our examples for the Proposed Titles database (PTDay13.nsf) and Titles in Development (TDDay13.nsf) in the Day13 folder of the CD.

13

DAY **14**

The Not So Secret Agents

By now you're probably asking yourself, "Where are the macros?" After all, macros are typically the way you automate your applications. With macros, you record steps that you expect to repeat often within your application, and run the macro when it is time to repeat those steps. Notes has macros, but doesn't call them that. Rather, it calls them *actions* or *agents*, depending on how you create them. In Lotus Notes and Domino, *actions* using *@Commands* handle repeat steps for you.

Notes and Domino also use *agents* to automate activities such as sending mail, changing fields in documents, or moving documents to a specified folder. You specify what the agent is to do and when it is to run.

By the time you complete this lesson, you will learn

- What an agent can do
- How to create an agent
- How agents and actions work together
- How to create and use a newsletter agent

What Are Agents and How Can You Use Them?

An agent is a small program that performs a task you define by setting simple actions or writing formulas or scripts. The agent can work on one database or on several. It can be confined to the user's workstation or run on the server.

Users can create their own agents, and designers can create agents for their applications. Where agents run and who can create them is, of course, limited by Domino's security measures (see "Secure Against Agents" later in this day for more details on security restrictions). Like views and folders, agents can be personal or shared. A personal agent is created and run by a user and isn't available to other users. A shared agent is available to other users.

Agents can be scheduled to run in the background at specified times, or the user can initiate the agent by clicking a button or making a selection from the menu. Other agents are triggered by a specific condition or occurrence, such as when new mail is received. Agents can even run other agents.

Although agents aren't associated with any specific design element, they can be replicated and therefore easily distributed.

When do you use an agent? You use agents for automating complicated tasks, especially those involving the entire database or several databases. Also use agents when you want to schedule tasks.

For example, your mail database has several agents (see Figure 14.1). The Out of Office agent alerts users that send you mail when you are not in the office (you have to specify the time period you're going to be away). The **Add Recipients\to new Group Calendar** entry agent and **Add Recipients\to new Group in Address Book** agent are practically self-explanatory.

FIGURE 14.1

Your mail database includes a number of agents, many of them hidden and working in the background.

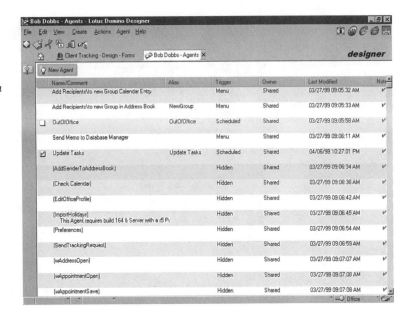

Create Agents

Before you start creating an agent, you need to ask yourself the following questions:

- What is going to trigger the agent? Will it be the arrival of mail, a newly modified document, or should it be run manually? Alternatively, is it going to be a scheduled agent?

- On which documents will the agent run—all documents, newly modified documents, or documents that are about the same subject?

- What is the agent going to do? Is it going to change the contents of one field, change the contents of many fields, or send a mail message?

After you have the answers to these questions, open the agent builder and create the agent.

Use the Agent Builder

To open the Agent Builder screen (see Figure 14.2), open the database and choose **Create, Agent** from the menu or open the database in Designer, choose **Agents**, and click the **New Agent** button on the Action Bar.

14

FIGURE 14.2

The Agent Builder leads you through the agent design process by asking questions you must answer. The bottom window is for the simple action, formula, or script you use to program the agent.

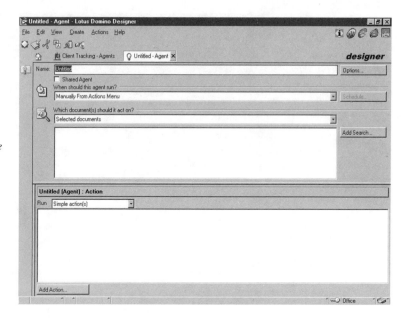

1. Enter a Name for the agent that is brief but descriptive. Use any combination of characters, including letters, numbers, spaces, and punctuation (note that names are case sensitive). If the agent is run manually, the name appears in the Actions menu. Try to be consistent in naming similar agents in different databases so that users can easily recognize them. You can also use an alias, specify shortcut keys by using the underscore before the key, or create cascading names on the menu using the backslash.

2. (Optional) If you plan to have the agent search for text in documents, click the **Options** button. When the Options dialog box appears (see Figure 14.3), select the appropriate options and then click **OK**.

    Show search in search bar menu—Displays your search query in the search bar.

    Store highlights in documents—Highlights search matches in the documents.

    Available to Publish Access Users—Users with No Access or Depositor access in the Access Control List of a database can be given limited access to specific pages, documents, forms, outlines, views, and folders. Provided they have public access to the documents the agent affects, selecting this option enables users with public access to run the agent manually from the menu.

    Comment—Any comments you enter display when you view the agents list.

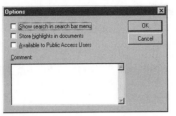

FIGURE 14.3

The Options dialog box enables you to set search options, or enables public access users to use the agent.

3. Check **Shared Agent** unless you're preparing a personal agent (a personal agent is run on your workstation and isn't available to other users). After you save the agent, you can't change this setting.

4. From the **When should this agent run?** drop-down list, select the appropriate option:

   Manually From Actions Menu—Enables users to activate the agent by choosing a menu command. You might want to use this option while the application is still being developed because agents that are triggered manually are run on your workstation and not on the server, which means you'll be testing your formula, script, or action instead of the trigger that sets off the agent. Testing on the server will occur after the application is transferred to the server for pilot testing.

   Manually From Agents List—For agents that are called by other agents or for agents still being developed.

   Before New Mail Arrives—For processing mail before it arrives in a database capable of receiving mail, such as moving incoming mail to a folder.

   After New Mail Has Arrived—For processing incoming mail, such as forwarding it, responding to it, or putting it in folders.

   If Documents Have Been Created or Modified—Useful for workflow applications, where a task is performed based on the creation of new documents or modification of existing documents.

   If Documents Have Been Pasted—Use to modify documents that are routinely pasted into the database.

   On Schedule More Than Once a Day—For databases that involve critical business processes or replicate frequently. Be careful not to schedule the agent to run so frequently that it seriously affects the server's performance (for example, running it every five minutes).

14

On Schedule Hourly—For business-critical databases. Be careful not to schedule the agent to run so frequently that it seriously affects the server's performance.

On Schedule Daily—For important activities, but not critical.

On Schedule Weekly—For routine tasks.

On Schedule Monthly—For maintenance tasks that are low priority.

On Schedule Never—Only for agents that shouldn't be run except in particular circumstances, such as an agent that's called by other agents.

Note

> Agents that are activated manually from the Actions menu are not supported on the Web. After all, the Actions menu doesn't exist in Web browsers. However, using an Action button to activate the agent *does* work. Triggering agents if documents are pasted or using agents that work on selected documents won't work in Web browsers either. Scheduled agents are not supported on the Web.

5. (Optional) If you selected a scheduled option, click the **Schedule** button. Set the options for running the agent in the Schedule dialog box (see Figure 14.4). From the Run on list, select the servers on which the agent is to run. Be careful about selecting **Any Server** because of the danger of creating replication conflicts; consult the Domino Administrator before specifying multiple servers. Select **Choose when agent is enabled** to prompt users to select a server when the agent is enabled (good idea for general use applications distributed to different groups of users). Click **OK**.

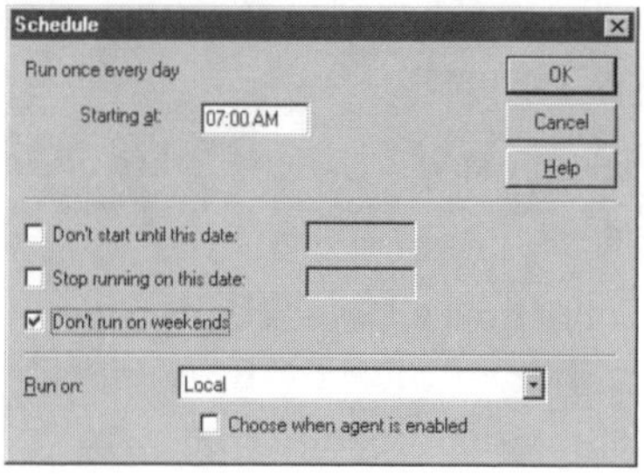

FIGURE 14.4

*If you select **Local** from the Run on list, the agent only runs on your workstation and Notes doesn't check security restrictions. You might want to use this option temporarily while testing, but eventually you'll have to change it so the agent can run on a server.*

6. Make a choice from the Which document(s) should it act on? list: **All new and modified documents since last run**, **All documents in view** (not supported on Web), **All unread documents in view** (not supported on Web), **Selected documents** (not supported on Web), **Pasted documents** (not supported on Web), or **Run once** (@Commands can be used). Not all these options are available in all circumstances, and sometimes none are available, depending on when the agent runs.

7. (Optional) If you chose Selected documents in step 6 or want to narrow the range of documents affected by the agent for some of the other options, click **Add Search** to specify which documents to select. The Search Builder opens (see Figure 14.5). Based on the Condition you select (**By Author, By Date, By Field, By Form, By Form Used, In Folder**, or **Words and Phrases**), the fields in the dialog box change. Click **OK** after you finish setting search options.

8. In the Programmer's Pane, select the method you want to use to program the agent from the Run list: **Simple action(s), Formula, LotusScript, Imported Java, or Java.**

9. If you selected Simple action(s) in step 8, click **Add Action** and select an action. Choose from **Copy to Database, Copy to Folder, Delete from Database, Mark Document Read, mark Document Unread, Modify Field, Modify Fields by Form, Move to Folder, Remove from Folder, Reply to Sender, Run Agent, Send Document, Send Mail Message, Send Newsletter Summary**, or @Function Formula. Then complete the other fields in the dialog box (see Figure 14.6) and click **OK**.

   For other selections, enter the formula or script needed to program the action.

10. Save the agent by choosing **File, Save** from the menu.

FIGURE 14.5

This search looks in the Attendees field for the name Bob Dobbs, so the agent only runs on documents that have an Attendees field that contains that name.

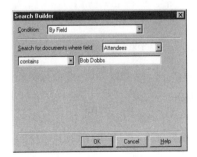

14

FIGURE 14.6

When you select the type of action, the fields in the box change. This one enables you to specify the contents of a particular field or several fields in a specified form.

Write an Agent Formula

Formulas for agents involve @Functions or @Commands. When the agent runs, it runs on each document completely before going on to the next document until the formula has been executed on all the documents.

While creating the agent, you select **Formula** from the Run drop-down list in the Programmer's Pane of the Agent Builder. Click the **Reference** tab in the Info List for lists of @Functions, @Commands, or database fields. At the bottom right of the Programmer's Pane, select the basic area in which the formula is to work: **Modify documents, Create new documents, or Select documents in view**. Click in the Script Area to write the formula.

For example, say your company wants to ensure that all new clients added to its client tracking database have a salesperson assigned to them. The database designer (you) created a formula-driven agent that finds new client forms that have no data in the Salesperson field. A prompt appears to the user to enter a salesperson's name (the user's name appears as the default). The agent is shown in Figure 14.7, and the prompt is displayed in 14.8.

The formula used in the Assign Salesperson agent is

```
SELECT Salesperson = "";
FIELD Salesperson := @Prompt([OKCANCELEDIT];
"Salesperson\'s Name for " + Company;
"Type the salesperson\'s name in the box below.";
@Name([CN]; @UserName));
Salesperson
```

It's even possible to combine simple actions with formulas. Set up the simple action, click **Add Action**, select @Function formula from the list of possible actions, and enter the formula in the editing window. However, you cannot combine formulas and LotusScript in an agent.

FIGURE 14.7

This agent runs manually, so the user can complete the prompts.

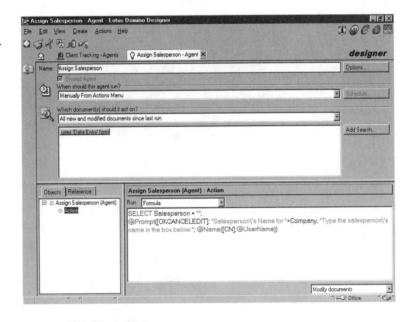

FIGURE 14.8

A prompt dialog box appears, asking for the name of a salesperson for the company, Zebley Zones.

To edit an existing agent, open the database in Designer and select **Agents**. Double-click the agent you want to change. The Agent Builder opens. Make any necessary modifications and then save the agent again.

Troubleshoot Agents

Always test an agent to see that it produces the desired result. From the Agents list, select the agent and then choose **Actions, Test**. The Test Run Agent Log reports the results of the test (see Figure 14.9).

The test, of course, only tells you that the agent *should* work. You still need to try it out with the working database to see if it gives you the desired result. Open the database in the Notes client and run the agent (this is why you set the agent to run manually during development). Check to see if the result you wanted occurs.

14

FIGURE 14.9

This test of the Assign Salesperson found two documents that matched the criteria set out in the agent builder. The log reports that the agent would have run on those two documents.

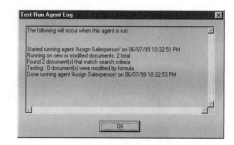

What do you do if your agent doesn't work, or if an existing agent fails or runs slowly? Well, remember seeing the Agent Log when you ran the test of your agent? The Agent Log also creates and records an entry each time an agent runs. Each new log entry overwrites the previous one, so you need to check the log immediately after running the agent to view the most current results. Information found in the log includes when the agent ran, the number of documents on which it ran, and what actions took place.

View the Agent Log by selecting the database and choosing **View, Agents** from the menu (or, in the Designer, open the database and select **Agents** in the Design Pane). Then select the agent for which you want to check the log and choose **Agent, Log** from the menu.

If the agent is not running, check to make sure the agent can run on the databases involved. The agent can't perform a task on a database to which it doesn't have access. See the section "Secure Against Agents" later in this day to learn about how access levels affect agents.

Some agents take too much time to run. This is especially true of LotusScript agents, which take longer to execute their many lines of code than formula agents. When the amount of time needed to run the agent exceeds the Max LotusScript/Java execution time set in the Server document (see Figure 14.10) in the Domino Directory, the agent can't complete its task. Ask the Domino Administrator to increase the time allotment, or rewrite the agent so that its task is run by several smaller agents.

When your agents do run but they run slowly, check to see how many agents you have running concurrently on the server. Change the scheduled agents to run at off-peak hours, such as nighttime. An alternative is to have the Domino Administrator allocate more resources to the Agent Manager by increasing the Max concurrent agents setting in the Agent Manager section of the Server document. The Administrator might be reluctant to do so, however, because other server processes might slow down as a result of shifting resources to the Agent Manager.

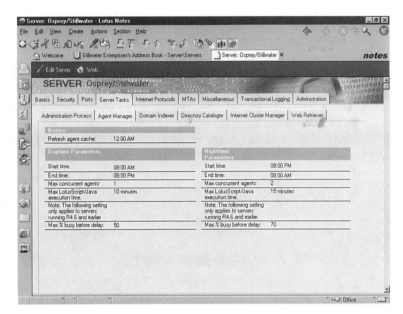

FIGURE 14.10

*To see the Agent Manager settings, open the Domino Directory, click **Server** and then **Servers**, and double-click the server in which you are interested. In the Server document, click the **Server Tasks** tab and then the **Agent Manager** tab.*

You need to become familiar with the server task called *Agent Manager*, which affects how agents on the server run. If the Agent Manager isn't scheduled to run during the same time period that your agent is due to execute, your agent won't work. Check the Server document to see the daytime and evening hours that are set for the Agent Manager. Make sure your agent runs during those hours, or have the Domino Administrator adjust the Agent Manager hours.

The Agent Manager can be your ally. It can record debug information about control parameters, events, loading reports, memory warnings, performance statistics, execution reports, and scheduling. For debugging information to be recorded, the Domino Administrator must add the Debug_AMgr = *option* statement to the Notes.ini file on the server. Options include

- **c**—List agent control parameters
- **e**—List Agent Manager event information
- **l**—List agent loading information
- **m**—List agent memory warnings
- **p**—List agent performance statistics
- **r**—List agent run-time reports
- **s**—List Agent Manager scheduling information

14

- **v**—List more information about agent loading, scheduling, and queues
- ***—List all information for all options

After you add the `Debug_AMgr` = *option* statement to Notes.ini and the agent runs on the server, check the Notes console and the Notes Log for the debugging information. To redirect the debugging information to another file, edit the Notes.ini and add the statement `Debug_Outfile=`*filename.* You must do this if you are running the agent on a database that is stored on your local workstation (the console is only on the server). Be warned that redirecting the debug information slows the performance of the agent.

For a solution to the problem of logging debugging information that doesn't degrade performance as much as `Debug_AMgr`, use `Log_AgentManager` in the Notes.ini file. However, this option records less information. To use this option, have the Domino Administrator edit the Notes.ini and add the statement `Log_AgentManager` = *option.* The options are

- **0**—Do not list debugging information
- **1**—List partial and complete information about successful agent runs
- **2**—List complete information about successful agent runs

Another recourse the Domino Administrator has to check why an agent isn't running properly—or at all—is to use one of three server console commands:

- `tell amgr schedule`—Lists each background agent that is scheduled to run on the current day. Using this command tells you whether your agent is scheduled properly.
- `tell amgr status`—Shows in which queue your agent is running and what parameters are in effect. Your agent won't be named, but you can see the number of agents waiting for events, the number of agents in queues waiting for a scheduled time to elapse, the time period (daytime or nighttime), or the maximum amount of time a LotusScript agent can run.
- `tell amgr debug`—Displays and changes the debugger settings for the debugger enabled in the Notes.ini.

Have the Domino Administrator run these commands to help you diagnose any problems with agents.

Agents and Actions

It sometimes seems that actions and agents are the same. Although they can perform similar tasks—sometimes even the same tasks—there are some basic differences.

An *action* is a menu command or button that is associated with either a view or a form. When activated by a user, the action performs a task that is programmed using formulas, simple actions, LotusScript, or JavaScript.

An agent, on the other hand, isn't tied to a button. It can be a menu command if the agent can be run manually by the user, but it can also work in the background, triggered by a schedule or a particular condition. Actions work only on the documents in a view or on documents created by the form in which the action resides. Agents run on any documents or subset of documents in the database, or multiple databases. Actions run on the workstation; agents run on the workstation or the server.

Actions can be used to activate agents. When you create an action for a view or form, select **Simple action(s)** from the Run list in the Programmer's Pane. Click **Add Action** to open the Add Action dialog box (see Figure 14.11). Select **Run Agent** as the Action, and then pick the Agent you want to run. Click **OK**.

FIGURE 14.11

One of the choices to make when using simple actions to define an action is to run an agent. The agent must already exist, and it must be one that is manually run.

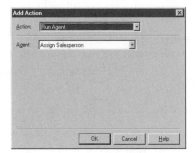

The agent then runs when the user selects the action from the menu or clicks the Action button.

Newsletter Agents

One of the simple actions to use with agents is Newsletter Summary. When you assign this simple action to an agent, the agent searches the database for documents that match the conditions you set in the agent. The agent then sends a summary document with links to the individual documents to the list of recipients you specify.

Use the following steps to create a newsletter agent:

1. Open the database in the Notes client and choose **Create, Agent** from the menu, or open the database in Designer, choose **Agents**, and click the **New Agent** button on the Action Bar.

14

2. Give the agent a name, define when it is to run, and select an option to choose the documents on which the agent is to run.

3. In the Programmer's Pane, select **Simple action(s)** from the Run list.

4. Click **Add Action** to open the Add Action dialog box (see Figure 14.12).

FIGURE **14.12**

In the Add Action dialog box, set up the recipients, subject, and message body to accompany the newsletter summary.

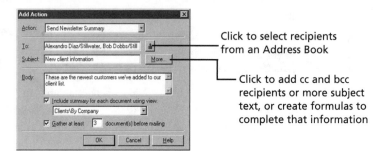

Click to select recipients from an Address Book

Click to add cc and bcc recipients or more subject text, or create formulas to complete that information

5. Select **Send Newsletter Summary** as the Action.

6. In the To field, enter the names of the recipients of your newsletter summary message. Click the **Address Book** button to select the names from a dialog box. Click **More** to select carbon copy (cc) and blind carbon copy (bcc) recipients, or use formulas to select recipients.

7. Enter a Subject. Click **More** to enter a longer subject or write a formula to create the subject.

8. In Body, enter the message you want to send with the newsletter summary.

9. To send a text summary for each document in a specified view, enable **Include summary for each document using view**. Then, select the view to use from the drop-down list. A snapshot of the way the document appears in the view is included as a summary. If you don't select this option, the recipients receive only document links to the documents.

10. Select **Gather at least** to specify how many documents must meet the summary conditions before the summary is sent. Don't select this option if the agent is connected to an action that acts on selected documents.

11. Click **OK**. Save the agent.

When the agent is run, a mail message is sent to each recipient listed in the agent (see Figure 14.13).

FIGURE 14.13

This message is the newsletter summary containing information on each document—a row from the selected view—plus a document link to the document.

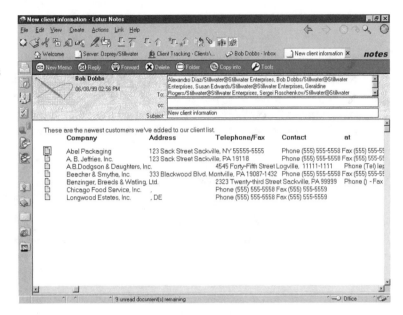

Archiving Agents

In some databases, you don't want to lose inactive documents by simply deleting them, but you *do* want to remove these documents from the database. One solution is to create an archive database in which to store the inactive documents in case they are needed at a later date.

First, you need to create a database in which to store the inactive documents. Choose **File, Database, New Copy** to create the database by copying the current database. Copy only the design to the new database. Give the new database a title that indicates that it is the archive database so you don't mistake it for the active database.

Second, you need to create an agent in the current database. Give the agent a name and decide when it is to be run (use run manually while in development). Then determine on which documents it is to be run. For example, to specify inactive documents, click **Add Search** and, in the Search Builder, set **By Date** as the Condition. Then search for documents whose date modified falls before a specified date.

From the Run list, select **Simple action(s)** and then click **Add Action**. Choose **Copy to Database** as the Action and select the archive database as the database into which the documents are to be copied.

Add a second action by clicking **Add Action** again. This time, select **Delete from Database** as the Action.

14

Save and close the agent. Then test it. If it works correctly, you might want to change your agent to make it scheduled instead of run manually.

Another way to archive documents is to use a field called Status (or something similar). Users mark the Status as **Closed** or **Inactive** when the document becomes inactive. In this case, the agent searches for documents in which the field named Status contains *Closed* or *Inactive*. When the agent runs, it locates these documents and copies them to the archive database, and then it deletes these documents from the active database.

Note

Notes does have an archiving tool that's accessible from Database Properties. Click the **Archive Settings** button on the Database Basics page of the Database Properties box. This tool enables you to set up archiving based on whether the documents have been read or accessed, or modified or updated, within a specified number of days. If you have marked documents as expired, you can also use the archiving tool on those documents. The archive database must be called a *filename* (the first six characters of the filename of the original database) and stored in an \archive directory. In the Advanced options of this tool, you can also set up a log of the archived documents which must be named l_*filename* (the first six characters of the filename of the original database) and stored in the \archive directory. Use the archiving tool for generalized archiving; use an agent to archive specific documents.

Secure Against Agents

Because agents are so powerful and flexible, they can have a wide range of effects on documents and databases. It's necessary, therefore, to restrict who can create them and where they can run.

Users can create their own personal agents that run on their own workstations. There are no restrictions on that. However, there are restrictions on who can create agents that run on servers, and these restrictions are found in the database access control list (see Figure 14.14):

- To create personal agents, the user must be assigned at least Reader access to the database and have Create personal agents enabled. These agents can only be run by the user who created them, but they are stored in the database on the server and run on the server copy of the database.

- A user needs at least Designer access to a database to create shared agents that use either simple actions or formulas. For agents that involve LotusScript or Java, a user must also have Create LotusScript/Java agents enabled.

FIGURE 14.14

The Access Control List defines who can create agents for the database and what type of agents they can create.

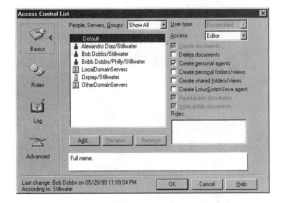

The Server document in the Domino Directory displays information about who can run agents on that server (see Figure 14.15). Open the Server document and select the **Security** tab. In the section on Agent Restrictions are several fields affecting the running of agents on the server:

- **Run personal agents**—If this is blank, anyone who can access the server can run personal agents that are stored on the server and involve server databases. If any names appear in the field, only the specified people can run personal agents.

- **Run restricted LotusScript/Java agents**—No one is allowed to run restricted LotusScript or Java agents if the field is blank. Only people named in this field can run these agents.

- **Run unrestricted LotusScript/Java agents**—No one is allowed to run unrestricted LotusScript or Java agents if the field is blank. Only people named in this field can run these agents.

What is the difference between restricted and unrestricted LotusScript/Java agents? Using either LotusScript or Java, a designer can write scripts in an unrestricted agent that access the server and manipulate file input/output, system time, and operating system commands. Restricted agents cannot perform these types of operations.

14

FIGURE **14.15**

The Server document determines who can write agents that run on the server, and overrides even if you have rights according to the Access Control List.

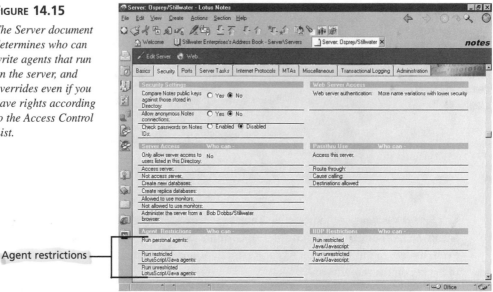

Agent restrictions

Agents and the Web

Both the Notes client and the Domino server can run agents, but Web browsers cannot. Therefore, if you want to use agents to process information when a Web browser is the client, Domino has to run the agents for the browser. Domino can run three kinds of agents for a Web browser:

- A WebQueryOpen agent, which the server runs before sending a form to the browser. You can use this kind of agent to preprocess the form before sending it to the browser.

- An agent triggered by an OpenAgent URL, which the Web user can trigger by clicking a hotspot on an HTML page. Use this kind of agent any time you want to do special processing as a result of a user request.

- A WebQuerySave agent, which the server runs when a browser submits a form to the server. Use this kind of agent to process the information in the submitted form.

The agents themselves are no different from any other agent you might create, except that they always run on the server, and never on the client. They must also be shared and be set to run manually. After creating the agent, set up its Web trigger as follows:

- **WebQueryOpen agent**—Open the WebQueryOpen event on a form. There you see the command `@Command([ToolsRunMacro]; "<Your agent goes here>")`. Substitute the name of your agent for the text between the quotation marks, and then save the form.
- **WebQuerySave agent**—Do the same thing, but in the WebQuerySave event instead of the WebQueryOpen event.
- **"OpenAgent URL" agent**—Create any kind of button or action or hotspot on a form, a view, or a page. The button/action/hotspot should produce a URL in the following form:
`http://www.planetnotes.com/dbname.nsf/agentname?OpenAgent`.

Summary

Agents automate tasks for you in a database (or in more than one database). They can be run on the workstation or on the server, with proper access levels. Agents have a trigger—a scheduled time, an event, or manual activation—that starts the agent running. Agents can therefore run in the background, unlike Actions. You also determine which documents in the database are to be affected by the agent.

You program agents by using simple actions, formulas, LotusScript, or Java. Use agents to modify fields, delete documents, move or copy documents, send mail, and more.

Whether your agents run on the server depends on the ACL settings for the database and also on the Security settings in the Server document.

If you want to use agents to process information when a Web browser is the client, Domino has to run the agents for the browser. Consider WebQueryOpen and WebQuerySave for this purpose.

Q&A

Q I have an agent that runs when a document opens, but now we're going to using the same application on the Web. How can I do the same thing for my Web users?

A You can create an agent to perform processes such as field validation before the Web users open documents or save them. Create an agent that runs manually. Then write a formula that uses `@Command([ToolsRunMacro])` to run the agent, and attach it to the WebQueryOpen or WebQuerySave form events.

14

Q **Does JavaScript work in agents?**

A Use JavaScript for actions (shared and unshared), buttons, action hotspots, and events. You can't use JavaScript for agents. You can use Java, Imported Java, and LotusScript for scripting agents.

Q **I have an agent that's producing some strange results. I don't want to delete it, but I need to stop it from running until I can fix it. What can I do?**

A You need to disable the agent (this only works for scheduled agents). In the Agents list in Designer, select the agent and then choose **Actions, Enable** from the menu to remove the check mark. If you need to disable all the agents in a database, choose **File, Database, Properties** to open the Database Properties box. Then select **Disable background agents for this database**. When you're ready to run the agent again, select the agent in the Agents list and choose **Actions, Enable** from the menu.

Q **I can't get the agents I write to work on my computer. What do I do?**

A If the agent you're trying to run is a scheduled agent, the problem might be that you haven't enabled scheduled agents to run on your workstation. Choose **File, Preferences, User Preferences**. Under Startup Options, select **Enable scheduled local agents**.

Workshop

In this workshop, you'll be adding agents to the Proposed Titles database that send a newsletter summary of titles under discussion, which notify someone that has been appointed as the acquisitions editor for a title, and that archive rejected titles. If you haven't been building the Proposed Titles database from workshop to workshop, use the PTDay13.nsf file from the Day13 folder on the CD.

Create a Newsletter Agent

Create a shared agent in the Proposed Titles database called Books Under Discussion. This agent should be run weekly, but for purposes of testing it you'll need to run it manually. The agent needs to be run on all documents in the view that have a status of "Under Discussion" (that value in the TStatus field has a synonym of 4).

Use a simple action, **Send Newsletter Summary**, to program this agent. Send the messages to the members of the EditBoard group. The subject of the message is "Titles Under Discussion", and the message needs to include a summary for each document using the view Books\By Title. There needs to be at least one title that meets the criteria before the summary is sent. The message should be similar to the following: `"These are the book titles currently under discussion in the Proposed Titles database."`

Click **OK** to return to the agent builder. Save the agent and test it.

Send Mail Memo to Editor

Create a shared agent named Appointed that runs weekly (run it manually at first). Run it on all documents that are new or modified since the agent last ran.

Use a simple action to program the agent. Select **Send Mail Message** as the simple action. The subject of the mail memo is "New Task." The body of the message is `"You have been appointed as the acquisition editor for the following title(s)."` Include a link to the document.

To address the message, click **More**. Select **Formula** under To. Enter or select the field name **TAcqEditor**. Click **OK**.

Click **OK** to return to the agent builder. Save the agent and test it.

Archive Rejected Titles

Create a shared agent called Archive Rejected that copies all titles that have a Rejected Status to the Rejected Titles database (use RTDay1.nsf in the Day1 folder of the CD if you didn't create a Rejected Titles database). The agent should be run weekly, but run it manually to test it.

The agent needs to act on all documents in the database for which the value of the TStatus field is Rejected (synonym is 2).

Use the Copy document simple action to copy the document to the Rejected Titles database. Then create a second simple action, Delete document, to remove the document from the current database.

Save and test the agent.

To see examples of the databases used in this workshop, open the Day14 folder of the CD, and then open PTDay14.nsf (Proposed Titles) and RTDay14.nsf (Rejected Titles). Note that the agents in our sample databases are still set to be manually run because they are not ready to be loaded on a server.

14

WEEK 3

Automate and Deliver

15

16

17

18

19

20

21

DAY 15

Incorporate Workflow

A business process involves a series of stages or steps in which ideas, paperwork, projects, and so forth flow from one stage to another. At some point, some parts of the process require approval before they can go on to the next stage. This movement from one stage to another is the *workflow*. Lotus Notes and Domino are particularly adept at business processes, or workflow.

It takes a workflow application to control a business process—making certain that steps are taken in the correct order, directing different elements to the correct people or departments, ensuring necessary approvals are made, and steering the consequences of those decisions and approvals to their appropriate next step.

Today you'll learn some strategies for automating workflow and how to enable those strategies using mail and agents.

Strategies for Automating Workflow

When creating a workflow application, it is extremely important to set out a plan of the flow beforehand. As part of the planning process you need to know

- What item or object is traveling through the flow (an order, expense form, project, and so on)
- Who or what starts the action
- The complete route the item follows, from start to finish
- Who or what receives workflow actions (by job function, not name or title)
- What decisions need to be made along the route (conditions for proceeding, and what to do when those conditions are not met)

The application you've been building in the workshops throughout this book is a workflow application designed for an imaginary book publishing company (see Figure 15.1). It works in this fashion:

1. Objects traveling through the workflow of this application are new book titles. These titles begin their route in a discussion database, where they are proposed and where their merits are discussed.

2. After 30 days of review by the editorial staff, a list of the new proposals are sent to the Executive Committee, who decides which titles they want to produce and which to reject.

3. Rejected titles are archived. Approved titles are mailed to the Titles in Development database.

4. A notice is sent to the Acquisitions Editor assigned to the new title, stating that it has been approved and is now in the Titles in Development database. This database tracks the steps in producing the book—assigning an author and editors, getting signed contracts, setting deadlines, and so forth. One of the first steps in Titles in Development is for the AE to find and contract an author for the book.

5. After the author contracts are signed, information about the book is sent to the Completed Titles database. Completed Titles is the Web application that displays Web pages about the books to the general public.

6. Submitted manuscript chapters are stored in a document library from which the editors can pull the manuscripts to work on them.

7. As manuscript chapters arrive, the Acquisitions Editor (AE) is notified. The AE then notes the completion of the manuscript in the Titles in Development database to track the progress of the book.

8. When the book is complete, additional information and chapters are posted in the Completed Titles database, where the public learns about books offered by the publisher.

FIGURE 15.1

This is a diagram of the workflow involved in book production, and is the example being used in the end of chapter workshops.

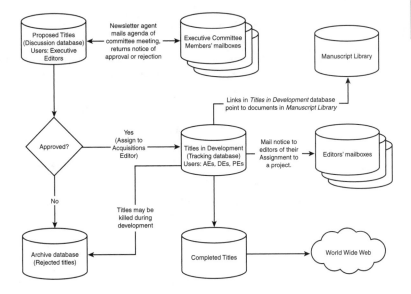

In a workflow application, you have to handle moving documents from one user to another or from one database to another, assigning people to tasks or assigning resources to accomplish the tasks, share information, and send reminders when the workflow slows or halts. Workflow strategies are the methods you employ to accomplish this.

- To move documents, you mail them to the next user or database. Alternatively, leave the documents in a central location, and notify the user that the documents are ready for the next step by mailing a reminder with a document link.

- To track the status of a document's process, create status-type fields and reports to show the current status. Don't overlook the importance of reports to track outstanding items.

- Use security measures at the database, document, and field levels to control who approves the document before passing it along. Define responsibilities by determining who can read for review and who can edit a document.

Mail Enable Databases

There are two ways to handle documents that will be used by different individuals in the workflow:

- Keep the documents in a central, shared database. Notify users when documents need their attention by sending mail messages that include document links (sending whole documents back and forth to users substantially increases the size of mail databases for the involved individuals, can slow performance, and makes it nearly impossible to control revisions). By using a central, shared database, you can create an agent or action that uses the Send Mail Message simple action and enables the Include link to document option. Another method is to use the Send Newsletter Summary simple action. A third method is to use an @MailSend formula with a flag that includes the document link (see the next section).

- Create databases for different purposes, and move the documents between the databases by mailing them. In this scenario, the receiving database must be enabled as a mail-in database.

When you decide to use a database that receives mail, the Domino Administrator must create a mail-in database document for the database (which must reside on the server). The mail-in database document resides in the Domino Directory, and the server's mail router consults that document for instructions on where to deliver documents for the database.

Use the following steps to create the mail-in database document:

1. Open the Domino Directory.
2. In the Navigation Pane, select **Servers**, and then **Mail-In Databases**.
3. Click the **Add Mail-In Database** button on the Action bar to create a new mail-in database document (see Figure 15.2).
4. Give the database a Mail-in name by which it can be identified in SendTo fields or in formulas.
5. Click the **Database Information** tab (see Figure 15.3). Enter the Domain name.
6. Type the hierarchical name of the Server on which the database is stored (such as Server1/Acme).
7. In Filename, enter the name of the directory in which the database is stored (if the database is in a subdirectory of the Notes\Data directory) and the filename of the database.

FIGURE 15.2

In the Mail-in name field, enter a name to use for the database in order to send mail to the database.

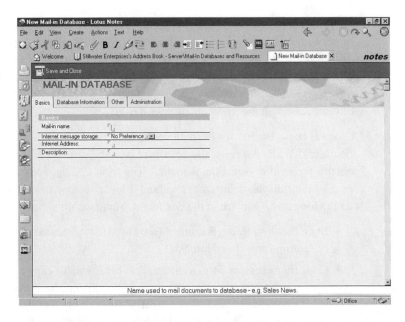

FIGURE 15.3

Enter the Domain, name of the server on which the database is stored, and path and filename of the database file.

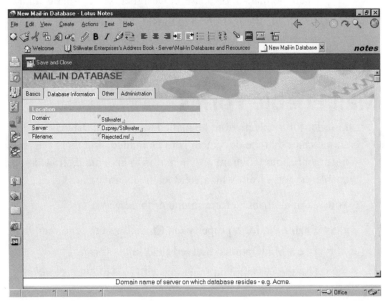

8. (Optional) Click the **Administration** tab and enter the names of people who can change the mail-in database document in Administrators.

9. Save and close the document.

Before you send any documents to this new mail-in database, you have to make sure that a replica of the database resides on the server (remember, up to now you've been working locally). If you don't have rights to do so yourself, have the Domino Administrator put a replica of the database on the server. Because you are still in development, you want to also make sure that access to the database is restricted to you, the Domino Administrator, and the members of your design team.

A second consideration for the mail-in database is this: How are you going to read the documents? Without a form, the document can't be displayed. Only the document, which contains the field information, is mailed. The form you used to create the document is not. You can't display a document without a form because the form provides the structure and the formatting you see in the document. You have three options:

- Store the form in the document (see Day 10, "Advanced Views," for a discussion on storing forms in documents).
- Copy the necessary form to the mail-in database. To copy a form, in Designer, open the database in which the original document was stored, select **Forms**, select the form you need, and choose **Edit, Copy** to copy the form to the Clipboard. Then open the mail-in database in Designer, select **Forms**, and choose **Edit, Paste**.
- Create an alternate form in the target database that uses all or some of the same fields used by the original form. Then change the contents of the Form field of the document when it arrives in the target database.

Mail Enable Forms

In order for a document to be mailed to a mail-in database or to a person, there has to be an indicator that the document is to be mailed, and there has to be information in the document about to whom or where it is to be mailed. To accomplish this, you mail-enable the form from which the documents are created.

You can mail-enable a form in one of three ways:

- Enable the form property On Close: Present send mail dialog.
- Use a MailOptions reserved field in the form.
- Use the @MailSend function, with or without arguments.

Address a Document

A mail memo has three main components:

- Recipients (who the memo is addressed to)—To, cc, and bcc
- Subject
- Message body, which can also include attachments or links

Documents you mail-enable also include these elements; but—most importantly—they must define the recipients. Carbon copy (cc) and blind carbon copy (bcc) recipients are always optional. It's the data in the To field of a mail memo that says to whom it's primarily addressed. The equivalent in a mail-enabled document is the SendTo field. SendTo is a reserved field name and can only be used to contain the names of people or mail-in databases who are to receive the mailed document.

The SendTo field can be an editable field that's completed by the user or a computed field where the result of the formula or script is the name of the recipient. There's no reason that the user has to see a SendTo field if you don't want him to know the document is being mailed. The SendTo field can be hidden.

With the exception of @MailSend (with arguments), a SendTo field is required for all methods of mail-enabling a document.

Other fields that control mailing options are listed in Table 15.1.

Table 15.1 Reserved Fields for Mailing Options

Field Name	Values
BlindCopyTo	The name of a person, group, or mail-in database.
CopyTo	The name of a person, group, or mail-in database.
DeliveryPriority	L, N, or H for low, normal, or high priority.
DeliveryReport	B, C, T, or N for create a report only if delivery fails (B), confirm successful and failed deliveries (C), trace failed deliveries (T), or never generate a report (N).
Encrypt	1 to encrypt mailed document, 0 to not encrypt.
MailFormat	B, E, M, or T for cc:Mail users to view Notes documents as both text and encapsulated (B), encapsulated in a Notes database that is attached to the cc:Mail memo (E), the body field of the document is pasted as text in the cc:Mail memo (M), or the contents of the document are converted to text and pasted into the body of the cc:Mail memo (T).

continues

Table 15.1   continued

Field Name	Values
MailOptions	1 for automatic mailing, 0 to not mail the document.
ReturnReceipt	1 to send a receipt when the document is opened by the recipient, 0 to not send a receipt.
SaveOptions	1 to save mailed documents, 0 to not save mailed documents.
SendTo	The name of a person, group, or mail-in database.
Sign	1 adds an electronic signature (applicable only if the form field contains enabled for signing), O to not add signature

Set the On Close Property

To make mailing of the document optional—that is, in the hands of the user—enable the **On Close: Present mail send dialog** in the Form Properties box (see Figure 15.4).

FIGURE 15.4

*In the Form Properties box, click the **Defaults** tab, and then check the **Present mail send dialog** option in the On Close section.*

The form must have a SendTo field that specifies the destination address for the document.

When the user saves a document created with that form, a dialog box appears (see Figure 15.5), displaying options to send and save a copy of the document, send the document only, save the document only, discard any changes, sign the document, or encrypt the document.

FIGURE 15.5

The dialog box presents options to send or save the document, and sign or encrypt it.

Note

A value of 1 in a Sign, Encrypt, or SaveOptions field overrides the choices
the user makes in the Close Window dialog box when the form property On
Close: Present mail send dialog is active.

15

Set Mail Options

Another method for sending a document is to use the reserved field MailOptions. When
MailOptions has a value of 1, mailing automatically takes place. The form must have a
SendTo field.

By making the MailOptions field an editable keywords field (such as radio buttons or a
dialog list), you give the user the choice of whether to mail the document. Because the
values returned for this field must be 1 or 0, use synonyms with the keywords (see
Figure 15.6).

FIGURE 15.6

*Use 1 as the synonym
to send the document
and 0 as the synonym
for not sending the
document.*

Note

When a MailOptions field has a value of 1, it overrides the choices made
by the user in the Close Window dialog box that appears when the form
property On Close: Present mail send dialog is selected. Users can only click
Yes to save the document, **No** to close without saving, or **Cancel** to return to
the document.

Use @MailSend

For agents, buttons, form actions, view actions, and SmartIcons, use the @MailSend function. The @MailSend function enables automatic mailing. There are two ways to use the @MailSend function:

- **Without parameters**—The @MailSend function sends the current document to the recipients in the SendTo field. The document must have a SendTo field.
- **With parameters**—The @MailSend function creates a new mail memo based on the arguments in the function and mails it to the recipients listed in the sendTo, copyTo, and blindCopyTo arguments.

Without parameters, @MailSend also causes the mail memo to route to recipients listed in CopyTo and BlindCopyTo fields in the document. If the document contains DeliveryPriority, DeliveryReport, or ReturnReceipt fields, these control the delivery priority, reports on delivery, and return receipts. Without these fields in the document, the defaults are normal priority, no delivery report, and no return receipt.

When used with parameters, @MailSend has the following syntax:

```
@MailSend(sendTo; copyTo; blindCopyTo; subject; remark;
bodyFields; [flags])
```

sendTo—Contains text or a text list for the primary recipients of the mail memo (separate members of the text list with colons).

copyTo—Contains text or a text list for the carbon copy recipients of the mail memo (separate members of the text list with colons).

blindCopyTo—Contains text or a text list for the blind carbon copy recipients of the mail memo (separate members of the text list with colons).

subject—An optional argument that contains text that is displayed in the Subject field of a mail memo. If you don't include a subject, put "" or **NULL** for that argument.

remark—An optional argument that contains any text you want to appear at the beginning of the memo's body field. If you don't include a remark, put "" or **NULL** for that argument.

bodyFields—Contains the names of one or more text fields from the current document that you want included in the mail memo. Enclose each field name in quotes. When listing multiple fields, use colons (:) to separate the items in the list.

[*flags*]—Indicate memo priority and security (see Table 15.2 for a complete list). Use square brackets around each flag. When listing multiple flags, separate the items in the list with colons.

Remember, the @MailSend function with parameters must have six arguments in order to pass the syntax check.

Table 15.2   Flags for @MailSend

DeliveryReportConfirmed	Notifies the sender whether the delivery was successful.
Encrypt	Encrypt the document using the recipient's public key, so only the recipient with a matching private key can read the document.
IncludeDocLink	Includes a link pointing to the document (you must include this flag if you want the document linked to the mail memo).
PriorityHigh	Sets a high priority for mail routing so the message is immediately routed to the next server (if necessary).
PriorityNormal	Sets a normal priority for mail routing as defined in the server's connection documents.
PriorityLow	Sets a low priority for mail routing so the message routes overnight to the next server, if necessary.
ReturnReceipt	Notifies the sender when each recipient reads the message.
Sign	Electronically sign the memo when mailing it, using information from the user's ID.

When using the [IncludeDocLink] flag, set the *bodyFields* parameter to NULL ("").

A rich text field can't be included in the *bodyFields* in an @MailSend formula. The fields in that parameter must be text fields, not rich text.

You can't use the @MailSend function in Web applications.

Don't use a MailOptions field and an @MailSend function in the same document. The mail gets sent twice when you do.

Write Agents for Automatic Replies

A person who receives a mail memo can determine whether to respond to the message, but a mail-in database can't make that decision. Therefore, you need to create an agent that automatically replies when mail is received by the database.

Use the following steps to create an agent that automatically replies to mail:

1. Open the mail-in database in Designer.
2. Select **Agents**.
3. Click the **New Agent** button on the Action Bar.
4. Give the agent a name.
5. Check **Shared Agent**.
6. Choose **After New Mail Has Arrived** from the When should this agent run? drop-down list.
7. From the Run drop-down list, select **Simple action(s)**.
8. Click **Add Action**.
9. In the Add Action dialog box (see Figure 15.7), select **Reply to Sender** from the Action drop-down list.
10. Select **Reply to sender only**.
11. If you want to include a message with your reply, type it in the Body box.
12. To include a copy of the document with your message, check **Include copy of document**.
13. If you think a person might be listed as a recipient more than once (in a group or in the carbon copy or blind carbon copy fields), check **Reply only once per person**.
14. Click **OK**. Save and close the agent.

FIGURE 15.7

An agent can respond to new mail to notify the sender that the document was received.

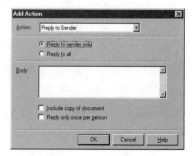

Add Agents that Mail Notices and Send Announcements

An agent can send a notice to a user that new mail was received by a mail-in database. Use an agent to notify specific users when changes in documents occur, or when conditions change in documents.

Triggers for agents include After New Mail Has Arrived and If Documents Have Been Created or Modified. Scheduled agents can periodically check documents for status changes, for instance.

A formula or script is not always necessary, either. The simple actions include Send Mail Message. When you select this simple action (see Figure 15.8), you build a mail memo to send. Including a document link or a copy of the document is also an option.

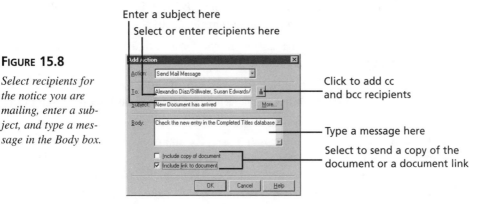

Enter a subject here
Select or enter recipients here

FIGURE 15.8

Select recipients for the notice you are mailing, enter a subject, and type a message in the Body box.

Click to add cc and bcc recipients

Type a message here

Select to send a copy of the document or a document link

Summary

Workflow applications require that copies of documents or document links get mailed to individuals so the individuals can act on the documents. An option is depositing the documents in a database that has been enabled to receive mail. Then a notice needs to be sent to concerned individuals to tell them that the documents are there so they can perform tasks on them.

For documents to be mailed, they must be mail-enabled: A SendTo field must be put in the form. Then, one of three methods can be used to mail-enable the form: The form property to present a mail send dialog box needs to be selected; a MailOptions field needs to be added to the form; or an @MailSend formula needs to be included in a view or form action, button, or agent.

When the mail send dialog box is presented, the user determines whether to save or send the document. With a MailOptions field, that choice can be given to the user in the form of an editable keywords field, or it can be automatic if the field is computed with a value of 1. An @MailSend formula automatically sends a mail message to the recipient in the SendTo field, unless it is used with parameters. In that case, all the elements of a mail message are included in the @MailSend formula.

Agents also provide a method for sending documents or notices, especially if triggered when new mail arrives or when documents are changed. The simple actions of replying to the sender or sending mail messages are enough to create agents for mailing.

Q&A

Q I want to create an agent that sends a notice when new mail arrives. However, the person to whom I want to send the mail is listed in a field of the document I'm sending. Can I use a simple action in the agent?

A You might be better off using an @MailSend formula in the agent that refers to the field name as the *sendTo* argument.

Q I'm creating an application that involves approval of expense accounts. I want to have the document mailed to the approver, but how do I get it routed to the next person?

A If you mail the document to the user who is the approver, put a button on the document to approve the expense account (add security so it is only available to the approver). When the button is clicked, use @MailSend in the button formula to send the document to the next person. Also have a button to reject the expense account and send it back to the person so they can fix any errors or explain them to the approver. The biggest problem in this system is defining who is the approver and who gets it after that. I hope you have that information in fields in the document.

Q How can I get workflow to work on the Web if I can't use @MailSend?

A You have to make a workaround solution. If the person who will access the document through the Web has an Internet email address, send a mail notice that the document is available in a database (include the Web address) and tell the person to check the document so it can go to the next stage. The Web user can open the database and the document. Have an action button for approval or setting status, so the Web user can click those.

Workshop

In this workshop, you are going to add some workflow features to your application. You will be working with the Proposed Titles database and the Titles in Development database. If you haven't created these databases and worked on them through the workshops, open the examples available on the CD. For the Proposed Titles database, use PTDay14.nsf in the Day14 folder; for the Titles in Development database, use PTDay13.nsf in the Day13 folder.

15

Part of what is needed for the application workflow was completed in Day 14, "The Not So Secret Agents." You created an agent to send a newsletter summary to the Editorial Board about the books that were currently under discussion. Another agent notified the Acquisitions Editor who is assigned to a new book. The Rejected agent archived rejected proposed titles and stored them in the Rejected Titles database, and then it deleted those titles from the Proposed Titles database.

Following are the tasks you need to accomplish in this workshop:

- Create a mail-in database document for the Titles in Development database.
- Modify an action so it uses @MailSend to send accepted titles to the Titles in Development database.
- Create an agent in the Manuscript Library database that sends a notice to the editors when a new chapter is stored there.
- Create an agent in the Titles in Development database that sends information about a book to the Marketing Department when an author signs a book contract and submits the Table of Contents. That information is to be used by the Marketing Department to create a book page in the Completed Titles database, which is the Web application we have yet to create.

Make a Mail-In Database Document

Up to this point in our application you've been able to create everything locally. We realize that not all our readers have access to a server, especially not to do the workshops in this book. When we create the agent that sends mail to the database, we'll give you a workaround if you don't have a server.

First, with the permission or assistance of your Domino Administrator, create a Mail-In Database document for the Titles in Development database in your Domino Directory. This means either your original database or a replica must reside on the server.

On the Basics tab, enter **Titles in Development** as the Mail-in name. On the Database Information tab, enter your domain, the name (in hierarchical form) of your server, and the file name of the database. Save and close the document. Exit the Domino Directory.

Send Accepted Documents

When the TStatus field in a Proposed Title document is changed to Accepted, the document is mailed from the Proposed Titles database to the Titles in Development database.

In Designer, open the Proposed Title form in the Proposed Titles database. At the bottom of the form, add a hidden field called **SendTo**. Make the field computed text, and enter **"Titles in Development"** as the formula (don't forget the quotes).

Open the Action Pane and select the **Set Status\Accepted** action. Currently, the action uses a simple action that modifies the TStatus field and sets the value as 1 (accepted). You want to leave that, but you also want to add an @MailSend function. Click **Add Action** in the Programmer's Pane and select **@Function Formula** as the Action. In the Formula window, enter **@MailSend**. Click **OK**.

Save the form. Test the action.

What's the workaround? If you can't mail, copy. Add an action to the agent that copies the document and pastes it in the Titles in Development database. Then add another action that deletes the document from the Proposed Titles database. You did the same thing to archive documents to the Rejected Titles database on Day 14. Just remember that you'll have to make some adjustments in later workshops because you copied instead of mailing.

Add an Agent to the Manuscript Library

On Day 1, "An Introduction to Lotus Notes and Domino 5 Development," you created a database called Manuscript Library (Manuscpt.nsf) as a place to store the book chapters as they are submitted by the author (if you don't have a copy of that database, use MSDay1.nsf in the Day1 folder on the CD).

A review cycle can be set for each type of document in the database (except the figures). When the review cycle is set, the reviewers of the document (in our case, the editors) are specified. The Reviewers field provides the names of the people who need to be notified that a chapter or set of figures is available.

Open the Manuscript Library in the Designer. Create a new shared agent called New Manuscript. Have the agent run more than once a day. Set the schedule to run every four hours starting at 9:00 a.m. and ending at 5:00 p.m. Don't run the agent on weekends. For testing purposes, run the agent manually at first.

Have the agent run on all new and modified documents since last run, but add two search criteria. First, select those documents by field—using the field Reviewers—that contain NULL. Click **OK** and then select only those created with the Document, MS Office\Word Document, and MS Office\Paintbrush Picture forms. The word **AND** needs to appear between the Search conditions.

Use an @MailSend formula for the agent that sends a message to the Reviewers with the subject "New Manuscript Arrived". Include the Subject field from the documents in the message (that contains the title of the document) and a document link.

Save the agent and test it.

Send a Mail Message to Marketing

Create a shared agent in the Titles in Development database. Call it **New Book to Sell**. Have the agent run weekly, even on weekends. Run it on all new and modified documents since last run, but add the search conditions that it only run on documents created using the New Title form, and that the field ActTOC is in the last seven days.

Create an @MailSend formula to send the message to the marketing department (create a group called "**Marketing**" in your Address Book). Use "**New Book to Sell**" as your subject. Your remarks should be, "**The Table of Contents is now available in the Manuscript Library database**". Include these fields: **TBookTitle, TProposedAuthors, TBookCategory, TAudience, and TDescription**.

Save the agent and test it.

To see examples of the databases from this workshop, open the Day15 folder on the CD and then open the Proposed Titles database (PTDay15.nsf), the Titles in Development database (TDDay15.nsf), and the Manuscript Library database (MSDay15.nsf).

15

DAY 16

List Processing

List processing provides a method of extracting and manipulating data when lists of items are stored in a field or returned by a formula.

On this day, you'll learn what lists are, how to work with them, how to extract information, and how to perform operations on lists.

What Are Lists and How Can You Use Them?

A list is a discrete entity that contains multiple values of the same data type. The simplest type of a list is a concatenation of items separated by colons, such as `"Miami" : "Toledo" : "San Francisco"`. Such a list might be the result of a value in a multivalue field. Lists also result from some @functions, especially those requiring user input.

Operations performed on lists are performed on each element of the list, one at a time. For example, if you want to be sure a list of cities (`"miami" : "tole-do" : "san francisco"`) appears with proper capitalization, you might write the following formula:

```
@ProperCase("miami" : "toledo" : "san francisco")
```

The result is a list: `"Miami, Toledo, San Francisco"` with the item separators you specify in the field or column properties (commas are used here). Remember, when writing lists of items in a formula, you separate the items with colons.

Manipulating Lists

There are a number of @functions that you use to manipulate lists. Table 16.1 lists the most commonly used functions, several of which are explained in the following sections. Some @functions that perform string operations can also be used with lists, but they perform the operation on each element in the list.

Table 16.1 Commonly Used List @Functions

@Function	Description
@Elements	Returns the number of elements in a list.
@Explode	Converts a text string into a text list.
@Implode	Converts a test list to a text string using spaces or a specified separator to separate list elements.
@IsMember	Determines if a string is an element of a list or if a list is contained in another list. Returns 1 (true) or 0 (false).
@IsNotMember	Determines if a string is not an element of a list or a list is not contained in another list. Returns 1 (true) or 0 (false).
@Keywords	Given two text lists, returns only those items from the second list that are found in the first list.
@Member	Determines the position (left to right) of an element in a string list and returns the number of that position.
@Replace	Does a find-and-replace operation on a text list.
@Select	Returns the list element that appears in a specified number position (left to right) in a list.
@Subset	Extracts a specified number of values from the list, counting left to right (use negative numbers to count right to left).
@Trim	Removes leading, trailing, and redundant spaces from a text string or from each element of a text list.
@Unique	Removes any duplicate values from a string list or returns a random, unique text value.

Add Entries

A numeric field that is empty is a NULL field. When the NULL field is specified in a formula, the formula might produce errors. In formulas, you can't mix data types, but Notes treats a NULL field as text, so you get a mixed data error. That's why it's important to use a default value in editable number fields. However, you don't always have that opportunity with new fields. One way around that is to first test if the field is empty and then add contents to the field:

```
FIELD Qty := @If(Qty = ""; 10 : 20; Qty : 10 : 20)
```

In this formula, using the FIELD keyword assigns a value to the field. If Qty is empty, the list 10 : 20 becomes the value of the field. If there is a value in Qty, the list of values includes that quantity in addition to the list 10 : 20.

For text lists, you can add values to the end of the list by using the FIELD keyword. If the field Candy already contains "licorice" : "mints" : "lollipops", the following formula line adds two items to the end of that list and puts the entire list in a new field called Sweets:

```
FIELD Sweets := Candy : "chocolate drops" : "lemon drops"
```

Use @Trim to ensure that the new list contains no NULL values:

```
FIELD Sweets := Candy : "chocolate drops" : "lemon drops";
@Trim(SweetList)
```

Remove Entries

When you remove list entries, use @Replace to replace elements in the list with NULL entries. Then use @Trim to remove any leading, trailing, or redundant spaces (in this case, the NULL entries).

The @Replace function has the following syntax:

```
@Replace(sourceList; fromList; toList)
```

    sourceList—The list that is scanned for the original set of values.

    fromList—The list of values you want to replace in the *sourceList*.

    toList—The list containing the replacement values.

For example, in a straight replacement, you might want to replace two names in a list of names contained in an Attendees field. That list includes James, Robert, Susan, Howard, and Peter. Robert and Peter need to be replaced by Harriet and Miriam. The formula might look like this:

```
@Replace(Attendees; "Robert" : "Peter"; "Harriet" : "Miriam")
```

On the other hand, if you want to remove Robert and Peter from the list but not replace them, the formula might be

```
NewAttendees := @Replace(Attendees; "Robert" : "Peter"; "" : "");
@Trim(NewAttendees)
```

The @Trim function removes the two NULL entries.

Insert Entries

Instead of adding entries at the end of a list, you might want to put new entries some-where in the middle of the list. To do this, you need to use more than one @function.

The first step is to determine what value in the existing list the new entry or entries will follow. Use the @Member function to do this:

```
@Member(value; stringlist)
```

> **value**—The element whose position in the stringlist you want to find.

> **Stringlist**—The text list.

The @Member function results in a number that represents the position of the value in the stringlist. The number 0 is returned if the value is not in the stringlist.

For example, to find the position of "Toledo" in the list "Miami" : "Toledo" : "San Francisco", the formula might be

```
CityList := "Miami" : "Toledo" : "San Francisco";
@Member("Toledo"; CityList)
```

The result of the formula is 2.

The second step in inserting new entries is to break the list into two. The first list con-sists of the elements up to and including the value that the new entries are to follow. The second list comprises the elements that follow the new entry point. Use the @Subset function to set up these two lists:

```
@Subset(list; number)
```

> **list**—The text list, number list, or time-date list from which you want the subset.

> **number**—The number of values from the list you want for the subset.

After you use @Member to find the location of the value you want the new entries to follow (in our example, "Toledo" is the value), the result is the *number* in the @Subset formula:

```
CityList := "Miami" : "Toledo" : "San Francisco";
Position := @Member("Toledo"; CityList);
@Subset(CityList; Position)
```

This formula returns the list `"Miami" : "Toledo"`.

To capture the second list, you need to know the total number of elements in the list and how many elements remain after removing the first subset. Count the number of elements in a list using the @Elements function:

```
@Elements(list)
```

> *list*—The text list, number list, or date-time list for which you want to know the total number of elements.

```
CityList := "Miami" : "Toledo" : "San Francisco";
Position := @Member("Toledo"; CityList);
FirstList := @Subset(CityList; Position);
NumCities := @Elements(CityList);
CitiesLeft := Position - NumCities;
@Subset(CityList; CitiesLeft)
```

After getting the two subsets, the third step is to assign the values you want to insert in the list, in this case `"New Orleans" : "Chicago"`.

The final step is to concatenate the three lists and assign that value to the field:

```
CityList := "Miami" : "Toledo" : "San Francisco";
Position := @Member("Toledo"; CityList);
FirstList := @Subset(CityList; Position);
NumCities := @Elements(CityList);
CitiesLeft := Position - NumCities;
SecondList := @Subset(CityList; CitiesLeft);
NewCities := "New Orleans" : "Chicago";
FIELD Cities := FirstList : NewCities : SecondList;
@Trim(Cities)
```

The final list of values is `"Miami" : "Toledo" "New Orleans" : "Chicago" : "San Francisco"`.

Find Values

At times, it's important to know if a value (or list) is part of a list. To determine this, use the @IsMember function, which returns 1 (true) if the value is a member of the list or 0 (false) if the value isn't a member of the list. The @IsMember syntax is slightly different, depending on whether you are working with a single value or a list of values:

```
@IsMember(textValue; textListValue)
```

```
@IsMember(textListValue1; textListValue2)
```

> *textValue*—The text value for which you are scanning the list.

> *textListValue*—The text list you are scanning.

16

textListValue1—The text list for which you are scanning another list to see if it's a member.

textListValue2—The second list you are scanning.

Usually, @IsMember is combined with another function, such as @If:

```
@If(@IsMember("San Francisco"; Cities); "California"; "")
```

This formula returns "California" if "San Francisco" is one of the values in the Cities field; otherwise, it returns a NULL value.

Frequently, a list displays values in date-time or number format and you need to translate that into words. For example, say you have a DueDate field that returns a date. You want to categorize a view by the month in which the DueDate falls. The result of @Month(DueDate) produces a number from 1 to 12. Using a list, use @Select to extract the text for the month based on the position of the month text in the list. The @Select function contains a list of arguments:

```
@Select(number; values)
```

number—The position (number) of the value you want to retrieve.

values—The list of values, separated by semicolons, from which you want to extract the value. These values can be single values or lists of values.

To return the month "May" for a due date of 5/31/99, the formula might be

```
MonthNum := @Month(DueDate);

@Select(MonthNum; "January"; "February"; "March"; "April";
"May"; "June"; "July"; "August"; "September"; "October";
"November"; "December")
```

Another function for extracting words is @Word.

```
@Word(string; separator; number)
```

string—The text string or text list you want to scan.

separator—The character that delimits words in the *string*.

number—The position (number) that indicates which word you want returned from the *string*.

For instance, say you want to display the weekday of the DueDate value. Your formula might look like this:

```
Weekday := "Sunday Monday Tuesday Wednesday Thursday Friday Saturday";
Number := @Weekday(DueDate);
@Word(Weekday; " "; Number)
```

The @Weekday function returns the number for the day of the week (1 is Sunday and 7 is Saturday). So, if the DueDate is 5/31/99, which was a Monday, the @Weekday function returns 2. The second value in the Weekday list is "Monday", which is the result of the formula.

Display List Values in Views

In views, some of your columns might display fields that contain multiple values. These multiple values are separated by the character you choose as the Multi-value separator in the Column Properties box (see Figure 16.1).

FIGURE 16.1

For multiple values, select New Line, Space, Comma, Semicolon, or None as the character to separate the values in the column.

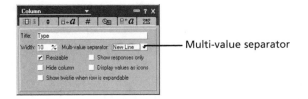

Multi-value separator

However, if you use a field with multiple values in a concatenation formula, the concatenation is applied to each element of the list of values. For example, for the following formula

```
"We are making plans to travel to " + City
```

the result is "We are making plans to travel to Miami, We are making plans to travel to Toledo, We are making plans to travel to San Francisco" if the list "Miami : Toledo : San Francisco" is the contents of the City field. Rather than have the concatenation formula return three separate statements for each city, use the @Implode function:

```
@Implode(list; separator)
```

The *list* argument is the name of the field that stores the list or the actual list text string; *separator* is the punctuation used to separate the members of the list. For example, the following formula returns "We are making plans to travel to Miami, Toledo, San Francisco":

```
@Implode(City; ",")
```

Create Dynamic Tables

A dynamic table has multiple rows of entries, but you don't specify the number of rows in advance. Instead, the table dynamically accepts data that is input. This is made possible by the use of lists.

For a dynamic table to work, you need the following:

- A results table that has one row for each set of unique values
- A data input area in which users select or input values
- A lookup area where the values the users select can be matched to additional values
- A button to process the data using list functions, and then to write the results to a line in the table

Results Table

The table that holds the results needs to have at least one row that has one field per cell (a first row might be the labels for the fields). The fields must be multivalue fields with a new line as the multiple value separator. Each field should be computed and evaluated to itself.

For example, in an order form for a hardware company, the fields are ItemName, UnitPrice, Qty, and Total (see Figure 16.2). The ItemName field is a computed text field. All the other fields are number computed fields. For each field, the **Allow multiple values** option is selected on the Field Info page of the Field Properties box. On the Advanced page, **New Line** is selected from the Display separate values with drop-down list. The formula for each field is the name of that field.

To display the total of the Total field, create a table of one cell immediately beneath the results table. Add a field to that table called GrandTotal. That field is a computed number field. The formula for the field is

```
@If(Total = ""; 0; @Sum(Total))
```

Data Input Area

At the top of the form is a hidden field called Hardware List. It is a computed text field. The contents of the field are the hardware items for sale in a list. It is at the top of the form, so it will be processed first.

FIGURE 16.2

The results table has two rows. One is for the field labels, and the other holds the fields. The number of columns in the table is equal to the number of fields displayed.

Field

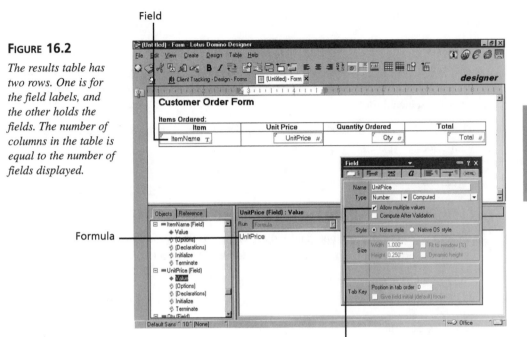

16

Formula

Allow multiple values selected

Above the results table is an input table, which consists of two rows and two columns. The first row contains the field labels. The second row contains two fields, each in its own cell. The first field, ItemInput, is an editable dialog list field (multiple values are not allowed, nor can the user add values not in the list). The choices for the field are determined by formula (see Figure 16.3), and the formula is Hardware. So the choices are the list of hardware items in the Hardware field ("hammer" : "screwdriver" : "plane" : "pliers" : "wrench").

FIGURE 16.3

*On the Control page of the Field Properties box, the **Use formula for choices** option is selected and Hardware is the formula.*

The InputQty field is an editable number field.

Lookup Area

The lookup area is a hidden field called LookupArea. This is a text field that is computed for display (the results aren't saved with the document). The **Allow multiple values** option is selected for this field.

The formula for this field is a text list that pairs the list of items in the Hardware field with prices. A space separates each item from its price:

```
"hammer 5.50" : "screwdriver 4.75" : "plane 3.75"
: "pliers 3.50" : "wrench 6.25")
```

List Processing Button

An Add button below the input and lookup areas processes the entries from the input area, looks up the appropriate values, and adds the results to the results tables.

The formula for the button is

```
REM" establish temporary variables to collect input information";
iQty := InputQty;
iItem := ItemInput;
iList := Hardware;
REM" determine the number of items in the hardware list";
ListLength := @Elements(iList);
REM" find the location in the Hardware list of the selected item";
iPosition := @Member(iItem; iList);
REM" If the item is last, get the last lookup item";
REM" If the item is first in the list, get the first lookup item";
REM" If the item is neither first nor last, create a list of the ";
REM" first n elements and then get the last element in that sublist";
iInfo := @If(iPosition = ListLength; @Subset(LookupArea; -1);
iPosition = 1; @Subset(LookupArea; 1); @Subset(@Subset(LookupArea;
iPosition); -1));
REM" Parse out the item and its price";
iPrice := @TextToNumber(@Word(iInfo; " "; 2));
REM" update the fields in the results table";
FIELD ItemName := @Trim(ItemName : iItem);
FIELD UnitPrice := @If(UnitPrice = ""; iPrice; UnitPrice : iPrice);
FIELD Qty := @If(Qty = ""; iQty; Qty : iQty);
FIELD Total := @If(Total = ""; iQty * iPrice; Total :
(iQty * iPrice));
@Command([FileSave])
```

The remark lines (REM) tell you what each step does—or is intended to do—in a long formula.

Figure 16.4 shows the end result of using the dynamic table.

FIGURE 16.4

Three items have been input, and you see the results in the table.

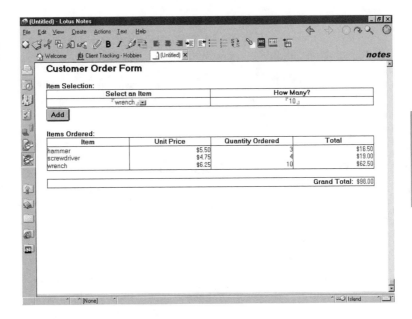

16

This example uses hard coded lists (Hardware and LookupArea), which work fine with small lists and lookups. For larger lists, a more flexible solution is to use lookup formulas such as @DbColumn and @DbLookup. Of course, such a solution requires a view in which the hardware items are listed, along with their prices. With the view in place, an @DbColumn formula can supply the hardware item choices for ItemInput. That can be presented to the user in a dialog box by using @Prompt. Then an @DbLookup formula can match the items with the prices, as was done in the LookupArea field.

Summary

Dealing with fields or formulas that return multiple values requires the use of list processing information. There are several @functions that work specifically with lists, and others that have some application to list processing. The FIELD keyword is also useful in assigning additional values to lists.

For removing items from lists, use @Replace to replace some members with NULL values and @Trim to remove the NULL values. Inserting members in a list requires a combination of functions—@Elements to count the number of members in the list, @Member to locate the breaking point in the list by position, and @Subset to break the list into two parts.

To find list elements, use @IsMember to see if an item is included in the list, @Word to extract an element from a text string or text list, and @Select to locate a text string when a number is returned in a formula.

The @Implode function is useful when concatenating formulas to group the list together with the text strings in the formula, rather than adding the text to each entry in the list.

Q&A

Q **Every time I bring in text from an Internet source, the carriage returns don't fit my current window. I want the text to wrap with the size of the window, but the hard returns in the imported text end lines in awkward places and wrap lines incorrectly. Can I use @Replace to replace carriage returns with a space?**

A The @Replace function works best with lists. However, there is a way to use it with any text string, as well as with lists: @Replace(`sourceList`; `fromList`; `toList`). If your imported text is in a field, use the name of that field as the `sourceList`. Use @NewLine as the `fromList` and a space (" ") as the `toList`. For example, if the imported text is in the Import field, the formula might be @Replace(`Import`; @NewLine; " "). The text wraps naturally afterwards.

Q **I tried using the @Keywords function mentioned in Table 16.1 to test text to see if it contained some of the words I was looking for, but it didn't work. Any idea why?**

A Without seeing your formula and the text, it is difficult to pinpoint the exact cause. However, the @Keywords function is case sensitive. Unless you standardize the case of the text you are scanning (use @UpperCase, @LowerCase, or @ProperCase), you have to be specific when you enter the list of words for which you are searching. Also, @Keywords has two syntaxes: @Keywords(`textList1`; `textList2`) or @Keywords(`textList1`; `textList2`; `separator`). In the second version, you must specify the separator character that appears between the words in the text string. That might not be uniform in the text you're searching. If you use the first version of the syntax, @Keywords will use any of the default delimiters as separators: `",?!;:[](){}<>` (double quotes, space, comma, question mark, exclamation point, semicolon, colon, brackets, parentheses, braces, or angle brackets).

Q **I have a field that has a list of words, but they don't appear in Notes list format. How do I make a list out of them so I can perform list operations on them?**

A Try using the @Explode(*string*) function, which returns a text list from a text string or date range. When it's used on a text string, @Explode recognizes a space, comma, or semicolon as a separator for words or phrases in the text string. As long as one of these characters separates the words in the field, you'll have the list you need. If another character separates the words, such as ~ or · or _, use the @Explode(*string; separator*). For example, if the words are separated by a dash and the fieldname is Words, the formula might be @Explode(Words; "-").

Workshop

In this workshop, you'll be working with the Titles in Development database. If you haven't been working on this database through the workshops, use the TDDay15.nsf file in the Day15 folder of the CD.

Open the Titles in Development database in Designer, and then open the New Title form. In this form, you are going to create a dynamic table that tracks the chapters, figures, and additional manuscript items that come in for a particular book.

Create the results table (place it below the Series Guidelines table). The table is 5 columns by 2 rows. The first row is labels: **Element #**, **Element**, **Page Equivalent**, **Quantity**, and **Total**. In the second row, create the following fields: **ElementNo**, **ElementName**, **PageEquiv**, **Qty**, and **Total**. ElementNo and ElementName are computed text fields. The other fields are computer number fields. All the fields accept multiple values and are set to display separate values as new lines. The formulas for these fields are the names of the fields.

Below the results table, place another table that is 1 column by 1 row. Add a computed number field to the table called **TotalPages**, plus any static text you want to act as the field label (our static text is "Total Number of Pages to date"). The formula for TotalPages is the sum of the Total field, if it isn't blank.

Above the table, you need to create a lookup area. Part of the lookup area is a set of page equivalent fields. These fields contain the factor you multiply times the number of typed pages or figures to calculate the number of actual printed pages they'll produce. You need four editable text fields for this, along with the static text that defines them:

- **ChapPg**—"Chapter Page"
- **FMPage**—"Front Matter Page"

16

- **GIPage**—"Glossary/Index Page"
- **FigPage**—"Figures"

Beneath these fields, but above the results table, you'll need three hidden fields (or place the hidden fields at the top of the form).

- **ElementList**—This is a computed text list. The value of this field is a list of elements: `"Chapter" : "Front Matter" : "Glossary or Index" : "Figures"`.
- **PageList**—This is a computed text list. The value of this field is a list of fields: `ChapPg : FMPage : GIPage : FigPage`.
- **ElementLookUp**—This is a computed text list. The value of this field is a concatenated list that combines the values of the previous two fields: `ElementList + "~" + PageList`. I used the tilde (~) to mark the separations in the list for easy lookup in building the dynamic table.

For the input area, create a table with two rows and three columns above the results table but below the hidden fields. In the first row, enter the following labels: **Element**, **Quantity**, and **Element #**. In the second row, enter three fields:

- **ElementInput**—This is an editable dialog list. It doesn't allow multiple values. Use a formula for the choices, and enter **ElementList** as the formula.
- **QtyInput**—This is an editable number field for the number of pages or figures to be entered.
- **ElementNoInput**—This is an editable text field for the number of the element being entered, such as the chapter number for the chapter pages and figures or IFC for Inside Front Cover (part of the front matter). It's an indicator for the editor, so he or she knows which chapter or other element the page count represents.

Below the table, I also entered another field to help the readers of the document know how current the figures are. The field is called **Modified**. It's a computed date/time field that's formatted to display date only. The formula is `@Modified`.

Finally, you need to add a hotspot button called **Add** above the results table. Use the example under "Create Dynamic Tables" to help you build the formula. I suggest you start by using the `@Command([ViewRefreshFields])` because you need to have the concatenation calculated for the ElementLookup field. Don't forget to also have the formula gather the input from the ElementNoInput field and put it in the ElementNo field in the results table.

To see how I handled the dynamic table in our database, open the TDDay16.nsf in the Day16 folder on the CD.

WEEK 3

DAY 17

Embed Objects in Your Application

Object Linking and Embedding (OLE)is a standard set of tools for integrating data from diverse programs, giving additional flexibility and functionality to your application. Spreadsheets, graphics, and other data sources provide objects that you can incorporate in your applications.

Designer gives you the capability to embed design elements in forms and pages that will give your applications consistency between Notes clients and Web browsers. By sharing elements throughout the database, you reduce the need to redesign the same element for use in different areas of your database.

This lesson explores the use of object linking and embedding to use objects from other applications, embedding design elements in pages and forms for dual-environment applications, embedding Java applets to give Web browsers more functions, and sharing resources throughout a database.

Employ OLE

Object linking and embedding, although available on other platforms, has the greatest range of options when used in Windows 95, Windows 98, and Windows NT. Designer supports the OLE2 (Object Linking and Embedding, Version 2) standard. That means you can either link to data created in another program or embed data created in another program in a form, and that the embedded or linked to data retains its identity with the program in which it was originally created. OLE can be a powerful design tool.

Linking

When you link to data created in another program, for example to cells in a Lotus 1-2-3 spreadsheet, the data appears in the form but actually continues to be stored in the 1-2-3 data file. All that is stored in the form is a pointer to the location of the 1-2-3 file.

Linking to data (the *object*) has its benefits. If someone updates the data in the spreadsheet file, the update appears automatically when a user opens or creates a document based on the form. Because the database file only contains a pointer to the original object, it doesn't get appreciably larger by including a linked object. The drawback to linking is that all users must have access to the file containing the linked data, as well as to the source application.

Use the following steps to link to an object in a form:

1. Open the source application and the file in which the data is stored (the data must already exist). Select or highlight the data you want to copy.

2. Copy the data to the Clipboard (**Edit, Copy**). The data is the object.

3. Open Designer.

4. Open the form and click where you want the linked object to appear.

5. Choose **Edit, Paste Special** from the menu to paste the object from the Clipboard.

6. In the Paste Special dialog box (see Figure 17.1), choose the type of object from the As list, select **Paste link to source,** and then click **OK**.

7. Adjust the size of the linked object to show the data you want the user to see, or at least a large enough area to display the data when it is available.

8. Save and close the form.

FIGURE 17.1

Paste link pastes a picture of the object in the form, but establishes a link to the original file so updates appear in the form. Paste places a picture of the object in the form that you can edit using the source application.

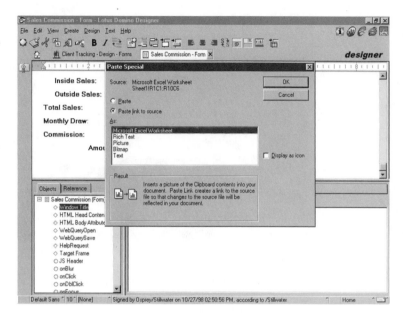

Embedding

When you embed data in a form, you insert a *copy* of the original data object, and Designer does not maintain a link to the original. If someone changes the original data, that change is not reflected in the copy embedded in your form. Users can modify and update the object from the form, but they are editing a copy only, not the original data.

Embedding data has its benefits. First, changes to the embedded data don't affect the original. Second, there is no link to the original data file. However, to view the object, users must have a compatible version of the source application or view the object via a viewer, such as the one that accompanies the Notes client.

Use the following steps to embed an object on a form:

1. Open the form in Designer.

2. Click where you want the object to appear on the form.

3. Choose **Create, Object** from the menu.

4. In the Create Object dialog box (see Figure 17.2) is a list of available applications that support OLE. Make sure the Create New value is Object. Select an application and click **OK**. Designer either launches the application into in-place edit or opens the application.

5. Adjust the size of the linked object to show the data you want the user to see, or at least a large enough area to display the data when it is available.

FIGURE 17.2

*Select **Object** under New and choose an Object Type that matches the object in the Clipboard.*

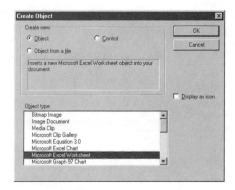

6. Create data in the application. Click outside the object if you are using an in-place edit, or exit the application and return to Designer.

7. Save and close the form.

When using objects in a workflow application, use LotusScript to create, manage, or update objects within documents.

Launching Objects

Both forms and pages have a launch property to determine what the user sees when the form or page is first launched. To set that property, click the **Launch** tab on the Page or Form Properties box (see Figure 17.3). Select **First OLE Object** from the Auto Launch drop-down list to have the object launch when the form or page launches (otherwise, the user double-clicks the object in edit mode to activate it).

FIGURE 17.3

The object can be launched in place, or the document can appear as a dialog box.

Decide whether to create an OLE object in the first rich text field in the form or to have an OLE object without it being displayed through a rich text field (select **None**). Then determine when you want the object launched—while the user is creating a document, editing it, reading it, or all of the above.

Embed Domino Elements

There are a group of objects and controls that can be embedded on a page, form, sub-form, or document. These include views, folders, outlines, navigators, and date pickers.

Why might you embed an element? You might want consistency in the display of your application between the Notes client and the Web browser. By embedding the element, you have better control over the display and functionality of the elements, so you minimize the differences that usually arise with the difference of environments. Web users get more of the functionality with embedded elements that Notes users already have. All this means to you is that it's easier to design an application for both types of users.

A side benefit of using embedded elements is that by combining elements on a page or form, you have the capability to use frames, tables, styled text, and graphics for better design.

Use the following steps to embed an element on a page or form:

1. In Designer, open the page, form, or subform in which you want to embed the element.

2. Position your cursor where you want to display the element.

3. Choose **Create, Embedded Element** from the menu and select the type of element to embed—Outline, View, Navigator, Import Navigator, Date Picker, Group Scheduler, File Upload, or Folder Pane. Not all of these are available for use on a page.

4. (Optional for some elements) Enter a formula that specifies when the embedded element displays or controls the content of the control (especially true for the group scheduler).

5. (Optional) Select the element by clicking it, and choose **Element, Element Properties** from the menu (the name of the embedded element is named in the menu). Set attributes for the embedded element in the Properties box.

6. Save the form, subform, or page.

17

Tip

To remove the embedded element, select it and choose **Edit, Clear** from the menu or press the **Delete** key.

Properties for embedded elements can include the name of the target frame (the frame in which the results of clicking on the embedded element display) and whether to display the element using HTML, a Java applet, or a current element property. The size of the element can also be set, and you can turn on scrollbars.

Embed a View

A Notes view might have a colored background and sometimes have alternating rows of color. These features aren't always available when views are displayed on the Web (see Figure 17.4).

FIGURE 17.4

Views displayed in Web browsers are very plain, acting only as links to documents.

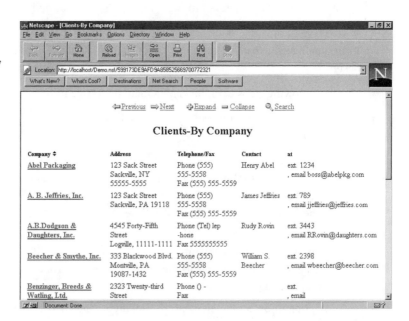

By embedding the view in a page or form, you have the opportunity to embellish the view (see Figure 17.5). The name of the company or a logo can appear with the view.

Notethat in Figure 17.5 you don't see the default view navigation bar. Domino doesn't add the bar to embedded views, so you have to provide a substitute by creating Action buttons to perform the same functions (Next, Prev, Expand, Collapse, Search). Table 17.1 lists the @Commands to use for the buttons.

FIGURE **17.5**

You won't see the view title or background color that is visible in the Notes client. Server settings determine how many lines are displayed.

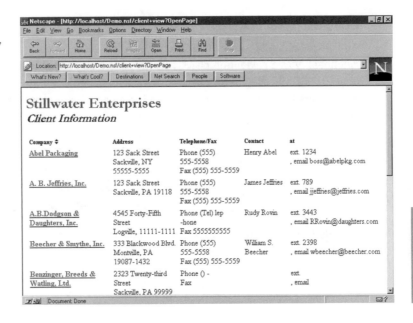

Table 17.1 Navigation Button Functions

Action button	Formula
Next	@Command([NavigateNext])
Prev	@Command([NavigatePrev])
Expand	@Command([ViewExpandAll])
Collapse	@Command([ViewCollapseAll])
Search	@Command([ViewShowSearchBar])

Note

In previous versions of Notes, the reserved field $$ViewBody held embedded views. For backward compatibility, this field still works on forms, as do the reserved fields $$ViewList (which contains an embedded folder pane) and $$NavigatorBody (which contains an embedded navigator).

One variation of the embedded view is to restrict the view to a single category—provided the view is categorized. After you insert the embedded view, select the **Show Single Category** event in the Objects list of the Programmer's Pane. Then enter a formula that evaluates to the category you want to show. Make the Show Single Category formula evaluate to an asterisk (*) if you want all the categories show.

Embed the Folder Pane

An embedded list of views and folders (the folder pane) gives Web browsers the same
functionality as a navigation page. This list can be embedded in a page or form (see
Figure 17.6). Choose **Create, Embedded Element, Folder Pane** to place the folder pane
at your cursor position. By embedding this element, you give a Web user some of the
functionality of the navigation pane.

FIGURE **17.6**

When included in a
frameset, this page
can open views that
can be seen in another
frame. Each item (view
name) in the list is a
link to a view.

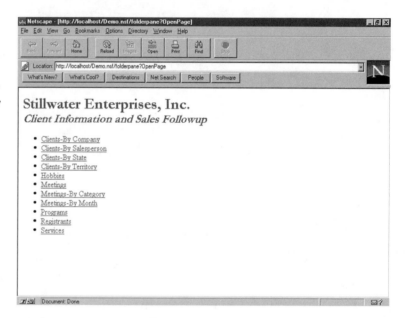

Only one view and one folder pane can be embedded on a page or form.

Embed an Outline

An outline is a graphic representation of an application or site (see Day 20, "The
Navigator Pane: Outlines and Graphical Navigators," to learn more about creating and
working with outlines). Using an outline for navigation in an application gives your users
a "site map" of the application.

Before the outline can be used as a navigation device, it must be embedded in a page, in
a form, or in the rich text field of a document. Embed the outline on a page so it can be
included in a frameset or part of the home page. When embedded on a form, each document created with the form displays the outline so users can navigate to other parts of the
application. Embedding the outline in the rich text field of a document enables other
users to find related elements from that document.

To embed the outline, open the page, form, or document and place your cursor where you want the outline to appear (in a document, it must be in a rich text field). Choose **Create, Embedded Element, Outline** from the menu. Select the outline to embed and click **OK** (see Figure 17.7).

FIGURE 17.7

Choose the outline to embed from a list of saved outlines.

To create a page and embed the outline at one time, open the outline you want to embed and click **Use Outline** on the Action Bar. The outline appears on the page. Save the page and give it a name.

How the embedded outline displays in the page or document depends on the formatting you apply to it. In the page or form, select the embedded outline and choose **Element, Outline Properties** to display the Embedded Outline Properties box (see Figure 17.8).

FIGURE 17.8

You set the basic style of the embedded outline by choosing Flat Style or Tree Style as the Type. The embedded outline in this form is the Tree Style.

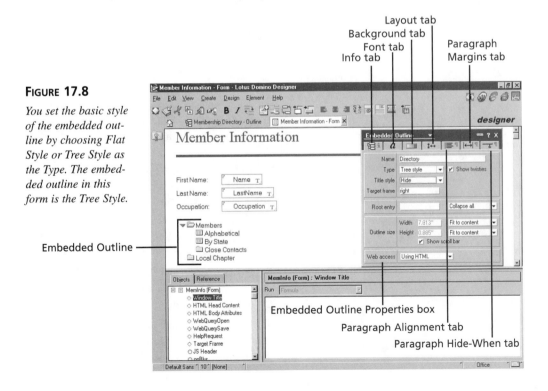

On the Info tab, select one of two Type styles: **Tree Style** displays the outline in a hierarchical format, and all the entries show. Where top-level entries exist with related sublevel entries, choose whether you want to see twisties. **Flat Style** only shows the top-level entries in the Outline, until the user clicks on one that has sublevel entries. If a top-level entry doesn't have sublevel entries, clicking it jumps to the link or performs the action assigned it. With Flat Style, however, you have the option of displaying the outline horizontally.

If you selected the **Flat Style**, we recommend you choose the **Simple Title Style**. This enables users to navigate back up to prior levels by displaying the parent of the current level. The other option for Title Style is **Hide**, which not only doesn't display the hierarchy, but also doesn't provide a way for users to navigate back up the hierarchy after they've gone down a level.

Table 17.2 lists some additional formatting choices available for embedded outlines that you might find helpful.

Table 17.2   Other Useful Embedded Outline Entry Properties

Tab	Property	Description
Info	Target Frame	Enter the name for the frame in which the results of the link or the named element appear. If the frameset hasn't been designed yet, enter the name you want to assign to that frame.
	Root Entry	Enter the name or alias of an entry to show only the children of the specified entry initially. When users click on one of the children, the children of that entry appear. If an entry has no children, nothing displays in the outline. Specify whether you want to show the Root Entry and its children collapsed or expanded. Root Entry only works if there is an alias in the entry in the outline and that alias value is put into this field.
		Unless you specify a Simple Title Style, users can't navigate back up the hierarchy to the root entry.
	Outline Size	Specifies the Width and Height of the embedded outline and whether you want a scroll bar to appear if the size you set doesn't display all the contents.
Font	Component name	Select Top-level or Sub- level to indicate which type of entry the font choices apply to. If the Title Style is Simple, you can also select Title Font.
	Normal	Select the normal color for the text.

Tab	Property	Description
	Selected	Select the color of the text when it's selected.
	Moused	Select the text color when the mouse passes over the entry.
Background	Component name	Select the component of the embedded outline to which the background options apply: Control Background, Title Background, Top-Level Background, or Sub-Level Background.
	Background Color	Select the Normal color for the background and the Moused color (when the mouse passes over the entry). For Control Background, only Normal shows; for Title Background, only Normal and Moused display; and for Top-Level and Sub-Level Backgrounds, Normal, Selected, and Moused display.
	Background Image	Click the Folder icon to select a shared image resource to use as a background, or click the @ button to write a formula to control the background. If the image is smaller than the area of the section, choose how you want the image to Repeat within the area.
Layout	Component name	Select the component of the embedded outline to which the layout options apply.
	Entry	Sets the Height of the section in relation to the entry and the Offset from the edge of the entry.
	Entry Label	Sets the position of the label within the entry and the Offset from the edge.
	OutlineEntry Image	Sets the position and Offset of the image in the entry.

Embed a Navigator

Navigators are comprised of graphics combined with hotspots, which enable users to move around an application by pointing and clicking. When you embed a navigator on a page or form, it can be combined with other objects—even other navigators.

To place an embedded navigator on a page or form, position your cursor where you want the navigator to display and choose **Create, Embedded Element, Navigator** from the menu. Then select the navigator you want to embed. Figure 17.9 shows a navigator embedded on a page.

FIGURE **17.9**

By embedding the navigator on the page, additional text identifying the company and application can be displayed.

Embed a Date Picker

Date pickers are calendar images from which users select a date (see Figure 17.10). They are useful when you need to create a custom calendar application.

FIGURE **17.10**

The date picker in the left frame is embedded on a page, and the page is displayed in a frameset. The target frame for selections in the date picker is the right frame, which displays a calendar view.

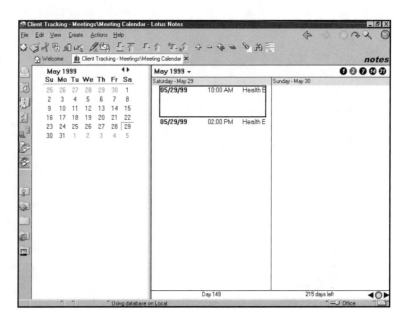

To add the date picker to a page, form, subform, or rich text field of a document, choose **Create, Embedded Element, Date Picker** from the menu. The date picker appears at your cursor location.

Unfortunately, this feature is not supported on the Web.

Embed a Group Scheduler

With an embedded group scheduler, you can design a form that displays user schedules (this doesn't work for the Web). Users can then check everyone's schedules when planning meetings and other joint events.

Start by creating the form and embedding the group scheduler element. Choose **Create, Embedded Element, Group Scheduler** from the menu to place the group scheduler at your cursor's location on the form. Don't be too disappointed—scheduling information won't appear while in Designer.

Next, you need to collect some basic information by using editable fields, formulas, or LotusScript. The data you need to collect is the name of the users or group whose schedule is to be displayed, what week the schedule information starts (date and time), and the number of hours per day to be displayed (an integer between 1 and 24).

The scheduler must be capable of getting the information from the fields. In the Programmer's Pane, click the **Objects** tab of the Info List, and expand the **Group Scheduler** object (see Figure 17.11). For each of the attributes, enter the field name in quotes in the Script Area.

- **Group Member Items**—Whose schedules are displayed
- **Start Time Item**—The week the scheduler display starts (specifies a date and time)
- **Duration Item**—The number of hours the scheduler displays

The embedded element also has properties to set—the size of the element in the form, a target frame for frameset purposes, and the colors for foreground, background, busy and free time, and unavailable time.

There are a couple of reserved fields you can create in the form that relate to the embedded group scheduler. Their use is optional, but you might find them helpful.

- **$GroupScheduleRefreshMode**—This field controls how the group scheduler refreshes the scheduling information from the mail servers of the group members. Normally, without this field, a user of the group scheduler document has to refresh the document to see the changes reflected in the scheduler if he changes the values of any of the fields used by the group scheduler. The default refresh is a full

17

refresh, which means retrieving scheduling data for all the group members. The $GroupScheduleRefreshMode field can have a value of 0 or 1. If the value is 0, the group scheduler only does a partial refresh. The partial refresh only refreshes data in the field that was changed. If the value is 1, the group scheduler updates all data for all members on refresh.

FIGURE 17.11

The Group Scheduler requires input about whose schedules to display, the starting week of the display, and the number of hours to show.

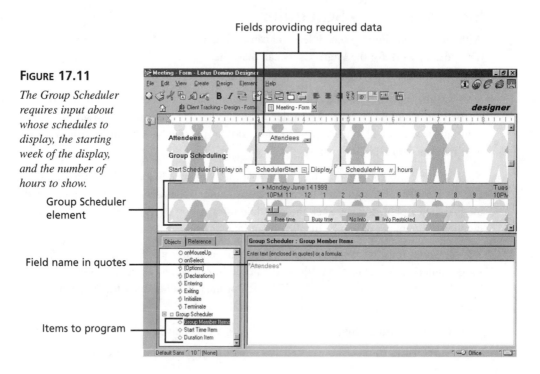

Fields providing required data

Group Scheduler element

Field name in quotes

Items to program

• **$GroupScheduleShowLegend**—This field controls whether the legend appears at the bottom of the schedule. The value of the field can either be 0 to not show the legend or 1 to show it.

 Caution

Are users complaining because they can't see the calendars for other users in their group? Remind them that a user has to be granted permission by another user to his/her calendar. A user grants that permission in mail preferences. You do not have control over who sets up their calendars to be viewed; you only control the programming that puts the group calendar in the form.

Embed a File Upload Control

Web users don't have all the functionality that is available to Notes users, and one of the missing functions is the ability to attach files to documents. Give them that capability by embedding a file upload control on a form. Then, when Web users create or edit a document, they can attach a file by typing the path and filename or by clicking **Browse** and selecting the file. The control only displays a field and a Browse button, so be sure to include some explanatory static text.

For the file upload control to work, the Domino Administrator must define a temp directory on the server.

To add the control to a form, click in the form where you want the control to appear and choose **Create, Embedded Element, File upload control**.

The file upload control isn't supported in the Notes client, so you'll have to hide it from Notes users.

17

Embed Java Applets

Most design elements in Domino are rendered in HTML when they are run in a Web browser. However, by using Java instead of HTML, certain elements achieve an interface that is closer to the one seen by the Notes client. Therefore, Domino provides some Java applets to achieve this interface. A Java applet is a small, self-contained application that can be embedded into forms or pages. You enable these applets at the same time you create the element.

The Domino applets that are available include

- **Action bar applet**—Enables users to scroll, view, and select actions from drop-down menus
- Editor applet—Makes it possible for Web users to change the font, color, size, and style of text in rich text fields
- **Outline applet**—Displays outlines embedded in forms or pages and enables Web users to navigate using the outline
- **View applet**—Gives Web users access to view features such as multiple document selection, column resizing, and collapse/expand of categories without generating new pages (the selection margin and alternating row colors aren't available in the view applet)

Although Domino provides Java applets, you can create or import applets for use in your Domino applications. A Java applet is a collection of files, and those files are attached as hidden files to the form, page, or document where you placed the applet. Another option is to link to an applet that is stored on the Web and provide a URL reference to the files in the form, page, or document in which you include the applet. A third option is to set up the applet as a shared resource (see more about this in the "Shared Resources" section later in this chapter).

 Note

> A Java applet's Java class is downloaded to the Web browser and run by the browser, so Java applets require Java support in the browser. Supported browsers include Internet Explorer 3.0 or 4.0 and Netscape 3.0 or 4.0.
>
> In order to use Java Applets in Designer, you must enable them for your workstation. Choose **File, Preferences, User Preferences**. On the Basics page, check **Enable Java applets** in the Additional Options list and click **OK**.

Action Bar Applet

The Action Bar contains buttons that users click to perform commands or run agents in the Notes client. When a form or view contains Action buttons, they display in a Web browser. However, they don't have that "button look".

Where you created Action buttons, you probably set properties for the individual buttons. However, you probably didn't bother setting properties for the Action Bar itself. Action bar properties include the alignment of the buttons on the bar, the bar background color, the bottom border attributes, button size and appearance, and button text attributes. One important property sets whether the Action Bar is displayed in a Web browser using HTML or using the Java applet (see Figure 17.12).

FIGURE 17.12

*To set Action Bar properties, open the Action Pane in Designer and then choose **Design, Action Bar Properties** from the menu.*

Select **Using Java applet** here

On the Action Bar Properties box, on the Action Bar Info page, select **Using Java applet** from the Web Access: Display drop-down list. Selecting **Using HTML** turns off the applet.

In Figure 17.13, you see a form with an Action Bar displayed using the Java applet.

FIGURE 17.13

When the mouse points to an Action button, it shows depth (as it does on the Action Bar in the Notes client).

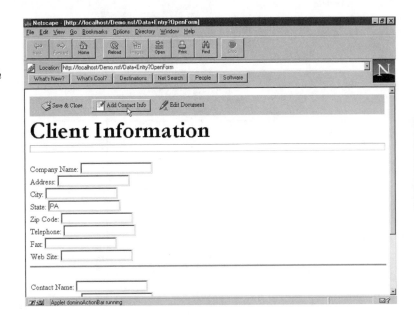

17

Editor Applet

In a Web application, a rich text field normally displays for editing within an HTML text area. You give the rich text field more functionality for the Web user by using the Editor applet to display the field.

When you use the Editor applet (see Figure 17.14), the images and formatting of the existing rich text field contents are preserved. The user can also create formatted content. The Editor applet supports the following formatting:

- bold
- italics
- underline
- single level indent
- ordered and unordered lists
- color selections

- limited size and font selection
- URL link hotspots

FIGURE **17.14**

The rich text field in the browser has buttons for applying formatting to the contents.

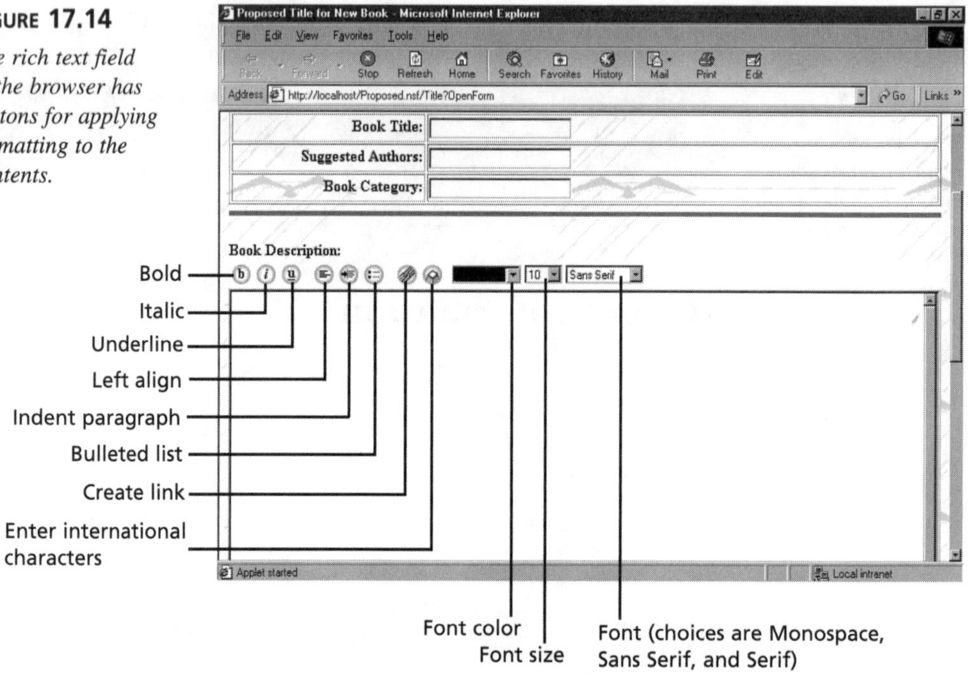

Bold
Italic
Underline
Left align
Indent paragraph
Bulleted list
Create link
Enter international characters

Font color
Font size
Font (choices are Monospace, Sans Serif, and Serif)

The Left align button shows the current alignment. Each time it's clicked, it cycles from Left align to Center to Right align. In a similar way, the single-level indent toggles with single-level outdent.

The Editor applet does not support tables, but instead displays them as HTML tags in lime green.

When the document is not being edited, the contents of the rich text field are shown in HTML.

To use the Editor applet in a Web application, create or select a rich text field in your form. Open the Field Properties box. On the Field Info tab, select the Web Access: Display option **Using Java applet** (see Figure 17.15).

FIGURE 17.15

*Select the **Using Java applet** option to activate the Editor applet for a rich text field.*

Outline Applet

The outline applet starts with an embedded outline, but it displays differently in a Web browser. Colors change for items during mouse-over, for instance, and you can see background images.

To make an embedded outline display using the applet (see Figure 17.16), select it in the form or page and choose **Element, Outline Properties** from the menu. On the Info page of the Embedded Outline Properties box, select **Using Java Applet** from the Web access drop-down list.

FIGURE 17.16

Selections from the outline Java applet in the left frame are displayed in the right frame.

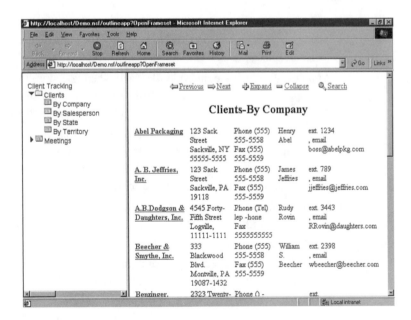

You learn more about outlines on Day 20.

View Applet

For Web users, the view applet gives them the capability to resize columns, collapse and expand views without generating a new page, select multiple documents, scroll vertically to see more documents, use F9 to refresh the view, and use Delete to mark documents for deletion.

To use a view applet, open a view in Designer and choose **Design, View Properties**. In the View Properties box, click the **Advanced** tab. Then select **Use applet in the browser**.

An embedded view can also be displayed as an applet. Open the page or form that contains the embedded view. Select the embedded view and choose **Element, View Properties** from the menu. On the Info tab, specify that the embedded view is to be displayed using a Java applet.

Shared Resources

In the Designer Pane for a database, you see an entry for Shared Resources (see Figure 17.17). This category expands to display a set of elements that can be shared throughout the database:

- **Images**—Graphic files available for use throughout the database, such as a logo. The images are in gif, jpeg, or bmp format. They can be used as graphics or icons on forms, pages, tables, action buttons, or documents.
- **Applets**—Can involve multiple files, and when you store the files as resources all the applets can use a single copy of the files rather than storing their own copies. Also, when you update one applet file, all the applets in the database are updated.
- **Subforms**—Can contain all the design elements that you put in a form, such as fields, graphics, and tables. When many of your forms contain similar elements, use one subform and insert it in the different forms. Changing the original subform modifies all the forms that use the subform.
- **Shared Fields**—Fields that can be used on more than one form, but only once on any one form. Shared fields share the same definition but not necessarily the same contents.
- **Script Libraries**—Used to store and share LotusScript programs and Java code. Any scripts in the database can share the script in a library.
- **Icon**—The icon displayed with the database bookmark. You'll learn more about the icon on Day 21, "Roll Out and Maintain Your Application."

- **"About Database" document**—Appears when a user opens a database for the first time or clicks the About button in the Open Database dialog box. It tells the user about the purpose of the database and very basic instructions for how to use it. You'll learn more about this document on Day 21.

- **"Using Database" document**—Provides information to a user about how to use a database. You'll learn more about this document on Day 21.

- **Database Script**—A collection of programming for events that are associated with the database rather than a specific design element. The programming can be either @formula language or LotusScript.

- **Shared Actions**—Form or view actions that you need to use frequently throughout the database. They aren't tied to a particular view or form. You define a shared action once. It can be used only once per form or view, but in as many forms or views in the database as you want. If you change the shared action, it is changed everywhere it is referenced.

17

FIGURE 17.17

Resources expands to display the types of shared resources you can create, store, and share for the entire database.

Resources ⎯

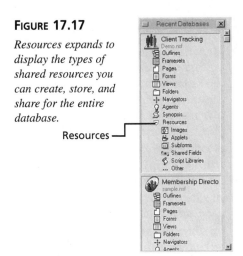

The purpose of these shared resources is to save the development time involved in creating the same element over and over again for different forms or views. Resources provides a single repository that you reference during development.

Images

By storing your images as resources you only store the image in one location, no matter how many times you use it in the database. When you paste or import images, a copy of the image is stored in each form or page in which you use it.

Use the following steps to create an image resource:

1. Open the database in Designer.
2. In the Design Pane, expand **Resources**, and then select **Images**.
3. Click the **New Image Resource** button.
4. In the Open dialog box (see Figure 17.18), select the drive or directory where the image is stored from the Look in drop-down list. Choose the type of image from the Files of type drop-down list—**BMP Image**, **GIF Image**, or **JPEG Image**. Select the graphic file, and click **Open**.
5. An entry for the graphic is added to the Images list.

FIGURE 17.18

If you don't see any image files listed at first, change the Files of type selection to the correct graphic format. To select multiple files, hold down Shift as you click to select adjacent files or Ctrl to select nonadjacent files.

Use the following steps to insert an image resource:

1. Open the form, page, or document in which you want to place the image.
2. Place your cursor where you want to put the image.
3. Choose **Create, Image Resource** from the menu.
4. Select the type of image (gif, jpeg, or all images) from the Image type list.
5. Choose the name of the image.
6. Click **OK**.

Changes to any image in Resources can be distributed to any place in the database where the image is used. Select the image in the Images list and choose **Resource, Refresh**. From the file system, select the updated version of the graphic file and then click **Open**. The image is automatically updated.

You've seen applications where the image changes as you pass the mouse over it or click on it. To do that with Designer, create a *horizontal image set*. First, decide how many states you want the image to display (you can use up to four—normal, mouse-over, selected, or clicked). Second, in a graphics program, create the number of variations of the image you need and put them in the normal, mouse-over, selected, clicked order from left to right. All the images must be the same size, so it's better to copy and paste duplicates of the original image and then change the colors (don't change an image if you don't want a change in state). Make one graphic file with the images lined up horizontally in it, separated by one pixel of space. Then create an image resource entry for that graphic file. Double-click the entry to open the Image Resource Properties box (see Figure 17.19). Enter the number of states you want to display in the Advanced: Images across box. Type **1** for normal (first image on left), **2** for mouse-over (second image), **3** for selected (third image), or **4** for clicked (fourth image). When you insert the image on a page, right-click on the inserted image to place the default hotspot around the picture.

FIGURE 17.19

The number of Images across corresponds to the number of states you want to display. In Images down, specify the number of images needed for a vertical image set.

Likewise, you can create a *vertical image set*, which represents the icons you add to the bookmark bar (you'll see an example if you right-click a bookmark icon and choose **Change Icon** from the menu). Because the bookmark bar can display small, medium, or large icons, you need to provide a graphic of three copies of the image (you'll need to do this in a decent graphics program where you can control pixels), going from small at the top to large at the bottom. The images must be lined up vertically, with one pixel between them. Then you create an image resource of the file, specifying **3** as the Images down number in the Image Resource Properties box.

The Colorize grays property on the Image Resource Property box is used to make the grays in the image correspond to the Lotus palette grays, based on the operating system color scheme. This helps the image blend in with other elements on the system.

Applets

The applets that Domino provides only demonstrate a small part of what Java applets can do for your applications. If you can create your own applets with an authoring program such as NetObjects BeanBuilder or can import them (see the Java Web site at java.sun.com), store them as resources. That way, all the applets can share the same files instead of storing their own copy of the files.

Use the following steps to create a shared applet resource:

1. In Designer, open the database in which you want to store the resource.

2. Expand **Resources** in the Design Pane and select **Applets**.

3. Click the **New Applet Resource** button. The Locate Java Applet Files dialog box opens (see Figure 17.20).

FIGURE 17.20

Locate and select the Java files you want to add as resources.

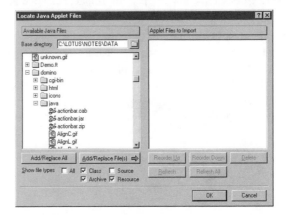

4. Select the path where the Java files are stored from the Base Directory field.

5. From the Available Java Files list, select the files you want to set up as shared resources. Click **Add/Replace File(s)**.

6. Click **OK**. Enter a name to use to refer to the shared resource.

7. Click **OK** to have Domino store the files as the shared resource.

Use the following steps to include a Java applet in a form or page:

1. Open the form or page and position your cursor where you want to place the applet.

2. Choose **Create, Java Applet** from the menu to open the Create Java Applet dialog box (see Figure 17.21). If Java Applet is grayed out, choose File, Preferences, User Preferences and make certain that under Additional Options you have selected **Enable Java applets.**

3. Select **Import an applet from the file system** if the shared resource doesn't have all the files required to locate the applet. If the shared resource does have the necessary fields, skip to step 6.

4. In the Base Directory box, enter the path for the applet files.

5. In the Class Name box, enter the name of the main class.

FIGURE 17.21

You must know where the Java applet files are stored in either the file system or in shared resources in order to complete this dialog box.

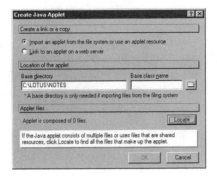

6. Click **Locate** to view all the related files and shared resources for the applet.

7. Choose **Local Filing System** in the Browse list and select any related applet files. Then click **Add/Replace File(s)**.

8. Select **Shared Resources** in the Browse list and select any related applet files. Then click **Add/Replace File(s)**.

9. Click **OK** twice.

Shared Fields

A shared field can be used on more than one form. You define the field once and use it again and again—but only once per form. Why might you use a shared field? One reason is to save time. For example, if you have a State field that is a dialog list field that includes all 50 states in the United States, you don't want to recreate that field in every form that involves an address in your database. Instead, create it once as a shared field and then insert it whenever you need it.

There are two ways to create a shared field. The first method is to use an existing field and convert it to a shared field. To do this, you select the field on the form and then choose **Design, Share This Field** from the menu. The shared field gets a dark, thick border around it in the form.

The second method for creating a shared field starts with the Design Pane, where you expand **Resources** and then select **Shared Fields**. Then click on the **New Shared Field** button. The Shared Field Properties box opens. Give the field a name and set the type of field, such as Text Editable. Enter any formulas you need for the field and set attributes such as keyword choices. Then close the box and save the shared field.

To use the shared field in a form, open the form and put your cursor where you want the field. Choose **Create, Insert Shared Field** from the menu. Select the name of the shared field and click **OK**. Apply attributes to the shared field as you would to any other field in the form.

Subforms

Subforms not only share fields with different forms; they can also include text, tables, graphics, and other elements that normally appear in forms. Use subforms to hold often used portions of forms (such as authoring information or approval data), or to provide different looks for different conditions (such as a Web banner and a Notes client banner).

Use the following steps to create a subform:

1. Open the database where you want to create the subform and expand **Resources** in the Design Pane. Then select **Subforms**.

2. Click the **New Subform** button.

3. Choose **Design, Subform Properties** from the menu to open the Subform Properties box (see Figure 17.22).

FIGURE 17.22

*Enable **Include in Insert Subform dialog** so designers will see it when they insert subforms. Select **Include in New Form dialog** to have a dialog box appear immediately when designers choose Create, Design, Form from the menu. The dialog box offers a list of subforms to insert in the new form.*

4. Add text, fields, and other elements to the subform.

5. Save and close the subform.

Use the following steps to include the subform in a form:

1. Open the form and place your cursor where you want to put the subform.

2. Choose **Create, Insert Subform** from the menu.

3. Select the name of the subform you want to insert (see Figure 17.23), or select **Insert Subform based on formula**.

FIGURE 17.23

When you choose to insert a subform based on a formula, you are creating a computed *subform.*

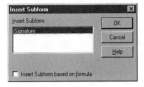

4. Click **OK**. The subform appears on the form with a border around it, unless you chose to create a computed subform. In that case, you see **<Computed Subform>** in your form and you must enter a formula that evaluates the name of a subform (see Figure 17.24).

FIGURE 17.24

This computed subform doesn't display if the user is a Web client, but the Signature subform displays for Notes clients.

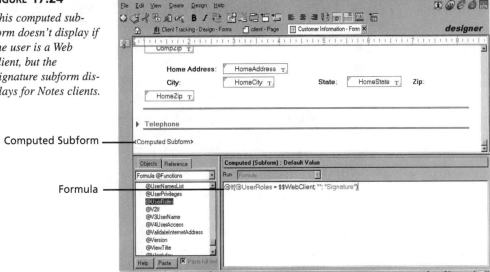

Computed Subform —

Formula —

Shared Actions

Shared actions are actions that aren't attached to views or forms. Instead, they are shared resources that you can use repeatedly, which saves you from creating the same action over and over. For example, each form needs an action button for saving the file; create a shared action and add it to every form.

Creating shared actions is very similar to creating view and form actions, except for where you do it.

Use the following steps to create a shared action:

1. Open the database in Designer. In the Design Pane, expand **Resources** and then select **Other**.

2. From the list of Other resources, double-click **Shared Actions**.

3. Select the **(Untitled)** action from the list.

4. In the Action Properties box (see Figure 17.25), enter a Name for the action and a Target Frame, if applicable.

FIGURE 17.25

The Action Properties box is the same one you saw when you created view and form actions.

Action names

Action Properties box

Formula

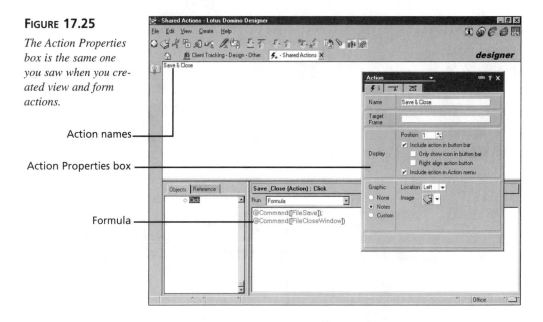

5. In the Display section, set the position of the button on the Action Bar and determine whether to include the action in the Action menu or in the Action Bar (note that the position can be individually overridden in each form or view).

6. Set the Graphic attributes of the button by using a Notes image or a Custom image that you select.

7. (Optional) To add another shared action, choose **Create, Shared Action** from the menu and repeat steps 3–6.

8. Save and close the shared actions.

To use a shared action in a form or view, open the Action Pane in the form or view and then choose **Create, Insert Shared Action**. Select the name of the action and click **Insert**. Repeat for as many actions as you want to insert; then click **Done**. Save the form or view.

Summary

Embedded objects give greater flexibility to your applications by incorporating the functions of other programs such as spreadsheets, presentations, flow charts, organization charts, graphs, and project management. After an object is embedded in a form, the user who opens the form to create a document has access to the embedded object. As long as the original (source) application is accessible to the users, they can use the menus and toolbars as the source application when working with the embedded object.

Design elements such as views, outlines, and navigators can also be embedded in pages and forms, which is especially useful in Web applications to give Web users some of the functionality available in the Notes client. This is especially true when the elements can be displayed using Java applets instead of HTML.

Designer has a central storage place for shared elements such as fields, actions, images, Java applets, and subforms. By using these shared resources, you save time by not having to repeatedly create them throughout the database, not to mention saving space by only storing these items once. Subforms give forms added flexibility because you can use formulas to determine which subform is to show in the form based on predetermined conditions.

17

Q&A

Q **My supervisor wants our logo to display on every document. Is using a shared image the best way to do that?**

A It could be. However, if you want additional text such as the name of the company or some other company information to appear with the logo, consider using a subform. Insert that subform in every form you create. Then, when you change the logo or company text, modify the subform, which automatically updates all the forms.

Q **I have this really neat layout region that I use as a banner for our documents. Now we want to open up our applications to users with Web browsers. What can I do?**

A Put the layout region in a subform. Create an alternative subform for the Web users. Insert a computed subform in your forms. Then use a formula that uses the layout region for Notes clients and the alternate subform for Web users. The key to that formula is the user role $$WebClient. Anyone accessing the database through a browser is assigned that role, which means you can use a formula such as
@If(@UserRoles = "$$WebClient"; "WebBanner"; "NotesBanner").

Q **I have a shared field that I'm using in one of our databases, but now I'm creating a new database and want to use the same shared field. Can I share fields across databases?**

A No, but you can copy and paste the shared field from one database to another.

Workshop

In this workshop, you'll be working with the Titles in Development database, and you'll be creating the Completed Titles database. If you haven't been building your databases as you went through the workshops, use the TDDay16.nsf file in the Day16 folder on the CD for the Titles in Development file.

The tasks you'll be working on include embedding a spreadsheet in the New Title form and embedding a group scheduler. Then you'll create the Completed Titles database, and design a Home Page for it, in which you embed an outline applet. You'll also design a form for new books, which includes the Action applet, and a view to display the books. A different subform appears for each book category.

Embed a Spreadsheet

In Designer, open the Titles in Development database. Then open the New Title form. There are two spreadsheet files—one saved as a Lotus 1-2-3 .wk1 file and the other as a Microsoft Excel .xls file (and a format file for the Excel worksheet). Depending on the application installed on your computer, select a spreadsheet file to embed. Place it near or beneath the page count area you created in the last workshop. The spreadsheet has column and row headings set up for the Development Editor to track when pieces of the book are due or received from the authors or other editors.

Embed a Group Scheduler

Editors need to get together from time or time to discuss planning and such. Embedding a group scheduler in the form where they store all their information is therefore a good idea, right?

Embed the group scheduler near or below the Editor Information table. You need to supply three pieces of information for the Group Scheduler: the names of the people in the group, the starting date for the calendar, and the number of hours per day to display in the calendar. Create the following fields so they appear above the group calendar:

- **SchedulerNames**—Use an editable dialog list that enables users to select names from the Address Book. For the default value, use **@UserName**.

- **SchedulerDate**—Make this an editable date field that displays both date and time.
- **SchedulerDuration**—Make this an editable text field, but you might include some help to tell users it's the number of hours per day to show.

For the group scheduler, enter the following formulas for the three events:

- Group Member Items: "**SchedulerNames**"
- Start Time Item: "**SchedulerDate**"
- Duration Item: "**SchedulerDuration**"

Save and test the form.

Create the Completed Titles Database

Create a new database based on a blank template and call it **Completed Titles**, with the filename **Completed.nsf**. Create a new form in the database, called **New Book|New**. Make it the default form for the database. Because this is going to be both a Web document (readers only) and a Notes document (input in Notes), you'll have to watch carefully not to include any features that appear in Notes only (or at least hide them).

On the Defaults tab of the Form Properties box, select **Treat document contents as HTML**.

On this form, include the following fields:

- TBookTitle
- TProposedAuthors
- TBookCategory
- TAudience
- TDescription

Those fields sound familiar? Well, all you have to do is copy them from either the Proposed Title form or the New Title form into the New Book form. Put the TBookCategory and TAudience fields at the top of the form and hide them when the form isn't being edited.

Add a new editable number field called **Price**. Format it to display as currency.

Add a new editable text field called **Software**. Hide this field when read, previewed, or printed. This field should contain the name of the software covered in the book. Make sure you include appropriate static text.

Add a rich text field near the title for the document author to insert a picture of the book cover. Call the field **BookCover**. Save the form.

17

Create Additional Forms

Create a new form called **Author Information** (alias Author). The Author form needs to have three fields: **FName, LName,** and **Biography.** FName is an editable text field that holds the first name of an author, and LName is an editable text field that contains the last name of an author. Biography is an editable text field with one or two paragraphs about the author.

Create a form to take book orders. Call the form **Book OrderForm**, alias Order. Add the following fields: **OName, OAddress, OPhone, OFax, OEmail, OCreditCard** (choices of MasterCard, Visa, American Express), **OCardNo, OCardExpireDate**, and **OBooksOrdered**. All are editable text fields except **OCreditCard**, which is a radio button field. Add a computed field for the order date called **ODate**. Add a **Submit** button to save the form that returns a message thanking the customer for the order and promising to return an email message confirming the order (use a **$$Return** field). For office use, add an editable date/time field called **OProcessed**. Hide that field from Web users.

Add a Shared Image

Add a shared image resource to the database. The filename is **Stillwater.gif**, and the file is currently stored in the Day17 folder on the CD.

Create a Subform

Create a subform to act as a letterhead/banner for the top of forms. Call it **Banner**. Insert a basic table that is one row by two columns. In the left cell, insert the Stillwater.gif shared image. In the right cell, insert the following text:

The best in computer training—books, videos, tapes, classroom curriculum, CBTs, and distance learningCall us at 555-555-5555

Format the text to make its appearance compatible with the picture, and then remove the cell borders from the table. Save the subform. Insert the subform at the top of the New Book form, the Author Information form, and the New Book Order form.

Create a Computed Subform

Create several subforms that are to automatically be inserted in the New Book form based on the choice in the TAudience field. Each subform includes a short piece of text to alert readers that this book is geared toward a specific audience. The names of the subforms roughly match the TAudience keywords:

- **Computer Literate**—"Just learning about computers? Go keystroke by keystroke, click by click with us."
- **Beginning**—"Know a little about computers? You won't be intimidated by this book. Learn step by step in easy stages."
- **Intermediate**—"Take what you know about computers one step further. Clear explanations and definitions of technical terms and subjects."
- **Advanced**—"One step beyond. Get the in-depth explanation of features and technical considerations that you need."
- **Super Advanced**—"A complete technical guidebook for advanced users. Tips and Techniques."

Insert the subforms based on a formula that is simply the field name TAudience.

Create Views

Create views to display the book documents alphabetically, by author, by category, by audience, and by software. Name them **New Books\by Title** (make this the default view), **New Books\by Author**, **New Books\by Category**, **New Books\by Level** (levels based on the audience level)**, and New Books\by Software**. The documents included in these views are those created using the New Book form. The columns need to include the book title, the author names, the book category, and the audience. Except for the **New Books\by Title**, the views need to be categorized as indicated in the name of the view. Only the **New Books\by Software** needs to have a column for the software name (the first one, which is also categorized).

Create a view called **Author Information** (alias Authors) to display author information documents. It should contain two columns. The first, which is sorted but hidden, uses **LName** as its formula. The second column, called **Author Name**, is a concatenation: FName + " " + LName.

Create a view that is to be hidden from Web users, called **Orders** (alias Orders). All saved orders will be displayed in this view. Make three columns in this view: Name (the name of the person ordering), Date Placed (date the order was submitted), and Date Processed (the date the office processed the order).

Embed a View Applet

On the Book Order Form, add a view applet that displays the **New Books\by Category** view. Place it near the **OBooksOrdered** field so that the users can look at the applet to find books they might want to order. Set the Web Access to **Using Java Applet**. Enable the scrollbars for the embedded view. Save the form.

Add Hotspot Links

On the New Book form, near the **TProposedAuthors** field, add a hotspot link that links to the Author Information view.

On the Banner subform, add a hotspot link to the Home Page.

To see examples of the workshop tasks, open the Titles in Development database TDDay17.nsf or the Completed Titles database CTDay17.nsf in the Day17 folder of the CD.

DAY 18

Introduction to JavaScript

What Is JavaScript?

JavaScript is an event-driven, object-based, cross-platform programming language used to control the display of information and behavior of a browser. The JavaScript programs are considered cross-platform because the same JavaScript program, without any changes or recompilation, will work on various operating system platforms, such as UNIX or Windows, as long as the browser or client supports JavaScript.

JavaScript started out as LiveScript (now defunct) from Netscape Communications Corporation (Netscape) and has evolved from version 1.0 to version 1.3. Domino R5.0 supports JavaScript 1.3, but earlier versions of JavaScript code will still run in the R5 browser. You should know that there are variants of JavaScript including JScript from Microsoft Corp. and ECMAScript is a language standard (see www.ecma.ch/stand/ecma-262.htm) from the ECMA, an international standards organization. Be warned that both Netscape and Microsoft have continued to enhance their languages beyond the 1997 adopted ECMAScript standard.

JavaScript is a fairly robust language and there are many books dedicated to it. Here, we give you a quick introduction and focus on integrating and using JavaScript with Domino applications.

Do not confuse *JavaScript* with *Java*. Java is a separate programming language that was designed by Sun Microsystems. It is designed to write entire applications, although it is most famous for writing Web applets.

Why Use JavaScript?

Have you ever filled in and submitted a registration form on the Web, just to get some dreaded error message saying your phone number is invalid or you forgot to enter your ZIP code, and then you had to start all over again? JavaScript will let you program field validation formulas to prevent the submission of incomplete information.

- JavaScript enables you to off-load processing from the main server to the browser. In this way, you can save your servers for critical processing.

- By moving the processing to the browser on the user's machine, you can provide help and cool visual effects.

- JavaScript enables you to manage cookies that contain information to reduce the amount of data entry the user has to make.

- JavaScript enables you to create a Web site that handles different browsers and gives the user the best possible experience at your site.

Understanding JavaScript Capabilities

You can use JavaScript in conjunction with the page HTML to implement

- **Graphic effects (image rollover)**—An image can change from gray to full color in response to the user dragging his mouse over it.

- **Form and field validation**—Users can receive meaningful help and error messages *before* they submit their forms. This includes making certain that required fields have valid entries and that a phone number has the appropriate number of digits.

- **Actions and buttons**—Create buttons that actually do something, not just another Submit button.

- **Perform numeric calculations**—Give the browser the ability to compute fields.

- **Perform text manipulation**—Parse, split apart, or combine pieces of information.

- **Dialog box simulations**—Display messages and ask for user input via a dialog box.
- **Dynamic content**—Change the content of the HTML page based on user information.
- **Frame management**—Determine what goes in each frame.
- **Cookies**—These will remember information about the user. JavaScript allows you to create, update, and remove cookies.
- **Activate a Java applet**—For example, invoke a video clip.

When you use JavaScript-aware browsers such as Lotus Notes R5 client, Netscape Navigator 2 or later, and Internet Explorer 3 or later, your applications are capable of

- Storing JavaScript programs
- Storing information about the browser content as objects
- Giving programs access to objects
- Associating the programs with particular events for particular objects, for example, do "xyz" when I click the Submit button
- Coordinating all the browser activities in a predictable way

In many ways the JavaScript-enabled browser, with coding by the programmer, can finally do what a Notes R5 client can do.

Object Model

There must be some consistent way for the program and the browser to refer to objects displayed on it. The object model is your roadmap to the standard names that you must use to manipulate (program) the browser.

What's an Object?

In our daily life, objects are things such as cars, houses, parrots, and so forth. Some objects are comprised of other objects; for example, a car includes objects such as tires, windows, an engine, and so forth. Likewise, a parrot has a beak, wings, tail, and eyes; a house has rooms, doors, windows, walls, floors, and ceilings.

But without descriptive details, objects can be ambiguous. For example, a parrot is an object, and a wing is an object but if I say, "Look! My parrot's wing is broken!" you might reply, "Which wing?" Had I originally said, "Look! My parrot's left wing is broken." you would have known where to look.

The same principle of defining objects applies to the JavaScript language. Objects in JavaScript include the images, the viewable form, and the form is further refined by elements such as fields. To make fields unambiguous, JavaScript allows you to refer to them by their own name, LName apart from FName. This example shows how to address the LName field. (This is not a legal statement by itself):

```
window.document.forms[0].LName
```

Let's dissect the statement:

- **window**—This is the starting point of the object model.
- **document**—This is the object that contains everything currently displayed on the browser.
- **forms[0]**—This is an array reference asking for the first form. The object model allows multiple forms to be defined for a document. The array subscript [0] is how you reference the first entry. Note that Domino, by default, creates only one form for a browser document. You must include the array subscript so the browser knows exactly which form you want.
- **LName**—This is the field name you want. The field is also an object.

Figure 18.1 shows the abbreviated object model for Domino. Please note that there are names that begin with a period (dot) in the figure. The *dot names* are the names always used to reference the object. Domino does not use the objects in the gray box.

How do you use the object model to come up with an object reference? You can start from the top with window. Next, do you want to access information in a frame or document? If you want a frame, note that there are multiple pictures shown for frame, so it is an array reference. You'll need to know which frame you want; we'll use the first, so the reference for it is: frames[0]. The combined reference is now

```
window.frames[0]
```

If you want to access the images on your document, the object statement would start with window, document, and then you would see that images are again stored as an array. If you want to access the first image the reference would be

```
window.document.images[0]
```

In Figure 18.1 you notice that .elements has object types associated with it, such as text, textarea, and button.

FIGURE 18.1

A simple map of the object model for JavaScript used by Domino. The names beginning with a dot are the names used to create an object reference.

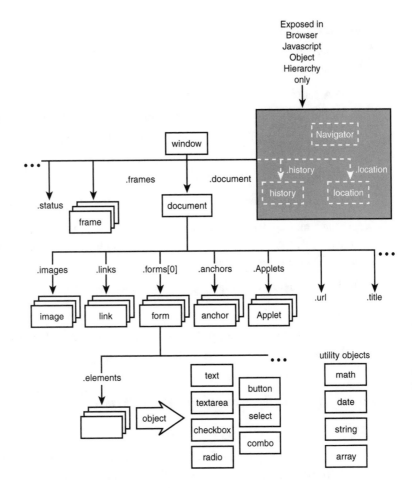

To reference an element you have several naming choices. We'll illustrate them using our LName field, which is a text object on a form. Please remember that these are still JavaScript fragments—they are not executable code:

- Instead of .elements use the object's name:

  ```
  window.document.forms[0].LName
  ```

- Use the field name as the array subscript for elements:

  ```
  window.document.forms[0].elements["LName"]
  ```

- You don't know how to determine this yet, but you can use a numeric subscript that represents the LName field. We'll arbitrarily say that it is 2 for this example:

  ```
  window.document.forms[0].elements[2]
  ```

What's a Property?

A *property* is a piece of information about an object similar to an adjective in English. For example,

- A car (object) is the color (property) blue (value of the property)
- The parrot (object) is the color (property) green and yellow (values of the property)
- The car (object) is of the type (property) of a stretch limousine (value of the property)
- The parrot (object) is the sex (property) female (value of the property)

A JavaScript text object has properties such as name (LName) and value (Claire Weber).

An object may contain other properties where those properties themselves are objects. For example, a car has tires. Tires are objects and they have properties also: color, size, thread depth, and air pressure.

The way to reference a property is to use the following dot notation:

```
<objectname>.<property>
```

To finally ask JavaScript for the value of our `LName` field, add `.value` to the examples used earlier:

```
window.document.forms[0].LName.value
```

```
window.document.forms[0].elements["LName"].value
```

What's a Method?

A method is a something an object can do. It is similar to a verb in English. The car *moves* (method); the parrot *flies* and *talks* (methods). Examples of JavaScript methods are `open()`, `close()`, and `write()`, which are methods for the *object* document.

The way to reference a method is to use the following dot notation:

```
<objectname>.<method>()
```

If you want to close a window (and your browser), enter

```
window.close()
```

It is important that you use the parentheses `()` whenever you reference a method. Sometimes there are argument values that are placed within the parentheses to give the method some more information about what you want to do. In this example you create a new browser window (you'll have two browsers running at the same time) that tries to open the `www.notes.net` site. The `open()` method for `window` takes up to three arguments: the first is the URL string you want to open, the second is the window name (no spaces allowed), and the third, which is optional, describes the window attributes. We use only the first two arguments:

```
window.open( "http://www.notes.net", "Notes_Net" )
```

Configuring Domino for JavaScript

Before you begin writing JavaScript, there are several setting changes you need to make in order to use JavaScript with Domino. These settings are all security related and often need to be coordinated with your Domino system administrator. Once you configure Domino for JavaScript, you can apply some of the basic skills you learned in this lesson.

Configuring the Notes Client and Domino Designer

As the developer you need to tell your own Domino Designer and Notes Client that you authorize JavaScript to be used on your own PC. In the Designer or Notes client select **File, Preferences, User Preferences** from the menu. Select the **Basics** tab, as shown in Figure 18.2, and scroll through the selections in window below the **Additional Options** label. You want to select the following:

- Enable JavaScript
- Enable Java access from JavaScript
- Enable JavaScript error dialogs

You may also want to select these options:

- Enable Java applets
- Accept Cookies

FIGURE 18.2

Select the JavaScript-related options in the Basics tab of the User Preferences dialog.

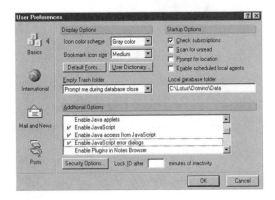

18

As your Domino development gets more advanced, you might want to change the Execution Control List (ECL) settings. The ECL settings initially protect your workstation from you. They are there to protect against accidents and malicious programs. Do not allow too many privileges. You can review the ECL settings for JavaScript by following these steps:

1. Select **File, Preferences, User Preferences.**

2. Select the **Basics** tab.

3. Click on the **Security Options** button.

4. The Workstation Security: Execution Control List dialog box appears, as shown in Figure 18.3.

5. Choose JavaScript security from the set of three radio buttons in the upper-right area of the dialog box.

6. You should review the settings for each entry in the **When signed by** area.

7. When you are finished with the review, click **OK**.

FIGURE 18.3

Shows the default Workstation Security: Execution Control List settings for JavaScript security.

When signed by:

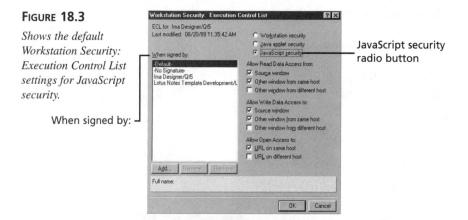

JavaScript security radio button

Configuring Database Settings for JavaScript

When you are designing a Domino database, you control whether the Domino HTTP process creates JavaScript when serving up the pages.

Database Settings

In the **Database Properties, Database Basics** tab, make certain that **Web access: Use JavaScript when generating pages** is selected.

When using JavaScript for your database, you are responsible for coding a **Submit** button or its equivalent. It should contain at least

```
@Command([FileSave]);
```

```
@Command([FileCloseWindow])
```

Notice that the Submit button is coded using the @Formula language. Domino converts it for you to JavaScript. You may have more than one button on a form that uses JavaScript. You might also see a performance improvement for databases that use navigators and complex hotspot formulas.

Form Settings

You need to decide on a form by form basis how to handle hidden fields. These settings are found on the **Form Properties, Defaults tab,** in the **On Web Access** group. In general for databases that use JavaScript you should select **Generate HTML for all fields** rather than Treat document contents as HTML. If your form has any Domino Designer created fields, including computed for display, you must not use Treat document contents as HTML setting because you will get an HTTP error.

Server Settings

There are security settings for each Domino Server that determines who may run JavaScript and LotusScript agents. You need to work with your Domino System Administrator to change these values. Please note that Unrestricted scripts are permitted to do file operations such as updating, writing, and deleting files. You should take great care in giving someone the authority to run Unrestricted scripts because they could accidentally erase your entire disk drive.

Using JavaScript in the IDE

Let the IDE be your guide to determining where you may code JavaScript. There are two ways to identify whether JavaScript is permitted: the first is the InfoList's Object tab, which shows a JavaScript icon (see Figure 18.4). The second way is to look at the Run drop-down list in the Programmers Pane. If the list includes JavaScript, you may select it.

The InfoList Reference tab allows you to switch between the browser-based Document Object Model and the Notes Domino Object Model (D.O.M.) to get to object names and then to the properties and methods associated with the object. Figure 18.5 shows the Reference Tab of the InfoList.

18

InfoList Objects tab

"Rush Delivery" button
that is being programmed

FIGURE 18.4

*The IDE is your guide
to using JavaScript.
This figure shows a
button. It may be pro-
grammed using
JavaScript. The
InfoList Objects show
JavaScript events
using a special icon.*

JavaScript Icon

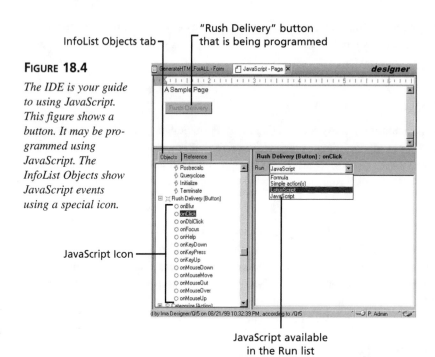

JavaScript available
in the Run list

Drop-down list to select either
Web or Notes D.O.M.

InfoList Reference tab

FIGURE 18.5

*The IDE is your guide
to using JavaScript
objects. The Reference
tab allows you to
select either the Notes
D.O.M. or the Web
D.O.M. Clicking on
the twistie allows you
to see the object's
properties and
methods.*

List of Form properties
and methods

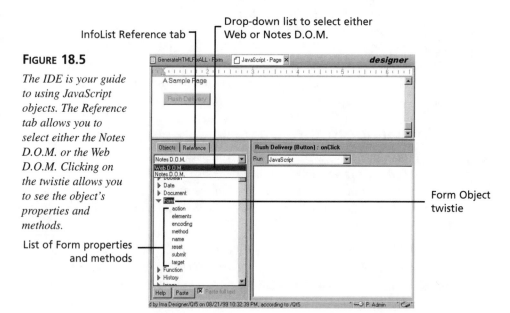

Form Object
twistie

Please note that the IDE does not automatically indent your JavaScript code you need to manage this yourself.

Understanding the JavaScript Language

To create a JavaScript program you need to understand the basic structure of a program. If you are already familiar with C, C++, or Java, the syntax and language structure is very similar. A program consists of statements that may use reserved words, variables, literal values, function definitions, function calls, and references to objects and their properties and methods. A program must follow the syntax rules of JavaScript.

Syntax

The language is case-sensitive, that is myName, MyName, and MYName are three different names. You must be consistent with your names or your program will not work.

Start new statements on a new line.

String Literals are defined by enclosing them in double quotes such as "This is a literal value".

Numeric values are entered as numbers with or without decimal points such as 5 or 1.456.

When you want to group a set of statements together, enclose them in meta-braces ({ }), also known as curly braces.

Parentheses are used in two ways:

- To define the order of calculation such as: 2 * 3 + 5 equals 11, but 2 * (3 + 5) equals 16 because the parentheses instruct JavaScript to add 3 to 5 before multiplying by 2.
- To enclose a set of arguments for a function call or function definition, such as window.open ("URL", "WindowName")

You can enter comments to help you remember what your code does. Comments are skipped by the language and do not affect the program operation.

- You can place a comment anywhere on a line by starting the comment with two forward slashes. You may have code preceding the comment or the comment may be on a line by itself.

  ```
  Example:  //This is my comment
  ```

- You may create a comment that spans multiple lines by starting the comment on the first line with forward-slash asterisk combination /* and ending it on the last line of the comment with a */.

18

Variables

The heart of programming is having a name in your program that stores different values during the execution of the program. The names are called variables and you should give them a name that accurately represents the information you want them to hold. By convention, JavaScript variables are named in a similar fashion to Java:

- Start with a lowercase letter (a–z)
- No spaces may be in the variable name, if you insist you may use an underscore (_) to simulate a space
- Follow the first letter with other letters, numbers, or underscores
- Each additional inner word of the variable should begin with a capital letter (A–Z)
- Examples: `myName`, `clientStreetAddress`, `counter3`, `clientOfficePhoneNumber`

Variables do not have to be declared before they are used; there are no "Dim" or "Declare" statements in JavaScript. The first reference to the variable name creates the variable, such as

```
myName = "Claire Weber"
```

```
myAge = 13.8
```

To make a variable *global*—accessible from any function in your program—you define it in the <HEAD> section and precede the first reference to the variable name with `var`.

```
var myName = "Sheila Galloway"
```

Data Types

No doubt you have noticed that `myAge` is assigned a numeric value and `myName` is assigned a string literal value. JavaScript determines the data type of the variable when it is assigned a value. You can change `myAge` to be a string by typing:

```
myAge = "I'm not telling"
```

This is not a good idea for you as a programmer. Whenever possible you should keep a variable one data type.

Table 18.1 lists the JavaScript data types.

Table 18.1 JavaScript Data Types

Type	Description	Examples
Numeric	Any number value. The numbers may be positive or negative values.	100 13.82 −1.62345
String	Anything you want to put between two double quote marks. If you put a number between double quote marks it will be treated as string and not as a number.	"Hi World!" "123" "What's the question?"
Boolean (Logic)	true or false (these are reserved words and must be lowercase). false is equivalent to zero in value.	((2+2) == 5) is false ((2+2) == 4) is true
Null	This is a special value that means that something is empty or doesn't exist. Test to see if a frame exists.	`if(window.frames[0] == null)`
Object	A reference to an object. This variable will let you access any of the object's properties or methods. It becomes an object variable for the first form object.	`f=window.document.forms[0]` `f.elements.length`

18

Arrays

It's cumbersome to create a separate variable for each piece of similar information; for example: `firstWkDay`, `secondWkDay`, `thirdWkDay`. Wouldn't it be nice to have one name for the information and a way to address each separate piece of information? You do this by using arrays. If you want to store the names of the days of the week you can do this:

```
daysOfWeek = new Array("Sunday", "Monday", "Tuesday", "Wednesday",
➥"Thursday", "Friday", "Saturday")
alert("The first day is: " + daysOfWeek[0])
```

Note that the subscript value to access the first value in an array is zero. You can have multidimensional arrays and arrays may contain any data type including objects.

Reserved Words

Reserved words should *not* be used as variable or function names. Reserved words have a special meaning that either controls program execution or names an object, property, or method. They include words such as for, var, if, and name. Please see the Q&A section at the end of this chapter for a list of reference books to help you learn about reserved words.

Operators

JavaScript has a rich set of operators. Table 18.2 describes the JavaScript arithmetic and string operators. Arithmetic operators are used to manipulate numbers, and string operators are used to manipulate text.

Note	The Result column in Table 18.2 is based on these variables and their assigned values: • a = 6 • b = 2 • firstName = "Joe" • lastName = "Programmer"

Table 18.2   JavaScript Arithmetic and String Operators

Operator	Description	Result
+	Numeric addition	a + b results in 8
+	String concatenation. Puts the second string immediately after the first.	firstName + " " + lastName yields Joe Programmer
-	Subtraction	a–b results in 4 b–a results in -4
*	Multiplication	a * b results in 12
/	Division	a / b results in 3
%	Modulus gives the remainder when two numbers are divided	a % b results in 0 b % a results in 2
++	Adds one to the variable (See the following Tip)	++a is equivalent to a = a + 1

Operator	Description	Result
--	Subtracts one from the variable (See the following Tip)	—b is equivalent to b = b–1
-	Unary minus. It is like multiplying a number by –1	–a results in –6 –b results in –2

Tip

++a and a++ are different when used in an equation:

a = 12.

b = a++ gives b the value 12 then increments a to be 13.

a = 12

b = ++a increments a to 13 first, then assigns b the value 13.

the -- operator works in the same fashion

18

JavaScript has many assignment operators as shown in Table 18.3. An assignment operator takes the final value of the statement on the right side of the assignment operator and puts that value into the variable on the left side of the assignment operator. You should just use the simple assignment operator (=) rather than the two character assignment operators to make your code easier to read, understand, and debug. For each row in the table assume that a starts out as 6 and b starts out as 2:

Table 18.3 JavaScript Assignment Operators

Example	Description	Result
a = b	Sets a to the value of b	a becomes 2
a += b	Same as: a = a + b	a becomes 8
a -= b	Same as: a = a–b	a becomes 4
a *= b	Same as: a = a * b	a becomes 12
a /= b	Same as: a = a / b	a becomes 3
a %= b	Same as: a = a % b	a becomes 0

You often want to know how one value compares with another. The comparison and logical operators allow you to make these comparisons. Table 18.4 shows JavaScript's comparison and logical operators. The end result of any comparison is a Boolean value, either true (non-zero value) or false (always a value of zero).

Table 18.4   JavaScript Comparison and Logical Operators

Example	When Does It Return True?
a == b	When a and b are exactly equal
a != b	When a and b are *not* equal
a > b	When a is greater than b
a >= b	When a is greater than or equal to b
a < b	When a is less than b
a <= b	When a is less than or equal to b
a && b	When both a and b are true
a ¦¦ b	When either a or b are true
	When both a and b are true
!a	When a is false

Functions

Functions allow you to write one set of code that can be reused. A function should perform one specific task. It often will require you to provide it some information to start its calculation. In this function example we calculate the payment for a loan:

```
function loanPayment( amount, periods, intPerPeriod ) {
//put the code here
        payment = (amount / periods ) * (1 + intPerPeriod)
        if ( payment >= 0 ) {
                return( payment )
        }
}
```

The function reserved word tells JavaScript that you are defining a function, loanPayment is the name of the function. The formal arguments: amount, periods, and intPerPeriod are used in the loanPayment code as variables for the calculation. Notice the line where we return the value payment. That is how you get the function to give the result back to the calling program. You invoke the function by coding:

```
myPayment = loanPayment( 10000, 5, 0.015 )
```

Program Flow and Control

JavaScript gives you ways to control your program's execution. The language lets you make decisions using **if** statements. If it is sunny, we will have fun, or else we will clean the garage.

Sometimes you need to do something over and over. Accomplish this using the iterative operator: for.

For example: If it is a sunny day we will drink five sodas otherwise we'll go clean the garage:

```
if ( todaysWeather == "Sunny" ) {
      for ( i=1; i <= 5; i++ ) {
            alert("Drinking soda number: " + i )
      }  // closes the for
}  // closes the if 'true'
else {
      alert("OKAY, I'll clean the garage!" )
}  // closes the if 'else'
alert( "That's all folks!" )
```

Coding JavaScript in Domino

The Lotus folks have done a lot in Release 5 to make programming with JavaScript easy for you. They have provided the following tools:

- **JS Header** event for forms, subforms, and pages that will place JavaScript code within the <HEAD> of your HTML document.

- **JavaScript event handlers** in the IDE Objects window. You can select an event handler name and write JavaScript code in the Programmer's Pane. The code will be placed in the <BODY> of your document.

- **HTML tab** in the properties box for most design elements. This is where you specify the object name for JavaScript. Domino does this automatically for fields, you must supply the name for buttons, pictures, hotspots, and actions.

- **Form** as a variable to reference the current window.document.forms[0].

JavaScript can be hand typed using a text editor or placed directly within HTML. You are permitted to hand code your <SCRIPT> in any HTML area, but we don't encourage you to do that because Domino, using the Domino supplied events, ensures the correct placement of the JavaScript code within the HTML. You may also place JavaScript code in any part of a form or page that is marked as Pass-Thru HTML. Although you may still use the field $$HTMLHead, we discourage its use because JS Header replaces it.

18

Domino does not provide JavaScript libraries as it does for LotusScript (as you will learn in Chapter 19, "Introduction to LotusScript") and Java.

How can you see that HTML and the <SCRIPT> code that Domino generates? You should test your form using **Design, Preview in Web Browser**, and then select your browser. Once you are in your browser, find where to view the source. In IE it is under **View, Source**; in Netscape it is under **View, Page Source.**

JS Header

JS Header is the primary place for you to write your JavaScript code for forms, subforms, and pages; it is where you put global variables and functions.

Events and Event Handlers

Events are the predefined times when you want something to occur, such as when the form loads, when you change the value of a field, or move the mouse onto or away from a hotspot. For each event you may write JavaScript code, but you don't have to write code for any of them. You get to choose which ones are useful to you. Table 18.5 lists the events that may appear in the IDE object list. There is a caveat: Even though an event is listed it may not be supported. For more detailed information, look in Domino Designer Help for a document entitled "Table of Supported JavaScript Objects for Automated Components" and in the release notes for Domino.

Table 18.5   Events for JavaScript

Event	Description
onBlur	When an object is exited (deselected)
onChange	When the object content has changed (Fields only)
onClick	When the object is selected (by any means, tabbed into, mouse click, cursor movement)
onDblClick	When the object is selected with a double-click
onFocus	When an editable object is selected
onHelp	When the user requests context-sensitive help (for example, Press F1)
onKeyDown	When a key is pressed down
onKeyPress	When a key is pressed
onKeyUp	When a key is released
onLoad	When a document is first opened by the browser
onMouseDown	When a mouse button is pressed down
onMouseMove	When the mouse is moved

Event	Description
onMouseOut	When the mouse moves so that it is outside of the object's area
onMouseOver	When the mouse moves so that it is inside of the object's area
onMouseUp	When a mouse button is released
onReset	When a document is reset (reloaded) (Forms only)
onSelect	When a value for a field is selected (Fields only)
onSubmit	Processed just before a document is submitted (Forms only)
onUnload	Processed just before a document is closed

Code for onClick event

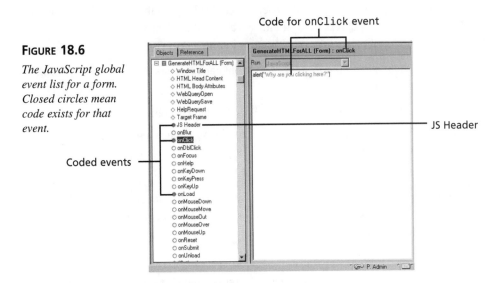

FIGURE 18.6

The JavaScript global event list for a form. Closed circles mean code exists for that event.

JS Header

18

Coded events

Putting It All together

The power of the Domino environment is that you use the IDE's graphical design to create the static text, fields, buttons, actions, hotspots, and images you want displayed. The IDE Object list and Programmers Pane allows you to add JavaScript to events. Domino takes the design and your code and generates the HTML to instruct the browser how to layout the form, defines the JavaScript and how to associate the document features with which coded events.

Domino creates the routine HTML entries for you. You do not have to code <SCRIPT LANGUAGE=JavaScript> or </SCRIPT> tags. You do not have to code <HEAD> or </HEAD> tags or <BODY> and </BODY> tags. Any code you put in JS Header will automatically be in the `<HEAD>` section. You also do not have to code the HTML start (`<! —`) and end comments (`—>`)to hide JavaScript from very old browsers, Domino does this for you.

Here are a few examples to assist you with learning:

Keyword Field

We simulate a keyword field that allows the user to make an entry not contained in our keyword list. On a new form define two editable fields: `IceCreamFlavors` and `MyIceCream`. The first field, `IceCreamFlavors`, is a List box with the first choice of `<Select a flavor>`, and then several flavors to choose from. You will put JavaScript code in the **onChange** event to copy the user-selected value into the second field. The second field, `MyIceCream` is a Text field. It either receives the select value from `IceCreamFlavors` or the user types their choice into it.

There are three equivalent coding solutions for `onChange` as described in the following list:

- **Fully-qualified object names**—Based on the standard object model.
- **Domino's `form` object variable**—Domino always creates a global object variable called `form` that references the current form.
- **`this`**—represents the current object.

Use the fully-qualified object solution. When you look at the Document Object Model this starts from the top with `window` and uses one object from each subsequent level to address the value:

```
window.document.forms[0].MyIceCream.value =
window.document.forms[0].IceCreamFlavors.options[
window.document.forms[0].IceCreamFlavors.selectedIndex].text
```

Use the `form` object variable that Domino creates. `form` replaces `window.document.forms[0]` from the fully-qualified solution:

```
form.MyIceCream.value =
form.IceCreamFlavors.options[form.IceCreamFlavors.selectedIndex].text
```

Use the `this` object variable for `IceCreamFlavors`. JavaScript provides shorthand for the current object. You use `this` to refer to the object you are currently programming in Domino:

```
form.MyIceCream.value = this.options[this.selectedIndex].text
```

Figure 18.7 shows all three coding solutions and the form design in Domino Designer.

IceCreamFlavors Choices

FIGURE 18.7

*Keyword with "allow"
not in list simulation.
The Programmers
Pane shows all three
solutions, but only the
last one is active; the
others are entered as
comments.*

IceCreamFlavors
List box field

onChange event

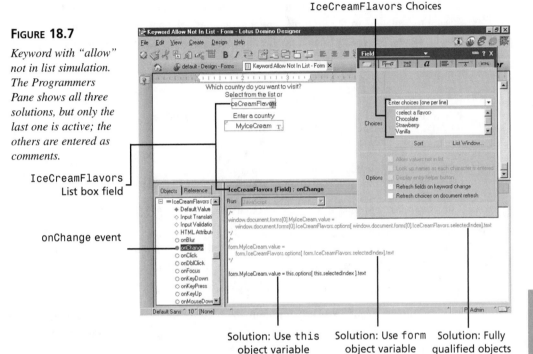

IceCreamFlavors Choices

Solution: Use this   Solution: Use form   Solution: Fully
object variable   object variable   qualified objects

18

Change Image with Mouse Movements

This example lets you change one graphic into another by moving the mouse. We will
replace a gray image with a full color image whenever the mouse is over the image area.

- Create the images as Image Resources
- Create a new Page (this will also work on a Form)
- On the page add some static text asking them to move the mouse onto and away
  from the image
- Place the gray Image Resource onto the Page
- Give the gray image on the page the HTML name of ShowMe by going to the
  Picture Extra HTML tab of the Picture Properties box and entering **ShowMe** in
  Name field.

In the **JS Header** you create space to store the two images and write a routine to handle swapping the images. In the Picture's **onMouseOver** and the **onMouseOut** events you will call **handleMouseMovement** to change the image on the screen. The JS Header code is

```
//Create two global variables that will hold the graphics
var graphic1 = new Image( )
var graphic2 = new Image( )
//Store the source name of the image resources.
//My database file name is: demo.nsf  Remember to use your image names
graphic1.src = "/demo.nsf/grayimage.gif?OpenImageResource"
graphic2.src = "/demo.nsf/colorful.gif?OpenImageResource"

function handleMouseMovement( whichGraphic, where ) {
//whichGraphic is the source of the graphic we want to display
//where will say to use the "ShowMe" location
    document.images[ where ].src = whichGraphic
}
```

The onMouseOut event tells the browser to show the original graphic when the mouse isn't over the graphic area (graphic1.src is the grayimage.gif).

```
handleMouseMovement( graphic1.src, "ShowMe" )
```

The onMouseOver event for the picture tells the browser that you want to show the second graphic when you move the mouse over the existing graphic area (graphic2.src is the fullcolor.gif).

```
handleMouseMovement( graphic2.src, "ShowMe" )
```

Change Page Content via a button

This example splits people into two groups based on their last name. If their last name starts with a letter from A to M, you will make the browser show on a new page: Welcome to the first half with a blue background, otherwise they will see Welcome to the better half with a yellow background.

What do we need?

- A form with an editable field called LName and static text asking the user to enter their name, and then click the button. Add a button to the form.
- Some code to determine which half they belong to. We'll do this with the function **selectGroup** entered in the **JS Header**.
- Some code to display the changed page. We'll do this with the function **changeDisplay** entered in the **JS Header**.
- Some code to make the button do something when clicked. We'll enter this in the **onClick** event for the button.

In the JS Header event for the form code enter the following:

```
function selectGroup( lastName ) {
    // get the first letter of the name
    lNameInitial = lastName.charAt(0).toUpperCase()
    if (lNameInitial >= 'A' && lNameInitial <= 'M' ) {
        return( 1 )
    }
    else {
        return( 2 )
    }
}


function changeDisplay( message, color ) {
    // Create the new window (in IE) with the
    // new background color
    window.document.write( message )
    window.document.bgcolor( color )
}
```

In the onClick event for the Button enter the following:

```
//Get the last name value.  Notice that JavaScript
// uses the same field name as Domino uses, but it
// is case sensitive (LName not lname )
myLastName = window.document.forms[0].LName.value
//Get the group by calling the function selectGroup
nameGroup = selectGroup( myLastName )
// Change the display with the correct message and color
if (nameGroup == 1 ) {
    changeDisplay( "Welcome to the first half", "blue" )
}
else {
    changeDisplay( "Welcome to the better half", "yellow")
}
```

What is happening? The JS Header functions are placed in the <HEAD> part of the document so that any field or button may use them. When you click the button the onClick code is run. It gets the value in the LName field, and asks selectGroup to figure out where in the alphabet our name lies. The selectGroup function takes the first character, makes it a capital letter and determines which half of the alphabet it is dealing with. It gives 1 as the value if you're A–M, otherwise it sends back to 2. The onClick routine uses an if statement to send the correct values to changeDisplay. It is handy to have one function that accepts argument values. Note that some older versions of Netscape will not show the text message, only the background color.

18

Handle a Cookie

In this very simplified cookie handler for the number of times someone has visited your site. The onLoad event calls a function handleCookie (coded in JS Header) that will retrieve the current cookie and update the site visit count. If no cookie exists, it creates one. On your form you will put some Pass-Thru HTML that calls the function getCount() to display an appropriate message referring to the number of visits. You code getCount() in **JS Header**. There is one global variable cookieName that holds the cookie's name.

The code for the JS Header defines the functions and global variables:

```
var cookieName = "TYR5in21"

function handleCookie() {
    restOfCookie = "; expires=Monday, 01-Jan-2001 17:00:00 GMT"
    index = -1   //Assume that the cookie does not exist
    if (document.cookie) {
        index = document.cookie.indexOf( cookieName )
    }
    //If the cookie exists, update it
    if (index != -1 ) {
        //Find the count.  It is between the = and ;
        countStart = (document.cookie.indexOf( "=", index ) + 1 )
        countEnd = document.cookie.indexOf( ";", index )
        if (countEnd == -1) {
            countEnd = document.cookie.length
        }

        //Get the count, convert it to a number, and increment
        curCount = document.cookie.substring( countStart, countEnd )
        newCount = eval( curCount ) + 1

        //Update the cookie
        document.cookie = cookieName + "=" + newCount + restOfCookie
    }
    else {
        //Create a new cookie because one did not exist
        document.cookie = cookieName + "=1" + restOfCookie
    }
}

function getCount() {
    //Find the cookie
    if (document.cookie) {
```

```
    index = document.cookie.indexOf( cookieName )
    if (index != 1 ) {
        //They have visited us before
        countStart = (document.cookie.indexOf( "=", index ) + 1 )
        countEnd = document.cookie.indexOf( ";", index )
        if (countEnd == -1 ) {
            countEnd = document.cookie.length
        }
        //Get the count and convert it to a number
        curCount = eval( document.cookie.substring( countStart, countEnd ) )
        if (curCount == 1 ) {
            return( "<b>You visited once before</b>")
        }
    else {
            return("<b>You visited " + curCount + " times before</b>" )
        }
    } //Visited us before
} //Cookie support
else {
    return("<H3><b>Thank you for visiting us for the first time</b></H3>" )
}
}
```

The onLoad event for the Form calls the function handleCookie():

```
handleCookie()
```

On the form you add this code as pass-thru HTML to call the getCount() function:

```
<script>

document.write( getCount() )

</script>
```

As the form is being prepared for display by the browser, the browser invokes the getCount() function, taking the result and putting it into the displayed information.

Summary

You have a very quick overview of JavaScript, its language and object model, and how to use it to build more robust Web browser run applications. You can now choose to program all your field enter, field exit, and field validation with JavaScript instead of the @Formula language because the Notes R5 client supports JavaScript.

18

Q&A

Q Where do I use JavaScript versus LotusScript?

A Use JavaScript wherever possible because it is the language that works with both browsers and the Notes R5 client. For more information, consult the Domino 5 Designer Help document "Table of Domino Objects," which lists the programmable objects in Domino, specifies the scope of each object, and tells whether an object supports simple actions, formulas, LotusScript, Java, or JavaScript.

Q Where do I find JavaScript information?

A Start with Domino 5 Designer Help and these references:

For JavaScript: *Special Edition Using JavaScript, Second Edition* by Andrew Wooldridge, et al., and for more advanced JavaScript with Domino topics: *Lotus Notes and Domino R5 Development Unleashed* by Debbie Lynd and Steve Kern or *Special Edition Using Lotus Notes and Domino R5* by Randy Tamura.

How Do I Get Started?

A few suggestions: Try doing some input validations. Pre-loading images and switching on mouse over is not a hard task, yet, it is one that makes you feel accomplished. Change the submit process. Most of all, have fun.

Workshop

Because we just introduced the subject of JavaScript with this chapter, we are only asking you to do a small task in this workshop. For more detailed information on how to use JavaScript, check out *Lotus Notes and Domino R5 Development Unleashed* by Debbie Lynd and Steve Kern and *Special Edition Using Lotus Notes and Domino 5* by Randy Tamura, et al.

For this task you need to open the Completed Titles database in Designer. If you didn't create one in the Day 17 workshop, open the Day17 folder on the CD, and then open CTDay17.nsf.

Open the Book Order Form. In the Programmer's Pane, select the **JS Header** event under **Order(Form)** in the Objects list. In the Script Area enter the following:

```
Alert("Thank you for ordering. If you need further assistance,
call our Customer Service Department at 1-800-555-5555")
```

This produces an alert box when the page first loads. The user clicks **OK** and proceeds to fill out the form. You've just entered your first JavaScript code!

To see how this works in the sample database, open the CTDay18.nsf database in the Day18 folder on the CD.

WEEK 3

DAY 19

Introduction to LotusScript

What is LotusScript?

Lotus Notes provides a set of objects that you use to build an application, and each of these objects has an associated set of events. An *event* is an action that has occurred in an application, such as clicking on a button. To define the responses to events, you use scripts. A set of statements in the LotusScript language is a *script*. A collection of scripts that have been compiled so the user can run them is one definition of an application.

You can attach scripts to agents, actions, forms, buttons, hotspots, elements on navigators, and fields.

LotusScript is a structured programming language built on BASIC that has a set of language extensions to enable object-oriented application development within and across Lotus products (Lotus Notes, Approach, Freelance Graphics, Word Pro, and 1-2-3).

Although it has been the primary programming language for Notes applications in the past, JavaScript is now the programming language of choice for Web-oriented applications. However, LotusScript's capability to manipulate the Domino back-end objects still makes it useful. There is also the need to support and update existing applications.

This lesson provides a basic overview of LotusScript, so you will be able to write simple scripts for your applications. To find more extensive and detailed explanations of scripting, refer to *Lotus Notes & Domino 5 Development Unleashed* or *Special Edition Using Lotus Notes and Domino 5*.

Why Would You Use LotusScript?

What are the advantages of using LotusScript?

- **Cross-platform**—LotusScript works with Windows, Macintosh, OS/2, UNIX, OS/390, and AS400. Scripts written in Windows execute on the other platforms without changes.

- **BASIC-compatible**—Like Visual Basic, LotusScript is an easy language to learn. It uses conditions, branches, subroutines, loops, and other conventions to develop sophisticated applications without using a programming language such as C or C++. For users of Visual Basic, the LotusScript learning curve is especially short because of the similarity of the languages.

- **Object-oriented**—Notes provides object classes that are available to LotusScript, so you can write scripts to manipulate these objects.

- **Supported by other Lotus products**—Because LotusScript is supported by Lotus products such as 1-2-3, Word Pro, Freelance Graphics, and Approach, you can use one language to write scripts in any of these products.

- **OLE**—In addition to the Lotus products, you can use LotusScript script to control and manipulate objects from other OLE-enabled applications, such as Microsoft Office.

When to Use Formula-Language or LotusScript?

There are some areas in which you can't use LotusScript. In designing views, you can't use LotusScript in form, selection, or column formulas. In Forms, LotusScript is not available for window titles, section titles, section access, inserting subforms, hiding paragraphs, or hide/show actions. You can't include LotusScript in default values, input translations, input validations, or computed values for fields. Keyword field formulas and SmartIcon formulas also can't use LotusScript.

However, there are areas where there is no appropriate formula language, so you must use a scripting language. For example, scripting is necessary when you want to

- Give users the rights to create or delete databases
- Read from or modify the access control list
- Locate and process a database when you don't know the name of the database
- Process field values on documents when you don't know the field names
- Create or update a full text index, manipulate external files on a disk
- Take action when a user enters or exits a field
- Add input/output to the underlying non-Notes file system
- Process rich text

When you aren't sure which to use—formulas or script—keep these guidelines in mind:

- If a specific @Function or @Command exists to do the task, use the formula.
- If the task involves complex procedural controls and conditional looping, use LotusScript.
- To access and manipulate stored document data, especially for cross-document and cross-database access, use LotusScript.
- For tasks the formula language doesn't support, use LotusScript.

Using the IDE

The Integrated Development Environment (IDE), or Designer, provides the tools for all your application development. That's also true for LotusScript. You open the database you want to work on in the Designer and select the type of design element you need to create or modify. You then open or create the specific design element.

Enter the script in the Programmer's Pane, but you must first select the object and event for which you are writing the script. To do this, click the Objects tab of the Info List if it isn't already open, and then click the plus sign (+) that appears beside the object on which you're working. A list of associated events shows beneath the object. You select the event that you want to script. A tiny scroll icon before the event indicates that it is a LotusScript event. For example, an Action is an object and the event you program with script is the Click event.

The Run drop-down list above the Programmer's Pane displays the language being used to manipulate or access the current object. The choices include Formula, Simple action(s), LotusScript, and JavaScript. Not all choices are available in every instance.

19

When you select LotusScript as the language you want to use, your screen is similar to the one shown in Figure 19.1. In that illustration, the application developer has just started creating an action button and has chosen LotusScript as the preferred language. In the Objects window of the Info List, the name of the object appears and the event (Click) is selected. The Programmer's Pane automatically displays the first and last lines of the script. You enter your script between these lines.

FIGURE 19.1

A new action is being created, and LotusScript is the chosen language to specify what is to occur in response to the Click event.

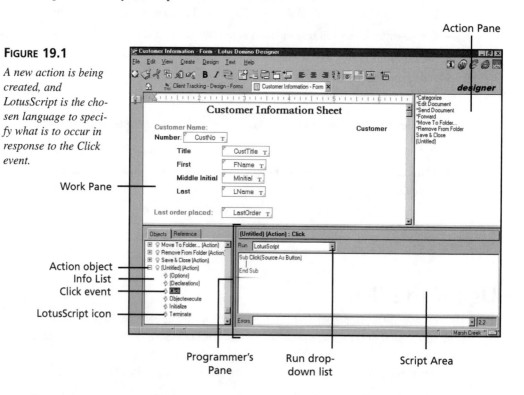

Action Pane

Work Pane

Action object
Info List
Click event

LotusScript icon

Programmer's
Pane

Run drop-
down list

Script Area

Designer displays different types of script statements in different colors. To assign the colors you want associated with various statements or to change the font of the Programmer's Pane (bigger is a good idea), right-click in the pane. Select **Programmer's Pane Properties** from the shortcut menu (see Figure 19.2).

FIGURE 19.2

Change the colors or font used in the Programmer's Pane to make your script easier to read as you work.

From the Reference window of the Info List, you can view or paste appropriate LotusScript language and script components such as Notes classes, Notes constants, Notes subs and functions, Notes variables, and OLE classes into the script. You can also read the Help text on any of these by selecting an item from the Reference window and clicking Help or pressing F1.

The code you enter is stored in a LotusScript module. Notes stores a separate module for each form, view, and agent that you design. To declare variables, subroutines, or functions that you want to be available for all the scripts within a module, enter them in the Globals section of the Objects window. You use the Options part to define options that affect the entire module, such as declaring all the variable names. In the Declarations section, you define the data types, constants, and variables used by your module.

As you enter your scripts, Notes might complete portions of it for you (such as entering Sub at the beginning and End Sub at the end when you start a subroutine). Notes also attempts to move blocks of code to the correct location.

When you save and close the design document, the script is compiled. Compiling translates the script into executable code. If the compiler finds an error in the script, a description of the error appears in the Error box (some errors are detected as you enter the script and appear in the Error box immediately because the script is partially compiled as you write it). The line of script where the error occurs changes color. You correct the error by editing the script in the Programmer's Pane. The design element has to be saved in order to compile the script again. You test script the same way you test any changes in your design—choose **Design, Preview in Notes** or **Preview in Web Browser** from the menu.

19

Writing Script

Like any programming language, LotusScript has a syntax and structure you need to learn to write scripts.

A script consists of one or more lines of text called *statements*. The statements are processed by the compiler in the order that you put them in the script, so the sequence of your statements is important. Blank lines are ignored, as are extra spaces and indents in your script.

Usually, each line of the script is a separate statement. Occasionally you might need to continue a statement on to the next line. To do that, you need to place a continuation character at the end of the line where the statement breaks to the next line. The line continuation character in LotusScript is the underscore (_). You must place the underscore at the end of the line, and there must be a space between the end of the text on the line and the underscore. For example, the following statement has been broken into two lines:

```
Dim db _
   AS NotesDatabase
```

You help yourself and others when you include comments in your code explaining what the code is doing. Just remember, it might be some time before you (or someone else) revisits the code, and by that time you won't remember why you wrote it that way or what it was intended to do. Documenting it as you are writing it is always a good idea.

To include comments in your script, begin the line with an apostrophe ('). The compiler ignores those lines. In fact, the compiler also ignores any text on the same line following an apostrophe; this means you can put the apostrophe and comment text on the same line with your code. Another way to indicate your comment text is to use %REM and %END REM to mark the beginning and end of the comment.

```
' A single comment line
' A second comment line
Const SIZE_SMALL = 1        ' a comment placed here is ignored by the compiler

%REM
The first line in a multi-line comment
followed by more information
and closed by
%END REM
```

| Tip | Be kind to maintenance programmers (and yourself) by commenting your code as you go. I tend to write a series of comments at the start of the script, explaining what the code does, before I begin entering the LotusScript. This helps me keep on track with what I need to do with the code. It also avoids the chore of having to add comments to your code after it has been written. |

The language elements that LotusScript uses to construct statements in scripts are identifiers, keywords, literals and constants, and operators.

Identifiers

Identifiers are the names given to elements in your scripts. You assign identifiers to variables, constants, and functions.

The following rules apply to identifiers you create:

- The first character must be a letter.
- Letters, digits, and the underscore character are all valid characters.

- You can use 1–40 characters in an identifier.
- Identifiers are not case sensitive, so NAME and Name are the same identifier (we suggest, however, that it's a good idea to be consistent with case—it will keep you in practice for other languages).

Keywords

Keywords are reserved for LotusScript's own use because they have a particular meaning or function. You don't use these words in any other context.

Keywords include

- Built-in constants, such as TRUE, FALSE, and NULL
- Built-in functions, such as MESSAGEBOX
- Data types, such as STRING
- Commands, such as the FOR statement

Literals and Constants

Literals are data values that don't change. They can be numbers (789) or strings ("Washington Township").

Constants represent unchanging values. They are names given to values, and those names cannot be changed while the application is running. Although you define many of your constants, LotusScript has a few built-in constants (see Table 19.1).

Table 19.1 LotusScript Built-In Constants

Constant	Description
EMPTY	An internal value that is the initial value of a Variant variable. If converted to a string, it's the empty string (""). If converted to a number, it is 0 (zero).
FALSE	The Boolean value false, represented by 0.
TRUE	The Boolean value true, represented by -1.
NULL	For variables of type Variant, NULL indicates that the variable does not have a value. It's usually used with missing or unknown data.
NOTHING	For variables that can refer to objects, NOTHING indicates that the variable does not currently refer to an object.
PI	The ratio of the circumference of a circle to its diameter (something such as 3.14159265358979).

19

LotusScript provides additional constants in a special file. You can substitute those constants for numeric arguments in certain statements in your script—such as `MessageBox`—so you don't have to specify a number to indicate the OK or Cancel buttons. The LSCONST.LSS file is stored in the program directory. To use the constants stored in that file, you need to include it in your script in the globals area—usually in the (Declarations) event—using the `%INCLUDE` directive.

```
%INCLUDE "LSCONST.LSS"
```

Other constants are user-defined. You define them in the script by using a `Const` statement. For example, the following statements define constants to represent product sizes:

```
Const SIZE_SMALL = 1
Const SIZE_MEDIUM = 2
Const SIZE_LARGE = 3
```

The convention in naming constants is to always put the names in uppercase.

Operators

Operators manipulate data in expressions (for example, the plus (+) and minus (-) in mathematical expressions). In LotusScript, there are four types of operators—arithmetical, logical, comparison, and string concatenation. Table 19.2 describes the operators.

Table 19.2   LotusScript Operators

Type	Operator	Description
Arithmetical	-	Negates a number
		Subtracts two numbers
	+	Adds two numbers
	*	Multiplies two numbers
	/	Divides two numbers
	\	Performs integer division on two numbers (16\5 results in 3)
	Mod	Performs modulo division on two numbers (16 Mod 5 results in 1)
	^	Raises a number to a power
Comparison	=	Returns True if two values are equal
	<> ><	Returns True if two values are not equal
	<	Returns True if the first value is less than the other

Type	Operator	Description
	>	Returns True if the first value is greater than the other
	>=	Returns True if the first value is greater than or
	=>	equal to the other
	<=	Returns True if the first value is less than or equal
	=<	to the other
	Is	Returns True if two object references refer to the same object (objX Is objY)
Logical	Not	Negation (not X is True if X is false)
	And	Considers both operands to meet conditions (X And Y is True if both X and Y are True)
	Or	Considers each operand separately (X Or Y is True if either X or Y is True)
	Xor	Exclusive Or (X Xor Y is True if either X or Y is True but not if both are True)
	Eqv	Equivalence (X Eqv Y is True if both X and Y are True or both X and Y are False, but False if either X or Y but not both is True)
	Imp	Implication (X Imp Y is True if X is False or both X and Y are True, but False if X is True and Y is False)
String	& +	Concatenates two strings("John" & "Smith")
	Like	Returns True if a string matches a supplied pattern ("XYZ" Like "X*" returns True)

19

Working with Variables

In LotusScript, as with all programming languages, *variables* are used to store and manipulate data. All variables in LotusScript have a type associated with them. The type defines how much storage LotusScript is to reserve for the data to be stored by the variable, and the types of statements in which you can use the variable.

Data Types

LotusScript recognizes numeric data (which can be used in calculations) and string data (data that represents any number of letters). These are scalar data types, and they are defined in Table 19.3. LotusScript also recognizes aggregate data types, such as arrays. Arrays are discussed later in this lesson.

Table 19.3 Scalar Data Types

Data Type	Suffix	Number of Bytes Stored	Description	Values
Integer	%	1	Whole numbers without fractional components	-32,768 to +32,767
Long	&	4	Large integers	-2,147,483,648 to 2,147,483,647
Single	!	4	Floating point values	+ or - 7 digits with a floating point
Double	#	8	Double-precision floating point values	+ or - 17 digits with a floating point
Currency	@	8	Numeric data, representing monetary values	Fixed-point format with up to 15 digits to the left of the decimal point and up to 4 digits to the right

Data Type	Suffix	Number of Bytes Stored	Description	Values
String	$	2 per char-acter	Character strings of variable length	0–2GB characters (GET and PUT statements severely limit this upper bound)
Fixed String		2 per char-acter	Character strings of a specified length	0–32k characters (consumes 64k bytes of memory)

There is a special data type called Variant. Variables of type Variant can hold values of any scalar data type, Boolean values, date/time values, arrays or lists, object references, NULL, or EMPTY. If you don't declare a data type for a variable, LotusScript automatically assigns Variant as the data type.

Declaring Variables

Variable declaration is the process of defining a variable name and its data type. When you declare a variable, you create an identifier, causing LotusScript to write an initial value to the memory location associated with that variable.

You declare a variable in your script with a Dim statement. There are two ways to write a Dim statement—using the keyword for the data type or using the suffix.

```
Dim variableName As dataType
Dim variableName(suffix)
```

For example, the first statement that follows declares the variable Size as an integer. The second statement does exactly the same:

```
Dim size As Integer
Dim size%
```

Tip

As a rule, don't use suffixes when declaring variables. It makes your code harder to understand for someone who doesn't immediately know, for example, that ! means a single value.

19

When declaring a fixed string, you need to specify the number of characters in the string.

```
' Declare the variable City as a string with a fixed length of
' 25 characters
Dim City As String*25
```

Strictly speaking, you don't have to declare variables in LotusScript because the first time you use a new variable, LotusScript automatically declares it for you and assigns it a type of Variant. However, it is good programming practice to always *explicitly* declare variable types, even when optional, because it removes any doubt about the type you intend to use and makes your program easier to maintain.

> **Note**   In the (Options) section, add Option Explicit to have the compiler force you to declare each variable before you use it. It helps catch typos.

Don't explicitly declare Variant as the data type unless you are unsure of the data type of the values your program is going to manipulate, such as dates and times that do not have a specific data type. Variants use more storage than other data types and are processed more slowly. You also run the risk of losing track of which type of data you're tracking. After you assign an actual value to the variable, LotusScript automatically determines its data type based on the value.

When creating the identifier for a variable, you need to follow the rules set out for identifiers earlier in this lesson. To help understand quickly what data type a variable is, you might want to follow the naming convention that includes a prefix in the name to indicate the data type. Table 19.4 contains a list of suggested prefixes.

Table 19.4   Suggested Prefixes for Variable Names

Data Type	Prefix	Example
Integer	i	iDocsDeleted
Long	l	lFileLength
Single	s	sWeightCoefficient
Double	d	dAcceleration
Currency	cur	curSalaryIncrease
String	str	strDocTitle
Variant	var	varName

Assigning Data

After a variable is declared, you can assign data to it once or many times. You assign data by using the assignment operator (=). In the following example, the variable City is declared as a String and then the value "Phoenix" is assigned to it.

```
Dim City As String
City = "Phoenix"
```

To have the user input information to assign data to the variable, you use a function called Inputbox. The syntax for this function is

```
InputBox("Prompt")
```

For example, to have the user assign a value to the variable Age, you might write the following script:

```
Dim Age As Integer
Age = Inputbox("Enter Your Current Age")
```

A dialog box appears, asking the user for his current age (see Figure 19.3). The user enters his age and clicks OK. The value he entered is assigned to the variable Age.

The Messagebox function opens a dialog box that displays information to the user, waits for the response, and returns information about the response. The syntax of the Messagebox function is

```
' To display a simple message
Messagebox("Prompt")

' To display buttons in the dialog box
Messagebox("Prompt", Buttons)
```

The buttons you want to show in the dialog box must be indicated by an integer, unless you have included the LSCONST.LSS file in your script. In that case, you can use the constant name for the buttons (see Table 19.5 for a list of button constants or integers).

```
' Displays a dialog box with Yes and No buttons but coded
' without constant file
Dim Close as Integer
Close = Messagebox("Do you want to close this session?", 4)

' Displays a dialog box with Yes and No buttons and is
' coded with constant file
```

19

```
%Include "lsconst.lss"
Dim Close as Integer
Close = Messagebox("Do you want to close this session?", MB_YESNO)
```

Note that the arguments in the Messagebox function are separated by a comma, not a semicolon as in formula language.

Table 19.5 MESSAGEBOX Button Constants

Buttons Displayed	Value	Constant
OK	0	MB_OK
OK and Cancel	1	MB_OKCANCEL
Abort, Retry, and Ignore	2	MB_ABORTRETRYIGNORE
Yes, No, and Cancel	3	MB_YESNOCANCEL
Yes and No	4	MB_YESNO
Retry and Cancel	5	MB_RETRYCANCEL

Converting Data Types

LotusScript recognizes numeric and string data, but the two aren't considered compatible in the same expression. When you combine the two types in an expression, LotusScript gives you a Type Mismatch error. This usually happens when you assign data of one type to a variable of a different type or when you concatenate data and one of the expressions isn't a string.

LotusScript automatically converts some data for you, following this sequence: Integer, Long, Single, Double, Currency. Therefore, if you combine a long value and a single value in the same expression, LotusScript converts the long value into a single value and then evaluates the expression.

There are several functions in LotusScript to enable you to convert a number into a string, a string into a number, or data of one type to another type. There is also a way to check the data type of a variable. Table 19.6 lists the commonly used data conversion functions available in LotusScript.

Table 19.6 Commonly Used Data Conversion Functions

Function	Description
CCur	Converts the supplied value to currency type
CDat	Converts the supplied value to Variant of type Date
CDbl	Converts the supplied value to Double data type

Function	Description
CInt	Converts the supplied value to Integer data type
CLng	Converts the supplied value to Long data type
CSng	Converts the supplied value to Single data type
CStr	Converts the supplied value to its string representation
TypeName	Returns a string representing the data type of the supplied value

In order to guarantee that the result of a calculation is a certain type, include a data conversion as part of the script.

```
Dim iQuantity as Integer
Dim curPrice as Currency
Dim curTotal as Currency
curTotal = CCur(iQuantity * curPrice)
```

When you use a Variant data type, you might have to check what data value or type has been assigned to it by LotusScript:

```
Dim x As Variant
Print TypeName(x)        ' Prints "EMPTY"
x = 1
Print TypeName(x)        ' Prints "INTEGER"
x = "welcome"
Print TypeName(x)        ' Prints "STRING"
```

Working with Arrays

19

A scalar variable names a single location in memory. An array variable, in contrast, names a set of locations in memory, each of which holds a value of the same type. Simply put, an *array* is a collection of values of the same data type. All the elements (values) in the array have the same variable name. Each element in the array is accessed individually by its position in the collection (called the *index* or *subscript*).

In the most basic terms, you can think of an array as a kind of *virtual table* (it's *virtual* in the sense that it exists only in RAM). Like a table or spreadsheet, a virtual table has rows and columns that can be used to store data. The intersection of a row and column is called an *element*. An array's dimensions tell you how many columns it has. A one-dimensional array has only one column, whereas a three-dimensional array has three columns. LotusScript arrays can have up to eight dimensions.

In LotusScript, you can declare two types of arrays: static and dynamic. A *static* array is an array of fixed size that contains a fixed number of elements (they are fixed in size at compile time by the programmer, but the values can change at any time the program runs). You can't add or delete elements. A *dynamic* array can be resized at any time; you make it larger or smaller by adding or removing elements. Table 19.7 shows the LotusScript functions you can use to work with arrays.

Table 19.7 Array-Handling Functions

Statement or Function	Description
Dim	Declares a static array and initializes its elements. For a dynamic array, you initially declare it via Dim, but without any bounds, as in Dim dimArray() as Integer
Erase	Reinitializes each array element (for fixed arrays). Removes all elements from the array (for dynamic arrays).
IsArray	Returns True (given a variable name or expression) if the supplied expression is an array.
LBound	Returns the lower bound of the dimension of the array (given an array name and an optional dimension of the array).
Preserve	Enables you to resize a dynamic array while maintaining its current values.
ReDim	Declares a dynamic array and allocates storage for its elements or changes the size of an existing dynamic array.
UBound	Returns the upper bound of the dimension of the array (given an array name and an optional dimension of the array).

You declare a static array by using the Dim statement. You specify the following:

- The number of dimensions for the array
- The subscript bounds for each dimension
- The type of data to be stored

Dim allocates storage for the array and initializes each element of the array to a default value. Unless you specify otherwise, the first element of an array has an index of 0. If necessary, you can change this default to 1 by using the Option Base 1 statement. The following declarations specify static arrays:

```
Dim strPrinterNames(9) As String       'Declares a one dimensional
                                        'string array with 10 elements,
                                        'bounds are 0 to 9
Dim strQueueNames(19) As String * 32    'Declares a one dimensional
                                        'string array with 32 characters
                                        'allotted to 20 elements,
                                        'bounds are 0 to 19
```

```
Dim iRoutingMatrix(9, 9) As Integer      'Declare a two dimensional
                                         'integer array of 100 elements
Dim iPrintJobIDs(1 To 50) As Integer     'Declares a one dimensional
                                         'string array of 50 elements,
                                         'bounds are 1 to 50
```

You can also use `Dim` to declare dynamic arrays. When you declare a dynamic array using `Dim`, however, you specify only the type. You don't specify the number of elements in the array, and no storage is allocated for the array. Before you can use a dynamic array, you have to use the `ReDim` statement to allocate some storage for its elements. For example, the following code shows how to declare a dynamic array and then allocate some storage for it:

```
Dim iDatabases As Integer          ' Declare the number of elements to use
Dim strDatabaseNames() As String   ' Declare a dynamic array
iDatabases = 25                    ' Initialize the number of elements
ReDim strDatabaseNames(iDatabases) ' Allocate storage for this
                                   ' 26 integer element in this one
                                   ' dimensional array
```

You can also declare and initialize an array using `ReDim`. To declare an array containing six elements of type `Integer` and initialize each element to 0, for example, use the following:

```
Option Base 1          ' Specify that the first element of any
                       ' array has an index of 1

ReDim varWidgets(6) As Integer    ' Declare a dynamic one dimensional
                                  ' integer array with 6 elements
```

You can use `ReDim` to change the size of a dynamic array with the option of preserving the existing contents of the array or reinitializing all elements. Suppose that you have a dynamic array, `iCustomerIDs`, containing 50 elements. You need to increase its size to 100 elements while preserving its current contents. You can use the following code:

```
ReDim Preserve iCustomerIDs(99)
```

If you need to find the size of a dynamic array at runtime, you can use the `LBound` and `UBound` functions. You supply these functions with the name of an array, and (optionally) with the dimension for which you are seeking the bounds. `LBound` returns the lower bound of the specified array dimension, and `UBound` returns the upper bound. After resizing the `iCustomerIDs` array, for example, `LBound(iCustomerIDs)` is 0 and `UBound(iCustomerIDs)` is 99.

You use the `Erase` statement to delete all the elements in a dynamic array and free up the storage the array uses. With a static array, you use `Erase` to reinitialize each element.

19

You can assign an entire array to a variable of type `Variant`. Consequently, you might need to check whether a variable contains an array by using the `IsArray` function. If the variable or expression you supply to `IsArray` is an array, the function returns True, as shown in this example:

```
Dim varIcons As Variant
Dim lIconIDs(255) As Long
Print IsArray(varIcons)         'False
varIcons = lIconIDs
Print IsArray(varIcons)         'True
```

Employing Lists

A *list* is similar to an array because it contains a set of elements. It differs from an array in the way you identify and work with its elements. With arrays, you identify the element with which you are working by using an index. With lists, you identify elements using a list tag. A *list tag* is simply a string used to uniquely identify a particular element in the list (think of the name=value pairs in the Notes.ini file). Table 19.8 describes the LotusScript functions used with lists.

Table 19.8 LotusScript List-Handling Functions

Statement or Function	Description
Dim	Declares a list.
Erase	Removes all elements from a list (for lists). Or, removes the element from a list (for list elements).
ForAll	Loops through the elements of a list.
IsElement	Returns True if the string is a list tag for any element in the list (given the name of a list and a string).
IsList	Returns True if the supplied expression is a list (given a variable name or expression).
ListTag	Returns the name of the element in the list that is being processed. Can be used only inside a ForAll block.

You use `Dim` to declare an empty list, as in the following example:

```
Dim curAmountOutstanding List As Currency
```

When you declare a list, it has no elements and no storage is allocated for it. You add elements to the list by assigning new list tags. For example, you can create two new elements in the list, with list tags ABC and XYZ, by using the following code:

```
curAmountOutstanding("ABC") = 12.99
curAmountOutstanding("XYZ") = 52.00
```

You use the tag to refer to a list element in much the same way you use an index to refer to an array element. To add the two list elements you just created, for example, use the following command:

```
Dim curTotal As Currency
curTotal = curAmountOutstanding("ABC") + curAmountOutstanding("XYZ")
```

Use Erase to delete specific elements from the list or to delete all elements. For example,

```
Erase curAmountOutstanding("ABC")
```

removes the ABC element from the list, whereas

```
Erase curAmountOutstanding
```

erases all elements from the list.

If you need to check whether you have already added an element to a list, you can use the IsElement function. You supply the list tag for the element for which you are looking, and the function returns True if the tag belongs to an element in the list. Continuing this example, the following code returns True:

```
IsElement(curAmountOutstanding("XYZ"))
```

In a similar way, you can use IsList to check whether a variable is a list. For example, the following returns True:

```
IsList(curAmountOutstanding)
```

To process elements in an array, you typically use a loop to step through each index in the array. When using lists, the list tag is the only way to identify an element. So how do you loop through all elements in a list? Use a ForAll loop with the ListTag function. For example, the following code prints all the elements in your example list:

```
ForAll varElement In curAmountOutstanding
    Print ListTag(varElement); " owes ";  varElement
End ForAll
```

You need to note a few things about using ForAll. In the example, the variable varElement is known as a *reference variable*. A reference variable is a special kind of

19

variable used by LotusScript in processing ForAll loops. In the body of the loop, each element in the list is assigned to the reference variable. You never have to declare a reference variable; LotusScript takes care of that for you and declares all reference variables to be of type Variant. In fact, if you do declare a reference variable, you'll get an error when you try to compile your script.

Inside a ForAll loop, you can use the ListTag function to find the list tag that corresponds to the current element. ListTag works only inside a ForAll loop.

Using Classes

In order to represent a real world object in script, LotusScript uses classes. A *class* includes the data necessary to represent the object and the subprograms used to manipulate the data. A database is an object, and you use the NotesDatabase class to represent it in script. The NotesView class corresponds to views, and the NotesDocument class corresponds to documents. A complete list of the Domino classes is available in Appendix D, "Frequently Used HTML."

For each class there are properties. A *property* is the attribute of a class, a variable that defines the object. A database, for example, has a title. Therefore, one of the properties of the NotesDatabase class is Title.

The behavior or action of the class is a *method*. Because one database can replicate with another, for example, the NotesDatabase class has a Replicate method.

There are two types of classes that enable you to work with Notes objects: front-end, or user interface (UI), classes and back-end classes (see Figure 19.4). *Front-end classes* enable you to work with databases, views, and documents that are displayed in the active Notes window. For example, you can work with the document that is currently onscreen using the NotesUIDocument class. The methods and properties of the front-end classes enable you to work with views and documents in the same way a user can—typing text into fields, moving the cursor around, using the Clipboards, and refreshing views. The front-end classes represent the Notes workspace, the current document, the current view, and the current database. Only workstation users can run scripts that access UI objects.

Back-end classes represent the constituent parts of Notes—named databases, views, documents, fields, sessions, collections of documents, and so on. Both workstation and server users can run scripts that access database objects.

To access and manipulate an object, you first need to declare an *object reference variable*. Next, you associate the variable with the instance of a class. Then you can access the properties and methods of that class to manipulate the object.

FIGURE 19.4

Many objects have properties that are object references to other objects. The Notes Object Model illustrates the hierarchy of references.

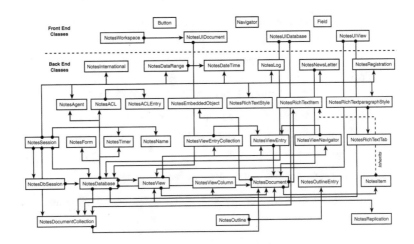

An object reference variable is not like other variables because it is associated with an object (instance of a class). Its data type is a class, but like any variable it names an area in memory storage. However, the value that is stored is not the object itself. The object and the data that compose it are stored in another area. What is stored in an object reference variable is a 4-byte pointer to the object data (called the *object reference*). LotusScript uses this pointer to access the object data. You bind the object reference to the object when you assign a value to the object reference variable.

You create an object reference with a DIM statement, in the following syntax:

```
Dim ObjectReferenceVariable As ClassName
```

For example, if you want to declare *x* as the object reference variable for the NotesDatabase class, you enter a statement in your script:

```
Dim x As NotesDatabase
```

The variable *x* is not a NotesDatabase object—it only points to an instance of the NotesDatabase class. Because the object doesn't exist yet, the variable is initialized to the value NOTHING.

You create objects using the NEW keyword. After declaring the object reference variable, you use a SET statement to create a new object and assign a reference to it. The argument list is optional, depending on the class.

```
Set ObjectReferenceVariable = NEW ClassName[(ArgumentList)]
```

19

For example, the following script declares the object reference variable *x* and then assigns the object reference *x* to the database `Clients`, which is located on the Sales server (to refer to a local database, use the empty string (`""`) in the server argument).

```
Dim x As NotesDatabase
Set x = NEW NotesDatabase("Sales", "Clients.nsf")
```

Now that you've associated the object reference with a class, you can access the properties and methods of that class. In writing script, you use the dot notation to refer to the members of classes.

```
ObjectReferenceVariable.MemberName[(ArgumentList)]
```

The following script declares an object reference variable and creates an instance of the `NotesDatabase` class. It then displays the title of the database in a dialog box.

```
Dim x As NotesDatabase
Set x = NEW NotesDatabase("Sales", "Clients.nsf")
Messagebox(x.title)
```

Because the `NotesUIWorkspace` class represents the current Notes workspace, you can use it to work with the document being displayed in the active window. The `NotesUIWorkspace` class has a property called `CurrentDocument`, which gives you access to the currently displayed document. After accessing the document, you can use the properties and methods of the `NotesUIDocument` class to work with it. For example, the following script uses the `GotoField` and `CreateObject` methods of the `NotesUIDocument` class to go to the rich text field called "Sheet" in the current document and create an Excel spreadsheet object from an existing file called Expenses.xls—all at the click of a button.

```
Sub Click(Source As Button)
        Dim uiWorkspace As New NotesUIWorkspace
        Dim uiDoc As NotesUIDocument
        Set uiDoc = uiWorkspace.CurrentDocument
        Call uiDoc.GotoField("Sheet")
        Call uiDoc.CreateObject("Expenses", "", "C:\Expenses.xls")
End Sub
```

It is critical that `"Expenses, "", "C:\Expenses.xls"` have `""` as the second argument, not a blank space.

Looping and Branching

LotusScript provides a variety of ways to control the flow of execution in a script. You can use loops to repeatedly execute a set of statements based on certain conditions being met. You can use branches to execute different parts of a script based on the results of comparisons or the value of variables.

For...Next Loops

You use the `For...Next` loop to execute a set of statements a specified number of times. You need to specify

- A control variable for the loop
- A start value for the variable
- An end value for the variable
- Optionally, a step value to add to the control variable after each execution of the loop (if you don't specify a value, the default is 1)

The first time the loop is executed, the control variable has the start value. After each execution of the loop, the control variable is updated by adding the step value to it. In the following example, the loop is executed five times, with `iCount` having the values 1, 3, 5, 7, and 9:

```
Dim iCount As Integer
For iCount = 1 to 10 Step 2
        ' Do something...
Next
```

ForAll Loops

You already had a sneak preview of the `ForAll` loop when you looked at using lists in LotusScript. However, you aren't restricted to using `ForAll` loops with lists. You can also use them with arrays and object collections. You can use a `ForAll` loop, for example, to loop through all elements in an array named `tCompanies`:

```
ForAll vElem In tCompanies
                ' Do something here
End Forall
```

Do...While Loops

`Do...While` loops repeatedly execute a block of statements while a specified condition is True. This type of loop is very handy when you need to process a nondiscrete number of items. Depending upon which construction is done, the control test is executed before the loop content is performed or after. If it evaluates to True, the block of statements within the loop is executed. If the condition evaluates to False, the loop is not executed and control passes to the next statement after the loop. The following loop, for example, executes three times and prints 17, 18, and 19:

```
Dim iCount As Integer
Dim iMax As Integer
iMax% = 20
iCount% = 17
```

19

```
Do While iCount% < iMax%
    Print iCount%
    iCount% = iCount% + 1
Loop
```

An alternative form of the Do...While loop tests the condition after the loop is executed, as shown here:

```
Dim iCount As Integer
Dim iMax As Integer
iMax% = 20
iCount% = 17
Do
    Print iCount%
    iCount% = iCount% + 1
Loop While iCount% < iMax%
```

The main difference between the two loops is that you can guarantee that the second loop is always executed at least once.

Do...Until Loops

A closely related type of loop is the Do...Until loop. With this kind of loop, the set of statements in the loop is executed until the loop condition evaluates to True. For example, if you change the first of the Do...While loops to a Do...Until loop, the statements inside this loop are never executed because the condition iCount% < iMax% is True before the loop is entered. Consider the following example:

```
Dim iCount As Integer
Dim iMax As Integer
iMax% = 20
iCount% = 17
Do Until iCount% < iMax%
    Print iCount%
    iCount% = iCount% + 1
Loop
```

The Do...Until loop also has an alternative form that checks the condition at the end of the loop:

```
Dim iCount As Integer
Dim iMax As Integer
iMax% = 20
iCount% = 17
Do
    Print iCount%
    iCount% = iCount% + 1
Loop Until iCount% < iMax%
```

This loop is executed only once and prints 17.

If...Then...Else Branches

You can use If...Then...Else statements to select which statements are executed based on a condition you specify. If the condition is True, one set of statements is executed; if the condition is False, a different set is executed, as demonstrated by this example:

```
If iCount% > iMax% Then
    Print "Too many items!"
Else
    Print "Processing "; iCount%; " item(s) . . ."
End If
```

You can omit the Else part of the statement if you only want to execute a set of statements when a condition is True, as shown in this example:

```
If iDaysOverdue% > 14 Then
    Print "Time to send a nastygram!"
End If
```

You can use the ElseIf statement with If to test multiple conditions, as shown in this example:

```
If iDaysOverdue% <= 7 Then
    Print "Time to send a reminder note!"
ElseIF iDaysOverDue% <=14 Then
    Print "Time to send a nastygram!"
ElseIF iDaysOverDue%<=21 Then
    Print "Time to put a lien on their property"
Else
    Print "Time to send Vito to break some kneecaps!"
End If
```

Select...Case Branches

Using the Select...Case statement is similar to using the ElseIf statement with If. It enables you to select a block of statements to execute based on the value of an expression. The primary difference between Select...Case and If/ElseIf is that Select...Case is faster and easier to code (and requires less typing!) because after a True condition is found, execution continues at the next line of code after the End Select statement. Consider the following example:

```
Select Case iBoxesOrdered%
    Case Is <= 0
        Call ProcessInvalidOrder(iBoxesOrdered%)
    Case 1
        Call ProcessSmallOrder(iBoxesOrdered%)
    Case 2 To 15
        Call ProcessMediumOrder(iBoxesOrdered%)
    Case 16 To 31
        Call ProcessLargeOrder(iBoxesOrdered%)
```

19

```
    Case Else
          Call ProcessHugeOrder(iBoxesOrdered%)
End Select
```

GoSub and On...GoSub

Within a sub or function, you can use GoSub and On...GoSub to branch to a specific label within the procedure. A *label* is simply a way of identifying a place in your code. The code at the label can execute a Return statement to branch back to the statement following the GoSub. The following code, for example, branches to the label lblLogError if the order quantity is negative:

```
Sub ProcessInvalidOrder(iOrderQuantity As Integer)
If iOrderQuantity% < 0 Then
    GoSub lblLogError
End If

Exit Sub

lblLogError:
Call LogError
Return
End Sub
```

You can use On...GoSub to branch to one of a number of labels based on a supplied value—for example, when the following statement is executed:

```
On iErrorNumber% GoSub lblA, lblB, lblC
```

If iErrorNumber% is 1, the program branches to lblA; if iErrorNumber% is 2, the program branches to lblB; and if iErrorNumber% is 3, the program branches to lblC. If iErrorNumber% is 0 or greater than 3, the On...GoSub statement is ignored.

GoTo and On...GoTo

GoTo and On...GoTo are similar to GoSub and On...GoSub because they enable you to branch to specific labels. However, GoTo statements are one-way branches. You cannot use a Return statement to return control back to the statement after the GoTo.

Note

It's generally frowned upon and considered bad form to use GoTo because it leads to fairly unstructured code that can be very difficult to follow and debug. The only exception is error-trapping routines because using On Error Goto is the only way to programmatically handle runtime errors.

Using Functions and Subroutines

In LotusScript, you can define functions and subroutines (*subs*) that you can call from within a script to perform specific functions. You can define a function to convert a date with a two-digit year into a date with a four-digit year, for example, and keep your boss happy well into the next century! The main difference between a function and a sub is that a *function* returns a value and a *sub* does not.

Declaring Functions and Subs

You declare a function by using the `Function` keyword:

```
Function fIsWeekend(iDay As Integer) As Integer
```

You give it a name and then define the list of arguments you are going to pass to it; finally, you define the type of value it is going to return. To set the return value, assign a value to the function name, as shown in the following example:

```
Function fIsWeekend(varDate As Variant) As Integer
If Weekday(varDate) = 1 Or Weekday(varDate) = 7 Then
    fIsWeekend = True
Else
    fIsWeekend = False
End If
End Function
```

You define subs in much the same way by using the `Sub` keyword. The only thing to remember is that you can't return a value from a sub, so you don't have to declare a return type. A typical sub declaration follows:

```
Sub GoToBeach(tResort As String, iMilesToResort As Integer)
```

To create a new sub, simply open any event that can be coded with LotusScript and begin typing in the new sub header. After you press Enter upon completion of the header, a new sub is added (as is an `End Sub` statement), and you're ready to code your sub. Functions work exactly the same way.

Calling Functions and Subs

To access the code you have written in a sub or function, you must *call* it. After a sub or function is called, program execution is transferred to the called routine. When the routine finishes, control is transferred back to the calling program, and execution continues at that point. To call a function, use it in a condition statement such as `if(fIsWeekend)`

19

then or in a select `case(fIsWeekend)` statement, or simply assign it to a variable, as in the following example:

```
Dim fGoToWork As Integer
Dim varToday As Variant
 ' Use the built in function Today to get today's date
varToday = Today
 ' Use the fIsWeekend function
fGoToWork = fIsWeekend(varToday)
```

To call a sub, you can use any of the following methods:

```
Call SubName(Arg1, Arg2 ...)
```

or

```
Call SubName arg1, arg2
```

or

```
SubName(Arg1, Arg2 ...)
```

The following example uses one of these methods:

```
If fIsWeekend(varToday) Then
    Call GoToBeach("Maui", 4000)
End If
```

When you pass values to subs and functions, you need to be aware of two ways in which LotusScript can pass arguments:

- **By reference**—LotusScript passes a reference to the argument. The function works with the argument. Any changes the function makes to the argument are reflected in the original. This is the default in all cases.

- **By value**—LotusScript passes a copy of the argument to the function. The function works with the copy. Any changes to the copy do not affect the original.

Some arguments—such as arrays, lists, and objects—are always passed by reference. With other arguments, you have a choice. If you always want an argument to be passed by value, use the `ByVal` keyword when you declare that argument in the function or sub declaration. In the following example, the second argument is always passed by value:

```
Sub DeleteDocument(iDocNumber As Integer, ByVal tDocTitle As String)
```

Script Libraries

To store code segments from scriptable objects that you want to use again within the application, you can create a script library. In a library, you can code options, declarations, an initialize subroutine, a terminate subroutine, and user scripts.

When you want to create a new script library, choose **Script Libraries** under Resources in the Design Pane and then click the **New Script Library** action button. Choose **[Options]**, **[Declarations]**, **Initialize**, or **Terminate** in the Object Pane and write your script in the Programmer's Pane. Then you need to save the script and give it a name.

The script library becomes one of the shared resources in the application. When you want to incorporate the code from the library into another script you are writing in that database, begin the module with a Use statement. The Use statement must appear before all implicit declarations within the module because LotusScript executes the Use statement before initializing the module and executing the module's Initialize sub (if one exists). The syntax of the Use statement is

```
Use useScript
```

where useScript is a String literal or constant that specifies the module to load. For example, you created a script library called "Declarations" that contains all the public declarations you want to use in most modules of the database. In designing a form, you decide to include that script in the global declarations for the form. The first line of your global declarations should be

```
Use "Declarations"
```

The script library saves you steps because you don't have to keep entering the same declarations in each script module you create.

19

Debugging Scripts

When you are trying to diagnose problems and need to examine the execution of your scripts, use the LotusScript debugger. Choose **File, Tools, Debug LotusScript** from the menu to enable the debugger (the same commands disable the debugger). Then run the application. When a script executes, the execution pauses at the first line of script and the Script Debugger opens (see Figure 19.5).

The debugger enables you to step through a script one line at a time, set breakpoints in the script so that the script temporarily stops executing at each breakpoint, and examine and modify the value of variables and properties.

Object box shows object   Line about to   Event box shows event
containing the script   be executed   containing the script

FIGURE 19.5

*The arrow points to the
line in the script where
the execution is
paused.*

Debug pane shows
script being debugged

Calls box displays a
list of subprograms
currently on the
execution stacks

Utilities pane

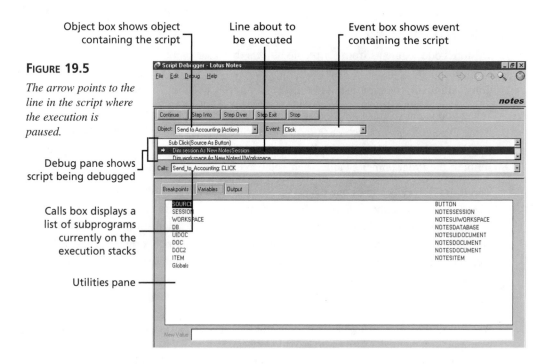

You control how the debugger steps through a script using the buttons at the top of the
screen:

- **Continue**—Continues execution of the script until you reach a breakpoint or the
  end of the script.
- **Step Into**—Executes the current statement and stops at the next one. If the current
  statement is a sub or function call, the debugger stops at the first executable statement in the sub or function.
- **Step Over**—Executes the current statement. If the current statement is a call to a
  sub or function, the debugger executes the sub or function and stops at the first
  statement immediately after the call. If the statement is not a sub or function call,
  the debugger executes the statement and stops at the next statement.
- **Step Exit**—Continues execution of the current sub or function until the end of the
  sub or function is reached, and then stops at the statement immediately following
  the one that called the sub or function.
- **Stop**—Stops executing the script.

Breakpoints are a way of interrupting the execution of a script at a specific line. When
the script has been interrupted, you can examine the current value of variables and

properties. To set a breakpoint, double-click in the debug pane the line that you want to be a breakpoint. A red stop sign appears to the left of the line. When you click on the Breakpoints tab (if that's not already the active tab), a list of breakpoints you've set appears in the utilities pane. Double-click the line containing the breakpoint to temporarily disable the breakpoint; double-click again to clear the breakpoint.

Click on the Variables tab to see all the defined variables, their current values, and their data types. Twisties are shown next to variables that represent objects or complex data structures. You use the twisties to expand a variable, showing its properties or component values. To change the value of a variable, type the new value in the New Value field.

If you used any Print statements in your script, click the Output tab to display the output from those statements. Putting Print statements into your script is a good way to test a script.

Summary

LotusScript gives you added flexibility in developing your application because you can program functionality that is not available with just the formula language. LotusScript can also deal with conditional loops that are too complex for formulas.

As with any programming language, syntax is important. The language elements that LotusScript uses to construct statements in scripts are identifiers, keywords, literals and constants, and operators. In the script statements you must declare variables and constants. Specify the data type of variables as Integer, Long, Single, Double, Currency, or String. Except for String, which is text data, the data types are numbers. After declaring variables, the data can be assigned to the variable at any time in the script. Data can also be stored in arrays, with many values assigned a single variable with a subscript to note the position of the data within the array.

Because LotusScript is an object-oriented language, you can access objects in Notes through classes, using the class properties and methods to manipulate the objects. You first need to declare an object reference variable. You create objects using the NEW keyword. After declaring the object reference variable, you use a SET statement to create a new object and assign a reference to it. By using a property or method of that class, you can access data or manipulate objects.

When you save your scripts, they are double-compiled. Any errors are immediately brought to your attention through color coding and error messages, so you can correct them and compile the script again. To spot more complex problems, use the LotusScript debugger.

19

Q&A

Q LotusScript has a set of data types you can use, but is it possible to define my own data type?

A Yes. LotusScript allows user-defined types. You define the new type using a Type statement. You give the new type a name and define one or more member variables for the type. A member variable is any variable included in a user-defined type. The following is an example of a new type with four member variables:

```
Type Customer
    lCustID As Long
    strCustFirstName As String
    strCustSurname As String
    curBalance as Currency
End Type
```

You can then declare variables as being the new type:

```
Dim custNew As Customer
```

To set the first name field to "Lucy", use

```
custNew.strCustFirstName = "Lucy"
```

Q You must use formulas to set the values that appear in columns in a view, but can you extract the values in columns using LotusScript?

A You can check the position of a column (make sure you add 1 to the array index to get the correct number because LotusScript arrays start at 0 and column numbering starts at 1) using the `NotesViewColumn` class Position property. The Title property returns the column title, and the `IsHidden` property enables you to check whether a column is hidden or not. You can also check whether a column is sorted or categorized by using the `IsSorted` and `IsCategory` properties. To get to the contents of the column for a document, use the `ColumnValues` property of `NotesDocument`.

Q How do I incorporate an existing spreadsheet object into a form using LotusScript?

A To open an existing object, use GetObject. You supply the path to the file containing the object, and LotusScript finds and opens the object. The following script opens a WordPro object:

```
Dim objDoc As Variant
Set objDoc = GetObject(C:\MyDocuments\Expenses.LWP")
```

Workshop

Because today's lesson is a simple introduction to LotusScript, our workshop is a simple and small LotusScript task. For more detailed information on how to use LotusScript, check out *Lotus Notes and Domino R5 Development Unleashed* by Debbie Lynd and Steve Kern and *Special Edition Using Lotus Notes and Domino 5* by Randy Tamura, et al.

For this task you need to open the Titles in Development database in Designer. If you haven't been building this database as you worked through the workshops, open the Day17 folder on the CD and then open TDDay17.nsf.

You are going to add a button to the form that asks the users how many chapters they expect the book to have, and then asks the total number of pages expected for the book. Based on that input a dialog box appears, displaying a message that displays the average size of a chapter.

Open the New Title form. Next to the ChapPg field, create a hotspot button called Chapter Count. In the Programmer's Pane, select **LotusScript** from the Run drop-down list. Select the **Click** event in the Objects list.

Enter the following in the Script Area:

```
Sub Click(Source As Button)
      Dim TotalChap As Single
      Dim TotalPg As Single
      Dim ChapCount As Single
      TotalChap = Inputbox("Enter the number of chapters expected")
      TotalPg = Inputbox("Total number of pages expected")
      ChapCount = TotalPg/TotalChap
      Messagebox("The average size of a chapter is " & ChapCount & " pages")
End Sub
```

To see how this works in our sample database, open the TDDay19.nsf database in the Day19 folder on the CD.

19

DAY **20**

The Last Minute Details: Outlines, Icons, Help

As your application pulls together, it's time to create elements such as the final outline (which can act as your site map), the icon for the database bookmark, any help pages you want to create to instruct users, and the About This Database and Using This Database documents.

Use Outlines

Navigation in an application usually begins at the Navigation Pane, which displays the standard Folders and Views navigator. The navigator and imagemap design elements (see Day 12, "Beautify Your Application"), which use graphic images with hotspots that link to important URLs, databases, views or documents, make navigation in your application easier, especially for Web browsers.

The *outline* is another design element that makes a great navigation tool. It combines the ease of use of a navigator with a flexible design that consists of jumps to views and folders in the database plus actions and links to other elements such as Web pages. An outline provides navigation through your entire application or site, or through only part of it (see Figure 20.1).

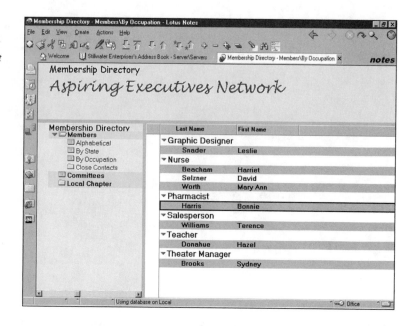

FIGURE 20.1

The outline in the left frame of this frameset is embedded in the home page.

From a designer's standpoint, outlines are easy to create and can be used to help plan an application as well as to navigate through existing elements. In planning, the outline becomes the skeleton of the application, with each outline entry representing a different design element or component.

After you create the outline, you embed it on a page or form to display it. By clicking on one of the entries, the users can jump to wherever they want to go.

Create an Outline

There are two approaches to creating outlines: Start from scratch or generate a default outline.

You start from scratch when you want to use the outline as a planning tool for your application. Add entries for each element you want in your navigation structure, whether you plan to use it as a navigator for Notes clients or a site map for a Web application. Include entries for jumps to pages, documents, views, folders, Web pages, or Domino databases. Other outline entries might be clickable actions. You might want some entries to act as categories for the entries below them. For a complex application, you might even create multiple outlines—one for each segment of the application.

Use the following steps to create an outline from scratch:

1. Select **Outlines** in the Design Pane.

2. Click the **New Outline** button on the Action Bar.

3. Choose **Design, Outline Properties** from the menu to open the Outline Properties box (see Figure 20.2).

FIGURE 20.2

Create a name for the outline, but also give it an alias for use in formulas and scripts.

4. Enter a Name for the outline and an Alias. Select **Available to Public Access Users** if you want users with No Access or Depositor access to be able to see the outline.

5. Add the outline entries (see instructions later in this section).

6. Click **Save Outline** on the Action Bar.

If you've already created some of your design elements or if your database was created from a template, a better approach might be to generate a default outline and then customize it. Generating the default outline creates entries automatically for all the folders and views in the database, including placeholders called *Other Folders*, *Other Views*, *Other Private Folders*, and *Other Private Views* (see Figure 20.3). To create a default outline, click **Generate Default Outline**.

Add Outline Entries

Whether you create your outline from scratch or generate a default outline, you need to add entries for all the elements you want to include in the navigation structure.

Use the following steps to add an outline entry:

1. Click the **New Entry** button on the Action Bar. The Outline Entry Properties box appears.

2. Enter the Label you want to appear in the outline. The Alias is recommended, but optional.

3. In Content, select the Type of element (see Figure 20.4). For an element that doesn't exist yet, a prompt shows to tell you that you need to create the element later.

20

FIGURE 20.3

The outline for this database was created using the Generate Default Outline method.

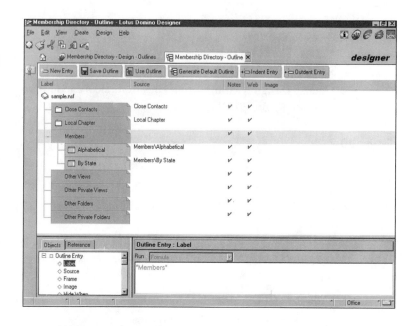

FIGURE 20.4

You can make Outline entries for elements that don't exist in the database. It helps you plan the elements you need to create. A warning will appear, however, telling you that it will have to be created later. Just make sure you remember to do it.

URL—Enter the entire URL, such as http://www.mcp.com. When users click this entry, it jumps them to the specified Web page.

Link—Use for database, view, document, or anchor links. Copy the link to the Clipboard. Then, in the Outline Entry Properties box, click the **Paste** button to paste the reference into the Value box. When users click this entry, it jumps them to the linked database, view, or document.

Named Element—Specify a page, form, frameset, folder, navigator, or view.

Enter the name of the element in the Value box, or click the **Folder** button to locate and select the element. Click the @ button to specify the Value based on a formula. The **Paste** button pastes an element you cut or copied to the Clipboard. When users click this entry, it jumps them to the specified element.

Action—Click the @ button and enter a formula for the action, such as @Command([Compose]; "CustInfo"), to create a Customer Information document. When users click the entry, Notes performs the action. In the sample case, a new Customer Information form opens.

(None)—Use to create a top-level entry, or category, for nesting entries.

4. (Optional) Enter the target frame for the jump or action. If the frameset hasn't been created yet, enter the name you plan to use or add this entry after you create the frameset.

5. (Optional) Select an image for the entry. Click the **Folder** icon to select a shared image resource; click the @ button to write a formula that controls which image displays. The graphics for entries need to be small, such as small icons or bullets. Check **Do not display an image** if you don't want to display a graphic on the outline entry.

6. Save the outline.

Reorder, Categorize, and Delete Entries

The default outline orders the entries based on the Folders and Views navigator, and you might need to change the order so it is the same order the user sees. Select one or more entries in the Design Pane and drag the selected entry (or entries) to a new position up or down the list.

The entries can be set in a hierarchy, with categories (top-level entries) and sublevel entries under them. To turn an entry into a sublevel entry, indent it by selecting the entry and clicking the **Indent Entry** button or pressing Tab. Pressing Shift+Tab or clicking the **Outdent Entry** button converts a selected sublevel entry to a top-level entry.

To remove an entry from the outline, select the entry and then press Delete or choose **Edit, Clear** from the menu.

20

Tip

To have an entry display only under special circumstances, click the **Hide** tab in the Outline Entry Properties box and select options for hiding the entry, or write a hide-when formula (see Day 9, "Forms on Steroids: Increase Form Performance," for more information on hiding objects).

Embed the Outline

Before the outline can be used as a navigation device, it must be embedded in a page, in a form, or in the rich text field of a document. Embed the outline on a page so it can be included in a frameset or part of the home page. When embedded on a form, each document created with the form displays the outline so users can navigate to other parts of the application. Embedding the outline in the rich text field of a document enables other users to find related elements from that document.

To embed the outline, open the page, form, or document and place your cursor where you want the outline to appear (in a document, it must be in a rich text field). Choose **Create, Embedded Element, Outline** from the menu. Select the outline to embed and click **OK** (see Figure 20.5).

FIGURE 20.5

Choose the outline to embed from a list of saved outlines.

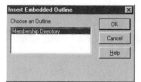

To create a page and embed the outline at the same time, open the outline you want to embed and click **Use Outline** on the Action Bar. The outline appears on the page. Save the page and give it a name.

Format the Embedded Outline

The formatting you apply to an embedded outline controls how the embedded outline displays in the page or document. In the page or form, select the embedded outline and choose **Element, Outline Properties** to display the Embedded Outline Properties box (see Figure 20.6).

On the Info tab, select one of two Type styles: **Tree Style** displays the outline in a hierarchical format and all the entries show. Where top-level entries exist with related sublevel entries, choose whether you want to see twisties. **Flat Style** only shows the top-level entries in the Outline until the user clicks on one that has sublevel entries. If a top-level entry doesn't have sublevel entries, clicking it jumps to the link or performs the action assigned to it. With Flat Style, however, you have the option of displaying the outline horizontally.

Paragraph Hide-When tab
Paragraph Margins tab
Paragraph Alignment tab
Layout tab
Background tab
Font tab
Info tab

FIGURE 20.6

You set the basic style of the embedded outline by choosing Flat Style or Tree Style as the Type. The embedded outline in this form is the Tree Style.

Embedded outline

Embedded Outline Properties box

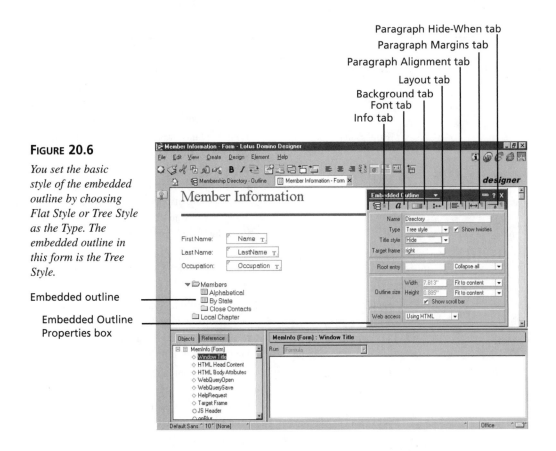

If you selected the Flat Style, we recommend you choose the **Simple** Title Style. This enables users to navigate back up to prior levels by displaying the parent of the current level. The other option for Title Style is **Hide**, which not only doesn't display the hierarchy but also doesn't provide a way for users to navigate back up the hierarchy after they've gone down a level.

Table 20.1 lists some additional formatting choices available for embedded outlines that you might find helpful.

20

Table 20.1   Other Useful Embedded Outline Entry Properties

Tab	Property	Description
Info	Target Frame	Enter the name for the frame where the results of the link or the named element appear. If the frameset hasn't been designed yet, enter the name you plan to assign to that frame.
	Root Entry	Enter the alias of an entry to show only the children of the specified entry initially. When users click on one of the children, the children of that entry appear. If an entry has no children, nothing displays in the outline. Specify whether you want to show the Root Entry and its children collapsed or expanded.
		Unless you specify a Simple Title Style, users cannot navigate back up the hierarchy to the root entry.
	Outline Size	Specify the Width and Height of the embedded outline and whether you want a scroll bar to appear if the size you set doesn't display all the contents.
Font	Component name	Select Top-level or Sub-level to indicate to which type of entry the font choices apply. If the Title Style is Simple, you can also select Title Font.
	Normal	Select the normal color for the text.
	Selected	Select the color of the text when it's selected.
	Moused	Select the text color when the mouse passes over the entry.
Background	Component name	Select the component of the embedded outline to which the background options apply: Control Background, Title Background, Top-Level Background, or Sub-Level Background.
	Background Color	Only a Normal color choice is available for the Control background. The Title Background has both Normal and the Moused color (when the mouse passes over the entry) available. Top-Level Background and Sub-Level Background both have Normal, Selected (when the item is selected) and Moused choices.

Tab	Property	Description
	Background Image	Click the Folder icon to select a shared image resource to use as a background or click the @ button to write a formula to control the background. If the image is smaller than the area of the section, choose how you want the image to Repeat within the area.
Layout	Component name	Select the component of the embedded outline to which the layout options apply.
	Entry	Set the Height of the section in relation to the entry and the Offset from the edge of the entry.
	Entry Label	Sets the position of the label within the entry and the Offset from the edge.
	Outline Entry Image	Sets the position and Offset of the image in the entry (not available for Title Layout).

Create Database Help

Your users have access to Notes 5 Help for instructions on using the Notes client, but you also need to provide assistance on how each custom database works and what you expect the user to do in certain situations.

There are two specialized documents that are designed to provide general help for a database: the About This Database document and the Using This Database document. You can also create context-sensitive help documents that open when a user presses F1. Adding field help tells your user how to complete the fields in documents (see Day 3, "Take a Field Trip: Add Fields").

About This Database

Unless you specified otherwise, the About This Database document appears by default the first time a user opens a database (see Figure 20.7). It also appears when a user looks up the database in the Database Catalog. Whenever users choose **File, Database, Open** to open a database, they can click **About** to see the About This Database document for the selected database. Users can also view this document if they choose **Help, About This Database** from the menu.

20

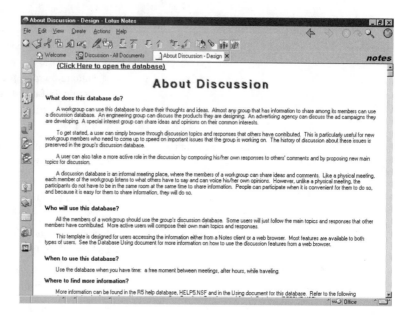

FIGURE 20.7

When you base your database on a template, such as in the discussion database pictured here, the About This Database might be prepared for you already. This particular document is a good model for what you need to put on your own About This Database document.

The About This Database document describes the purpose of the database. It should also explain who is to use the database and why. There need to be some general guidelines for the use of the database. Lotus also suggests that you include the name of the database manager and that person's telephone number. However, in many cases using the name of an actual person can be a problem if that person leaves or is assigned other job duties. Therefore, instructions on how to reach a help desk or what to do in case of questions is probably a better idea.

If there are any requirements for using the database, such as a network connection, those requirements need to also appear in the About This Database document.

Use the following steps to create the About This Database document:

1. Open the database in Designer.
2. Expand **Resources** in the Design Pane.
3. Select Other.
4. Double-click **"About Database" Document** to open it.
5. Add the text or other elements to the document.
6. Close and save the document.

The About This Database document is like a page. You can add text (or edit existing text), links, buttons, hotspots, and attachments. The text can be formatted. However, you cannot use fields in this document. You can embed elements.

You control whether the About This Database document displays when the database opens. Open the Database Properties box and select **Show "About Database" document when database is opened for the first time** (see Figure 20.8). **Open "About Database" document** is also a launch option when the database is opened in the Notes client, as well as when the database is opened in a browser. In R4 Web applications, you might even see the About This Database document used as the home page for the database.

FIGURE 20.8

On the Launch tab of the Database Properties box, you have the option to open the About This Database when the database is opened the first time or whenever the About This Database document changes. Opening the document whenever the database is launched is also an option in the When opened in the Notes client drop-down list. If selected, the check-box options disappear, as they do when Open designated Navigator in its own window, Launch first attachment in "About database", or Launch first doclink in "About database" options are selected.

20

Using This Database

The Using This Database document is meant to supply help information to the user (users access this document by choosing **Help, Using This Database** from the menu). In this document (see Figure 20.9), include a brief description of the database, how it works, and what it is intended to do. Explain what each form is and how it is to be used, and do the same for the views and any shared folders. You might even want to provide instructions for filling out each form.

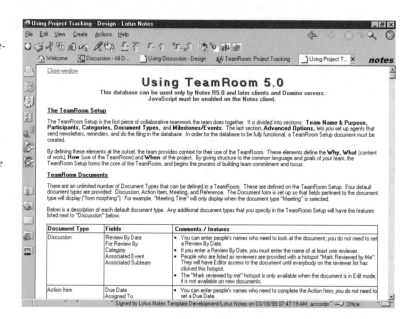

If this application follows a work process, make it clear what the process is and what steps the user is to follow—and in what order.

Each agent needs to be described and its purpose explained, along with instructions on when to run the agent.

Use the following steps to create the Using This Database document:

1. Open the database in Designer.

2. Expand **Resources** in the Design Pane.

3. Select Other.

4. Double-click **"Using Database" Document** to open it.

5. You can add text (or edit existing text), links, buttons, hotspots, and attachments to the document. The text can be formatted.

6. Save and close the document.

Context-Sensitive Help

In complex applications, it's a good idea to provide help documents in the database (or in a separate help database). These documents provide the detailed documentation needed to complete steps, fill in forms, and so on. You don't need to provide documents for basic Notes functions—those are in the Notes 5 Help database. After you have the documents in place, you create the necessary formulas to link to the correct document when the user presses F1 (don't worry, your help documents won't interfere with help in dialog and property boxes).

One way to create your help documents is to start with a form called "Help" to which you add any appropriate fields, such as the title of the help document and a rich text body field. Put *Help* in the Window title, too. Save the form. Then use the form to create the documents you need. After you're finished with the documentation, open the form again and make sure it's no longer included in the menu (you don't want users creating help documents) by deselecting **Include in Menu** in Form Properties.

You also need to create a help view. In that view, the first column needs to contain the title or subject of the help document. That column must be sorted.

A help document can be associated with each page, form, subform, view, or folder in an application by including a formula for the HelpRequest event. Then use the @Command([OpenHelpDocument]) function to open the appropriate help document (see Figure 20.10). For Web users, create an action button that uses the function—this might not be a bad idea for Notes clients, as well.

FIGURE 20.10

A formula for the HelpRequest event refers the user to the "Add Client" help document in the "Help" view of the current database.

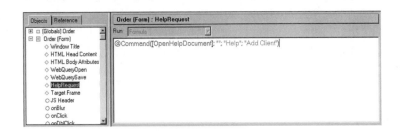

20

The syntax for the function is

```
@Command([OpenHelpDocument]; server : database; viewname; key)
```

> **server**—The name of the server where the database resides
>
> **database**—The path and filename of the database you want to open
>
> **viewname**—The name of the view that contains the help documents
>
> **key**—A text value that appears in the first sorted column of the help document view, such as the name of the help document

To access documents in the Notes 5 Help database, use the following syntax:

```
@Command([OpenHelpDocument]; [ClientHelp]; viewname; key)
```

> **Tip**
>
> When working with Web applications, you might want to use pages instead of documents (although either works). In that case, use the @Command([OpenPage]) function to open the appropriate page.

Where you anticipate that there will be different needs in different situations, you might include the @Command([OpenHelpDocument]) function in an @If formula, such as

```
@If(@IsDocBeingEdited; @Command([OpenHelpDocument]; ""; "Help";
"Data Entry"); @Command([OpenHelpDocument]; ""; "Help";
"Client Information")
```

Use this for situations in which it might be helpful to have users select from several help documents. Use a dialog box to present the choices.

Another idea is to place the help text on the form or page and hide it. Have the RequestHelp formula make the text available. Or, when you need users to choose from a list of help documents, put that list in a hidden field that becomes available when help is requested.

Note

> If you decide to create a separate database for your help documentation, use the @Command([OpenHelpDocument]) function to open its documents from the application. The advantage of using a help database is that you can have the help documents appear in a separate window for the users. The database must be stored in the Domino data directory (you can store it locally if you're developing locally, but it must be moved to the server when the application is). To have the database listed in the Database Catalog, open the Database Properties box for your help database, click the **Design** tab, and select **List in Database Catalog** (enter **NotesHelp** as the category for the database).

Design a Database Icon

The *database icon* is the small picture that appears next to the name of the database in the bookmarks. It helps users quickly identify a database. Generally, the icon reflects the purpose of the database, such as the open book used for Address Books.

Where do you get the icon pictures? You can copy an icon from another database, copy a bitmap from a graphics program, or draw one in Designer. Just be sure not to infringe on any trademarks or copyrights.

Create a New Icon

The Designer does have some limited facilities to create or change an icon. For a simple icon, these facilities can be enough to do the job.

Use the following steps to create the icon from scratch:

1. Open the database in Designer.

2. In the Design Pane, expand **Resources** and select **Other**.

3. Double-click **Icon** to open the Design Icon dialog box (see Figure 20.11).

4. (Optional) Click **Clear** to remove an icon if one is already in the drawing area. If you don't clear the drawing area, you can modify the current icon.

5. Use the drawing tools on the left to create the icon, pixel by pixel.

6. Click **OK**.

20

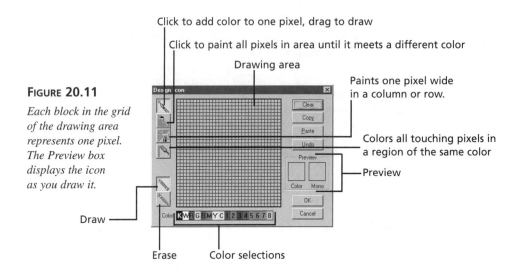

Click to add color to one pixel, drag to draw

Click to paint all pixels in area until it meets a different color

Drawing area

Paints one pixel wide in a column or row.

FIGURE 20.11

Each block in the grid of the drawing area represents one pixel. The Preview box displays the icon as you draw it.

Colors all touching pixels in a region of the same color

Preview

Draw

Erase   Color selections

Copy a Bitmap from a Graphics Program

For a unique icon, either draw the icon in a graphics program or use the program's clipart. The picture must be a bitmap (usually in .bmp, .gif, or .jpg format). It doesn't matter if the picture is in color or black and white. However, the picture you want to copy must be only 1/2 inch square (32× 32 pixels). You either have to draw it in that size or reduce it to that size in the graphics program because there are no facilities in Designer for making a bitmap smaller. Designer simply cuts off any part of the picture that extends beyond the specified size.

Use the following steps to copy a bitmap from a graphics program:

1. In the graphics program, select the icon picture and choose **Edit, Copy**.
2. In Designer, open the database into which you want to paste the icon.
3. From the Design Pane, expand **Resources** and select **Other**.
4. Double-click **Icon** to open the Design Icon dialog box.
5. Click **Paste**.
6. Click **OK**.

Copy an Icon from Another Database

As long as you can find an icon that suggests the database purpose (usually from a similar type of database), it makes sense to copy that icon and then paste it into the database. It's already the right size and close at hand. You won't have to do any drawing, either.

Use the following steps to copy another database's icon:

1. In Designer, open the database from which you want to copy the icon.
2. From the Design Pane, expand **Resources** and select **Other**.
3. Double-click **Icon**.
4. Click **Copy** and then close the Design Icon dialog box.
5. Open the database into which you want to paste the icon.
6. From the Design Pane, expand **Resources** and select **Other**.
7. Double-click **Icon** to open the Design Icon dialog box.
8. Click **Paste**.
9. Click **OK**.

Summary

Outlines provide a navigation method for your application, pointing to different segments of the application or to the total application. Entries in the outline can be links to views, documents, and databases, as well as open Web pages or any named element in a database. You can even add actions to the entries to perform @Commands. When embedded on a page, the outline can be incorporated into a frameset.

Providing your users with help on how the application works can be done with the About This Database and Using This Database documents. For context-sensitive help, create documents or pages with help information. Then write a formula for the HelpRequest event of pages, forms, views, and other elements that uses the @Command[OpenHelpDocument]) or @Command([OpenPage]) functions.

For quick identification of the database in the bookmarks, create or copy a database icon. When you copy the icon, use an icon from another database or a picture from a graphics program. To use a picture, keep it small (1/2-inch square) and use a bitmap. Copy the picture or icon to the Clipboard and paste it into the Design Icon dialog box. If you want to create your own icon, draw it in the Design Icon dialog box with the tools provided.

20

Q&A

Q I embedded an outline in my home page, but in my frameset it comes up empty in a preview with a browser. What's the trouble?

A On the Embedded Outline Properties box Info page, try selecting **Using Java Applet** instead of **Using HTML** for Web access. In User Preferences, make sure you select **Enable Java Applets** in the Additional Options so the Java applets work on your workstation.

Q **I changed the database icon for an existing database, but it didn't change on the other servers.**

A Icon changes don't replicate, and icons aren't affected by replacing or refreshing the design unless you modify the design document properties. You'll have to copy the icon to each database.

Q **What's the advantage of using a help form and documents over using pages for your help? It seems like more trouble, with having to create a view and all.**

A By using a form you can keep the look of the help documents consistent. Also, the help view is available to users, so they can look up items even if they don't need help on a particular page. However, in a Web application, having the view might not be that helpful. Pages are probably a better idea. For a mixed application, stick to the documents. Just remember to include action buttons that open the help documents for Web users or use the onHelp JavaScript event for IE browsers. You program the message, and when a user presses F1 the form/page help comes up, and then the overall system help displays.

Workshop

In this workshop you'll be putting some final touches on the Completed Titles database and adding help documentation to Proposed Titles and Titles in Development. If you haven't been building these databases all along, use the Proposed Titles database (PTDay15.nsf) in the Day15 folder on the CD, the Titles in Development (TDDay19.nsf) in the Day19 folder, and the Completed Titles (CTDay18.nsf) in the Day18 folder.

The Completed Titles database needs an outline, which you will embed on a home page, and a frameset that will appear when the database launches on a Web browser. All three databases need About This Database and Using This Database documents. Plus, in the Proposed Titles database, you'll add online help. All three databases also need icons.

Create an Outline and Embed It

Open the Completed Titles database in Designer. Create an outline called **Home**. Add the following entries:

- **New Books**—Content: None.
- **by Author**—Content: View New Books\by Author. Indent under New Books.
- **by Category**—Content: View New Books\by Category. Indent under New Books.
- **by Level**—Content: View New Books\by Level. Indent under New Books.

- **by Software**—Content: View New Books\by Software. Indent under New Books.
- **by Title**—Content: View New Books\by Title. Indent under New Books.
- **About Our Authors**—Content: View Author Information. Outdent.
- **Create an Order**—Content: Action. Formula: `@Command([Compose]; "Order")`.

Save the outline and then click **Use Outline** on the Action bar to create a page and embed the outline.

Name the page **Home Page**. Name the embedded outline **Home Page**. Set it up in **Tree Style**, show twisties, and select the **Hide** title style. Set the Outline Size, Height to **Fit to Content**. From Web Access, select **Using Java Applet**.

Create a Frameset

Create a new shared image resource using the SmallName.gif file located in the Day20 folder on the CD. Create a page called **Company** and place the new image on the page. Save the page.

Create a frameset called **Home**. Set it up with three frames—two on the left and one on the right. In the upper-left frame (called Left Top), put the Company page. In the lower-left frame (called Left Bottom), put the Home Page and make the default target the Right frame. The third frame, called Right, will contain the New Books\by Category view as the default.

Save the frameset. For Web browsers, have the database automatically open to the Home frameset (Database Properties, Launch tab).

Create Database Icons

Create an icon for each database in the application. For extra credit, make one for the Rejected Titles and Manuscript Library too.

Create the About and Using Documents

Create the About This Database and Using This Database documents for the Proposed Titles, Titles in Development, and Completed Titles databases.

Create Online Help

In the Titles in Development database, create a new form called **Database Help**. That form has two fields: **HelpTopic** (editable text) and **HelpText** (rich text). Save the form.

Create a view called **Database Help** that contains only Database Help documents. It has one column called **Open document to get help on**. The formula for that column is `HelpTopic`. The column must be sorted. Save the view.

20

In the New Title form, select **HelpRequest** from the Objects list in the Programmer's Pane. In the Script Area, enter the following formula:

```
@Command([OpenHelpDocument]; "":""; "Database Help"; "New Title form")
```

Save the form.

To see examples of how we completed these tasks, open PTDay20.nsf, RTDay20.nsf, MSDay20.nsf, TDDay20.nsf, or CTDay20.nsf in the Day20 folder on the CD.

DAY 21

Roll Out and Maintain Your Application

You're finally close to getting your application out to your users. There are some final checklists that you need to run through, and then the application can be copied over to a production server and opened to a limited number of people for testing. When you have user feedback and have incorporated the needed changes into the application, you create a design template to control future design changes. The application is then ready to be made available to the full user population.

Check Your Design

As you are designing, it's hard to keep an eye out for everything that you need to change in the final version. Some things might work when you create them, but later design elements can affect how they work. That's why you need to check through your design one last time before you make your application available to a test group. Checking the design is particularly important when you have more than one designer working on an application, to make sure the design is consistent and that all the parts work together.

Start with Fields

Go through your forms with the eyes of a new user. Look for any potential problems, but also make sure that everything works the way you intended (and the way your users asked to have it). Make sure you use a computer of the same speed as your users typically have, with a monitor of the same screen size and resolution. Use this list of questions as a guide in examining your work:

- **Do you have a help description for every editable field?** Sometimes you don't add field help for obvious fields (watch yourself—they might be obvious to you, but not to your users). Add any missing help descriptions now, and make sure that all the field help text uses consistent language. Are you using full sentences, commands, or punctuation?

- **Do your fields show the correct data when you open a form?** Check your default value formulas.

- **Are all your editable fields available to users?** If they can't enter data, it might be because you defined the field as computed by mistake.

- **Can users see text, fields, or sections that should appear when specific options are selected?** Make sure you set the option to refresh on keyword change.

- **Are hidden fields and text appearing at inappropriate times?** Check your hide-when formulas. Very often, developers reverse the hide-when—try making it NOT equal instead of equal.

- **After you save a document, are the editable fields formatted correctly?** Also try editing the same document and saving it again because formatting errors sometimes don't appear until a document is saved again. Check your input translation formulas. You might need to add @If statements to specify the state of the document or field before applying the formatting.

- **Can you enter invalid data in some editable fields or leave some required fields blank?** Check your input validation formulas.

- **When you try saving a document without completing required fields, do input validation formulas display an appropriate message?** Add input validation formulas or correct the existing ones.

- **Are your computed fields producing expected results? Are the results of the appropriate data type?** Your formulas might need a data conversion function such as @Text or @TextToNumber.

- **Do your date/time fields display the correct date and time?** Check your time zone settings in the Field Properties box.

- **In documents that inherit field values, are the fields inheriting data correctly from the parent document?** Check the default value formula for editable fields and the value formulas for computed fields. If the field is computed, when composed, it might not pick up changes made later in the parent document. Consider using @GetDocField for response documents.

- **Do your fields align properly when your forms are displayed on different monitors or in different window sizes?** Either change your tab settings or use a table instead of tabs.

- **Can users who have encryption keys access encrypted fields? Are users without encryption keys unable to access encrypted fields?** Check your encryption settings. Make sure the encryption keys are distributed to the proper users and that unauthorized users don't have access to the keys. You might have to create a new encryption key and distribute that to the authorized users.

Look at Your Forms

For every form in your database, make at least two or three test documents. Enter different information to test all the conditions within the form. Use the following questions to catch any potential problems:

- **Did you specify a default form for the database?** In the list of forms in Designer, a blue arrow points to the default form. If there isn't one, open the form that is supposed to be the default and choose Design, Form Properties. On the Form Info tab, select Default database form.

- **Do the names of the forms appear correctly on the Create menu, in the correct order, and with appropriate shortcut keys?** Check the names of the incorrectly listed forms in the Form Properties box to see that they are entered properly, with an underscore before the desired shortcut key. Add numbers or letters to force the order of the forms in the menu. For forms not showing on the menu, select **Include in Menu** (if you have more than nine forms, you have to click **Other** in the Create menu to see the rest of your forms). If you have such a large number of forms, consider using cascading form names.

- **Are there window titles for each form? Do they display correctly for all conditions?** Check your window title formulas.

- **Did you group related fields on the form?** Because it makes reading and entering data easier, move the fields and their associated static text to logically group them (for example, putting the name and address together).

- **Do your forms print properly? Did you add page numbers for long forms? Did you use headers and footers?** Check the Printing tab on the Form Properties box.

21

- **Do you have Names fields on forms for tracking authors and editors of documents?** Add one to each form in which it's appropriate.

- **Did you define a read or write access list for the form?** If you want to restrict who can create documents or who can read documents created with the form, click the Security tab on the Form Properties box and select the appropriate users, servers, and groups. Also, if you created these lists during development, you might need to update the lists for production use.

- **Are your forms used on more than one operating system (platform)? Do the forms display properly on all platforms? Did you use fonts that are available on all platforms?** Try to make multiple-platform forms as generic as possible. To display or hide parts of forms or subforms based on the platform, use @Platform to determine which platform the user has.

Check Out Your Views

Open each of the views in the database to make sure your design works. Test any action buttons you've added to the views. Following are some questions you might ask yourself as you're looking at the views:

- **Is one of the views designated as the default view?** In the list of views in Designer, a blue arrow points to the default view. If you don't have a default view, double-click on the view that is supposed to be the default to open it. Choose **Design, View Properties** to open the View Properties box. Click the **Options** tab and select **Default when database is first opened**.

- **Have you designated the view to use as the default design for all new views and folders?** This is the view whose name appears automatically as the Copy style from view in the Create View dialog box. To set a view as the default design view, open the view in Designer and choose **Design, View Properties** to open the View Properties box. Click the **Options** tab and select **Default design for new folders and views**.

- **Do all your views display correctly in the View menu? Are they in the correct order? Do they have the correct shortcut keys?** Check the names of each of the incorrectly listed views in the View Properties box to see that they are entered properly, with an underscore before the desired shortcut key. Add numbers or letters to force the order of the views in the menu. Consider cascading some of the views if they are related. For views not showing on the menu, select **Show in View Menu** on the Options tab of the View Properties box.

- **Are your views easy to read, or are the columns too close together?** Widen the columns or align the column contents (left, right, center) to allow more space between column text.

- **Do the appropriate documents appear in the view, or are there too few or too many documents showing?** Check your view selection formulas to better define which documents are to appear in the view.

- **Are your response documents showing in hierarchical format (indented under the associated main document)?** On the Options tab of the View Properties box, make sure **Show response documents in a hierarchy** is checked.

- **Are the response documents not showing at all or are there blank lines in the view where the responses are supposed to be?** Check your selection formula first to see that you added @AllChildren or @AllDescendents to the formula. Then make sure you added a Responses-only column to the view.

- **Do the categories display properly?** You might have to add a sorted, categorized column that shows a choice from a keyword field.

- **Is your application used on different platforms?** Make sure that the views appear correctly on all platforms. Be sure that the fonts you chose are available on the other platforms.

- **Does the view need a read access list?** Check to see if one was added and that the correct names or roles are listed. Look on the Security tab of the View Properties box.

- **Are the columns displaying the appropriate information?** Check the formulas to correct them, if necessary.

- **Are the columns displaying values of the proper data type?** Some data conversion might be necessary. You might have to use the @Text function to convert numbers and dates to text where you have mixed data types, such as in a concatenation. Try not to convert dates unless there is no other solution so you don't create Y2K type problems.

- **Can you see all the information in each column?** You might need to widen a column, change the number of lines allowed in each row, or change the font or font size.

- **In your date columns, have you set the dates up to display 4-digit years when necessary?** Do it before the year 2000 rolls around.

- **Have you aligned the contents of the columns appropriately?** Numbers need to be right-aligned; text needs to be left-aligned or centered.

- **In the columns that contain numbers, are the numbers right-aligned? Do they have the appropriate number of digits to the right of the decimal point?** Check your number format settings for the decimals and column alignment settings to properly align the numbers.

21

- **Are the documents displaying in the correct order?** Make sure you sorted the columns and that the most important columns for sorting are on the left.
- **Do you need to have the documents in the view numbered?** Add a column that uses @DocNumber for its formula and is sorted in ascending order. Put that column in the leftmost position if you want to sort the view in number order.

Double Check Your Security

You need to check the security settings you've made for your application, especially if you've been developing locally. Even if you've had your application databases on a server during development, you are now about to put it on a production server and you have to be sure you have it right. This is a time when you might want to sit down with the Domino Administrator as you check through the application.

Some of the things you need to check include

- Make sure that in the Access Control List, Default is not assigned Designer (or worse, Manager) level access. Default access is usually Reader or Author access, and sometimes Editor access. It might be No Access, which excludes most of your users.
- Are the entries in the ACL in acceptable format? Acceptable entries include user, server, and groupnames, database replica IDs, the Anonymous name for Internet users and anonymous Notes user access, Internet clients' user and groupnames, and alternate names. The maximum length of each name is 255 characters. Are your user and server names in hierarchical format? The ACL works better if they are.
- Are the groups in your ACL assigned the proper access privileges? Many companies have a policy that individual names are not permitted in the ACL. Only group names are allowed. Assigning rights to those groups is then even more important.
- The Domino Administration and anyone acting as the Database Manager needs to be assigned Manager access to the database.
- Unless you'll be taking on a Manager role, assign yourself Designer access.
- If Web users are going to use the database, have you added Anonymous as an entry? Unless you intend for anyone to have access to any part of the database, set the access level for Anonymous as No Access or Reader access.

- For users who use name-and-password authentication and access the database via a Web browser, or for users who access the server anonymously over the Internet, have you set the Maximum Internet name & password access on the Advanced page of the ACL?

- Make sure that any groups you need for the ACL are added to the Domino Directory, if they aren't already there.

- Have you added all the roles you need for the application to the ACL and assigned those roles to users, servers, or groups? Make certain the registration server is assigned to every role.

- Does the Domino Administrator or the database manager have a copy of any encryption keys you used for the application?

- Check any access lists for forms or views in which you specified who can read or edit the form or read the view. Make sure you selected the correct roles, servers, groups, or users.

- Do you have any Readers or Authors fields in any of the forms? Make sure you granted read and edit access to the correct users. If you can't open documents you created to test these forms, it means you excluded yourself.

- Are the correct IDs specified for signatures in the ECL?

- Do you have any agents that need to run on the server? Make sure that the Domino Administrator makes the appropriate entries in the Server document so your agents can run on the server, or that the agent is saved with an approved ID that has permission to run restricted or unrestricted access to the production server.

Test Your Application

Now comes the time when you pilot test your application with a select group of users. It's important that people who will eventually use your application are the ones who test it. They need to see if the application fits into and helps with day to day operations. Because they have a different perspective, they are more likely to discover problems with the application that you might never uncover and make suggestions about improvements that didn't occur to you.

Although you don't always have a choice regarding who is included in the test group, the ideal is for you to get a cross-section of the normal user group. That way you get people at all levels, and they approach the application from the viewpoint of getting their own

21

work done. If you only get systems people to test an application, for example, your application might not address the barely computer-literate users who will eventually have to use the application. If you have only support people in the pilot test, the needs of salespeople might not be addressed.

It's very important that your instructions to the test group be very clear. You have to be certain that the problems lay in the application and not in your instructions.

Provide some instrument for your users to provide feedback on the application, both good and bad. Think about creating a discussion database for them to bring up questions and suggestions, to which others in the group can respond. The easier it is for the pilot group to give you feedback, the more likely it is that you'll get feedback. The database can also act as a problem-reporting forum, where you can respond when you've fixed the problem. If you don't want to create a whole database, incorporate forms and a view or two in the application database for comments, questions, and suggestions.

Don't replicate your application databases to the production server. In case of problems, you want to keep the original version of the application clean—you don't want errors to replicate back to your copy of the database. Instead, make a new copy of the databases for use on the server (choose **File, Database, New Copy** from the menu). Your copy then becomes the backup. For Web applications, make sure the Domino Administrator specifies the Web site home page in the Server document. You'll also want to create the first full-text index. If this is a new database that will participate in an existing Web site, you have to contact the Web site home page manager, or manager of the page from which you want to be accessed, and ask them to provide a link to your new database.

Make sure you add the pilot test group to the ACL and assign them appropriate access levels. During the test period, you need to retain manager access, and the Domino Administrator should also be a manager. That way, either of you can quickly correct ACL problems. The Domino Administrator also makes sure that you and the test group have appropriate access to the server.

Even if you plan to have the application on several servers when it's rolled out, use only one server for the test period. Don't replicate the databases yet. After the initial test period and the "clean up" of the application, test replication with one or two servers or with mobile users to be sure the replication settings work properly. If you do have replication problems, make certain that every server that contains a replica and the servers through which the database must replicate (pass-thru servers) are included in the ACL with at least designer access (if you want to distribute design changes from the main database).

Address design problems as soon as possible after becoming aware of them. Then handle suggestions. Communicate with your users, telling them about problems that were reported and fixed. When you incorporate one of the suggestions into the application, tell your users that you've made changes so they know to test that portion of the application.

At the end of the test period, collect all the questions people had about the function or use of the database and include them and the answers in the Using This Database document. The same questions should guide the preparation of any training materials.

Use the Design Synopsis

Even if you keep users from making design changes to your application, other designers and managers can make modifications. Many organizations fall prey to the "too many cooks" problem, where changes aren't announced before they happen or documented after they do. That's why a backup of the design is essential, so you can undo any unwise modifications. At the very least, document your application when it is ready for release to the general user population. The documentation also helps you later when you have to make changes and can't remember what you did.

Your documentation in Domino development is the Design Synopsis. With the Design Synopsis you get a detailed report on a selected database. Not only can you gather information about the database, but you can select which design elements you want the report to cover. By selecting what you want to see, you can create reports at different times on different parts of the database, so you don't have to read one long report. Also, you can choose to have the report on the screen, printed, saved to a file, or stored in a specified database.

Start by opening the database about which you want the report. Then choose **File, Database, Design Synopsis** from the menu (or select **Synopsis** from the Design Pane in Designer). The Design Synopsis dialog box has four tabs (see Figure 21.1). Table 21.1 describes the types of information that can be included in the report, depending on the choices you make in the Design Synopsis dialog box.

FIGURE 21.1

The Design Elements tab of the Design Synopsis dialog box is where you choose the elements to include in the report.

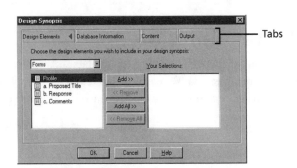

Tabs

21

Table 21.1 Design Synopsis Information to Request

Tabs in Design Synopsis Dialog Box	What to Do
Design Elements	Select each type of element (one at a time) that you want covered in the report, or select **All** to see all of them.
	For each element you select, choose the specific named elements and click **Add** to include the ones you select in the report or **Add All** to include all of them.
Database Information	Click **General information** to get information such as the database title, location, and categories.
	Click **Space usage** to get information about file size, number of documents, and space used by the database.
	Click **Replication** to get information on the replication settings for the database.
	Click **Access List** to see a list of users, groups, and servers in the ACL and their assigned access levels and roles.
Content	For each type of design element, select the details you want to see reported on that type of element.
	Select **Include subcomponents, Include LotusScript code, Include Java code,** or **Include JavaScript and HTML** to receive information.
Output	Select either **Blank line** or **Page break** as report separators.
	Check **Write Output to Database** if you want to write the report to a database. When you check this option, a new dialog box appears so you can specify the database in which you want to write the output.

When you click **OK**, the report shows in a new window unless you chose to write it to a database. From that window (see Figure 21.2), the report can be printed or saved to a file.

Create Master Templates

A template holds only the design structure for a database, and this design structure is imprinted on a new database that's created with a template. Templates are useful because they help give consistency to databases, and because it's easier to create a new database using a template.

FIGURE 21.2

The design synopsis showing in this window is for the Proposed Titles database.

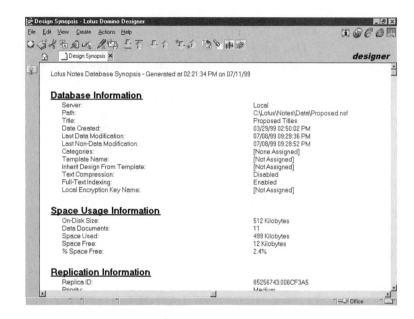

Domino provides a set of templates for you to use when creating new databases. These templates can be customized to fit the needs of your organization. It's best to create a copy of the template that you can customize without changing the original template. Use **File, Database, New Copy** to copy the original template and inherit its design, and then give the template a different name.

Before putting your application databases out for general use, make a template copy of the databases. In addition to preserving the design portion of the database, you can make design changes to the template without interfering with the actual data. Either set the template so you can replace the design of the databases manually, or make it a *master*, or design, template that links to the databases to provide automatic design updates.

Make a Master Template

In terms of maintaining database design, having a template gives you an "isolated" place to work on the design. Any documents you create in the template to test your design are not copied to the database, and database documents aren't copied to your template. In other words, when a template is in place, there is no longer any reason to make design changes in the database itself. When you designate a database copy as your template, set it up as a master template that distributes design changes automatically to all databases created from it or linked to it, courtesy of a nightly server task.

21

Use the following steps to create a master template:

1. Select the database and then choose **File, Database, New Copy** from the menu to open the Copy Database dialog box (see Figure 21.3).

FIGURE 21.3

When entering the File Name of the template, you don't want to add a path to a subdirectory. Store the template in the default data directory so it is available if you want users to be able to choose this as a template for building a new database.

2. In the Server box, select the name of a server where you want to store the template.

3. Enter a Title for the template.

4. The File Name appears automatically as you enter the title for the template. Reduce the size of the name to limit it to eight characters and change the file extension to **.ntf**.

5. Select **Database design only**. You don't want to copy the documents to your template.

6. Select **Access Control List**.

7. Click **OK**.

8. Open the template and then choose **File, Database, Properties** from the menu.

9. On the Design tab of the Database Properties box, select **Database is a template**. Then, in Template name, enter the filename of the template (see Figure 21.4). The template name needs to be something meaningful, such as Lotus's StdR5MailTemplate.

10. (Optional) If you want to hide the template from casual use (unless users select **Show advanced templates** in the New Database dialog box), select **List as advanced template in 'New Database' dialog**.

FIGURE 21.4

A template name must be assigned to the file. The Design tab provides the field in which you supply the template name.

Make a Design Copy

If you don't want the database to automatically inherit design changes via the nightly server task, make a design copy of the database instead. That preserves the design, and you still can work on design without working directly in the database. Either don't put the template on a server running the nightly update task or don't set the property that sets the database as a template. The properties of the databases also have to be set to not automatically inherit the design. When you don't use the nightly server task to update the design of the database, you have to distribute changes manually using the Replace Design command.

Use the following steps to make a design copy of the database:

1. Select the database and then choose **File, Database, New Copy** from the menu.

2. In the Server box, select **Local** to store the template on your workstation or select the name of a server on which you want to store the template.

3. Enter a Title for the template.

4. The File Name appears automatically as you enter the title for the template. Reduce the size of the name to limit it to eight characters and change the file extension to **.ntf**.

5. Select **Database design only**.

6. Deselect **Access Control List.** When setting up the ACL after the template is created, define who has access to the template instead of access to the database created from the template. Specify Manager access for yourself and the database manager, Reader access for LocalDomainServers (the template isn't going to be replicated), and No Access for OtherDomainServers, [Default], and [Anonymous].

21

7. (Optional) Click **Encryption** to encrypt the database, which protects its contents from being accessed at the operating system level. Select a level and then click **OK**. Don't do this if you plan to automatically update database design based on this template.

8. Click **OK**.

Link a Database to a Template

A database won't receive the nightly design updates unless it is linked to a master template.

Use the following steps to link a database to a template:

1. Open or select the database and then choose **File, Database, Properties** from the menu.

2. Click the **Design** tab (see Figure 21.5).

FIGURE 21.5

If you can't remember the name to enter in the Template Name box, copy the filename of the template from the Design tab of the template's Database Properties box.

3. Select **Inherit design from template**.

4. In the Template Name box, enter the name of the template file.

Any new replicas automatically link to the same template that the original database uses. When you create a new database, selecting **Inherit future design changes** in the New Database box creates the link.

Link Design Elements to a Template

A form, view, navigator, page, or other design element can be linked to a template. Any time you copy an individual design element from a template, or from a database that inherits its design from a template, the element can automatically link to the template. All you have to do when you paste it into another database is answer **Yes** to the prompt about inheriting future design changes. Although it's unusual, a design element can even be linked to a template that's different than the one defined in the Database Properties Design tab.

But what about existing elements? You can link an element without the rest of the database design elements being linked. After linking the element, the design is changed when the Design task runs on the server or when the design is manually refreshed. From then on, the design element remains synchronized with the template.

Use the following steps to link an existing element to a different template:

1. You need to know the filename of the master template, so open the template and choose **File, Database, Properties**. Click the **Design** tab, and copy the contents of the Template name box to the Clipboard.

2. In Designer, open the database that contains the design element you want to link to the template.

3. From the Design Pane, select the type of element so you can view all the items of that type (for example, to link to a view, select **Views** in the Design Pane).

4. From the list of design elements, select the name of the one you want to link (for example, click the name of the view).

5. Select **Design, Design Properties** (or Agent, Agent Properties if the element is an agent).

6. In the Design or Agent Properties box, select the **Design** tab (see Figure 21.6).

FIGURE 21.6

Under Inherit from the design template, enter or paste the name of the template to which you want to link the element.

7. Click in the box below **Inherit from the design template**. Paste the name of the template there.

21

Distribute New Design Changes

After your application is running on the server and available to users, you have some choices to make if you want to modify the design. You need to decide where to make the changes and how to distribute them. You can do one of three things:

- **Make the changes directly in the database, which eliminates the distribution problem**—Do this only for a single database that resides on only one server and doesn't have a large user group.
- **Change the design in a template and use the Replace Design command to distribute the modifications to the database**—Design changes are replicated to other server replicas (provided the servers have at least Design access to the database).
- **Modify the design in a master template**—Rely on the Design server task to update the design nightly at 1:00 a.m. (by default), or use the Refresh Design command to distribute your design changes in an orderly manner.

For automatic updating to work, the template and the databases linked to it must reside on the same server.

Update Design in Replicas

When templates aren't involved, any changes to the design and any document modifications in a database are automatically replicated to any replicas—provided the servers have at least Designer access to the database. When you aren't using templates to control design, it's recommended that only one Designer or database manager make design changes. The changes need to be made to only one database on one server. Otherwise, you might run into problems with unexpected modifications or replication conflicts. Replication does the work of distributing the design changes to other replicas.

Things work differently when you use templates. For each server that has a replica of a database that inherits its design from a template, you must put a replica of the template on that server. For the replica templates, servers need to have Designer or greater access in the ACL. You still need to confine any changes to one template on one server. Replication distributes the design changes to the other template replicas, and the linked databases' designs are updated by the template on that same server. For the sake of efficiency, have the Domino Administrator schedule the replication of the templates prior to the 1:00 a.m. run time of the Design task.

Refresh a Design

You need to refresh the design of a database manually when you're storing the database locally (you can't rely on the Design server task in that case), or when you need to distribute design changes prior to the scheduled update. Refreshing a design only works for databases that are linked to a template.

Refreshing a design, either manually or automatically, only affects the following components:

- Agents
- Database Properties, except the advanced template option
- Event scripts
- Fields
- Folders
- Form actions
- Forms
- Framesets
- Navigators
- Pages
- Shared fields
- View actions
- Views

The following components are not updated during either the manual or automatic design refresh:

- Individual elements whose design is protected from updates ("Prohibit design refresh or replace to modify property" is selected in the Design Properties box of the element)
- The "List as advanced template in New Database" property
- The database ACL and encrypted database settings
- The database icon (unless the "Prohibit design refresh or replace to modify" is deselected in the Design Properties box for the element)
- The database title and category
- Using This Database and About This Database documents (unless the "Prohibit design refresh or replace to modify" is deselected in the Design Properties box for the element)

21

Use the following steps to manually refresh a database's design:

1. Select the database you want to update.
2. Choose **File, Database, Refresh Design** from the menu.
3. Select the name of the Domino server on which the template resides, or **Local** if the templates are on your workstation.
4. Click **OK**. Then click **Yes** to confirm.

Replace a Design

For databases that don't inherit their changes from a template, you have to use the Replace Design command to distribute design changes. When you use the Replace Design command, the database design becomes identical to the specified template.

The following components are replaced during Replace Design:

*   Agents
*   Database Properties, except the advanced template option
*   Event scripts
*   Fields
*   Folders
*   Form actions
*   Forms
*   Framesets
*   Navigators
*   Pages
*   Shared fields
*   View actions
*   Views

However, Replace Design doesn't affect the following components:

*   Individual elements whose design is protected from updates ("Prohibit design refresh or replace to modify property" is selected in the Design Properties box of the element)
*   The "List as advanced template in New Database" property
*   The database ACL and encrypted database settings

- The database icon (unless the "Prohibit design refresh or replace to modify" is deselected in the Design Properties box for the element)
- The database title and category
- Using This Database and About This Database documents (unless the "Prohibit design refresh or replace to modify" is deselected in the Design Properties box for the element)

Tip

Just in case, you might want to back up the database before you replace the design.

To replace the design of a database, use the following steps:

1. Select the database on the server.
2. Choose **File, Database, Replace Design** from the menu.
3. Make certain you select the correct **Template Server**.
4. Click **Show advanced templates** (if necessary).
5. Click **About** and read the About This Database document if you have any doubt that you've selected the correct template.
6. Select the template whose design you want to use.
7. Click **Replace** and then click **Yes** to confirm.

Update Documents After Form Changes

Redesigning a form might require that you update any pre-existing documents in order to see the change there. Some form changes won't appear in these documents until you manually edit and resave the documents. That can be quite time-consuming if you have to change 100 or more documents. The alternative is to run an agent that does it for you.

You don't have to update documents for every change. When you change a static text, pop-ups, text properties and formats, form actions and buttons, or graphics, you don't have to update the documents. The changes display automatically when users open the documents, as long as the forms don't have the "Store form in documents" property selected. Even changing the form name doesn't require an update, as long as you include the previous name in the synonyms.

21

Note
> Our Tech Editor recommends that you run an agent to recalculate computed fields if the computed field is used in views or in search values. Always consider carefully whether the computed fields require an update.

You have to update the documents whenever you add a new field, change the field data type, change a field name, delete a field, change the form name without including the previous name in the synonyms, change the form type, or change a form that has the property "Store form in document" selected.

When you have many documents to change, it makes sense to use an agent. Because these are generally single-use agents, don't share the agents and run them manually. Table 21.1 describes some formulas or functions you can use in agents to update your documents.

Table 21.2   Agents to Update Documents Affected by Form Changes

To	Include this function/formula
Edit and save documents	`@Command([ToolsRefreshAllDocs])` or `@Command([ToolsRefreshSelectedDocs])`
Insert a newly created field into existing documents	`FIELD NewFieldName := Value`
	NewFieldName is the name of the new field you want to add to the document.
	Value is the value you want the field in the documents to have. It can be the default value or a formula that calculates the value or a NULL value that inserts the field but doesn't provide a value.
Remove field data from all documents (existing documents still store deleted fields and their values)	`FIELD FieldName := @DeleteField`
	FieldName is the name of the deleted field.
	Compact the database after you run the agent to reduce the size of the database.

To	Include this function/formula

Rename a field (existing documents continue to refer to the old field name)	```FIELD NewFieldName := OldFieldName;```
	```FIELD OldFieldName := @DeleteField```
	
	NewFieldName is the new name for the field.
	
	OldFieldName is the original name of the field.

Remove a stored form from documents and all its related internal fields	```SELECT $TITLE = "Old Form Name";```
	```FIELD $TITLE := @DeleteField;```
	```FIELD $INFO = @DeleteField;```
	```FIELD $WINDOWTITLE := @DeleteField;```
	```FIELD $BODY := @DeleteField;```
	```FIELD $ACTIONS := @DeleteField;```
	```FIELD FORM := "New Form Name"```
	
	Old Form Name is the name of the form used to create the documents.
	
	New Form Name is the new form that is used to display the documents in the future.
	
	Compact the database after you run this agent to reduce the actual size of the database.

Reassign documents to another form (if you deleted a form, users see a notice that the form can't be found when they try to open a document)	In the Agent Builder, have the agent run on all documents in the database, but click **Add Search** and select **By Form Used**. Select the name of the old form and click **OK**. (By Form Used might work if you've already deleted the form from the design, in which case you have to code a formula such as ```SELECT Form = "Old Form Name"```. In the Programmer's Pane, enter the following formula: ```FIELD Form := "Reassigned Form Name"``` *Reassigned Form Name* is the name of the form that the documents are to use.

21

Preserve Your Design

An important decision you must make before final rollout is how open you want to make the design. Do you want users to update forms and views? Should users pass along design changes? Or do you want the application used as it is presented without any users having access to design elements? Do you want to keep even users with Designer or Manager access from modifying the design?

If you *do* give developers and managers some level of access to the design, there's no guarantee that some design element won't be deleted accidentally, or some important formula lost in error. You need to back up your design and document it.

Prevent Design Changes

There are three methods that you can use when you want to protect your design from accidental changes. However, these changes won't keep someone with Designer or Manager access to the database from changing the design. You'll have to hide the database design to do that (see "Hide Your Design" later in this day).To prevent overwriting a design element when running Replace Design and to protect an element in a database that's linked to a template, open the Design Properties box for the element (or Agent Properties box for an agent). On the Design tab (see Figure 21.7) select **Prohibit design refresh or replace to modify**.

FIGURE 21.7

To open the Design Properties box, open the database in Designer, select the type of element from the Design Pane, click the listed design element, and choose **Design, Design Properties**.

Note

Using Prohibit is a last resort and should not be done lightly. It is very easy to forget that you've set this value and when you, the designer, want to change the design it will drive you crazy that something isn't working.

To break the link between a design element and a template, remove the name of the template from the box under Inherit from the design template on the Design tab of the Design Properties box. You might want to do this after copying an element from a template from which you don't want to inherit future design changes.

To break the link between a database and a template, open the Database Properties box for the database (**File, Database, Properties**). Click the **Design** tab and deselect **Inherit design from template**. You might want to do this when you decide to customize the entire design of the database and you no longer want the database to inherit design changes from the template. For example, you start building a new database by using the Discussion Template provided by Lotus, but then you decide to customize the database. That's when you need to break the link.

Hide Your Design

One way to prevent users from making design changes to the application databases is to hide the database design. This disables all design operations and hides all formulas and scripts. Hiding the database design also keeps users with Designer or Manager access from making design changes.

After hiding the database design, users cannot view the settings for design elements because the **View, Design** menu command is no longer available. Users cannot take any of the following actions:

- Modify, add, or delete fields, forms, navigators, pages, or subforms.
- Modify or delete existing views.
- View, delete, or modify existing agents or add shared agents.
- View or modify formulas, LotusScript programs, or formulas associated with simple actions.
- Change the Database Open properties.
- Display a synopsis of the design.
- Reveal the design of the database by making a copy or replica of it.

Depending on the ACL settings, users can add personal agents, personal folders, and views, and create and delete documents.

Before you take these steps, create a design template from which the database inherits. Then be sure that you've thoroughly reviewed, debugged, and tested the template before you hide the database design.

21

If you have any agents that require user input, such as changing schedule options, select the agent schedule option **Choose when agent is enabled**. Then create a button, form, or view action (whichever is most appropriate for that agent) that uses the function @Command([AgentEnableDisable]) to enable the agent automatically.

Use the following steps to hide the database design:

1. Create a new database that is based on the template.
2. Select the new database and choose **File, Database, Replace Design** from the menu.
3. In the Replace Database Design dialog box (see Figure 21.8), select the template (click **Template Server** and choose the server on which the template is stored if the template isn't listed).

FIGURE 21.8

Select the design template you created for the application database.

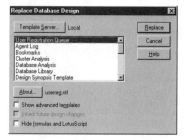

4. Select **Hide formulas and LotusScript** and **Inherit future design changes**.
5. Click **Replace** and then **Yes** to confirm.

Although you've hidden the database design, you have a design template for the database (see the "Make a Master Template" section in this day). Any design modifications that are required after you hide the database can be made to the template. Because the database is linked to the design template, any design changes are transferred to the database when you refresh the database design.

Train the Users

Your application is on the server and ready to go into production. However, except for the users included in your pilot test, no one knows how to use the application or why they need to use it.

The users need training on the new application. They need not only to understand the step by step mechanics of the application, but to know where it fits in their normal workload. Training is half knowledge of the mechanics and half sales to get the users to "buy into" the new application. If the users don't see the benefit of it or don't think that when they get the steps down it will work better than what they are currently doing, they might not use it.

Don't expect someone in the department to train everyone else. People have their own workload, and training tends to be shoddy or half-hearted when the "trainer" is also trying to keep up with their own work. Unless the application is simple and totally self-explanatory (your help documents better be good), you can't just expect people to figure it out on their own.

Have a knowledgeable person who is accustomed to training people facilitate the training. Bring users to a room away from their desks for training so that interruptions can be kept to a minimum. Give each user a chance to use a computer on which the application is running. Provide training materials with the step by step information users need to work with the application and that they can take back to their desks. With complicated applications, use a training database for the users to try for a few days at their own desks before you put them on the "real" application.

Always provide a help desk for the application. People will always have questions, especially at the beginning. Plus, the help desk acts as a clearance area for any additional problems that come up with the design—no matter how well you tested it, you can't anticipate what can happen in every single instance. Users need to know it's a bug and not them. After help requests dwindle, the help desk personnel can be shifted to help in other areas not related to the application.

Coupled with the training is making the application available for newly trained users. Where before you only had the select pilot testing group assigned access levels so they could work with the database, now access has to be assigned to the complete user population. Sometimes this is done by training class—only giving them access after they attended training. Another strategy is to assign access for everyone, but only notify small groups of users at a time that the database is available (send a mail message with a database link to the new application). Whatever you do, don't make it haphazard.

Create a Design Library Template

Did this application design have some elements that might be helpful in preparing other applications? The more you work in application design, the more you realize how often you use similar elements.

Keep all these great design ideas in one place. Make yourself a design library template. In that template, store all the design elements you think you might use again. You can to copy stored design elements to other templates or databases. Then, when you make

21

design changes, they'll be propagated to all the databases or design elements that inherit from the template.

To create a design library template, start by creating a new blank database. Give it an appropriate filename, but add an .ntf extension. Copy the design elements you want to save into the template. Then, on the Database Properties box for the template, click the Design tab and select **Database is a template**. Enter the name of the template file.

For every database that you want to link to the design library template, select **Inherit design from template** in the Database Properties box and enter the template name.

Summary

Do a final check of your application prior to putting it into production to be sure your fields, forms, actions, views, agents, and security settings are all ready to go. Make a copy of the database and put it on the production server. Give access at first to only a small group of users, who will test the application for you.

After incorporating any suggestions and repairing any problems, the application is ready to go. Create a design synopsis so you have a complete report on all the design elements in the database. Then make a template in which you'll do your design work in the future. Link the template to the database if you want to update the database nightly with any design changes.

To protect certain elements in your design from changing during design refreshing or replacement, change the design element's properties to prohibit changes. For complete protection, hide the design from the users. The master template becomes the only way to modify the design.

Train your users to use the application, and then make the necessary changes to the ACL to open up the application to all the users who need it.

Q&A

Q The design synopsis sounds like a great tool. Do I have to wait until the application is finished to use it?

A No. It's also a great way to document as you go. Particularly when you have more than one developer for the application, you can look to see what someone else did before you make changes.

Q **Usually our IS department does the pilot testing. You advised against that. Why?**

A Go ahead and use the IS department for the first pass. They'll catch some of the glaring mistakes, and it'll help them become familiar with the application. However, they won't be using the application with real data in real situations. You need to see that your application can deal with the normal course of business, plus anything bizarre that crops up. That means getting users to test the application. Otherwise, you'll have a lot of errors being reported when the application is released to the users.

Workshop

In this workshop you'll be winding up your application chores and cleaning up any design elements that need it before your application goes into production. If you haven't been working on your own databases through the workshop, all the databases are stored in the Day20 folder on the CD.

Carefully check all elements of your design, including security, to be sure they are ready to be put on the server for testing. Create a design synopsis. If you can load the application on a server, make new copies of the databases on the server and then make design templates for the Proposed Titles, Titles in Development, and Completed Titles databases. Hide the design if you want.

We did create an agent in Titles in Development to remove the stored form from the mailed in Proposed Title documents and replace the form with the New Title form. Then we removed the Form formula from the Titles view and replaced it with a selection condition specifying documents created with the New Title form.

By the way, if you disabled the encryption on the TStatus field so you can manually change the field value while testing documents, you'd better enable it again. Also, change any agents you tested by running manually to their proper schedule.

In the Day21 folder on the CD, you will find the design templates for the Proposed Titles, Titles in Development, and Completed Titles databases.

21

Appendixes

A

B

C

D

E

APPENDIX **A**

Find Help

Several Help Databases typically accompany a new release of Domino: the R5 users help database, called Notes 5 Help (help5_client.nsf); the R5 help database for developers, "Domino 5 Designer Help" (help5_designer.nsf); and the R5 administrators help database "Domino 5 Administration Help" (help5 admin.nsf). The Help Database that is accessed from the Designer menu is the Domino 5 Designer Help, and it contains information that is important to the developer. Release Notes for developers can be found on the R5 CD. Also, be sure to look for current information at the following sites: the Lotus Development Corporation home page (www.Lotus.com) and developer sites such as www.notes.net and www.lotus-developer.com. These sites also contain links to Iris Web sites for up-to-the-minute help, particularly if you are working in a .0 release of software, such as 5.0.

In the printed books version of Help, you'll find the complete Programmer's Guide. This includes information and help with LotusScript, Notes programming language, formulas, and formula syntax. This book is particularly useful when you are writing formulas using @Functions because it explains each function and provides examples of how the function is used. The functions are organized in alphabetical order for easy reference.

You will also find the Application Developer's Guide under the Printed Books view of the Help database. This guide, which is organized by subject, provides information on building applications.

You can visit Lotus's Web site at `www.Lotus.com`. Like all sites, the information changes frequently here. Search for application development, development, and Iris as keys for finding design and development assistance.

APPENDIX B

@Functions

The Formula tools of Lotus Notes and Domino are an important part of application development. The @Functions are specialized formulas that handle a wide variety of situations. Domino has more than 200 @Functions. This appendix lists only the most commonly used @Functions. A full listing is available in Lotus's Release 5 Programmer's Guide, Part 2, or in the Designer 5 Help database. The Help database also includes a table that displays how you can use @Functions (formulas for buttons, SmartIcons, view selection, view columns, agents, hide-when situations, sections, and more). You can also learn more about the new @functions for R5 in Que's *Special Edition, Using Lotus Notes and Domino R5* by Randy Tamura.

Table B.1 lists the most commonly used @Functions in alphabetical order, the formula syntax, and the purpose of the function. @Functions marked with an asterisk (*) indicate that new functionality has been added in Release 5 of Domino. Table B.2 lists some of the new @Functions found in Release 5 of Domino.

Table B.1 Frequently Used @Functions

Frequently Used @Functions and the context in which they work. Bolded @functions are not supported on the Web. Note that this table does NOT include all purposes or examples for each @function listed. To learn more about each @function, see the Domino help databases.

@Function	Purpose
@AddToFolder("FolderNameToAddTo"; "FolderNameToRemoveFrom")	Adds the current document to a folder and removes it from its existing folder. For example, @AddToFolder ("Current";"Future") moves the currently selected document to the folder Current from the folder Future. Can be used with a Null string; for example, @AddToFolder("Current";"") adds the currently selected document to the folder Current. If the document exists in folder Future, it is unaffected. Use this formula in SmartIcons, Buttons, and Agents.
@Adjust(DateValue; years; months; days; hours; minutes; seconds; [dst])	Adjusts a date value, forward or backward, by the amount specified in the years, months, days, hours, minutes, or seconds arguments (you must use a zero for arguments you aren't using in the adjustment). Use negative numbers to adjust the date backward. Use the optional keyword [dst] if you want to adjust for daylight savings time. Typically used for calculating due dates, such as @Adjust(InvoiceDate; 0; 0; 30; 0; 0; 0), which adds 30 days to the invoice date. Values for [dst] are: [InLocalTime], [InGMT] (where [InGMT] means do not adjust for daylight savings time).
@All	Returns the value True (1). Used most frequently in selection formulas, such as in the view selection formula SELECT @All, which indicates that all database documents are to be included in the view.
@AllChildren	Used in selection formulas to include all response documents. The view selection formula SELECT MainTopic ¦ @AllChildren displays all the MainTopic documents and any first level responses to those documents, but not responses to response documents.

@*Function*	*Purpose*
`@AllDescendents`	Used in selection formulas to include all response and response-to-response documents. The view with the selection formula `SELECT MainTopic ¦ @AllDescendents` displays the MainTopic documents, their immediate responses, and the responses to those responses.
`@Author`	Returns a list of names included in the first author's field in a document. If the document doesn't have an author's field, @Author returns a list from the From field. If the document has no From field, the name of the user who last modified the document is listed. For an unsaved document, @Author returns the name of the current user. The list of names appears in abbreviated form, such as Bob Dobbs/Stillwater, instead of the full canonical form.
`@BrowserInfo(` `"propertyname" )`	Returns information about the browser. Syntax is `@BrowserInfo("PropertyName")`. It recognizes three types of browsers: Internet Explorer, Netscape Navigator, and Lotus Notes Web Navigator. Can be used in all types of formulas except view column and view selection formulas; for example, `@BrowserInfo("Frames")` returns `1[True]` if the browser supports the HTML <Frame> tag, otherwise returns `0 [False]`. For a complete list of Property names, see the Designer Help file.

`@Contains(string;`
`substring)`
	Returns a `True` value (1) if the specified substring is included in the text string. For example,
	
	`@If(@Contains(City; "Philadelphia" : "New York" :`
	`"Boston"); "Office Account"; "")`
	
	Returns `"Office Account"` if one of the cities listed in the City field was Boston.

`@Created`	Use this function to show the date or time when the document was created.
`@Date(Time-` `DateValue)`	Returns only the date portion of a date-time value. For example `@Date(@Created)` returns `01/16/99` instead of showing the complete value of `01/16/99 10:25:03 PM`.

continues

Table B.1   continued

@Function	Purpose
@Day(Time-DateValue)	Returns the day of the month from the specified date. The formula @Day(Holiday) returns 4 if the holiday is the Fourth of July.
@DbColumn(class : "NoCache"; server : database; view; column#)	Used mainly to provide a list of selections for keyword fields, this formula pulls a column of information from a view or folder in the specified database. For example, in the formula @DbColumn(""; "":"Contacts.nsf"; "Contacts by Territory"; 2), the data is in a Notes database so the class is "" (you could use "Notes"). Because "NoCache" isn't used, the results of the lookup are automatically cached ("NoCache" is an optional keyword). The database is on the current server, so "" replaces the server name. The name of the database appears in quotes, as does the name of the view (use either the full name or the synonym). The data returned is in the second (2) column from the left. This function doesn't work in column or selection formulas.
@DbLookup(class: "NoCache"; server : database; view; key; fieldname) or @DbLookup(class: "NoCache"; server : database; view; key; column#)	Finds all the documents in a view that match the key in the first sorted column in the view and returns the contents of the specified field or column. On a sales report document, the formula @DbLookup("":"NoCache";""; "Contacts by Company Name"; SubmittedBy; Salesperson) returns a list of documents from the Contacts by Company Name view in the current Notes database, in which the name in the Salesperson field is the same as the name of the person submitting the report (the value of the SubmittedBy field). The results aren't cached. If the Salesperson information appeared in the third column of the view, you could also write the formula as @DbLookup("" : "NoCache"; ""; "Contacts by Company Name"; SubmittedBy; 3). This function doesn't work in column or selection formulas.
@DialogBox(form; [AutoHorzFit] : [AutoVertFit] : [NoCancel] : [NoNewFields] : [NoFieldUpdate] : [ReadOnly]; SizeToTable; NoOKCancel; Title)	Useful for action buttons, especially with forms that contain layout regions, because a dialog box appears that displays the current document using a specified form. If the specified form has fields in common with the current document, the field values are displayed in the dialog box and the user can change the values. For example, a button in the Company form has a formula that reads @DialogBox("CompInfo"; [AutoHorzFit] :

@Function	Purpose
	[AutoVertFit]). Both the Company and the CompInfo forms have fields for the Company Name, Address, and Contact Name. When the button is activated, a dialog box appears that displays the document in a dialog box that uses the layout region from the CompInfo form. The user can change the company information and click OK to also change the document created from the Company form. Check Domino 5 Designer Help for a complete description of all the keywords available for this function.
@DocumentUniqueID	Finds the unique document ID (UNID) for a document, which is useful in linking parent and child documents so field information can be inherited. The $Ref internal field in a response document contains the UNID for the parent document. In order to perform lookups on parent documents, you can create a hidden view with @Text(@DocumentUniqueID) as a column formula. In displaying it, make the column at least 32 characters wide (the length of the UNID).
@Elements(List)	Returns the number of text, number, or time-date values in a list. If you have an Invitees field that lists the individuals who are invited to a meeting, the formula @Elements(Invitees) returns the number of people invited to the meeting. When the list is empty, this formula returns a zero.
@Environment (variable) or @Environment (variable; value)	For use in field and form formulas, buttons, SmartIcons, and agents, this function returns an environmental variable stored in the Notes.ini file. If you are storing an invoice number in the Notes.ini file, @Environment("InvoiceNumber") returns that number. To place an invoice number variable into the Notes.ini file and assign it the value zero, use a formula such as @Environment("InvoiceNumber"; "0"). Note that @environment stores and retrieves all values as text.
@Failure("string")	Used in validation formulas, @Failure returns a message if the entered value doesn't meet the validation requirements. For example, to be sure the ZipCode field is completed, write a validation formula such as @If(ZipCode != ""; @Success; @Failure ("You must enter a zip code")).

continues

Table B.1 continued

@*Function*	*Purpose*
@FontList	Returns a text list of available fonts. For example, @FontList returns a list containing information such as "Arial"; "Courier", and so forth. Useful in a keyword formula to enable users to select a preferred font.
@GetDocField (documentUNID; "fieldname")	Returns values in a field from the document identified by the unique document ID. For example, to get the subject from a parent document if the selected document is a response document, use a formula such as @If(@IsResponseDoc; @GetDocField($Ref; "Subject"); "ResponseSubject").
@HardDeleteDoc	Used to physically delete a document from the database. See also @UnDeleteDocument and @DeleteDocument.
@If(Condition1; Action1; Condition2; Action2;...; Condition99; Else_action)	When you need to evaluate a condition, use the @If function. If the first condition is true, Notes performs the action that immediately follows it Action99; and does not evaluate any other part of the formula. If it is not true, Notes evaluates the next condition. Notes continues to evaluate each pair of conditions and actions until it finds a condition that is true; if no condition is true, Notes performs the Else_action. An @If formula must have an odd number of arguments. For example, the formula @If(Month = 1, "January"; Month = 2; "February"; "March") returns "January" if the Month value is 1, "February" if the Month value is 2, or "March" is the Month value is not 1 or 2.
@IsMember(TextValue; TextListValue) or @IsMember (TextListValue1; TextListValue2)	Returns True (1) if the text value or text list is part of another text list. This formula is case sensitive. The @IsMember function is often combined with @If formulas, such as @If(@IsMember(@UserName; Advisors); "Sales Contact List"; ""). This will return "Sales Contact List" if the current Notes user is one of the advisors.

@Function	Purpose
@IsNewDoc	Indicates whether a document being edited has been saved yet. Returns True (1) if the document hasn't been saved. The function is usually combined with an @If formula, such as the window title formula @If(@IsNewDoc; "New Response"; "Response to " + Subject).
@IsNumber(value)	Returns True (1) if the value is a number or list of numbers. This function is often used as a condition in an @If formula, such as @If(@IsNumber(Quantity); Quantity; @TextToNumber(Quantity)).
@IsResponseDoc	Returns True (1) if a document is a response to another document. The document type has to be response or response-to-response. This function is often used in combination with an @If formula, such as in the window title formula @If(@IsResponseDoc, "Response to " + Subject; Subject).
@IsText(value)	Returns True (1) if a value is text. This function is often used as a condition in an @If formula, such as @If(@IsText (PhoneNumber); "My phone number is " + PhoneNumber; "My phone number is " + @Text(PhoneNumber)).
@IsTime(value)	Returns True (1) if a value is a time-date value or list. This function is often used as a condition in an @If formula, such as @If(@IsTime(DueDate); DueDate; @TextToTime(DueDate)).
@Left(SearchString; #Characters) or @Left(SearchString; Substring)	Searches a string of characters (SearchString) and returns the leftmost number of characters you specified. For example, @Left(PhoneNumber; 3) returns the first three digits of the phone number, which is the area code. To find the first name of the document author, search for all the characters to the left of the space between the first and last names, such as @Left(DocumentAuthor; " "). For the author "Bob Dobbs," this formula would return "Bob".
@LowerCase(string)	Converts all the uppercase letters in the specified text string to lowercase. For example, @LowerCase(DocumentAuthor) converts "Bob Dobbs" to "bob dobbs".

continues

Table B.1 continued

@Function	Purpose
@MailSend or @MailSend(SendTo; CopyTo; BlindCopyTo; Subject; Remark; BodyFields;[flags])	Without arguments, @MailSend mails the current document to the recipients indicated in the SendTo field of the document. The document must have a SendTo field. With arguments, @MailSend creates a mail memo based on the information you put in the arguments. For example, @MailSend("Bob Dobbs/Stillwater"; ""; ""; "New Book Idea"; "How about a computer cookbook"; ""; [Encrypt] : [IncludeDocLink]) sends a mail memo to Bob Dobbs with the subject "New Book Idea" and the remark "How about a computer cookbook." The mail message is encrypted and a document link is included, linking back to the document that was selected or open when @MailSend was evaluated. Other flags you can include in an @MailSend formula include [Sign], [PriorityHigh], [PriorityNormal], [PriorityLow], [ReturnReceipt], and [DeliveryReportConfirmed]. To use more than one flag, format them as a list with each entry separated by colons, and each flag must appear in square brackets.
@Max(Number1; Number2)	Returns the larger of two numbers or two lists of numbers. To find the larger of salary paid versus commission earned, the formula would be @Max(Salary; Commission). Caution: This function does *not* return the single largest value from a list of numbers.
@Min(Number1; Number2)	Returns the smaller of two numbers or two lists of numbers. To find the smaller of the salary paid versus commission earned, the formula would be @Min(Salary; Commission). Caution: This function does *not* return the single smallest value from a list of numbers.
@Modified	Returns the date-time value when the document was last modified and saved. If the document was last edited and saved on March 10, 1998 at 10:00 p.m., @Modified returns 03/10/98 10:00:00 PM. Only works correctly in view columns. In existing documents, usually shows the next-to-the-last time the document was saved.
@Month(DateTime)	Returns the number of the month from a date-time value. If a document was last edited and saved on March 10, 1998 at 10:00 p.m., the formula @Month(@Modified) returns 3. @Month starts at 1 for January.

@Function	Purpose
@Name([Action]; Name) *	Use @Name to expand, abbreviate, or manipulate hierarchical names. For example, @Name([CN]; @UserName) returns the common name of the current user. The common name is the first and last name. Other actions you can use include [Abbreviate] to remove the component labels, [C] to return the country component, [Canonicalize] to expand the abbreviated name, [G] to return the given name (first name), [I] to return the initials, [O] to return the organization name, [OUn] to return the organizational unit component (*n* can be a number from 1 to 4), [Q] to return the generational component such as Jr., and [S] to return the surname (last name). Please see Domino Help database for more information on this function.
@NewLine	Inserts a carriage return, or new line, into a text string, so when you want the text to continue on the next line you add an @NewLine formula where you want the line break. For example, in a concatenation formula where you want the city and state on a separate line following the name, you write FirstName + " " + LastName + @NewLine + City + ", " + State. This function doesn't work in selection, hide-when, column, window title, or form formulas. It also doesn't work inside an @Prompt formula, in which case our Tech Editor suggests you use @Char(0) or @Char(13) instead.
@No	Returns the value 0 (zero). Used frequently in @If formulas where a 1 or 0 result is required, such as @If(Salary>Commission; @No; @Yes).
@NoteID	Returns the unique document ID number of the current document. Useful in column formulas in hidden views where you need to look up a document by its unique document ID. Caution: the NoteID is different for the same document in each replica. Only the DocumentUniqueID (UNID) is the same across all replicas for the same document.
@Now	Returns the current date-time. The time and date that are returned are based on the user's computer clock. For example, you can use @Now to calculate a due date within 45 days for an assignment, such as @Adjust(@Now; 0; 0; 45; 0; 0; 0).

continues

Table B.1 continued

@*Function*	*Purpose*
@Pi	Returns the constant value of pi (π).
@PickList*([Custom]; Server : File; View; Title; Prompt; Column; CategoryName) or @PickList([Name] : [Single])	Displays either a dialog box that contains a view you specify (from which a user can select one or more documents) or a window that shows information from all available Directories(from which the user selects one or more person, group, or server names). To choose a document from a Sales Contact view, the formula might be @PickList([Custom]; ""; "Sales Contact"; "Select a Company"; "Select the company name you want to appear in this document"; 4). When the formula evaluates in the document, a dialog box titled "Select a Company" appears, and the user is prompted to "Select the company name to appear in this document." The company names are listed from column 4 of the specified view. To pick items from a Directory, use the keyword [Name] to indicate you want an address book and the optional keyword [Single] to display only a single Address dialog box. An enhancement of @PickList that is available in R5 is the capability to substitute the replica ID for the server and file name to identify the database you want to search. Also, two new keywords, [Room] and [Resource], enable you to open dialog boxes for selecting rooms and resources as in the formula @PickList([Room]). CategoryName is an optional para- meter that displays the specified category in the view (the view must be categorized).
@PostedCommand ([Command]; Parameters)	Executes a Notes command. Used for SmartIcons, buttons, hotspots, and actions. In a formula, @PostedCommand executes after all formulas have been been evaluated. For example, @PostedCommand([FileCloseWindow]) closes the active window. See Appendix C to learn more about @PostedCommand and @Command functions.
@Prompt([Style]: [No Sort]; Title; Prompt; DefaultChoice; ChoiceList)	Use in field formulas, buttons, SmartIcons, manual agents, form actions, or view action formulas to display a dialog box from which the user makes choices. The styles of dialog boxes include Ok (title, prompt, and OK button), YesNo (title, prompt, Yes and No buttons), YesNoCancel (title, prompt, and Yes, No, and Cancel buttons),

@Function	Purpose
	OkCancelEdit (title, prompt, text box for user input, OK and Cancel buttons), OkCancelList (title, prompt, list of choices, OK and Cancel buttons), OkCancelCombo (title, prompt, list of choices, OK and Cancel buttons), OkCancelEditCombo (title, prompt, list of choices with text box, OK and Cancel buttons), OkCancelListMult (title, prompt, list of choices, OK and Cancel buttons), and Password (title, prompt, text that accepts and hides user input, OK and Cancel buttons). Use the optional [NoSort] keyword to have the members of the ChoiceList appear in the order you entered them. The DefaultChoice is the value that appears as the user's input and can be accepted or refused. The formula @Prompt([YesNo]; "Accept Terms"; "Do you accept the terms listed above?") causes the Accept Terms dialog box to appear with a prompt that asks if the user accepts the terms. The user selects Yes or No. The [LocalBrowse]; *title*; *filetype*) displays a box that enables the user to select names from the local file system. Filetype specifies .nsf if LocalBrowse is 1, .ntf if it's 2, or 3 for all other files.
@ProperCase(string)	Converts a text string to lowercase, with the first letter of each word becoming uppercase. For example, @ProperCase(Location) changes the entry from PHILADEL-PHIA, PA to Philadelphia, Pa.
@Replace(SourceList; FromList; ToList)	Replaces the SourceList text string entries that match those in the FromList with those in the ToList. For example, @Replace(Territory; "Unassigned"; TerritoryAssigned) replaces any "Unassigned" entries in the Territory field with the value in the Territory Assigned field. Works on list items: vs.@replaceSubString will change parts of words.
@Return(Value)	Stops the execution of a formula and returns the specified value. For example, the formula @If(Continue = "Yes"; @Command([FileSave]); @Return(@Command([FileCloseWindow]))) makes Notes save the file if the user selects "Yes" but closes the window if the answer is not "Yes."

continues

B

Table B.1   continued

@Function	Purpose

`@Right(SearchString;`
`#Char)`
or
`@Right(SearchString;`
`Substring)`
	Searches a string of characters (SearchString) and returns the rightmost number of characters you specified, as in `@Right(Address; 5)`, which returns the zip code from the address "515 Manly Terrace, Keatsville, Pa 19073." Or, to find the last name of the person in the Name field, use the formula `@Right(Name; " ")`.

`@Round(Number)`
or
`@Round(Number;`
`Factor)`
	Rounds the specified number to the nearest whole number or, if an additional factor is specified, to the nearest factor of the number. For example, `@Round(125.6)` returns `126`, but `@Round(125.6; 10)` returns `130`.

`@Select(Number;` `Values)`	Returns the value that appears in the position specified by the number. Values is a list of items. For example, the formula `@Select(@Month(Due); "January" :` `"February" : "March")` returns `"March"` if the @Month formula result is 3.

`@SetDocField`
`(DocumentUNID;`
`Fieldname; NewValue)`
	Sets a specific field on the document identified by the unique document ID (UNID) to the specified NewValue. For example, `@SetDocField($Ref; "Status";`
	`"Complete")` would set the Status field on the parent document to "Complete."

`@SetTargetFrame`	Followed by the target frame identifier, `@SetTargetFrame(targetframe)`, enables designers to specify a target frame when opening design notes. For example, `@SetTargetFrame("Frame A"); @Command` `([OpenView]; "Touring")` opens the "Touring" view in frame A. Can be used with nested frames, as in `@SetTargetFrame("Frame B":` `"FrameA");@Command([Compose;"Registration")`.
`@Subset(List; Number)`	Searches through the specified list and returns the number of values you specify (reading the list from left to right). For example, whereas the field CitiesVisited can contain multiple values, the formula `@Subset(CitiesVisited; 3)` would return only the first three cities listed. @Subset(CitiesVisited; -3) would return only the last three cities listed.
`@Success`	Used with validation formulas, this function returns `True` (1) if the validation condition is met. For example, if the validation formula reads `@If(Name != "";` `@Success;`

@Function	Purpose
	@Failure("You must enter a name before you can save this document")) and a name appears in the Name field, the validation is True and the document can be saved. Otherwise, the user sees a prompt noting the required information.
@Sum(Numbers)	Calculates the sum of a set of numbers or number lists. For example, to calculate the number of items ordered from three categories of products, the formula would read @Sum(PaperProd : ComputerProd : FurnitureProd).
@Text(Value; FormatString)	Converts a value to a text string. For example, to change the date a document was created to text, write @Text(CreateDate). However, to have that date formatted so only the date appears and it displays the year, month, and day, write @Text(CreateDate; "D0S0"). To have a number appear as text with currency formatting and no decimal places in the number, write @Text(Price; "C,0"). The format strings must appear in quotes and include D0 (year, month and day), D1 (month and day, and year if not the current year), D2 (month and day), D3 (year and month), T0 (hour, minute, and second), T1 (hour and minute), Z0 (Always convert time to this zone), Z1 (Display zone only when it's not this time zone), Z2 (always display zone), S0 (date only), S1 (time only), S2 (date and time), S3 (Date, time, Today, or Yesterday), Sx (for unpredictable formats where value is known to be a date or time), G (general number format), F (fixed format), S (scientific format), C (currency format, including the thousands separator, and no decimal places), , (punctuated at thousands with a comma), % (percentage format), ((parentheses around negative numbers), or the number of digits for the number of decimal places you want to display.
@TextToNumber(String)	Converts a text string to a number, as in the formula @TextToNumber(Price) * Qty.
@TextToTime(String)	Converts a text string to a time-date value, as in @TextToTime(Birthdate).
@Today	Returns today's date without time. Use @Now to return time.

continues

Table B.1 continued

@Function	Purpose
@UndeleteDocument	When database property has soft deletes enabled, this command removes the soft deleted status from a soft deleted document. Use in SmartIcons, or in button or agent formulas. There are no parameters; for example, @UndeleteDocument removes the soft deleted status from any documents that have been soft deleted.
@UpperCase(String)	Converts lowercase letters to uppercase, as in @UpperCase(State), which you might use as an input translation formula to ensure that the state abbreviations are entered in uppercase letters.
@UserName*	Returns the name of the current user as identified by the user ID. For example, @UserName returns CN=Bob Dobbs/O=Stillwater. @UserName(Index) returns the user's primary name if the Index value is 0 and the alternate name if the Index is 1. Caution: for server-based agents the server is considered the user, so @UserName returns the name of the server.
@UserNamesList	If "Enforce a consistent Access Control List across all replicas" is enabled, @UserNamesList returns a text list containing the current name, group names, and roles. Returns a null value ("") when "Enforce a consistent Access Control List across all replicas" is not enabled. Does not work in column, selection, mail agent, or scheduled agent formulas. Example: @If(@IsMember("Sales Force"; @UserNamesList); "Sales Header"; "Generic Header").
@UserRoles	Returns a list of roles assigned the current user, as defined in the access control list of that database. For example, @UserRoles != "Supervisor" might be the hide-when formula for a section that can be seen only by users who have been assigned the Supervisor role for purposes of approving documents. @UserRoles will return the NULL string on local databases unless "Enforce a consistent Access Control List across all replicas" is selected for the ACL.

@Function	Purpose
@ValidateInternetAddress ([KEYWORD]; Address)	Validates an Internet address. If used with [Address821] as the KEYWORD the function validates the address based on the RFC821 Address Format Syntax (the address appears as JCalabri@Stillwater.com). If KEYWORD is [Address822], the function validates based on the RFC822 Address Format Syntax (the address appears as "Calabria, Jane (Indianapolis)"<Jcalabri @Stillwater.com>). Returns NULL if the validation is successful or an error message if it isn't.
@Weekday(Date-Time)	Returns a number that identifies the day of the week for a specified date-time value. Sunday is Day 1, Monday Day 2, and so forth. For example, to calculate what day of the week January 1, 2000 will fall on, write @Select(@Weekday([01/01/2000]); "Sunday" : "Monday" : "Tuesday" : "Wednesday": "Thursday" : "Friday" : "Saturday"). The @Weekday function returns 7, which selects the seventh text string: "Saturday".
@Year(Time-Date)	Extracts the year from a date-time value. For example, @Year(12/14/97) returns 1997.
@Yes	Often included in an @If formula, this function returns the value True (1). For example, @If(Price > 500; @Yes; @No).

@Name enhancement for R5 returns the following new actions: [HierarchyOnly] strips the CN component of a hierarchical name and returns the remaining components. See the Help file for more information.

@Picklist enhancement for R5 can use keywords to open dialogs for selecting rooms and resources from the Name and Address book. For example, @Picklist ([Room]). See the Help file for more information.

@UserName enhancements include a new parameter, "index", which is used to return the user name, alternate user name, or server name indicated by parameter "index". See the Help file for more information.

APPENDIX C

@Commands

The @Command functions are specialized @Function formulas that enable you to access the command structure of Notes and Domino. They are most commonly used in actions, buttons, and agents. There are two classes of @Commands: @Commands and @PostedCommands. This appendix lists only the most commonly used @Command functions, which can also be @PostedCommands, and doesn't provide all the details about using the command. A full listing with details is available in the Designer 5 Help database (we also don't include functions relating to system administration and many agent-related commands, but those commands are available and you probably want to look at them if you are a Domino Administrator as well as an application developer). For more information on @Commands, see Day 11, "Help the User: Design Interface Enhancements."

[AddBookmark]

@Command([AddBookmark]; Urlstring)
@Command([AddBookmark]; Urlstring; Title)
@Command([AddBookmark]; Urlstring; Title; Folder)

Adds a bookmark with the specified URL or with the current object. Use Title to specify a title for the bookmark (optional), and specify the folder in which you want to place the bookmark (if you specify NULL, either an open bookmark page or a default bookmark folder is selected).

[AddDatabase]

@Command([AddDatabase]; Server : Database; Bookmark)

Adds the icon for the database to the user's workspace but doesn't open the database. The Bookmark value is optional—if it's left off or has a value of 0 it adds the database to the Databases folder. If the Bookmark value is 1 Notes displays the Add Bookmark dialog. For example, to have the Sales Contact database added to the user's workspace, use the following command:

```
@Command([AddDatabase]; "Server1/Acme" : "Contacts.nsf")
```

[AttachmentDetachAll]

@Command([AttachmentDetachAll])

Opens the Save Attachments To dialog box so the user can specify a location for storing the attachments in the current open document. If there's only one attachment, it displays the Save Attachment dialog box instead.

[AttachmentLaunch]

@Command([AttachmentLaunch])

Opens the application in which the selected attachment was created (if available) and launches the selected attachment.

[AttachmentView]

@**Command([AttachmentView])**

For a document in read or edit mode, this command launches the Viewer so the user can view the contents of the attachment without opening the source application.

[CalendarGoTo]

@**Command([CalendarGoTo]; TimeDate)**

Displays the View Calendar Go To dialog box if no parameters are specified. With parameters, this moves the view focus to the requested date, as in

```
@Command([CalendarGoTo]; [10-19-98])
```

A calendar view must be open.

[ChooseFolders]

@**Command([ChooseFolders])**

For a document the user has open in edit mode, this command displays the Folders dialog box so the user can select a folder in which to file the document.

[Compose]

@**Command([Compose]; Server: Database; Form; width: height)**

Opens the designated form so the user can create a new, blank document in the specified database. For example, to open the form needed to create a new contact document in the Sales Contact database on Server1, the formula is

```
@Command([Compose]; "Server1/Acme" : "Contacts.nsf"; "New Contact")
```

It isn't necessary to specify the server if the formula refers to a database on the current server. It isn't necessary to add the width and height if you don't need to specify a window size for the document.

C

[EditBottom]

@Command([EditBottom])

Moves the insertion point to the last editable field or button on a form or document.

[EditClear]

@Command([EditClear])

Marks for deletion a selected document from a view, folder, or document in read mode. This command also removes a selected database icon from the workspace. For a document in edit mode, it deletes the currently selected text, tables, graphics, links, file attachments, and objects. Because it immediately deletes a document if invoked from the Web, you might consider using [MoveToTrash] instead if you have Web users.

[EditCopy]

@Command([EditCopy])

Copies selected documents or highlighted data to the Clipboard.

[EditCut]

@Command([EditCut])

Removes selected documents or highlighted data and stores them in the Clipboard.

[EditDeselectAll]

@Command([EditDeselectAll])

Deselects all selected documents or highlighted data.

[EditDetach]

@Command([EditDetach])

or

@Command([EditDetach]; SourceFile; TargetFile)

Detaches a file attachment to a specified location. Without parameters, it opens the Save Attachment dialog box so the user can specify the storage location. With parameters, it detaches the SourceFile and stores it in the TargetFile location. For example, to detach the word processing file TOC.doc from a document and store it in the My Documents folder, type the following:

```
@Command([EditDetach]; "TOC" ; "c:\\My Documents\\TOC.doc")
```

Note that the double backslash is needed in the path. Backslash is a special "escape" character that tells Notes that the character following it is to be used as is, not as the special character. Use a backslash before a double-quote or backslash that you want to include in the text."

C

[EditDocument]

@Command([EditDocument])

or

@Command([EditDocument]; mode)

Places a document into edit mode or a document that is being edited into read mode. With the parameter, it places the document into the specified mode ("1" for edit or "0" for read mode). To open the document in edit mode, type the following:

```
@Command([EditDocument]; "1")
```

[EditFind]

@Command([EditFind])

Displays the Find dialog box in a view, or the Find and Replace dialog box in a document.

[EditFindNext]

@Command([EditFindNext])

Highlights the next document in a view that contains the search string. Highlights the next occurrence of the search string in a document.

[EditGoToField]

@Command([EditGoToField]; Fieldname)

When a document is in edit mode, this command places the insertion point in the specified editable field.

[EditHeaderFooter]

@Command([EditHeaderFooter])

Displays the document or form Property box to let the user set header, footer, and print attributes. However, the Printer tab of the Property box is not automatically selected.

[EditHorizScrollbar]

@Command([EditHorizScrollbar])

Is a toggle command that displays the horizontal scrollbar if currently hidden; otherwise, this command hides it.

[EditInsertFileAttachment]

@Command([EditInsertFileAttachment]; File; Compress)

Without a File parameter, Notes displays the Create Attachment dialog box so the user can specify the filename and location of the file to attach. With the File parameter, Notes attaches the specified file to the document automatically. The Compress parameter is optional: Use "1" to compress the attachment or "0" to not compress it. The document must be in edit mode with the insertion point in a rich text field for this function to work. To attach the file Contacts.xls to a document, use the following formula:

```
@Command([EditInsertFileAttachment]; "c:\\my documents\\Contacts.xls";
➥ "1")
```

[EditInsertObject]

@Command([EditInsertObject]; Object)

Without the Object parameter, the Insert Object dialog box displays. With the Object parameter specified, Notes attempts to insert a copy of the object into the document. The document must be open in edit mode with the insertion point in a rich text field. For example, the following formula inserts an Excel worksheet object in the document:

```
@Command([EditInsertObject]; "Microsoft Excel Worksheet")
```

This is supported only by the Windows platforms. The object name must match a registered name (Excel).

[EditInsertPageBreak]

@Command([EditInsertPageBreak])

Inserts a page break into the document at the insertion point. The document must be in edit mode.

[EditInsertTable]

@Command([EditInsertTable])

Opens the Create Table dialog box so the user can set the number of rows and columns for the new table. The document must be in edit mode with the insertion point in a rich text field.

[EditMakeDocLink]

@Command([EditMakeDocLink])

Creates a link to the current document (either selected in a view or open in read or edit mode) and stores it in the Clipboard so the user can paste it into any rich text field.

[EditOpenLink]

@Command([EditOpenLink])

Opens the selected link.

[EditPaste]

@Command([EditPaste])

Pastes the contents of the Clipboard.

[EditPasteSpecial]

@Command([EditPasteSpecial])

If a document is in edit mode and the insertion point is in a rich text field, this command displays the Paste Special dialog box. The Paste Special dialog box allows the user to determine how to represent the Clipboard content. Some choices are Rich Text, Picture (excludes the text), Bitmap, and Text (excludes the picture).

[EditTableDeleteRowColumn]

@Command([EditTableDeleteRowColumn])

Opens the Delete Row/Column dialog box so the user can set the number of rows or columns to delete from the current table. The insertion point must be in a table, and the document must be in edit mode.

[EditTableFormat]

@Command([EditTableFormat])

For a document in edit mode with the insertion point in a table, this command displays the properties box for the table.

[EditTableInsertRowColumn]

@Command([EditTableInsertRowColumn])

Opens the Insert Row/Column dialog box so the user can set the number of rows or columns to insert in the current table. The insertion point must be in a table, and the document must be in edit mode.

[EditTop]

@Command([EditTop])

In a document in edit mode, moves the insertion point to the first editable field or button, whichever is uppermost in the document.

[EditUndo]

@Command([EditUndo])

Undoes the previous operation, providing that the operation is reversible, such as creating tables, removing attachments, and adding OLE objects. For buttons and actions, it can be used only from the view level to undelete a document that's marked for deletion.

[Execute]

@Command([Execute]; Application; Filenames)

Launches the application (specify the executable file) and loads the specified files. For example, to open the Newslett.doc document file located in the Data folder into Microsoft Word, use the following formula:

```
@Command([Execute]; "C:\\Program Files\\MSOffice\\Office\\Winword.exe";
➥ "C:\\Data\\Newslett.doc")
```

[FileCloseWindow]

@Command([FileCloseWindow])

Closes the active Notes window and prompts the user to save the document if it hasn't been saved. Regardless of where this command is in your formula, it executes last.

[FileExit]

@Command([FileExit])

Closes Notes and all its open windows. If an open document has not been saved, a prompt appears. Regardless of where this command is in your formula, it executes last.

C

[FileExport]

@Command([FileExport]; FileType; FileName)

Exports a view or document. For example, to export the selected document in Word for Windows 6.0 format as the file Schedule.doc, use the following formula:

```
@Command([FileExport]; "Word for Windows 6.0"; "C:\\Data\\Schedule.doc")
```

See the Designer 5 Help documentation for a list of valid file types.

[FileImport]

@Command([FileImport]; FileType; FileName)

Imports a specified file into a document or view. For example, to import a Lotus 1-2-3 worksheet named Schedule.wk1 into a view, use the following formula:

```
@Command([FileImport]; "Lotus 1-2-3"; "c:\\data\\Schedule.wk1")
```

Usually used at the view level, FileImport can also be used for a document in edit mode when the insertion point is in a rich text field.

[FileOpenDatabase]

@Command([FileOpenDatabase]; Server : Database; View; Key; NewInstance; Temporary)

or

@Command([FileOpenDatabase]; Server : Database; Navigator; Solo; NewInstance; Temporary)

Opens a specified database to a specified view or navigator and highlights the first document that has a value in the sort column that matches the key. For example, the following formula opens the Contacts.nsf database on Server1 to the Contacts by Company view and scrolls to the first document that's category is Northeast Territory:

```
@Command([FileOpenDatabase]; "Server1": "Contacts.nsf";
➥"Contacts by Company"; "Northeast Territory"; ""; "")
```

A value of 1 in NewInstance indicates that you want the view to open in a new window; 0 indicates that you only want a window open if necessary. The empty Temporary string means you want to add the database to the user's workspace (use 1 if you don't). A Solo value of 1 means that you want the navigator to open in its own window.

All parameters are optional except the name of the server and the database name.

[FilePageSetup]

@Command([FilePageSetup])

Displays the Page Setup dialog box so the user can specify print settings for the selected database.

[FilePrint]

@Command([FilePrint]

or

@Command([FilePrint]; NumCopies; FromPage; ToPage; "draft"; "printview"; FormName; "pagebreak"; "resetpages";startdate; enddate)

Prints the currently open or selected documents or the current view. Use the optional print parameters and keywords to specify how the printing job is to be done. For example, the following formula will print three copies of the current view with a page break between each document:

```
@Command([FilePrint]; "3"; ""; ""; ""; "printview"; ""; "pagebreak";
➥"resetpages")
```

Each document will start numbering with Page 1, instead of numbering all the printed pages consecutively starting with the first page printed. By specifying an empty string for FromPage and ToPage, you indicate that you want to print all the pages. "Draft" means you want draft quality printing. Specify the name of a form if you want to print a document using a form other than the current form.

[FileSave]

@Command([FileSave])

Saves an open document (in edit mode) as if the user had selected File, Save from the menu commands.

[Folder]

@Command([Folder]; FolderName; MoveOrCopy)

Moves or copies the selected document to a folder. You can't omit the FolderName parameter; you must enter NULL or "" to hold the parameter's place. When you don't enter a FolderName, the Move to Folder dialog box displays so the user can specify a folder.

Use "1" in the MoveOrCopy parameter to indicate a move; use "0" to copy the document to the folder (the Move button is dimmed). When you use this function, a saved document must be open or selected in a view. The following formula moves the selected document to the Important folder:

```
@Command([Folder]; "Important"; "1"
```

[HelpTableOfContents]

@Command([HelpTableOfContents])

Displays the table of contents from the Help database. The user can select a topic to read. Although this command is no longer listed in Domino 5 Designer Help, it still works.

[MailComposeMemo]

@Command([MailComposeMemo])

Creates a blank mail memo document for the user to complete and send.

[MailOpen]

@Command([MailOpen])

Opens the user's mail database.

[MailSend]

@Command([MailSend])

Displays the Mail Send dialog box so the user can choose encryption, signing, and how to send a mail memo. The underlying document must have a field named SendTo in it to successfully execute this command.

[MoveToTrash]

@Command([MoveToTrash])

Marks the currently selected document for deletion. This command is the same as [EditClear], except that on the Web [MoveToTrash] doesn't delete the current document. Because this command works consistently in both environments, use it whenever you have Web users involved. By the way, you can use this command to program the view applet.

[NavigateNext]

@Command([NavigateNext])

Goes to the next document, response document, or response-to-response document in the current view or folder. Regardless of where this command is in the code, it executes last.

[NavigateNextMain]

@Command([NavigateNextMain])

Goes to the next *main* document in the current view. Regardless of where this command is in the code, it executes last.

[NavigatePrev]

@Command([NavigatePrev])

Goes to the previous document in the current view or folder. Regardless of where this command is in the code, it executes last.

[NavigatePrevMain]

@Command([NavigatePrevMain])

Goes to the previous *main* document in the current view or folder. Regardless of where this command is in the code, it executes last.

[OpenFrameset]

@Command ([OpenFramset]; Frameset)

Opens a defined frameset for the current database. Frameset is the name of a frameset, defined for the current database.

[ObjectOpen]

@Command([ObjectOpen])

Opens a selected OLE object for editing on Windows platforms only.

C

[OpenCalendar]

@Command([OpenCalendar]; Username)

Opens the mail file for the Username person to the Calendar view. If a name isn't specified, the name picker displays. After a name is selected, that person's mail opens to the Calendar view.

[OpenDocument]

@Command([OpenDocument]; WriteOrReadOnly; UNID; width : height)

Opens a document. Use the optional parameter WriteOrReadOnly to open the document in edit mode by specifying "1" as the parameter; use "0" to open the document in read-only mode. To open a document other than the currently selected document, specify the unique document ID as the UNID parameter.

[OpenHelpDocument]

@Command ([OpenHelpDocument]; "Server" : "Database"; "Viewname"; "Key")
@Command([OpenHelpDocument; [ClientHelp]; "Viewname"; "Key")
@Command([OpenHelpDocument; [DesignerHelp]; "Viewname"; "Key")
@Command([OpenHelpDocument; [AdminHelp]; "Viewname"; "Key")

Enables users to press F1 and access the help files created by application developers or the help files in one of the R5 Help databases (specified in keyword). Works in conjunction with the HelpRequest event available for forms. Use this in a hotspot or a button on the Web.

[OpenNavigator]

@Command([OpenNavigator]; Navigator; Solo)

Opens the specified navigator. Use a value of "1" for the optional parameter Solo to open the navigator in its own window.

[OpenView]

@Command([OpenView]; ViewName; Key; NewInstance)

Opens the specified view from the current database. The default view for the database opens if you omit the ViewName parameter. Use the optional Key parameter to indicate the document you want to scroll to when the view opens. The Key is a value that appears in the first sorted column of the view. Specify "1" as the NewInstance parameter if you want the view to open in a new window. For example, the following formula opens the Company by Territory view and selects the first document that's value begins with "Northeast":

```
@Command([OpenView]); "Companies by Territory"; "Northeast")
```

[RefreshParentNote]

@Command([RefreshParentNote])

Sends the values entered in a dialog box to the parent document (the document that was active when the dialog box was opened). When using this command, the parent note is updated without your having to click OK in the dialog box.

[RemoveFromFolder]

@Command([RemoveFromFolder])

Removes a selected document from the current folder. This command can be used with the view applet.

[ShowHidePreviewPane]

@Command([ShowHidePreviewPane]; ShowOrHide)

Displays or hides the document preview pane. Specify a value of "1" as the ShowOrHide parameter to show the document in the preview pane; "0" hides it. Omit the parameter to toggle from the current state of display.

C

[TextAlignCenter]

@Command([TextAlignCenter])

Horizontally centers the current text. The document must be in edit mode with the insertion point in a rich text field.

[TextAlignFull]

@Command([TextAlignFull])

Aligns the text at the left and right edges of the field. The document must be in edit mode with the insertion point in a rich text field.

[TextAlignLeft]

@Command([TextAlignLeft])

Aligns the text along the left margin but leaves the ends of the lines ragged on the right side. The document must be in edit mode with the insertion point in a rich text field.

[TextAlignNone]

@Command([TextAlignNone])

Reverses the previous text alignment. The document must be in edit mode with the insertion point in a rich text field.

[TextAlignRight]

@Command([TextAlignRight])

Aligns the text along the right margin. The document must be in edit mode with the insertion point in a rich text field.

[TextBold]

@Command([TextBold])

Makes selected text—and any text that follows—bold. Use the same command to turn off the boldface. The document must be in edit mode with the insertion point in a rich text field.

[TextBullet]

@Command([TextBullet]; OnOff)

Applies bulleting to any selected text or text that is subsequently added. Specify "1" as the OnOff parameter to turn the bullets on and "0" to turn the bullets off. The document must be in edit mode with the insertion point in a rich text field.

[TextEnlargeFont]

@Command([TextEnlargeFont])

Increases to the next point size any selected text or any subsequently added text. The document must be in edit mode with the insertion point in a rich text field.

[TextFont]

@Command([TextFont])

Displays the Text Properties box so the user can select the typeface, size, color, and style for the selected text or the text that is about to be typed. The document must be in edit mode with the insertion point in a rich text field.

[TextItalic]

@Command([TextItalic])

Italicizes the selected and subsequently added text. Use the same command to turn off the Italic attribute. The document must be in edit mode with the insertion point in a rich text field.

[TextNormal]

@Command([TextNormal])

Removes all style attributes from selected text and text that is entered subsequently. The document must be in edit mode with the insertion point in a rich text field.

[TextNumbers]

@Command([TextNumbers]; OnOff)

Applies paragraph numbering to any selected text or text that is subsequently added. Specify "1" as the OnOff parameter to turn the numbering on and "0" to turn it off. The document must be in edit mode with the insertion point in a rich text field.

[TextReduceFont]

@Command([TextReduceFont])

Decreases to the next lower point size any selected text or text subsequently added. The document must be in edit mode with the insertion point in a rich text field.

[TextSetFontColor]

@Command([TextSetFontColor]; [Color])

Changes the color attributes of selected text. The document must be in edit mode with the insertion point in a rich text field. The following formula sets the text color to dark magenta:

```
@Command([TextSetFontColor]; [DarkMagenta])
```

The other color choices include Black, Red, Green, Blue, Magenta, Yellow, Cyan, White, Gray, DarkRed, DarkGreen, DarkBlue, Brown, and DarkCyan. Note: Don't put quotes around the square brackets.

[TextSetFontFace]

@Command([TextSetFontFace]; Typeface)

Sets the selected text to the specified font (which must be available as a font choice on the user's computer). For example,

```
@Command([TextSetFontFace]; "Times New Roman")
```

sets the typeface to Times New Roman. The document must be in edit mode with the insertion point in a rich text field.

[TextSetFontSize]

@Command([TextSetFontSize]; Size)

Sets the specified point size for the selected text. The following formula sets the size of the selected text to 12 points:

```
@Command([TextSetFontSize]; "12")
```

The document must be in edit mode with the insertion point in a rich text field or have selected text in a rich text field.

[TextSpacingDouble]

@Command([TextSpacingDouble])

Sets the line spacing for the selected text to double-spacing. The document must be in edit mode with the insertion point in a rich text field.

[TextSpacingSingle]

@Command([TextSpacingSingle])

Sets the line spacing for the selected text to single-spacing. The document must be in edit mode with the insertion point in a rich text field.

[TextUnderline]

@Command([TextUnderline])

Underlines selected text or any text that is subsequently entered. The document must be in edit mode with the insertion point in a rich text field.

[ToolsCall]

@Command([ToolsCall])

Opens the Call Server dialog box so the user can select a server and dial into it.

[ToolsHangUp]

@Command([ToolsHangUp])

Opens the Hang Up dialog box so the user can disconnect from the server.

[ToolsMarkAllRead]

@Command([ToolsMarkAllRead])

Marks all the documents in a database as read if the database is open at the view or folder level or if a document is open.

[ToolsRefreshAllDocs]

Refreshes the fields of the documents in a view or folder.

[ToolsRefreshSelectedDocs]

Refreshes the fields of all the selected documents in a view or folder.

[ToolsReplicate]

@Command([ToolsReplicate]; RepMethod)

Opens the Replicate dialog box for the open or selected database. Use a value of "1" for the RepMethod to enable the user to set the replication options; use "0" to replicate with current settings. Omit the RepMethod parameter to cause a prompt to appear, asking the user to select the method.

[ToolsRunMacro]

@Command([ToolsRunMacro]; Agent)

Executes the agent you specify, as in the following formula, which runs the Archive Rejected Books agent:

```
@Command([ToolsRunMacro]; "Archive Rejected Books")
```

[ToolsSpellCheck]

@**Command**([**ToolsSpellCheck**])

Starts the spell checker if the document is in edit mode.

[ViewChange]

@**Command**([**ViewChange**]; **ViewName**)

Opens the specified view or folder in the current database. If the view or folder isn't specified, the View menu displays so the user can select a view. This command doesn't work from within a document or form. For example, the following formula changes the open view to the Company by Territory view:

```
@Command([ViewChange]; "Company by Territory")
```

[ViewHorizScrollBar]

@**Command**([**ViewHorizScrollBar**])

Hides or shows (this is a toggle) the horizontal scrollbar in a view or folder.

[ViewNavigatorsFolders]

@**Command**([**ViewNavigatorsFolders**])

From a view or folder, switches to the Folders and Views navigator in the Navigator Pane and opens the view or folder that the user had open most recently.

[ViewRefreshFields]

@**Command**([**ViewRefreshFields**])

Recalculates the fields in the current document (in edit mode) or updates the current view or folder, like pressing F9. For Web applications, you must set the database property **Web Access: Use JavaScript when generating pages**. You can program the view applet using this command, in which case the Use JavaScript property doesn't have to be selected.

C

[ViewShowRuler]

@Command([ViewShowRuler])

Displays or hides (a toggle command) the ruler when the document is in edit mode. Despite its name, this command does not operate on a view, only in documents.

[ViewShowSearchBar]

@Command([ViewShowSearchBar]; OnOff)

Displays the full text search bar at the top of the view. Specify "1" as the OnOff parameter to show the search bar and "0" to hide it. If this parameter is omitted, the formula toggles the display.

[ViewSwitchForm]

@Command([ViewSwitchForm]; FormName)

Changes the form that is used to display the current document, as in

```
@Command([ViewSwitchForm]; "Contacts")
```

If the FormName is omitted, a dialog box appears with a list of forms available in that database. This command does not work if the document has a form stored in it.

[WindowWorkspace]

@Command([WindowWorkspace])

Makes the workspace the active window.

APPENDIX **D**

Frequently Used HTML

Although you will rarely have to use HTML tags directly in Domino applications, you might have to do so occasionally, and you will probably want to at times. To give you an overview of what you can accomplish with HTML tags, we have provided several tables. Domino R5 supports HTML 4.0 and because this is a rapidly changing area you will want to frequently visit two sites: www.w3.org/MarkUp for the latest spec on HTML and the Lotus site www.lotus.com to see if Domino supplies any updates regarding HTML.

In Table D.1, we've listed the tags used in the Head sections of HTML documents. In Table D.2, we've listed the most commonly used tags that can appear in the Body section of an HTML document. In Table D.3, we've listed the tags that can appear in an HTML form.

If our overview of HTML is not enough to satisfy your craving for expertise, you'll find that *Sams Teach Yourself HTML 4 in 24 Hours*, Third Edition, by Dick Oliver can provide you with a thorough grounding in the fundamentals of HTML.

Table D.1   HTML Tags Used in the Head Sections of HTML Documents

Element	Type	Description
BASE	empty	Base context document.
HEAD	container	Document head.
META	empty	Additional information about the document. Also used to enter keywords for search engine categories, including the facility to specify keywords in different languages.
SCRIPT	container	Used to specify script language, as in <SCRIPT LANGUAGE="JavaScript">. Also used to enter script code.
STYLE	container	Used for cascading style sheet definitions.
TITLE	container	Document title.

Table D.2   HTML Tags Used in the Body Sections of HTML Documents

Tag	Type	Description
A	container	Anchor. Can be either the source or the destination of a hypertext link.
ADDRESS	container	Address, signature, or byline for a document. Usually appears in Italics at the bottom of the document.
B	container	Boldface text
BLOCKQUOTE	container	Quoted paragraph that the browser would usually display indented further than standard paragraphs.
BODY	container	The body of a document.
BR	empty	A line break but not a paragraph break. No white space appears between the lines.
CITE	container	Title of a cited document. Usually appears italicized.
CODE	container	Text of programming code. Usually appears in monospaced font.
LI	empty	List item.
DL	container	Definition list or glossary. See DT and DD.
DT	empty	Defined term. See DL and DD.

Tag	Type	Description
DD	empty	Definition of a term. Appears in a Definition List. See DL and DT.
EM	container	Emphasized text. Usually appears italicized.
H1 through H6	container	Heading paragraph, levels 1 (most general, main headings) through 6 (most specific, sub-headings). Can be used to outline a document. Appear in progressively smaller fonts with progressively less emphasis.
HR	empty	Horizontal rule. A line across the screen.
I	container	Italics.
IMG	empty	Contains the URL of any image or icon to be embedded in an HTML document.
KBD	container	Used to denote any keyboard input to be entered by the user. Usually appears in a monospace font.
OL	container	Ordered list. Appears as a numbered list. Use the LI tag to delimit the listed items.
UL	container	Unordered list. Appears as a bulleted list. Use the LI tag to delimit the listed items.
P	empty (but optionally can take a </P> tag)	Paragraph break. Similar to the tag, but defines a new paragraph. A line of white space appears between the paragraphs.
PRE	container	Contains *pre*formatted text. Appears as a monospace font. Extra spaces between characters are preserved to maintain column formatting. (Normally, HTML removes extra spaces.)
STRONG	container	An alternative to <EM>. Usually displayed in boldface.
TT	container	Typewriter text. Appears in monospace font. Like <PRE>, permits column formatting because extra spaces between characters are preserved.
TABLE	container	Defines an HTML table.
TH	container	Defines a header row at the top of a table or header column down the left side of a table.
TR	container	Defines a standard row in a table.
TD	container	TD stands for *Table Data*. Defines a cell in a table row.

D

Table D.3   HTML Tags Used in HTML Forms

Tag	Type	Description
FORM	container	Defines an input form. Appears within the Body section of an HTML document. The other form tags, listed as follows, must appear within the <FORM>…</FORM> container.
INPUT	empty	One-line form input field. Can be of types Text, Password, Checkbox, Radio, Reset, or Submit. Text is the default and appears as a box into which the user can enter text. Password is also a text box, but nothing appears on the screen when the user enters text into the field. Checkbox and Radio both present lists. Reset and Submit both present clickable buttons.
TEXTAREA	empty	Multiline form input field. Defines a rectangular area into which the user can enter lines of text.
SELECT	empty	Pick-list form input field. Appears either as a pop-up menu or a scrollable list of choices.

Understanding Color Attributes in HTML

HTML 4.0 supports 16 primary colors, as described in Table D.4. Within HTML it is highly recommended that the names (not case sensitive) are used. The RGB color scheme is also available where it is of the format #RRGGBB where each of RR, GG, and BB are replaced by a hexadecimal number from zerozero (00) to FF. It is probably best to set the Use Web Palette under File, Preferences, User Preferences, Additional Options. Also, you need to restrict yourself to defining your own colors in style sheets only.

Table D.4   HTML Colors and Their sRGB Value

Black	#000000
Silver	#C0C0C0
Gray	#808080
White	#FFFFFF
Maroon	#800000
Red	#FF0000
Purple	#800080
Fuchsia	#FF00FF

Green	#008000
Lime	#00FF00
Olive	#808000
Yellow	FFFF00
Navy	000080
Blue	0000FF
Teal	008080
Aqua	00FFFF

A good book on the topic of using color and graphics in Web design is *Designing Web Graphics.2* by Lynda Weinman, New Riders Publishing, Indianapolis, IN, 1996.

Creating Hypertext Links

Creating hypertext links in HTML is a simple matter of inserting an HTML *Anchor* tag pair:

```
<A HREF="URL">URL highlighted text or graphic goes here</A>
```

The `<A>` tag begins the Anchor. The `</A>` tag ends it. The text or picture in between is what the Web user clicks on to activate the link. If it is text, it appears in the browser as either underlined text or in a different color than the surrounding text, or perhaps both, depending on how the browser works and how the user has configured the browser. A graphic link won't appear different from any other graphic in the browser, but when the user points at it, the mouse pointer icon changes from an arrow to a pointing hand.

The `<A>` tag includes an `HREF` attribute, which is set equal to the name and location (that is, the URL) of the file to which the anchor links.

The preceding syntax points to a file, and when a Web user clicks on the link, her browser retrieves that file, formats it, and displays it with the beginning of the file at the top of the browser's screen. If a given HTML page is many screens in length, you can set up hypertext links to different places on the page. You can do this by inserting anchors with Name attributes on the page at the positions to which you want to link and then pointing to those anchors by name.

A Name anchor looks something like this:

```
<A NAME="XYZ">XYZ</A>w
```

D

A hypertext link that points to it looks something like this:

```
<A HREF="#XYZ">Go to XYZ</A>
```

Note that *XYZ* in the preceding HREF is preceded by a pound sign (#). This is the tip-off to the browser that the HREF refers to a named anchor rather than a file, and that the browser is to search through the current page for an anchor with NAME="XYZ" as one of its attributes.

If the named anchor is in a different file, use the following syntax:

```
<A HREF=#URL#AnchorName>…</A>
```

For an example of the use of named anchors, take an HTML page that consists of an alphabetical listing of people's names. You can divide it up alphabetically by inserting name anchors at the beginning of each letter break in the list. At the beginning of the document you can insert a list of pointers to the letters of the alphabet. The user can click on a letter in the list at the top of the page; the browser then jumps to that point in the alphabet. The raw HTML might look something like this:

```
<HTML>
<HEAD>
<TITLE>Friends of Bill</TITLE>
</HEAD>
<Body>
<CENTER><H1>Friends of Bill</H1></CENTER><P><P>
Click on a letter below to jump to that part of the alphabet:<P>
<A HREF="#A">A  </A>
<A HREF="#B">B </A>
<A HREF="#C">C </A>
…
<A HREF="#Z">Z </A>
<P><HR><P>
<CENTER><H2><A NAME="A">A</A></H2></CENTER><P>
Aardvark, Alvin<BR>
Abate, Mary<BR>
Accardo, Ricardo<BR>
…
Azzolino, Nina<P><P>
<DIV align="center"><H2><A NAME="B">B</A></H2></CENTER><P>
Babbage, Bob<BR>
…
</BODY>
</HTML>
```

APPENDIX E

Formulas and Scripts by Task

Here are some great ideas for adding features or functionality to your application, listed by task.

Great Window Titles

The window title displays information about what is in the window. In the Notes client, the window titles can be the name of the form you're using to create a document or simply "Lotus Notes"—which conveys little meaning. To make your window titles more useful, try some of our suggestions. You specify the window title by selecting Window Title in the Objects list of the Programmer's Pane and then entering the formula in the Script Area.

Shows the Number of Responses

When you have a discussion database, use this window title formula for the main topic document. For an existing document, it displays the number of responses the topic has; for a main topic document you are creating, it displays the type of document (in the case of our Proposed Titles database, that is "Proposed Title"):

```
@If(@IsNewDoc; "New Proposed Title"; Title +
@DocDescendants(" - No Responses"; " - 1 Response"; " - %Responses"))
```

Displays the Number of the Current Response

In a discussion database, when a new response or response-to-response document is created, the window title in this formula displays "New Response to" and the subject. After the document is saved, the window title includes the total number of responses for that topic and the number of the response that is open:

```
@If(@IsNewDoc; "New Response to " + Subject; "Response " +
@DocNumber("") + " of " + @DocSiblings + " to " + Subject
```

Add the Date Created

This formula creates a window title that displays the name of the Company (in the CompanyName field) and the date the document was created:

```
"Information Sheet for " + CompanyName + " created on " +
@Text(@Created; "D0S0")
```

The format string `"D0S0"` displays the date only in Month-Day-Year format.

Include the Name of the Form

Instead of including the words *Information Sheet* as part of the window title, use the name of the form. That way, if the form name changes, the window title does too.

```
Form + " for " + CompanyName
```

Write an Agent to Delete a Field

When you need to remove a field, delete it on the form. However, the documents you already created with that form retain that field data. That's why you need the *agent*, which you run manually to remove the field data from existing documents. For the documents on which you want the agent to run, select **Run Once (@Commands may be used)**.

The formula for the agent is

```
FIELD fieldname := @DeleteField;
@Command([ViewRefreshFields])
```

where *fieldname* represents the name of the field you want to delete.

Save a Document with Field Validations

When you have a form to which you added the typical Save and Close Action buttons, you sometimes have problems when the form also requires several field validations. With each field validation that doesn't pass comes another @Failure message, followed by a Do you want to save the document type of message. That can get tedious after a while. Wouldn't it be better to only get the save prompt once? You do if you use this formula for the Save and Close action:

```
@If(@Command([FileSave]); @Command([FileCloseWindow]); @Return(""))
```

This suggestion comes our way from the 2Cool4Domino electronic newsletter. Check out their Web site at www.lotus411.com for other cool suggestions and to sign up for their newsletter.

Help Web Users Get to the Top

You see it fairly often on the Web that a page has a link you click to take you back to the top of the page, or one at the top to take you to the bottom. With longer pages, this is really helpful. With a Domino application, this becomes really important because the Action buttons on the Web are at the top of the page, and you can't see them after you scroll down the page.

The easiest way to handle this is to create an anchor link to some hidden text at the top of the page. Then, at the bottom of the page, paste the link with related text. Do the same thing in reverse to go to the bottom of the page. You can use a hotspot link too.

E

Validate a Telephone Number

Telephone numbers need to have 10 digits, with dashes properly placed. You can create an input translation formula that adds the dashes, which only works if the user doesn't add the dashes. This validation formula makes sure the number of digits is correct and that the dashes are properly placed—or else the user gets a message saying the number was not entered properly:

```
@If(@Matches(Phone; "{0-9}{0-9}{0-9}-{0-9}{0-9}{0-9}-
{0-9}{0-9}{0-9}{0-9}"); @Success; @Failure("Make sure
you enter the ten-digit telephone number in this
format XXX-XXX-XXXX"))
```

Use a Password Field

When a user enters a password in a password field, all anyone sees is a set of asterisks. For further security on the password, the application should not save the field after the password has been verified. One way to do this is to use an Input Translation formula that matches the input password with the HTTP password in the user's Person document in the Domino Directory. If it matches, a prompt says that the password was accepted; if not, a prompt says the password is incorrect. The password field is then deleted.

The formula looks like this:

```
Temp := @DbLookup(""; "Osprey/Stillwater":"names.nsf"; "($Users)";
@UserName; "HTTPPassword");
@If(@IsError(Temp); @Prompt([OK]; "Error"; "Error");
@Password(Password) = Temp; @Prompt([OK]; "Password";
"Password is correct"); @Prompt([OK]; "Password";
"Password is Incorrect"));

@Unavailable
```

Force Web User Authentication

Anonymous users aren't always prompted for a name and password when they enter a Web site. If you want to make your Web users authenticate no matter what their ACL status, add a Login argument to the end of a Domino URL.

Your URL looks like this:

```
http://Host/DatabaseDirectory/DatabaseFileName?OpenDatabase&login
```

or

```
http://Host?OpenServer&login
```

For example, to open the Completed Titles database in the Books directory for Stillwater's Web site, the URL might be

```
http://www.Stillwater.com/books/completed.nsf?OpenDatabase&login
```

Let Web Users Send Documents

For your Web users who have mail databases on a Domino server to participate in mail processes, you have to supply a substitute for any menu commands (no Notes menus on the Web!) or system actions. *System actions* are the default set of actions that Designer makes available for every form or view.

Instead, use a form or view action. The buttons are a shortcut for the Notes user and a necessity for the Web users. A Send Document action, for example, uses an @MailSend function.

Convert Date/Time Values to Text

When you concatenate fields and text, but also when performing calculations, data type compatibility is a problem. You don't want to see an error message saying `Date expected` or `Text expected`.

To avoid compatibility problems, convert any dates in concatenations to text using the `@Text(value; format-string)` function.

The problem most designers encounter when dealing with @Text is getting the correct format string.

The first part of the format string defines what you want displayed: `D` for date, `T` for time, `Z` for time zone, or `S` to display only one portion of the date/time value. Combine the letter with a number that indicates which format you want to see. For example, `D0` displays the year, month, and day of the date, whereas `D3` shows the year and the month. When you put one of the date (`D`) or time (`T`) strings in the argument, adding a zone (`Z`) string further defines the time value. The string formats (`S`) indicate whether you want just the time or just the date to display.

With that explanation, use Table E.1 to work on your date to text conversions.

E

Table E.1 Date to Text Conversion Format Strings

String	Displays
D0	Year, month, day
D1	Month and day (year only if it isn't the current year)
D2	Month and day
D3	Year and month
T0	Hour, minute, and second
T1	Hour and minute
Z0	Zone (always convert time to this zone)
Z1	Zone (only when not this zone)
Z2	Zone (always shown)
S0	Date only
S1	Time only
S3	Date, time, Today, or Yesterday
Sx	Time, date, or both (depending on the value passed—use only when you aren't sure of the format)

Therefore, when you want to see the month, day, and year of a date but you don't want to see the time portion, the format string is `"D0S0"`.

For example, if you concatenate text with the date, it might look like this:

```
"This document was submitted on " + @Text(@Created; "D0S0")
```

Convert Numbers to Text

Another data compatibility problem occurs when combining number and text fields. Again, you must convert the number to text using the @Text function. Table E.2 shows the number format strings.

Table E.2 Number-to-Text Conversion Format Strings

String	Returns Format
%	Percentage
(	Puts parentheses around negative numbers
,	Adds thousands separator
C	Currency
F	Fixed (set decimal places)
G	General (significant digits only)
S	Scientific (E notation)
number	Number of decimal places

A concatenation including data from a number field (such as Age) might look like this:

```
"We congratulate you on your " + Age + "th Birthday"
```

E

GLOSSARY

.gif   The filename extension for GIF (Graphic Interchange Format), a graphic file format with widespread use on the Internet. .gif files are compressed graphic files that can be animated and can have transparent backgrounds. See also *.jpg or .jpeg*.

.jpg or .jpeg   The filename extension for the Joint Photographic Experts Group format. One of two graphic files formats in use on the Internet. See also *.gif*

.nsf   The filename extension for a Domino Database (as in `Mail.nsfd`). The letters are short for Notes Storage Facility.

.ntf   The filename extension for a Domino Database design template (as in `perweb.ntf`). The letters are short for Notes Template Facility.

@command   A built-in formula that runs a Notes command. Commands include menu commands and specialized commands.

@function   A commonly used or complex formula that is built in to Notes.

About this Database document   A special document that describes the purpose of a Domino database. The document can be viewed from the Help menu. The database designer can work with the document from the Resources, Other menu in the Domino Designer client.

Accelerator key   See *Hotkey*.

Access Control   See *Access Control List*.

Access Control List (ACL)   A list of users, groups, and servers and their rights and access privileges to a Domino database.

Access control section   Within a Notes form, a section where the capability to edit can be restricted to specific individuals. An individual must already have the right to edit the document in the ACL before he can be granted the privilege to edit an access-controlled section. Other users can still read the section.

Access level   A security feature that defines the degree of access to a database granted to a user, group, or server. There are seven levels of access: No Access, Depositor, Reader, Author, Editor, Designer, and Manager.

ACL   See *Access Control List*.

ACL Monitor   A statistical report document that can be set up in the Domino Directory to monitor all changes to ACLs.

Action Bar   Also called a button bar, this nonscrolling region at the top of a view or form contains predefined Actions for that form or view.

Action Buttons and Hotspots   The preprogrammed areas of a view or form that users click on to automate.

Address bar   The area of a window that shows the current file path or Web page address (URL). New file or address requests are entered here.

Address Books   See *Personal Address Book* and *Domino Directory*.

Adjacent Domain Document   A document in the Domino Directory used to restrict mail routing from one Domino domain to adjacent (connected) and non-adjacent (not connected) Domino domains.

Administration Process   A process on the Domino Server (adminp) that automates the completion of changes initiated by the Domino Administrator, such as name changes, recertification of IDs, and moving databases.

Agent (macro)   A program that consists of and performs a series of automated tasks. An agent can be initiated by the user or can run on a scheduled basis. It is comprised of three parts: 1. When it acts (the trigger); 2. What it acts on (the search); and 3. What it does (the action). Agents are written in the Lotus Formula language, LotusScript, JavaScript, or Java.

Agent Builder   The window in Notes where users create and test agents.

Agent Manager   The server program that runs and controls the agents (macros) on a server.

Alarm   In Domino, an automated notification that a triggering event has occurred. For example, a calendar event can notify a user that he has a meeting in 30 minutes, or a server event can trigger an alarm to the Domino administrator that a performance threshold has been reached.

Alias   In Domino, an additional name for a Notes form by which the element can be referred to in formulas. By referencing an alias in formulas, the full name can be changed as it appears in places such as on menus or in selection boxes without having to change all the formulas.

Anonymous Access   The unauthenticated access to a Domino Server by a Notes or Web user. Usually used on public access databases where an Anonymous entry in the ACL enables people to view the database without having to verify their identity with the server.

API (Applicaton Programming Interface)   A set of functions that give programmers access to Notes and Domino internal features from within their own applications.

Applets   See *Java Applets*

Application Proxy   A firewall configuration that controls the flow of information between internal and external clients and servers, based on the type of information in a packet and whether the network allows delivery of packets to the destination.

Applications   A collection of programs and design objects that enable users to interact with data.

Array   A collection of similar data items. In LotusScript, lists and other objects are treated as arrays. To create an array in LotusScript, use the DIM statement.

Attachment   A file attached to a document or form.

Authenticate   In Domino, to exchange identifying information in such a way that the identity of both parties is established.

Author access   A level of security (defined in the Access Control List) that permits a user or server to create and edit his own documents.

Authors field   A field that contains the name of the author of a document. When combined with author access to the database, an Authors field can be used to grant editor access to users who are not authors of the document.

Autolaunch   Automatically launches an attachment or embedded object in its native format when a Notes document is opened.

Autoregistration   The automated process of adding databases when the type of database and the path are provided during a connection.

Billing   In Domino, a server task that collects and reports data that can be used when billing for connect time and/or data access.

Binary Tree Server Topology   A type of topology where servers connect to each other in a branching tree. The first server connects to two others, and those two each connect to two others, and so on. Information can flow up or down the branches.

Bookmark   In Domino, a link that references a document or a location in a document on the Web or in a Domino database.

Bookmark folder   A folder on the bookmark bar that holds bookmarks linking to Domino databases, Notes views or documents, or Web pages.

Broadcast meeting   A type of calendar entry that invites people to a meeting but to which no response is required.

Browser   A graphical interface that enables users to interact with the World Wide Web on the Internet.

Button Bar   See *Action Bar.*

Button Hotspot   Also known as a pushbutton, actions that appear in the form of a clickable button that can be added to forms, subforms, pages, and documents.

CA (Certificate Authority)   The issuer of certificates that guarantees a certificate's authenticity.

Calendar   In Domino, the calendaring views, forms, and documents built in to the Notes mail template; it is used to make and track events such as appointments, meetings, and anniversaries. The calendar function also includes the scheduling of shared resources and tracking freetime for meeting scheduling and group calendaring.

Calendar profile   A document that defines how the Notes calendar should handle different types of calendar events on a Notes client.

Canonical format   The format in which Notes stores hierarchical names internally, with each hierarchical component identified by a one- or two-character code. For example, CN=John Smith/OU=East/O=Acme/C=US.

Cascading Falling from. In cascading *menu*, a collection of menu items that fall under a single prompt in a parent menu. The File, Database menu prompt is an example. In cascading *actions*, a collection of actions that appear under a single action button in the Action Bar.

Category In Domino, a word, number, or phrase used to group Notes documents in a view.

CDSA (Common Data Security Architecture) Provides an open software structure for making computer platforms more secure. Relates to securing, applications, electronic commerce, communications, and so on.

Certificate A file that verifies the identity of a computer when two computers communicate. Certificates are used to verify the identify of an email sender and to exchange and authenticate identifies with an Internet server. In Domino, an electronic stamp that becomes part of a server or user ID. The certificate is unique to the certifier ID that was used to create the certificate.

Certificate Authority Certificate (CA) A binary file containing a name, a public key, and a digital signature. The certificate resides on the CA server and is used to establish the authenticity of a Domino or third-party Certificate Authority.

Certification In Domino, the process of issuing a certificate to a Domino server or a Notes user so that he can authenticate with other Domino servers that have a certificate created using the same Certifier ID.

Certifier ID A file that is used to register users and servers into specific hierarchical groups used in the authentication process. There are two types of Certifier IDs: the organization certifier (O level) and the organizational unit certifier (OU level).

CGI (Common Gateway Interface) A standard for external gateway programs to interface with information servers such as HTTP servers.

Chain server topology A Domino Server topology where servers are connected in a single chain. Communication moves along the chain and back again.

Channel A Web site designed to deliver content from the Internet to your computer, similar to subscribing to a favorite Web site.

Checkbox fields In Domino, a keyword field type that presents a list of choices to the user in a checkbox format. Users make a choice by clicking the checkbox, which places an × in the box. This keyword field is used where multiple choices can be made, as in a checklist.

Child document   A Notes document created using a Response-type form. The child document inherits data from its parent document and is permanently associated with that parent. If the parent document is deleted, the child document will be orphaned unless it is also deleted.

Classes   A self-contained unit able to describe itself and have certain responsibilities that it can carry out alone or in collaboration with other objects. Classes contain properties and methods.

Client certificate   An electronic certificate used when sending encrypted and signed S/MIME messages to a server using SSL.

CLS file (Country Language Services file)   A file that defines the parameters (such as sorting order and character substitutions) to be used when converting currency and alphabet characters from another country.

Clustering   As it relates to the Domino server, clustering is an enhancement available in the Domino Advanced Services package that enables Domino servers to replicate with other Domino servers for redundancy in the event of failure. See also *failover*.

Collapse   In Domino, to condense a view so that it displays only categories or only main documents (with the responses hidden). The term is also used when sections within documents are condensed so that only the section header is displayed.

Combobox field   A keyword field type that presents a list of choices to the user in a drop-down list format.

Command key   A keyboard shortcut for performing an immediate action. For example, to print a document, you can use Ctrl+P in Windows (Command+P on a Macintosh).

Common Name   The first element in the X.500 naming convention. Each name requires at a minimum the Common Name element (CN) and the Organization element (O). This field contains the user's full first and last name.

Compact   In Domino, to compress a database by removing any white space created when documents were deleted.

Computed Field   A type of field that is calculated when a document is originally created or edited. The result is stored with the document and recalculated when the document is opened again. Values in these fields appear automatically—they are based on formula calculations, or they are pulled from other systems or database information.

Computed for Display Field   A type of field whose value is calculated every time the document containing the field is opened for reading purposes and whenever the document recalculates (by pressing F9, for example). The results of this calculation are not stored in the document when it is saved; hence, these fields cannot be used in a view.

Computed Text   The text produced as a result of a formula.

Computed when Composed Field   A type of field whose value is computed and assigned when the document is first created.

Concatenation   The stringing together of field names and text constants. For example, if your form has City, State, and Zip fields but you want a column in a view to show a combination such as "Philadelphia, PA 19101," you need a concatenation formula: City + ", " + State + " " + Zip. Do not confuse concatenation with addition. They both use plus (+) signs, but addition is a mathematical function.

Connection document   A Domino document that defines the connection properties between two servers. For two servers in separate domains to communicate, a connection document must exist in the PAB. It is required to transfer mail between adjacent domains.

Context Pane   The area of the Notes Window in which a document (such as a Mail Memo) is displayed when creating a response to that document or a Mail Memo.

Context-sensitive   A term used to describe menus and help screens that change depending on the task or function being performed in the program.

CORBA (Common Object Request Broker Architecture)   A standard for handling requests to distributed objects and returning the results of the request.

Criteria   The information used to filter data on the system, for example, to select which documents appear in a view.

Cross-certificate   A certificate issued by another hierarchical organization, enabling a user or server from outside the organization to authenticate with one or more servers.

Data directory   The top-level directory in which local Domino databases and templates are stored, along with DESKTOP.DSK, CACHE.DSK, and CLS files. Partitioned NT servers and also UNIX and OS/2 also store the NOTES.INI file in the data directory. By default, the directory is called DATA and is directly under the Notes or Domino directory.

Data type   The type of data a specific field on a Notes form can contain—for example, text, rich text, numbers, and names.

Database cache   A portion of the memory on a server where open databases are temporarily stored for quick access.

Database Catalog   A database that lists information about databases on a Domino server, in a group of Domino servers, or in a Domain.

Database library   A database that lists information about selected databases on a workstation or shared databases on a server.

Database Manager   In Domino, a person who has been granted Manager access in the database ACL. The manager can edit the ACL and can delete the database, as well as performing all database design and edit functions.

Database replica   A database created using replication. A database replica has the same ID as the database from which it was created and can exchange information with the original database through replication.

Date/Time field   A field defined with the date/time data type. The field can only store data that is entered using date/time formats via user input or formulas.

DDE   See *Dynamic Data Exchange.*

DECS (Domino Enterprise Connectivity Services)   A program enabling access to data sources external to the Domino server, such as SQL Server, Oracle, and Sybase.

Default   The setting, direction, or choice made by a program unless intervention is made by the user. Built in to an application or program when values or options are necessary for the program to function.

Default Form   The form that is used when a document is opened or a new document is created. Also used unless programming specifies which form to use when creating, editing, and reading documents.

Default Value (for fields)   The value displayed in an editable field when a document is first created. For example, a default value formula can insert today's date in a field that the user has the option of changing.

Default view   The view that is displayed when a database is first opened.

Depositer access   The level of security (defined in the Access Control List) that enables users or servers to create but not see or edit any documents.

Design document   An element in a Domino database that defines the design object. Properties of the design document can be viewed from the work pane in Domino Designer when an object is selected.

Design pane   The navigator area of the Domino Designer.

Design template   A collection of design objects that can be used to create and maintain the design of other databases. These special databases are usually designated by the filename extension .NTF (Notes Template Facility).

Designer Access   The level of security (defined in the Access Control List) that enables users or servers to modify the design of a database. Designer Access does not permit changes to the database Access Control List.

desktop.dsk   A file that stores the options selected for the Notes client desktop. Also stores unread marks and private views in some cases.

Detach   In Domino, to save to a disk drive a copy of a file that appears as an attachment in a Notes document.

Dialog box   A box that is displayed on the screen so the user can provide further information when it is required before the system can continue.

Dialog list field   A keyword field type that presents a list of choices to the user in the notes client. This field appears with the entry helper button by default. In a Web client, this is presented as a combobox. See also *Combobox field*.

Dial-up   A type of connection in which you connect to a server or network using a modem over a telephone line.

Digital speech synthesizer   A device that translates what is on the screen into voice output; used as a way for the blind to get information from the computer screen.

DIIOP (Domino Internet Inter-ORB Protocol)   A task that runs on the Domino Server to allow Java applets created using the Notes Java classes to communicate with the Domino Server. This task works in conjunction with the Domino Object Request Broker to enable Browser users and Domino servers to communicate.

Directory   In Domino, an address book. See also *Domino Directory*.

Directory Assistance   A Domino feature that enables searches and authentication using multiple directories, including Domino directories and LDAP directories.

Directory Assistance database   The database used to set up Directory Assistance. The database serves a directory to the other Domino directories and LDAP directories that are to be used for searching.

Directory Catalog   A condensed version of information such as person and group names and email addresses from one or more Domino Directories. This is used primarily to provide quick lookups in multiple directories for mobile users.

DNS   The Domain Name System used by the Internet to associate a domain name (for example, www.lotus.com) with a specific IP address to which domain requests are routed.

Document   A type of form independent of all others. It does not respond to other forms. It is sometimes referred to as a main document.

Document ID   See *NoteID* or *Universal ID*.

Document Object Model (DOM)   In Javascript, the collection of classes that comprise a document.

Domain   In relation to the Internet, the last part of an Internet address (for example, .gov and .com). In networks, a group of connected computers that share the same security system so a user has to use only one ID and password to access resources within the Domain. In Domino, an address book. See also *Domino Directory*.

Domino (also Domino Server)   The server component in a Lotus Notes environment.

Domino application server   A Domino server used primarily to provide access to Domino databases for Lotus Notes clients.

Domino database   A container for both data and program code. (Note that this does not match the definition used for Relational Databases, which are a collection of related tables.)

Domino Designer   The name of the software program used by application developers and programmers to create Domino databases.

Domino Directory   The public address book stored on the Domino server containing names and addresses of people and servers in that Domino Domain. This address book is accessible to all individuals in the Domain.

Domino Enterprise Server   A Domino Server license type that provides the tools for scaling the Domino Application Server to a wider enterprise with clustering, load balancing, and failover.

Domino Mail Server   A Domino server license type for a server whose primary use is for mail routing and hosting Notes mail databases.

Domino Object Model   The collection of classes within Domino.

Dual key encryption   An encryption using two types of keys—a private and a public key used to encrypt and decrypt.

Dynamic Data Exchange (DDE)   A method of displaying data created in another application so there is a link to the live data. When the data is displayed in Notes, the information is dynamically updated to reflect what is currently stored in the original application.

ECL (Execution Control List)   A list of security settings that users control to enhance the security of workstation data; accessed through the User Preferences dialog box.

Edit mode   The condition in which a document can be modified or created.

Editable field   A field in which the user can enter or change values. The database designer might manipulate user input with formulas such as default value formulas, input translation formulas, or input validation formulas.

Editor access   The level of security (defined in the Access Control List) that enables users or servers to create, read, and edit documents in a database, regardless of whether they created the original document.

Electronic signature   See *Signature, Electronic.*

Email signature   See *Signature, email.*

Embedded Element   The design objects embedded in forms and pages.

Embedded objects and controls   The information created in another application that exists only in the container (such as a Notes document).

Encryption   The scrambling or encoding of data to make it unreadable. Encrypted data must be decrypted to read it. Encryption and decryption involve the use of keys associated with or assigned by the software. Domino uses both public and private encryption keys and both single- and dual-key encryption methods.

Events   In LotusScript, occurrences that cause Domino databases to respond as in Enter and Exit events, input translation, and validation events for fields. Also, in the calendar, an appointment with a minimum time value of one day, such as a vacation or all-day meeting.

Export   To Save a Lotus Notes document or view in a file format other than Notes (.nsf).

Extended accelerator key   The keys used to access bookmarks and task buttons. To view the extended accelerator keys, press and hold down the Alt key.

External Directory   In a Domino domain, a directory that is not part of the Domino domain. External directories might not be accessible via Notes RPC. LDAP is the only guaranteed way to access an External Directory.

Extranet   A group of interconnected intranets with extended access, usually protected by a firewall. For example, companies in business with each other might form extranets in order to share certain types of information as in the case of a manufacturer and a parts supplier. See also *Intranet*.

Failover   The redirection of a client request from one server to another server in a cluster when the first server becomes unavailable.

Field   An area of a form that can contain a single data type of information, such as numbers, graphics, and rich text.

Field data type   The classification of data a field is designed to accept. Examples of field data types are text, date/time, numbers, rich text, and names.

Field value   The value stored in a field in a saved document.

File Transfer Protocol (FTP)   A protocol designed for transferring large messages (files) between two points on the Internet, providing error-checking functions so that the entire data file arrives intact.

Firewall   A system designed to control unauthorized access to a private network from the Internet.

Folder   A container similar to a view into which the user can place documents for later reference. The user can move documents into and out of a folder, whereas a view depends on a formula to determine which documents are displayed.

Folder pane   The workspace area that shows the folders and views available in the opened database.

Form   An item used for collecting and displaying information in a Domino application. Forms can contain subforms, graphics, fields, links, embedded elements, and so on. Forms are used to create and display documents. There are three types of forms: Document, Response, and Response to Response.

Formula   A collection of commands and variables to effect a result. Formulas can be written for numerous events in Domino, such as views, Input validation, default value, and so forth.

Formula field   A field used to populate a subscription list. Subscription lists are used by the Headlines database.

Formula Pop-up Hotspot   The collection of commands and variables (*formula*) that compute the text that appears on screen (*pop-up*) when a mouse is held over an area of the screen (*hotspot*).

Frames One of the panes of a frameset that can contain pages, documents, forms, links, views, and so forth.

Framesets A collection of frames. Each frame within the frameset can work independent of the other frames.

FTP See *File Transfer Protocol.*

Full-text index A series of files containing the indexes to text in a database, enabling Notes to process user search queries.

Full-text search A search option supporting word and phrase searches of Domino databases as well as advanced searches, such as logical expressions.

Group In Domino, a list of users and/or servers used for addressing, access control lists, and address books.

Groupware A loosely defined term that refers to applications that enable groups of people to work together in a collaborative environment.

Hierarchical Having a structure with gradations. See *Hierarchical Naming.*

Hierarchical naming A naming system in which an entity's name includes the names of the entity's antecedents. As used in Notes, your hierarchical name includes at least the name of the organization to which you belong and might also include the names of sub-units within the organization and the country in which you reside. For example: Bob Dobbs/Sales/Stillwater/US. The benefit of hierarchical naming is that it increases security by providing a standard way of distinguishing between people who might otherwise have the same name. Thus, Bob Dobbs/Sales/Stillwater is not the same person as Bob Dobbs/Acctg/Stillwater.

Hierarchical view A view that displays response documents indented and directly beneath the documents to which they respond.

Home page The first page that displays when a user visits an Internet or intranet site. The home page of a site usually contains a company logo, a welcome message, and links to the other pages within the site. In Notes, it is the first database that is displayed upon opening the Notes client.

Home server The term used for the Domino server on which your mail database resides.

Hop A mail stop along the delivery path of routed mail when the recipient's and sender's servers are not directly connected.

Hotkey   The underlined letter in a menu used to select a menu command; also referred to as accelerator key.

Hotspot   The graphics or text contained in a rich text field that users click to follow a link, perform an action, or run a formula or script. Hotspots can be attached in text or graphics, such as Action Hotspots, Formula Pop-up Hotspots, Button Hotspots, and Link Hotspots.

HTML   See *Hypertext Markup Language.*

HTTP   See *Hypertext Transfer Protocol*

Hub-spoke server topology   A mail routing or replication scheme in which one server is designated the hub and all other servers are spokes. The spoke servers replicate only with the hub, not with each other directly, or they route mail to and receive it from the hub only. Hub-spoke is the most efficient topology in a domain that includes more than a few servers.

Hunt group   A group of servers that share the same phone number(s). Users dial the hunt group rather than any one server, and deal with whatever server responds. This is a load-balancing technique for passthru servers.

Hyperlink   A block of text (usually colored and underlined) or a graphic that represents a connection to another place in the same or a separate document. Clicking the hyperlink opens the document to which it is linked. See also *Link.*

Hypertext   The special text contained in a Web page that, when clicked on, takes the user to a related Web page. Hypertext often appears as blue underlined text that changes to purple text when clicked. See also *Link.*

Hypertext Markup Language (HTML)   A collection of instructions or tags that tell a browser program how to display a document—as in when to bold or italicize. HTML tags typically appear embedded within a document, set apart from the document text by angle brackets.

Hyptertext Transfer Protocol (HTTP)   A protocol that defines how HTML files are sent and received via the Internet. See also *Hypertext Markup Language.*

IIOP (Internet Inter-ORB Protocol)   An Internet protocol that implements CORBA solutions over the Web. IIOP lets browsers and servers exchange complex objects, unlike HTTP, which only supports transmission of text.

Image map   A special kind of graphics object that can contain multiple hotspots linking to other objects or URLs.

IMAP, IMAP4   See *Internet Message Access Protocol.*

Input Translation   A Domino field level event that modifies the contents of an editable field to a specified value or format.

Input Validation   A Domino field level event that validates information entered into a field.

Instances   In scripting languages, a specific use of a class. The class contains a definition of an object; to use a class you instantiate it, assigning it to a variable.

Internal field   In Domino, fields that are created by Lotus and are reserved for use by the Domino program.

Internet Message Access Protocol (IMAP, IMAP4)   A protocol enabling mail clients to access their mail and bulletin board messages over the Internet or an intranet.

Internet Protocol (IP)   The system that defines the location, or IP address, of the networks that comprise the Internet. See also *TCP.*

Internotes Server   A Domino Server process that retrieves Web pages and stores them in a Server Web Browser database so that users can retrieve the pages to their Personal Web Browser database without having to connect to the Internet.

Intranet   A restricted-access network that shares information intended for internal use within a company, although intranets might span the globe. Similar to the Web, intranet software enables the routing of HTML documents that are read using a Web browser. See also *Extranet* and *Web.*

ISDN (integrated services digital network)   A communications standard describing digital transmission over ordinary phone lines.

ISP (Internet Service Provider)   A company that provides access to the Internet.

Items   Otherwise known as fields, the internal representation of data objects in a document.

Java   An interpreted programming language developed by Sun Microsystems. A Java program is delivered in textual, compressed, or tokenized form from an Internet server to a computer. The Java interpreter or "Java virtual machine" (such as the one which comes with Internet Explorer) interprets and executes the program as though it were stored on the receiving computer's hard drive. Java makes possible the transmission of logical and often user-tailored content (such as a desktop stock ticker), whereas HTML by contrast is merely a system for the formatting and display of text and graphics.

Java Applets   The small, self-contained applications that can be embedded into forms.

Javascript   A scripting language that permits access to the Document Object Model (DOM) and runs on both Notes and Web clients.

Key ring file   A binary file that contains one or more server or CA certificates, is protected by a password, and is stored on the server hard drive. Not applicable to client certificates.

Keyboard shortcut   A combination of keys used to perform a command in lieu of selecting an item from the menu. For example, Ctrl+P is the keyboard shortcut for printing.

Keyword Field   A multiple choice field that presents users with a list of choices in checkbox, combobox, dialog list, listbox, or radio button format.

Labels   In database design, text accompanying a field which indicates the use or intended contents of the field. By convention field labels are usually positioned to the left or above the field. See also *Static text*.

LAN   See *Local Area Network*.

Layout Region   In Domino, a fixed-length area on a form or subform that combines text and graphics and is the only place on a form where you can insert dialog boxes. Layout regions are not supported in Web browsers.

LDAP (Lightweight Directory Access Procotol)   A protocol that defines a standard way for directory servers and clients to exchange data. Domino 4.6 and later are optionally LDAP-compliant directory servers.

Letterhead   The manner (style) in which your name, date, and time appear at the top of a mail message.

Library   A database that contains lists of other databases and links to them. Library databases provide a method for informing users about the applications available to them, describing the applications, and making them easy to open.

Link   A pointer to a block of data, graphic, or a page in an external file or document. On the Web, a link can reference another Web page, a file, or a program, such as a Java program. In Domino, links can open other views, databases, or documents without closing the object containing the link.

Link Hotspot   In Domino, an area that when clicked links to other Domino objects or URLs. Link hotspots can be text, graphics, or regions of a graphic object.

List concatenation   The process of combining and linking two lists. For example, concatenating A,B,C and 1,2,3 can yield A1,B1,C1, A2,B2,C2, A3,B3,C3.

Listbox field   A keyword field type that presents choices to the user in a scrollable list.

Lists   A list contains data elements of a similar type. Multi-valued fields are lists of data elements. See also *Multi-valued fields.*

Load Balancing   The passing off of server requests from one server in a cluster to another to help even out the cluster workload.

Local Area Network (LAN)   A network that connects a group of computers located within an immediate area, such as the same building. Computers are connected to each other by network cable.

Location document   A document stored in the Personal Address Book that contains settings that determine how Notes communicates with servers from a specific location.

LotusScript   A version of the BASIC programming language that is included in Notes (as well as other Lotus products) and that includes language extensions that enable object-oriented development of Notes applications.

LS:DO (LotusScript Data Object)   An object that provides properties and methods for accessing and updating tables in external databases through the ODBC (Open Database Connectivity) version 2.0 standard. Consists of three LotusScript classes: ODBCConnection, ODBCQuery, and ODBCResultSet.

Macro   See *Agent.*

Mail database   In Lotus Notes, a database designed to store a person's mail, calendar, and to-do documents. Your mail database is stored on your home server. (See also *Outgoing mail database.*)

Manager access   A level of security (defined in the Access Control List) that gives all rights to a database, including the right to modify a database Access Control List and to delete a database. All other access levels (Designer, Editor, Reader, and so forth) fall under the level of Manager, and the Manager has the rights defined in all those other access levels.

Methods   In scripting languages, actions available to a specific class.

MIME   See *Multipurpose Internet Mail Extensions*

Modem   A piece of hardware, either internal or external that allows one to send data via the telephone lines by converting digital signals to analog signals.

MSAA (Microsoft Active Accessibility)   A Microsoft-defined technology for enabling handicapped people to use Windows-based computers.

MTA (Message Transfer Agent)   A program that transfers messages from one place to another. Domino MTAs also translate messages between different formats (for example, Notes–cc:Mail, Notes–SMTP, and Notes–X.400).

Multi-valued fields   The fields that contain more than one element of the same data type. See also *Lists*.

Multipurpose Internet Mail Extensions (MIME)   An Internet standard method (RFC1521 and RFC1522) for converting nontext files to ASCII format and attaching the converted files to ASCII files, such as with SMTP email messages and HTML Web pages.

NAB   The acronym for Lotus Notes Name and Address Book prior to Release 5. In Release 5, address books are called the Personal Address Book and the Domino Directory.

Named element   All design elements in a database, including forms, views, folders, navigators, and so on.

Named style   A collection of formats that you can apply to one or more paragraphs in a rich text field. All text and paragraph formats can be included in a named style.

Names field   A field of Names data type. It can hold the names of people, servers, and groups.

Navigation buttons   The browser-like buttons in Notes that enable a person to navigate among open database documents or Web pages. Functions include Back, Forward, Stop, Refresh, Search, and Go.

Navigation pane   The left pane of a Notes screen that displays either the currently selected navigator or icons for all views, folders, and agents in a database.

Navigator   In Notes, a menu made up of hyperlinked rich text, or hotspots. When clicked, the links or hotspots perform certain actions or access other documents. Netscape also has a Web browser called Netscape Navigator.

Negotiated session key   An encryption key that is generated at the beginning of an SSL session and used by the parties to the session to encrypt all communications during the session. The key is discarded at the end of the session.

Nested table   The tables that reside within (or inside) other tables.

Network News Transfer Protocol (NNTP)   The protocol of Usenet Newsgroups. Defines how newsgroup lists and articles will be transferred between NNTP servers and between NNTP servers and newsreaders.

Newsfeed   The NNTP equivalent to Notes server-to-server replication. NNTP servers use newsfeeds to transfer newly posted news articles to each other, as well as changes and deletions.

Newsgroups   The online discussion groups on the Internet. Messages posted to a newsgroup can be read and responded to by others.

Newsreader   An NNTP client program that enables a user to browse, subscribe to, and unsubscribe from newsgroups; it also enables a user to read, create, and print newsgroup articles.

NNTP   See *Network News Transfer Protocol.*

NNTP server   A server that handles newsgroup messages using NNTP, or Network News Transfer Protocol.

No Access   A database access level. Entities having no access to a database cannot, in general, see or add to the contents of a database or for that matter, even add a shortcut for the database to their desktops. An exception to this rule is public documents. Users assigned No Access can still be permitted either to create or to read public documents in the database.

NoteID   An identification number that Notes/Domino assigns to every note in a database. The NoteID is unique within the database. But when the note is replicated or copied, it receives a new NoteID. Compare with a Universal ID, which is only reissued after a copy but retained during replication.

Notes Client   The software designed for use by Lotus Notes users; enables the user to access a Domino server, send mail, and browse the Web.

Notes RPC (Notes Remote Procedure Call)   A proprietary protocol defining how Domino servers and Notes clients transfer information among each other. It is derived from RPC (Remote Procedure Call), which is a well-established, standard method for programs to transfer information back and forth.

Notes/FX (Field Exchange)   A standard method for Notes and desktop applications such as word processors and spreadsheet applications to read data from and write it to each other's fields.

notes.ini　A text file that consists of a list of variables and their values, each recorded on a separate line in the form *variable=value*. Notes and Domino refer to the settings in notes.ini when loading into memory and periodically while they are running to determine how to do various things.

NotesNIC　An Internet-based service offered by Lotus in which companies can add one or more Internet-based Domino servers to the "Net" domain that is maintained by Lotus. It provides a way for companies to route mail to and replicate with each other over the Internet because they each have servers on the Net domain. To learn more about it, connect to the Internet, and from within Notes open the Domino server called home/notes/net.

NSF (Notes Storage Facility)　The name of the filename extension that identifies a Notes database file.

NTF (Notes Template Facility)　The name of the filename extension that identifies a Notes template file. A template is a Notes database that usually stores only design elements and is used as a model for production Notes databases (NSF files).

Number field　In Notes, a field designated to hold a numerical value.

Objects　In object-oriented programming, the basic building blocks of programs and systems. Objects provide reusable components from which developers can build and evolve applications. Java is an example of an object-oriented programming language.

ODBC (Open Database Connectivity)　A Microsoft-developed standard that permits database programs to share data with or receive data from other programs.

ODS (On Disk Structure)　The format in which a Notes database is physically stored on disk. Notes 3.x uses ODS version 17. Notes 4.x uses ODS version 20 but also recognizes earlier ODS versions. Notes 5.x uses ODS version 41 and recognizes earlier ODS versions.

Operands　In programming, the data that will be "operated on" by the operator.

Operators　The "verbs" in a formula. In programming, operators manipulate data or perform certain operations (add, subtract, multiply, and so on) on operands. In "2 + 2," the "+" is the operator, and each "2" is an operand.

ORB (Object Request Broker)　An intermediary or middleman between a requesting client and a variety of services provided by application servers. Services can include database queries, component location (via directory servers), notifications, and transactions.

Outgoing mail database   A Notes database that temporarily stores mail while it is en route to its final destination. Unlike most Notes databases, it does not use the `.nsf` filename extension. Rather, its filename is `mail.box` or if a Domino server uses multiple outgoing mail databases, `mailn.box` (where *n* is an integer).

Pages   In Notes, a design element that is used to display information but is not used to create documents by users. In Web browsers, individual HTML documents that can display text, links to other documents, forms, and graphics.

Pane   A portion of a window, usually divided from the remainder of the window by a movable border.

Parent Document   In Domino, a document from which information is derived or inherited by another document, such as a response document. All response and response-to-response documents have a parent document.

Partitioned server   A Domino feature that lets you run multiple Domino servers on a single computer. By creating partitioned servers, you can overcome certain architectural limitations of Domino 4.x to increase the number of users that a given computer can accommodate.

Passthru Server   A Domino server used to receive incoming calls from mobile Notes users, to authenticate those users, and to enable them to access and authenticate with target servers to which they are not directly connected. Passthru server is also used so that a client that runs only one type of protocol, such as SPX, can access servers that don't run that protocol. The client connects to a passthru server running both SPX and TCP/IP, and the passthru server connects to the other servers only running TCP/IP.

Peer-to-peer server topology   A network architecture where every server is an equal and is connected directly to every other server in the network.

Permanent pen   A toggle feature of the Lotus Notes client software that enables users to enter text in rich text fields using a font and or font color different from the default font without affecting the default font settings.

Personal Address Book   A database designed for each Notes user that contains contact information entered by that user.

Personal Web Navigator   The Web browser function of Notes; also the name of the database in which the Notes browser stores retrieved Web pages.

POP3 (Post Office Protocol Version 3)   A protocol that specifies how an email client will access and download messages from a POP3 mail server.

Preview Pane   A window in which you view documents selected in the View pane without opening those documents. This pane is sizable (adjustable).

Private folder   A folder that users can create for their own exclusive use.

Private key   The secret half of the public/private key pair that every Notes certifier, user, and server has. It is stored in the Notes ID file. Because it is private and unique to its owner, the private key makes possible Notes authentication, electronic signature, and mail encryption. See also *public key*.

Private view   In Notes, a view of Notes documents that is accessible only to the user who created it. Sometimes also known as a *personal view*.

Properties   The settings that control the behavior or appearance of Notes elements, documents, or databases. In LotusScript, a property is a characteristic of an object. Also a class in LotusScript.

Protocol   In networking, the established rules that servers and applications follow to communicate across networks. For example, the Internet Protocol (IP) describes how two computers will connect and exchange information over the Internet. FTP and HTTP are also examples of protocols.

Proxy servers   The intermediary servers that provide controlled access through a firewall. Instead of enabling direct connections, proxy servers connect to the intended destination and handle data transfers.

Public key   The public half of the public/private key pair that every Notes certifier, server, and user has. Your public key is unique to you and the certificates in your ID file attest to that fact. You publish your public key in the Domino Directory so that others can use it to encrypt documents that they want to send you and to decrypt your signature on documents you send them.

Pull-Down Menu   A list of related commands or actions that expand when activated by the mouse or keyboard.

Radio Button   In window interfaces, radio buttons are small round selection boxes that enable users to indicate their choice of an item in a list.

Read access list   A list of authorized readers of a document or of documents created using a given form. Reader access lists can be defined in two places, either on the Security pane of Form and Document Properties boxes or in fields of Readers data type in forms and documents.

Read Marks   See *Unread marks*.

Reader access In the Access Control List of a database, the access level that enables users to read the contents of the database.

Readers field In Notes, the readers field contains a list of individuals and groups who will be enabled to read the document in question.

Referral The URL of an LDAP directory that a Domino LDAP server might return to an LDAP client in lieu of an answer to the query. The LDAP client would then refer its query to the referral server. The Domino LDAP server returns a referral if the server cannot itself answer an LDAP client query but if an entry in the Master Address Book indicates that another LDAP directory might be able to answer it.

Replica ID A 16-character combination of letters and numbers that represents a Notes database and its replicas. This ID differentiates between database copies and database replicas and is required in order to replicate a database.

Replica One of multiple copies of a single database that maintains a link to the original database on a server for the purpose of replicating or synchronizing information.

Replica Stub In Notes, an empty replica or copy of a database template. The design of the database is replicated, but not the contents.

Replicate See *Replication*.

Replication The process of synchronizing the same databases on different computers.

Replication Conflict An error that occurs when two users using different replica copies of the database edit and save the same document and then the database is replicated. One version of the document becomes the main document, and the other becomes the "Replication or Save Conflict" document. Someone, usually the Notes administrator, has to resolve the conflict by editing one of the documents to include the changes made in the other. Then, one of the documents gets deleted. See also *Save Conflict*.

Replication Monitor A document in the Statistics and Events database (events4.nsf) that tells the Event task on a server to monitor a specific database and to notify an administrator if the database does not replicate within a defined time period.

Replicator A Domino server task that replicates databases between servers.

Replicator page The page in Notes where the user manages the replication process.

Reserved Field A predefined field used by Notes. The field's name is also reserved and cannot be used to label another field.

Resources   The components and requirements needed or used to run a Notes system. Typically used in the phrase "system resources" to describe the processing power, disk space, or RAM being used.

Response Form or Document   A Notes form or document created with the form that is always subordinate to and dependent on the form type Document. A Response form typically appears in views indented beneath its parent, the Document form.

Response-to-Response Form or Document   A Notes form or document created with the form that is always subordinate to and dependent on its parent: the Document, Response, or Response-to-Response form. A Response-to-Response form also appears in views indented beneath its parent.

Rich text field   A type of field that accepts multiple data types and text formatting.

Ring server topology   A Domino replication or mail-routing topology in which servers replicate databases or route mail one-to-one in a circle with the ends connected (A–B–C–D–A). See also *Chain server topology*, in which servers are connected one-to-one but with the ends unconnected (A–B–C–D).

Role   A database-specific group or variable created to simplify the maintenance of a database. Roles enable a database manager to define who has access to restricted fields, documents, forms, and views without having to change the design of the database.

SASL (Simple Authentication and Security Layer)   An Internet protocol that provides for authentication and secure communication between LDAP servers and clients.

Save Conflict   An error that occurs when two users on the same network edit and save the same document at the same time. See also *Replication conflict*.

screen reader   A device that reads what is displayed on the computer screen. See *digital speech synthesizer*.

Scripted actions, buttons, and events   The instructions that will guide actions triggered by certain occurrences, such as mouseovers, button clicks, or the passing of a specified period of time.

Search engine   A special program that enables users to find information on the Internet by typing a key word or phrase. The search engine searches the Internet for pages containing the key word or phrase. The search engine then returns a list of Web addresses to the browser that are active links to pages on which the key word or phrase was found. Notes has a search engine used to query databases that have been Full Text Indexed. The Global Directory uses search engines to search Notes, files, and sites for information.

Sections   The collapsible areas of a document. Helpful for managing large documents. When collapsed, sections display one line of information; when expanded, sections reveal their entire contents.

Serif/Sans Serif   The short, horizontal bars at the top and bottom of text characters. If a typeface has serifs, it's known as a serif typeface or serif font. If it does not have serifs, it's known as a sans serif font.

Server   A computer that's purpose is to store files or programs and provide file, program, and resource access to clients.

Server certificate   An affirmation, electronically signed by a certifier, that a given public key is that of a named server. Domino server certificates are stored in a server's ID file. X.509 server certificates are stored in an ID file. SSL certificates are stored in a key ring file.

Server command   A command that you issue to a Domino server, in response to which the server will perform a task. You can issue server commands at the server console, the remote server console, or a command prompt. You can also issue server commands from within Domino Administrator or by creating Program documents in the Domino Directory.

Server connection   A document in a user's Personal Address Book that defines how Notes should connect to another server. Also, a document in the Domino Directory that defines how one Domino server should connect to another Domino server.

Server task   A program running on a Domino server. Domino servers consist of a series of programs or tasks that work together to accomplish the server's mission.

Shared field   A special kind of Notes field that exists independently of any form and can be re-used on multiple Notes forms. Shared fields streamline the Notes application development process by eliminating the need to re-create the same field in multiple forms.

shared mail   A feature of Domino servers by which they can store in a central database a single copy of any messages addressed to more than one user on a mail server. This is a space-saving feature. Shared mail is also known as the Single Copy Object Store (SCOS).

Shared, Private on First Use View   A view that is shared at first but when accessed by a user, becomes Private for that user.

Shared views   The views that are public and accessible to multiple users.

Shortcut Keystroke   A keystroke or combination of keystrokes that perform a task without using a mouse.

Sibling document   In a hierarchical view or folder, all documents at a given level under a parent document are siblings of each other.

Sign   The act of attaching an electronic signature to a document. The signature assures that the document originated with the signing party and that the signed document is unaltered since being signed.

Signature, electronic   An encryption method that enables Notes users to verify the identity of the author of a document or of a section in a document. At times, Domino applies signatures to documents automatically; other times, users can manually apply signatures.

Signature, email   The text or object appended to the end of a mail message used in the way you would close a letter with your handwritten signature. Signatures can contain a name, along with email, phone, address, and other pertinent information.

Single copy object store (SCOS)   A shared mail database on a Domino server. See *Shared mail.*

Single Key Encryption   A data security method that enables a single key to encrypt and decrypt private documents.

SLIP/PPP   These are two different dial-up protocols. SLIP (Serial Line Internet Protocol) is the older of the two protocols and supports only IP. PPP (Point-to-Point Protocol) supports IP, IPX, and NetBEUI and is the preferred protocol of the two. Use either one (whichever is supported by your software) to establish dial-up connections to remote networks.

SmartIcons   Lotus' name for icons located on the Notes client and Designer software toolbars.

S/MIME (Secure/MIME)   A version of the MIME protocol that incorporates security features. S/MIME-compliant mail programs can send encrypted and electronically signed messages to each other.

SMTP (Simple Mail Transfer Protocol)   The Internet's mail transfer protocol. SMTP hosts connect to each other over the Internet.

SOCKS server   A type of proxy server that can accommodate any kind of TCP-based traffic. Contrast it to an application-level proxy server (such as a Domino passthru server) that can accommodate only traffic related to a particular application. A SOCKS server handles Internet requests from clients inside a company's firewall and either accepts or rejects those requests based on the destination or user identification.

SSL (Secure Sockets Layer)   An Internet security protocol that provides authentication between two communicating computers and secures all transmissions between them so that the transmitted data can't be read or tampered with by third parties.

Stacked icon   A database icon that represents more than one replica of a database. A stacked database icon has a small button in its upper right corner that, when clicked, displays a list of the represented replicas.

Static text   The unchanging text on a form. The title, field labels, and so on. See also *Labels*.

Subform   A form fragment, stored as a separate design element, that becomes part of another form when the other form is called into use. Subforms can appear in forms based on conditions (formulas). For example, if a user places an X in a field indicating they are a first time visitor to your site, a subform opens in the current form asking them to supply registration information.

Subscription   A Web page, channel, Domino database, or Active Desktop item that's information is updated on a computer at pre-set intervals determined by the user. Subscriptions also apply to newsgroups.

Surfing   Browsing the Internet, similar to browsing or "surfing" channels on cable TV.

System Administrator   The person who oversees and manages a network. The administrator can grant a user permission to access certain files and resources, troubleshoot problems with the network, and control each computer on the network. The administrator has the capability to track each user's activities on the network.

TCP/IP [also TCP] (Transmission Control Protocol)   The protocol that defines how data should be sent from point to point over the Internet. Following TCP protocol, data is broken into packets that are flushed through the Internet in the general direction of their recipient. There, they are collected and reorganized into their original sequence. Because TCP and IP protocols work hand-in-hand, people refer to them together as TCP/IP.

Template   A Notes database that usually contains only design elements and is intended to provide the starting design of a production database.

Text constants   A fixed value (text) that does not change.

Text Field   In a Notes form, a field that can hold and display text. Notes rich text fields can hold attachments, graphics, and code in addition to plain text.

Text Pop-up Hotspot   The text that appears when a user holds his mouse over or clicks on a specially marked or highlighted object. Text pop-ups are used to provide additional information to the user about the object. Text pop-ups are popular for parenthetical or extraneous information.

Trigger   See *Agent*.

Trusted root   A Certificate Authority's certificate merged into the Domino Directory, client's browser , or the server's key ring file that enables clients and servers to communicate with any client or server that has that Certificate Authority's certificate marked as trusted.

Twistie   The name of icon that when clicked expands and collapses a Domino document section or view.

UI (User Interface)   The onscreen environment that gives the user the capability to control and view the actions of an application.

UNID   See *Universal ID*.

Uniform Resource Locator   See *URL*.

Universal ID   Also known as a "UNID," this is an identification number that Notes/Domino assigns to every note in a database. The note retains this number when replicated to other copies of the database, and Notes/Domino uses it to recognize when notes are replicas of each other. If a note is copied (not replicated) to another database or copied and then pasted back into the same database, it gets a new UNID (and is therefore not a replica of the original note from which it was copied). Compare with a NoteID, which is replaced after both replication and copying.

Unread Marks   The characters (stars) that appear in a Domino database used to indicate when a document has not been read. Unread documents also appear in red text in a view. After documents have been read, the unread marks disappear, and the document text appears in black in a view.

URL (Uniform Resource Locator)   A pointer to the location of an object, usually the address of an Internet resource. URLs conform to a standard syntax. See also *Web*.

User ID   A file that uniquely identifies every user and server to Lotus Notes and Domino.

Using This Database document   A document that explains how the database works. Specifically, it provides users with instructions on using various forms, views, and navigators in the database. See also *About This Database Document*.

Value   See *Field value*.

Variables   In programming, changeable values (numbers, text) used by the application to perform certain functions.

View   In Notes, the method for grouping and sorting documents for display in table format like a table of contents. Documents are selected for views based on their characteristics (Field contents, Subject, Name, Date, and so on).

WAN (Wide Area Network)   A network (usually private to a single company) that connects users and network components spread over a large geographical region.

Web   The *World Wide Web* (or just *Web*) is a component of the Internet. It is a collection of HTML documents accessible through the Internet. It uses the following syntax:

`[protocol]://[host].[domain].[superdomain]/[directory]/[file]`

`[protocol]` is a standard Internet protocol such as HTTP, FTP, or NNTP; `[host]` is the name of a computer; `[domain]` is a registered domain name; `[superdomain]` is a super-domain such as com, gov, edu, mil, us, uk, and so on; `[directory]` is a subdirectory or perhaps a directory mapping on the host computer; and `[file]` is a file on the host computer.

Welcome page   The opening screen in the Lotus Notes client. This page is customizable, contains a search bar, and links to major tasks such as sending mail and using the calendar. See also *Home Page*.

Window tab   A tabbed page that represents an open window in Notes that is used to switch back and forth between open windows.

Workgroup   A group of people working together and sharing computer data, often over a company intranet.

Workstation   Any networked computer.

INDEX

A